FEAR ITSELF
THE HOME FRONT

WRITER
CHRISTOS GAGE

ARTIST
MIKE MAYHEW

COLOR ARTIST
RAIN BEREDO

"THE AGE OF ANXIETY"
WRITER
PETER MILLIGAN

ARTIST
ELIA BONETTI

COLOR ARTIST
JOHN RAUCH

"THE CHOSEN"
WRITER
FRED VAN LENTE

ARTIST
ALESSANDRO VITTI

COLOR ARTIST
JAVIER TARTAGLIA

FEAR ITSELF: THE HOME FRONT. Contains material originally published in magazine form as FEAR ITSELF: THE HOME FRONT #1-7. First printing 2012. ISBN# 978-0-7851-5667-3. Published by MARVEL WORLDWIDE, INC., a subsidiary of MARVEL ENTERTAINMENT, LLC. OFFICE OF PUBLICATION: 135 West 50th Street, New York, NY 10020. Copyright © 2011 and 2012 Marvel Characters, Inc. All rights reserved. $24.99 per copy in the U.S. and $27.99 in Canada (GST #R127032852); Canadian Agreement #40668537. All characters featured in this issue and the distinctive names and likenesses thereof, and all related indicia are trademarks of Marvel Characters, Inc. No similarity between any of the names, characters, persons, and/or institutions in this magazine with those of any living or dead person or institution is intended, and any such similarity which may exist is purely coincidental. **Printed in the U.S.A.** ALAN FINE, EVP - Office of the President, Marvel Worldwide, Inc. and EVP & CMO Marvel Characters B.V.; DAN BUCKLEY, Publisher & President - Print, Animation & Digital Divisions; JOE QUESADA, Chief Creative Officer; TOM BREVOORT, SVP of Publishing; DAVID BOGART, SVP of Operations & Procurement, Publishing; RUWAN JAYATILLEKE, SVP & Associate Publisher, Publishing; C.B. CEBULSKI, SVP of Creator & Content Development; DAVID GABRIEL, SVP of Publishing Sales & Circulation; MICHAEL PASCIULLO, SVP of Brand Planning & Communications; JIM O'KEEFE, VP of Operations & Logistics; DAN CARR, Executive Director of Publishing Technology; SUSAN CRESPI, Editorial Operations Manager; ALEX MORALES, Publishing Operations Manager; STAN LEE, Chairman Emeritus. For information regarding advertising in Marvel Comics or on Marvel.com, please contact Niza Disla, Director of Marvel Partnerships, at ndisla@marvel.com. For Marvel subscription inquiries, please call 800-217-9158. Manufactured between 9/12/2012 and 10/15/2012 by R.R. DONNELLEY,

ARTIST
PEPE LARRAZ
COLOR ARTIST
CHRIS SOTOMAYOR

"BETWEEN STATIONS"
WRITER
CORINNA BECHKO
ARTIST
LELIO BONACCORSO
COLOR ARTIST
BRIAN REBER

"BREAKDOWN"
WRITER
BEN McCOOL
ARTIST
MIKE DEL MUNDO

"LEGACY"
WRITER
KEVIN GREVIOUX
PENCILER
MC WYMAN
INKER
JOHN WYCOUGH
COLORIST
WIL QUINTANA

ARTIST
JASON LATOUR

"FEAR & SELF-LOATHING
IN WISCONSIN"
WRITER
ELLIOTT KALAN
ARTIST
TY TEMPLETON
COLOR ARTIST
DAVID CURIEL

"HOME FRONT LINES"
WRITER
BRIAN CLEVINGER
ARTIST
PABLO RAIMONDI
COLOR ARTIST
VERONICA GANDINI

"A MOMENT WITH..."
WRITER & ARTIST
HOWARD CHAYKIN
COLOR ARTIST
EDGAR DELGADO

LETTERERS
DAVE LANPHEAR & TROY PETERI
COVER ARTIST
MARKO DJURDJEVIC
ASSISTANT EDITOR
JOHN DENNING
EDITORS
LAUREN SANKOVITCH & RACHEL PINNELAS
EXECUTIVE EDITOR
TOM BREVOORT

COLLECTION EDITOR: CORY LEVINE • ASSISTANT EDITORS: ALEX STARBUCK & NELSON RIBEIRO
EDITORS, SPECIAL PROJECTS: JENNIFER GRÜNWALD & MARK D. BEAZLEY
SENIOR EDITOR, SPECIAL PROJECTS: JEFF YOUNGQUIST • SENIOR VICE PRESIDENT OF SALES: DAVID GABRIEL
SVP OF BRAND PLANNING & COMMUNICATIONS: MICHAEL PASCIULLO
BOOK DESIGN: JEFF POWELL

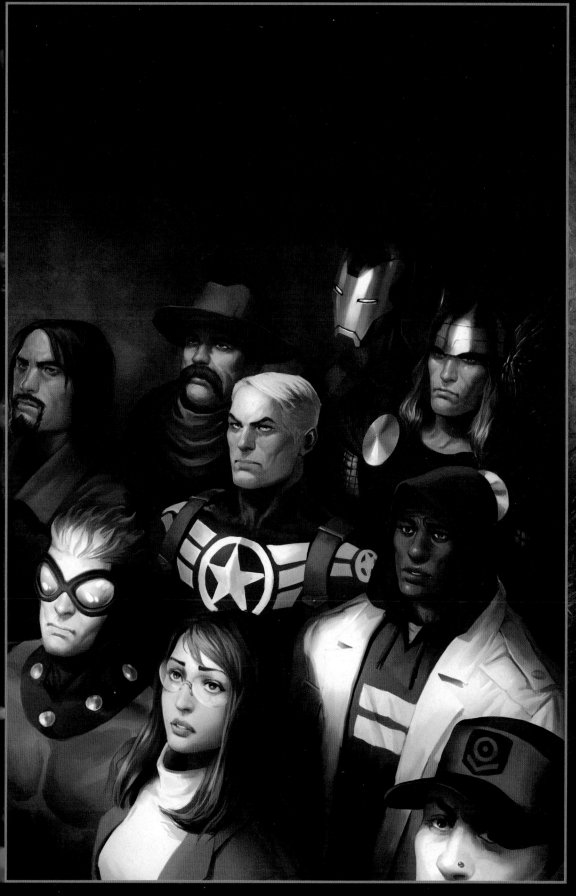

FEAR ITSELF: THE HOME FRONT #1

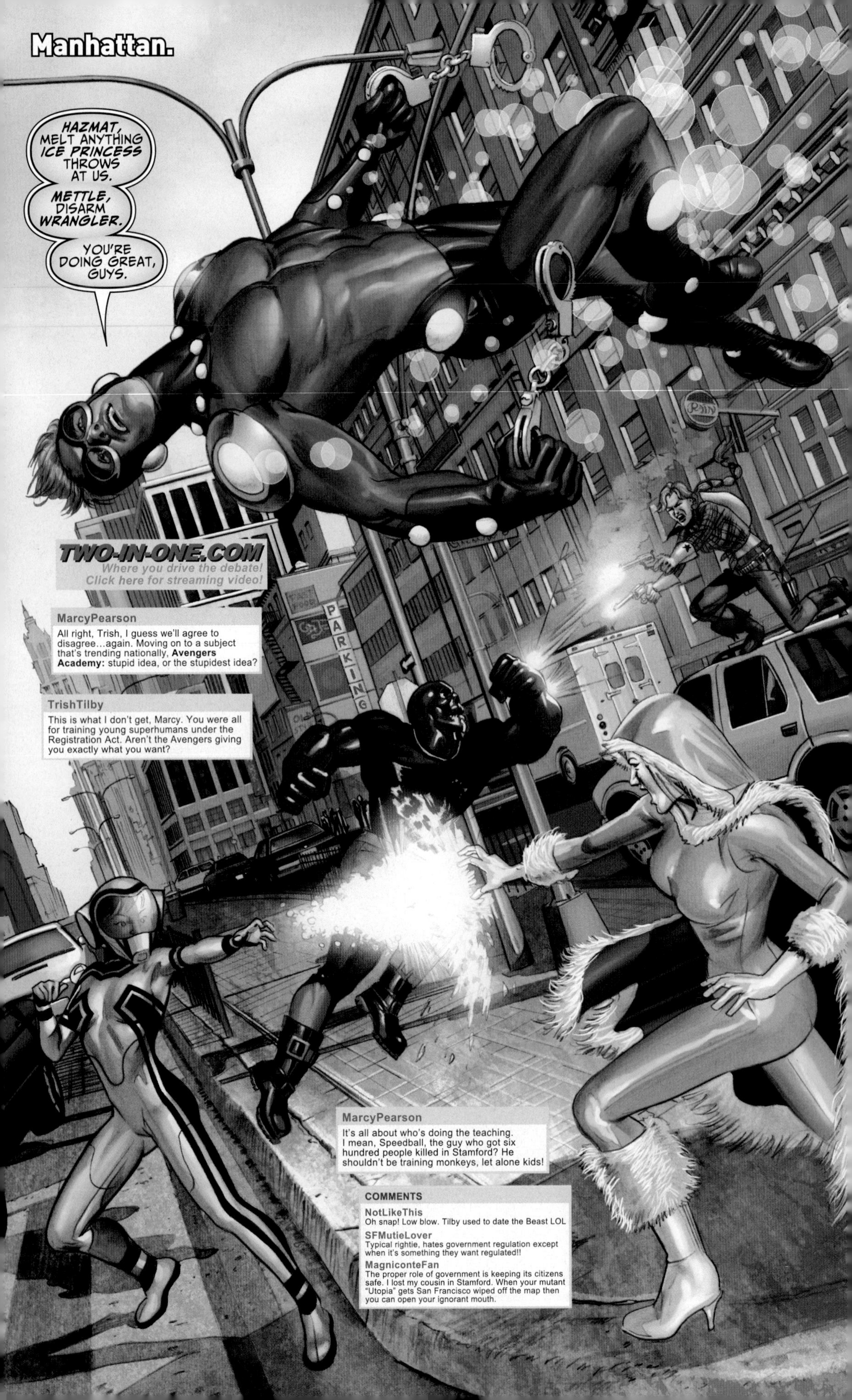
Manhattan.
HAZMAT, MELT ANYTHING ICE PRINCESS THROWS AT US.
METTLE, DISARM WRANGLER.
YOU'RE DOING GREAT, GUYS.
TWO-IN-ONE.COM
Where you drive the debate!
Click here for streaming video!
MarcyPearson
All right, Trish, I guess we'll agree to disagree...again. Moving on to a subject that's trending nationally, **Avengers Academy:** stupid idea, or the stupidest idea?
TrishTilby
This is what I don't get, Marcy. You were all for training young superhumans under the Registration Act. Aren't the Avengers giving you exactly what you want?
PARKING
MarcyPearson
It's all about who's doing the teaching. I mean, Speedball, the guy who got six hundred people killed in Stamford? He shouldn't be training monkeys, let alone kids!
COMMENTS
NotLikeThis
Oh snap! Low blow. Tilby used to date the Beast LOL
SFMutieLover
Typical rightie, hates government regulation except when it's something they want regulated!!
MagniconteFan
The proper role of government is keeping its citizens safe. I lost my cousin in Stamford. When your mutant "Utopia" gets San Francisco wiped off the map then you can open your ignorant mouth.

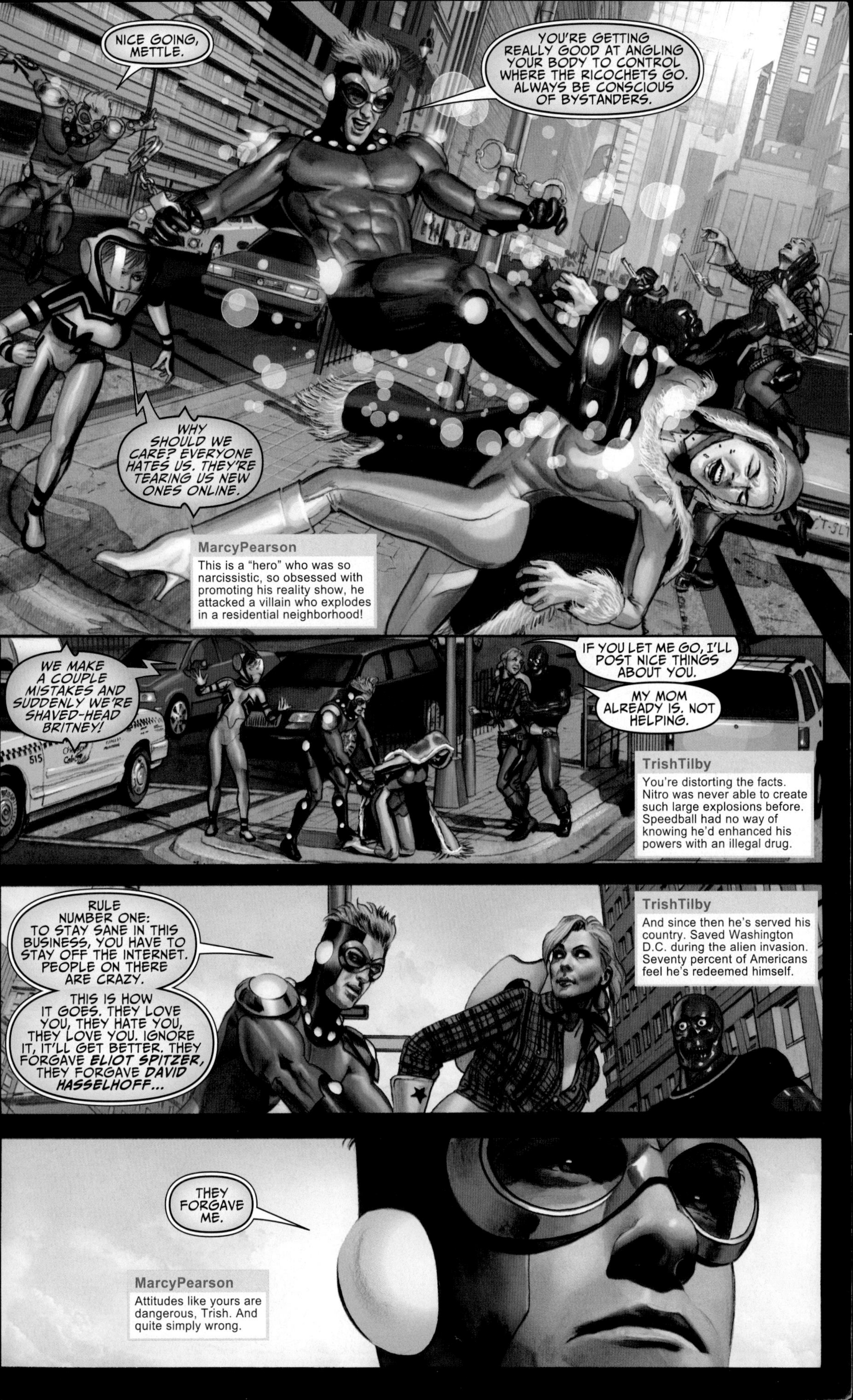
NICE GOING, METTLE.
YOU'RE GETTING REALLY GOOD AT ANGLING YOUR BODY TO CONTROL WHERE THE RICOCHETS GO. ALWAYS BE CONSCIOUS OF BYSTANDERS.
WHY SHOULD WE CARE? EVERYONE HATES US. THEY'RE TEARING US NEW ONES ONLINE.
MarcyPearson
This is a "hero" who was so narcissistic, so obsessed with promoting his reality show, he attacked a villain who explodes in a residential neighborhood!
WE MAKE A COUPLE MISTAKES AND SUDDENLY WE'RE SHAVED-HEAD BRITNEY!
IF YOU LET ME GO, I'LL POST NICE THINGS ABOUT YOU.
MY MOM ALREADY IS. NOT HELPING.
TrishTilby
You're distorting the facts. Nitro was never able to create such large explosions before. Speedball had no way of knowing he'd enhanced his powers with an illegal drug.
RULE NUMBER ONE: TO STAY SANE IN THIS BUSINESS, YOU HAVE TO STAY OFF THE INTERNET. PEOPLE ON THERE ARE CRAZY.
THIS IS HOW IT GOES. THEY LOVE YOU, THEY HATE YOU, THEY LOVE YOU. IGNORE IT, IT'LL GET BETTER. THEY FORGAVE ELIOT SPITZER, THEY FORGAVE DAVID HASSELHOFF...
TrishTilby
And since then he's served his country. Saved Washington D.C. during the alien invasion. Seventy percent of Americans feel he's redeemed himself.
THEY FORGAVE ME.
MarcyPearson
Attitudes like yours are dangerous, Trish. And quite simply wrong.

Infinite Avengers Mansion.
Temporary holding cells.
The next morning.

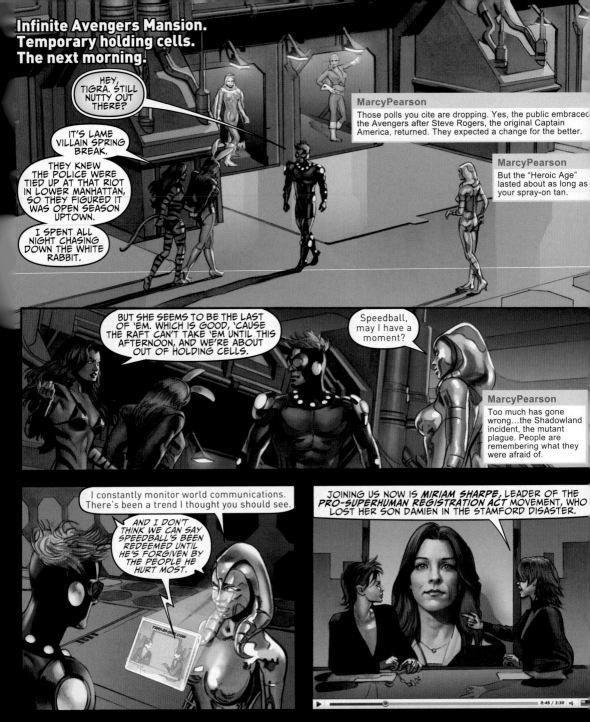

HEY, TIGRA. STILL NUTTY OUT THERE?

IT'S LAME VILLAIN SPRING BREAK.

THEY KNEW THE POLICE WERE TIED UP AT THAT RIOT IN LOWER MANHATTAN, SO THEY FIGURED IT WAS OPEN SEASON UPTOWN.

I SPENT ALL NIGHT CHASING DOWN THE WHITE RABBIT.

MarcyPearson
Those polls you cite are dropping. Yes, the public embraced the Avengers after Steve Rogers, the original Captain America, returned. They expected a change for the better.

MarcyPearson
But the "Heroic Age" lasted about as long as your spray-on tan.

BUT SHE SEEMS TO BE THE LAST OF 'EM. WHICH IS GOOD, 'CAUSE THE RAFT CAN'T TAKE 'EM UNTIL THIS AFTERNOON, AND WE'RE ABOUT OUT OF HOLDING CELLS.

Speedball, may I have a moment?

MarcyPearson
Too much has gone wrong...the Shadowland incident, the mutant plague. People are remembering what they were afraid of.

I constantly monitor world communications. There's been a trend I thought you should see.

AND I DON'T THINK WE CAN SAY SPEEDBALL'S BEEN REDEEMED UNTIL HE'S FORGIVEN BY THE PEOPLE HE HURT MOST.

JOINING US NOW IS *MIRIAM SHARPE*, LEADER OF THE *PRO-SUPERHUMAN REGISTRATION ACT* MOVEMENT, WHO LOST HER SON DAMIEN IN THE STAMFORD DISASTER.

0:45 / 2:30

MIRIAM, THANKS FOR YOUR TIME...AND AGAIN, OUR DEEPEST CONDOLENCES. WHAT ARE YOUR FEELINGS ABOUT SPEEDBALL TEACHING YOUNG SUPERHUMANS?

I THINK IT'S APPALLING. A SLAP IN THE FACE TO THOSE OF US WHO LOST LOVED ONES.

I REALIZE *NORMAN OSBORN* USED THE REGISTRATION ACT TO COMMIT CRIMES, AND HE WAS PROPERLY JAILED FOR IT. BUT REPEALING THE ACT WAS THROWING THE BABY OUT WITH THE BATHWATER.

NOW *IRON MAN*, WHO CLAIMED TO FAVOR ACCOUNTABILITY FOR SUPERHUMANS, HAS FORGOTTEN HIS PROMISE.

HE AND STEVE ROGERS ARE THE BEST OF FRIENDS AGAIN.

EVERYTHING'S BACK TO THE WAY IT WAS FOR THEM. LIKE NOTHING EVER HAPPENED.

WELL, MY SON IS STILL DEAD.

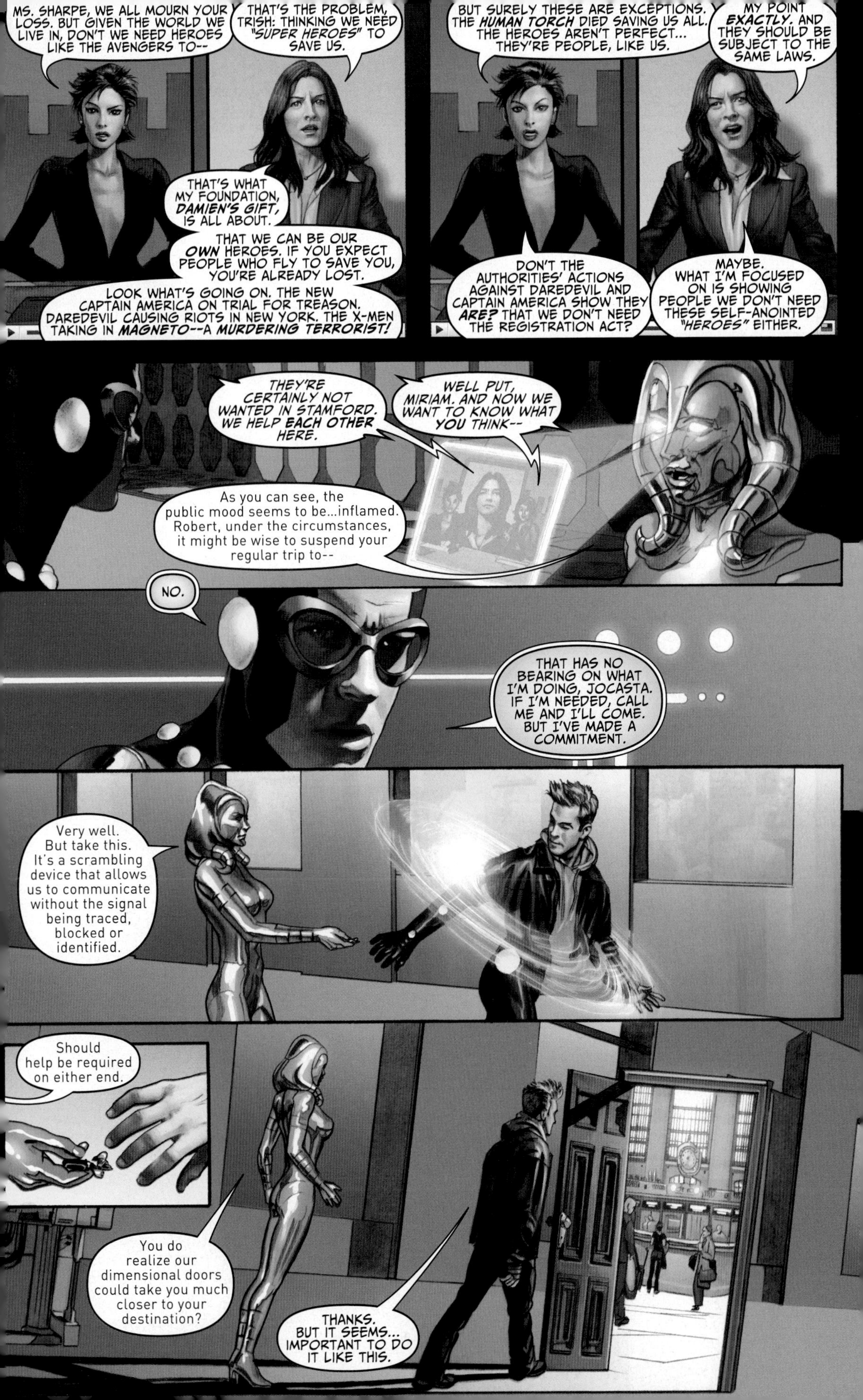
MS. SHARPE, WE ALL MOURN YOUR LOSS. BUT GIVEN THE WORLD WE LIVE IN, DON'T WE NEED HEROES LIKE THE AVENGERS TO--
THAT'S THE PROBLEM, TRISH: THINKING WE NEED "SUPER HEROES" TO SAVE US.
THAT'S WHAT MY FOUNDATION, DAMIEN'S GIFT, IS ALL ABOUT.
THAT WE CAN BE OUR OWN HEROES. IF YOU EXPECT PEOPLE WHO FLY TO SAVE YOU, YOU'RE ALREADY LOST.
LOOK WHAT'S GOING ON. THE NEW CAPTAIN AMERICA ON TRIAL FOR TREASON. DAREDEVIL CAUSING RIOTS IN NEW YORK. THE X-MEN TAKING IN MAGNETO--A MURDERING TERRORIST!
BUT SURELY THESE ARE EXCEPTIONS. THE HUMAN TORCH DIED SAVING US ALL. THE HEROES AREN'T PERFECT... THEY'RE PEOPLE, LIKE US.
MY POINT EXACTLY. AND THEY SHOULD BE SUBJECT TO THE SAME LAWS.
DON'T THE AUTHORITIES' ACTIONS AGAINST DAREDEVIL AND CAPTAIN AMERICA SHOW THEY ARE? THAT WE DON'T NEED THE REGISTRATION ACT?
MAYBE. WHAT I'M FOCUSED ON IS SHOWING PEOPLE WE DON'T NEED THESE SELF-ANOINTED "HEROES" EITHER.
THEY'RE CERTAINLY NOT WANTED IN STAMFORD. WE HELP EACH OTHER HERE.
WELL PUT, MIRIAM. AND NOW WE WANT TO KNOW WHAT YOU THINK--
As you can see, the public mood seems to be...inflamed. Robert, under the circumstances, it might be wise to suspend your regular trip to--
NO.
THAT HAS NO BEARING ON WHAT I'M DOING, JOCASTA. IF I'M NEEDED, CALL ME AND I'LL COME. BUT I'VE MADE A COMMITMENT.
Very well. But take this. It's a scrambling device that allows us to communicate without the signal being traced, blocked or identified.
Should help be required on either end.
You do realize our dimensional doors could take you much closer to your destination?
THANKS. BUT IT SEEMS... IMPORTANT TO DO IT LIKE THIS.

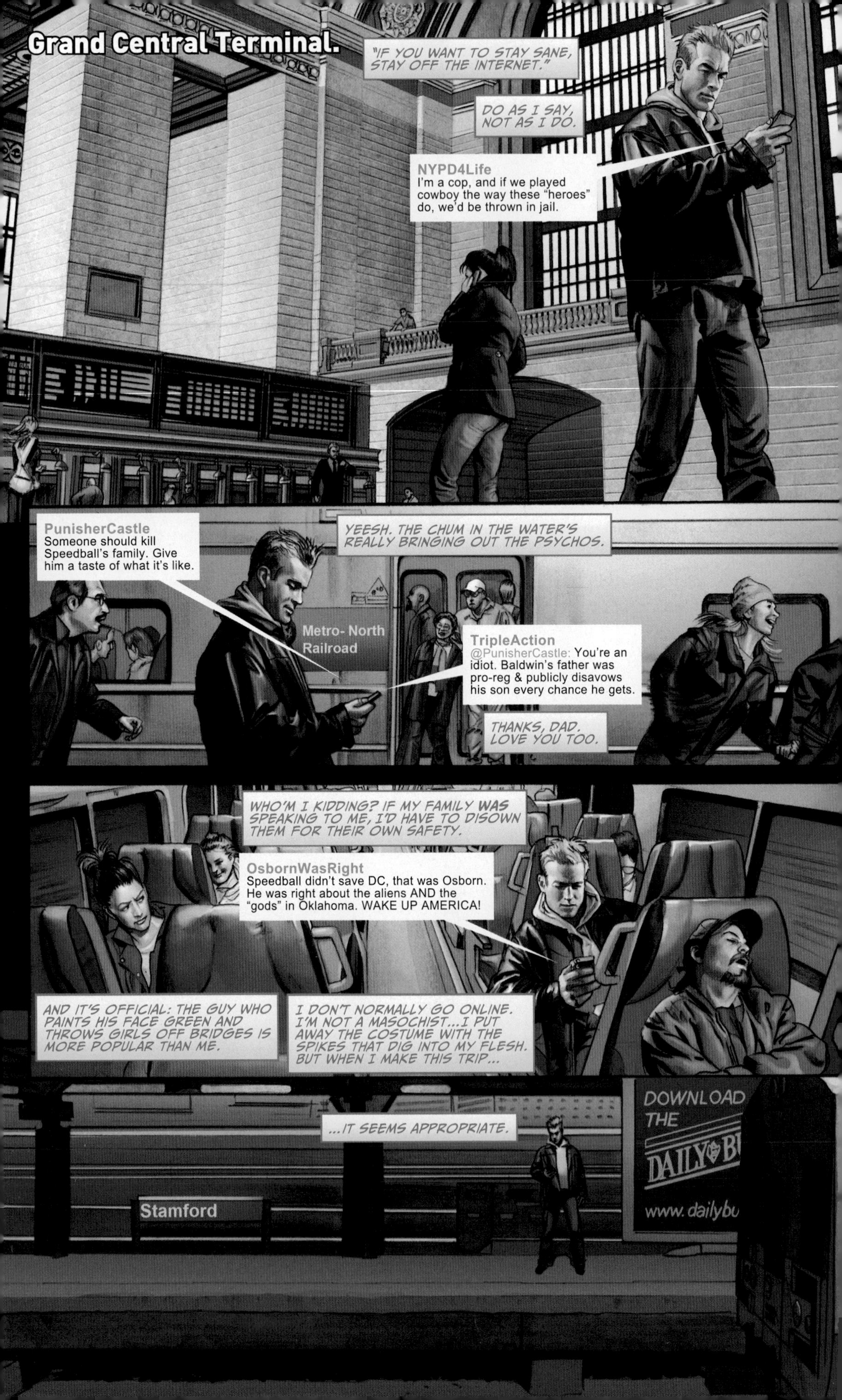
Grand Central Terminal.
"IF YOU WANT TO STAY SANE, STAY OFF THE INTERNET."
DO AS I SAY, NOT AS I DO.
NYPD4Life
I'm a cop, and if we played cowboy the way these "heroes" do, we'd be thrown in jail.
PunisherCastle
Someone should kill Speedball's family. Give him a taste of what it's like.
YEESH. THE CHUM IN THE WATER'S REALLY BRINGING OUT THE PSYCHOS.
Metro- North Railroad
TripleAction
@PunisherCastle: You're an idiot. Baldwin's father was pro-reg & publicly disavows his son every chance he gets.
THANKS, DAD. LOVE YOU TOO.
WHO'M I KIDDING? IF MY FAMILY WAS SPEAKING TO ME, I'D HAVE TO DISOWN THEM FOR THEIR OWN SAFETY.
OsbornWasRight
Speedball didn't save DC, that was Osborn. He was right about the aliens AND the "gods" in Oklahoma. WAKE UP AMERICA!
AND IT'S OFFICIAL: THE GUY WHO PAINTS HIS FACE GREEN AND THROWS GIRLS OFF BRIDGES IS MORE POPULAR THAN ME.
I DON'T NORMALLY GO ONLINE. I'M NOT A MASOCHIST...I PUT AWAY THE COSTUME WITH THE SPIKES THAT DIG INTO MY FLESH. BUT WHEN I MAKE THIS TRIP...
...IT SEEMS APPROPRIATE.
DOWNLOAD THE
Stamford
www. dailybu

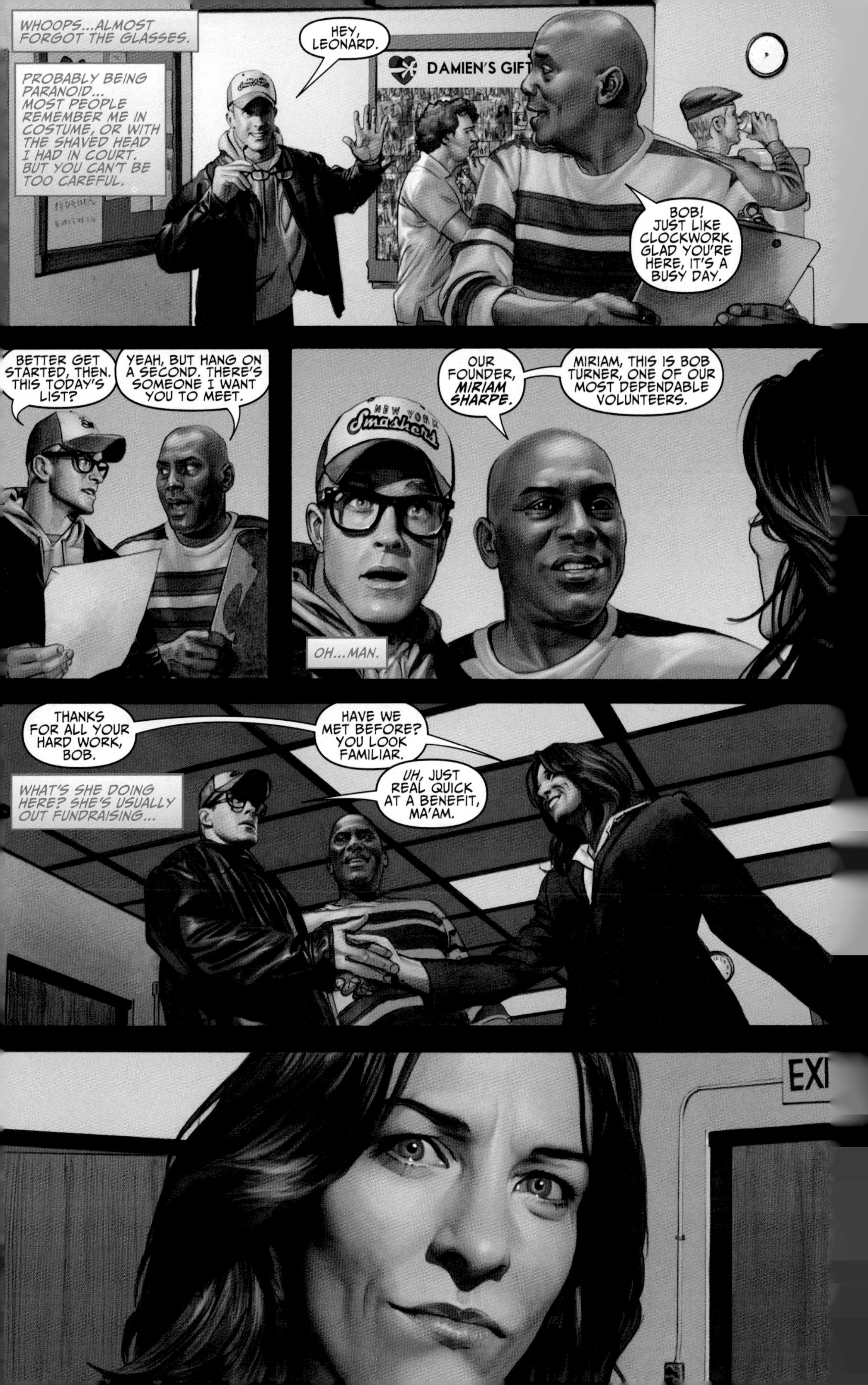
WHOOPS...ALMOST FORGOT THE GLASSES.
PROBABLY BEING PARANOID... MOST PEOPLE REMEMBER ME IN COSTUME, OR WITH THE SHAVED HEAD I HAD IN COURT. BUT YOU CAN'T BE TOO CAREFUL.
HEY, LEONARD.
DAMIEN'S GIFT
BOB! JUST LIKE CLOCKWORK. GLAD YOU'RE HERE, IT'S A BUSY DAY.
BETTER GET STARTED, THEN. THIS TODAY'S LIST?
YEAH, BUT HANG ON A SECOND. THERE'S SOMEONE I WANT YOU TO MEET.
OUR FOUNDER, MIRIAM SHARPE.
MIRIAM, THIS IS BOB TURNER, ONE OF OUR MOST DEPENDABLE VOLUNTEERS.
NEW YORK Smashers
OH...MAN.
THANKS FOR ALL YOUR HARD WORK, BOB.
HAVE WE MET BEFORE? YOU LOOK FAMILIAR.
WHAT'S SHE DOING HERE? SHE'S USUALLY OUT FUNDRAISING...
UH, JUST REAL QUICK AT A BENEFIT, MA'AM.
EXI

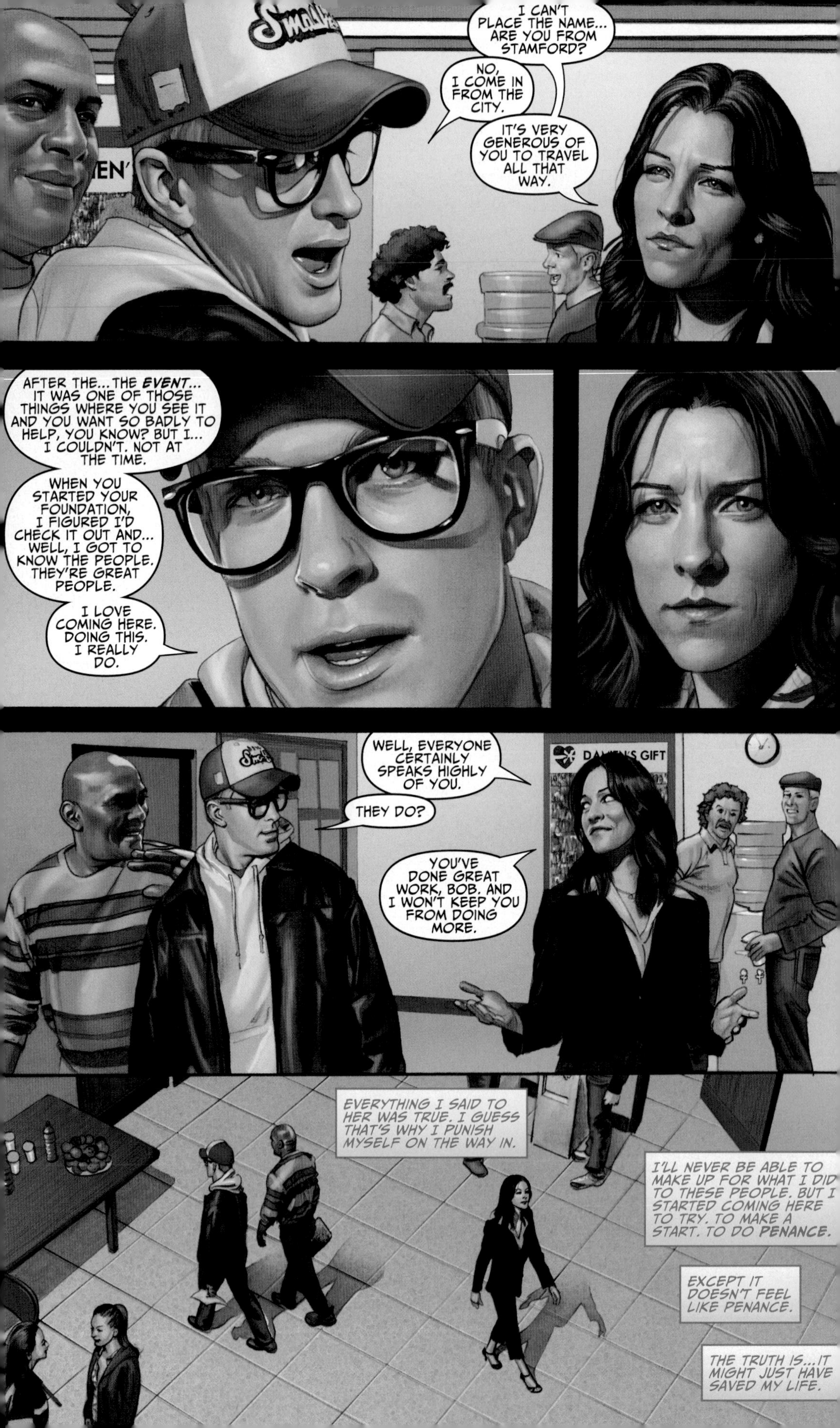
I CAN'T PLACE THE NAME... ARE YOU FROM STAMFORD?
NO, I COME IN FROM THE CITY.
IT'S VERY GENEROUS OF YOU TO TRAVEL ALL THAT WAY.
AFTER THE...THE *EVENT*... IT WAS ONE OF THOSE THINGS WHERE YOU SEE IT AND YOU WANT SO BADLY TO HELP, YOU KNOW? BUT I... I COULDN'T. NOT AT THE TIME.
WHEN YOU STARTED YOUR FOUNDATION, I FIGURED I'D CHECK IT OUT AND... WELL, I GOT TO KNOW THE PEOPLE. THEY'RE GREAT PEOPLE.
I LOVE COMING HERE. DOING THIS. I REALLY DO.
WELL, EVERYONE CERTAINLY SPEAKS HIGHLY OF YOU.
THEY DO?
YOU'VE DONE GREAT WORK, BOB. AND I WON'T KEEP YOU FROM DOING MORE.
EVERYTHING I SAID TO HER WAS TRUE. I GUESS THAT'S WHY I PUNISH MYSELF ON THE WAY IN.
I'LL NEVER BE ABLE TO MAKE UP FOR WHAT I DID TO THESE PEOPLE. BUT I STARTED COMING HERE TO TRY. TO MAKE A START. TO DO **PENANCE**.
EXCEPT IT DOESN'T FEEL LIKE PENANCE.
THE TRUTH IS...IT MIGHT JUST HAVE SAVED MY LIFE.

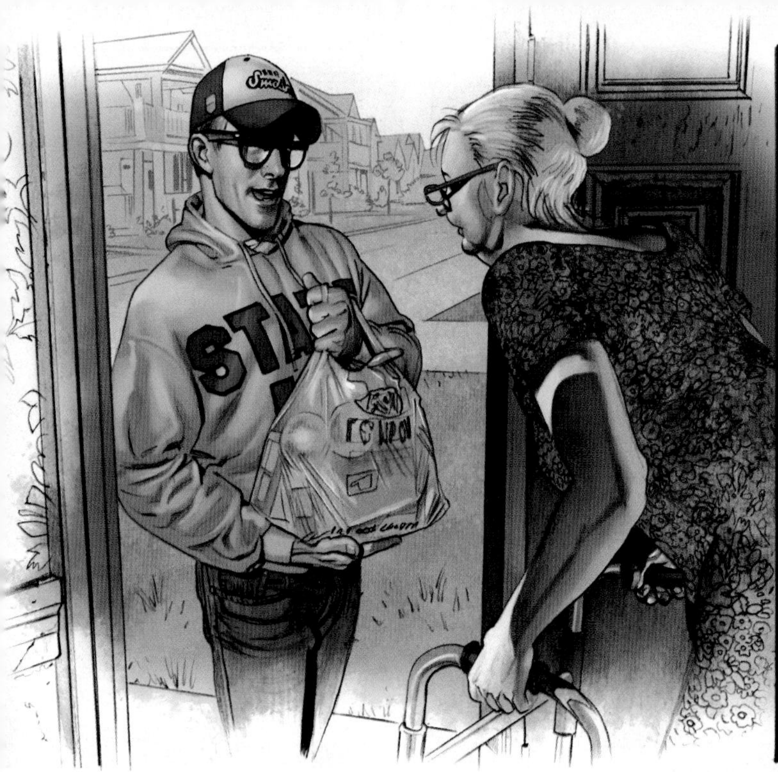

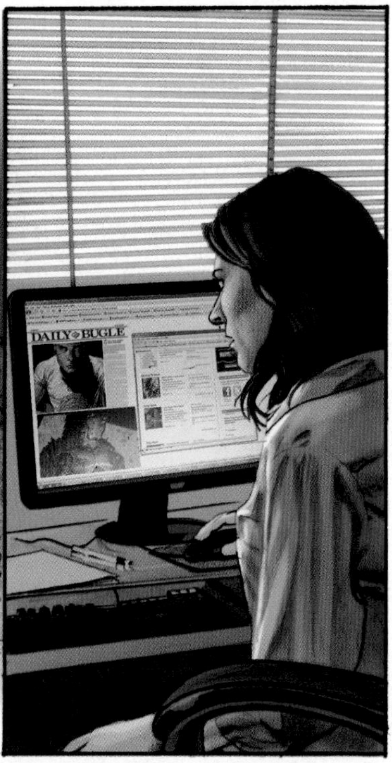
DAILY BUGLE

THESOAPBOX.COM

MANHATTAN RIOT RULE, NOT EXCEPTION

Yesterday's riot in Manhattan has tongues wagging because Steve Rogers, our nation's living legend, was hit with a brick. Some are shocked the original Captain America couldn't calm the crowd. But anyone who pays attention to world politics shouldn't be surprised. Riots are the new normal. Austerity measures in Greece, food price inflation in Algeria, uprisings in the Middle East...these are frightening times. And making it worse is the fact that, in our wired world, the fear and anger feed off each other regardless of geographic distance. Now, more than ever, violence begets violence. MORE...

THE HINDSIGHT REPORT

ASGARDIANS ABANDON EARTH?

Reports are coming out of Oklahoma that the Asgardian "gods," whose number include the Avenger known as Thor, have left Earth. No statements were made or reasons given. If true, the timing is highly unusual, as it immediately follows an announcement by the Avengers that Tony Stark's company, Stark Resilient, will rebuild the Asgardians' home in Broxton. What could make an entire city of godlike beings run like scared rabbits? And why won't they tell us? CONT.

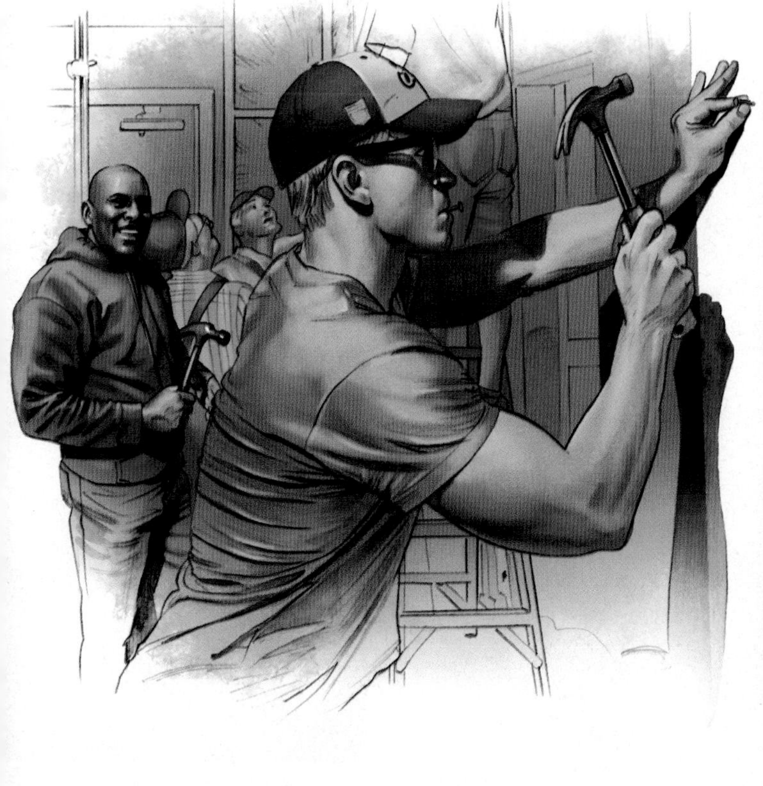

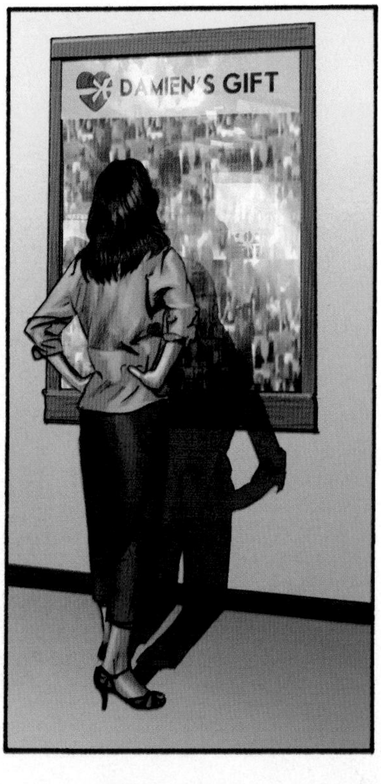
DAMIEN'S GIFT

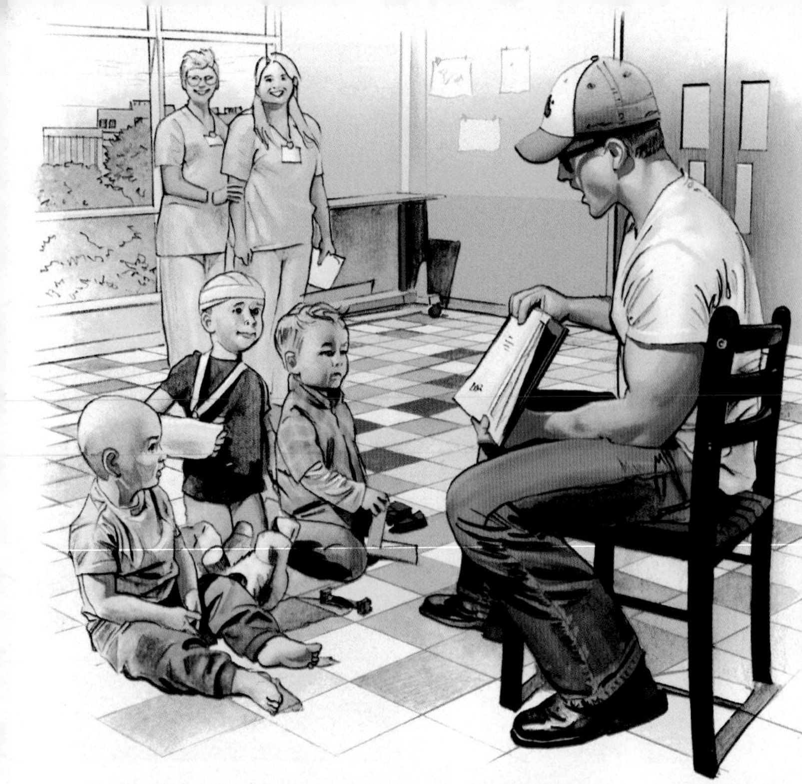

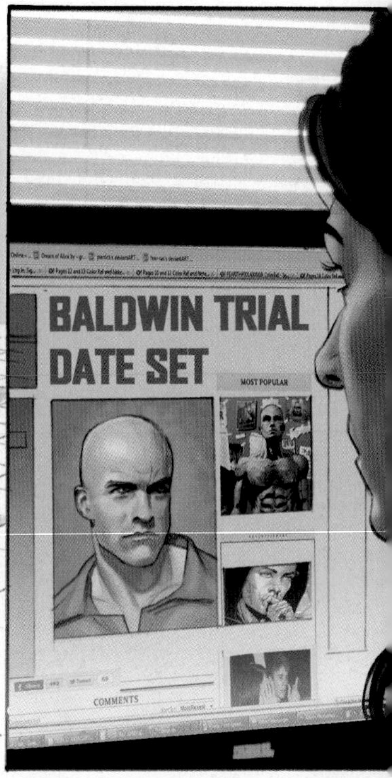
BALDWIN TRIAL DATE SET
MOST POPULAR
COMMENTS

BLACK-HELICOPTER.COM

THIRD MASS SUICIDE TODAY

Local news outlets in Nevada are reporting the suicide of six members of the Ascendant Light commune. What the Mainstream Media is choosing to ignore is that this is the third such incident IN THE SAME DAY, at roughly THE SAME TIME. Because these are small-scale suicides, not on the level of Heaven's Gate or Jonestown, they're being dismissed by authorities as coincidence, or prearranged copycat behavior. But anyone with any sense knows these groups had nothing to do with each other, and I don't have to tell you my feelings on coincidence. So the question I pose to you, my vigilant readers, is: what did these people know that we don't?

THE DAILY BUGLE ONLINE

LIGHTS IN SKY PANIC MILLIONS

Astronomers have no explanation as yet for seven fiery streaks of light that originated in outer space and appear to have struck Earth. "The descent was too controlled to be meteors," said Dr. Gruenwald, director of Project P.E.G.A.S.U.S. "Of course, the immediate concern is another alien invasion, but the proper authorities are investigating, and until we know more, we mustn't jump to conclusions." Nevertheless, widespread panic has affected...

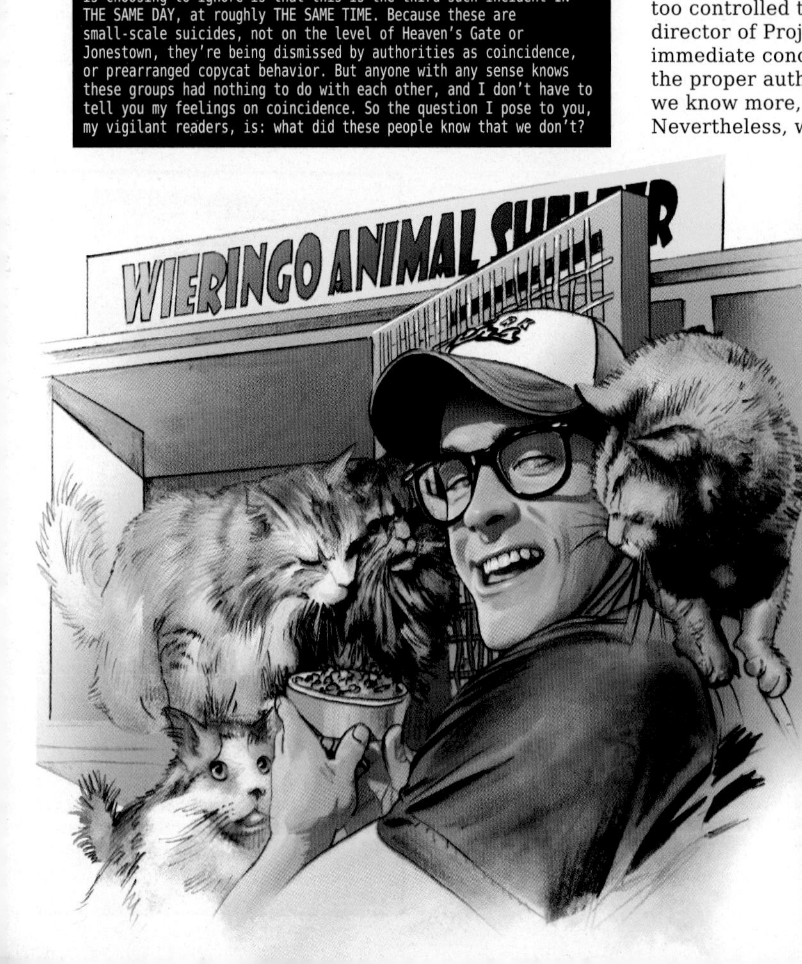
WIERINGO ANIMAL

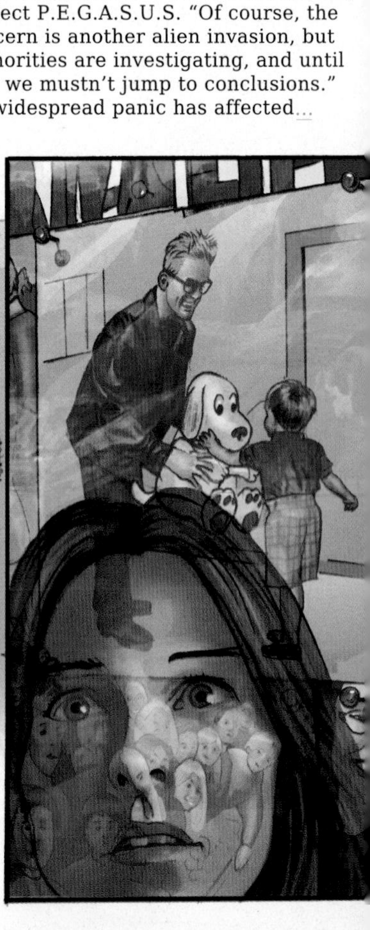

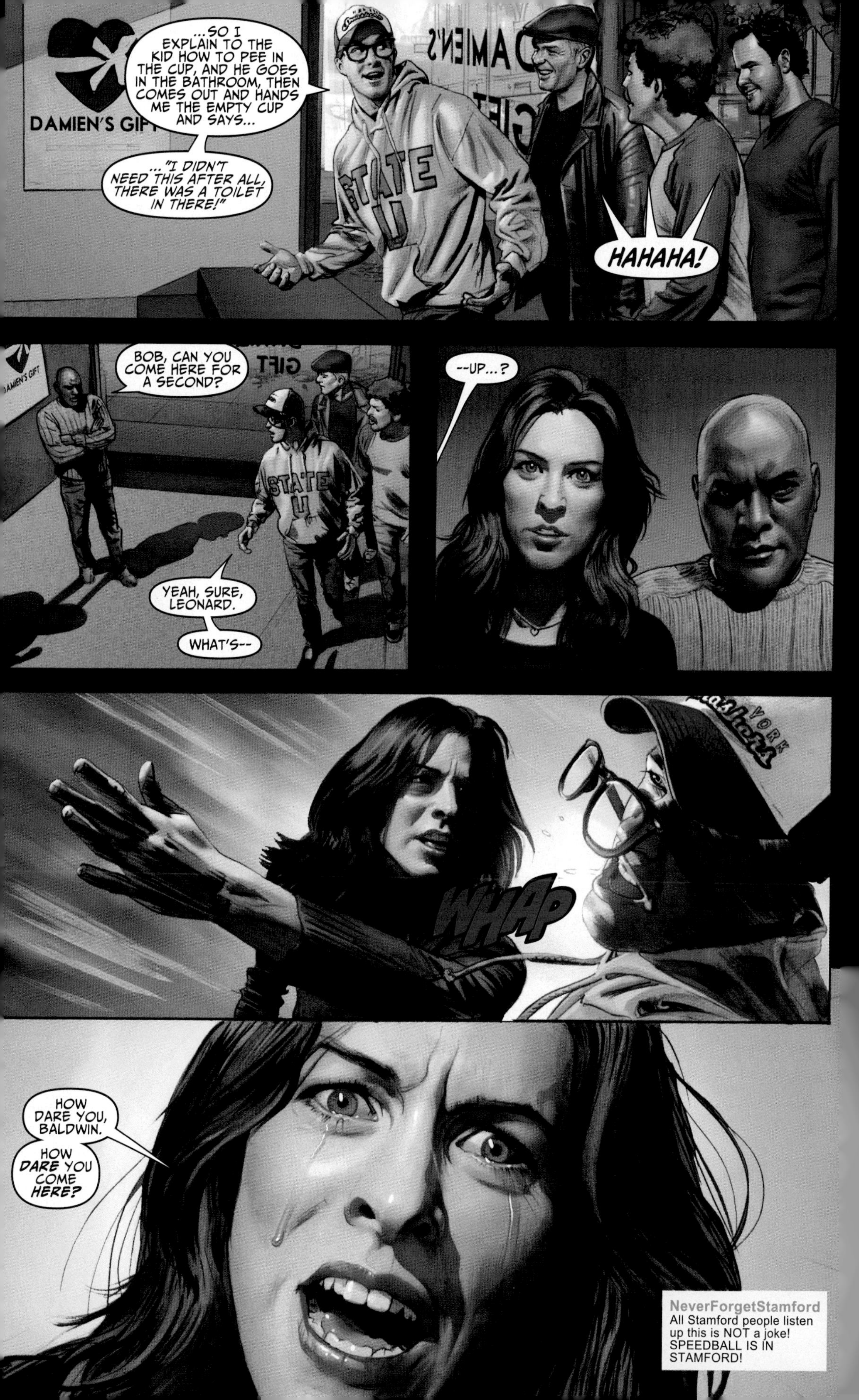

DAMIEN'S GIFT
...SO I EXPLAIN TO THE KID HOW TO PEE IN THE CUP, AND HE GOES IN THE BATHROOM, THEN COMES OUT AND HANDS ME THE EMPTY CUP AND SAYS...
..."I DIDN'T NEED THIS AFTER ALL, THERE WAS A TOILET IN THERE!"
HAHAHA!
BOB, CAN YOU COME HERE FOR A SECOND?
YEAH, SURE, LEONARD.
WHAT'S--
--UP...?
WHAP
HOW DARE YOU, BALDWIN.
HOW *DARE* YOU COME *HERE?*
NeverForgetStamford
All Stamford people listen up this is NOT a joke! SPEEDBALL IS IN STAMFORD!

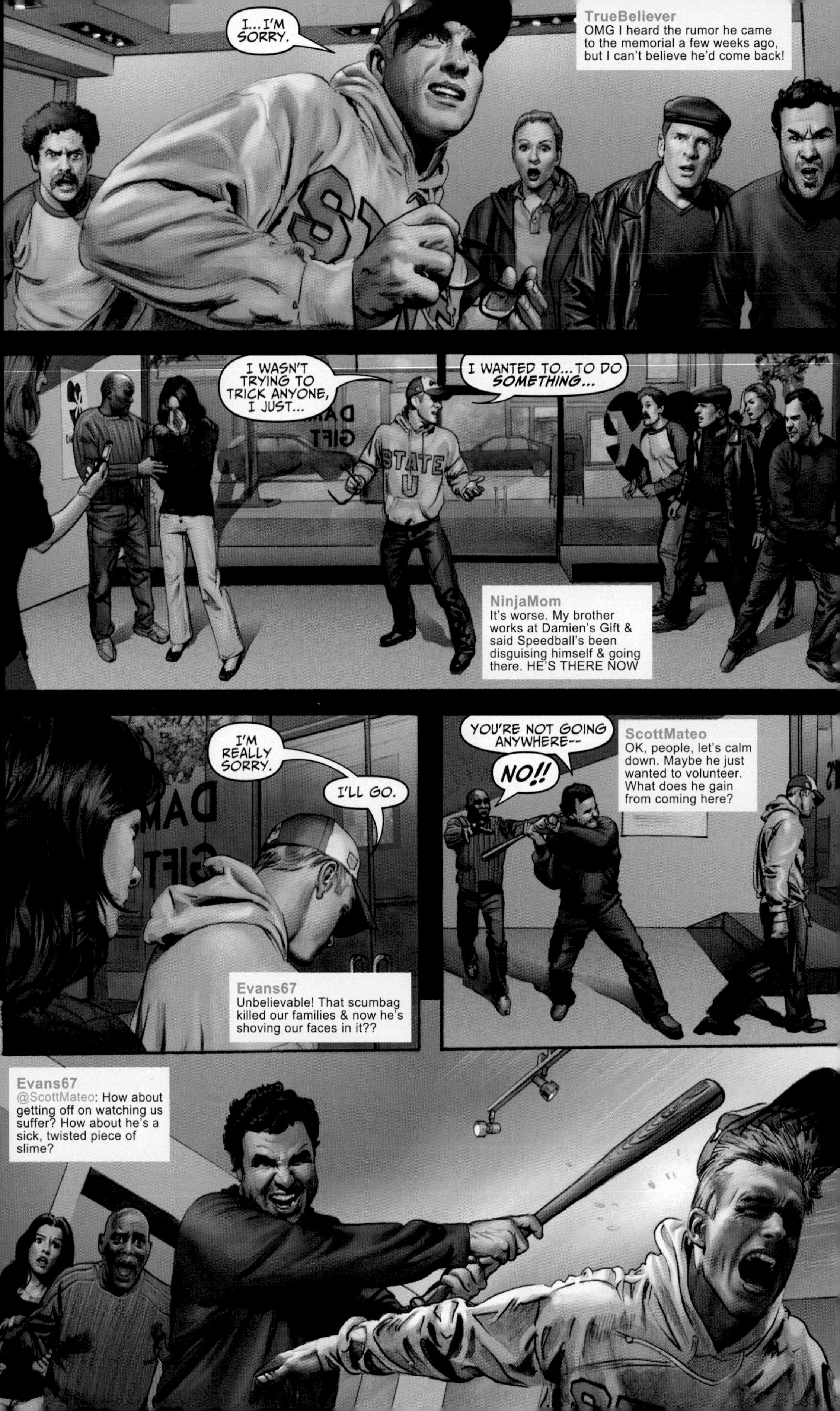
I...I'M SORRY.
TrueBeliever
OMG I heard the rumor he came to the memorial a few weeks ago, but I can't believe he'd come back!
I WASN'T TRYING TO TRICK ANYONE, I JUST...
I WANTED TO...TO DO SOMETHING...
NinjaMom
It's worse. My brother works at Damien's Gift & said Speedball's been disguising himself & going there. HE'S THERE NOW
I'M REALLY SORRY.
I'LL GO.
Evans67
Unbelievable! That scumbag killed our families & now he's shoving our faces in it??
YOU'RE NOT GOING ANYWHERE--
NO!!
ScottMateo
OK, people, let's calm down. Maybe he just wanted to volunteer. What does he gain from coming here?
Evans67
@ScottMateo: How about getting off on watching us suffer? How about he's a sick, twisted piece of slime?

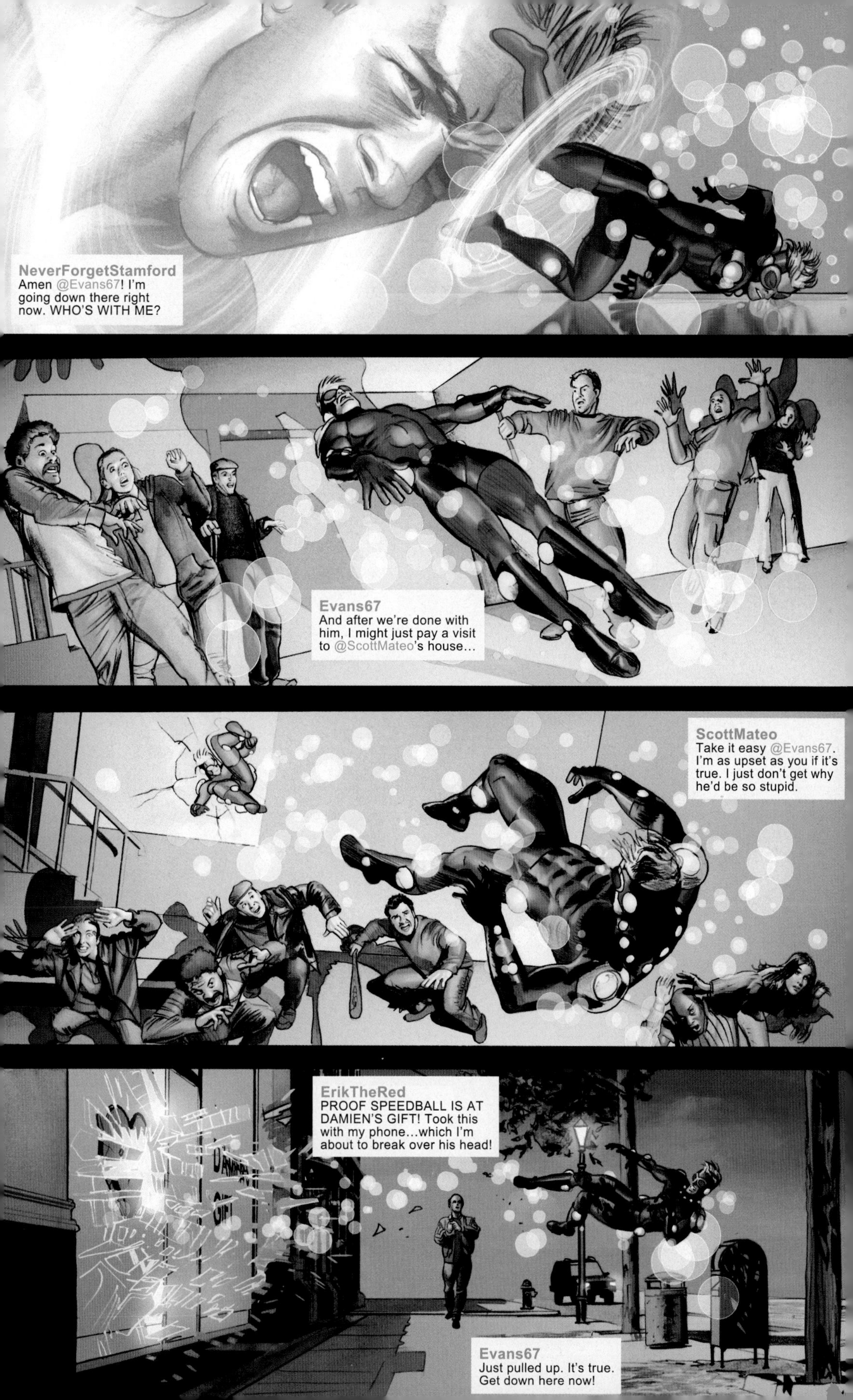
NeverForgetStamford
Amen @Evans67! I'm going down there right now. WHO'S WITH ME?
Evans67
And after we're done with him, I might just pay a visit to @ScottMateo's house...
ScottMateo
Take it easy @Evans67. I'm as upset as you if it's true. I just don't get why he'd be so stupid.
ErikTheRed
PROOF SPEEDBALL IS AT DAMIEN'S GIFT! Took this with my phone...which I'm about to break over his head!
Evans67
Just pulled up. It's true. Get down here now!

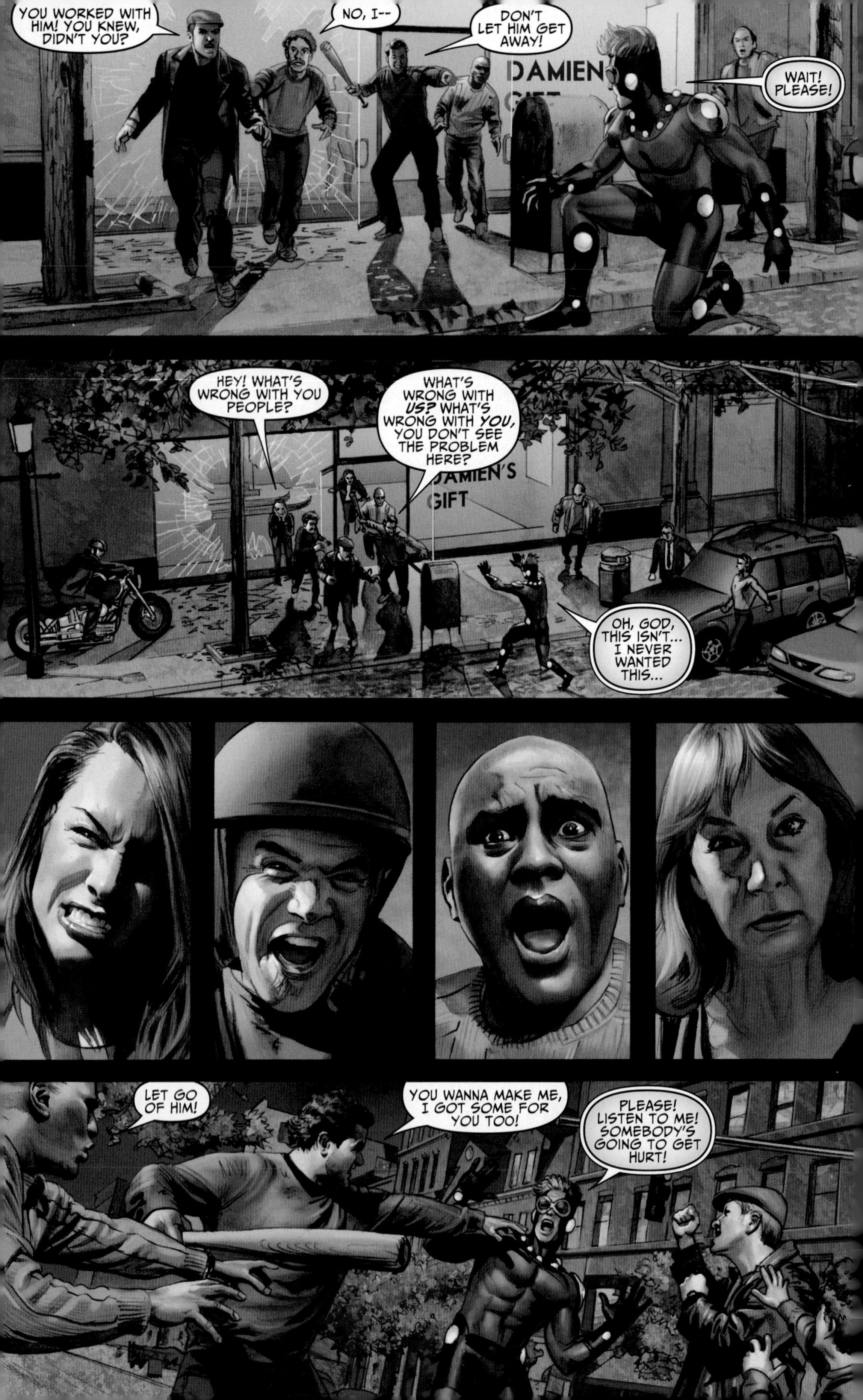
YOU WORKED WITH HIM! YOU KNEW, DIDN'T YOU?
NO, I--
DON'T LET HIM GET AWAY!
DAMIEN
WAIT! PLEASE!
HEY! WHAT'S WRONG WITH YOU PEOPLE?
WHAT'S WRONG WITH US? WHAT'S WRONG WITH YOU, YOU DON'T SEE THE PROBLEM HERE?
DAMIEN'S GIFT
OH, GOD, THIS ISN'T... I NEVER WANTED THIS...
LET GO OF HIM!
YOU WANNA MAKE ME, I GOT SOME FOR YOU TOO!
PLEASE! LISTEN TO ME! SOMEBODY'S GOING TO GET HURT!

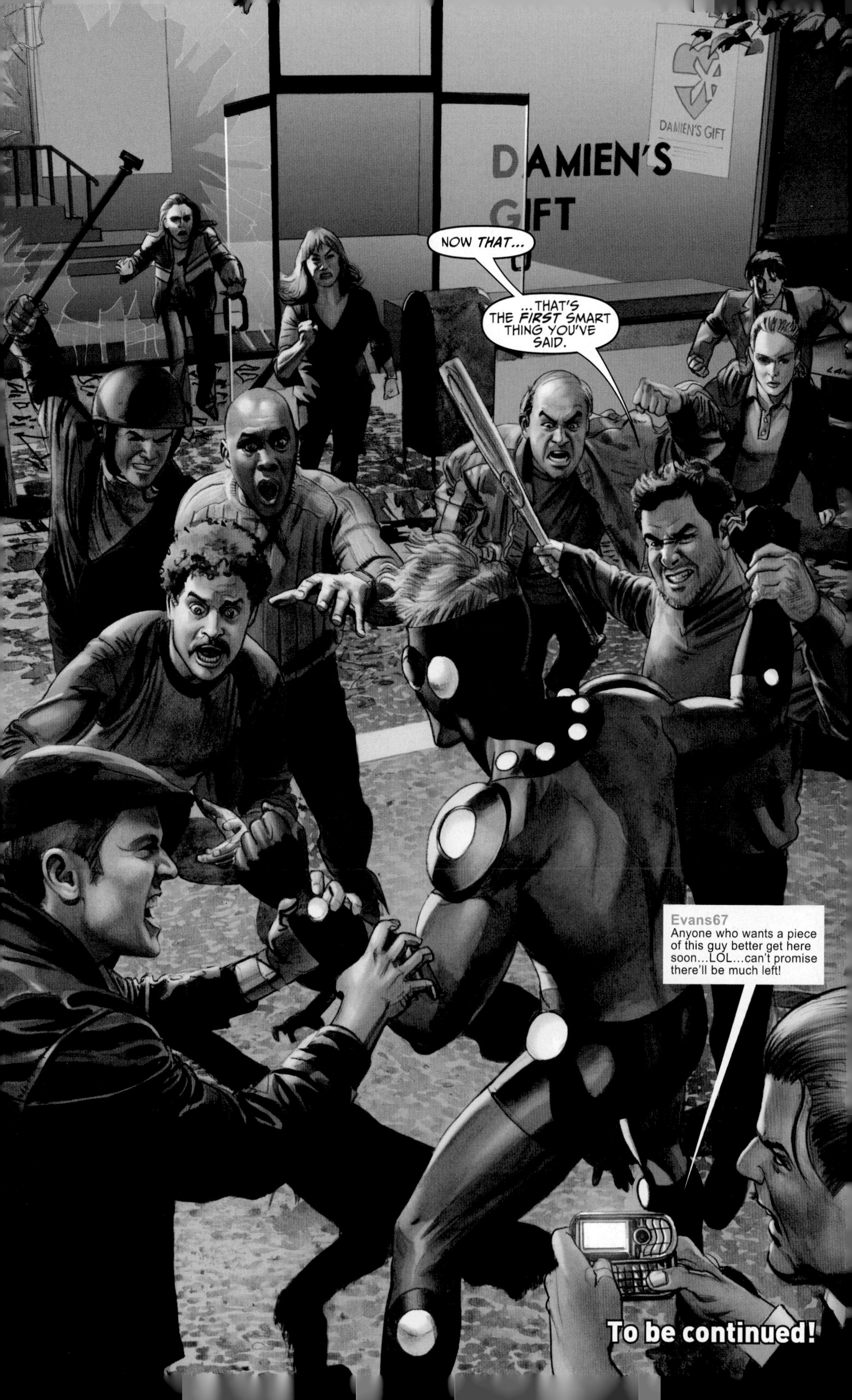
DAMIEN'S GIFT
DAMIEN'S
GIFT
NOW THAT...
...THAT'S THE FIRST SMART THING YOU'VE SAID.
Evans67
Anyone who wants a piece of this guy better get here soon...LOL...can't promise there'll be much left!
To be continued!

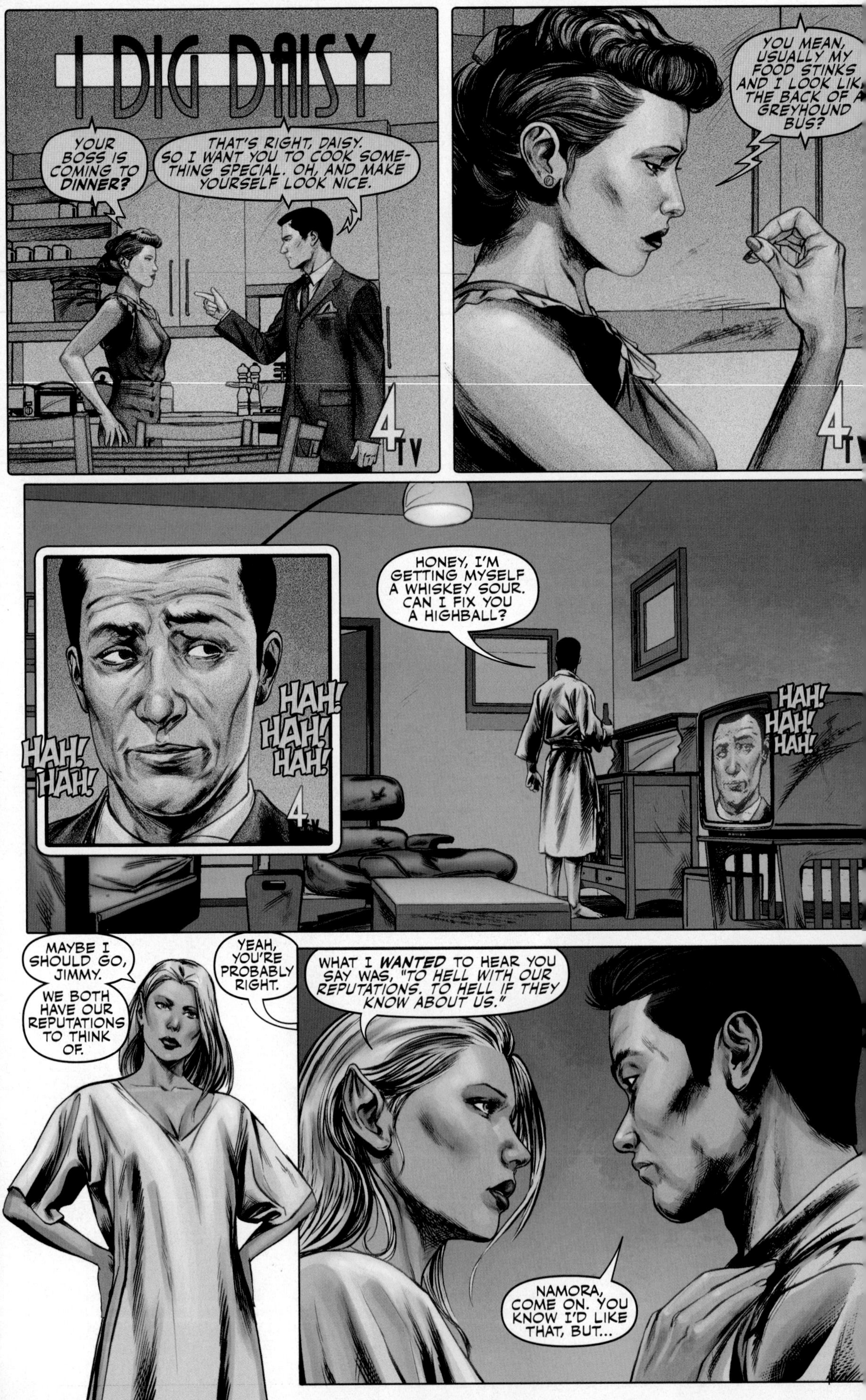
I DIG DAISY
YOUR BOSS IS COMING TO DINNER?
THAT'S RIGHT, DAISY. SO I WANT YOU TO COOK SOMETHING SPECIAL. OH, AND MAKE YOURSELF LOOK NICE.
4TV
YOU MEAN, USUALLY MY FOOD STINKS AND I LOOK LIKE THE BACK OF A GREYHOUND BUS?
4TV
HONEY, I'M GETTING MYSELF A WHISKEY SOUR. CAN I FIX YOU A HIGHBALL?
HAH! HAH!
HAH! HAH! HAH!
4TV
HAH! HAH! HAH!
MAYBE I SHOULD GO, JIMMY.
WE BOTH HAVE OUR REPUTATIONS TO THINK OF.
YEAH, YOU'RE PROBABLY RIGHT.
WHAT I WANTED TO HEAR YOU SAY WAS, "TO HELL WITH OUR REPUTATIONS. TO HELL IF THEY KNOW ABOUT US."
NAMORA, COME ON. YOU KNOW I'D LIKE THAT, BUT...

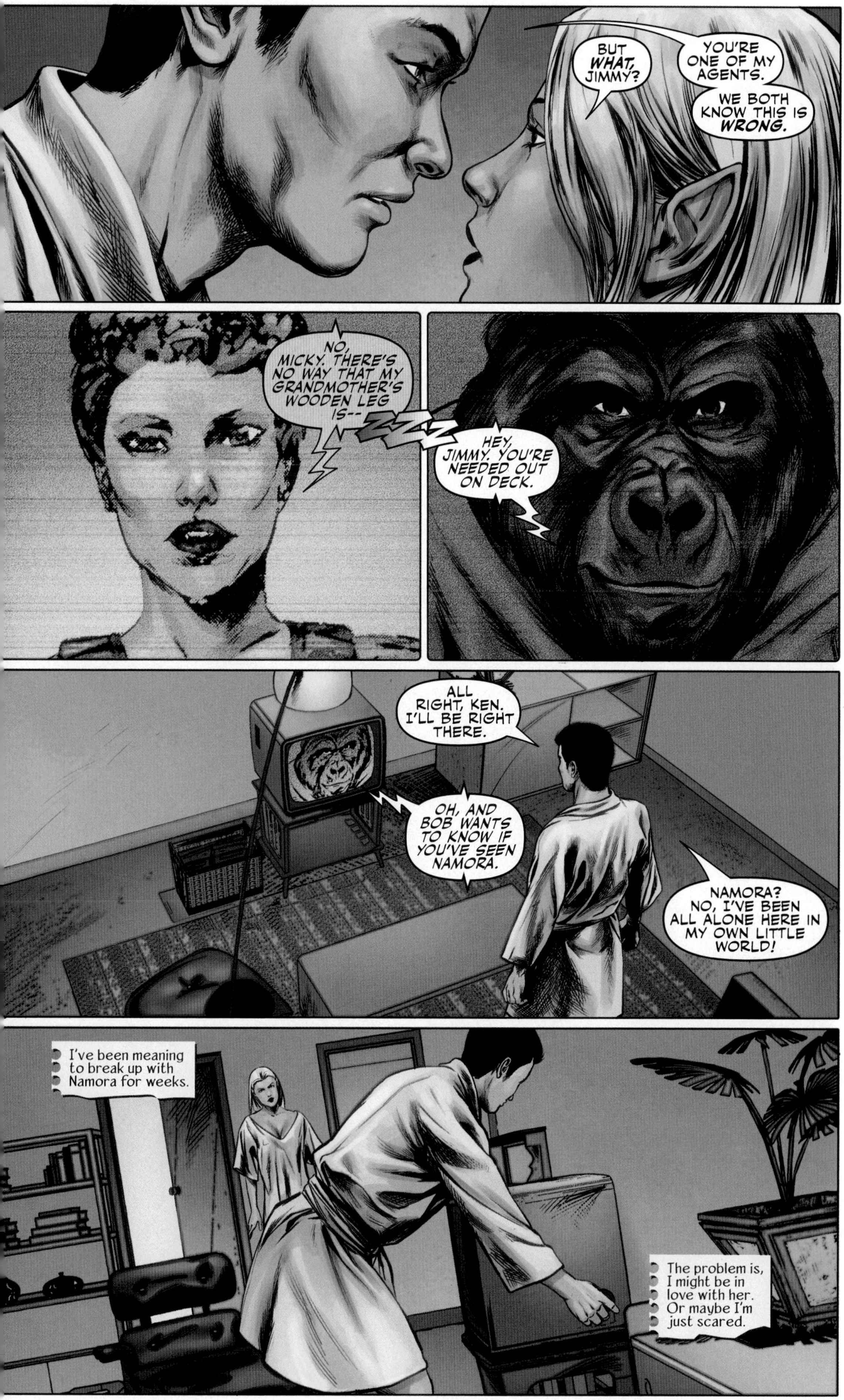
BUT WHAT, JIMMY?
YOU'RE ONE OF MY AGENTS.
WE BOTH KNOW THIS IS WRONG.
NO, MICKY. THERE'S NO WAY THAT MY GRANDMOTHER'S WOODEN LEG IS--
ZZZ
HEY, JIMMY. YOU'RE NEEDED OUT ON DECK.
ALL RIGHT, KEN. I'LL BE RIGHT THERE.
OH, AND BOB WANTS TO KNOW IF YOU'VE SEEN NAMORA.
NAMORA? NO, I'VE BEEN ALL ALONE HERE IN MY OWN LITTLE WORLD!
I've been meaning to break up with Namora for weeks.
The problem is, I might be in love with her. Or maybe I'm just scared.

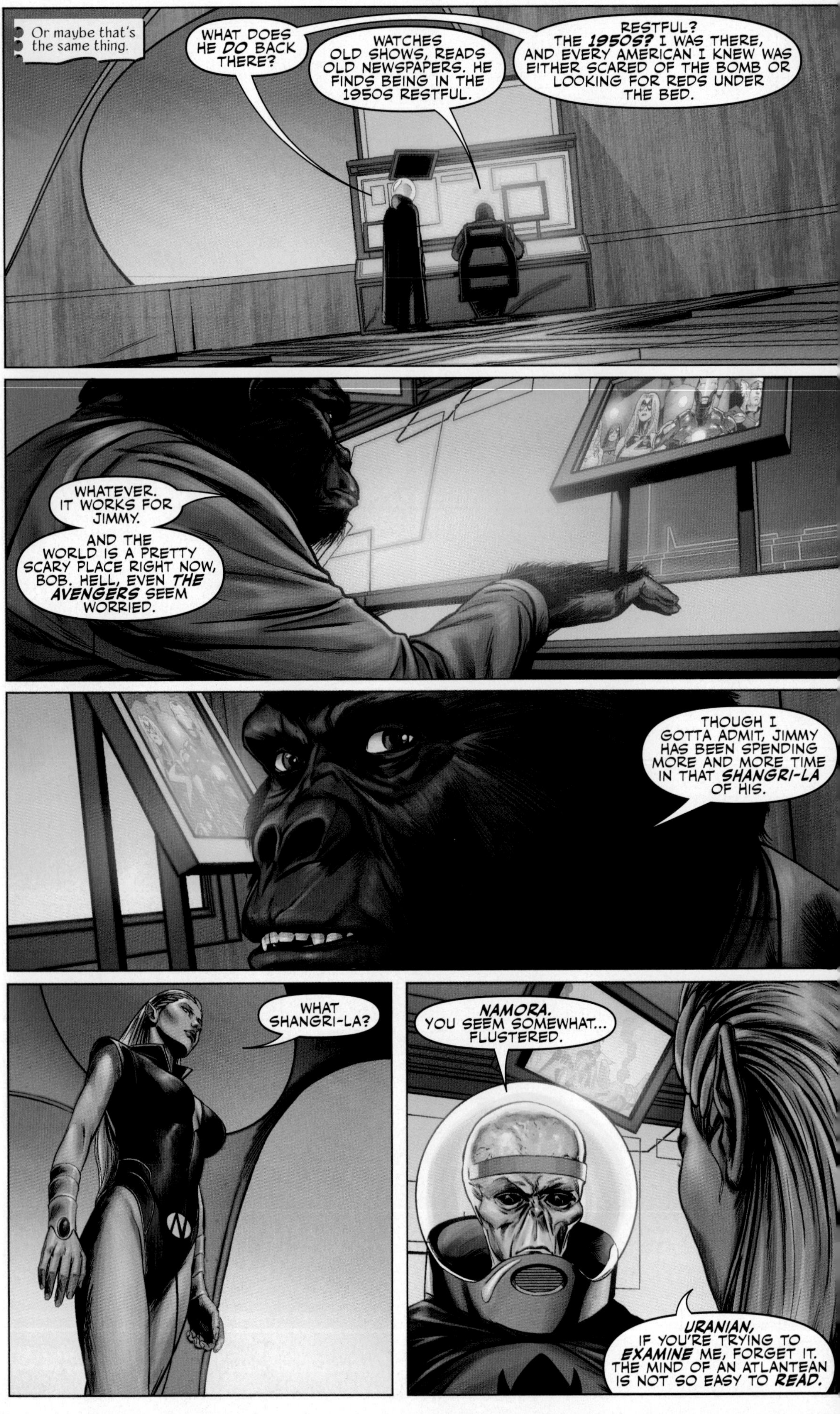
Or maybe that's the same thing.
WHAT DOES HE *DO* BACK THERE?
WATCHES OLD SHOWS, READS OLD NEWSPAPERS. HE FINDS BEING IN THE 1950S RESTFUL.
RESTFUL? THE *1950S?* I WAS THERE, AND EVERY AMERICAN I KNEW WAS EITHER SCARED OF THE BOMB OR LOOKING FOR REDS UNDER THE BED.
WHATEVER. IT WORKS FOR JIMMY.
AND THE WORLD IS A PRETTY SCARY PLACE RIGHT NOW, BOB. HELL, EVEN *THE AVENGERS* SEEM WORRIED.
THOUGH I GOTTA ADMIT, JIMMY HAS BEEN SPENDING MORE AND MORE TIME IN THAT *SHANGRI-LA* OF HIS.
WHAT SHANGRI-LA?
NAMORA. YOU SEEM SOMEWHAT... FLUSTERED.
URANIAN, IF YOU'RE TRYING TO *EXAMINE* ME, FORGET IT. THE MIND OF AN ATLANTEAN IS NOT SO EASY TO *READ.*

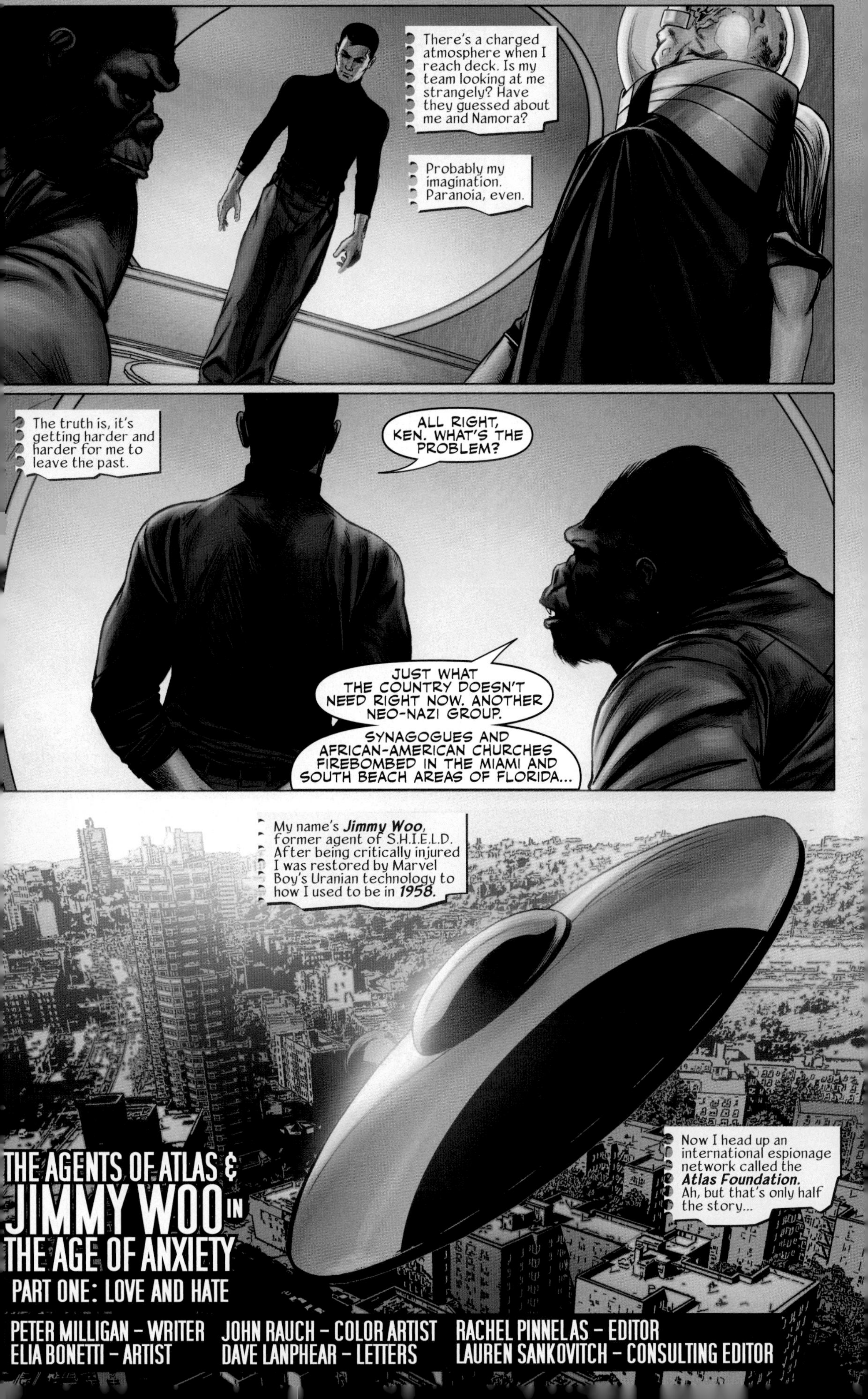
There's a charged atmosphere when I reach deck. Is my team looking at me strangely? Have they guessed about me and Namora?
Probably my imagination. Paranoia, even.
The truth is, it's getting harder and harder for me to leave the past.
ALL RIGHT, KEN. WHAT'S THE PROBLEM?
JUST WHAT THE COUNTRY DOESN'T NEED RIGHT NOW. ANOTHER NEO-NAZI GROUP.
SYNAGOGUES AND AFRICAN-AMERICAN CHURCHES FIREBOMBED IN THE MIAMI AND SOUTH BEACH AREAS OF FLORIDA...
My name's *Jimmy Woo*, former agent of S.H.I.E.L.D. After being critically injured I was restored by Marvel Boy's Uranian technology to how I used to be in *1958*.
Now I head up an international espionage network called the ***Atlas Foundation.*** Ah, but that's only half the story...
THE AGENTS OF ATLAS & JIMMY WOO IN THE AGE OF ANXIETY
PART ONE: LOVE AND HATE
PETER MILLIGAN - WRITER
ELIA BONETTI - ARTIST
JOHN RAUCH - COLOR ARTIST
DAVE LANPHEAR - LETTERS
RACHEL PINNELAS - EDITOR
LAUREN SANKOVITCH - CONSULTING EDITOR

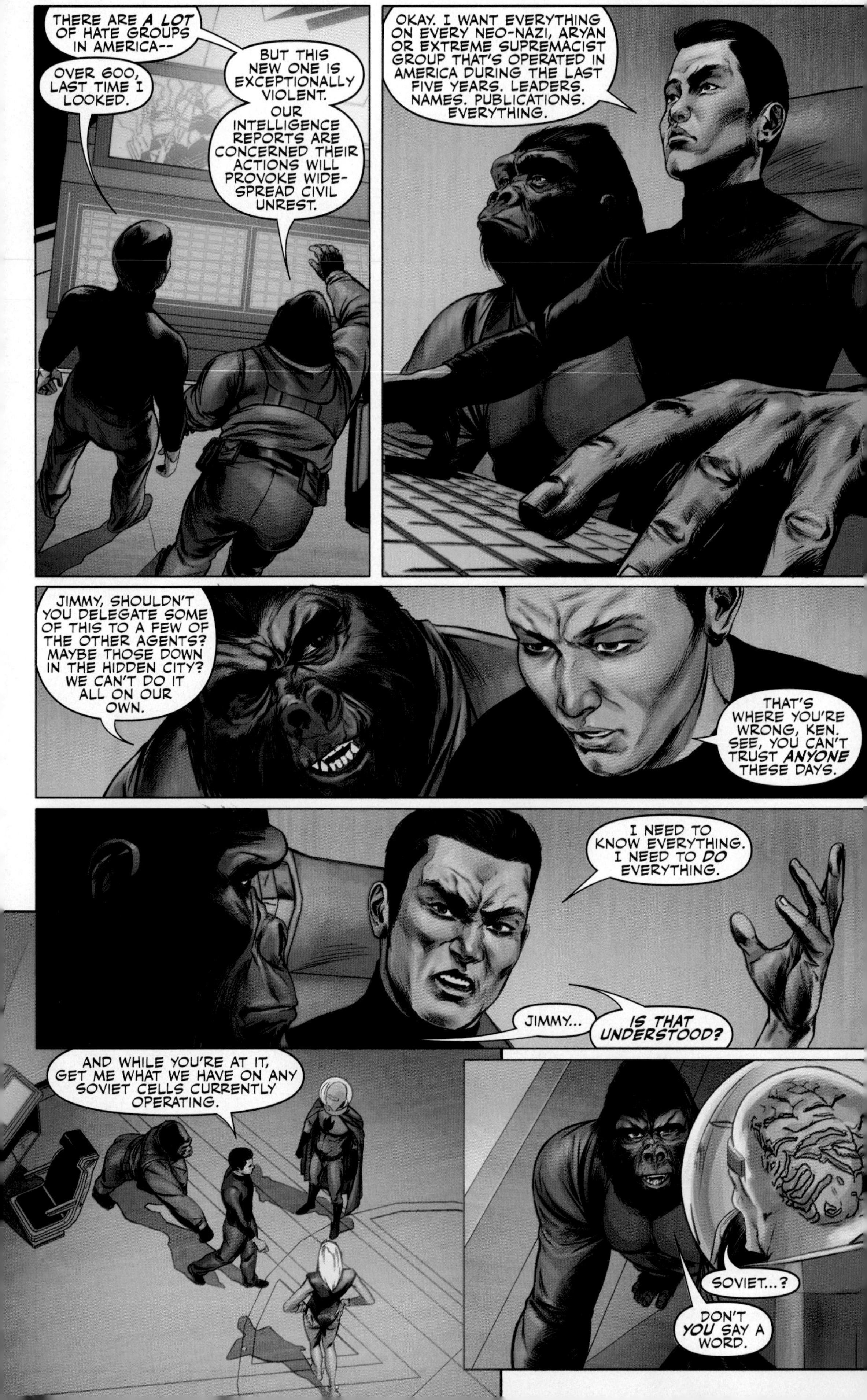
THERE ARE *A LOT* OF HATE GROUPS IN AMERICA--
OVER 600, LAST TIME I LOOKED.
BUT THIS NEW ONE IS EXCEPTIONALLY VIOLENT.
OUR INTELLIGENCE REPORTS ARE CONCERNED THEIR ACTIONS WILL PROVOKE WIDE-SPREAD CIVIL UNREST.
OKAY. I WANT EVERYTHING ON EVERY NEO-NAZI, ARYAN OR EXTREME SUPREMACIST GROUP THAT'S OPERATED IN AMERICA DURING THE LAST FIVE YEARS. LEADERS. NAMES. PUBLICATIONS. EVERYTHING.
JIMMY, SHOULDN'T YOU DELEGATE SOME OF THIS TO A FEW OF THE OTHER AGENTS? MAYBE THOSE DOWN IN THE HIDDEN CITY? WE CAN'T DO IT ALL ON OUR OWN.
THAT'S WHERE YOU'RE WRONG, KEN. SEE, YOU CAN'T TRUST *ANYONE* THESE DAYS.
I NEED TO KNOW EVERYTHING. I NEED TO *DO* EVERYTHING.
JIMMY...
IS THAT UNDERSTOOD?
AND WHILE YOU'RE AT IT, GET ME WHAT WE HAVE ON ANY SOVIET CELLS CURRENTLY OPERATING.
SOVIET...?
DON'T *YOU* SAY A WORD.

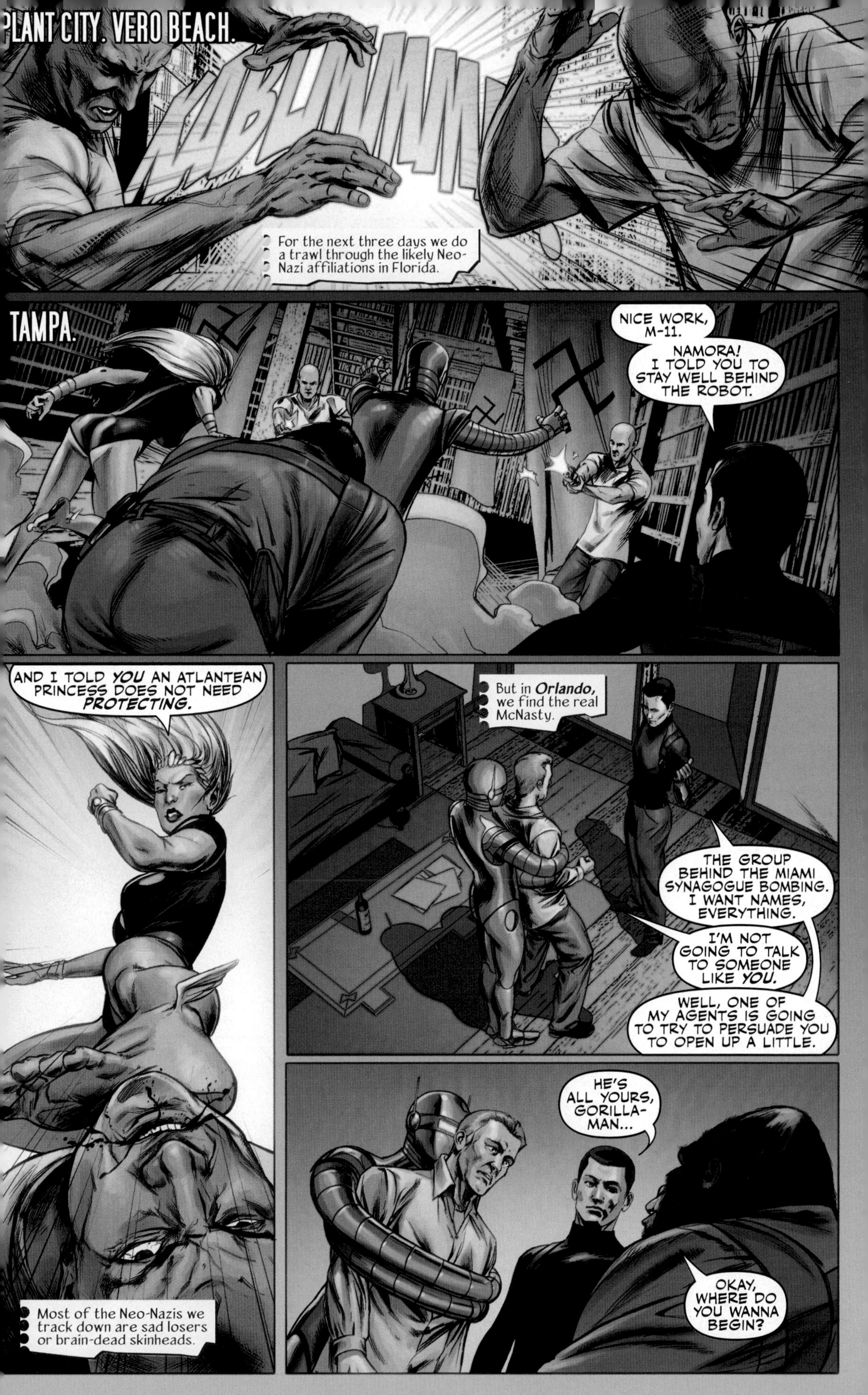
PLANT CITY. VERO BEACH.
KABUMMM
For the next three days we do a trawl through the likely Neo-Nazi affiliations in Florida.
TAMPA.
NICE WORK, M-11.
NAMORA! I TOLD YOU TO STAY WELL BEHIND THE ROBOT.
AND I TOLD YOU AN ATLANTEAN PRINCESS DOES NOT NEED PROTECTING.
Most of the Neo-Nazis we track down are sad losers or brain-dead skinheads.
But in Orlando, we find the real McNasty.
THE GROUP BEHIND THE MIAMI SYNAGOGUE BOMBING. I WANT NAMES, EVERYTHING.
I'M NOT GOING TO TALK TO SOMEONE LIKE YOU.
WELL, ONE OF MY AGENTS IS GOING TO TRY TO PERSUADE YOU TO OPEN UP A LITTLE.
HE'S ALL YOURS, GORILLA-MAN...
OKAY, WHERE DO YOU WANNA BEGIN?

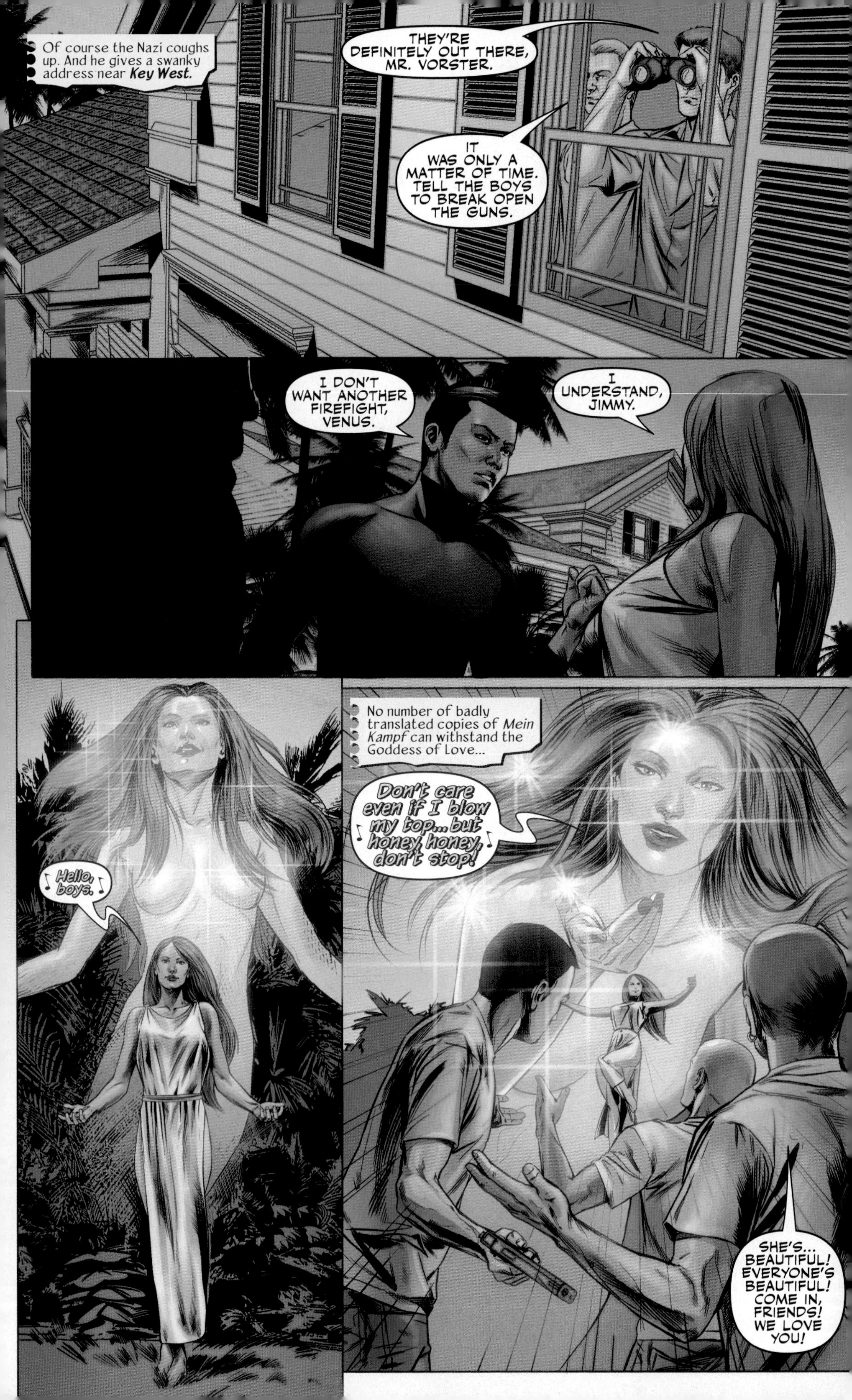
Of course the Nazi coughs up. And he gives a swanky address near Key West.
THEY'RE DEFINITELY OUT THERE, MR. VORSTER.
IT WAS ONLY A MATTER OF TIME. TELL THE BOYS TO BREAK OPEN THE GUNS.
I DON'T WANT ANOTHER FIREFIGHT, VENUS.
I UNDERSTAND, JIMMY.
Hello, boys.
No number of badly translated copies of Mein Kampf can withstand the Goddess of Love...
Don't care even if I blow my top... but honey, honey, don't stop!
SHE'S... BEAUTIFUL! EVERYONE'S BEAUTIFUL! COME IN, FRIENDS! WE LOVE YOU!

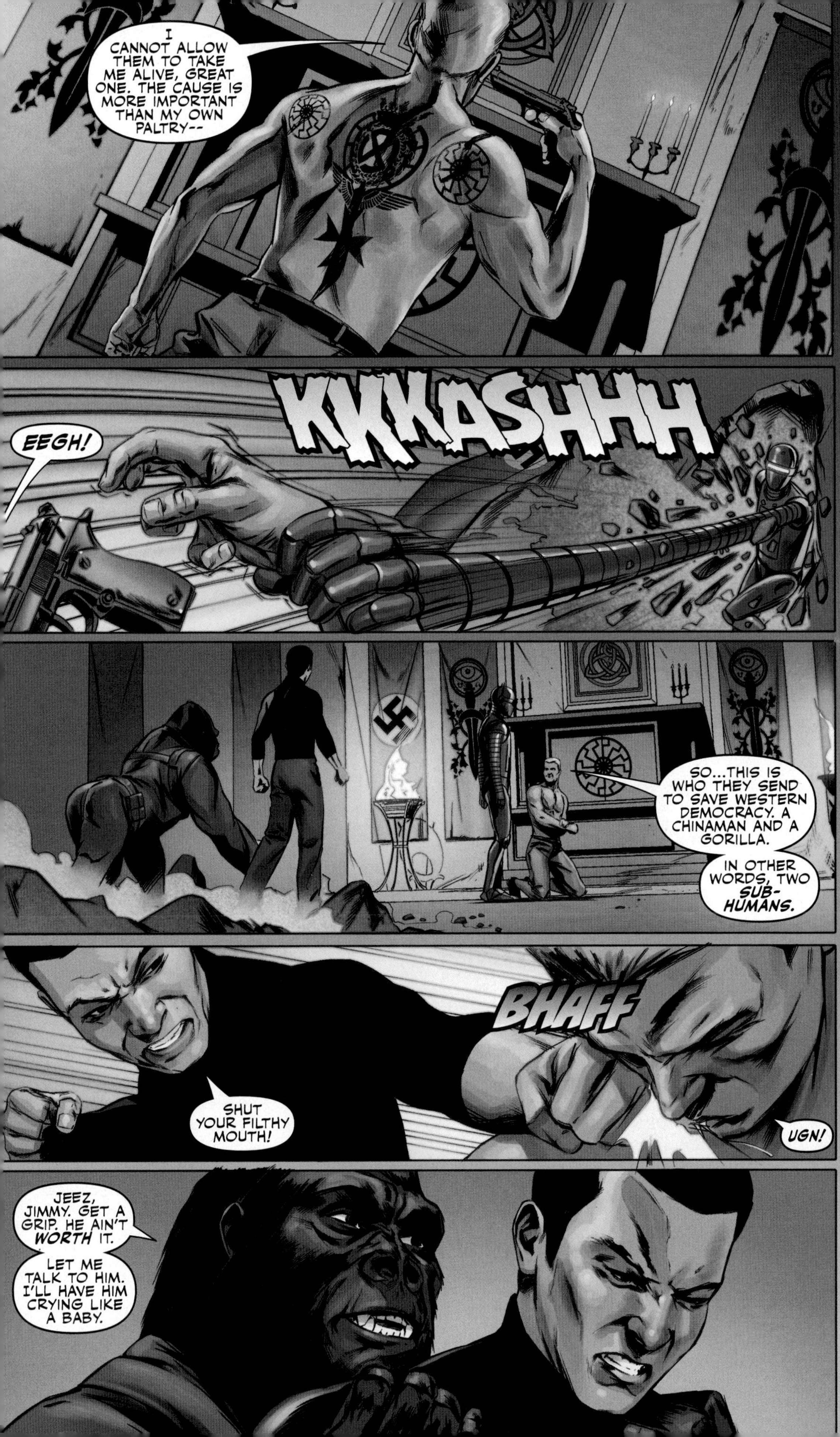
I CANNOT ALLOW THEM TO TAKE ME ALIVE, GREAT ONE. THE CAUSE IS MORE IMPORTANT THAN MY OWN PALTRY--
KKKASHHH
EEGH!
SO...THIS IS WHO THEY SEND TO SAVE WESTERN DEMOCRACY. A CHINAMAN AND A GORILLA.
IN OTHER WORDS, TWO SUB-HUMANS.
BHAFF
SHUT YOUR FILTHY MOUTH!
UGN!
JEEZ, JIMMY. GET A GRIP. HE AIN'T WORTH IT.
LET ME TALK TO HIM. I'LL HAVE HIM CRYING LIKE A BABY.

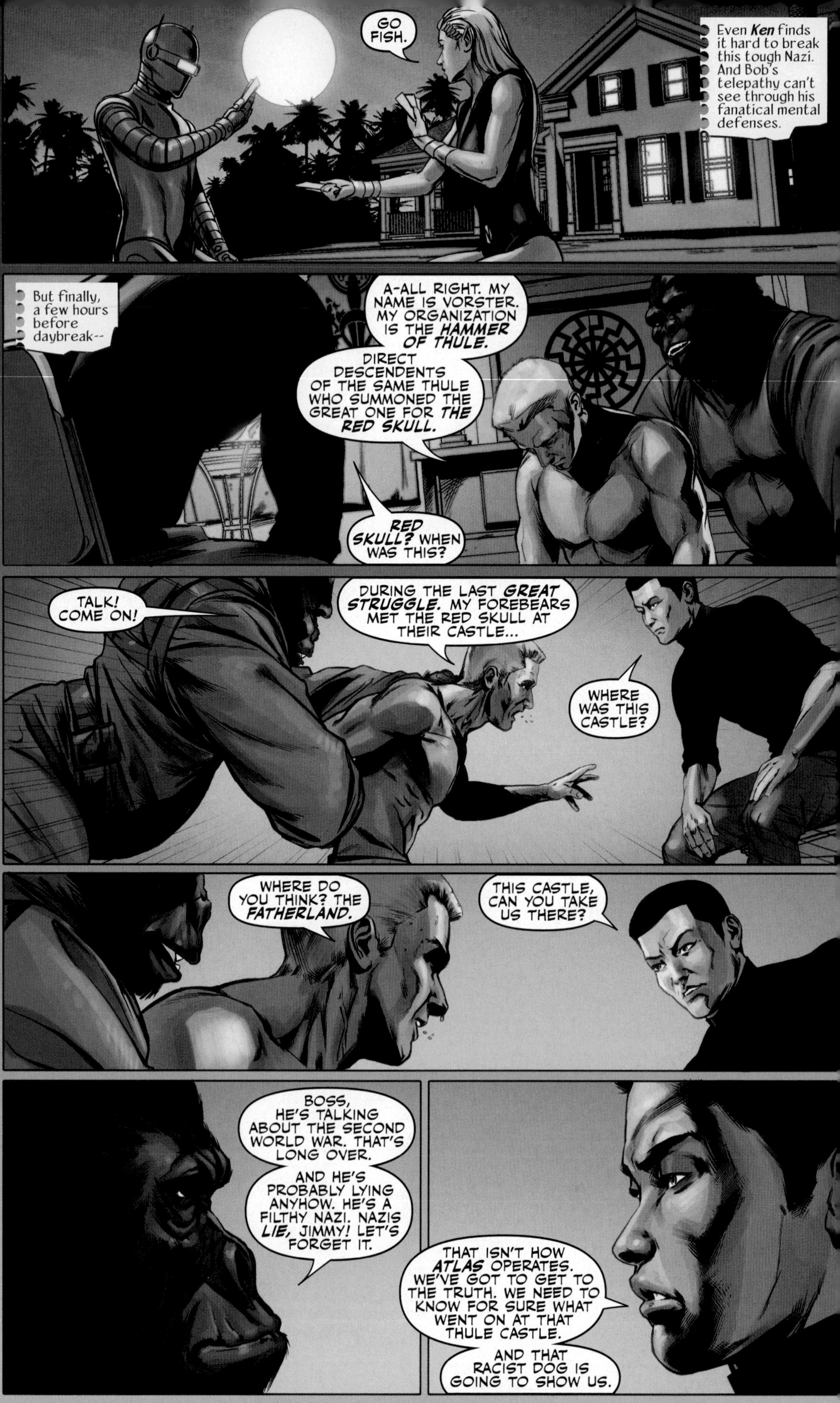
GO FISH.
Even Ken finds it hard to break this tough Nazi. And Bob's telepathy can't see through his fanatical mental defenses.
But finally, a few hours before daybreak--
A-ALL RIGHT. MY NAME IS VORSTER. MY ORGANIZATION IS THE HAMMER OF THULE.
DIRECT DESCENDENTS OF THE SAME THULE WHO SUMMONED THE GREAT ONE FOR THE RED SKULL.
RED SKULL? WHEN WAS THIS?
TALK! COME ON!
DURING THE LAST GREAT STRUGGLE. MY FOREBEARS MET THE RED SKULL AT THEIR CASTLE...
WHERE WAS THIS CASTLE?
WHERE DO YOU THINK? THE FATHERLAND.
THIS CASTLE, CAN YOU TAKE US THERE?
BOSS, HE'S TALKING ABOUT THE SECOND WORLD WAR. THAT'S LONG OVER.
AND HE'S PROBABLY LYING ANYHOW. HE'S A FILTHY NAZI. NAZIS LIE, JIMMY! LET'S FORGET IT.
THAT ISN'T HOW ATLAS OPERATES. WE'VE GOT TO GET TO THE TRUTH. WE NEED TO KNOW FOR SURE WHAT WENT ON AT THAT THULE CASTLE.
AND THAT RACIST DOG IS GOING TO SHOW US.

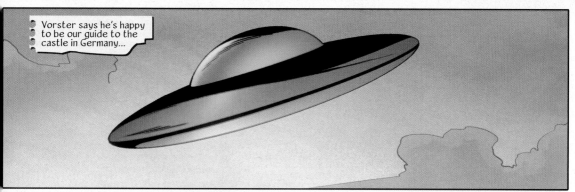

Vorster says he's happy to be our guide to the castle in Germany...

IN FACT, I'M *MORE* THAN HAPPY. BECAUSE I'M GOING TO WATCH YOU ALL *DIE* THERE!

AND DON'T THINK YOUR PRECIOUS *ATLAS* WILL SAVE THE WORLD, EITHER.

WHAT DO YOU KNOW ABOUT ATLAS?

PLENTY. AFTER THE WAR MY THULE FOREBEARS WENT UNDERGROUND...

...AND INFILTRATED MANY LARGE ESPIONAGE ORGANIZATIONS. INCLUDING *YOUR OWN.*

M--MY GOD. IF THAT WERE TRUE...

C'MON, JIMMY. HE'S FULL OF CRAP. WHAT D'YA EXPECT FROM A CLAPPED-OUT *BROWNSHIRT?*

M--MAYBE I'LL...I'LL JUST GO AND SPEND A LITTLE TIME IN MY QUARTERS.

YOU MEAN YOU'LL RUN AWAY BACK TO THE *PAST?*

JIMMY, THIS IS THE PRESENT. YOU MIGHT NOT *LIKE* IT, BUT YOU'RE GOING TO HAVE TO *DEAL* WITH IT.

SHE'S RIGHT, BOSS. IF YOU GO BACK THERE NOW... YOU MIGHT *NEVER* RETURN.

Heck, all this fuss. And all I wanted was a *whiskey sour!*

TO BE CONTINUED...

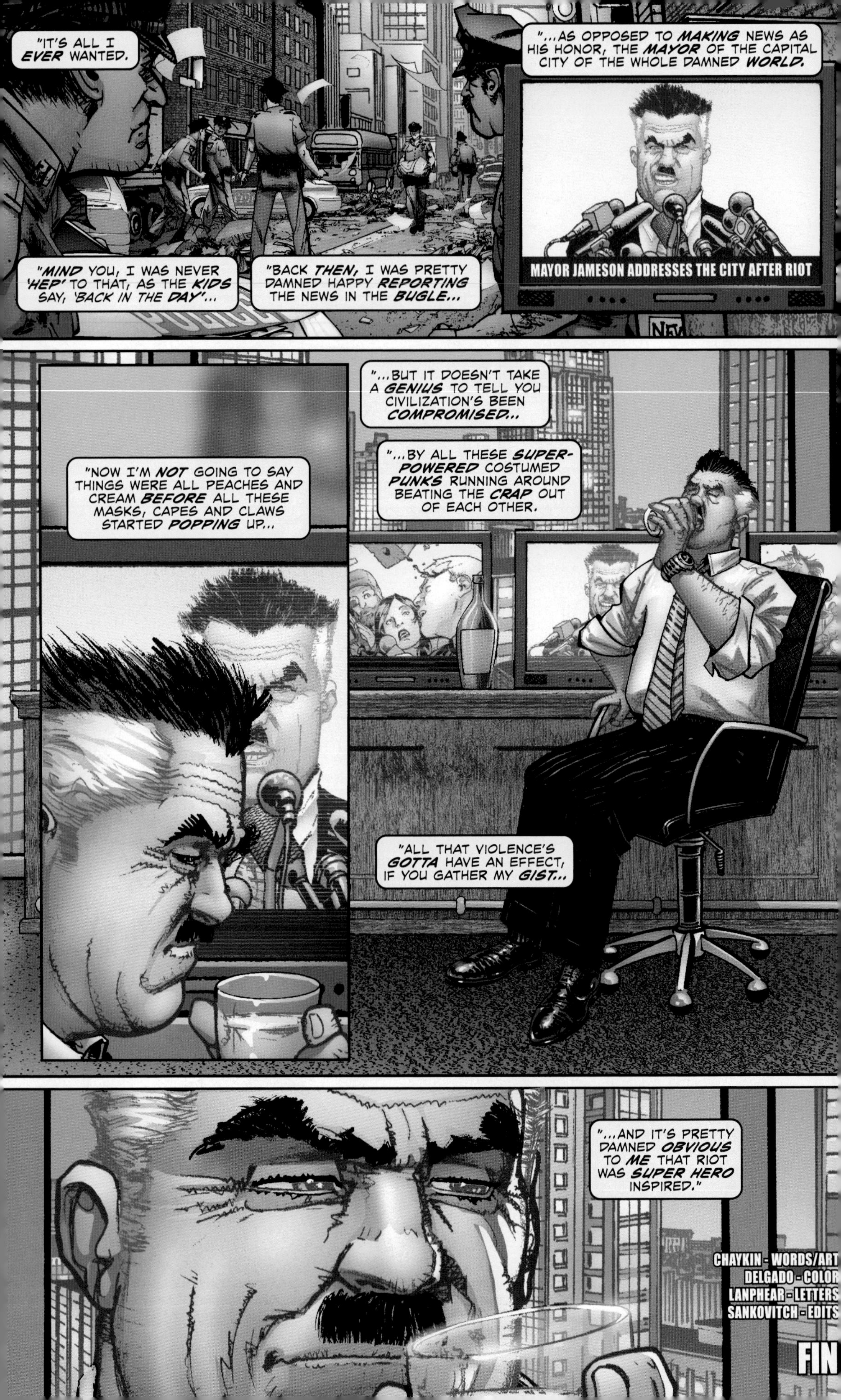

"IT'S ALL I EVER WANTED.
"MIND YOU, I WAS NEVER 'HEP' TO THAT, AS THE KIDS SAY, 'BACK IN THE DAY'...
"BACK THEN, I WAS PRETTY DAMNED HAPPY REPORTING THE NEWS IN THE BUGLE...
"...AS OPPOSED TO MAKING NEWS AS HIS HONOR, THE MAYOR OF THE CAPITAL CITY OF THE WHOLE DAMNED WORLD.
MAYOR JAMESON ADDRESSES THE CITY AFTER RIOT
"NOW I'M NOT GOING TO SAY THINGS WERE ALL PEACHES AND CREAM BEFORE ALL THESE MASKS, CAPES AND CLAWS STARTED POPPING UP...
"...BUT IT DOESN'T TAKE A GENIUS TO TELL YOU CIVILIZATION'S BEEN COMPROMISED...
"...BY ALL THESE SUPER-POWERED COSTUMED PUNKS RUNNING AROUND BEATING THE CRAP OUT OF EACH OTHER.
"ALL THAT VIOLENCE'S GOTTA HAVE AN EFFECT, IF YOU GATHER MY GIST...
"...AND IT'S PRETTY DAMNED OBVIOUS TO ME THAT RIOT WAS SUPER HERO INSPIRED."
CHAYKIN - WORDS/ART
DELGADO - COLOR
LANPHEAR - LETTERS
SANKOVITCH - EDITS
FIN

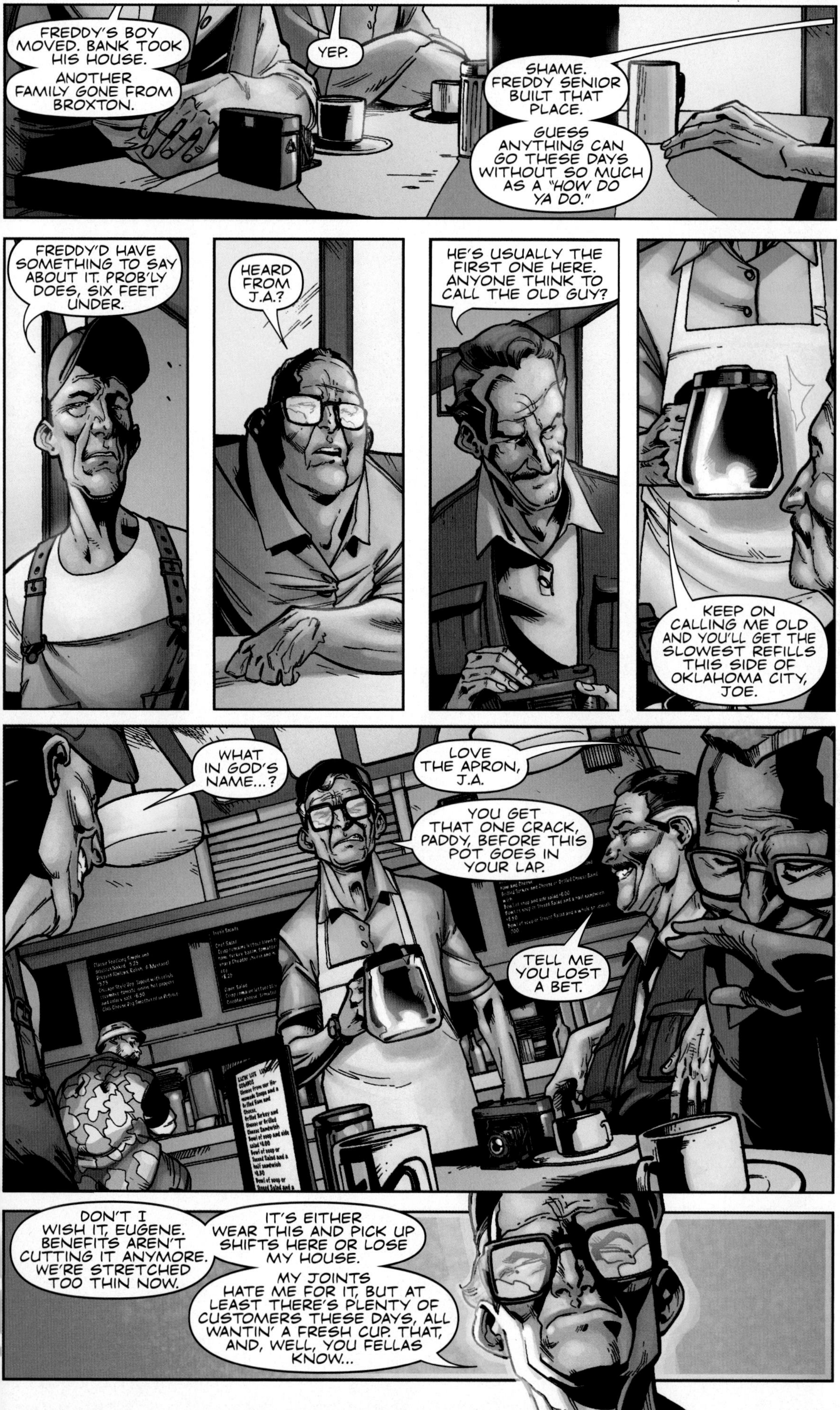
FREDDY'S BOY MOVED. BANK TOOK HIS HOUSE.
ANOTHER FAMILY GONE FROM BROXTON.
YEP.
SHAME. FREDDY SENIOR BUILT THAT PLACE.
GUESS ANYTHING CAN GO THESE DAYS WITHOUT SO MUCH AS A "HOW DO YA DO."
FREDDY'D HAVE SOMETHING TO SAY ABOUT IT. PROB'LY DOES, SIX FEET UNDER.
HEARD FROM J.A.?
HE'S USUALLY THE FIRST ONE HERE. ANYONE THINK TO CALL THE OLD GUY?
KEEP ON CALLING ME OLD AND YOU'LL GET THE SLOWEST REFILLS THIS SIDE OF OKLAHOMA CITY, JOE.
WHAT IN GOD'S NAME...?
LOVE THE APRON, J.A.
YOU GET THAT ONE CRACK, PADDY, BEFORE THIS POT GOES IN YOUR LAP.
TELL ME YOU LOST A BET.
DON'T I WISH IT, EUGENE. BENEFITS AREN'T CUTTING IT ANYMORE. WE'RE STRETCHED TOO THIN NOW.
IT'S EITHER WEAR THIS AND PICK UP SHIFTS HERE OR LOSE MY HOUSE.
MY JOINTS HATE ME FOR IT, BUT AT LEAST THERE'S PLENTY OF CUSTOMERS THESE DAYS, ALL WANTIN' A FRESH CUP. THAT, AND, WELL, YOU FELLAS KNOW...

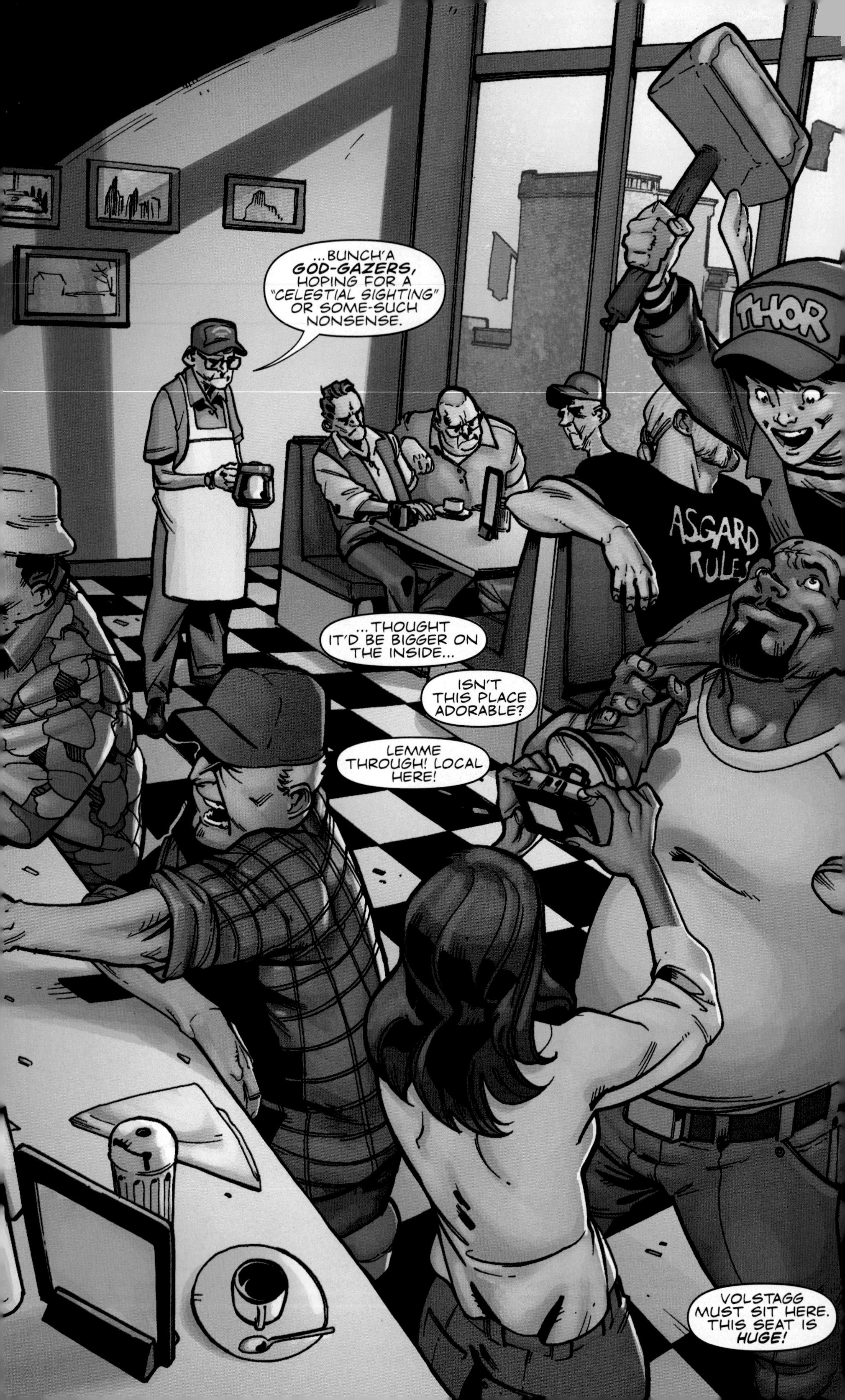

...BUNCH'A **GOD-GAZERS,** HOPING FOR A "CELESTIAL SIGHTING" OR SOME-SUCH NONSENSE.
THOR
ASGARD RULES
...THOUGHT IT'D BE BIGGER ON THE INSIDE...
ISN'T THIS PLACE ADORABLE?
LEMME THROUGH! LOCAL HERE!
VOLSTAGG MUST SIT HERE. THIS SEAT IS ***HUGE!***

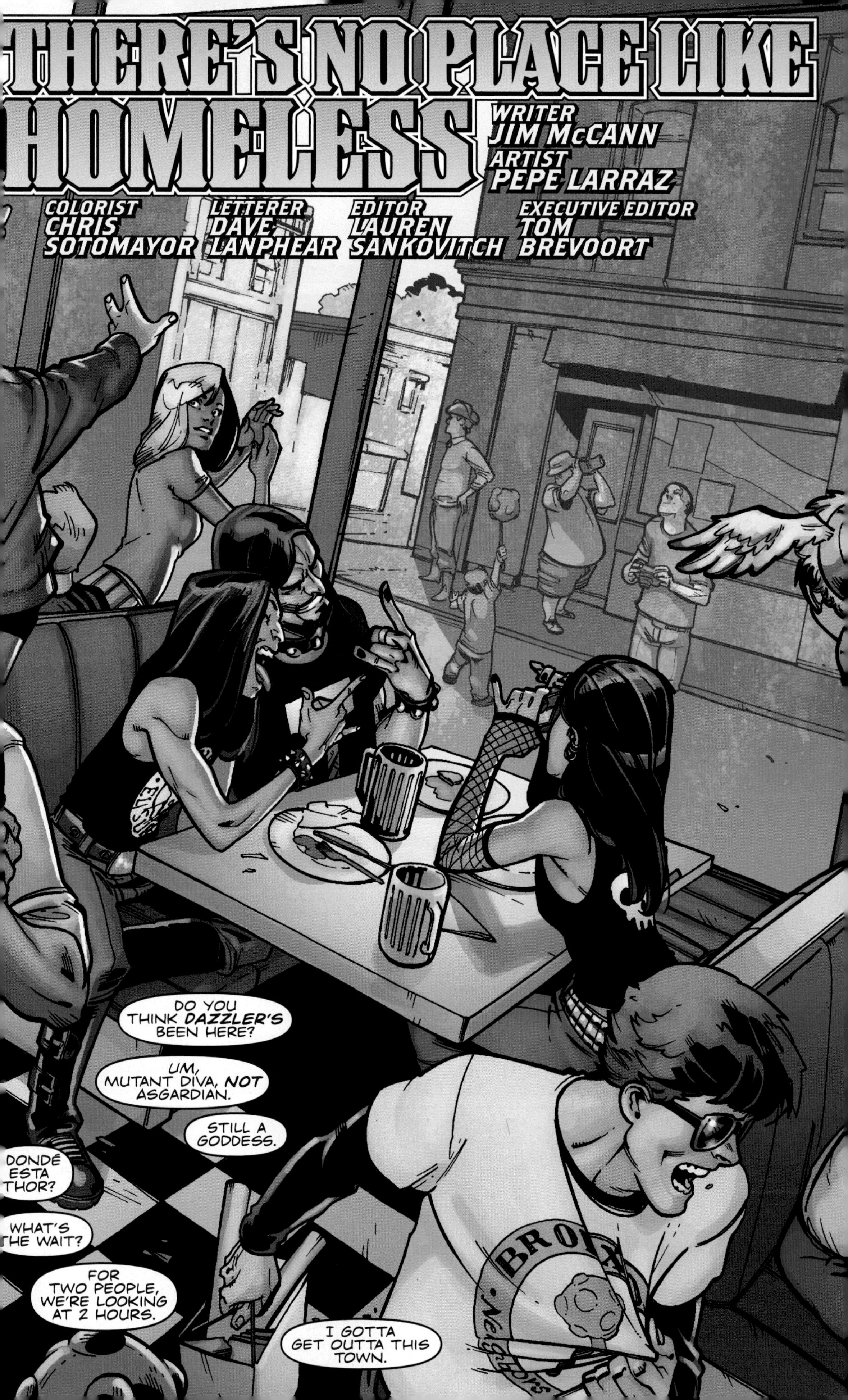
THERE'S NO PLACE LIKE HOMELESS
WRITER JIM McCANN
ARTIST PEPE LARRAZ
COLORIST CHRIS SOTOMAYOR
LETTERER DAVE LANPHEAR
EDITOR LAUREN SANKOVITCH
EXECUTIVE EDITOR TOM BREVOORT
DO YOU THINK DAZZLER'S BEEN HERE?
UM, MUTANT DIVA, NOT ASGARDIAN.
STILL A GODDESS.
DONDÉ ESTA THOR?
WHAT'S THE WAIT?
FOR TWO PEOPLE, WE'RE LOOKING AT 2 HOURS.
I GOTTA GET OUTTA THIS TOWN.

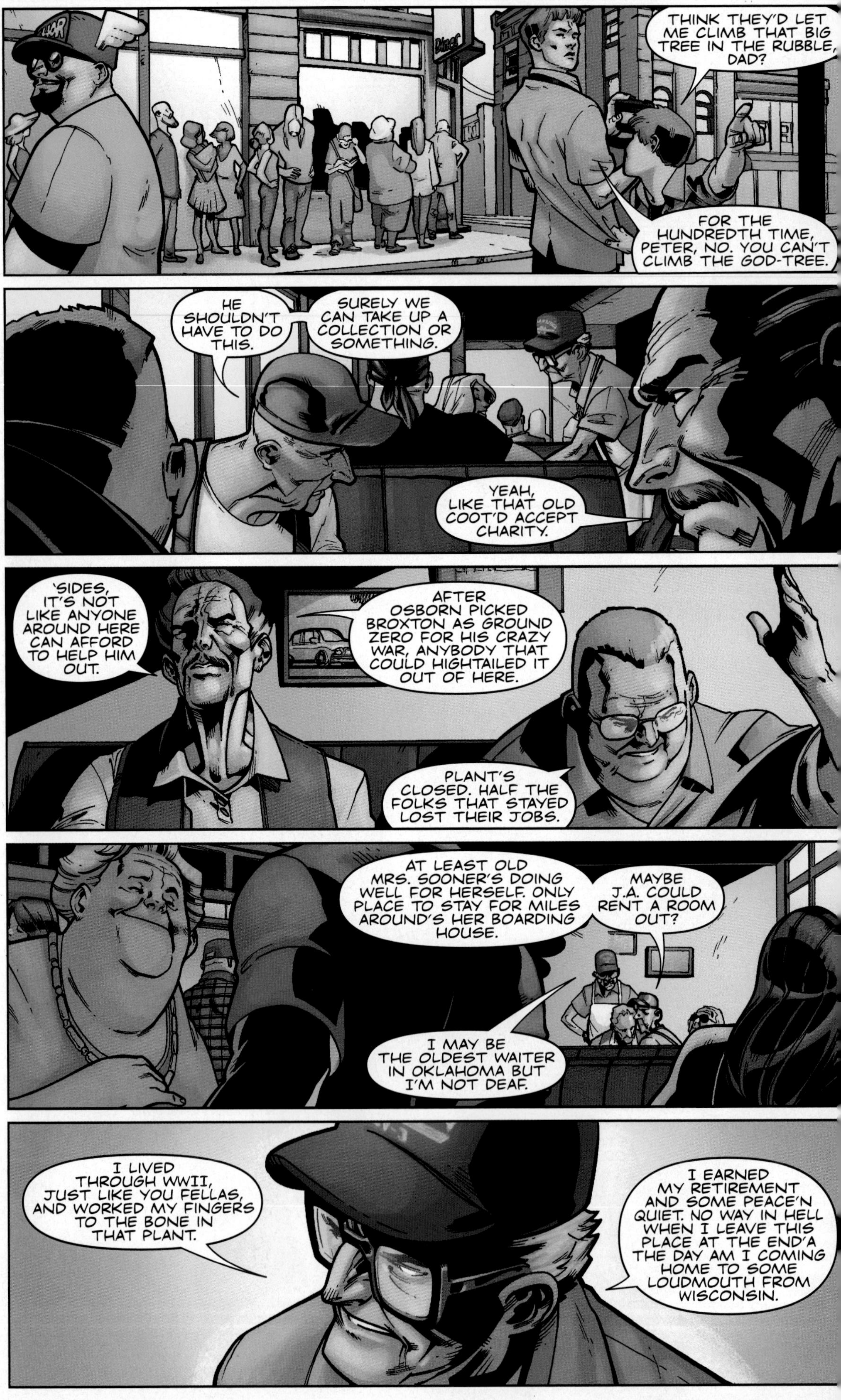

THINK THEY'D LET ME CLIMB THAT BIG TREE IN THE RUBBLE, DAD?
FOR THE HUNDREDTH TIME, PETER, NO. YOU CAN'T CLIMB THE GOD-TREE.
HE SHOULDN'T HAVE TO DO THIS.
SURELY WE CAN TAKE UP A COLLECTION OR SOMETHING.
YEAH, LIKE THAT OLD COOT'D ACCEPT CHARITY.
'SIDES, IT'S NOT LIKE ANYONE AROUND HERE CAN AFFORD TO HELP HIM OUT.
AFTER OSBORN PICKED BROXTON AS GROUND ZERO FOR HIS CRAZY WAR, ANYBODY THAT COULD HIGHTAILED IT OUT OF HERE.
PLANT'S CLOSED. HALF THE FOLKS THAT STAYED LOST THEIR JOBS.
AT LEAST OLD MRS. SOONER'S DOING WELL FOR HERSELF. ONLY PLACE TO STAY FOR MILES AROUND'S HER BOARDING HOUSE.
MAYBE J.A. COULD RENT A ROOM OUT?
I MAY BE THE OLDEST WAITER IN OKLAHOMA BUT I'M NOT DEAF.
I LIVED THROUGH WWII, JUST LIKE YOU FELLAS, AND WORKED MY FINGERS TO THE BONE IN THAT PLANT.
I EARNED MY RETIREMENT AND SOME PEACE'N QUIET. NO WAY IN HELL WHEN I LEAVE THIS PLACE AT THE END'A THE DAY AM I COMING HOME TO SOME LOUDMOUTH FROM WISCONSIN.

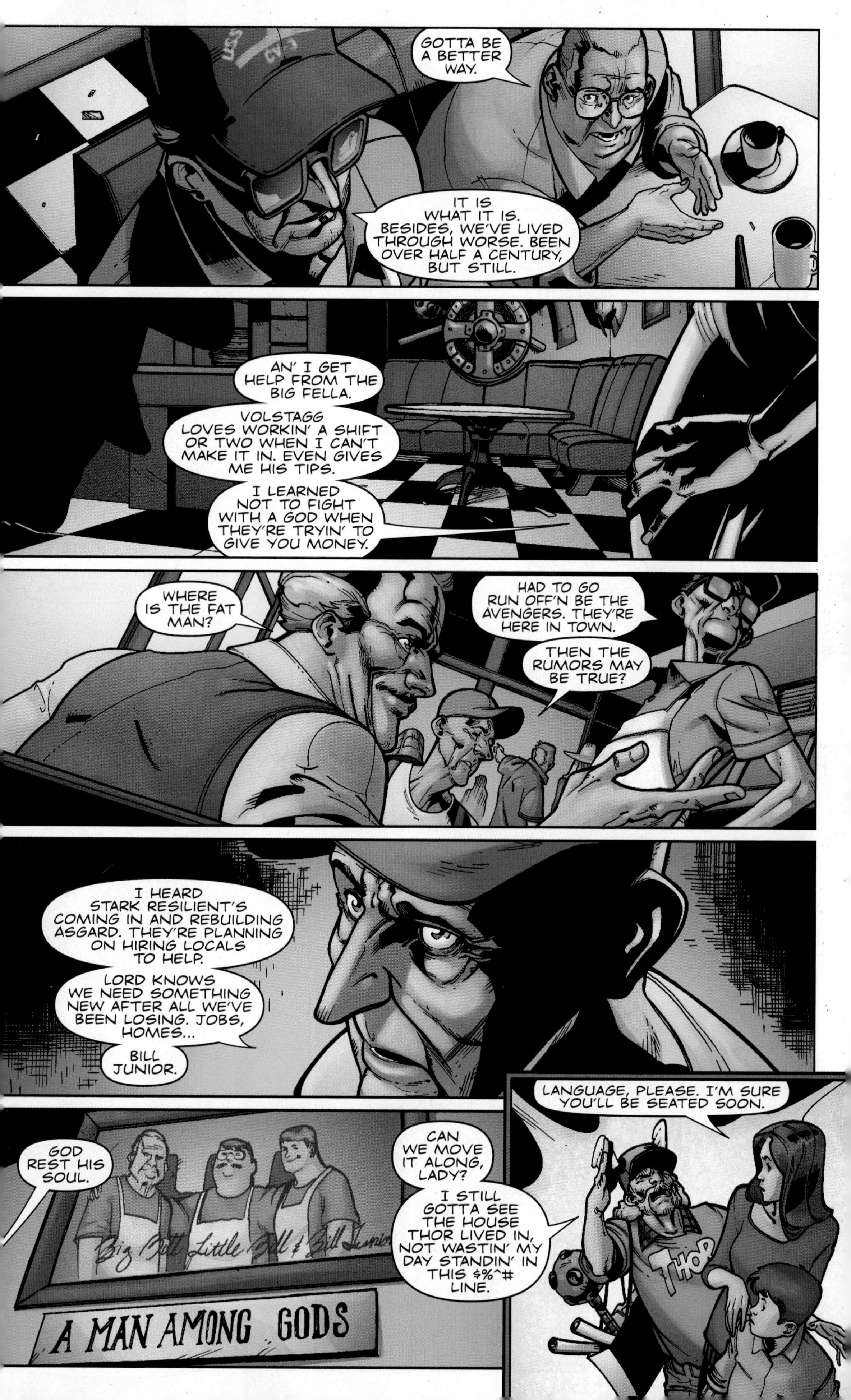
GOTTA BE A BETTER WAY.
IT IS WHAT IT IS. BESIDES, WE'VE LIVED THROUGH WORSE. BEEN OVER HALF A CENTURY, BUT STILL.
AN' I GET HELP FROM THE BIG FELLA.
VOLSTAGG LOVES WORKIN' A SHIFT OR TWO WHEN I CAN'T MAKE IT IN. EVEN GIVES ME HIS TIPS.
I LEARNED NOT TO FIGHT WITH A GOD WHEN THEY'RE TRYIN' TO GIVE YOU MONEY.
WHERE IS THE FAT MAN?
HAD TO GO RUN OFF'N BE THE AVENGERS. THEY'RE HERE IN TOWN.
THEN THE RUMORS MAY BE TRUE?
I HEARD STARK RESILIENT'S COMING IN AND REBUILDING ASGARD. THEY'RE PLANNING ON HIRING LOCALS TO HELP.
LORD KNOWS WE NEED SOMETHING NEW AFTER ALL WE'VE BEEN LOSING. JOBS, HOMES...
BILL JUNIOR.
GOD REST HIS SOUL.
Big Bill Little Bill & Bill Junior
A MAN AMONG GODS
CAN WE MOVE IT ALONG, LADY?
I STILL GOTTA SEE THE HOUSE THOR LIVED IN, NOT WASTIN' MY DAY STANDIN' IN THIS $%^# LINE.
LANGUAGE, PLEASE. I'M SURE YOU'LL BE SEATED SOON.
THOR

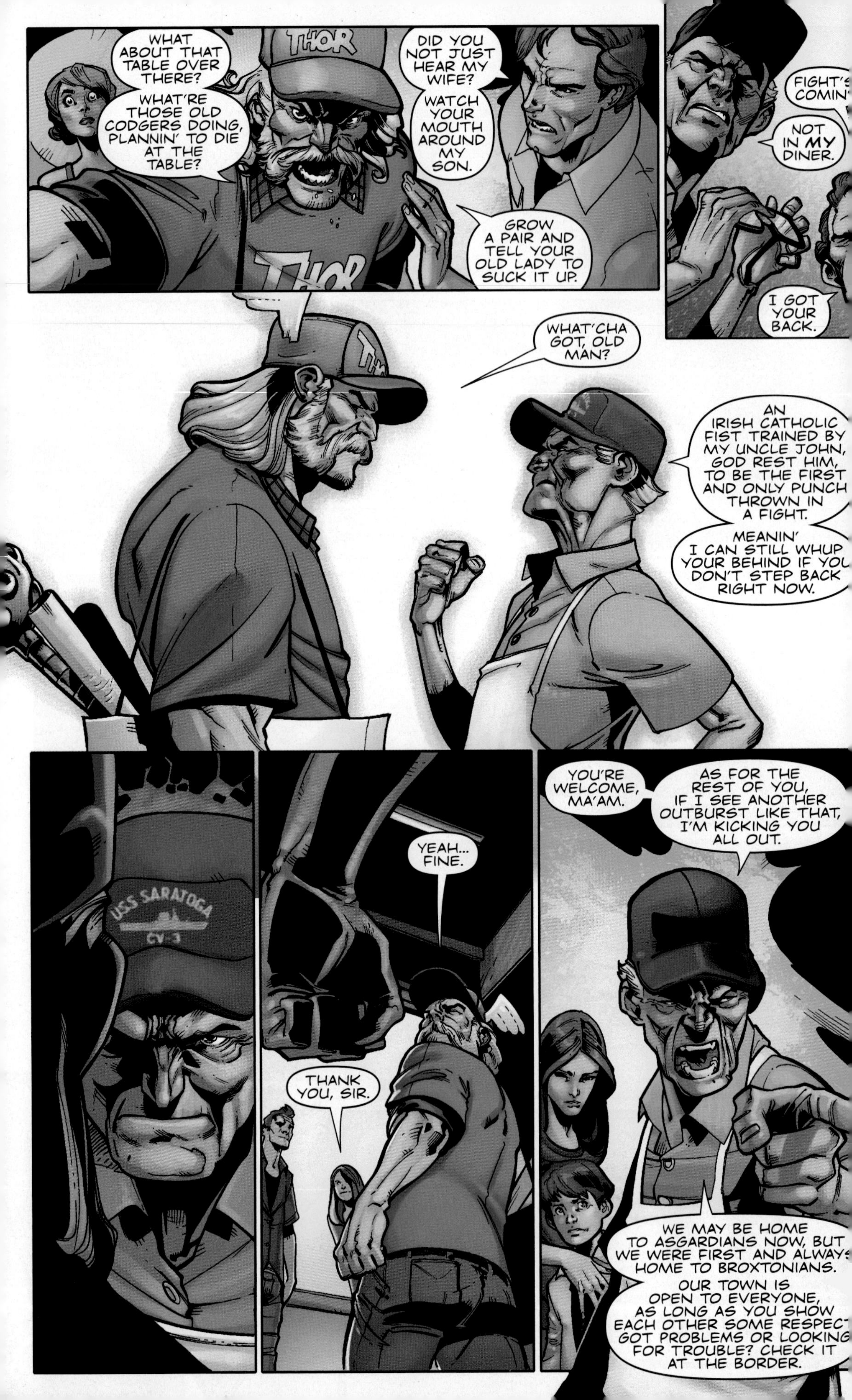

WHAT ABOUT THAT TABLE OVER THERE?
WHAT'RE THOSE OLD CODGERS DOING, PLANNIN' TO DIE AT THE TABLE?
THOR
DID YOU NOT JUST HEAR MY WIFE?
WATCH YOUR MOUTH AROUND MY SON.
GROW A PAIR AND TELL YOUR OLD LADY TO SUCK IT UP.
THOR
FIGHT'S COMIN'
NOT IN MY DINER.
I GOT YOUR BACK.
WHAT'CHA GOT, OLD MAN?
AN IRISH CATHOLIC FIST TRAINED BY MY UNCLE JOHN, GOD REST HIM, TO BE THE FIRST AND ONLY PUNCH THROWN IN A FIGHT.
MEANIN' I CAN STILL WHUP YOUR BEHIND IF YOU DON'T STEP BACK RIGHT NOW.
USS SARATOGA
CV-3
YEAH... FINE.
THANK YOU, SIR.
YOU'RE WELCOME, MA'AM.
AS FOR THE REST OF YOU, IF I SEE ANOTHER OUTBURST LIKE THAT, I'M KICKING YOU ALL OUT.
WE MAY BE HOME TO ASGARDIANS NOW, BUT WE WERE FIRST AND ALWAYS HOME TO BROXTONIANS.
OUR TOWN IS OPEN TO EVERYONE, AS LONG AS YOU SHOW EACH OTHER SOME RESPECT. GOT PROBLEMS OR LOOKING FOR TROUBLE? CHECK IT AT THE BORDER.

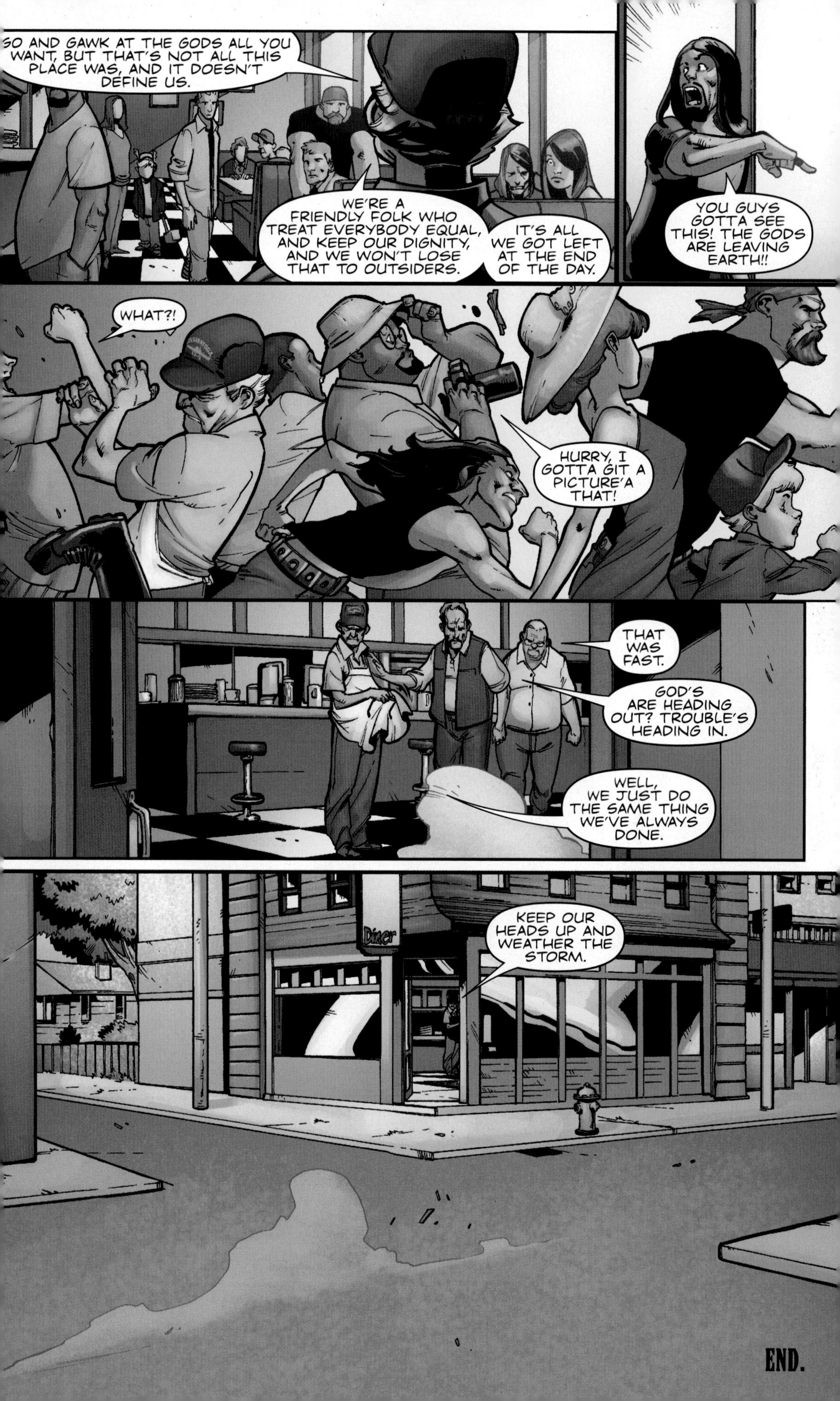
GO AND GAWK AT THE GODS ALL YOU WANT, BUT THAT'S NOT ALL THIS PLACE WAS, AND IT DOESN'T DEFINE US.
WE'RE A FRIENDLY FOLK WHO TREAT EVERYBODY EQUAL, AND KEEP OUR DIGNITY, AND WE WON'T LOSE THAT TO OUTSIDERS.
IT'S ALL WE GOT LEFT AT THE END OF THE DAY.
YOU GUYS GOTTA SEE THIS! THE GODS ARE LEAVING EARTH!!
WHAT?!
HURRY, I GOTTA GIT A PICTURE'A THAT!
THAT WAS FAST.
GOD'S ARE HEADING OUT? TROUBLE'S HEADING IN.
WELL, WE JUST DO THE SAME THING WE'VE ALWAYS DONE.
KEEP OUR HEADS UP AND WEATHER THE STORM.
Diner
END.

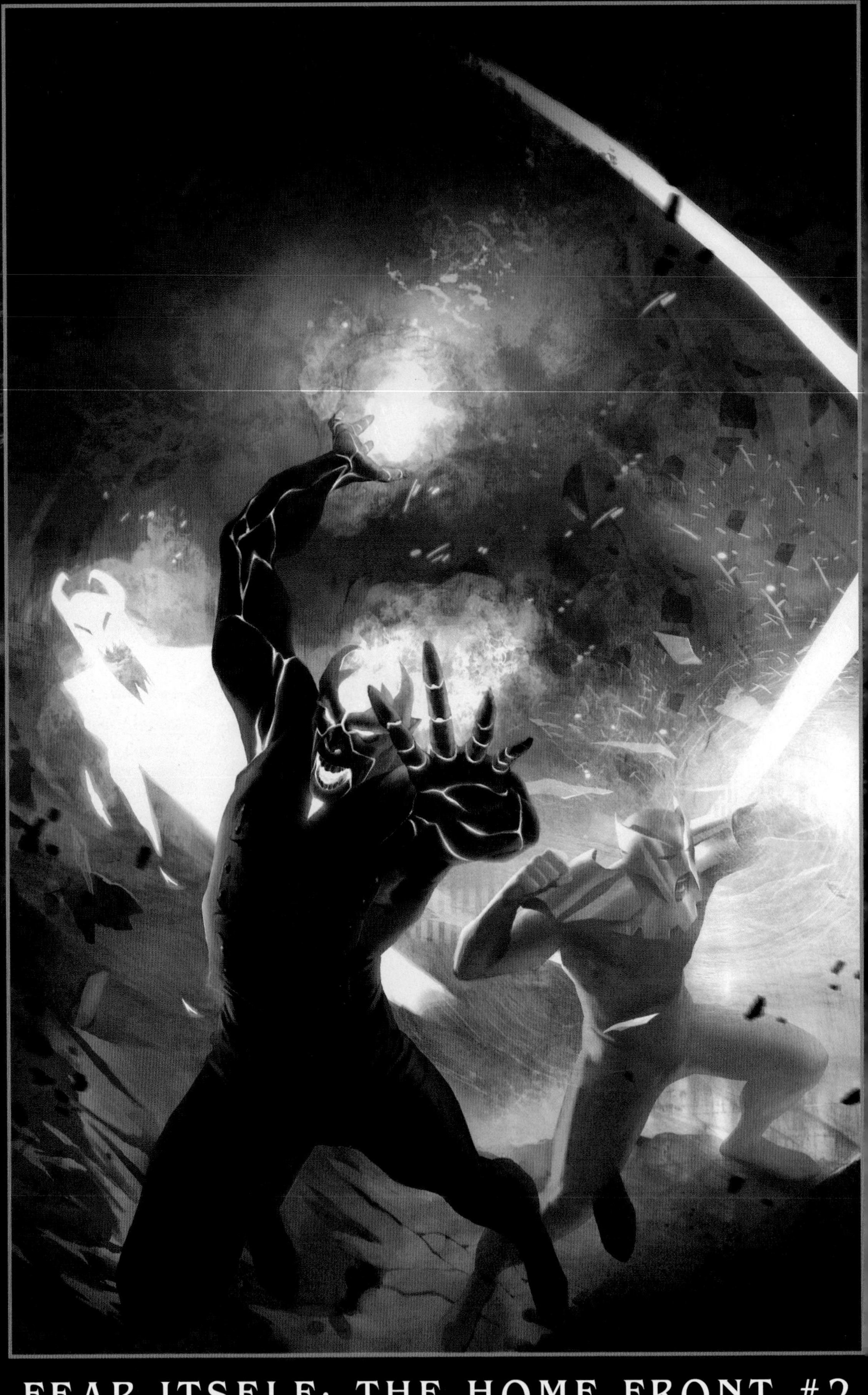

FEAR ITSELF: THE HOME FRONT #2

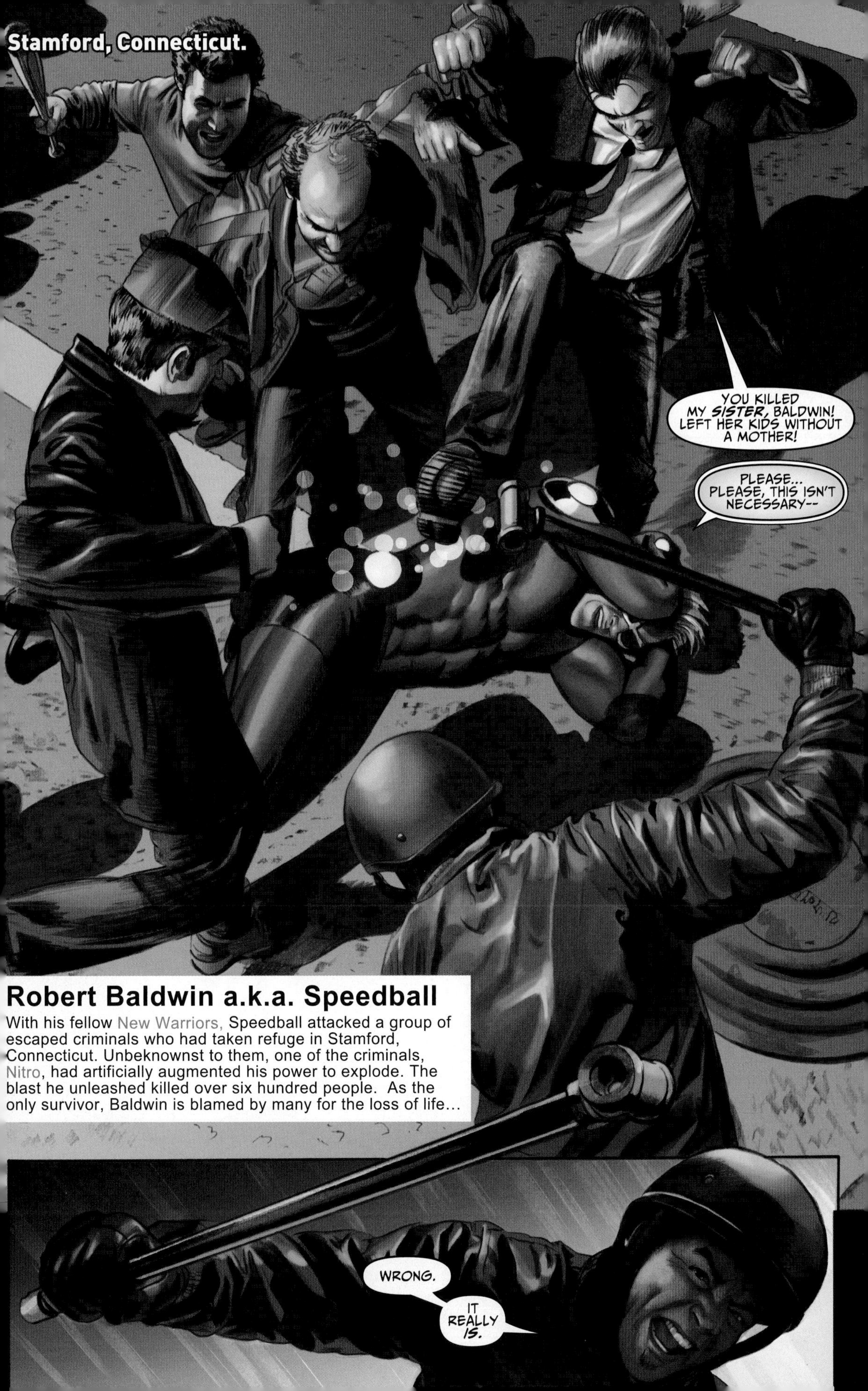
Stamford, Connecticut.
YOU KILLED MY *SISTER,* BALDWIN! LEFT HER KIDS WITHOUT A MOTHER!
PLEASE... PLEASE, THIS ISN'T NECESSARY--
Robert Baldwin a.k.a. Speedball
With his fellow New Warriors, Speedball attacked a group of escaped criminals who had taken refuge in Stamford, Connecticut. Unbeknownst to them, one of the criminals, Nitro, had artificially augmented his power to explode. The blast he unleashed killed over six hundred people. As the only survivor, Baldwin is blamed by many for the loss of life...
WRONG.
IT REALLY *IS.*

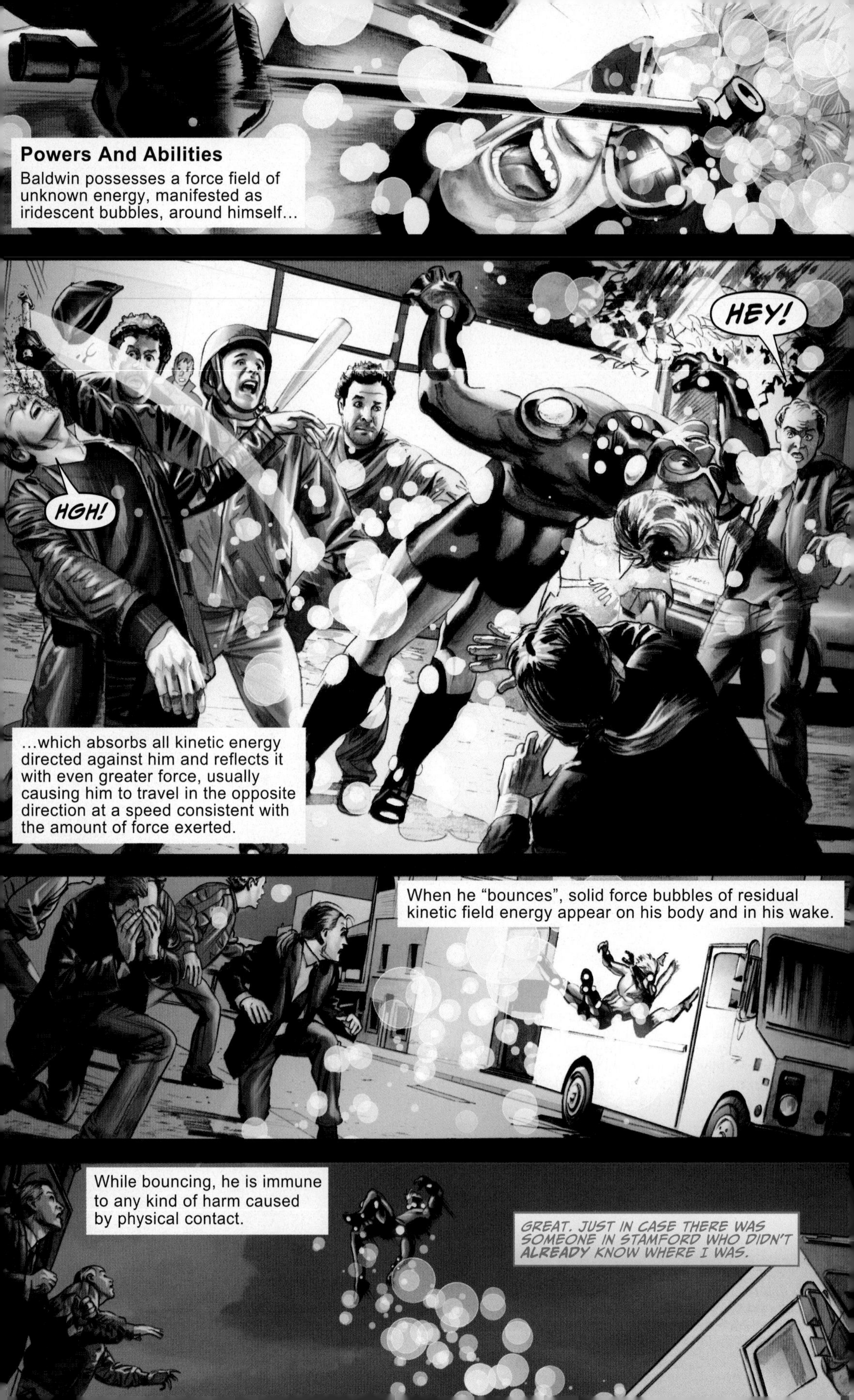
Powers And Abilities
Baldwin possesses a force field of unknown energy, manifested as iridescent bubbles, around himself…
HEY!
HGH!
…which absorbs all kinetic energy directed against him and reflects it with even greater force, usually causing him to travel in the opposite direction at a speed consistent with the amount of force exerted.
When he "bounces", solid force bubbles of residual kinetic field energy appear on his body and in his wake.
While bouncing, he is immune to any kind of harm caused by physical contact.
GREAT. JUST IN CASE THERE WAS SOMEONE IN STAMFORD WHO DIDN'T ALREADY KNOW WHERE I WAS.

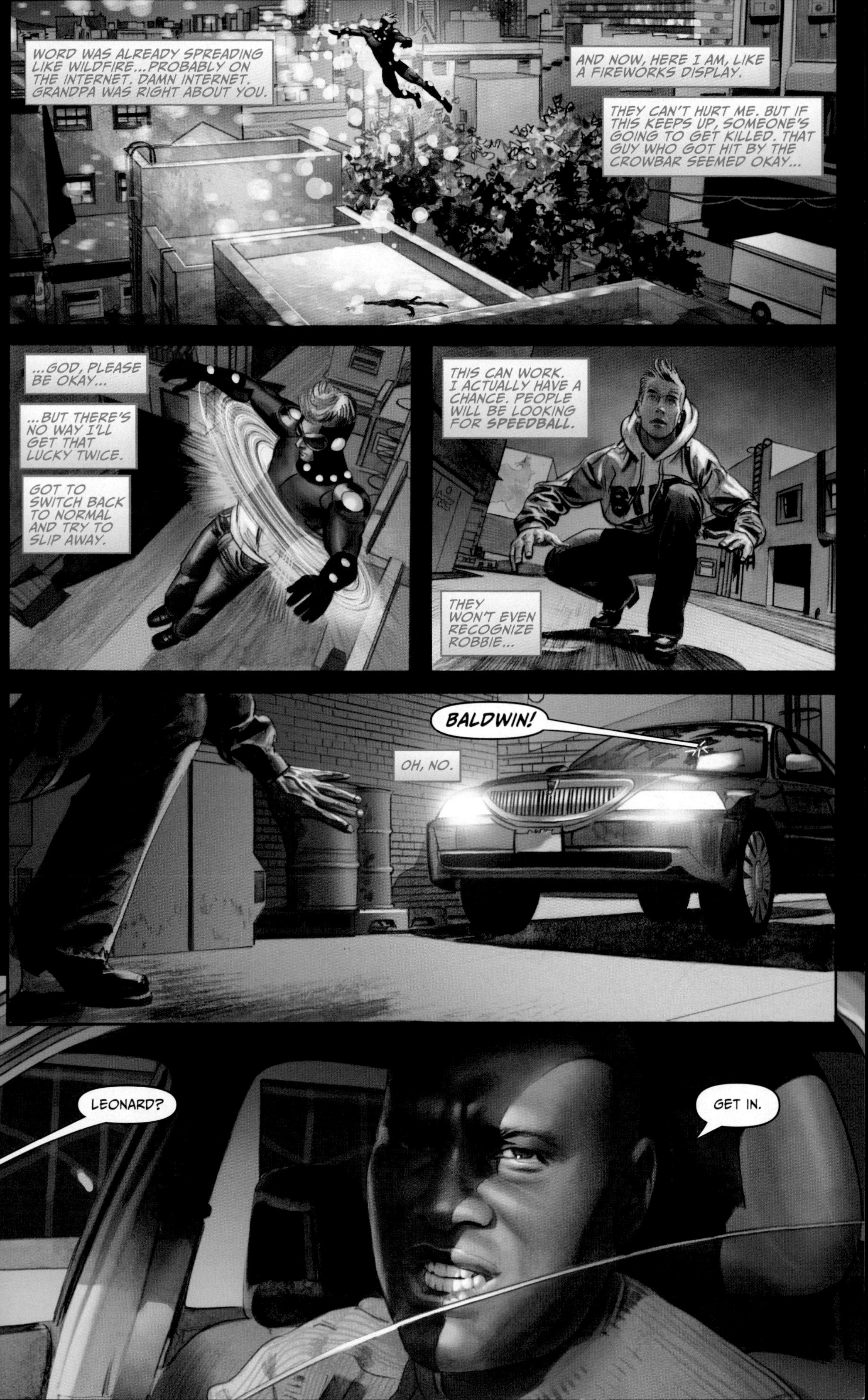

WORD WAS ALREADY SPREADING LIKE WILDFIRE...PROBABLY ON THE INTERNET. DAMN INTERNET. GRANDPA WAS RIGHT ABOUT YOU.
AND NOW, HERE I AM, LIKE A FIREWORKS DISPLAY.
THEY CAN'T HURT ME. BUT IF THIS KEEPS UP, SOMEONE'S GOING TO GET KILLED. THAT GUY WHO GOT HIT BY THE CROWBAR SEEMED OKAY...
...GOD, PLEASE BE OKAY...
...BUT THERE'S NO WAY I'LL GET THAT LUCKY TWICE.
GOT TO SWITCH BACK TO NORMAL AND TRY TO SLIP AWAY.
THIS CAN WORK. I ACTUALLY HAVE A CHANCE. PEOPLE WILL BE LOOKING FOR SPEEDBALL.
THEY WON'T EVEN RECOGNIZE ROBBIE...
BALDWIN!
OH, NO.
LEONARD?
GET IN.

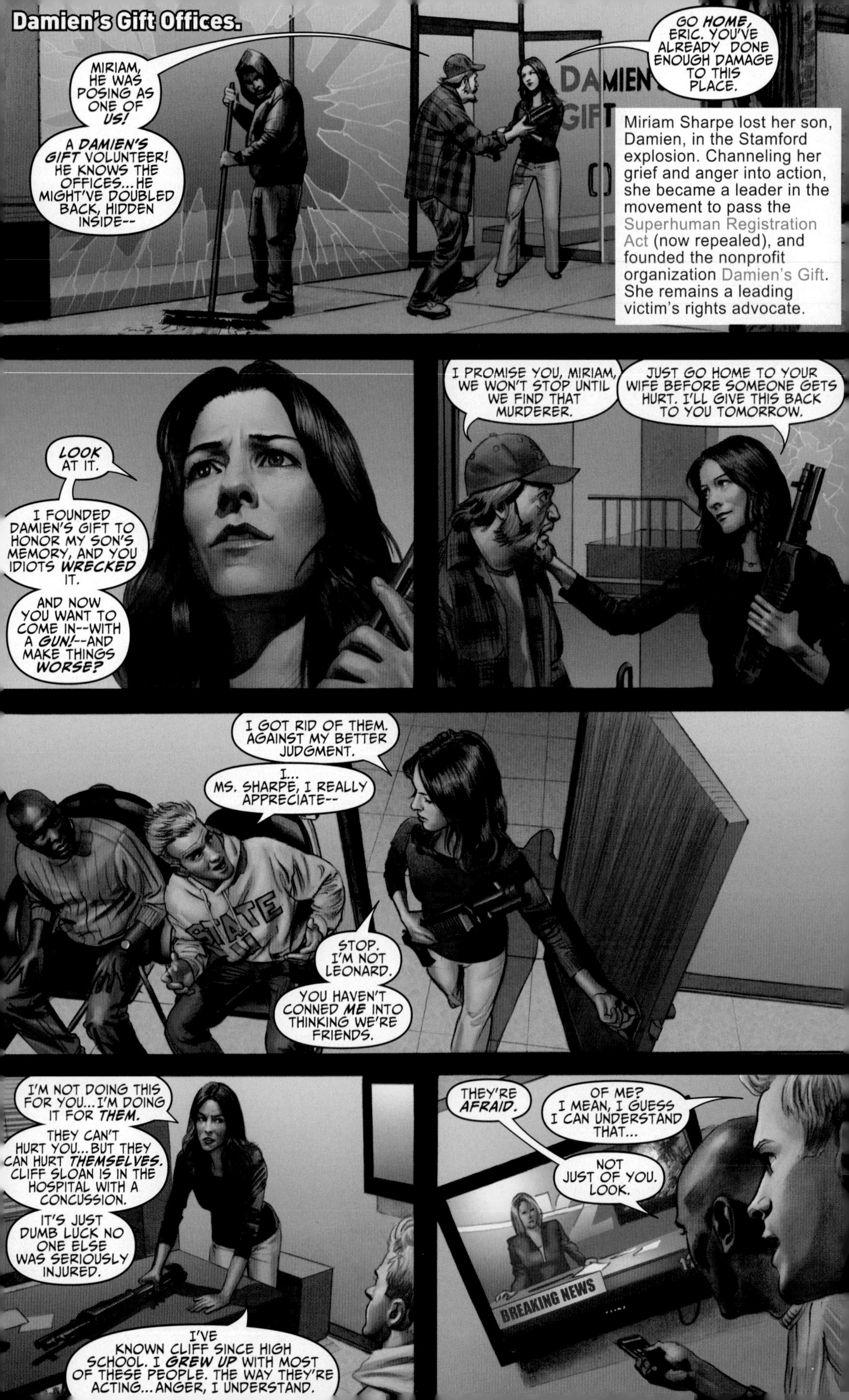
Damien's Gift Offices.
MIRIAM, HE WAS POSING AS ONE OF US!
A DAMIEN'S GIFT VOLUNTEER! HE KNOWS THE OFFICES... HE MIGHT'VE DOUBLED BACK, HIDDEN INSIDE--
GO HOME, ERIC. YOU'VE ALREADY DONE ENOUGH DAMAGE TO THIS PLACE.
DAMIEN'S GIFT
Miriam Sharpe lost her son, Damien, in the Stamford explosion. Channeling her grief and anger into action, she became a leader in the movement to pass the Superhuman Registration Act (now repealed), and founded the nonprofit organization Damien's Gift. She remains a leading victim's rights advocate.
LOOK AT IT.
I FOUNDED DAMIEN'S GIFT TO HONOR MY SON'S MEMORY, AND YOU IDIOTS WRECKED IT.
AND NOW YOU WANT TO COME IN--WITH A GUN!--AND MAKE THINGS WORSE?
I PROMISE YOU, MIRIAM, WE WON'T STOP UNTIL WE FIND THAT MURDERER.
JUST GO HOME TO YOUR WIFE BEFORE SOMEONE GETS HURT. I'LL GIVE THIS BACK TO YOU TOMORROW.
I GOT RID OF THEM. AGAINST MY BETTER JUDGMENT.
I... MS. SHARPE, I REALLY APPRECIATE--
STOP. I'M NOT LEONARD.
YOU HAVEN'T CONNED ME INTO THINKING WE'RE FRIENDS.
STATE
I'M NOT DOING THIS FOR YOU... I'M DOING IT FOR THEM.
THEY CAN'T HURT YOU... BUT THEY CAN HURT THEMSELVES. CLIFF SLOAN IS IN THE HOSPITAL WITH A CONCUSSION.
IT'S JUST DUMB LUCK NO ONE ELSE WAS SERIOUSLY INJURED.
I'VE KNOWN CLIFF SINCE HIGH SCHOOL. I GREW UP WITH MOST OF THESE PEOPLE. THE WAY THEY'RE ACTING... ANGER, I UNDERSTAND.
THEY'RE AFRAID.
OF ME? I MEAN, I GUESS I CAN UNDERSTAND THAT...
NOT JUST OF YOU. LOOK.
BREAKING NEWS

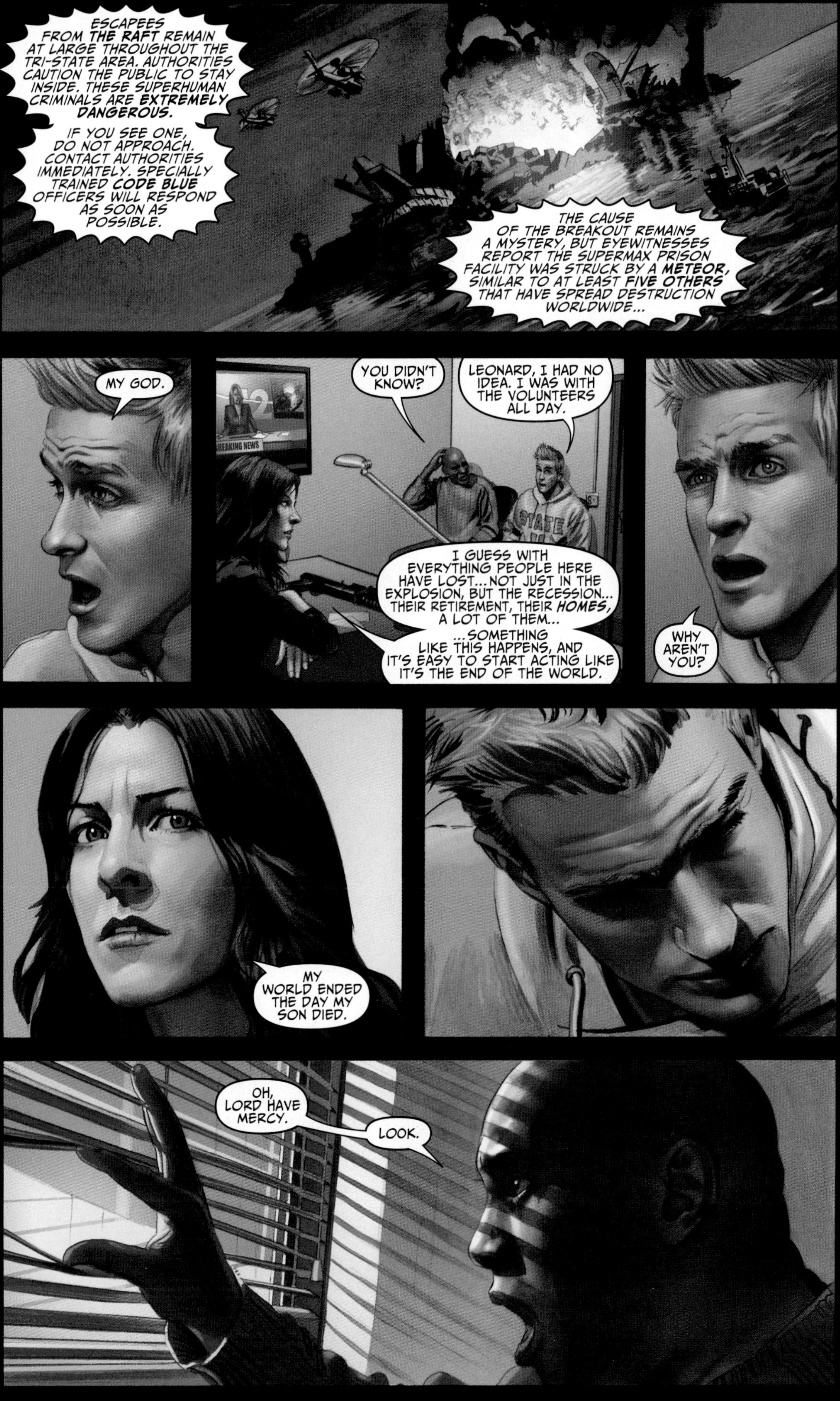
ESCAPEES FROM THE RAFT REMAIN AT LARGE THROUGHOUT THE TRI-STATE AREA. AUTHORITIES CAUTION THE PUBLIC TO STAY INSIDE. THESE SUPERHUMAN CRIMINALS ARE EXTREMELY DANGEROUS.
IF YOU SEE ONE, DO NOT APPROACH. CONTACT AUTHORITIES IMMEDIATELY. SPECIALLY TRAINED CODE BLUE OFFICERS WILL RESPOND AS SOON AS POSSIBLE.
THE CAUSE OF THE BREAKOUT REMAINS A MYSTERY, BUT EYEWITNESSES REPORT THE SUPERMAX PRISON FACILITY WAS STRUCK BY A METEOR, SIMILAR TO AT LEAST FIVE OTHERS THAT HAVE SPREAD DESTRUCTION WORLDWIDE...
MY GOD.
BREAKING NEWS
YOU DIDN'T KNOW?
LEONARD, I HAD NO IDEA. I WAS WITH THE VOLUNTEERS ALL DAY.
I GUESS WITH EVERYTHING PEOPLE HERE HAVE LOST...NOT JUST IN THE EXPLOSION, BUT THE RECESSION... THEIR RETIREMENT, THEIR HOMES, A LOT OF THEM...
...SOMETHING LIKE THIS HAPPENS, AND IT'S EASY TO START ACTING LIKE IT'S THE END OF THE WORLD.
WHY AREN'T YOU?
MY WORLD ENDED THE DAY MY SON DIED.
OH, LORD HAVE MERCY.
LOOK.

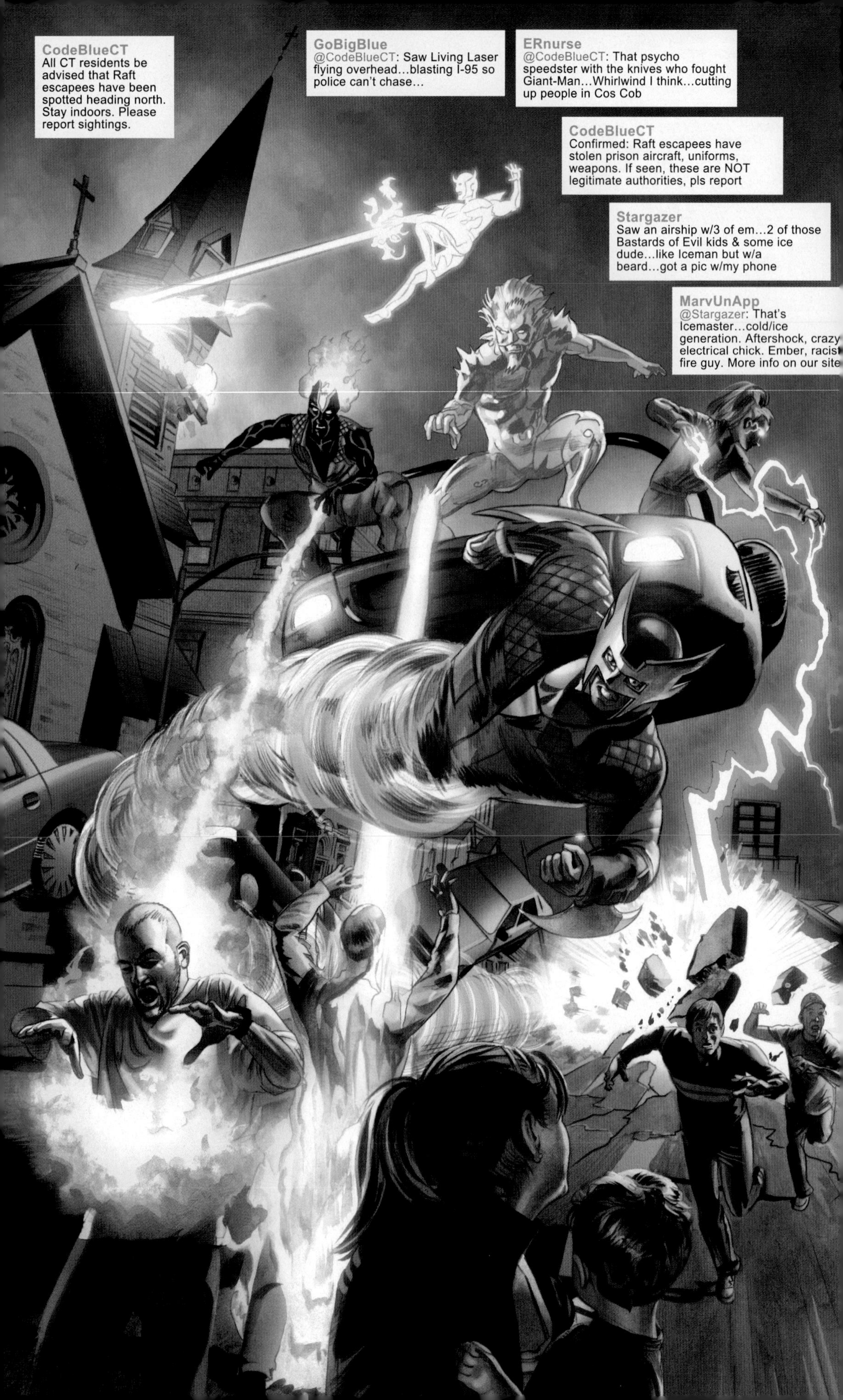
CodeBlueCT
All CT residents be advised that Raft escapees have been spotted heading north. Stay indoors. Please report sightings.
GoBigBlue
@CodeBlueCT: Saw Living Laser flying overhead…blasting I-95 so police can't chase…
ERnurse
@CodeBlueCT: That psycho speedster with the knives who fought Giant-Man…Whirlwind I think…cutting up people in Cos Cob
CodeBlueCT
Confirmed: Raft escapees have stolen prison aircraft, uniforms, weapons. If seen, these are NOT legitimate authorities, pls report
Stargazer
Saw an airship w/3 of em…2 of those Bastards of Evil kids & some ice dude…like Iceman but w/a beard…got a pic w/my phone
MarvUnApp
@Stargazer: That's Icemaster…cold/ice generation. Aftershock, crazy electrical chick. Ember, racist fire guy. More info on our site

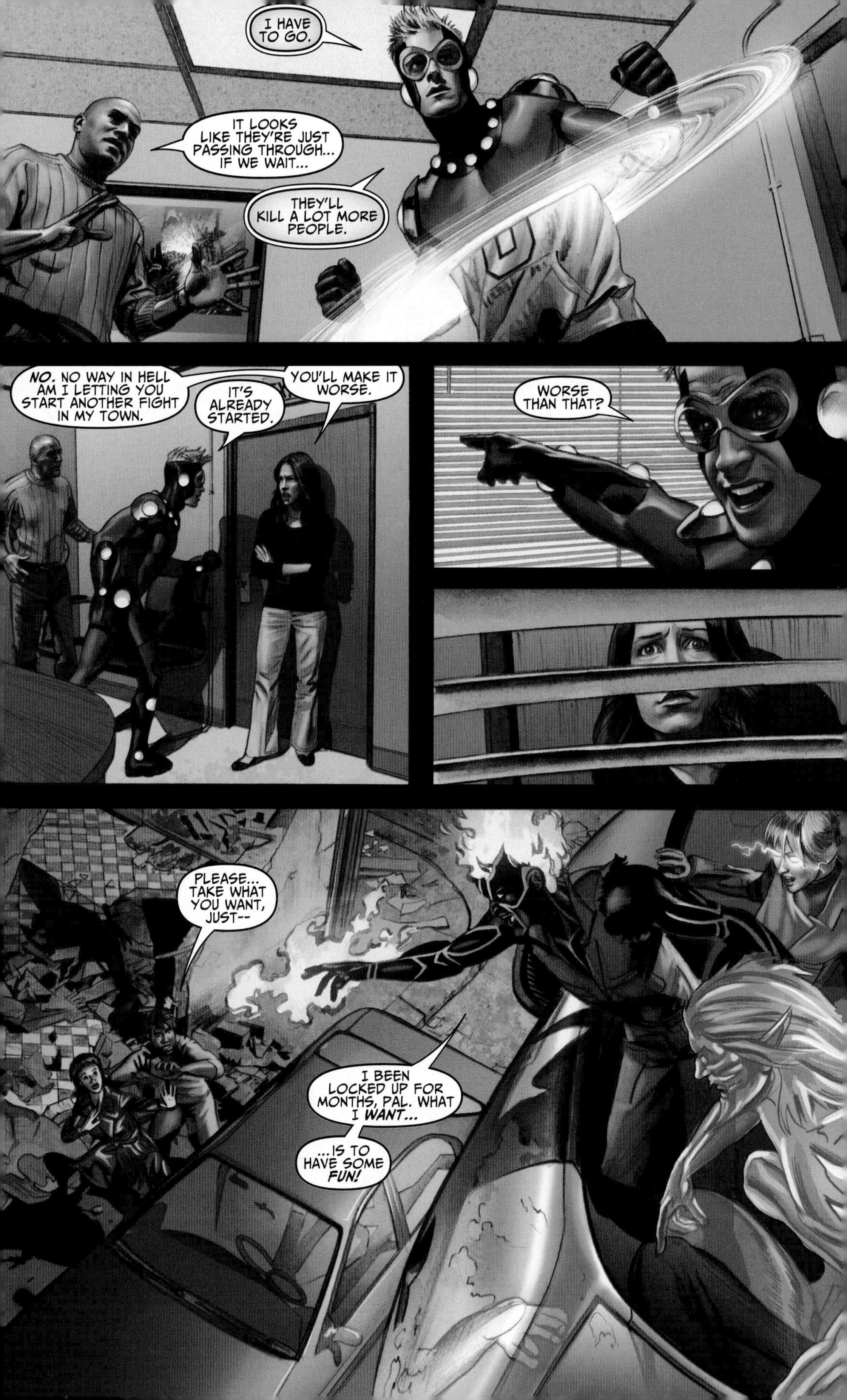
I HAVE TO GO.
IT LOOKS LIKE THEY'RE JUST PASSING THROUGH... IF WE WAIT...
THEY'LL KILL A LOT MORE PEOPLE.
NO. NO WAY IN HELL AM I LETTING YOU START ANOTHER FIGHT IN MY TOWN.
IT'S ALREADY STARTED.
YOU'LL MAKE IT WORSE.
WORSE THAN THAT?
PLEASE... TAKE WHAT YOU WANT, JUST--
I BEEN LOCKED UP FOR MONTHS, PAL. WHAT I WANT...
...IS TO HAVE SOME FUN!

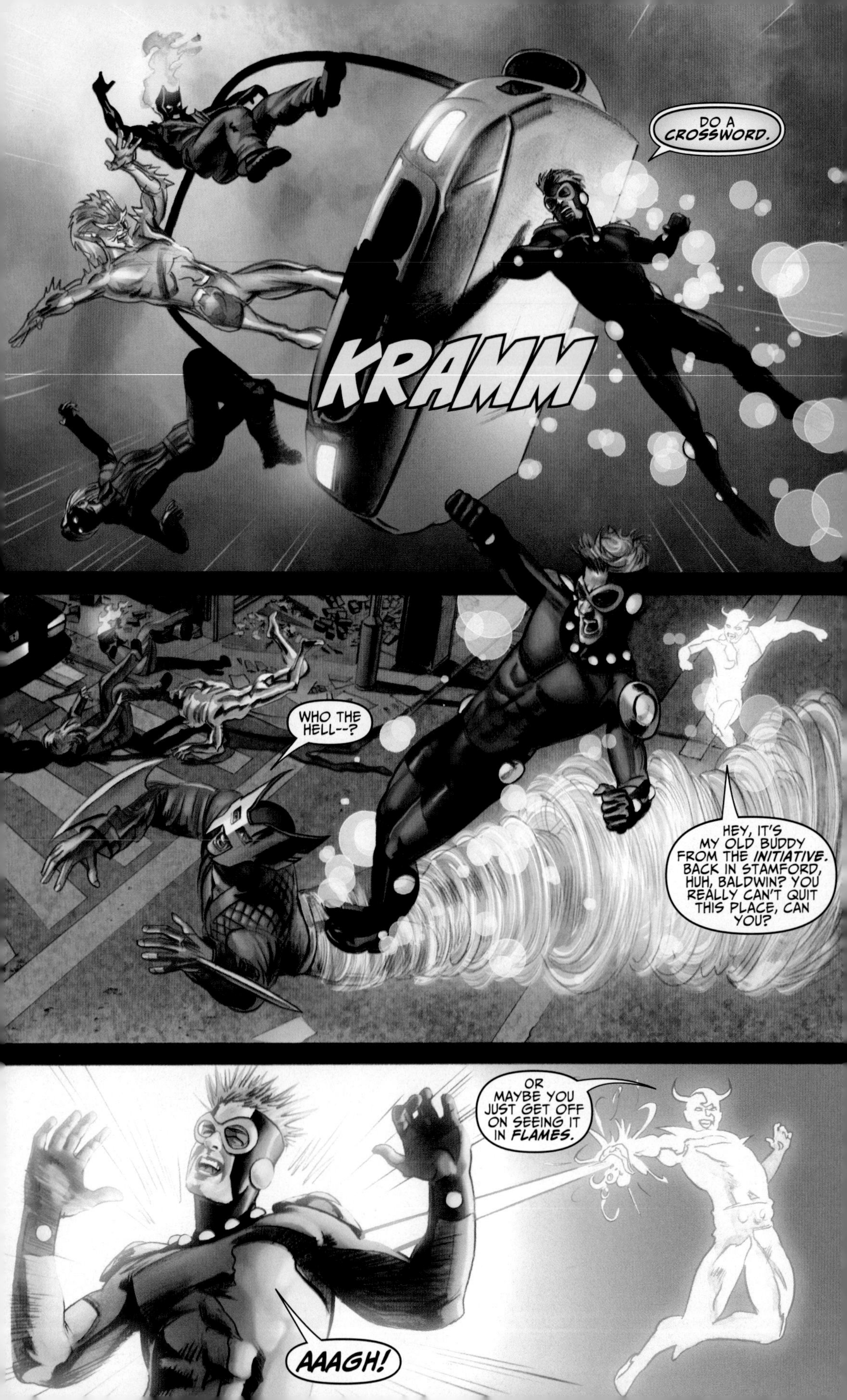
DO A CROSSWORD.
KRAMM
WHO THE HELL--?
HEY, IT'S MY OLD BUDDY FROM THE *INITIATIVE.* BACK IN STAMFORD, HUH, BALDWIN? YOU REALLY CAN'T QUIT THIS PLACE, CAN YOU?
OR MAYBE YOU JUST GET OFF ON SEEING IT IN *FLAMES.*
AAAGH!

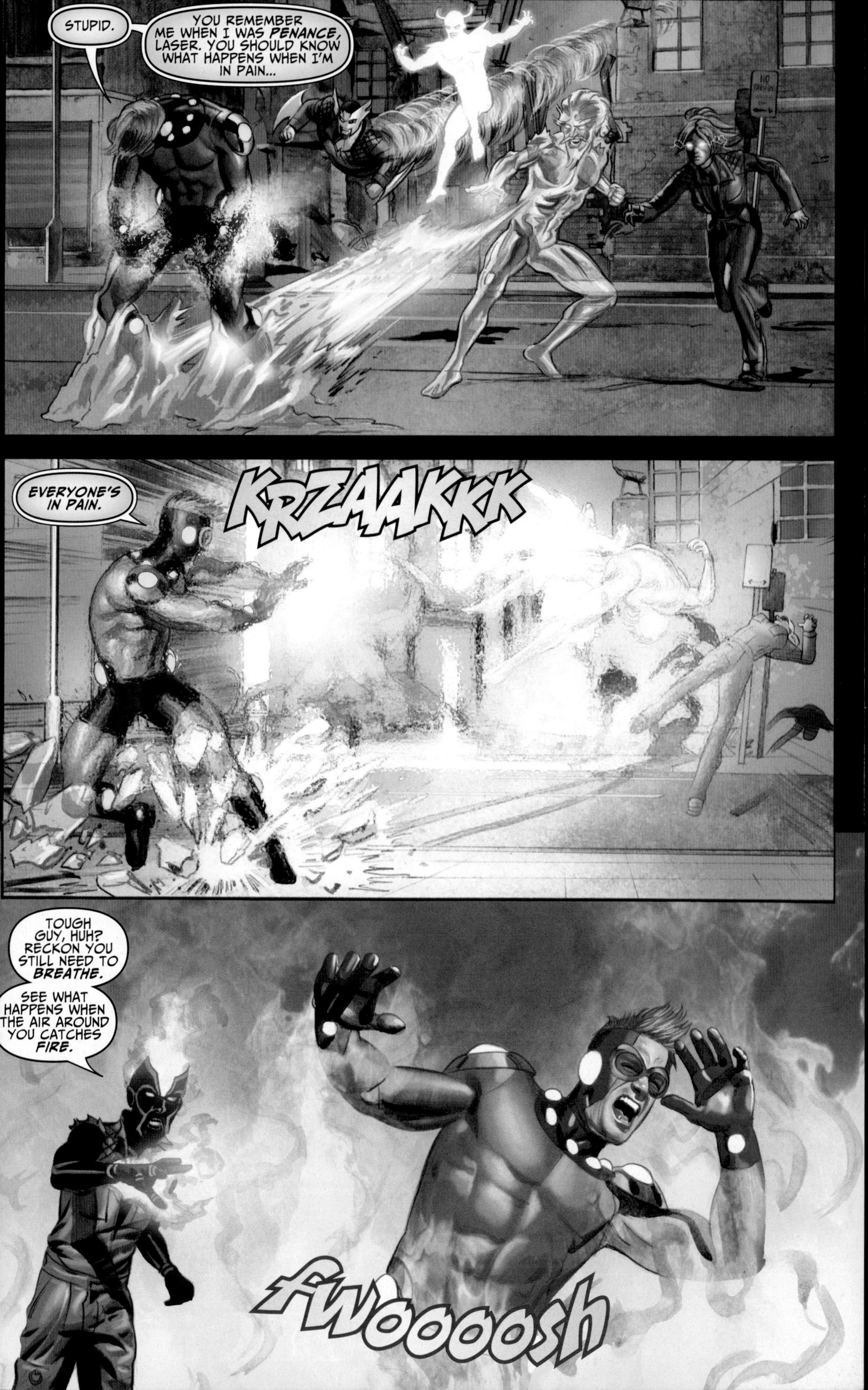
STUPID.
YOU REMEMBER ME WHEN I WAS PENANCE, LASER. YOU SHOULD KNOW WHAT HAPPENS WHEN I'M IN PAIN...
EVERYONE'S IN PAIN.
KRZAAKKK
TOUGH GUY, HUH? RECKON YOU STILL NEED TO BREATHE.
SEE WHAT HAPPENS WHEN THE AIR AROUND YOU CATCHES FIRE.
fwoooosh

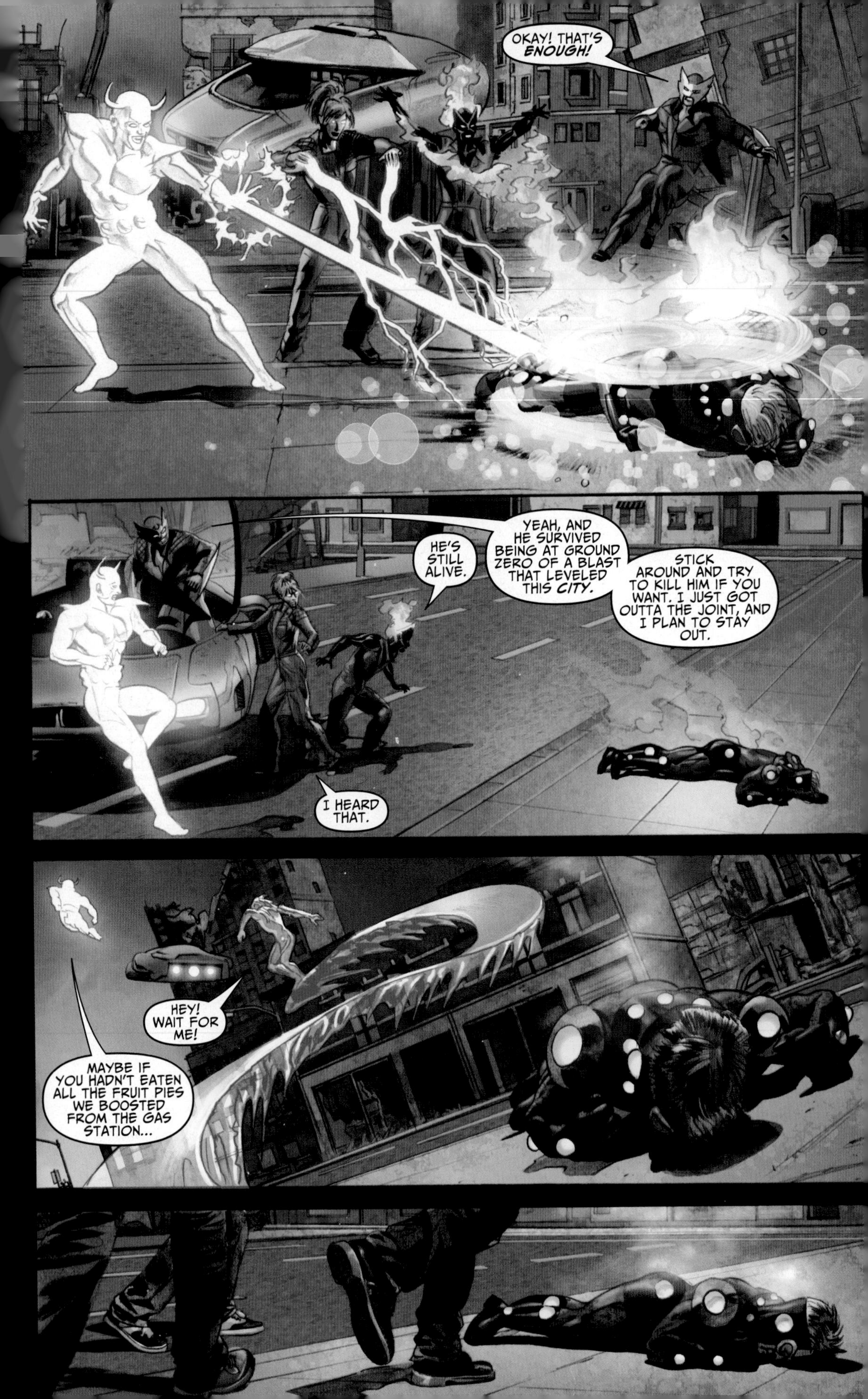
OKAY! THAT'S *ENOUGH!*
HE'S STILL ALIVE.
YEAH, AND HE SURVIVED BEING AT GROUND ZERO OF A BLAST THAT LEVELED THIS *CITY*.
STICK AROUND AND TRY TO KILL HIM IF YOU WANT. I JUST GOT OUTTA THE JOINT, AND I PLAN TO STAY OUT.
I HEARD THAT.
HEY! WAIT FOR ME!
MAYBE IF YOU HADN'T EATEN ALL THE FRUIT PIES WE BOOSTED FROM THE GAS STATION...

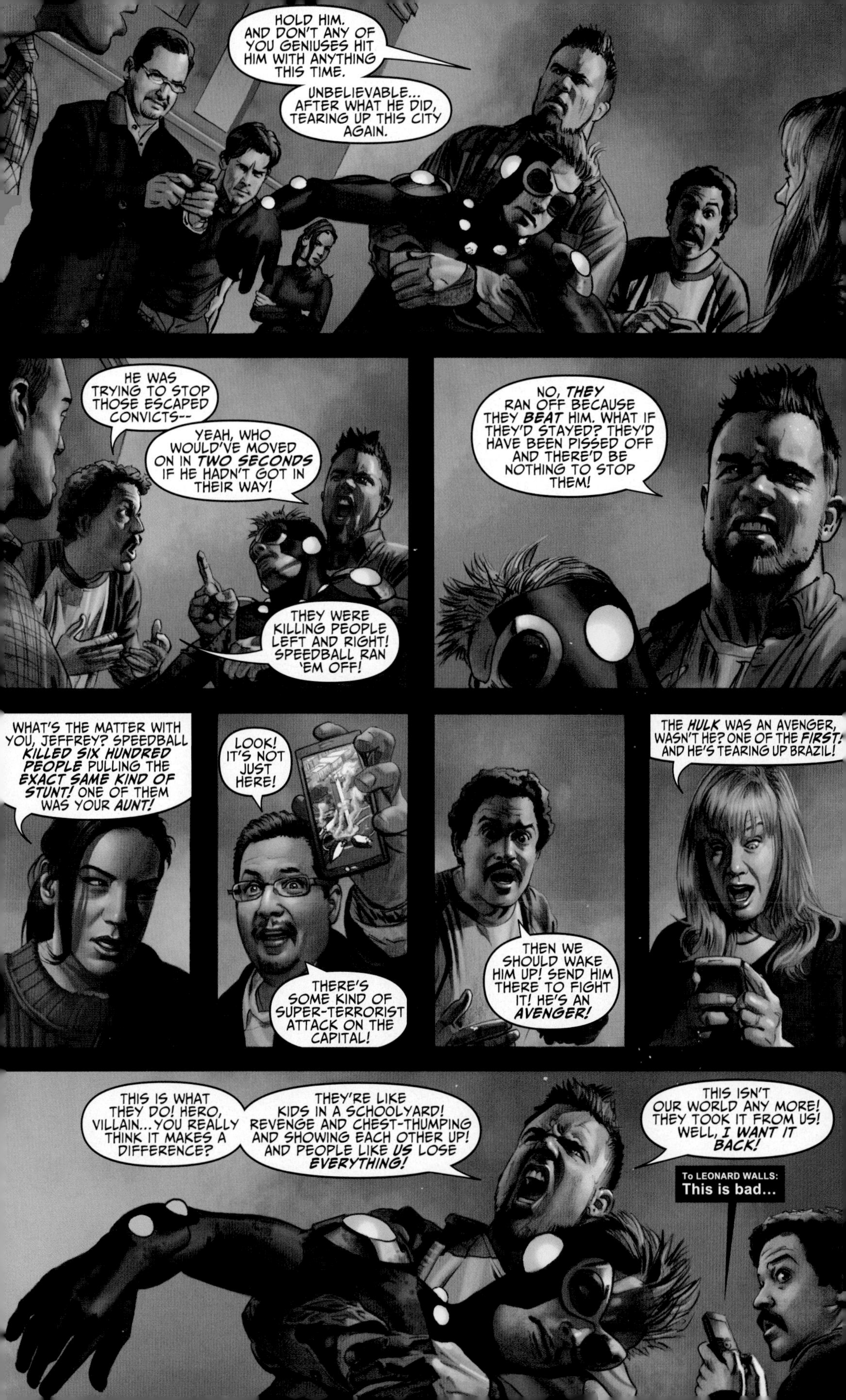
HOLD HIM. AND DON'T ANY OF YOU GENIUSES HIT HIM WITH ANYTHING THIS TIME.
UNBELIEVABLE... AFTER WHAT HE DID, TEARING UP THIS CITY AGAIN.
HE WAS TRYING TO STOP THOSE ESCAPED CONVICTS--
YEAH, WHO WOULD'VE MOVED ON IN TWO SECONDS IF HE HADN'T GOT IN THEIR WAY!
THEY WERE KILLING PEOPLE LEFT AND RIGHT! SPEEDBALL RAN 'EM OFF!
NO, THEY RAN OFF BECAUSE THEY BEAT HIM. WHAT IF THEY'D STAYED? THEY'D HAVE BEEN PISSED OFF AND THERE'D BE NOTHING TO STOP THEM!
WHAT'S THE MATTER WITH YOU, JEFFREY? SPEEDBALL KILLED SIX HUNDRED PEOPLE PULLING THE EXACT SAME KIND OF STUNT! ONE OF THEM WAS YOUR AUNT!
LOOK! IT'S NOT JUST HERE!
THERE'S SOME KIND OF SUPER-TERRORIST ATTACK ON THE CAPITAL!
THEN WE SHOULD WAKE HIM UP! SEND HIM THERE TO FIGHT IT! HE'S AN AVENGER!
THE HULK WAS AN AVENGER, WASN'T HE? ONE OF THE FIRST! AND HE'S TEARING UP BRAZIL!
THIS IS WHAT THEY DO! HERO, VILLAIN...YOU REALLY THINK IT MAKES A DIFFERENCE?
THEY'RE LIKE KIDS IN A SCHOOLYARD! REVENGE AND CHEST-THUMPING AND SHOWING EACH OTHER UP! AND PEOPLE LIKE US LOSE EVERYTHING!
THIS ISN'T OUR WORLD ANY MORE! THEY TOOK IT FROM US! WELL, I WANT IT BACK!
To LEONARD WALLS:
This is bad...

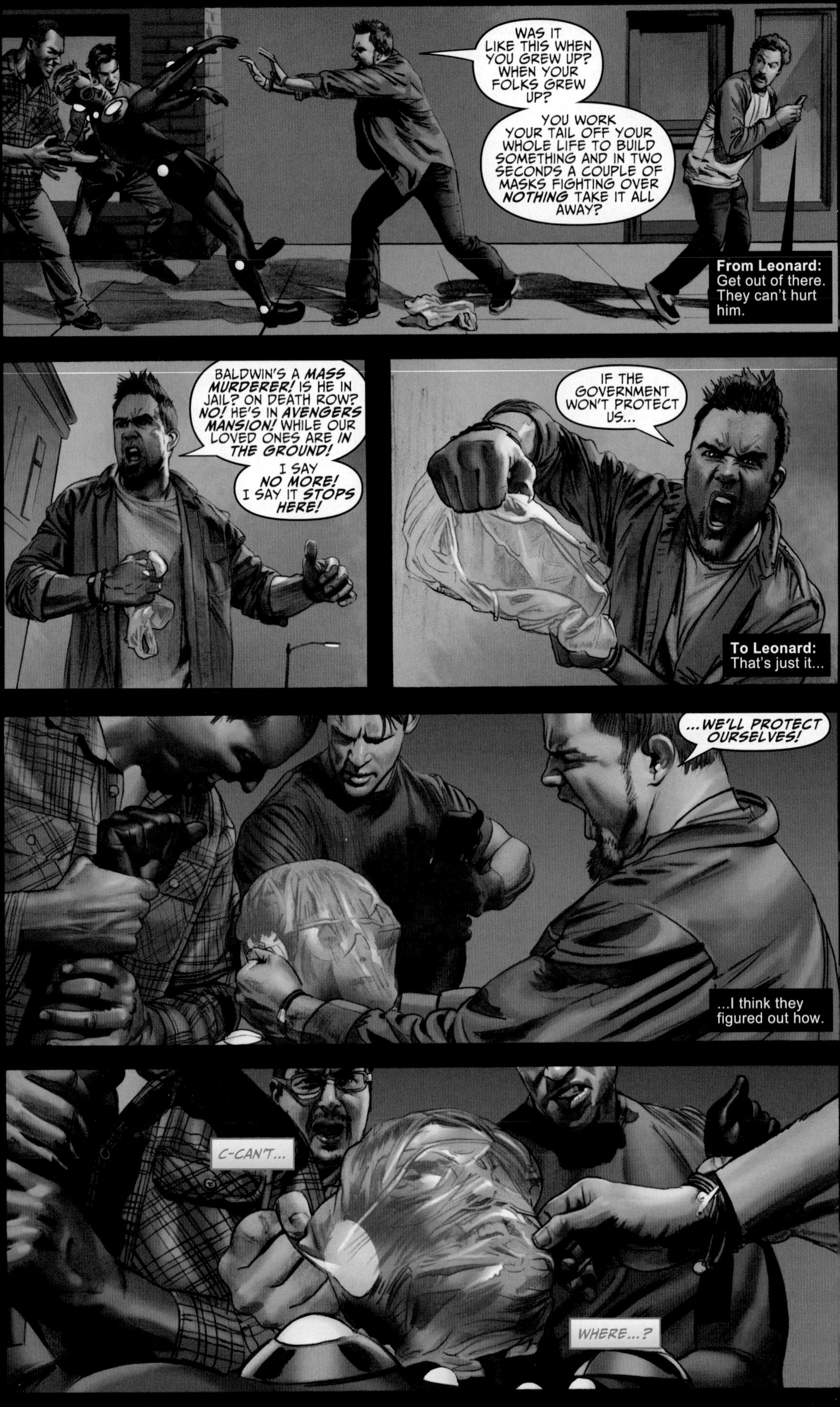
WAS IT LIKE THIS WHEN YOU GREW UP? WHEN YOUR FOLKS GREW UP?
YOU WORK YOUR TAIL OFF YOUR WHOLE LIFE TO BUILD SOMETHING AND IN TWO SECONDS A COUPLE OF MASKS FIGHTING OVER NOTHING TAKE IT ALL AWAY?
From Leonard: Get out of there. They can't hurt him.
BALDWIN'S A MASS MURDERER! IS HE IN JAIL? ON DEATH ROW? NO! HE'S IN AVENGERS MANSION! WHILE OUR LOVED ONES ARE IN THE GROUND!
I SAY NO MORE! I SAY IT STOPS HERE!
IF THE GOVERNMENT WON'T PROTECT US...
To Leonard: That's just it...
...WE'LL PROTECT OURSELVES!
...I think they figured out how.
C-CAN'T...
WHERE...?

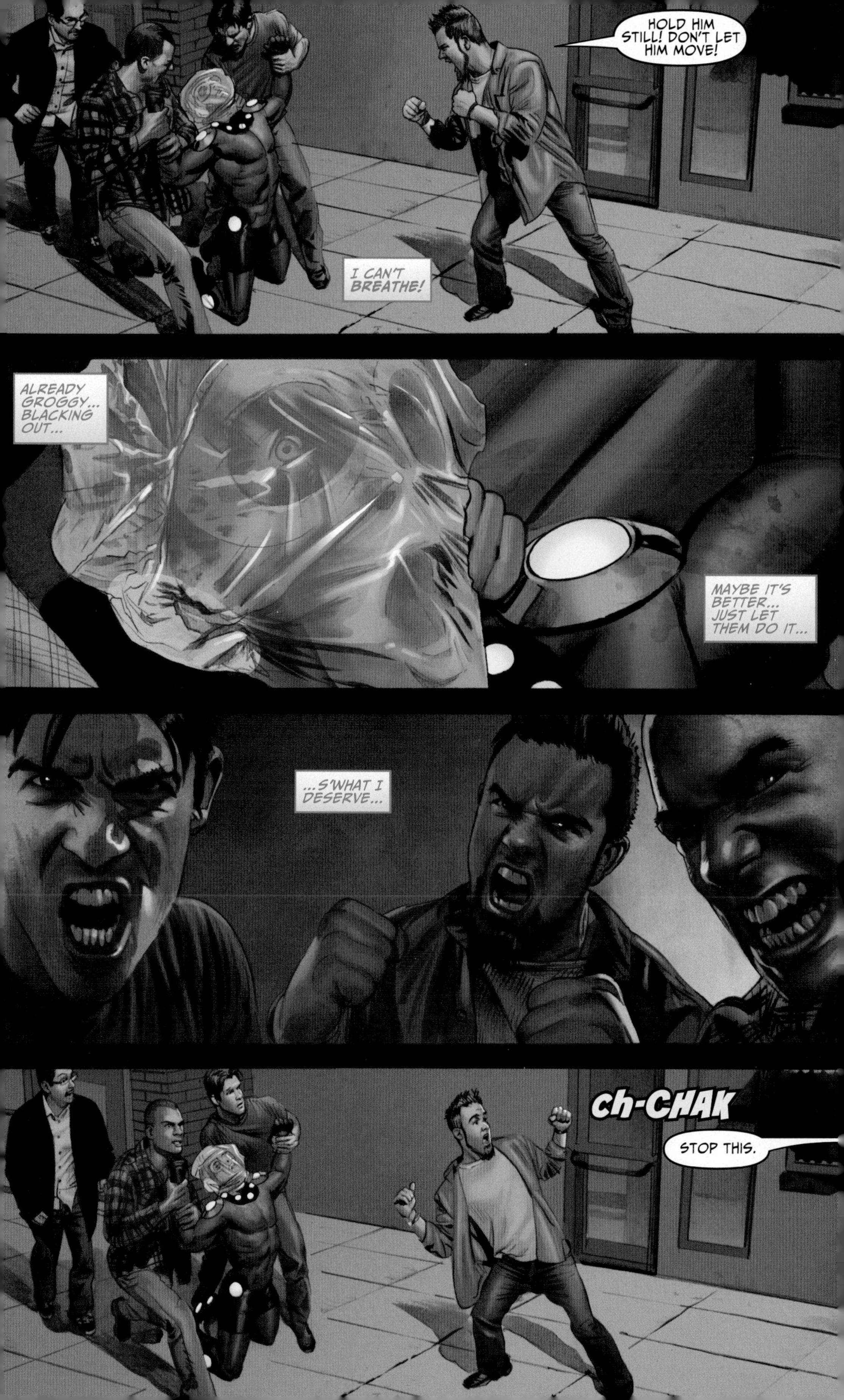
HOLD HIM STILL! DON'T LET HIM MOVE!
I CAN'T BREATHE!
ALREADY GROGGY... BLACKING OUT...
MAYBE IT'S BETTER... JUST LET THEM DO IT...
...S'WHAT I DESERVE...
Ch-CHAK
STOP THIS.

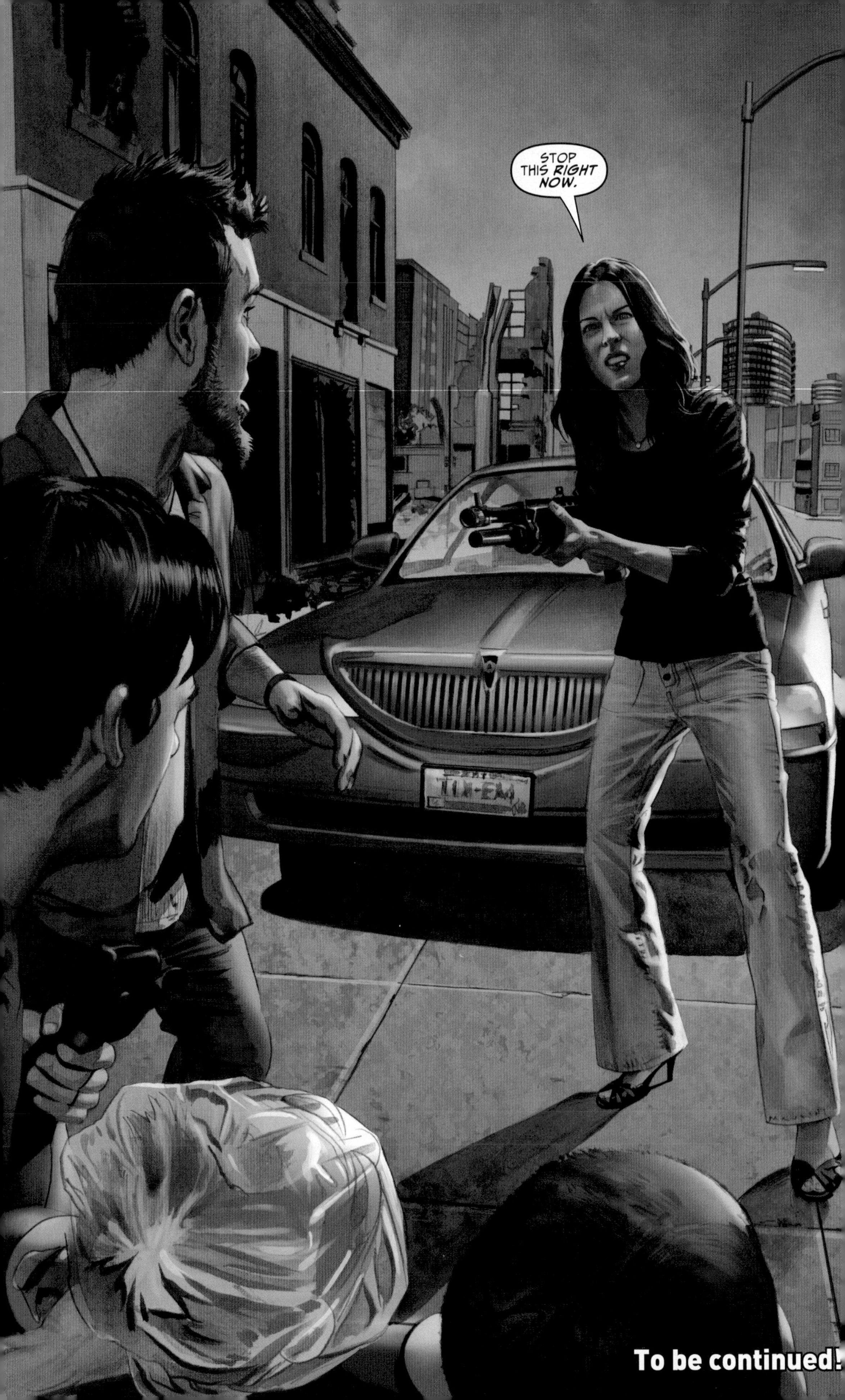
STOP THIS RIGHT NOW.
To be continued!

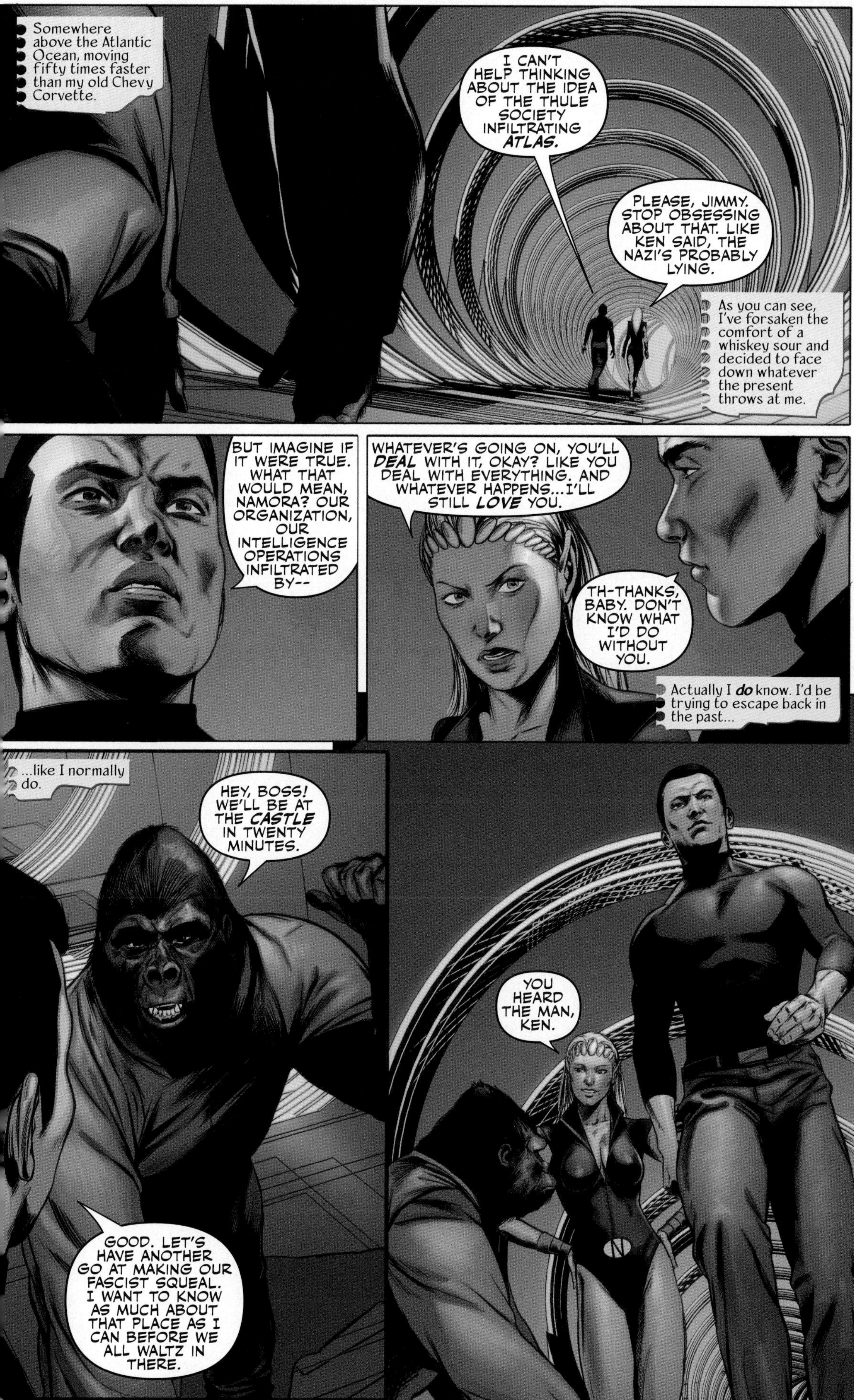
Somewhere above the Atlantic Ocean, moving fifty times faster than my old Chevy Corvette.
I CAN'T HELP THINKING ABOUT THE IDEA OF THE THULE SOCIETY INFILTRATING *ATLAS.*
PLEASE, JIMMY. STOP OBSESSING ABOUT THAT. LIKE KEN SAID, THE NAZI'S PROBABLY LYING.
As you can see, I've forsaken the comfort of a whiskey sour and decided to face down whatever the present throws at me.
BUT IMAGINE IF IT WERE TRUE. WHAT THAT WOULD MEAN, NAMORA? OUR ORGANIZATION, OUR INTELLIGENCE OPERATIONS INFILTRATED BY--
WHATEVER'S GOING ON, YOU'LL *DEAL* WITH IT, OKAY? LIKE YOU DEAL WITH EVERYTHING. AND WHATEVER HAPPENS...I'LL STILL *LOVE* YOU.
TH-THANKS, BABY. DON'T KNOW WHAT I'D DO WITHOUT YOU.
Actually I ***do*** know. I'd be trying to escape back in the past...
...like I normally do.
HEY, BOSS! WE'LL BE AT THE *CASTLE* IN TWENTY MINUTES.
GOOD. LET'S HAVE ANOTHER GO AT MAKING OUR FASCIST SQUEAL. I WANT TO KNOW AS MUCH ABOUT THAT PLACE AS I CAN BEFORE WE ALL WALTZ IN THERE.
YOU HEARD THE MAN, KEN.

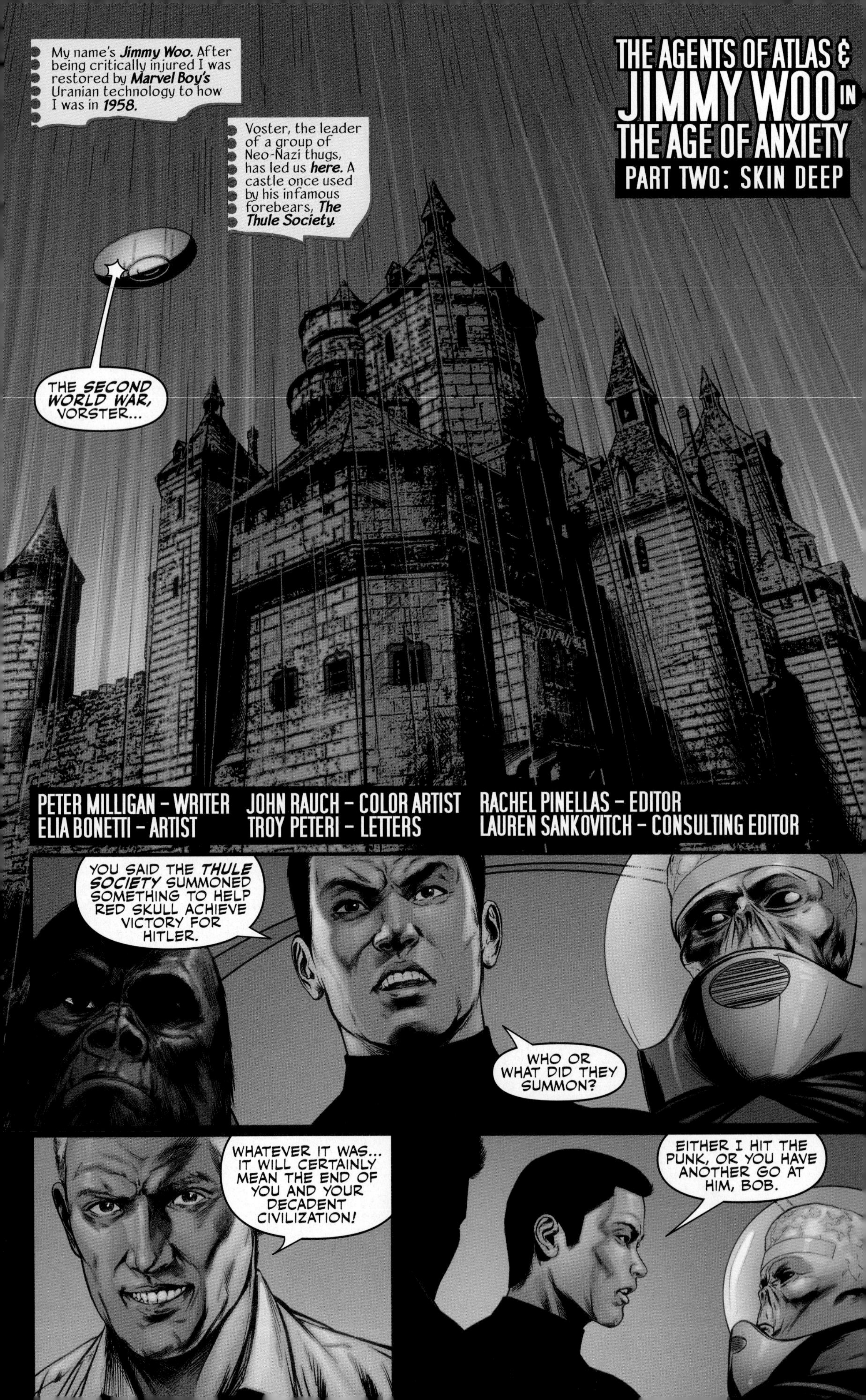
My name's Jimmy Woo. After being critically injured I was restored by Marvel Boy's Uranian technology to how I was in 1958.
THE AGENTS OF ATLAS & JIMMY WOO IN THE AGE OF ANXIETY
PART TWO: SKIN DEEP
Voster, the leader of a group of Neo-Nazi thugs, has led us here. A castle once used by his infamous forebears, The Thule Society.
THE SECOND WORLD WAR, VORSTER...
PETER MILLIGAN – WRITER
ELIA BONETTI – ARTIST
JOHN RAUCH – COLOR ARTIST
TROY PETERI – LETTERS
RACHEL PINELLAS – EDITOR
LAUREN SANKOVITCH – CONSULTING EDITOR
YOU SAID THE THULE SOCIETY SUMMONED SOMETHING TO HELP RED SKULL ACHIEVE VICTORY FOR HITLER.
WHO OR WHAT DID THEY SUMMON?
WHATEVER IT WAS... IT WILL CERTAINLY MEAN THE END OF YOU AND YOUR DECADENT CIVILIZATION!
EITHER I HIT THE PUNK, OR YOU HAVE ANOTHER GO AT HIM, BOB.

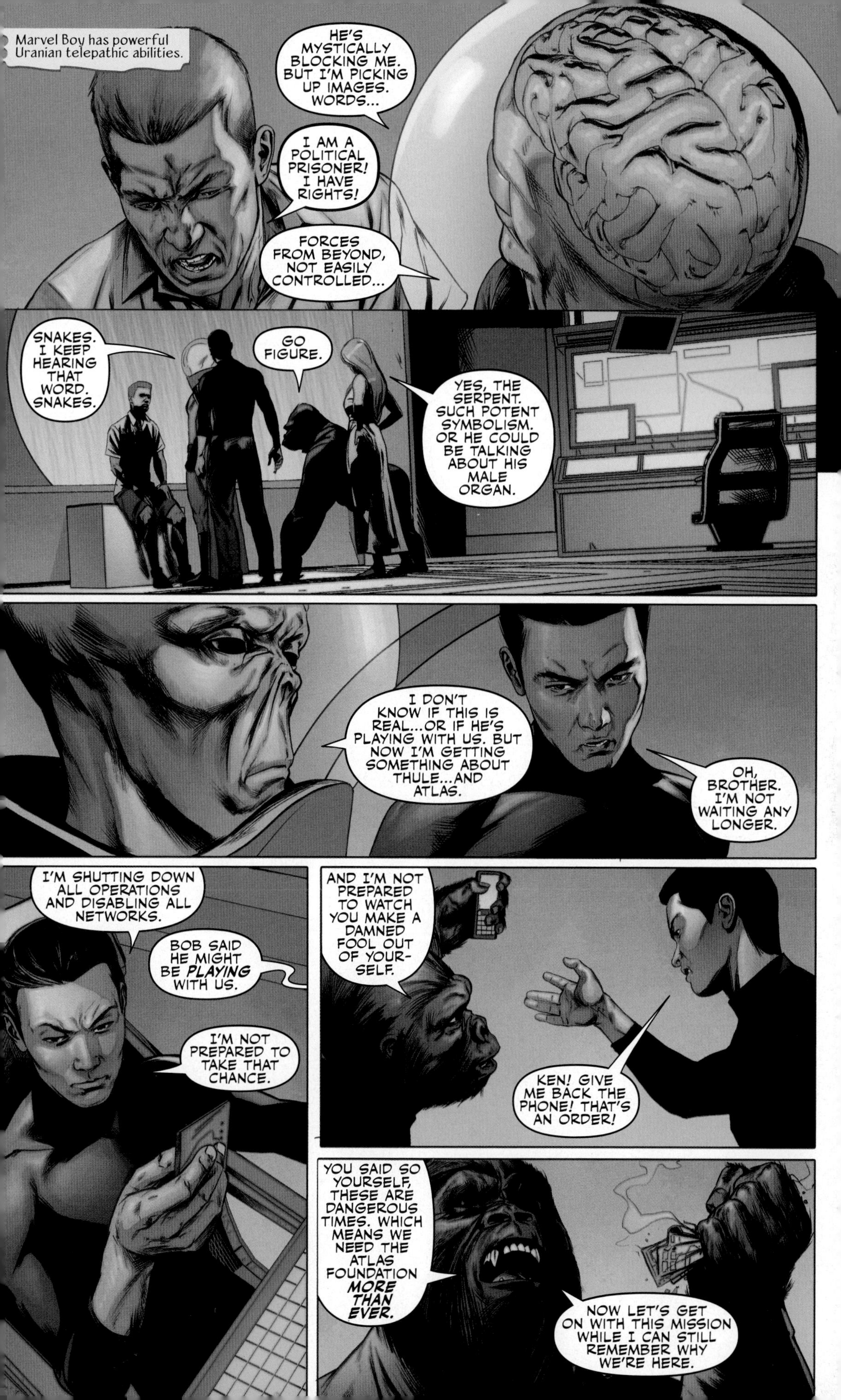
Marvel Boy has powerful Uranian telepathic abilities.
HE'S MYSTICALLY BLOCKING ME. BUT I'M PICKING UP IMAGES. WORDS...
I AM A POLITICAL PRISONER! I HAVE RIGHTS!
FORCES FROM BEYOND, NOT EASILY CONTROLLED...
SNAKES. I KEEP HEARING THAT WORD. SNAKES.
GO FIGURE.
YES, THE SERPENT. SUCH POTENT SYMBOLISM. OR HE COULD BE TALKING ABOUT HIS MALE ORGAN.
I DON'T KNOW IF THIS IS REAL...OR IF HE'S PLAYING WITH US. BUT NOW I'M GETTING SOMETHING ABOUT THULE...AND ATLAS.
OH, BROTHER. I'M NOT WAITING ANY LONGER.
I'M SHUTTING DOWN ALL OPERATIONS AND DISABLING ALL NETWORKS.
BOB SAID HE MIGHT BE *PLAYING* WITH US.
I'M NOT PREPARED TO TAKE THAT CHANCE.
AND I'M NOT PREPARED TO WATCH YOU MAKE A DAMNED FOOL OUT OF YOUR-SELF.
KEN! GIVE ME BACK THE PHONE! THAT'S AN ORDER!
YOU SAID SO YOURSELF, THESE ARE DANGEROUS TIMES. WHICH MEANS WE NEED THE ATLAS FOUNDATION ***MORE THAN EVER.***
NOW LET'S GET ON WITH THIS MISSION WHILE I CAN STILL REMEMBER WHY WE'RE HERE.

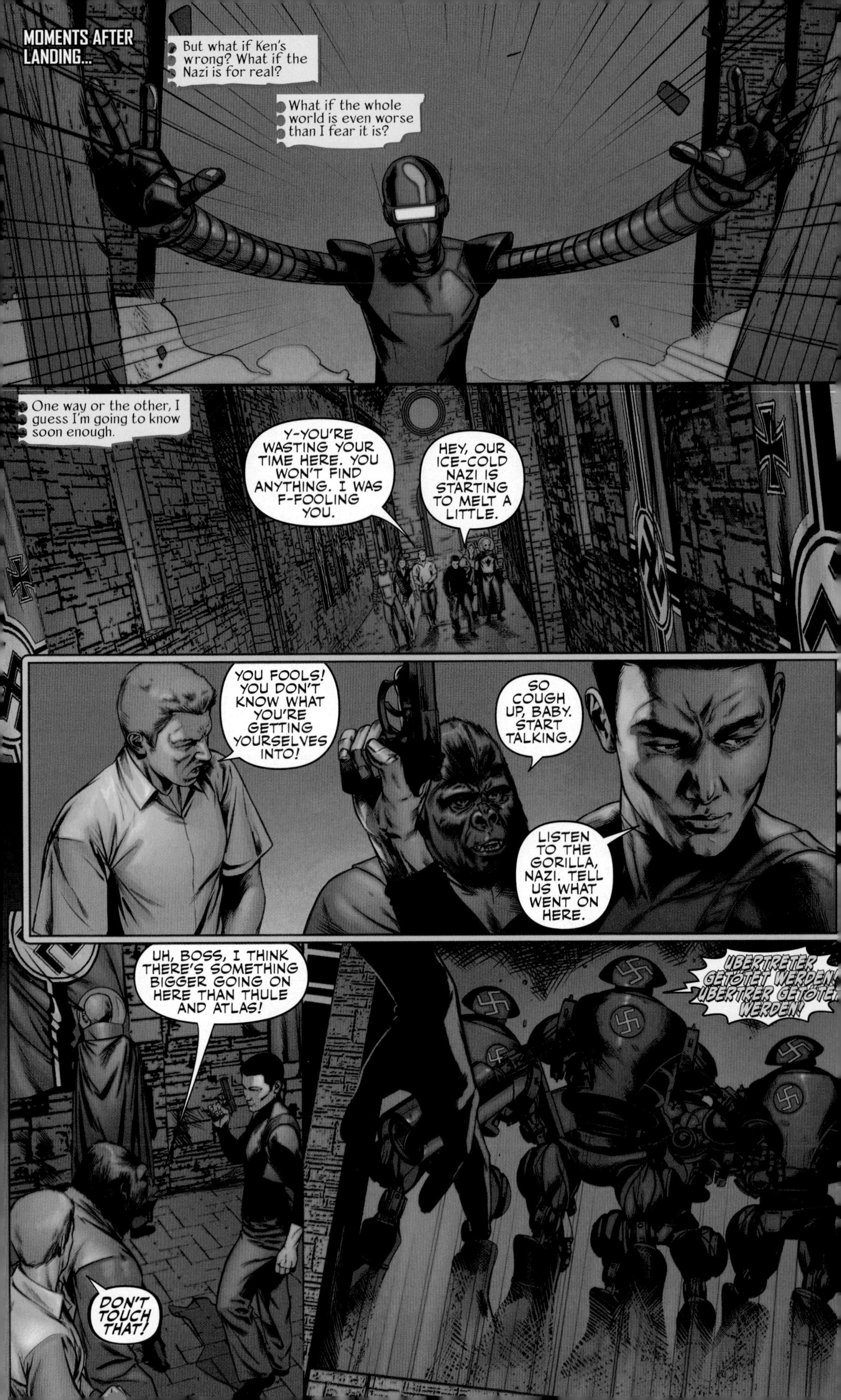
MOMENTS AFTER LANDING...
But what if Ken's wrong? What if the Nazi is for real?
What if the whole world is even worse than I fear it is?
One way or the other, I guess I'm going to know soon enough.
Y-YOU'RE WASTING YOUR TIME HERE. YOU WON'T FIND ANYTHING. I WAS F-FOOLING YOU.
HEY, OUR ICE-COLD NAZI IS STARTING TO MELT A LITTLE.
YOU FOOLS! YOU DON'T KNOW WHAT YOU'RE GETTING YOURSELVES INTO!
SO COUGH UP, BABY. START TALKING.
LISTEN TO THE GORILLA, NAZI. TELL US WHAT WENT ON HERE.
UH, BOSS, I THINK THERE'S SOMETHING BIGGER GOING ON HERE THAN THULE AND ATLAS!
DON'T TOUCH THAT!
UBERTRETER GETÖTET WERDEN! UBERTRER GETÖTET WERDEN!

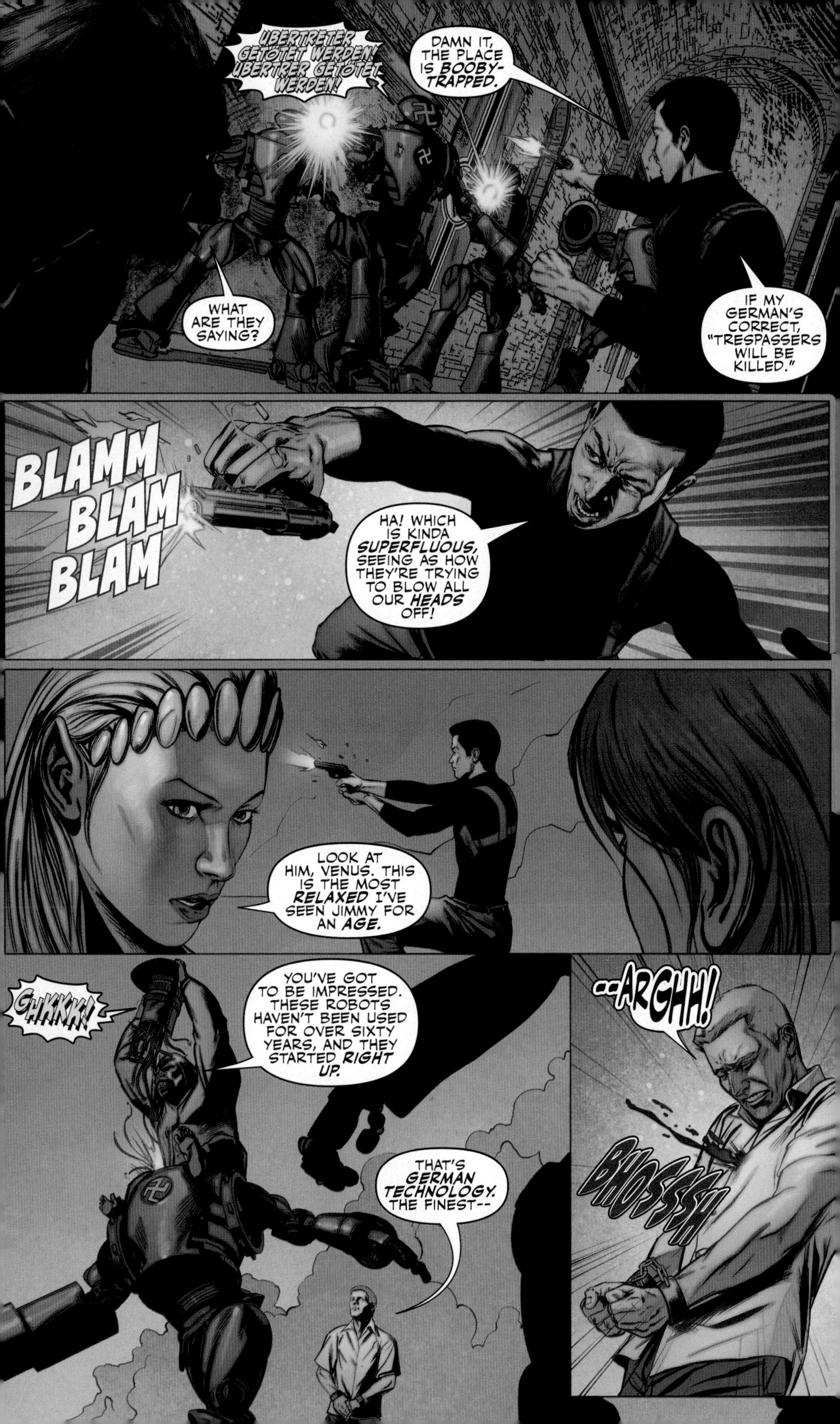

UBERTRETER GETÖTET WERDEN! UBERTRER GETÖTET WERDEN!
DAMN IT, THE PLACE IS BOOBY-TRAPPED.
WHAT ARE THEY SAYING?
IF MY GERMAN'S CORRECT, "TRESPASSERS WILL BE KILLED."
BLAMM BLAM BLAM
HA! WHICH IS KINDA SUPERFLUOUS, SEEING AS HOW THEY'RE TRYING TO BLOW ALL OUR HEADS OFF!
LOOK AT HIM, VENUS. THIS IS THE MOST RELAXED I'VE SEEN JIMMY FOR AN AGE.
GHKKK!
YOU'VE GOT TO BE IMPRESSED. THESE ROBOTS HAVEN'T BEEN USED FOR OVER SIXTY YEARS, AND THEY STARTED RIGHT UP.
THAT'S GERMAN TECHNOLOGY. THE FINEST--
--ARGHH!
BHOSSSH

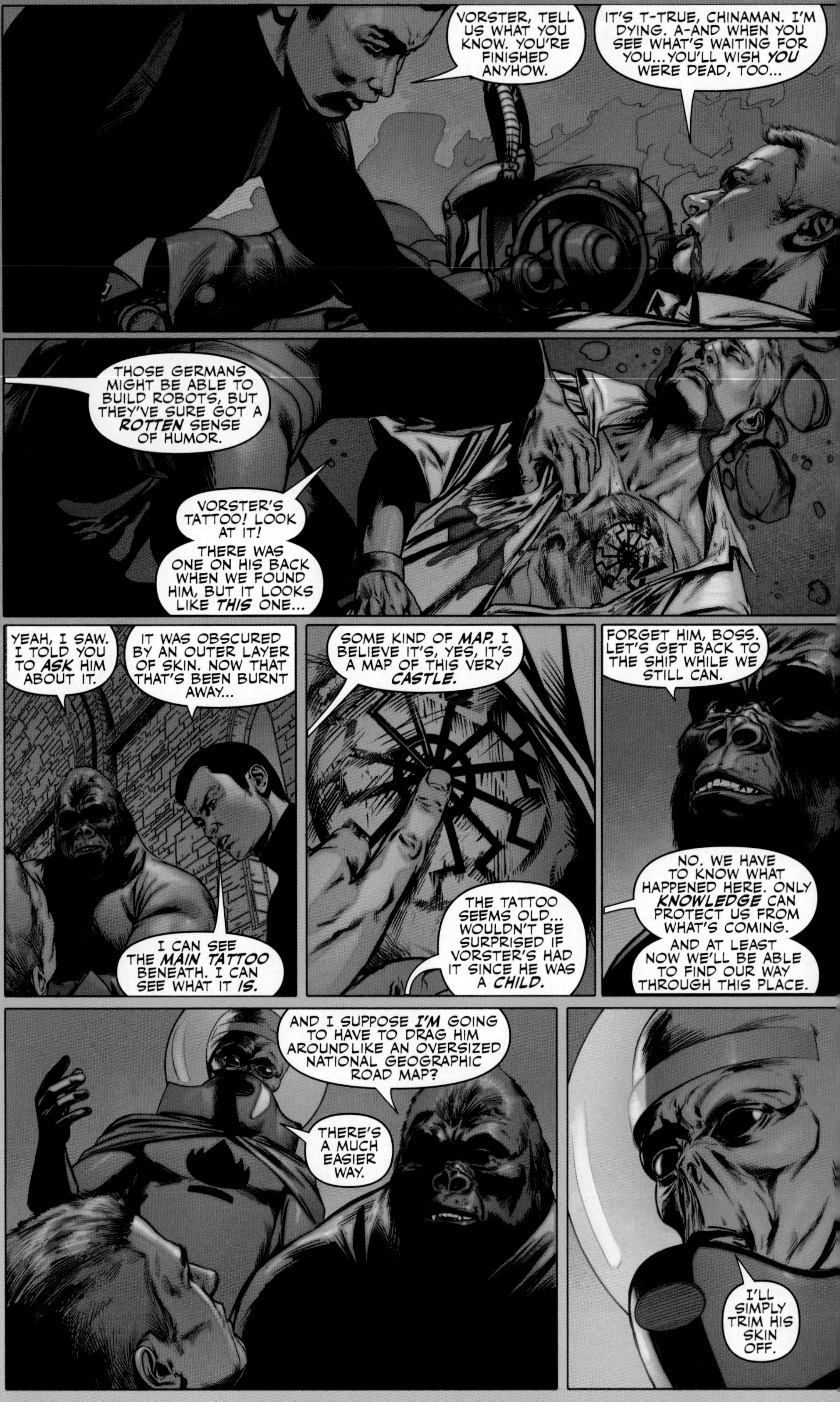
VORSTER, TELL US WHAT YOU KNOW. YOU'RE FINISHED ANYHOW.
IT'S T-TRUE, CHINAMAN. I'M DYING. A-AND WHEN YOU SEE WHAT'S WAITING FOR YOU...YOU'LL WISH YOU WERE DEAD, TOO...
THOSE GERMANS MIGHT BE ABLE TO BUILD ROBOTS, BUT THEY'VE SURE GOT A ROTTEN SENSE OF HUMOR.
VORSTER'S TATTOO! LOOK AT IT!
THERE WAS ONE ON HIS BACK WHEN WE FOUND HIM, BUT IT LOOKS LIKE THIS ONE...
YEAH, I SAW. I TOLD YOU TO ASK HIM ABOUT IT.
IT WAS OBSCURED BY AN OUTER LAYER OF SKIN. NOW THAT THAT'S BEEN BURNT AWAY...
I CAN SEE THE MAIN TATTOO BENEATH. I CAN SEE WHAT IT IS.
SOME KIND OF MAP. I BELIEVE IT'S, YES, IT'S A MAP OF THIS VERY CASTLE.
THE TATTOO SEEMS OLD... WOULDN'T BE SURPRISED IF VORSTER'S HAD IT SINCE HE WAS A CHILD.
FORGET HIM, BOSS. LET'S GET BACK TO THE SHIP WHILE WE STILL CAN.
NO. WE HAVE TO KNOW WHAT HAPPENED HERE. ONLY KNOWLEDGE CAN PROTECT US FROM WHAT'S COMING.
AND AT LEAST NOW WE'LL BE ABLE TO FIND OUR WAY THROUGH THIS PLACE.
AND I SUPPOSE I'M GOING TO HAVE TO DRAG HIM AROUND LIKE AN OVERSIZED NATIONAL GEOGRAPHIC ROAD MAP?
THERE'S A MUCH EASIER WAY.
I'LL SIMPLY TRIM HIS SKIN OFF.

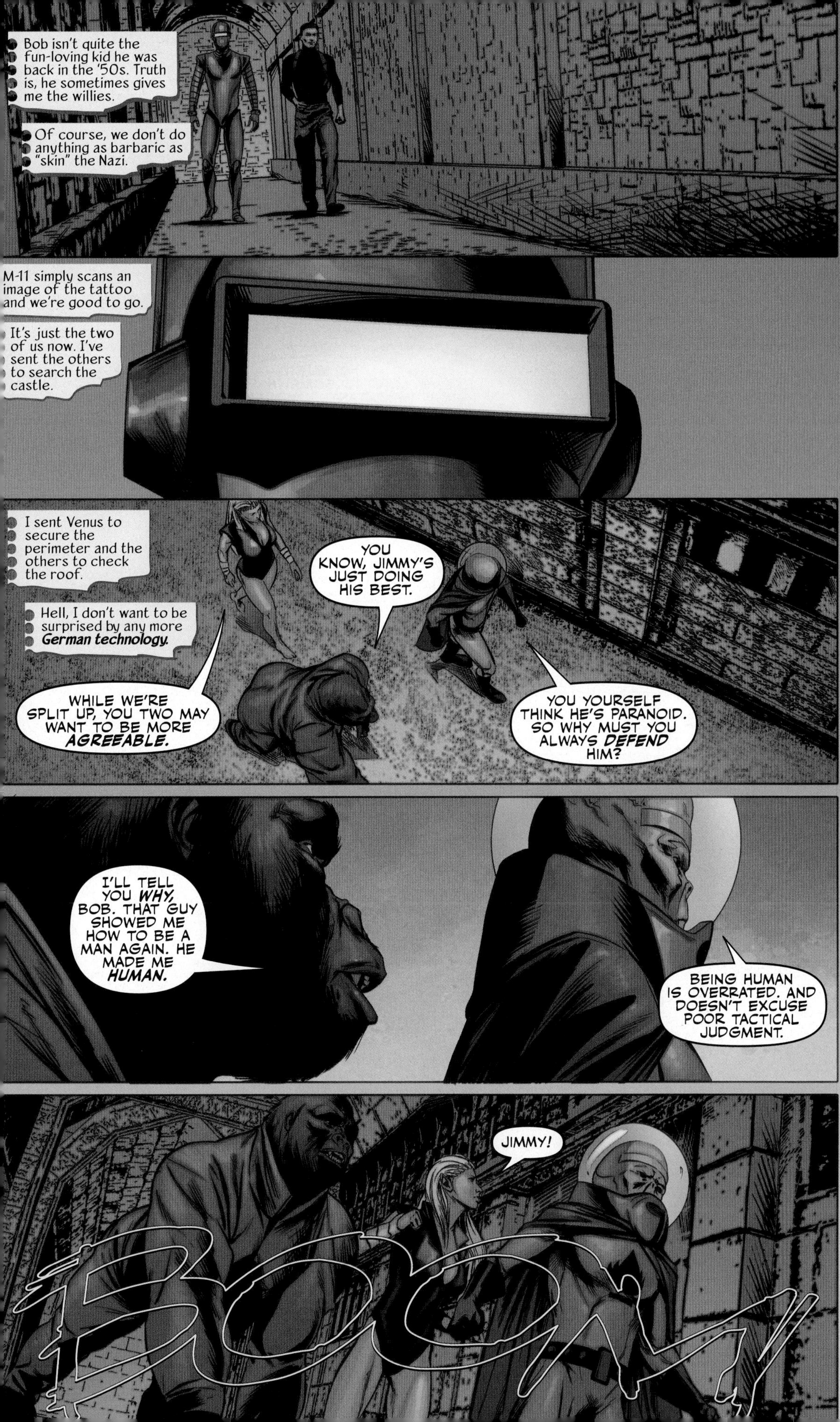
Bob isn't quite the fun-loving kid he was back in the '50s. Truth is, he sometimes gives me the willies.
Of course, we don't do anything as barbaric as "skin" the Nazi.
M-11 simply scans an image of the tattoo and we're good to go.
It's just the two of us now. I've sent the others to search the castle.
I sent Venus to secure the perimeter and the others to check the roof.
Hell, I don't want to be surprised by any more German technology.
YOU KNOW, JIMMY'S JUST DOING HIS BEST.
WHILE WE'RE SPLIT UP, YOU TWO MAY WANT TO BE MORE AGREEABLE.
YOU YOURSELF THINK HE'S PARANOID. SO WHY MUST YOU ALWAYS DEFEND HIM?
I'LL TELL YOU WHY, BOB. THAT GUY SHOWED ME HOW TO BE A MAN AGAIN. HE MADE ME HUMAN.
BEING HUMAN IS OVERRATED. AND DOESN'T EXCUSE POOR TACTICAL JUDGMENT.
JIMMY!
BOOM!

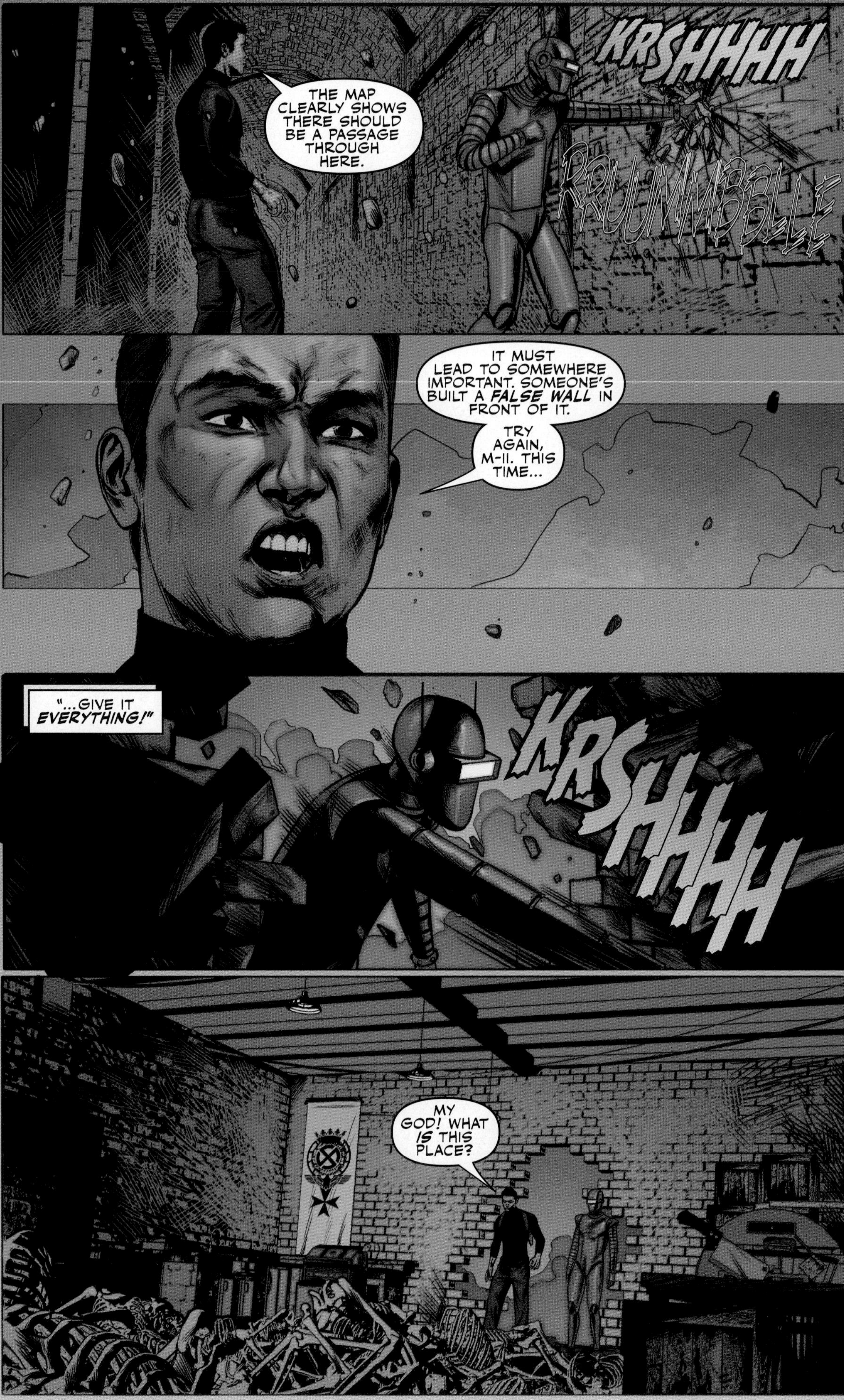
THE MAP CLEARLY SHOWS THERE SHOULD BE A PASSAGE THROUGH HERE.
KRSHHHH
RRUMMBBLE
IT MUST LEAD TO SOMEWHERE IMPORTANT. SOMEONE'S BUILT A FALSE WALL IN FRONT OF IT.
TRY AGAIN, M-11. THIS TIME...
"...GIVE IT EVERYTHING!"
KRSHHHHH
MY GOD! WHAT IS THIS PLACE?

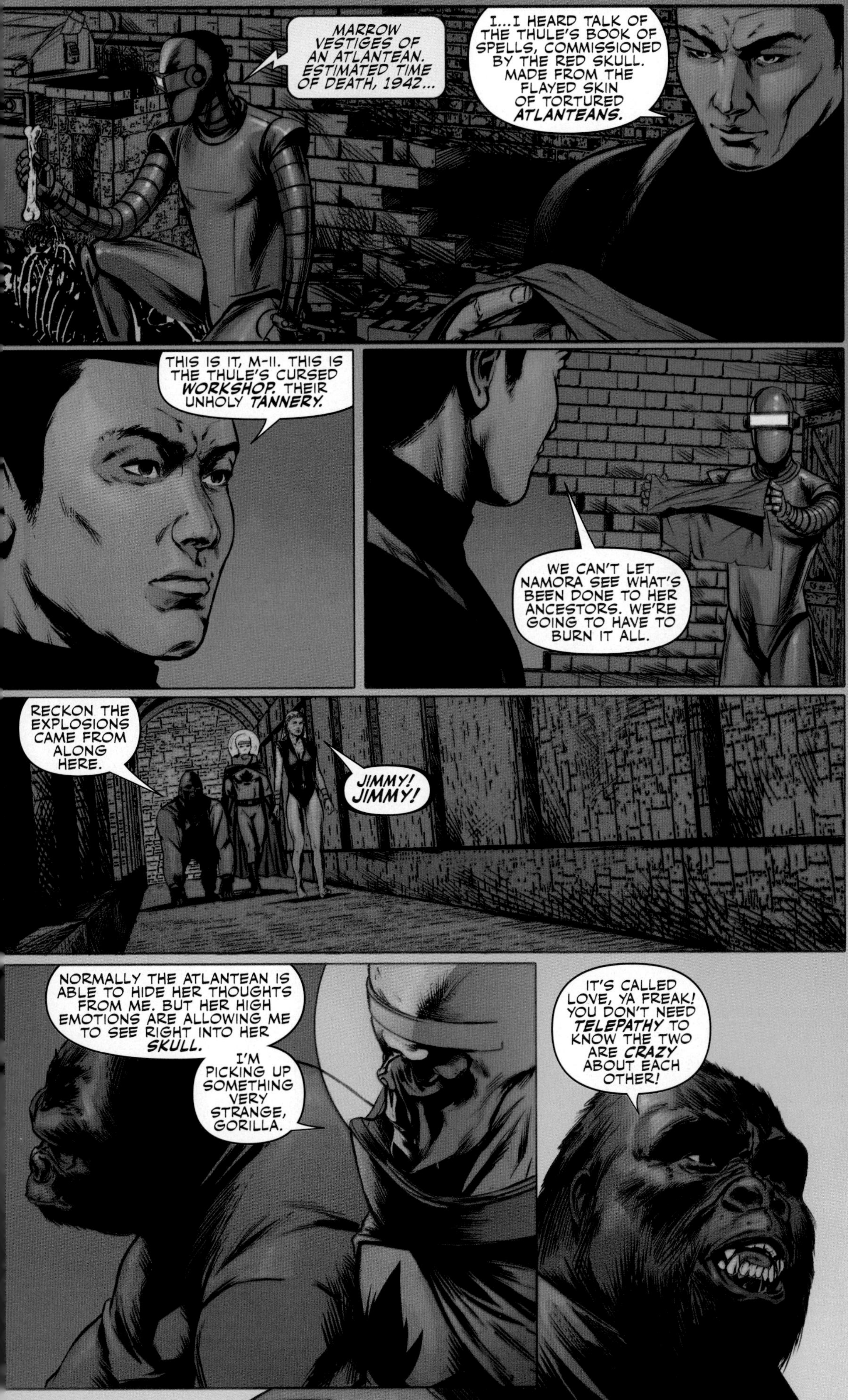
MARROW VESTIGES OF AN ATLANTEAN. ESTIMATED TIME OF DEATH, 1942...
I...I HEARD TALK OF THE THULE'S BOOK OF SPELLS, COMMISSIONED BY THE RED SKULL. MADE FROM THE FLAYED SKIN OF TORTURED ATLANTEANS.
THIS IS IT, M-11. THIS IS THE THULE'S CURSED WORKSHOP. THEIR UNHOLY TANNERY.
WE CAN'T LET NAMORA SEE WHAT'S BEEN DONE TO HER ANCESTORS. WE'RE GOING TO HAVE TO BURN IT ALL.
RECKON THE EXPLOSIONS CAME FROM ALONG HERE.
JIMMY! JIMMY!
NORMALLY THE ATLANTEAN IS ABLE TO HIDE HER THOUGHTS FROM ME. BUT HER HIGH EMOTIONS ARE ALLOWING ME TO SEE RIGHT INTO HER SKULL.
I'M PICKING UP SOMETHING VERY STRANGE, GORILLA.
IT'S CALLED LOVE, YA FREAK! YOU DON'T NEED TELEPATHY TO KNOW THE TWO ARE CRAZY ABOUT EACH OTHER!

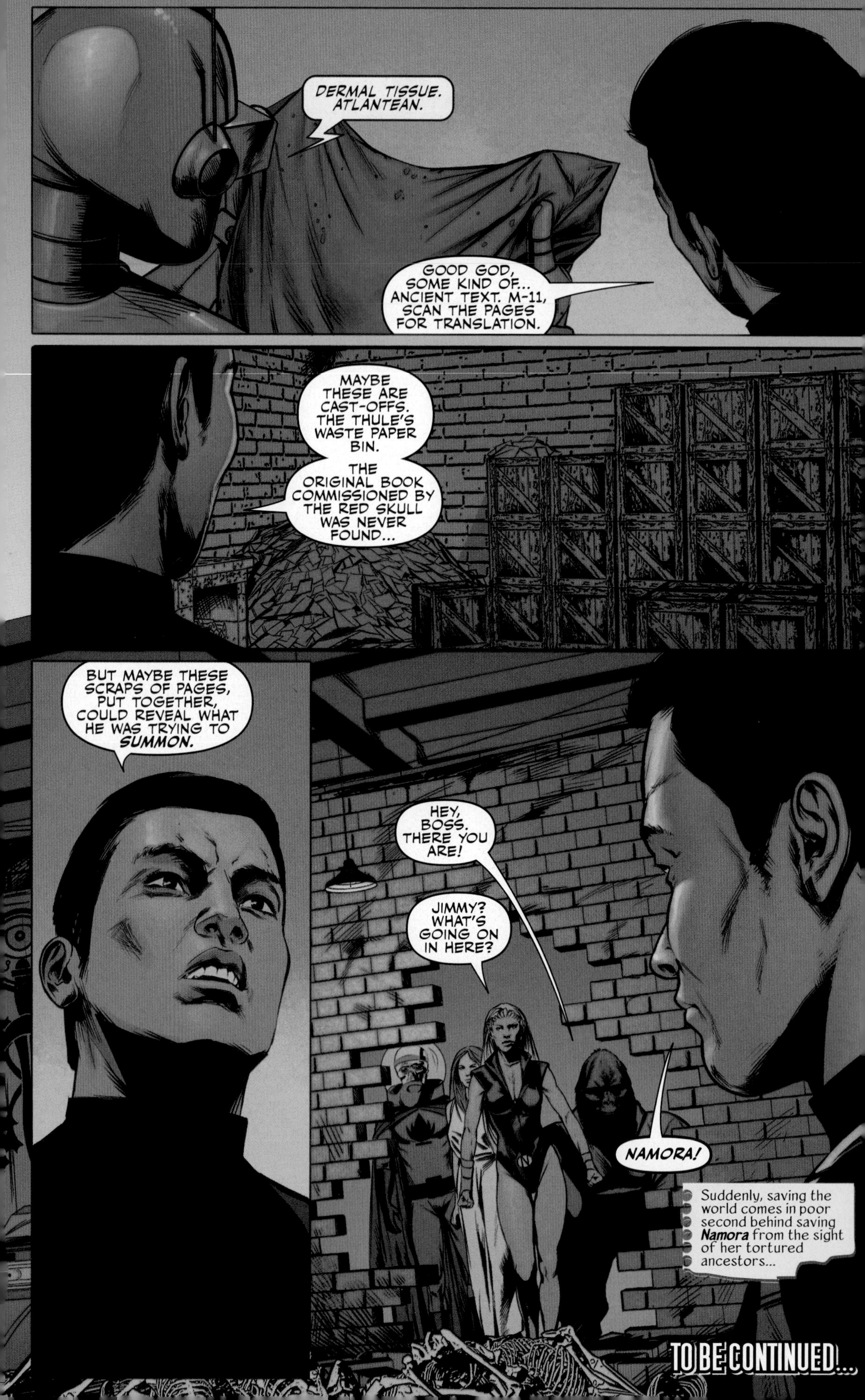
DERMAL TISSUE. ATLANTEAN.
GOOD GOD, SOME KIND OF... ANCIENT TEXT. M-11, SCAN THE PAGES FOR TRANSLATION.
MAYBE THESE ARE CAST-OFFS. THE THULE'S WASTE PAPER BIN.
THE ORIGINAL BOOK COMMISSIONED BY THE RED SKULL WAS NEVER FOUND...
BUT MAYBE THESE SCRAPS OF PAGES, PUT TOGETHER, COULD REVEAL WHAT HE WAS TRYING TO *SUMMON.*
HEY, BOSS. THERE YOU ARE!
JIMMY? WHAT'S GOING ON IN HERE?
NAMORA!
Suddenly, saving the world comes in poor second behind saving *Namora* from the sight of her tortured ancestors...
TO BE CONTINUED...

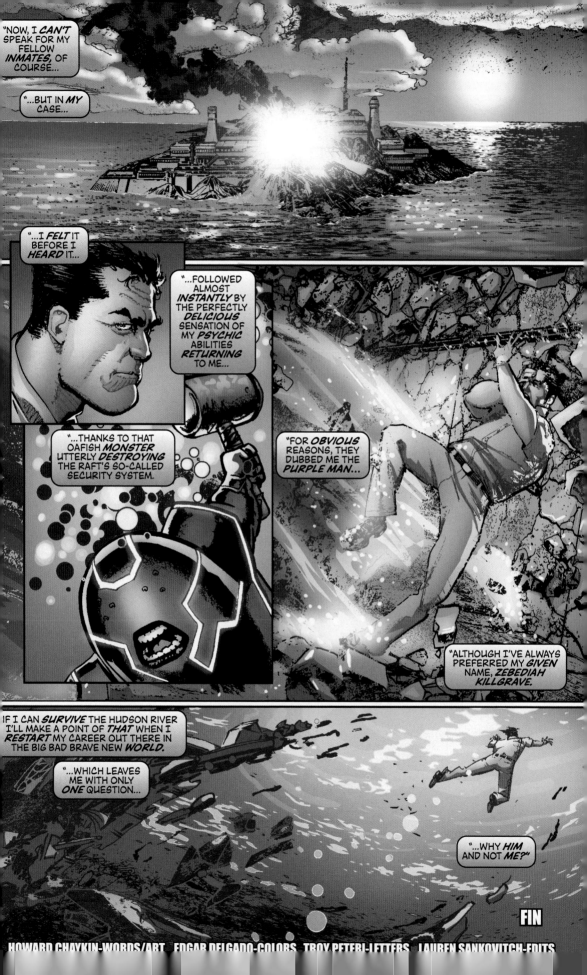

"NOW, I *CAN'T* SPEAK FOR MY FELLOW *INMATES*, OF COURSE...

"...BUT IN *MY* CASE...

"...I *FELT* IT BEFORE I *HEARD* IT...

"...FOLLOWED ALMOST *INSTANTLY* BY THE PERFECTLY *DELICIOUS* SENSATION OF MY *PSYCHIC* ABILITIES *RETURNING* TO ME...

"...THANKS TO THAT OAFISH *MONSTER* UTTERLY *DESTROYING* THE RAFT'S SO-CALLED SECURITY SYSTEM.

"FOR *OBVIOUS* REASONS, THEY DUBBED ME THE *PURPLE MAN*...

"ALTHOUGH I'VE ALWAYS PREFERRED MY *GIVEN* NAME, *ZEBEDIAH KILLGRAVE.*

IF I CAN *SURVIVE* THE HUDSON RIVER I'LL MAKE A POINT OF *THAT* WHEN I *RESTART* MY CAREER OUT THERE IN THE BIG BAD BRAVE NEW *WORLD.*

"...WHICH LEAVES ME WITH ONLY *ONE* QUESTION...

"...WHY *HIM* AND NOT *ME?*"

FIN

HOWARD CHAYKIN-WORDS/ART   EDGAR DELGADO-COLORS   TROY PETERI-LETTERS   LAUREN SANKOVITCH-EDITS

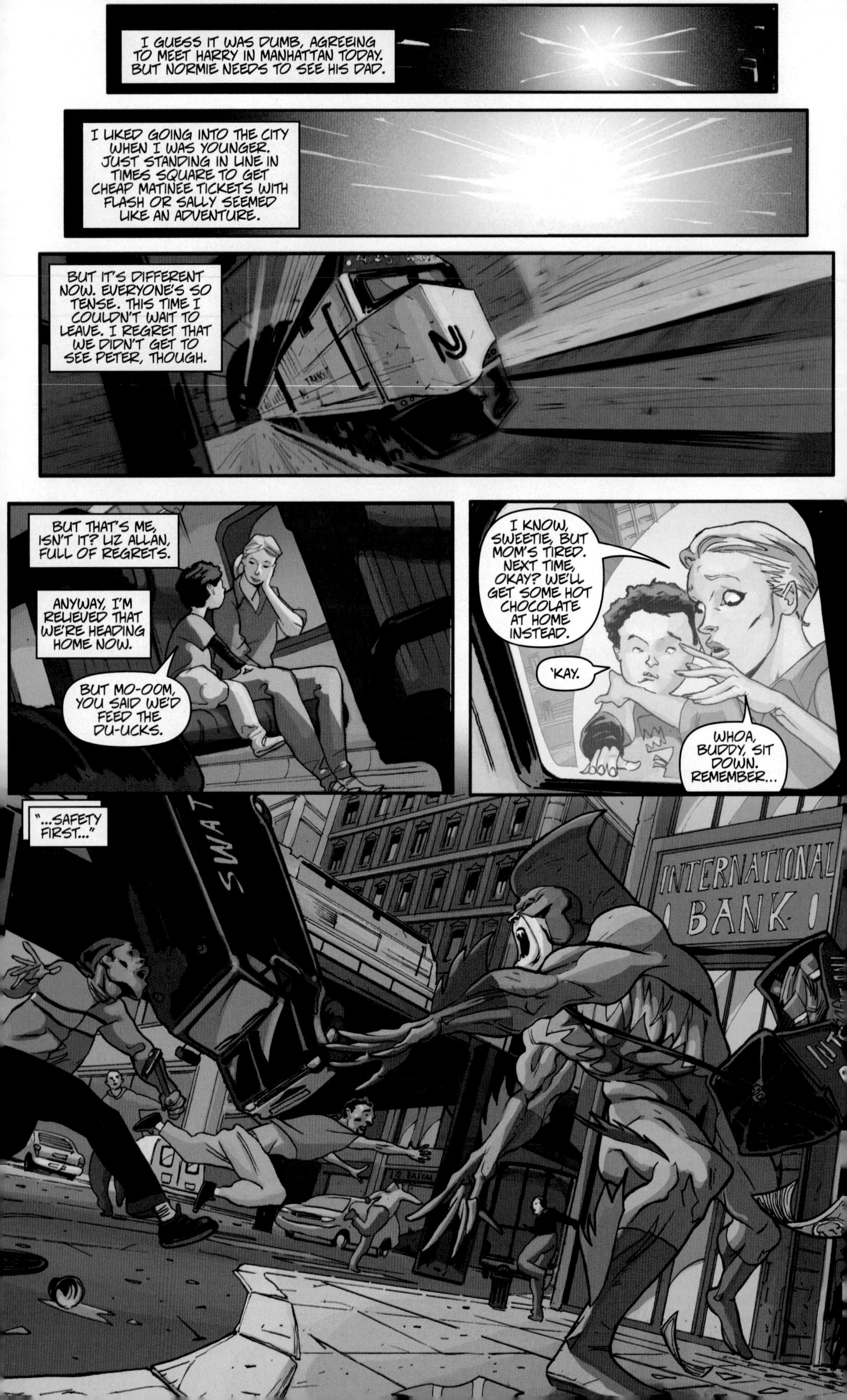
I GUESS IT WAS DUMB, AGREEING TO MEET HARRY IN MANHATTAN TODAY. BUT NORMIE NEEDS TO SEE HIS DAD.
I LIKED GOING INTO THE CITY WHEN I WAS YOUNGER. JUST STANDING IN LINE IN TIMES SQUARE TO GET CHEAP MATINEE TICKETS WITH FLASH OR SALLY SEEMED LIKE AN ADVENTURE.
BUT IT'S DIFFERENT NOW. EVERYONE'S SO TENSE. THIS TIME I COULDN'T WAIT TO LEAVE. I REGRET THAT WE DIDN'T GET TO SEE PETER, THOUGH.
BUT THAT'S ME, ISN'T IT? LIZ ALLAN, FULL OF REGRETS.
ANYWAY, I'M RELIEVED THAT WE'RE HEADING HOME NOW.
BUT MO-OOM, YOU SAID WE'D FEED THE DU-UCKS.
I KNOW, SWEETIE, BUT MOM'S TIRED. NEXT TIME, OKAY? WE'LL GET SOME HOT CHOCOLATE AT HOME INSTEAD.
'KAY.
WHOA, BUDDY, SIT DOWN. REMEMBER...
"...SAFETY FIRST..."
SWAT
INTERNATIONAL BANK

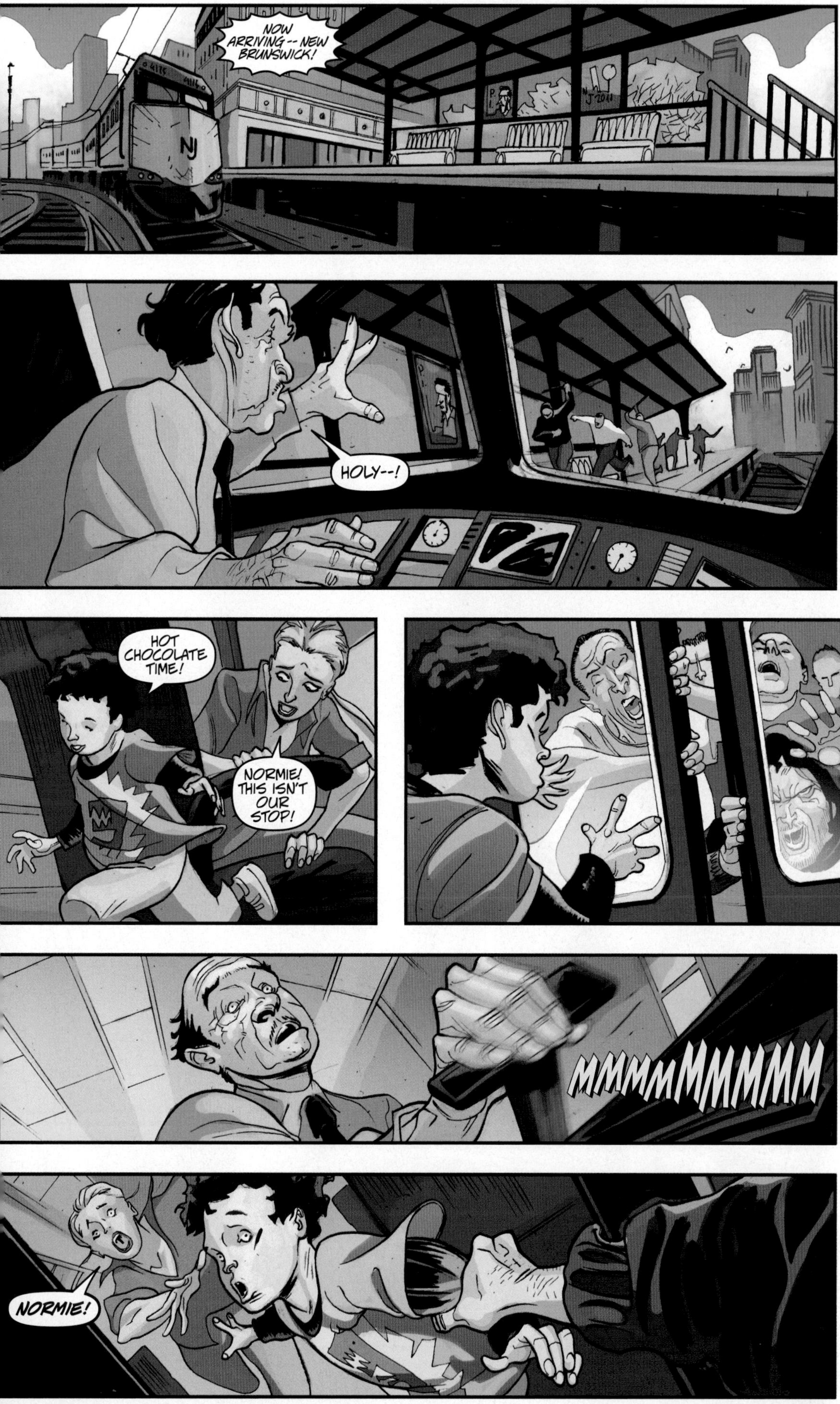
NOW ARRIVING -- NEW BRUNSWICK!
HOLY--!
HOT CHOCOLATE TIME!
NORMIE! THIS ISN'T OUR STOP!
MMMMMMMMMM
NORMIE!

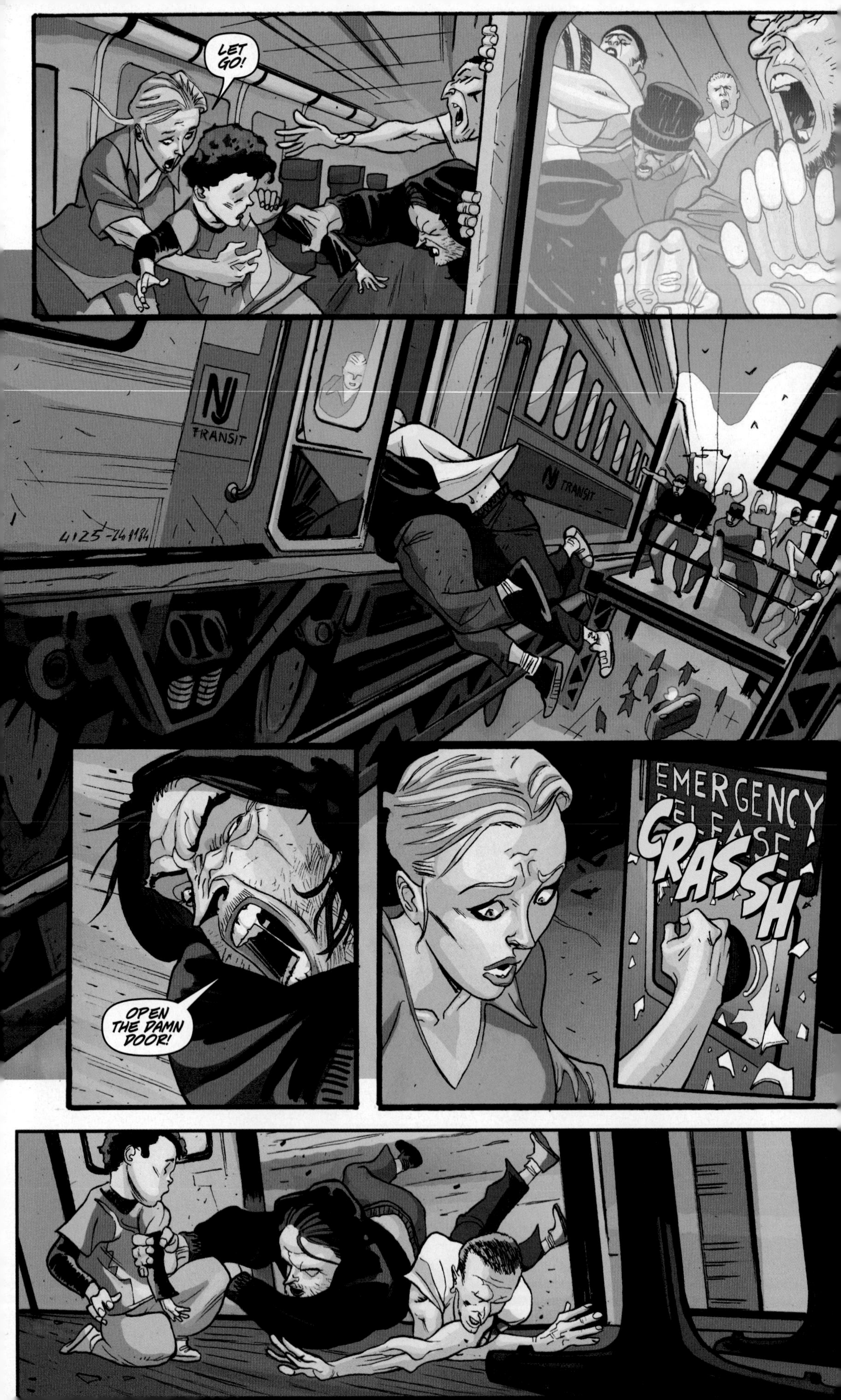
LET GO!
NJ TRANSIT
4125-26 1184
OPEN THE DAMN DOOR!
EMERGENCY
CRASSH

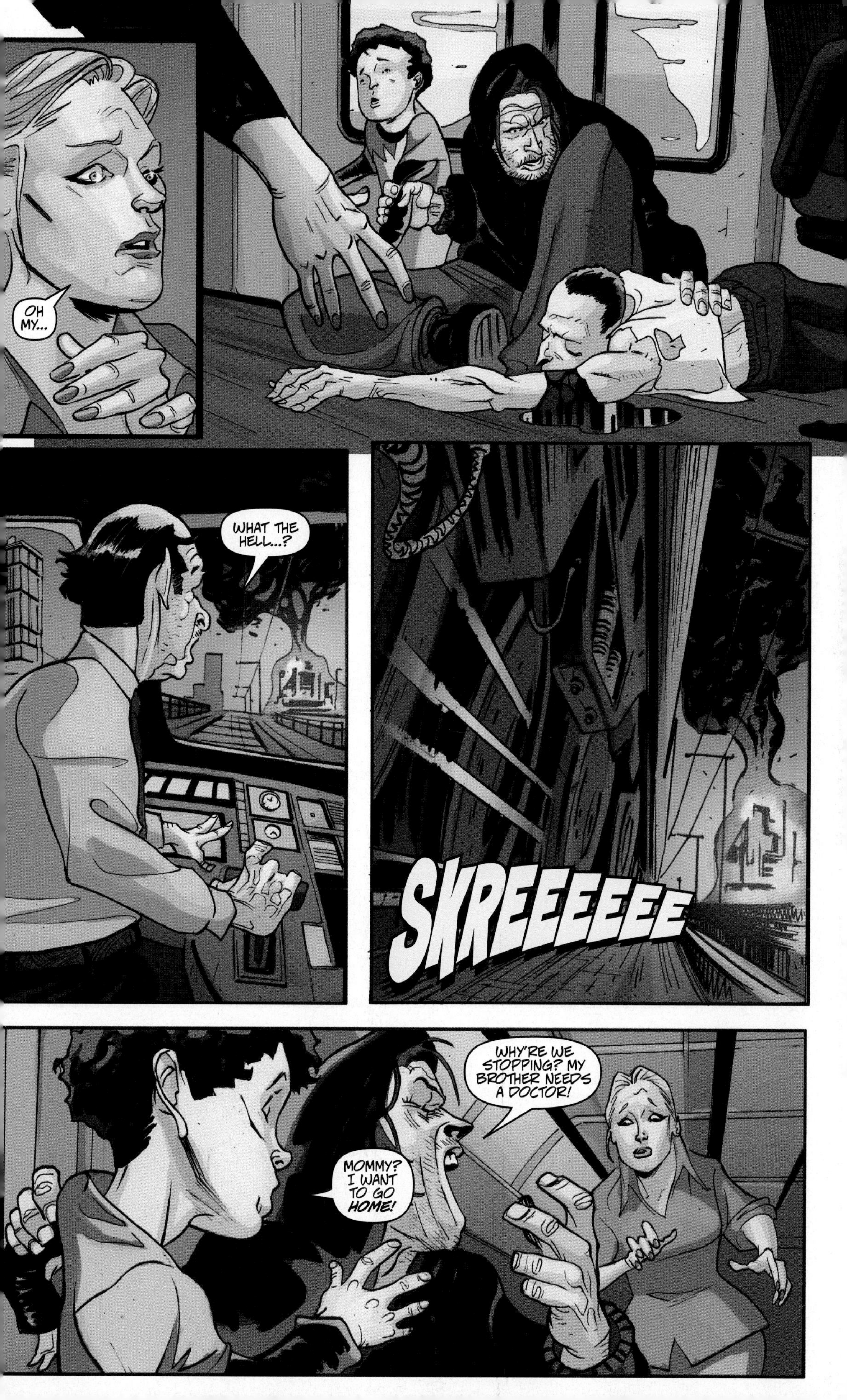
OH MY...
WHAT THE HELL...?
SKREEEEEEE
WHY'RE WE STOPPING? MY BROTHER NEEDS A DOCTOR!
MOMMY? I WANT TO GO HOME!

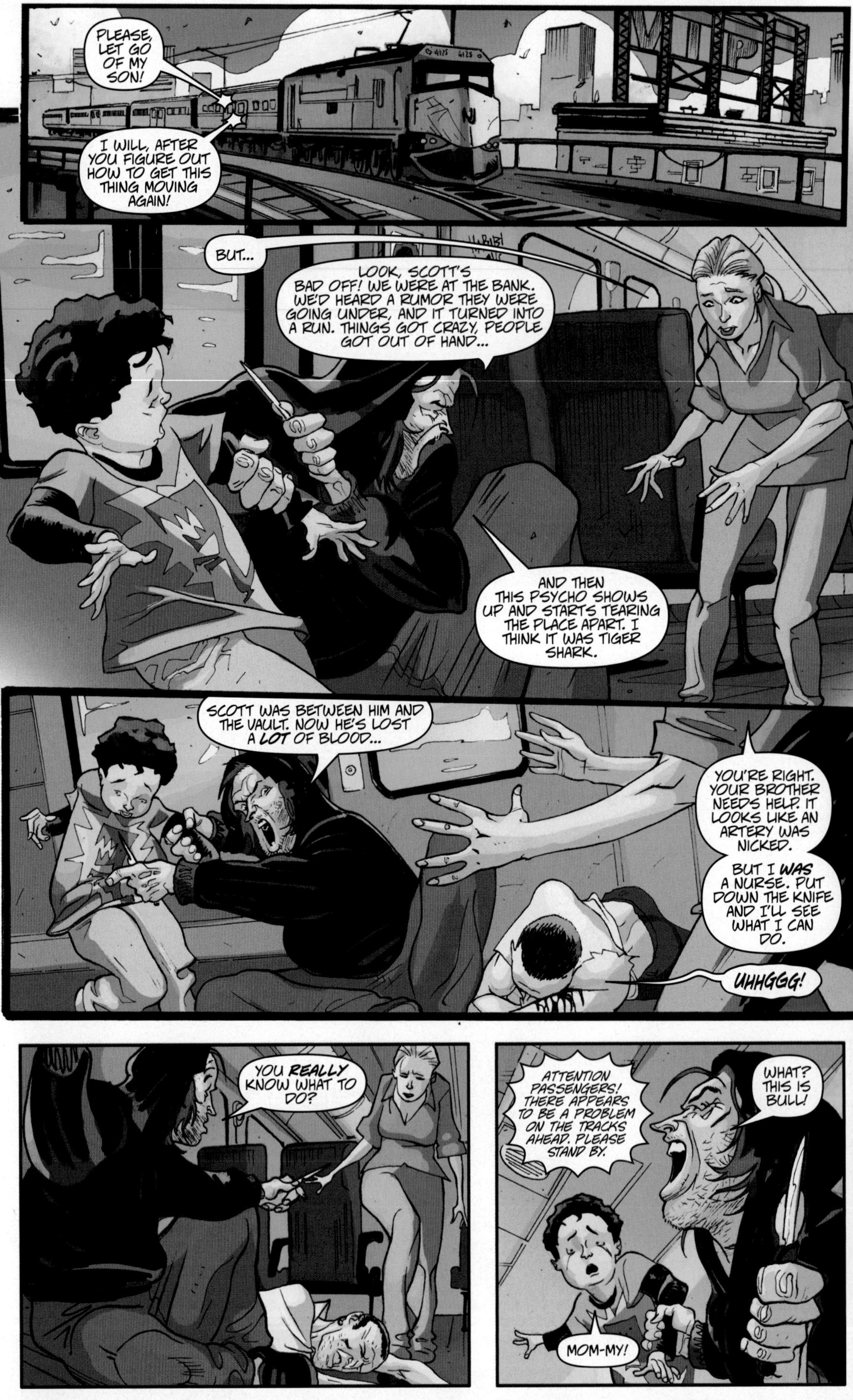
PLEASE, LET GO OF MY SON!
I WILL, AFTER YOU FIGURE OUT HOW TO GET THIS THING MOVING AGAIN!
BUT...
LOOK, SCOTT'S BAD OFF! WE WERE AT THE BANK. WE'D HEARD A RUMOR THEY WERE GOING UNDER, AND IT TURNED INTO A RUN. THINGS GOT CRAZY, PEOPLE GOT OUT OF HAND...
AND THEN THIS PSYCHO SHOWS UP AND STARTS TEARING THE PLACE APART. I THINK IT WAS TIGER SHARK.
SCOTT WAS BETWEEN HIM AND THE VAULT. NOW HE'S LOST A LOT OF BLOOD...
YOU'RE RIGHT. YOUR BROTHER NEEDS HELP. IT LOOKS LIKE AN ARTERY WAS NICKED.
BUT I WAS A NURSE. PUT DOWN THE KNIFE AND I'LL SEE WHAT I CAN DO.
UHHGGG!
YOU REALLY KNOW WHAT TO DO?
ATTENTION PASSENGERS! THERE APPEARS TO BE A PROBLEM ON THE TRACKS AHEAD. PLEASE STAND BY.
WHAT? THIS IS BULL!
MOM-MY!

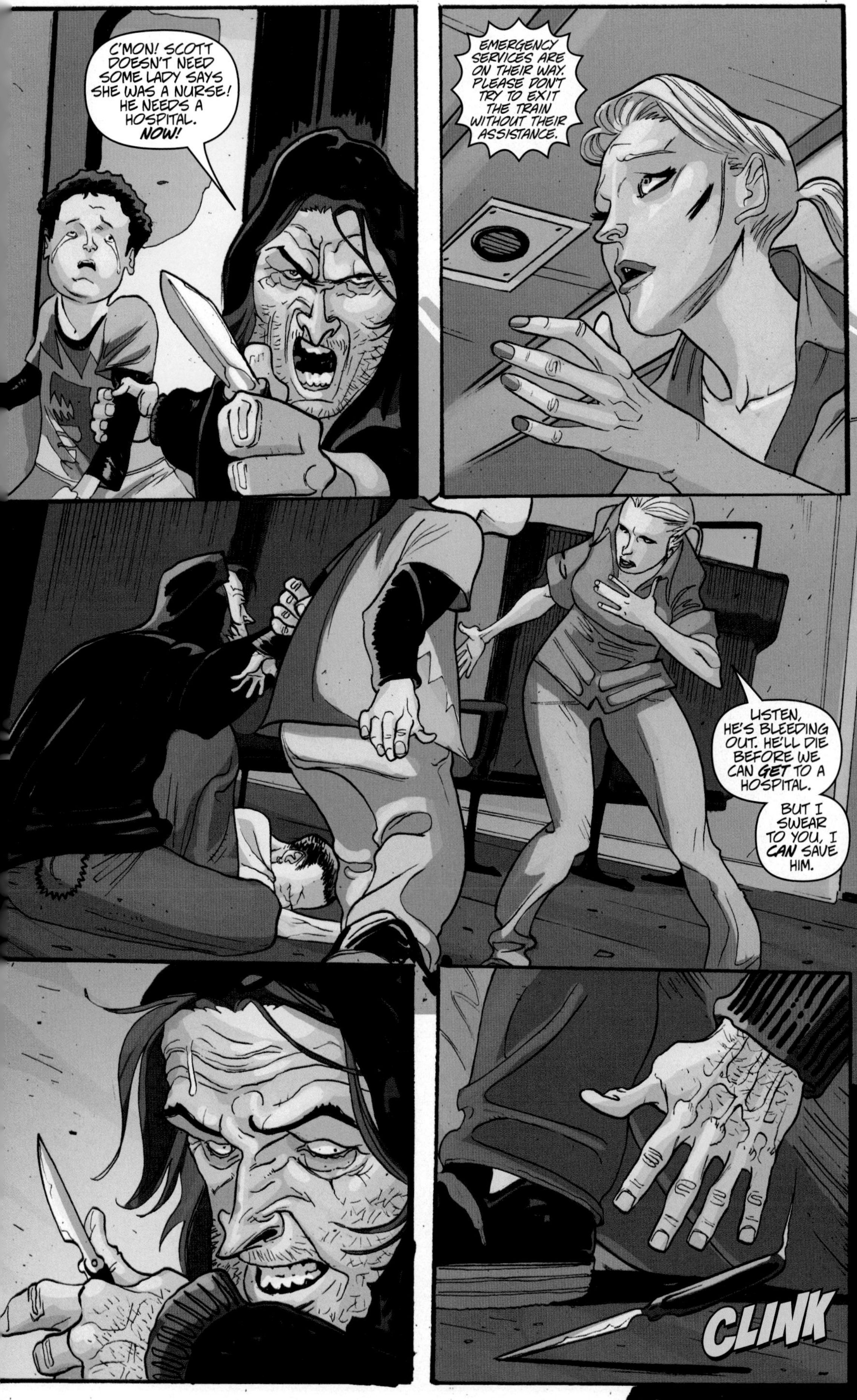
C'MON! SCOTT DOESN'T NEED SOME LADY SAYS SHE WAS A NURSE! HE NEEDS A HOSPITAL. NOW!
EMERGENCY SERVICES ARE ON THEIR WAY. PLEASE DON'T TRY TO EXIT THE TRAIN WITHOUT THEIR ASSISTANCE.
LISTEN, HE'S BLEEDING OUT. HE'LL DIE BEFORE WE CAN GET TO A HOSPITAL.
BUT I SWEAR TO YOU, I CAN SAVE HIM.
CLINK

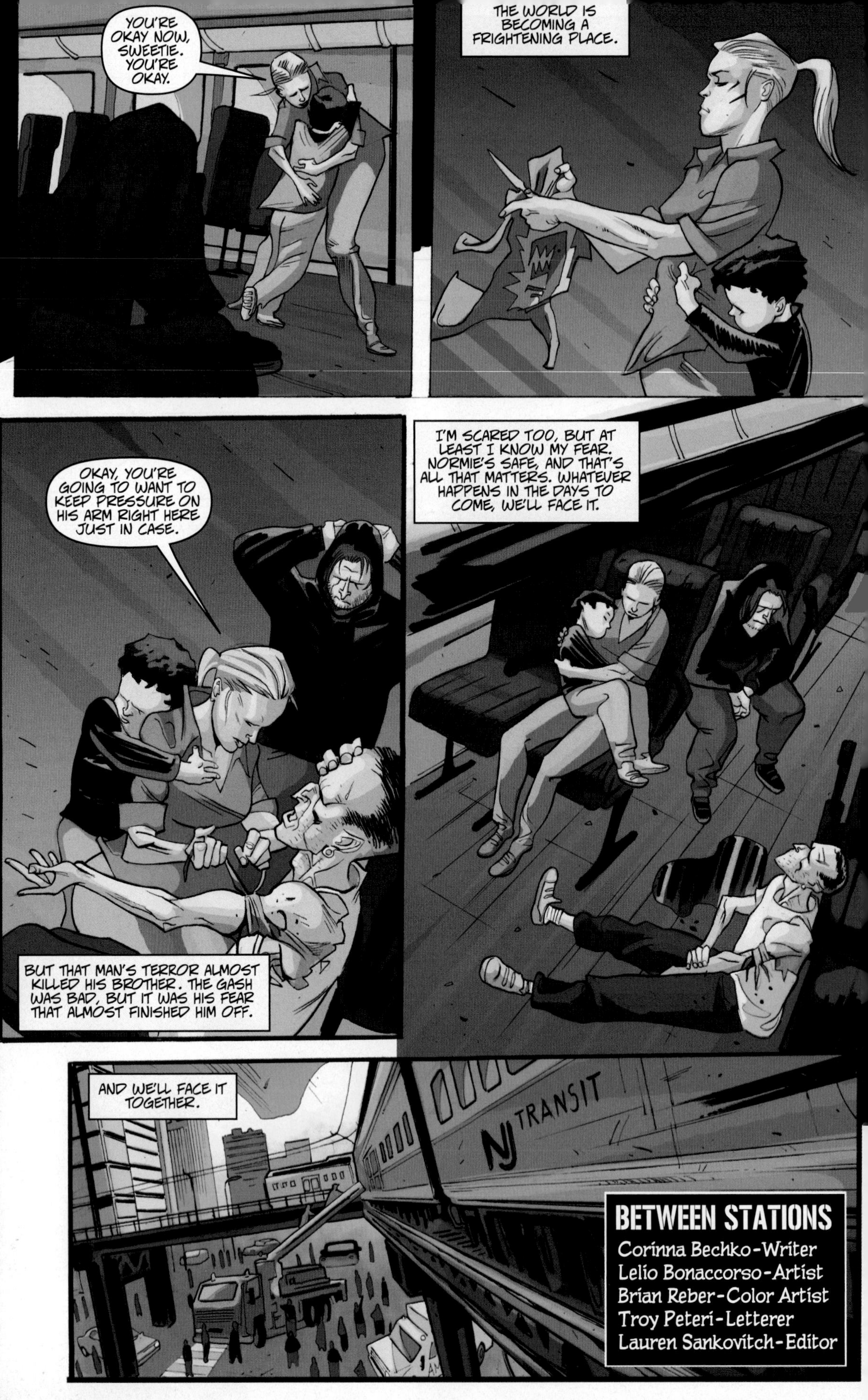
YOU'RE OKAY NOW, SWEETIE. YOU'RE OKAY.
THE WORLD IS BECOMING A FRIGHTENING PLACE.
OKAY, YOU'RE GOING TO WANT TO KEEP PRESSURE ON HIS ARM RIGHT HERE JUST IN CASE.
BUT THAT MAN'S TERROR ALMOST KILLED HIS BROTHER. THE GASH WAS BAD, BUT IT WAS HIS FEAR THAT ALMOST FINISHED HIM OFF.
I'M SCARED TOO, BUT AT LEAST I KNOW MY FEAR. NORMIE'S SAFE, AND THAT'S ALL THAT MATTERS. WHATEVER HAPPENS IN THE DAYS TO COME, WE'LL FACE IT.
AND WE'LL FACE IT TOGETHER.
NJ TRANSIT
BETWEEN STATIONS
Corinna Bechko-Writer
Lelio Bonaccorso-Artist
Brian Reber-Color Artist
Troy Peteri-Letterer
Lauren Sankovitch-Editor

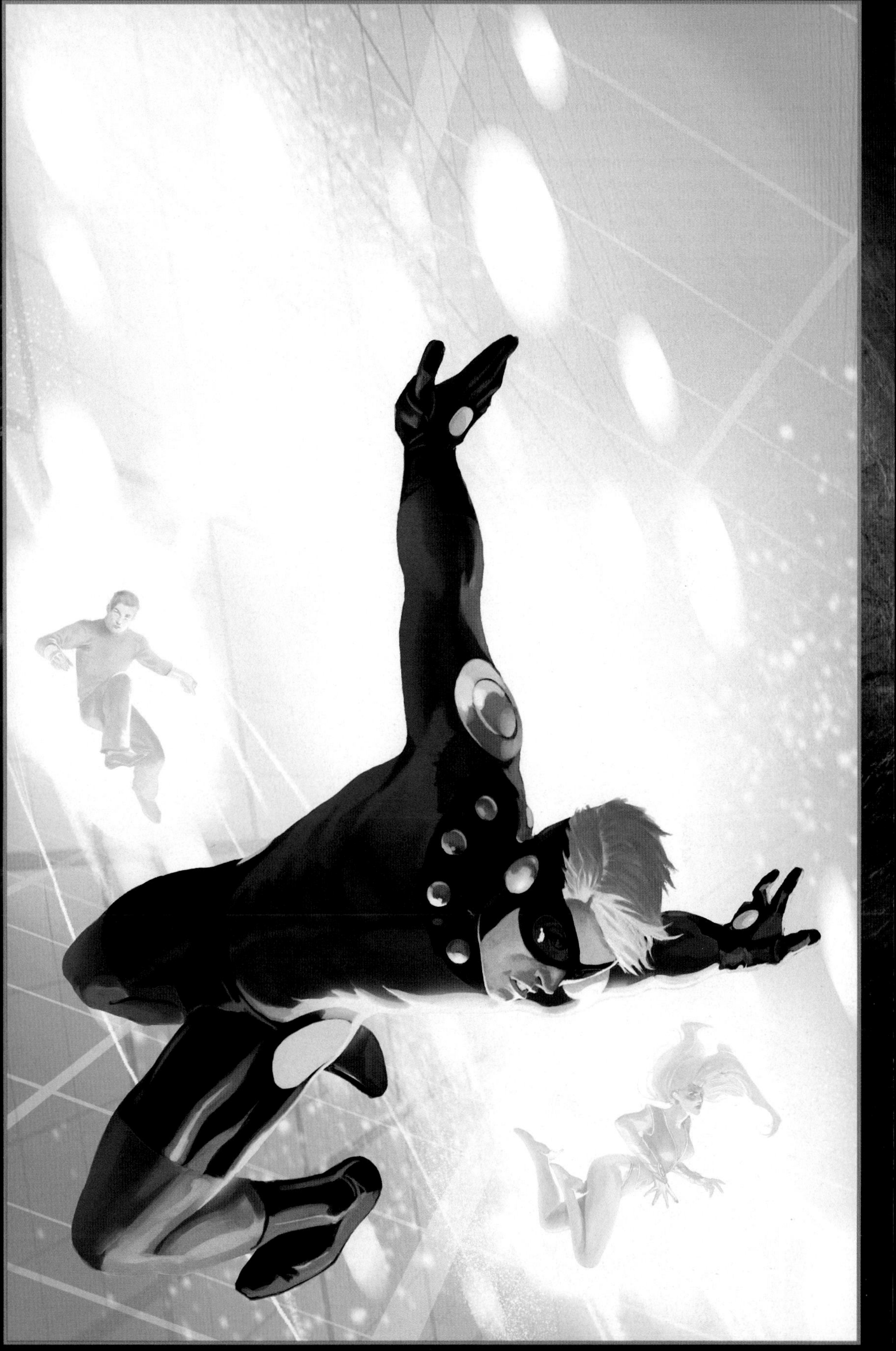

FEAR ITSELF: THE HOME FRONT #3

Stamford, Connecticut.

It's not surprising Miriam Sharpe emerged as the chief critic of Speedball's role as a teacher of young superhumans in Avengers Academy. Sharpe began her activism after her son, Damien, was killed in the Stamford explosion caused by a battle between Speedball's team of New Warriors and superhuman criminals.

As a result, some have dismissed her arguments as stemming from personal hatred of the young hero. But one must admit, if she is biased, she certainly has a compelling reason…

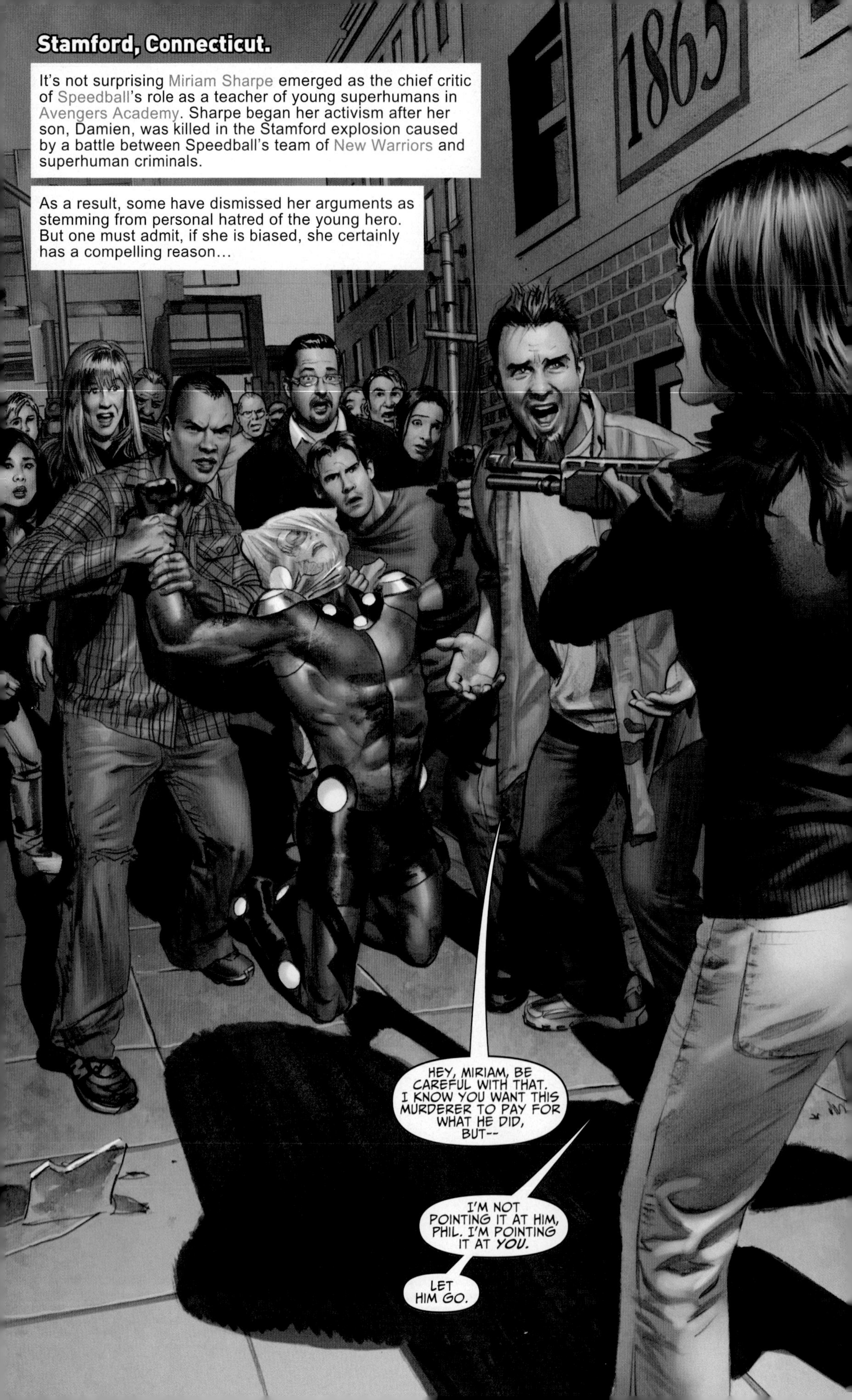

HEY, MIRIAM, BE CAREFUL WITH THAT. I KNOW YOU WANT THIS MURDERER TO PAY FOR WHAT HE DID, BUT--
I'M NOT POINTING IT AT HIM, PHIL. I'M POINTING IT AT *YOU.*
LET HIM GO.

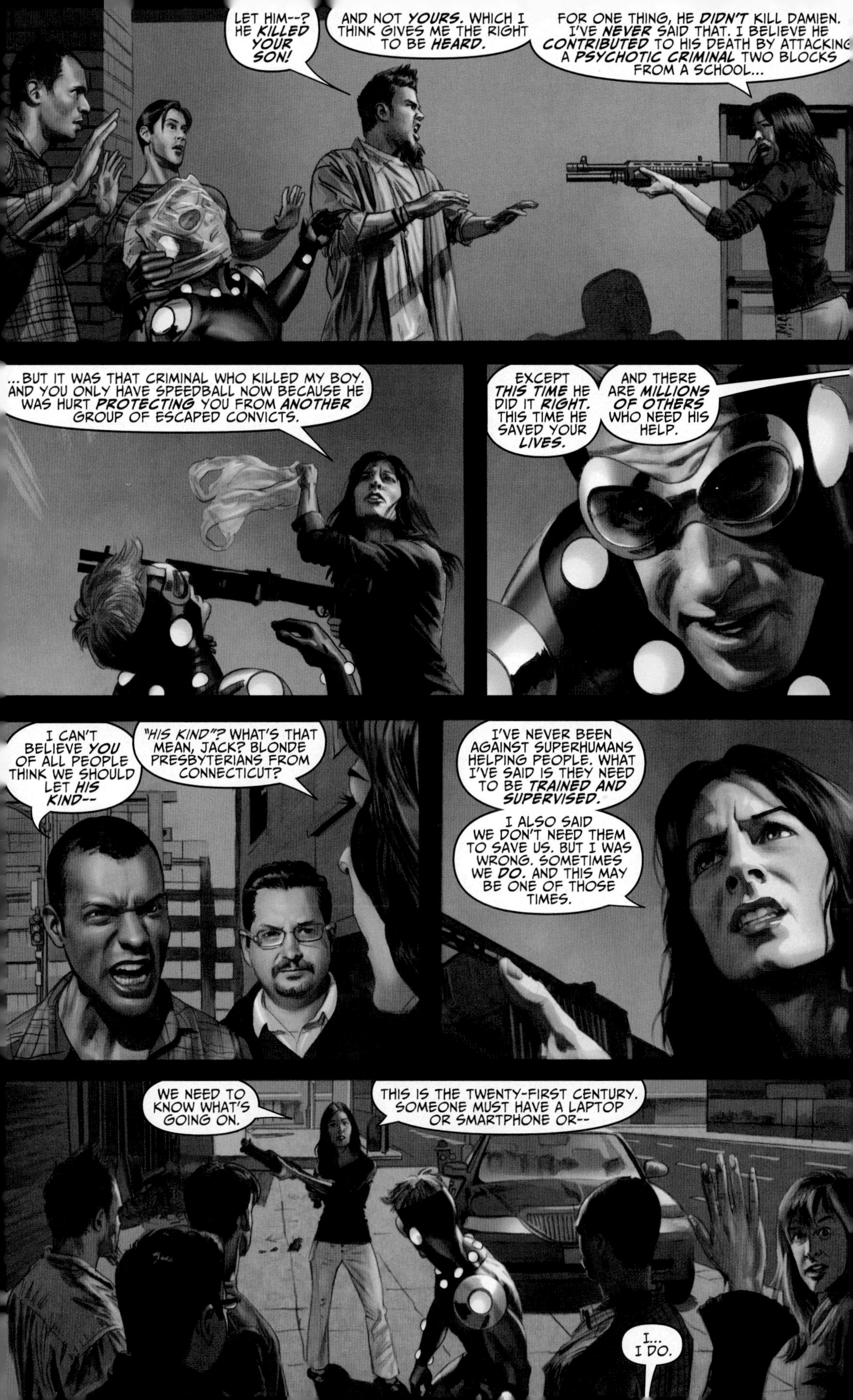
LET HIM--? HE KILLED YOUR SON!
AND NOT YOURS. WHICH I THINK GIVES ME THE RIGHT TO BE HEARD.
FOR ONE THING, HE DIDN'T KILL DAMIEN. I'VE NEVER SAID THAT. I BELIEVE HE CONTRIBUTED TO HIS DEATH BY ATTACKING A PSYCHOTIC CRIMINAL TWO BLOCKS FROM A SCHOOL...
...BUT IT WAS THAT CRIMINAL WHO KILLED MY BOY. AND YOU ONLY HAVE SPEEDBALL NOW BECAUSE HE WAS HURT PROTECTING YOU FROM ANOTHER GROUP OF ESCAPED CONVICTS.
EXCEPT THIS TIME HE DID IT RIGHT. THIS TIME HE SAVED YOUR LIVES.
AND THERE ARE MILLIONS OF OTHERS WHO NEED HIS HELP.
I CAN'T BELIEVE YOU OF ALL PEOPLE THINK WE SHOULD LET HIS KIND--
"HIS KIND"? WHAT'S THAT MEAN, JACK? BLONDE PRESBYTERIANS FROM CONNECTICUT?
I'VE NEVER BEEN AGAINST SUPERHUMANS HELPING PEOPLE. WHAT I'VE SAID IS THEY NEED TO BE TRAINED AND SUPERVISED.
I ALSO SAID WE DON'T NEED THEM TO SAVE US. BUT I WAS WRONG. SOMETIMES WE DO. AND THIS MAY BE ONE OF THOSE TIMES.
WE NEED TO KNOW WHAT'S GOING ON.
THIS IS THE TWENTY-FIRST CENTURY. SOMEONE MUST HAVE A LAPTOP OR SMARTPHONE OR--
I... I DO.

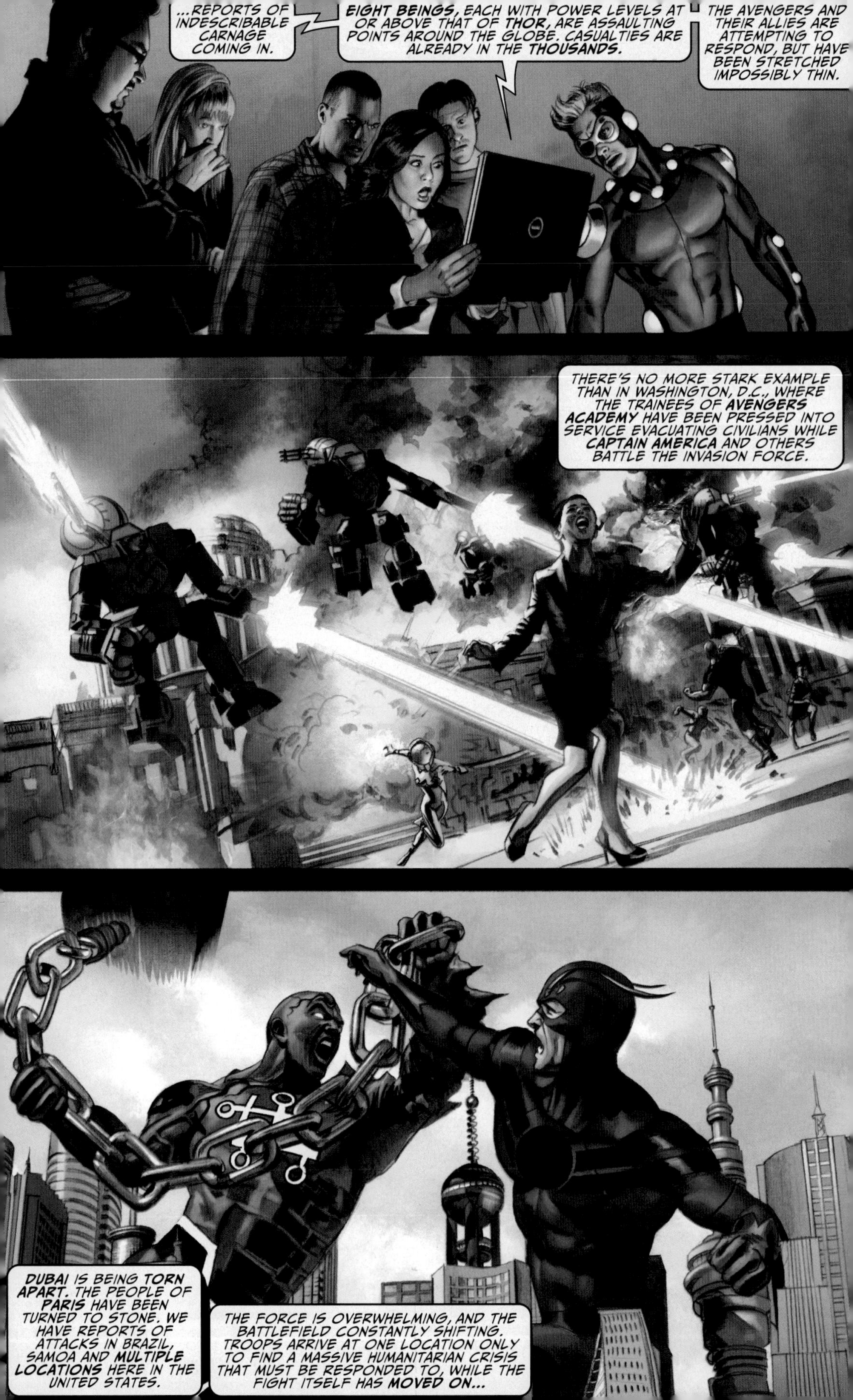

...REPORTS OF INDESCRIBABLE CARNAGE COMING IN.
EIGHT BEINGS, EACH WITH POWER LEVELS AT OR ABOVE THAT OF THOR, ARE ASSAULTING POINTS AROUND THE GLOBE. CASUALTIES ARE ALREADY IN THE THOUSANDS.
THE AVENGERS AND THEIR ALLIES ARE ATTEMPTING TO RESPOND, BUT HAVE BEEN STRETCHED IMPOSSIBLY THIN.
THERE'S NO MORE STARK EXAMPLE THAN IN WASHINGTON, D.C., WHERE THE TRAINEES OF AVENGERS ACADEMY HAVE BEEN PRESSED INTO SERVICE EVACUATING CIVILIANS WHILE CAPTAIN AMERICA AND OTHERS BATTLE THE INVASION FORCE.
DUBAI IS BEING TORN APART. THE PEOPLE OF PARIS HAVE BEEN TURNED TO STONE. WE HAVE REPORTS OF ATTACKS IN BRAZIL, SAMOA AND MULTIPLE LOCATIONS HERE IN THE UNITED STATES.
THE FORCE IS OVERWHELMING, AND THE BATTLEFIELD CONSTANTLY SHIFTING. TROOPS ARRIVE AT ONE LOCATION ONLY TO FIND A MASSIVE HUMANITARIAN CRISIS THAT MUST BE RESPONDED TO, WHILE THE FIGHT ITSELF HAS MOVED ON...

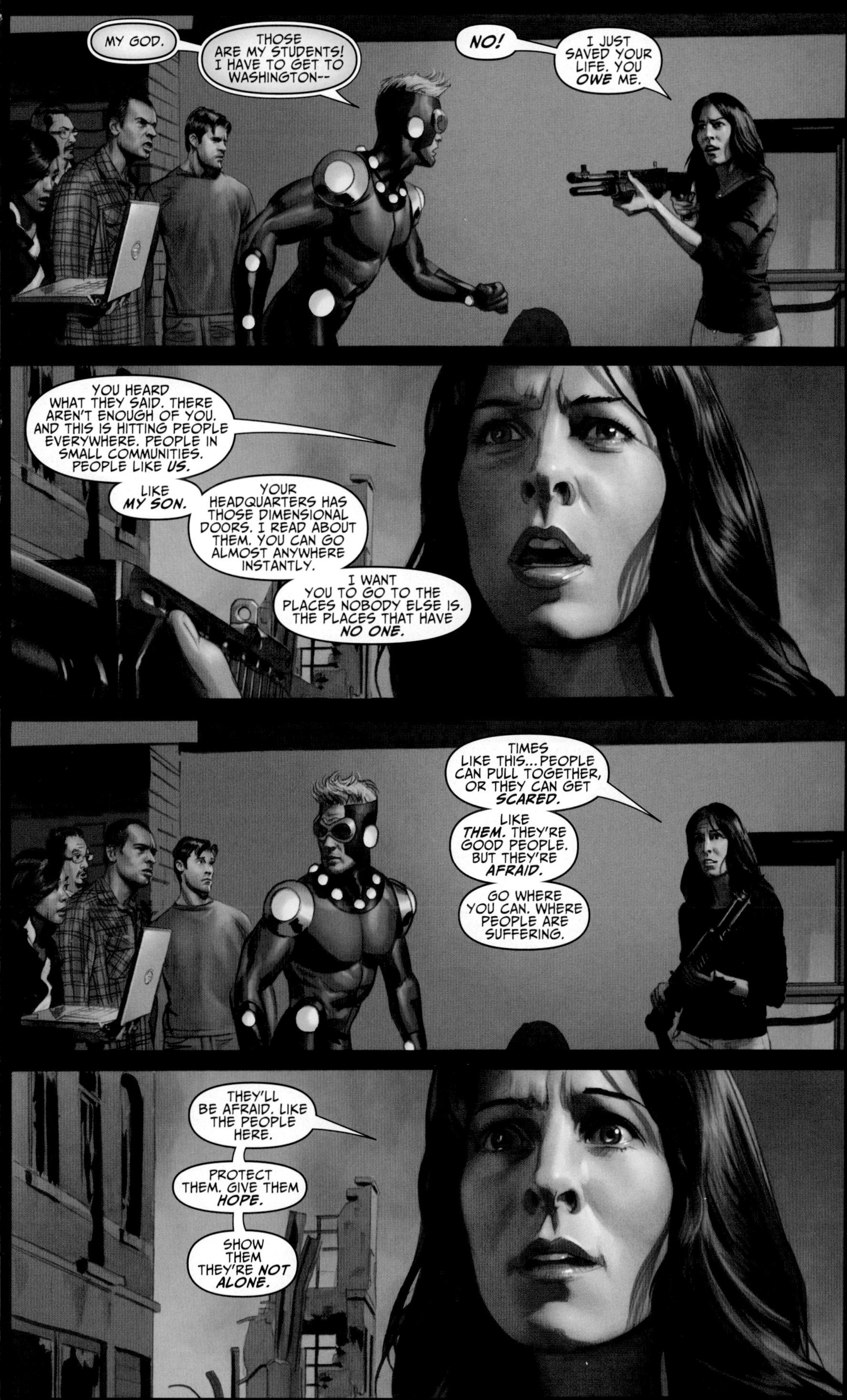
MY GOD.
THOSE ARE MY STUDENTS! I HAVE TO GET TO WASHINGTON--
NO!
I JUST SAVED YOUR LIFE. YOU OWE ME.
YOU HEARD WHAT THEY SAID. THERE AREN'T ENOUGH OF YOU. AND THIS IS HITTING PEOPLE EVERYWHERE. PEOPLE IN SMALL COMMUNITIES. PEOPLE LIKE US.
LIKE MY SON.
YOUR HEADQUARTERS HAS THOSE DIMENSIONAL DOORS. I READ ABOUT THEM. YOU CAN GO ALMOST ANYWHERE INSTANTLY.
I WANT YOU TO GO TO THE PLACES NOBODY ELSE IS. THE PLACES THAT HAVE NO ONE.
TIMES LIKE THIS...PEOPLE CAN PULL TOGETHER, OR THEY CAN GET SCARED.
LIKE THEM. THEY'RE GOOD PEOPLE. BUT THEY'RE AFRAID.
GO WHERE YOU CAN. WHERE PEOPLE ARE SUFFERING.
THEY'LL BE AFRAID. LIKE THE PEOPLE HERE.
PROTECT THEM. GIVE THEM HOPE.
SHOW THEM THEY'RE NOT ALONE.

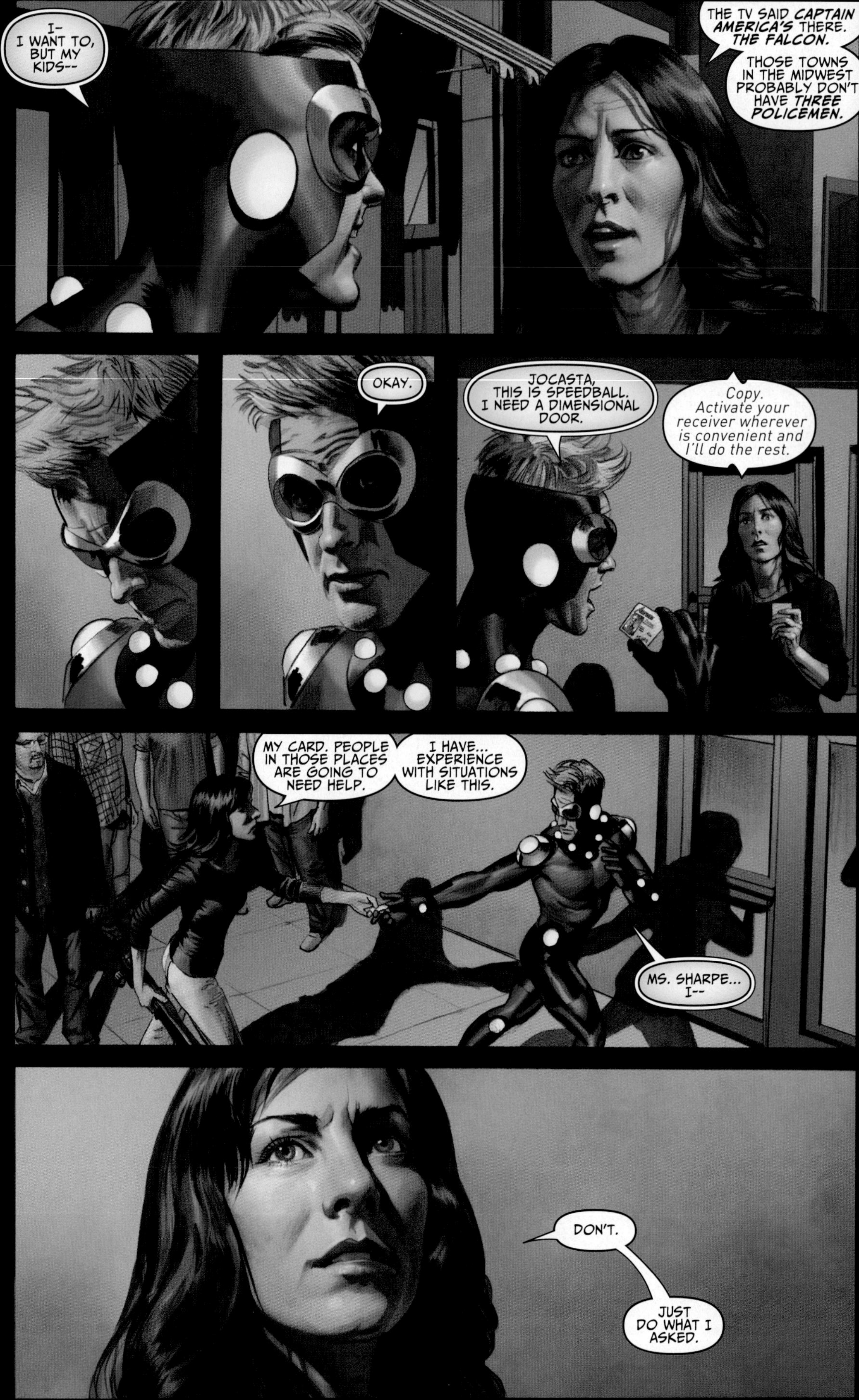
I- I WANT TO, BUT MY KIDS--
THE TV SAID CAPTAIN AMERICA'S THERE. THE FALCON.
THOSE TOWNS IN THE MIDWEST PROBABLY DON'T HAVE THREE POLICEMEN.
OKAY.
JOCASTA, THIS IS SPEEDBALL. I NEED A DIMENSIONAL DOOR.
Copy. Activate your receiver wherever is convenient and I'll do the rest.
MY CARD. PEOPLE IN THOSE PLACES ARE GOING TO NEED HELP.
I HAVE... EXPERIENCE WITH SITUATIONS LIKE THIS.
MS. SHARPE... I--
DON'T.
JUST DO WHAT I ASKED.

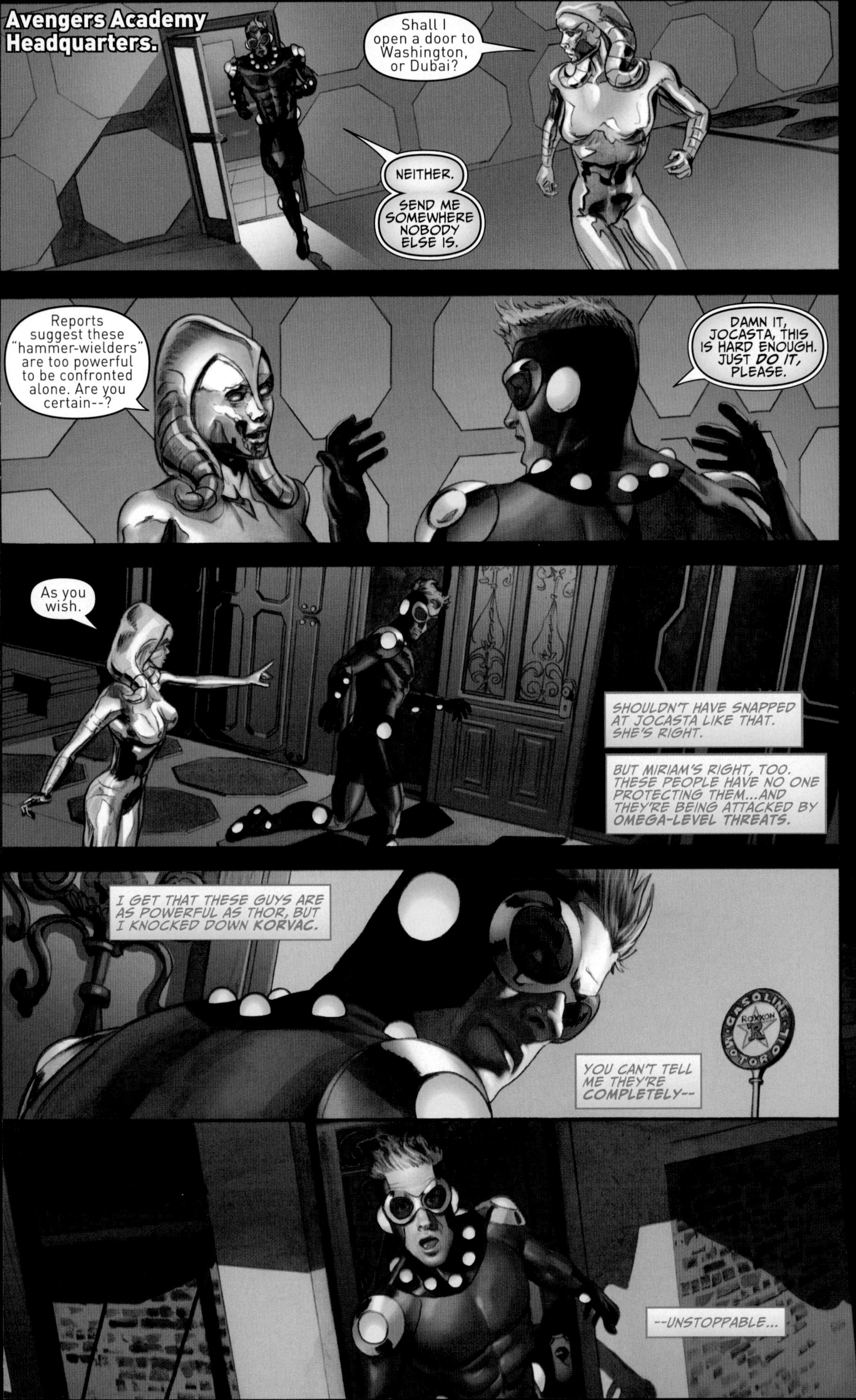
Avengers Academy Headquarters.
Shall I open a door to Washington, or Dubai?
NEITHER.
SEND ME SOMEWHERE NOBODY ELSE IS.
Reports suggest these "hammer-wielders" are too powerful to be confronted alone. Are you certain--?
DAMN IT, JOCASTA, THIS IS HARD ENOUGH. JUST DO IT, PLEASE.
As you wish.
SHOULDN'T HAVE SNAPPED AT JOCASTA LIKE THAT. SHE'S RIGHT.
BUT MIRIAM'S RIGHT, TOO. THESE PEOPLE HAVE NO ONE PROTECTING THEM...AND THEY'RE BEING ATTACKED BY OMEGA-LEVEL THREATS.
I GET THAT THESE GUYS ARE AS POWERFUL AS THOR, BUT I KNOCKED DOWN KORVAC.
GASOLINE ROXXON MOTOR OIL
YOU CAN'T TELL ME THEY'RE COMPLETELY--
--UNSTOPPABLE...

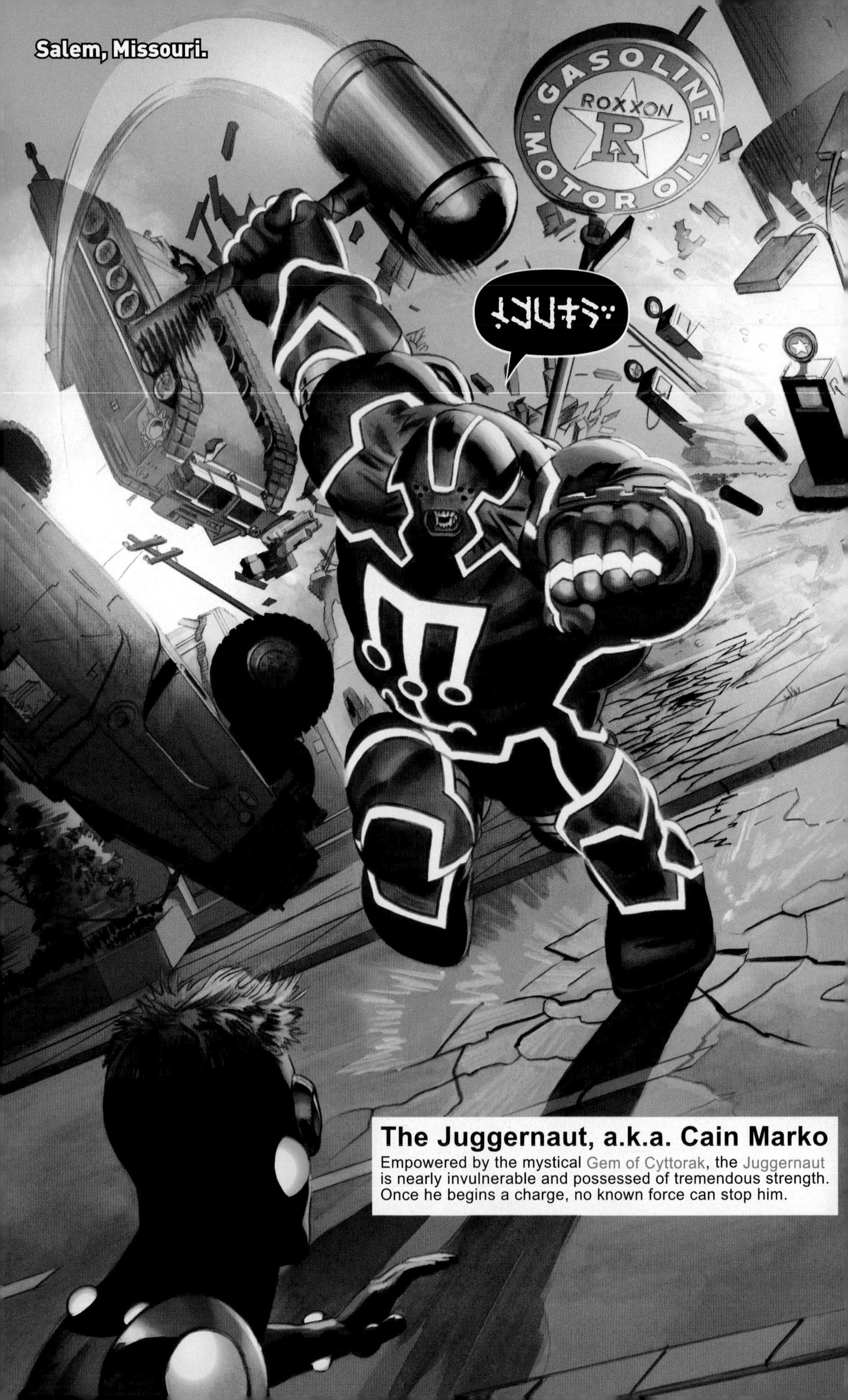
Salem, Missouri.
ROXXON
GASOLINE
MOTOR OIL
The Juggernaut, a.k.a. Cain Marko
Empowered by the mystical Gem of Cyttorak, the Juggernaut is nearly invulnerable and possessed of tremendous strength. Once he begins a charge, no known force can stop him.

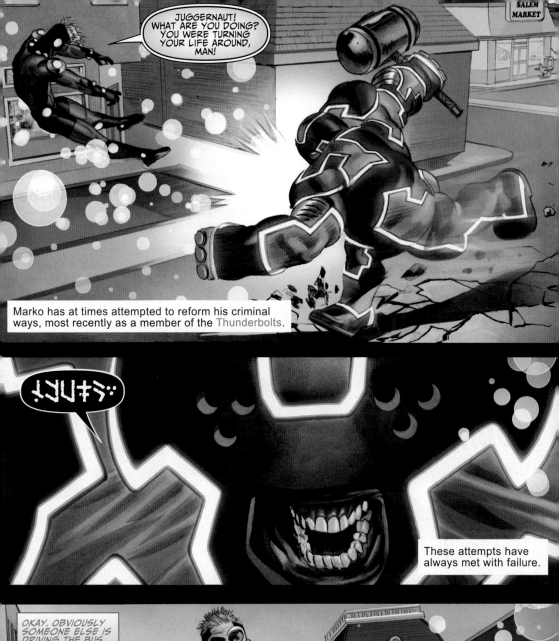

JUGGERNAUT! WHAT ARE YOU DOING? YOU WERE TURNING YOUR LIFE AROUND, MAN!

Marko has at times attempted to reform his criminal ways, most recently as a member of the Thunderbolts.

These attempts have always met with failure.

OKAY. OBVIOUSLY SOMEONE ELSE IS DRIVING THE BUS.

HE'S HEADED FOR TOWN, SO IT'S TIME TO SHUT UP AND...AND TRY TO STOP THE UNSTOPPABLE.

I'M STILL IN ENOUGH PAIN TO ACCESS MY PENANCE POWERS...

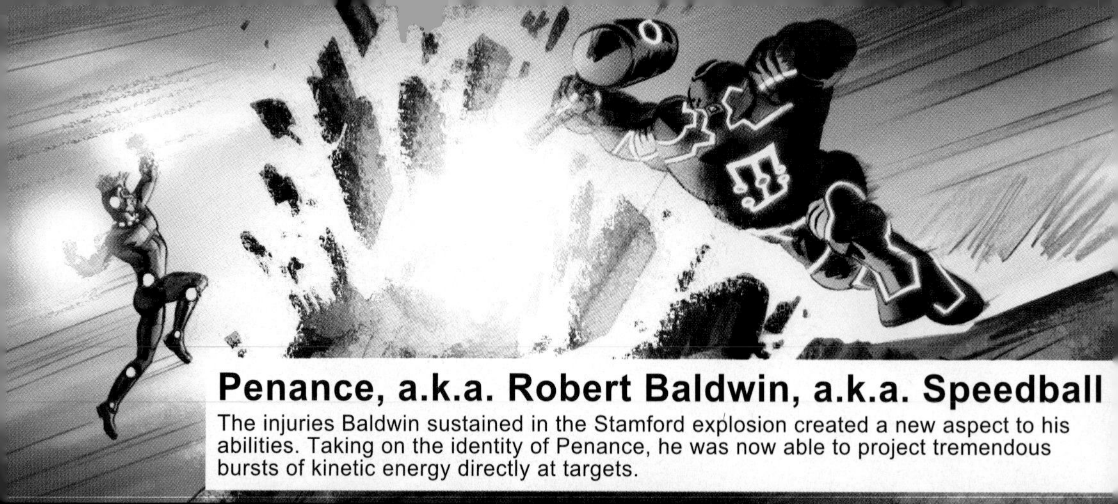
Penance, a.k.a. Robert Baldwin, a.k.a. Speedball
The injuries Baldwin sustained in the Stamford explosion created a new aspect to his abilities. Taking on the identity of Penance, he was now able to project tremendous bursts of kinetic energy directly at targets.

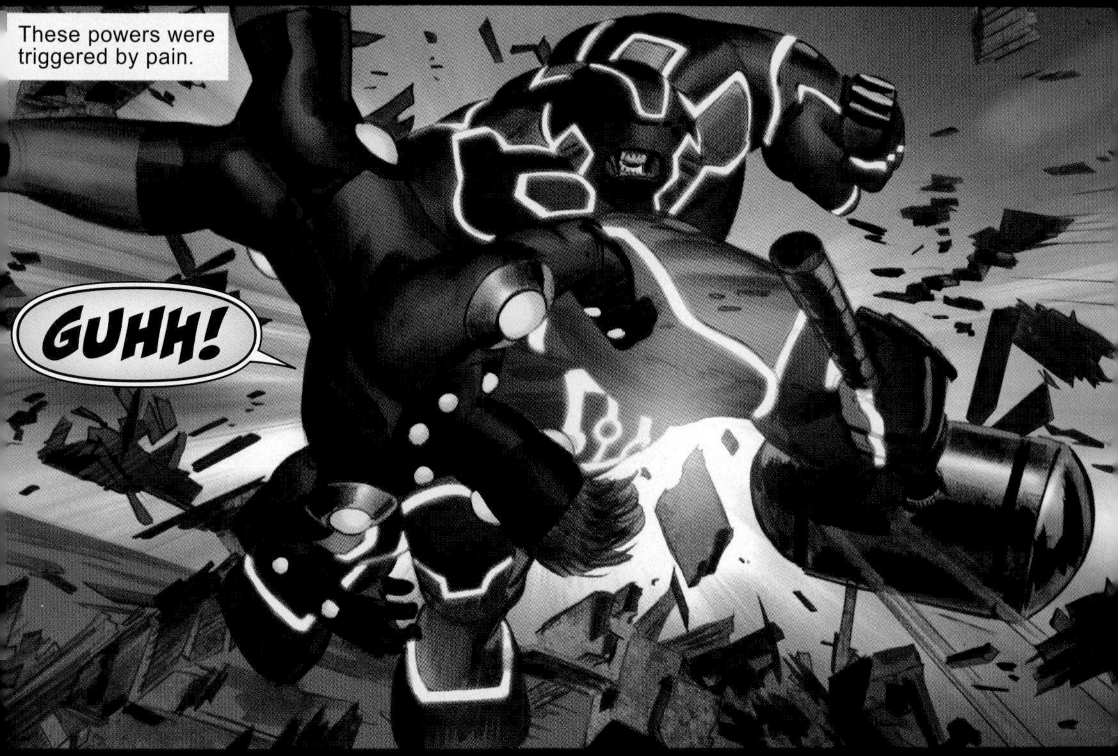
These powers were triggered by pain.
GUHH!

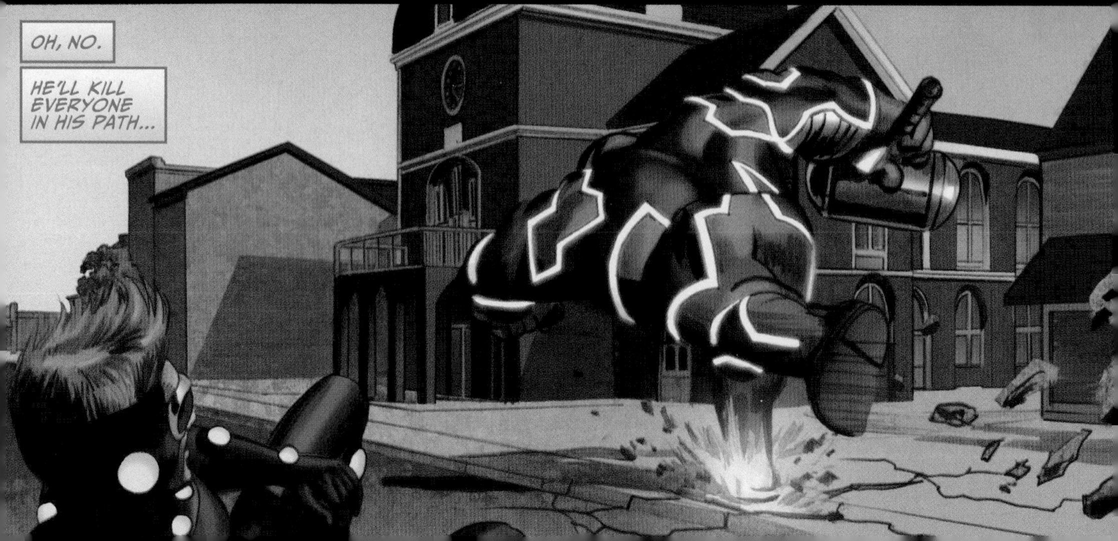
OH, NO.
HE'LL KILL EVERYONE IN HIS PATH...

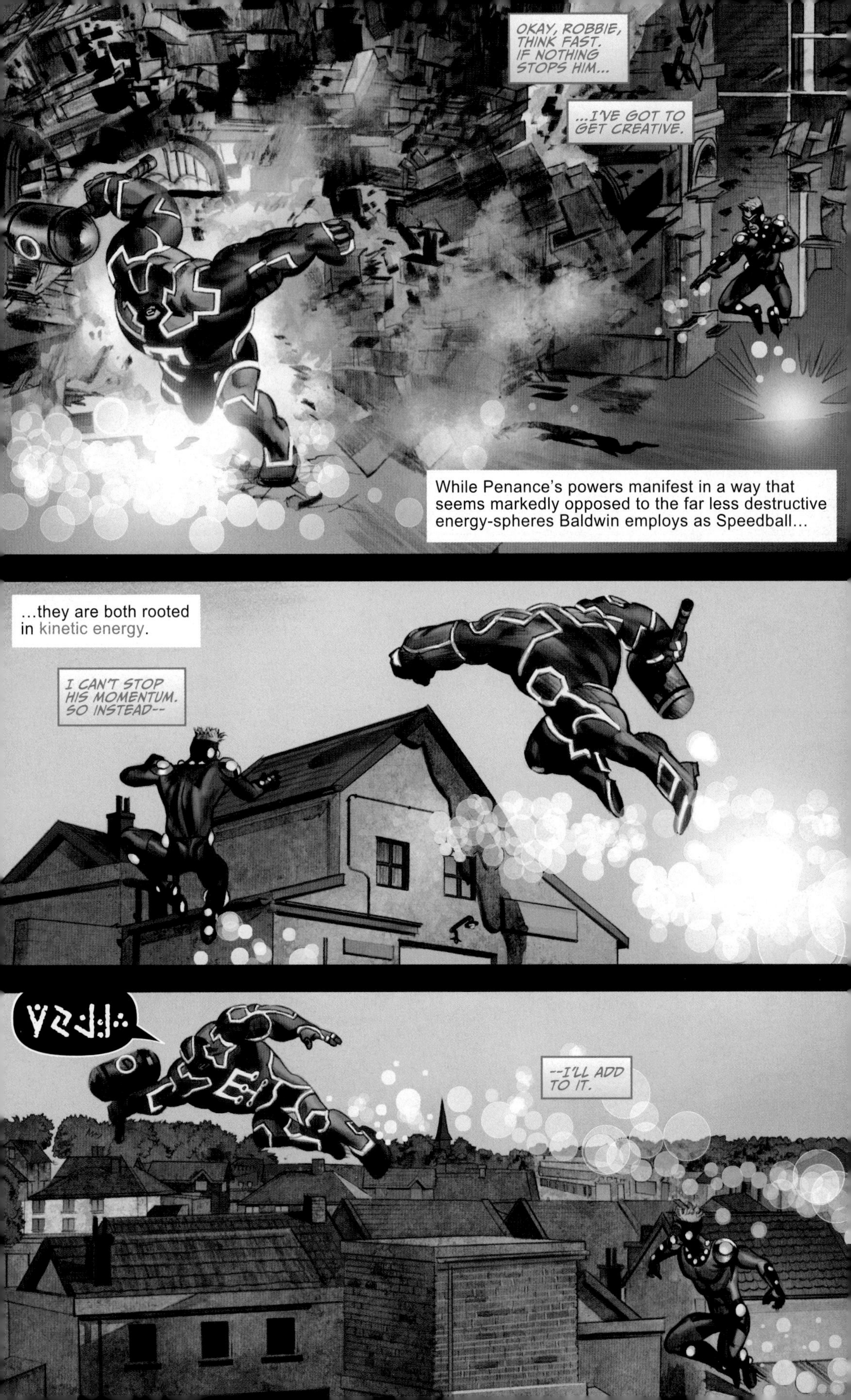
OKAY, ROBBIE, THINK FAST. IF NOTHING STOPS HIM...
...I'VE GOT TO GET CREATIVE.
While Penance's powers manifest in a way that seems markedly opposed to the far less destructive energy-spheres Baldwin employs as Speedball...
...they are both rooted in kinetic energy.
I CAN'T STOP HIS MOMENTUM. SO INSTEAD--
--I'LL ADD TO IT.

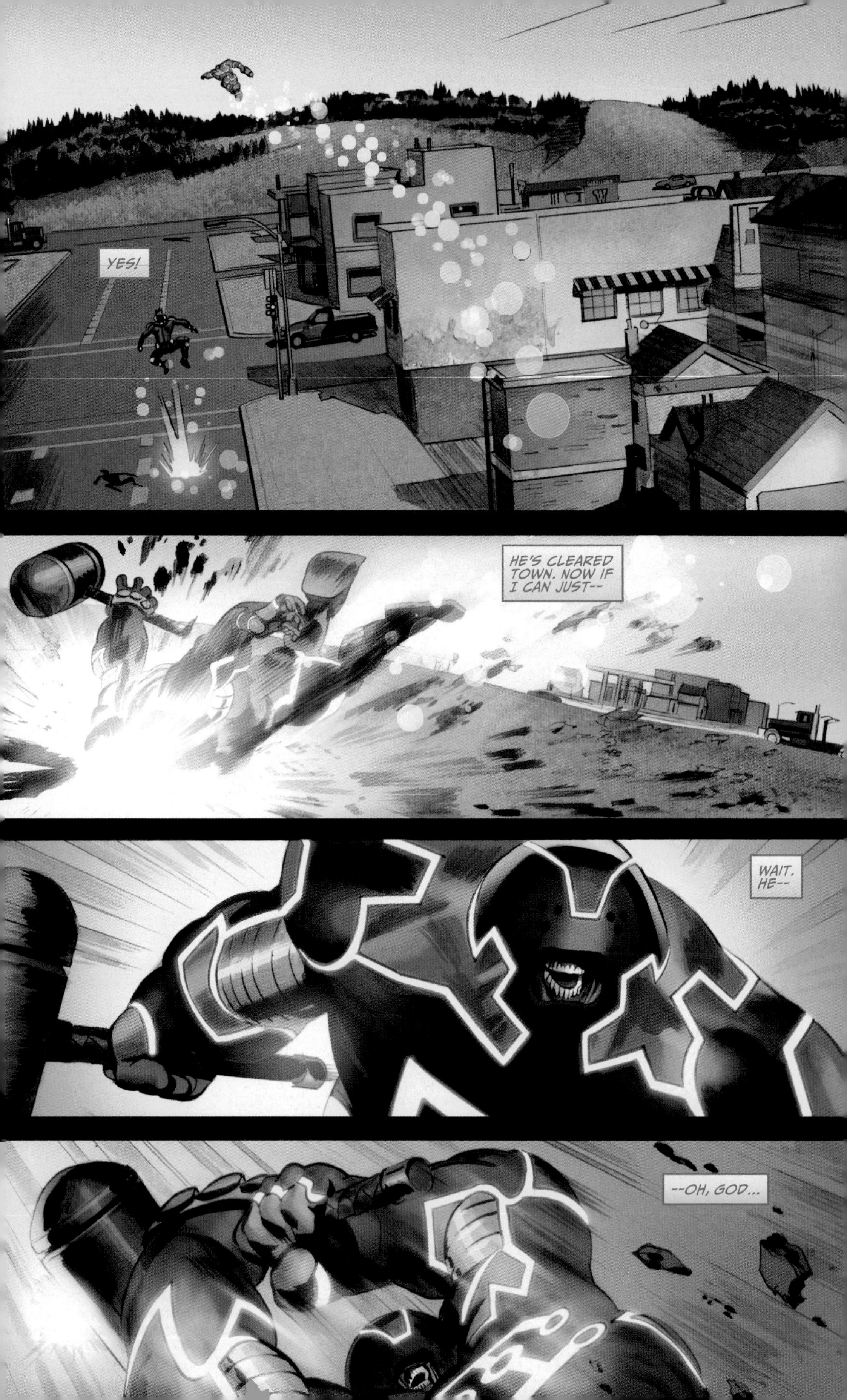
YES!
HE'S CLEARED TOWN. NOW IF I CAN JUST--
WAIT. HE--
--OH, GOD...

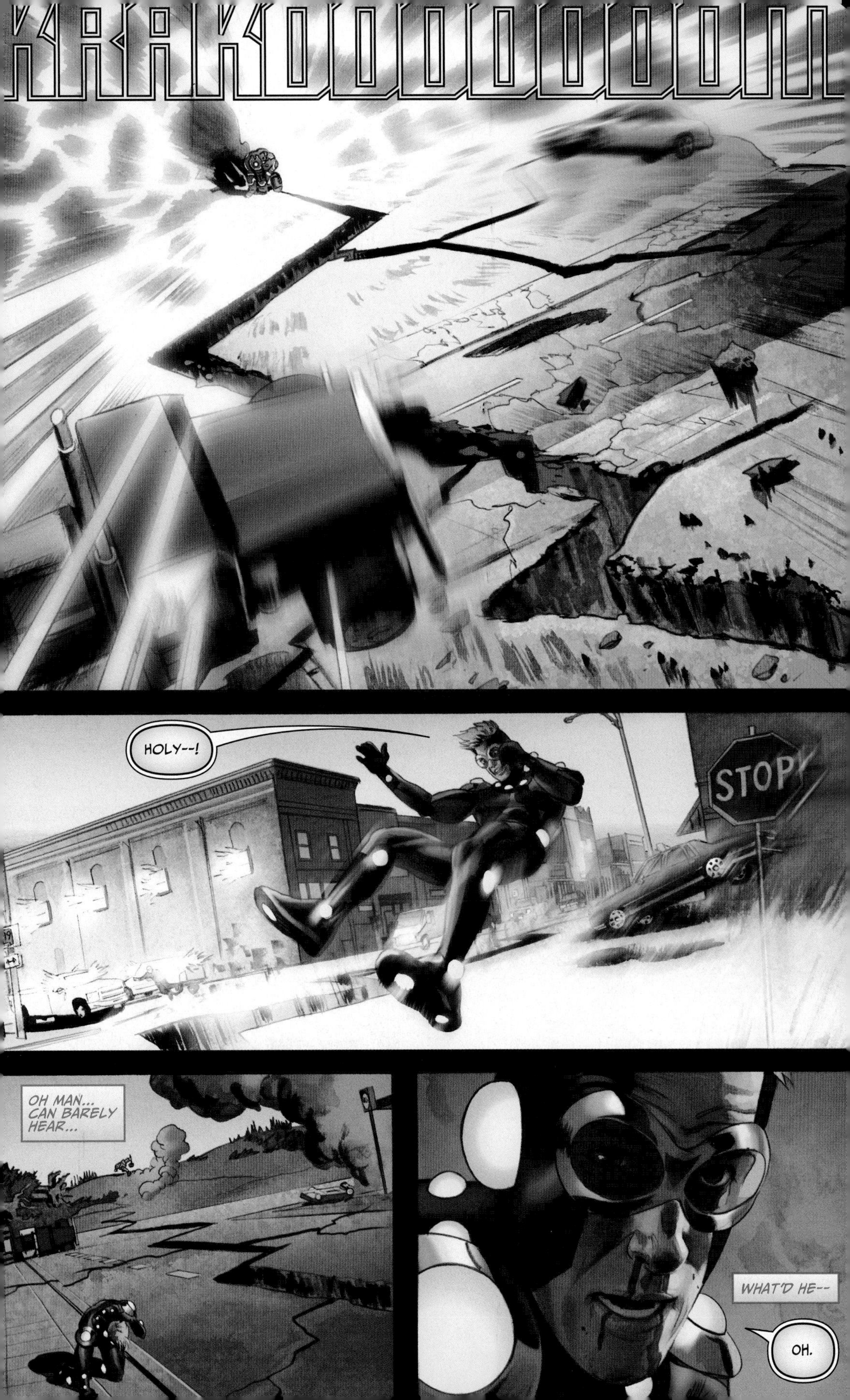
KRAKOOOOOOOM
HOLY--!
STOP
OH MAN... CAN BARELY HEAR...
WHAT'D HE--
OH.

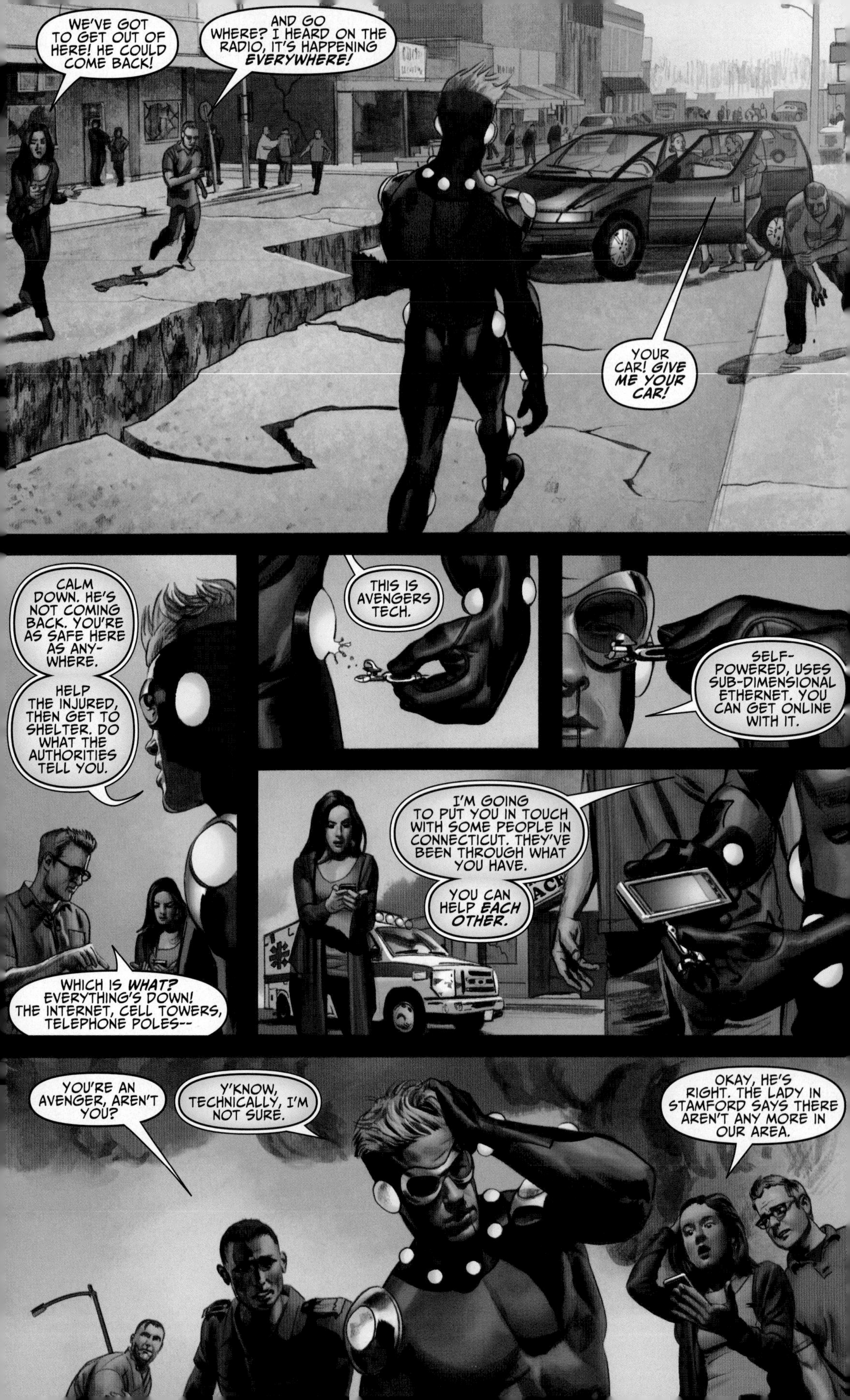
WE'VE GOT TO GET OUT OF HERE! HE COULD COME BACK!
AND GO WHERE? I HEARD ON THE RADIO, IT'S HAPPENING EVERYWHERE!
YOUR CAR! GIVE ME YOUR CAR!
CALM DOWN. HE'S NOT COMING BACK. YOU'RE AS SAFE HERE AS ANY-WHERE.
HELP THE INJURED, THEN GET TO SHELTER. DO WHAT THE AUTHORITIES TELL YOU.
THIS IS AVENGERS TECH.
SELF-POWERED, USES SUB-DIMENSIONAL ETHERNET. YOU CAN GET ONLINE WITH IT.
WHICH IS WHAT? EVERYTHING'S DOWN! THE INTERNET, CELL TOWERS, TELEPHONE POLES--
I'M GOING TO PUT YOU IN TOUCH WITH SOME PEOPLE IN CONNECTICUT. THEY'VE BEEN THROUGH WHAT YOU HAVE.
YOU CAN HELP EACH OTHER.
YOU'RE AN AVENGER, AREN'T YOU?
Y'KNOW, TECHNICALLY, I'M NOT SURE.
OKAY, HE'S RIGHT. THE LADY IN STAMFORD SAYS THERE AREN'T ANY MORE IN OUR AREA.

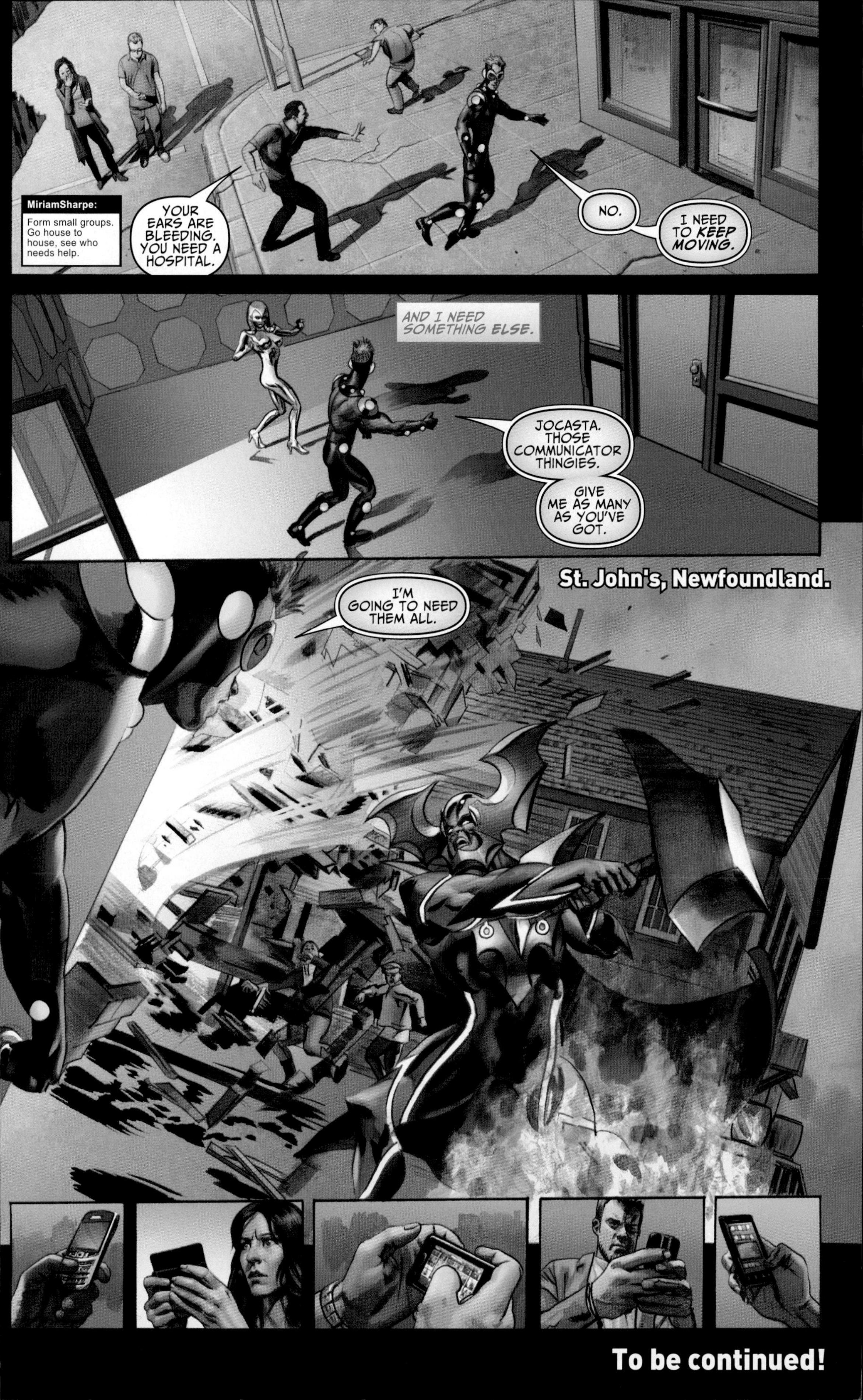

MiriamSharpe:
Form small groups. Go house to house, see who needs help.
YOUR EARS ARE BLEEDING. YOU NEED A HOSPITAL.
NO.
I NEED TO KEEP MOVING.
AND I NEED SOMETHING ELSE.
JOCASTA. THOSE COMMUNICATOR THINGIES.
GIVE ME AS MANY AS YOU'VE GOT.
St. John's, Newfoundland.
I'M GOING TO NEED THEM ALL.
To be continued!

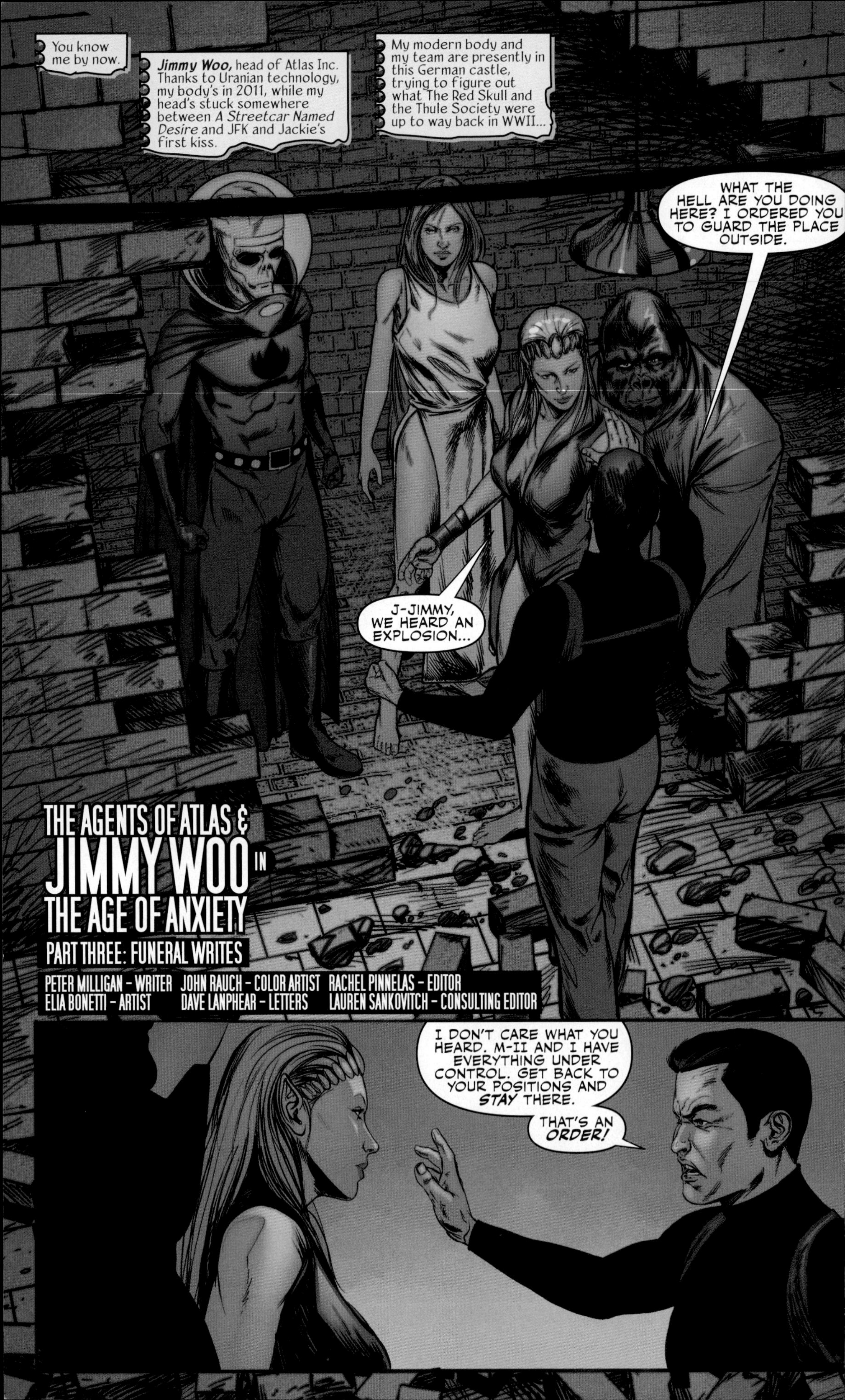
You know me by now.
Jimmy Woo, head of Atlas Inc. Thanks to Uranian technology, my body's in 2011, while my head's stuck somewhere between A Streetcar Named Desire and JFK and Jackie's first kiss.
My modern body and my team are presently in this German castle, trying to figure out what The Red Skull and the Thule Society were up to way back in WWII...
WHAT THE HELL ARE YOU DOING HERE? I ORDERED YOU TO GUARD THE PLACE OUTSIDE.
J-JIMMY, WE HEARD AN EXPLOSION...
THE AGENTS OF ATLAS &
JIMMY WOO IN
THE AGE OF ANXIETY
PART THREE: FUNERAL WRITES
PETER MILLIGAN - WRITER
ELIA BONETTI - ARTIST
JOHN RAUCH - COLOR ARTIST
DAVE LANPHEAR - LETTERS
RACHEL PINNELAS - EDITOR
LAUREN SANKOVITCH - CONSULTING EDITOR
I DON'T CARE WHAT YOU HEARD. M-II AND I HAVE EVERYTHING UNDER CONTROL. GET BACK TO YOUR POSITIONS AND STAY THERE.
THAT'S AN ORDER!

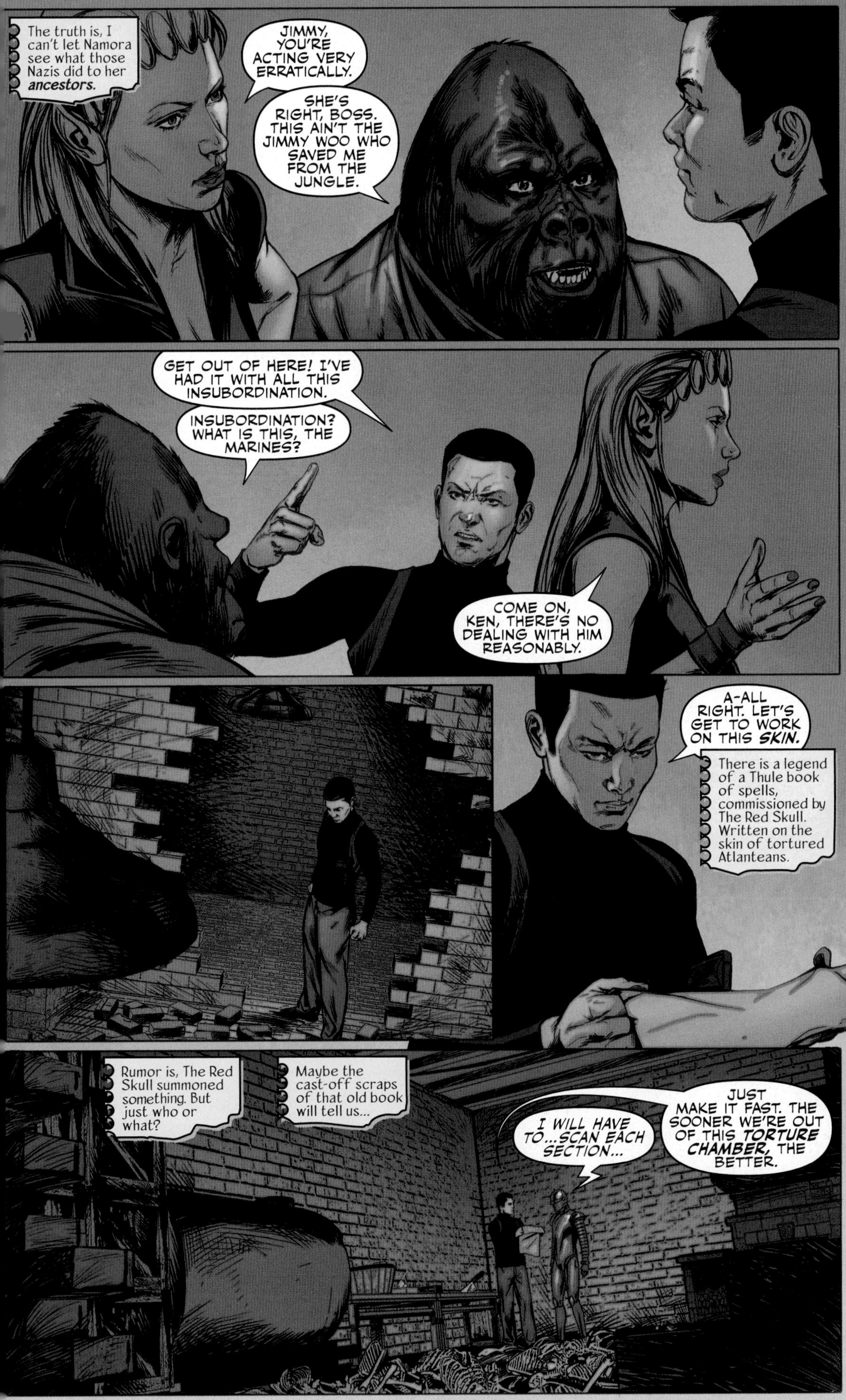
The truth is, I can't let Namora see what those Nazis did to her *ancestors*.
JIMMY, YOU'RE ACTING VERY ERRATICALLY.
SHE'S RIGHT, BOSS. THIS AIN'T THE JIMMY WOO WHO SAVED ME FROM THE JUNGLE.
GET OUT OF HERE! I'VE HAD IT WITH ALL THIS INSUBORDINATION.
INSUBORDINATION? WHAT IS THIS, THE MARINES?
COME ON, KEN, THERE'S NO DEALING WITH HIM REASONABLY.
A-ALL RIGHT. LET'S GET TO WORK ON THIS *SKIN*.
There is a legend of a Thule book of spells, commissioned by The Red Skull. Written on the skin of tortured Atlanteans.
Rumor is, The Red Skull summoned something. But just who or what?
Maybe the cast-off scraps of that old book will tell us...
JUST MAKE IT FAST. THE SOONER WE'RE OUT OF THIS *TORTURE CHAMBER*, THE BETTER.
I WILL HAVE TO...SCAN EACH SECTION...

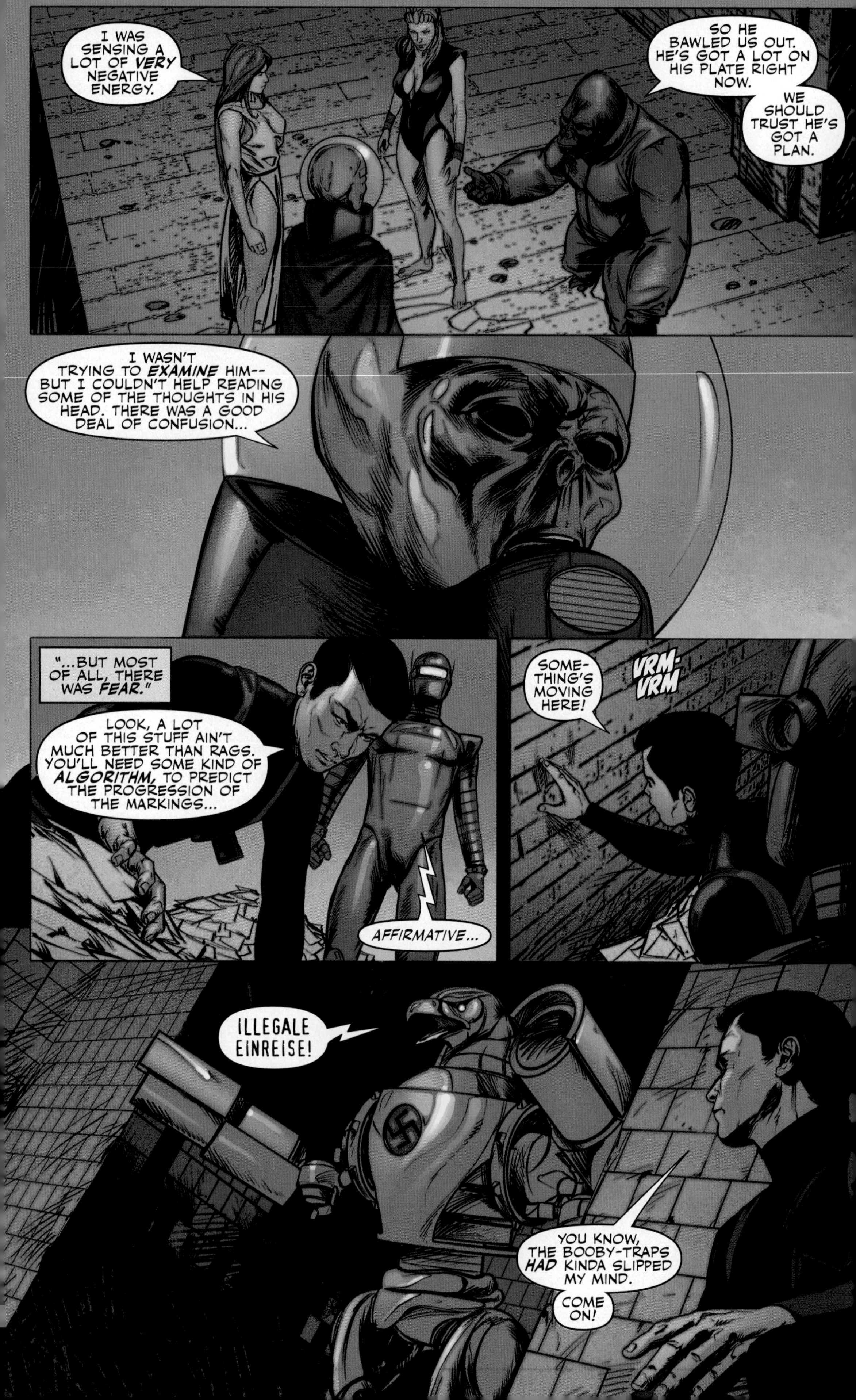
I WAS SENSING A LOT OF *VERY* NEGATIVE ENERGY.
SO HE BAWLED US OUT. HE'S GOT A LOT ON HIS PLATE RIGHT NOW.
WE SHOULD TRUST HE'S GOT A PLAN.
I WASN'T TRYING TO *EXAMINE* HIM--BUT I COULDN'T HELP READING SOME OF THE THOUGHTS IN HIS HEAD. THERE WAS A GOOD DEAL OF CONFUSION...
"...BUT MOST OF ALL, THERE WAS *FEAR.*"
LOOK, A LOT OF THIS STUFF AIN'T MUCH BETTER THAN RAGS. YOU'LL NEED SOME KIND OF *ALGORITHM,* TO PREDICT THE PROGRESSION OF THE MARKINGS...
AFFIRMATIVE...
SOME-THING'S MOVING HERE!
VRM-VRM
ILLEGALE EINREISE!
YOU KNOW, THE BOOBY-TRAPS *HAD* KINDA SLIPPED MY MIND.
COME ON!

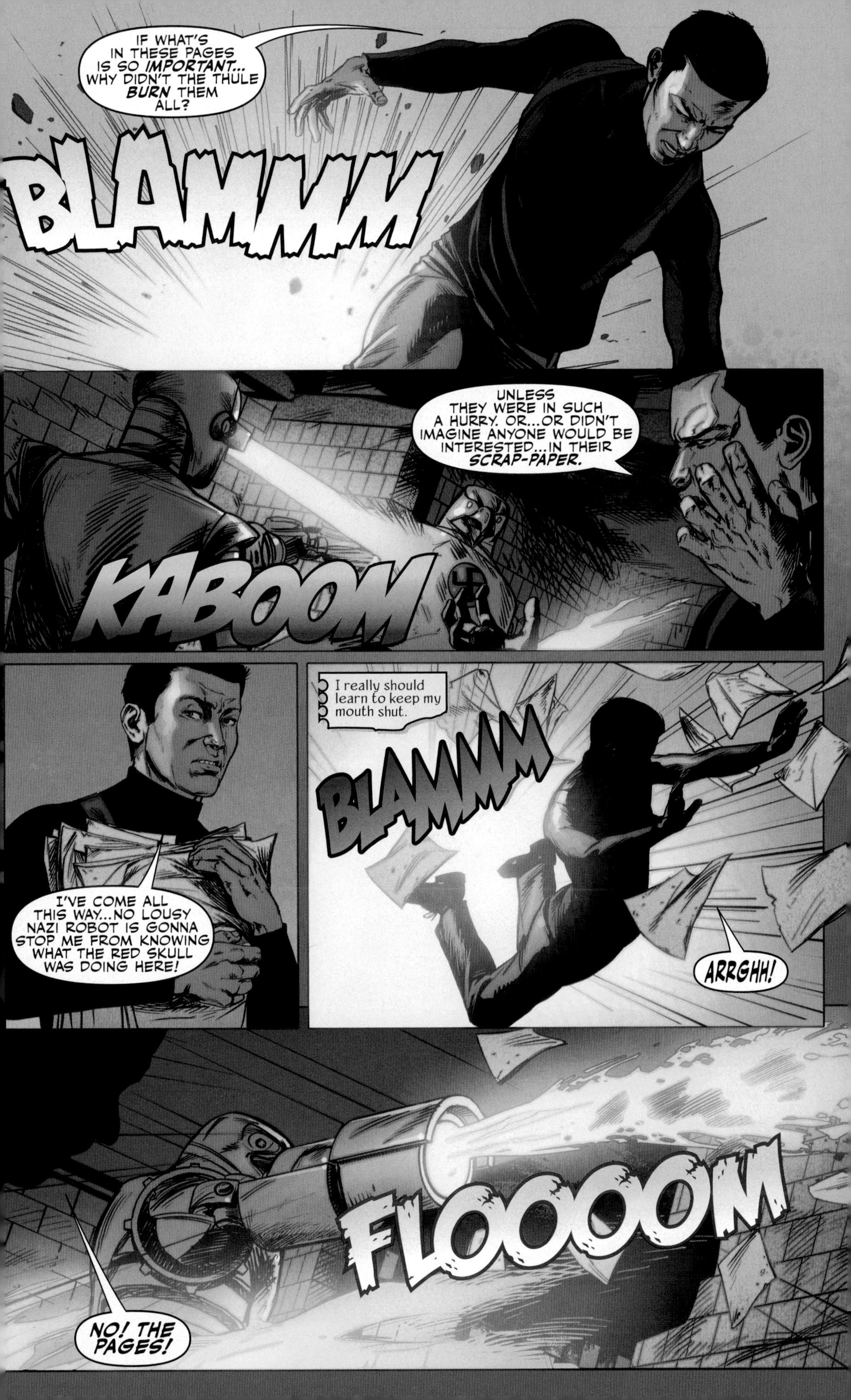
IF WHAT'S IN THESE PAGES IS SO IMPORTANT... WHY DIDN'T THE THULE BURN THEM ALL?
BLAMMM
UNLESS THEY WERE IN SUCH A HURRY. OR...OR DIDN'T IMAGINE ANYONE WOULD BE INTERESTED...IN THEIR SCRAP-PAPER.
KABOOM
I'VE COME ALL THIS WAY...NO LOUSY NAZI ROBOT IS GONNA STOP ME FROM KNOWING WHAT THE RED SKULL WAS DOING HERE!
I really should learn to keep my mouth shut.
BLAMMM
ARRGHH!
FLOOOOM
NO! THE PAGES!

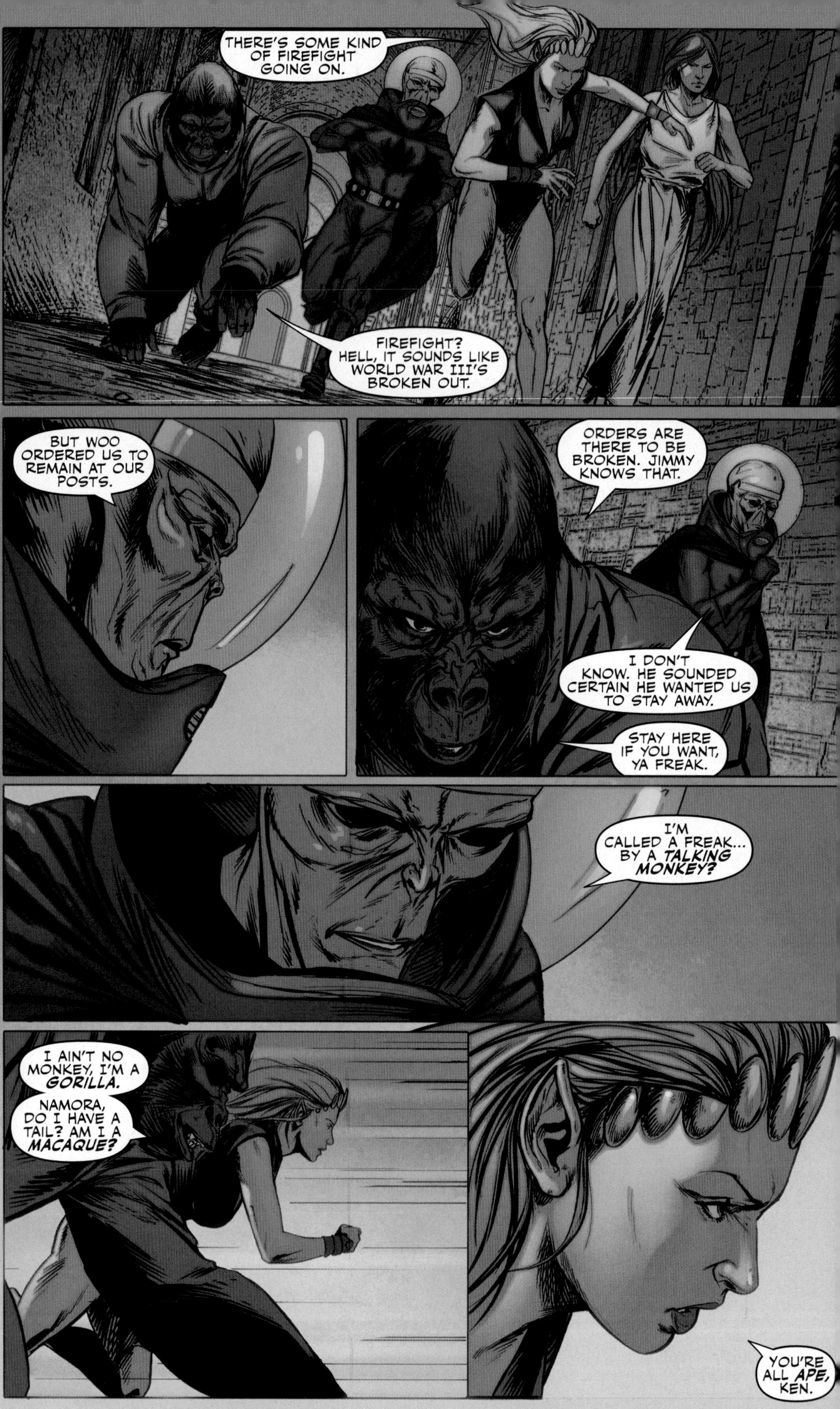
THERE'S SOME KIND OF FIREFIGHT GOING ON.
FIREFIGHT? HELL, IT SOUNDS LIKE WORLD WAR III'S BROKEN OUT.
BUT WOO ORDERED US TO REMAIN AT OUR POSTS.
ORDERS ARE THERE TO BE BROKEN. JIMMY KNOWS THAT.
I DON'T KNOW. HE SOUNDED CERTAIN HE WANTED US TO STAY AWAY.
STAY HERE IF YOU WANT, YA FREAK.
I'M CALLED A FREAK... BY A *TALKING MONKEY?*
I AIN'T NO MONKEY, I'M A *GORILLA.*
NAMORA, DO I HAVE A TAIL? AM I A *MACAQUE?*
YOU'RE ALL *APE*, KEN.

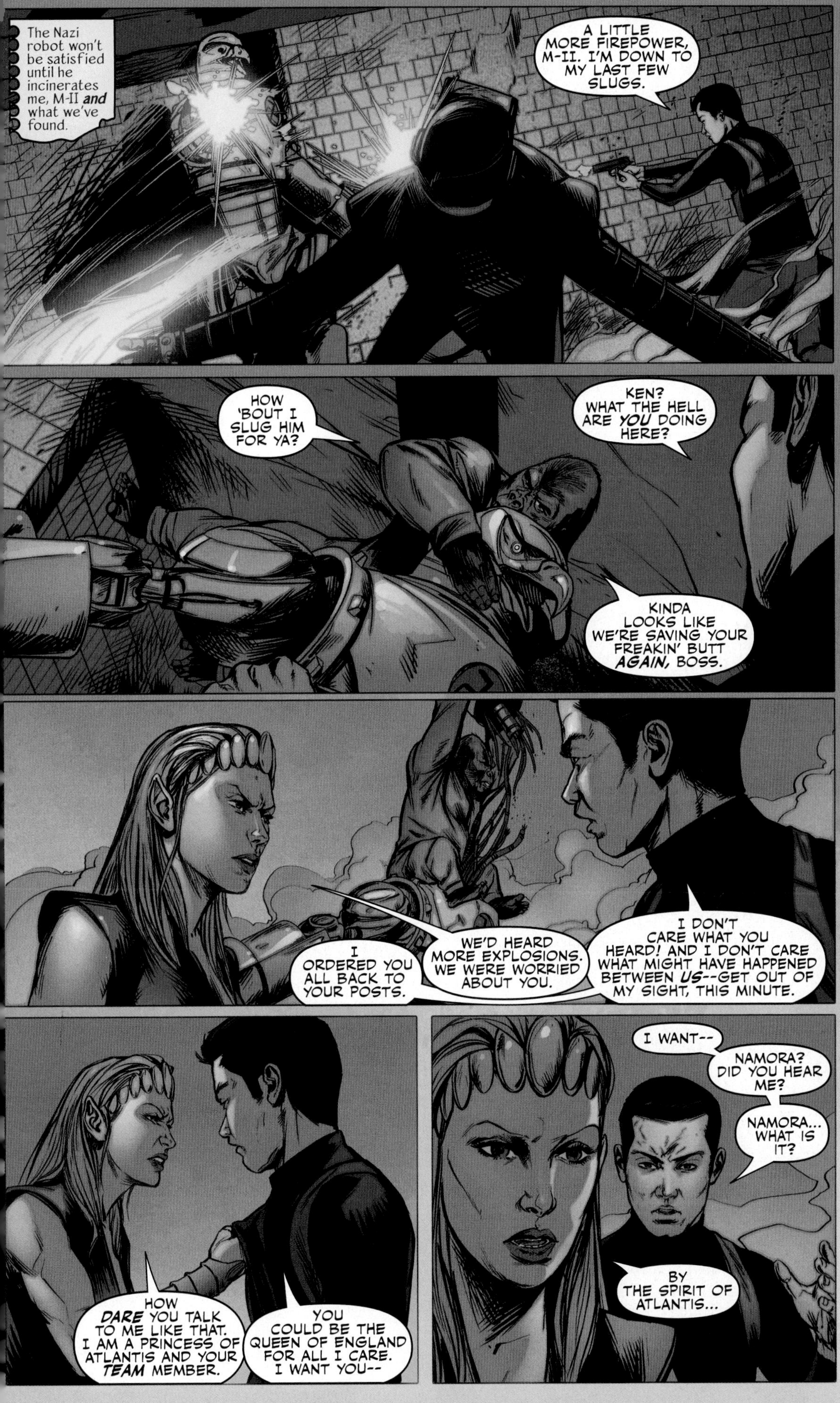

The Nazi robot won't be satisfied until he incinerates me, M-II **and** what we've found.
A LITTLE MORE FIREPOWER, M-II. I'M DOWN TO MY LAST FEW SLUGS.
HOW 'BOUT I SLUG HIM FOR YA?
KEN? WHAT THE HELL ARE ***YOU*** DOING HERE?
KINDA LOOKS LIKE WE'RE SAVING YOUR FREAKIN' BUTT ***AGAIN,*** BOSS.
I ORDERED YOU ALL BACK TO YOUR POSTS.
WE'D HEARD MORE EXPLOSIONS. WE WERE WORRIED ABOUT YOU.
I DON'T CARE WHAT YOU HEARD! AND I DON'T CARE WHAT MIGHT HAVE HAPPENED BETWEEN ***US***--GET OUT OF MY SIGHT, THIS MINUTE.
HOW ***DARE*** YOU TALK TO ME LIKE THAT. I AM A PRINCESS OF ATLANTIS AND YOUR ***TEAM*** MEMBER.
YOU COULD BE THE QUEEN OF ENGLAND FOR ALL I CARE. I WANT YOU--
I WANT--
NAMORA? DID YOU HEAR ME?
NAMORA... WHAT IS IT?
BY THE SPIRIT OF ATLANTIS...

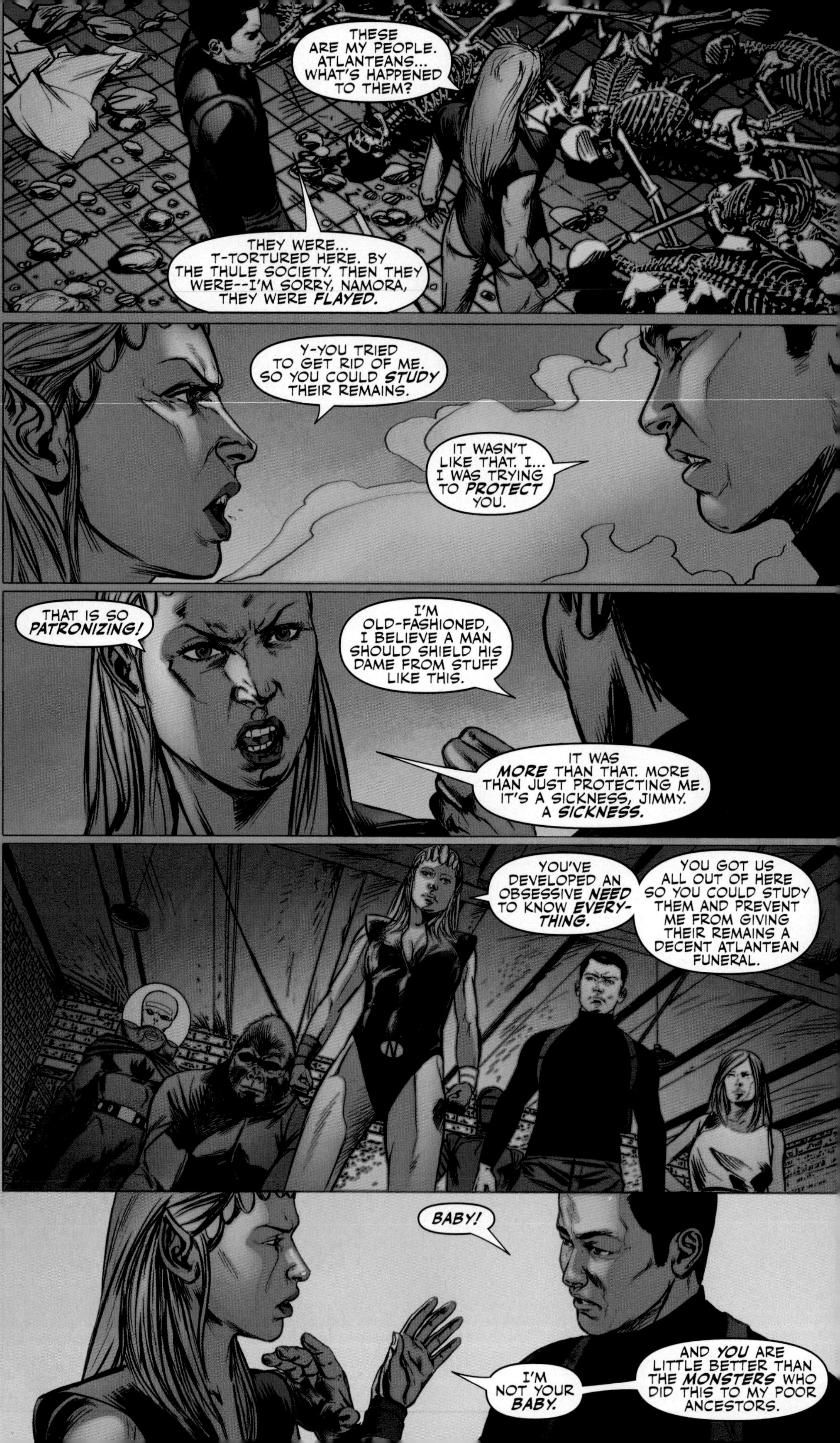

THESE ARE MY PEOPLE. ATLANTEANS... WHAT'S HAPPENED TO THEM?
THEY WERE... T-TORTURED HERE. BY THE THULE SOCIETY. THEN THEY WERE--I'M SORRY, NAMORA, THEY WERE *FLAYED.*
Y-YOU TRIED TO GET RID OF ME. SO YOU COULD *STUDY* THEIR REMAINS.
IT WASN'T LIKE THAT. I... I WAS TRYING TO *PROTECT* YOU.
THAT IS SO *PATRONIZING!*
I'M OLD-FASHIONED, I BELIEVE A MAN SHOULD SHIELD HIS DAME FROM STUFF LIKE THIS.
IT WAS *MORE* THAN THAT. MORE THAN JUST PROTECTING ME. IT'S A SICKNESS, JIMMY. A *SICKNESS.*
YOU'VE DEVELOPED AN OBSESSIVE *NEED* TO KNOW *EVERY-THING.*
YOU GOT US ALL OUT OF HERE SO YOU COULD STUDY THEM AND PREVENT ME FROM GIVING THEIR REMAINS A DECENT ATLANTEAN FUNERAL.
BABY!
I'M NOT YOUR *BABY.*
AND *YOU* ARE LITTLE BETTER THAN THE *MONSTERS* WHO DID THIS TO MY POOR ANCESTORS.

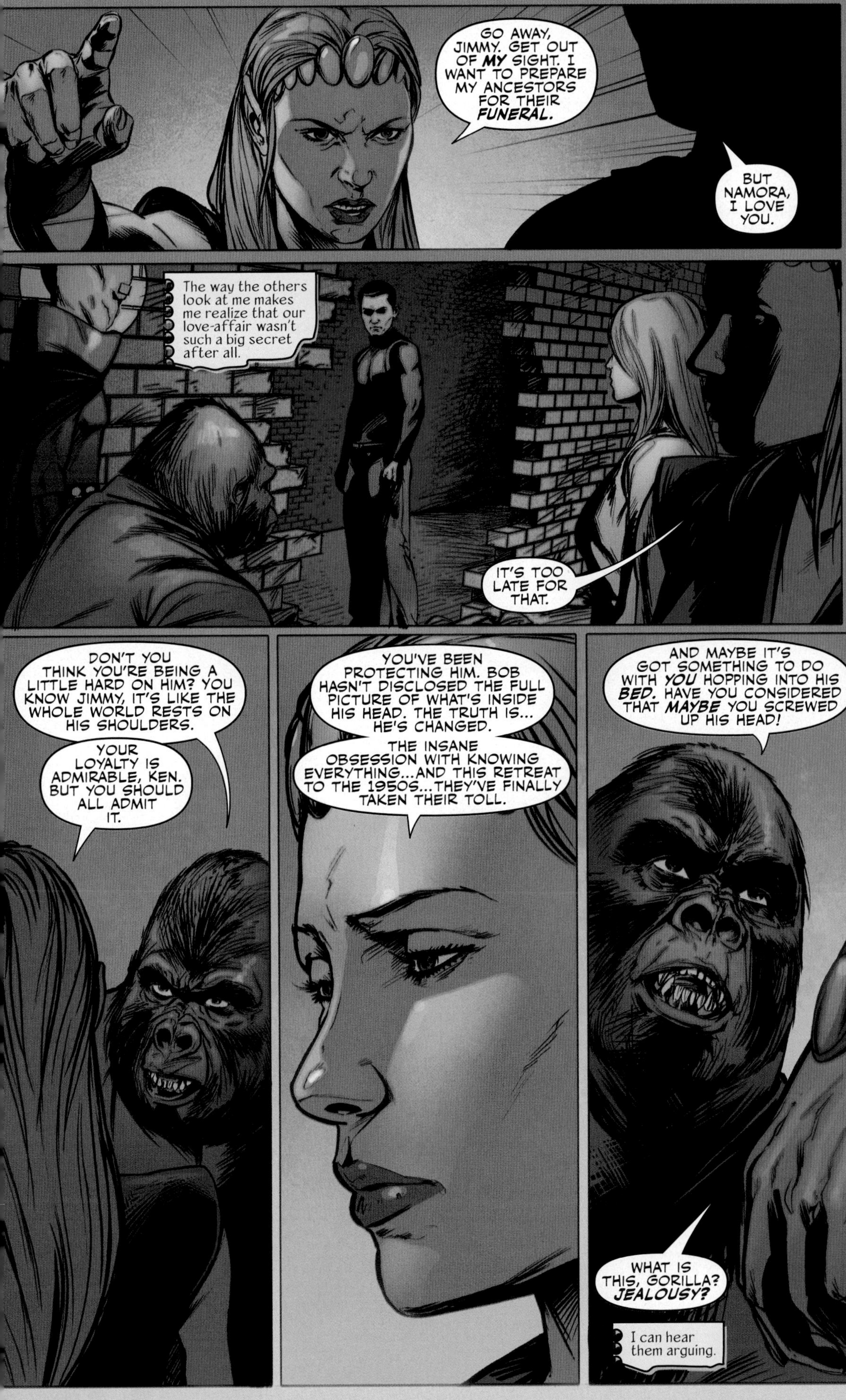
GO AWAY, JIMMY. GET OUT OF MY SIGHT. I WANT TO PREPARE MY ANCESTORS FOR THEIR FUNERAL.
BUT NAMORA, I LOVE YOU.
The way the others look at me makes me realize that our love-affair wasn't such a big secret after all.
IT'S TOO LATE FOR THAT.
DON'T YOU THINK YOU'RE BEING A LITTLE HARD ON HIM? YOU KNOW JIMMY, IT'S LIKE THE WHOLE WORLD RESTS ON HIS SHOULDERS.
YOUR LOYALTY IS ADMIRABLE, KEN. BUT YOU SHOULD ALL ADMIT IT.
YOU'VE BEEN PROTECTING HIM. BOB HASN'T DISCLOSED THE FULL PICTURE OF WHAT'S INSIDE HIS HEAD. THE TRUTH IS... HE'S CHANGED.
THE INSANE OBSESSION WITH KNOWING EVERYTHING...AND THIS RETREAT TO THE 1950S...THEY'VE FINALLY TAKEN THEIR TOLL.
AND MAYBE IT'S GOT SOMETHING TO DO WITH YOU HOPPING INTO HIS BED. HAVE YOU CONSIDERED THAT MAYBE YOU SCREWED UP HIS HEAD!
WHAT IS THIS, GORILLA? JEALOUSY?
I can hear them arguing.

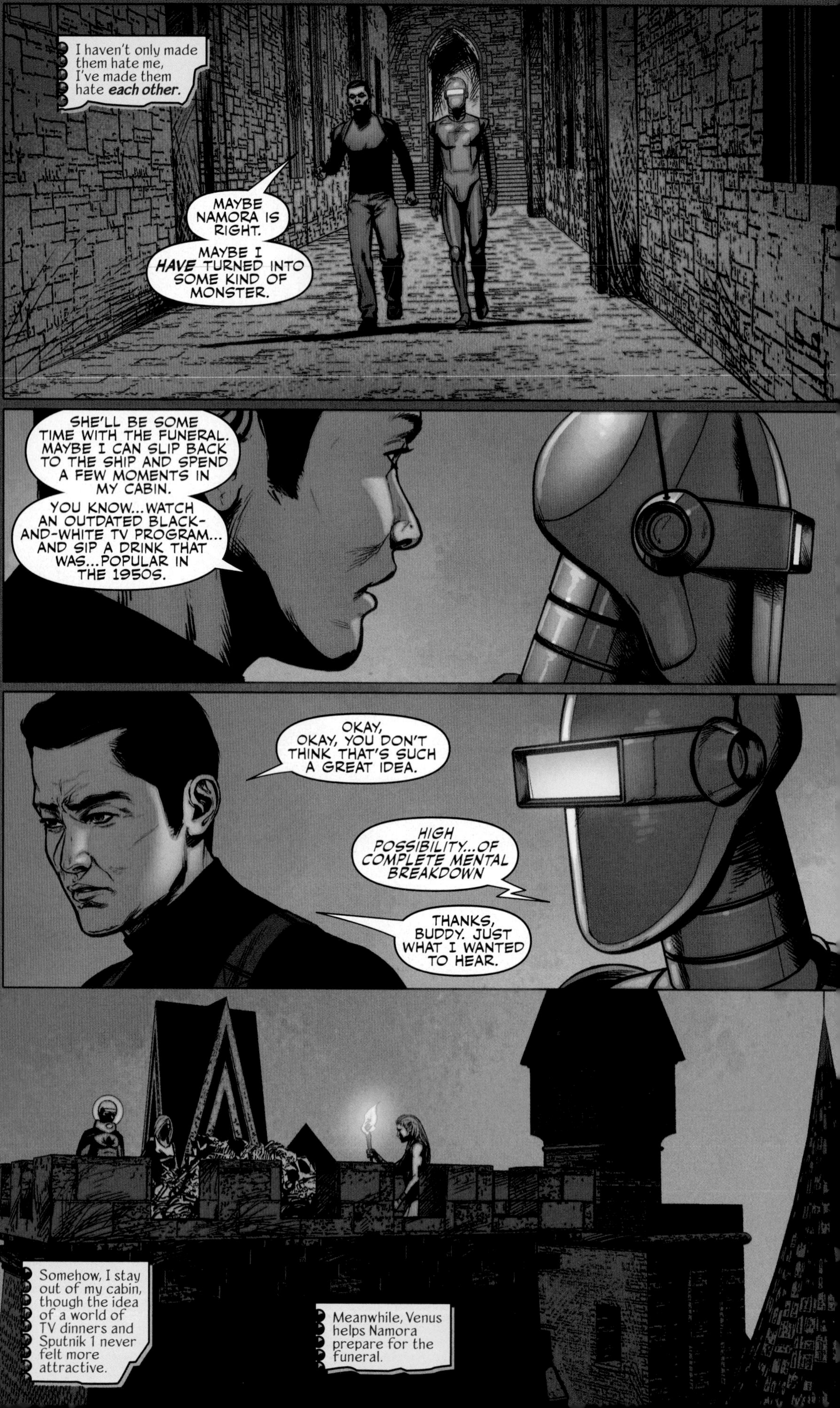
I haven't only made them hate me, I've made them hate *each other*.
MAYBE NAMORA IS RIGHT.
MAYBE I *HAVE* TURNED INTO SOME KIND OF MONSTER.
SHE'LL BE SOME TIME WITH THE FUNERAL. MAYBE I CAN SLIP BACK TO THE SHIP AND SPEND A FEW MOMENTS IN MY CABIN.
YOU KNOW...WATCH AN OUTDATED BLACK-AND-WHITE TV PROGRAM... AND SIP A DRINK THAT WAS...POPULAR IN THE 1950S.
OKAY, OKAY, YOU DON'T THINK THAT'S SUCH A GREAT IDEA.
HIGH POSSIBILITY...OF COMPLETE MENTAL BREAKDOWN
THANKS, BUDDY. JUST WHAT I WANTED TO HEAR.
Somehow, I stay out of my cabin, though the idea of a world of TV dinners and Sputnik 1 never felt more attractive.
Meanwhile, Venus helps Namora prepare for the funeral.

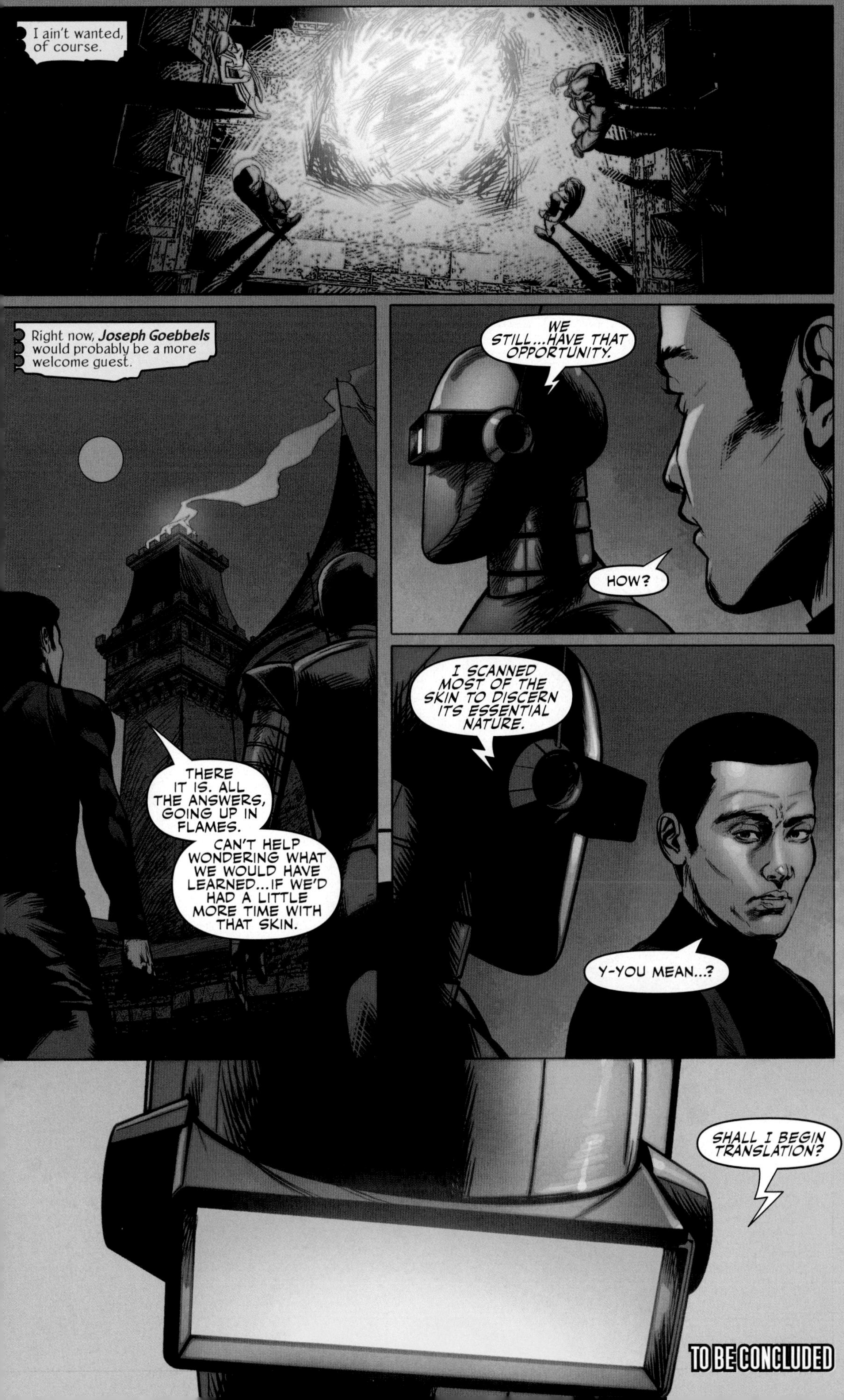
I ain't wanted, of course.
Right now, Joseph Goebbels would probably be a more welcome guest.
THERE IT IS. ALL THE ANSWERS, GOING UP IN FLAMES.
CAN'T HELP WONDERING WHAT WE WOULD HAVE LEARNED...IF WE'D HAD A LITTLE MORE TIME WITH THAT SKIN.
WE STILL...HAVE THAT OPPORTUNITY.
HOW?
I SCANNED MOST OF THE SKIN TO DISCERN ITS ESSENTIAL NATURE.
Y-YOU MEAN...?
SHALL I BEGIN TRANSLATION?
TO BE CONCLUDED

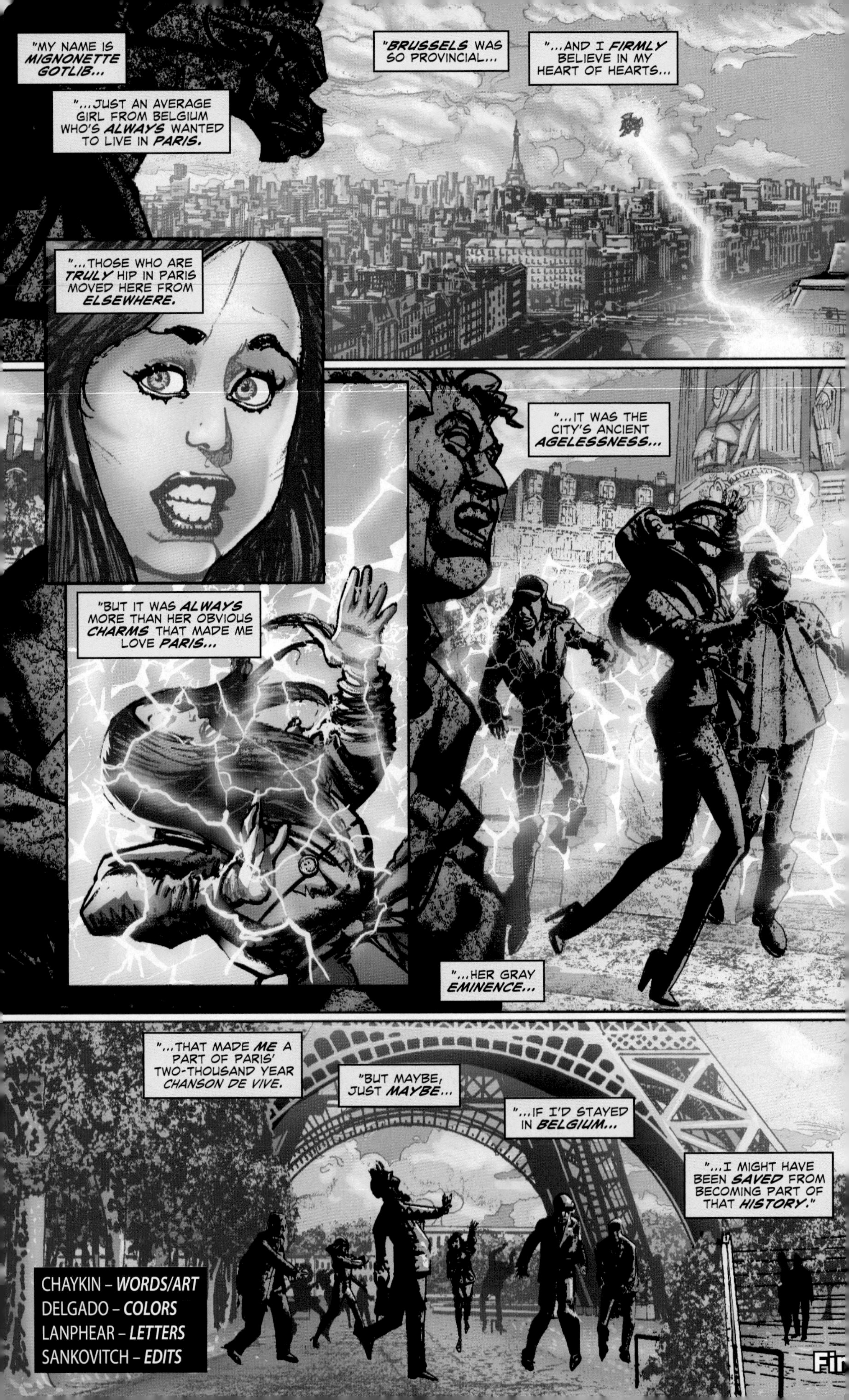
"MY NAME IS MIGNONETTE GOTLIB...
"...JUST AN AVERAGE GIRL FROM BELGIUM WHO'S ALWAYS WANTED TO LIVE IN PARIS.
"BRUSSELS WAS SO PROVINCIAL...
"...AND I FIRMLY BELIEVE IN MY HEART OF HEARTS...
"...THOSE WHO ARE TRULY HIP IN PARIS MOVED HERE FROM ELSEWHERE.
"BUT IT WAS ALWAYS MORE THAN HER OBVIOUS CHARMS THAT MADE ME LOVE PARIS...
"...IT WAS THE CITY'S ANCIENT AGELESSNESS...
"...HER GRAY EMINENCE...
"...THAT MADE ME A PART OF PARIS' TWO-THOUSAND YEAR CHANSON DE VIVE.
"BUT MAYBE, JUST MAYBE...
"...IF I'D STAYED IN BELGIUM...
"...I MIGHT HAVE BEEN SAVED FROM BECOMING PART OF THAT HISTORY."
CHAYKIN – WORDS/ART
DELGADO – COLORS
LANPHEAR – LETTERS
SANKOVITCH – EDITS

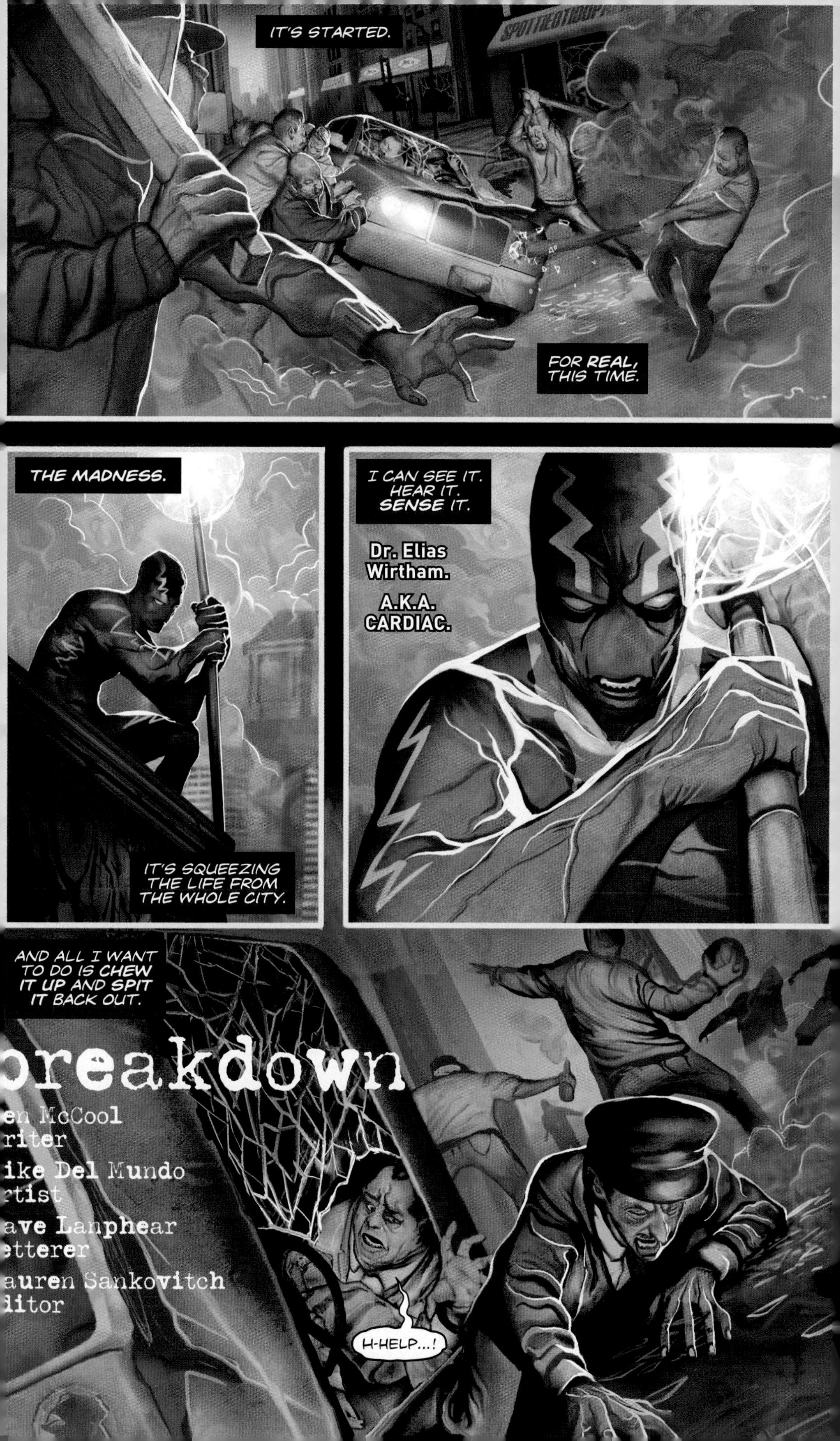

IT'S STARTED.
FOR REAL, THIS TIME.
THE MADNESS.
IT'S SQUEEZING THE LIFE FROM THE WHOLE CITY.
I CAN SEE IT. HEAR IT. SENSE IT.
Dr. Elias Wirtham.
A.K.A. CARDIAC.
AND ALL I WANT TO DO IS CHEW IT UP AND SPIT IT BACK OUT.
reakdown
en McCool
riter
ike Del Mundo
rtist
ave Lanphear
etterer
auren Sankovitch
ditor
H-HELP...!

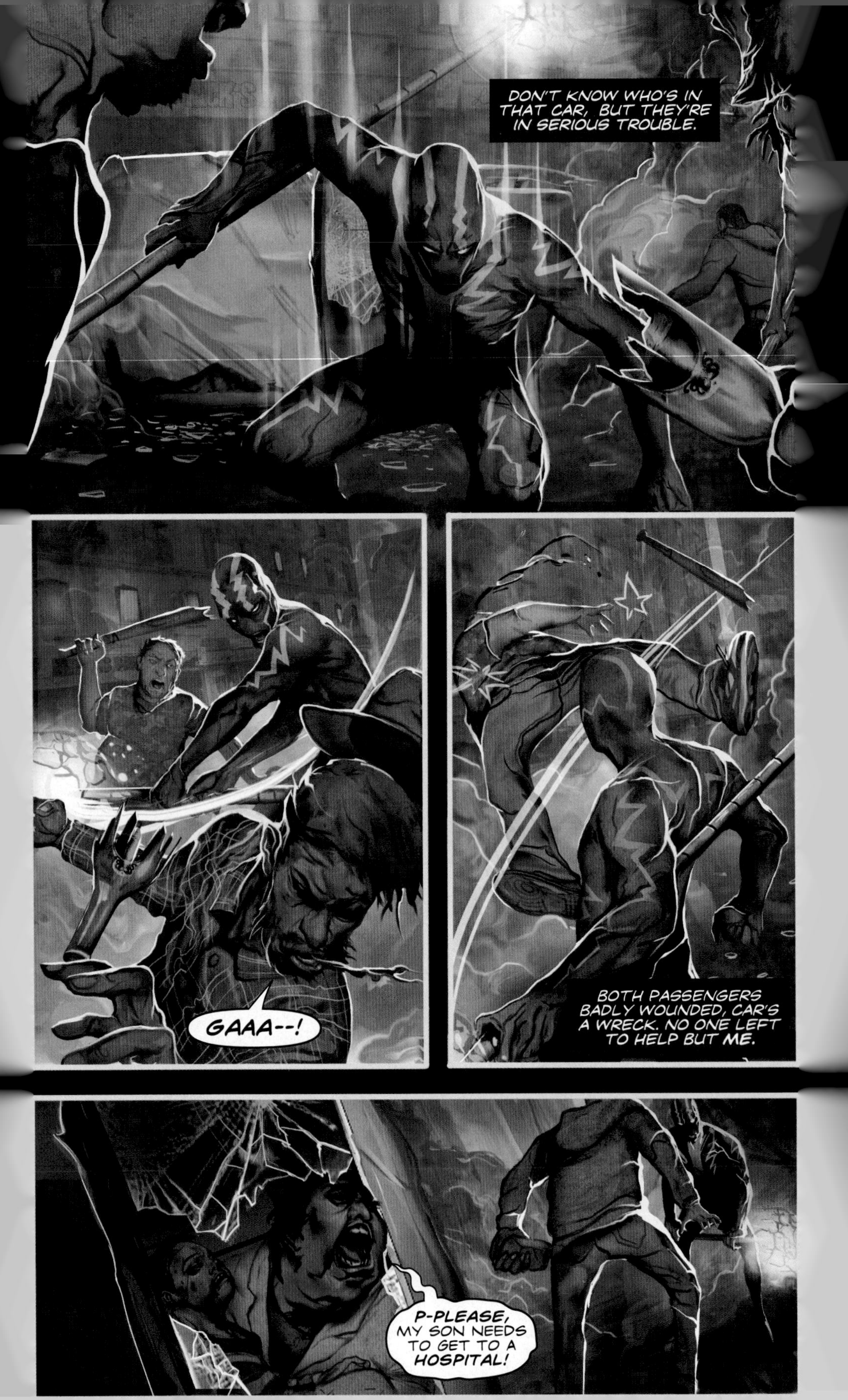
DON'T KNOW WHO'S IN THAT CAR, BUT THEY'RE IN SERIOUS TROUBLE.
GAAA--!
BOTH PASSENGERS BADLY WOUNDED, CAR'S A WRECK. NO ONE LEFT TO HELP BUT ME.
P-PLEASE, MY SON NEEDS TO GET TO A HOSPITAL!

IF W-WE DON'T GET HIM TO THE EMERGENCY ROOM **FAST** H-HE'S GONNA DIE!

⊰OOOF⊱

HOSPITAL'S ALMOST A MILE AWAY. NO TIME TO LOSE.

WHAT'S WRONG WITH THE BOY?

M-MENINGITIS, AND HE NEEDS **IMMEDIATE** CARE!

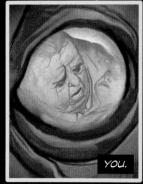

YOU.

CHARLES DAVIES. CEO OF JERIXO HEALTHCARE.

THREE PRODUCTS RECALLED IN THE PAST TWELVE MONTHS, **NINE** RECORDED FATALITIES.

NO CHARGES FILED, DESPITE **GLARING** MALPRACTICE.

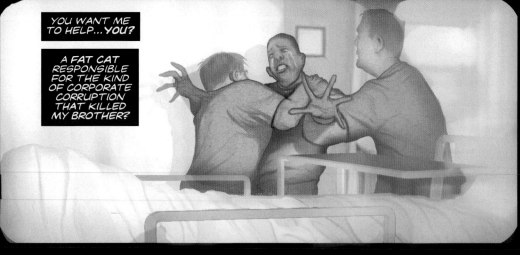

YOU WANT ME TO HELP...*YOU?*

A FAT CAT RESPONSIBLE FOR THE KIND OF CORPORATE CORRUPTION THAT KILLED MY BROTHER?

I LOST JOSHUA TO A DISEASE FOR WHICH I LEARNED A PHARMACEUTICAL COMPANY HAD A *CURE,* EMBARGOED DUE TO AN UNFAVORABLE ECONOMIC CLIMATE.

I ENDED MY LIFE AS *ELIAS WIRTHAM* AND BECAME *CARDIAC.*

THE BETA ENERGY THAT NOW PULSATES THROUGH MY BODY ENSURES NO CRIMINAL IS SAFE.

W-WE'RE RUNNING OUT OF *TIME!*

LEGAL TECHNICALITIES SHIELD MONSTERS LIKE DAVIES FROM JUSTICE.

BUT THEY DON'T PROTECT HIM FROM ME.

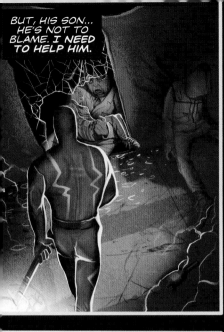

BUT, HIS SON... HE'S NOT TO BLAME. I NEED TO HELP HIM.

PART OF ME'S SAYING THIS IS A BAD IDEA. THAT THE BOY'S GUILTY BY ASSOCIATION.

WHAT KEPT YOU, DAMMIT?

BUT I CAN'T LET THE DARK SIDE TAKE COMPLETE CONTROL.

HE'S LOST CONSCIOUSNESS.

EMERGENC

DOESN'T HAVE MUCH LONGER WITHOUT MEDICAL AID.

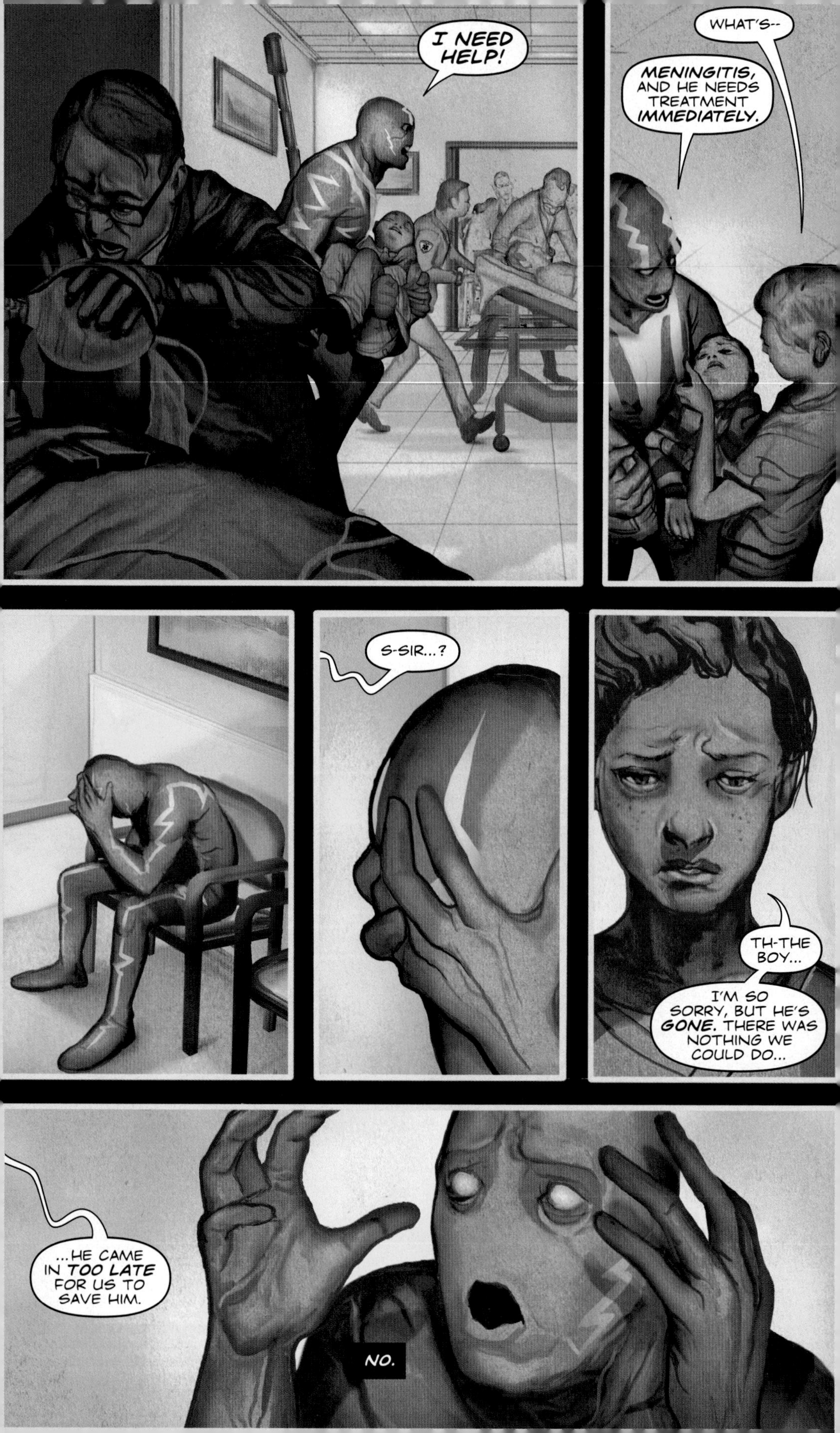
I NEED HELP!
WHAT'S--
MENINGITIS, AND HE NEEDS TREATMENT IMMEDIATELY.
S-SIR...?
TH-THE BOY...
I'M SO SORRY, BUT HE'S GONE. THERE WAS NOTHING WE COULD DO...
...HE CAME IN TOO LATE FOR US TO SAVE HIM.
NO.

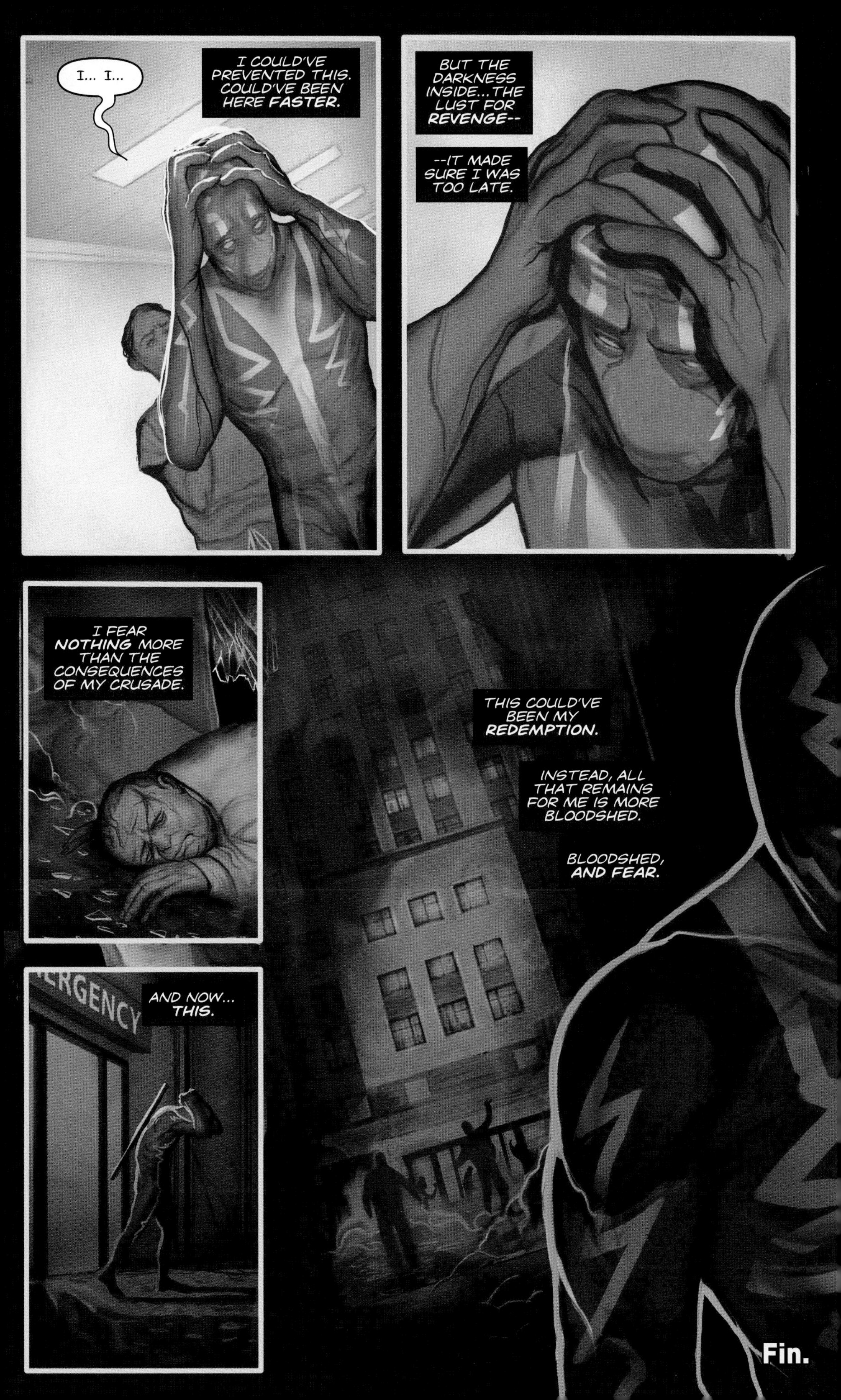
I... I...
I COULD'VE PREVENTED THIS. COULD'VE BEEN HERE FASTER.
BUT THE DARKNESS INSIDE...THE LUST FOR REVENGE--
--IT MADE SURE I WAS TOO LATE.
I FEAR NOTHING MORE THAN THE CONSEQUENCES OF MY CRUSADE.
ERGENCY
AND NOW... THIS.
THIS COULD'VE BEEN MY REDEMPTION.
INSTEAD, ALL THAT REMAINS FOR ME IS MORE BLOODSHED.
BLOODSHED, AND FEAR.
Fin.

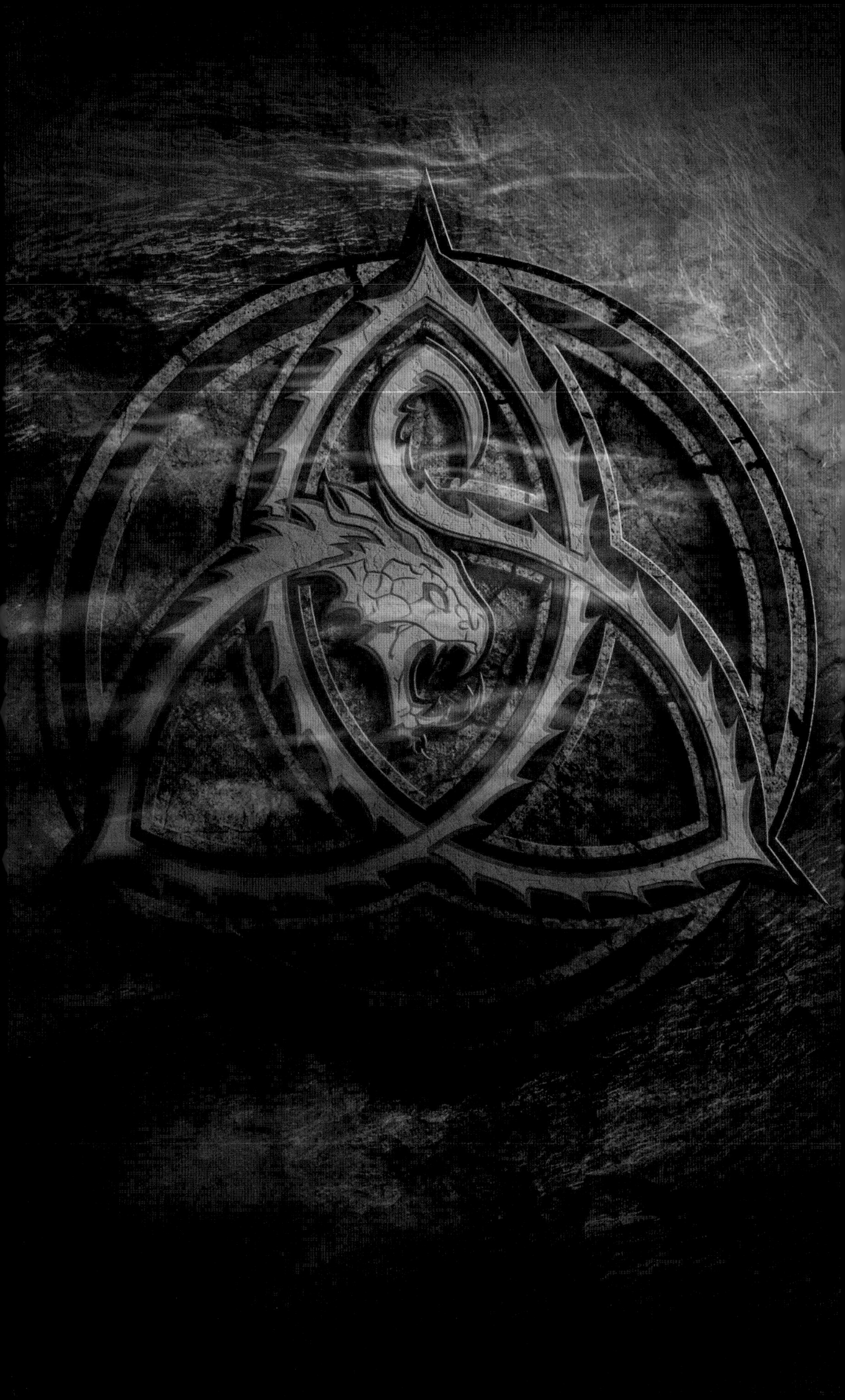

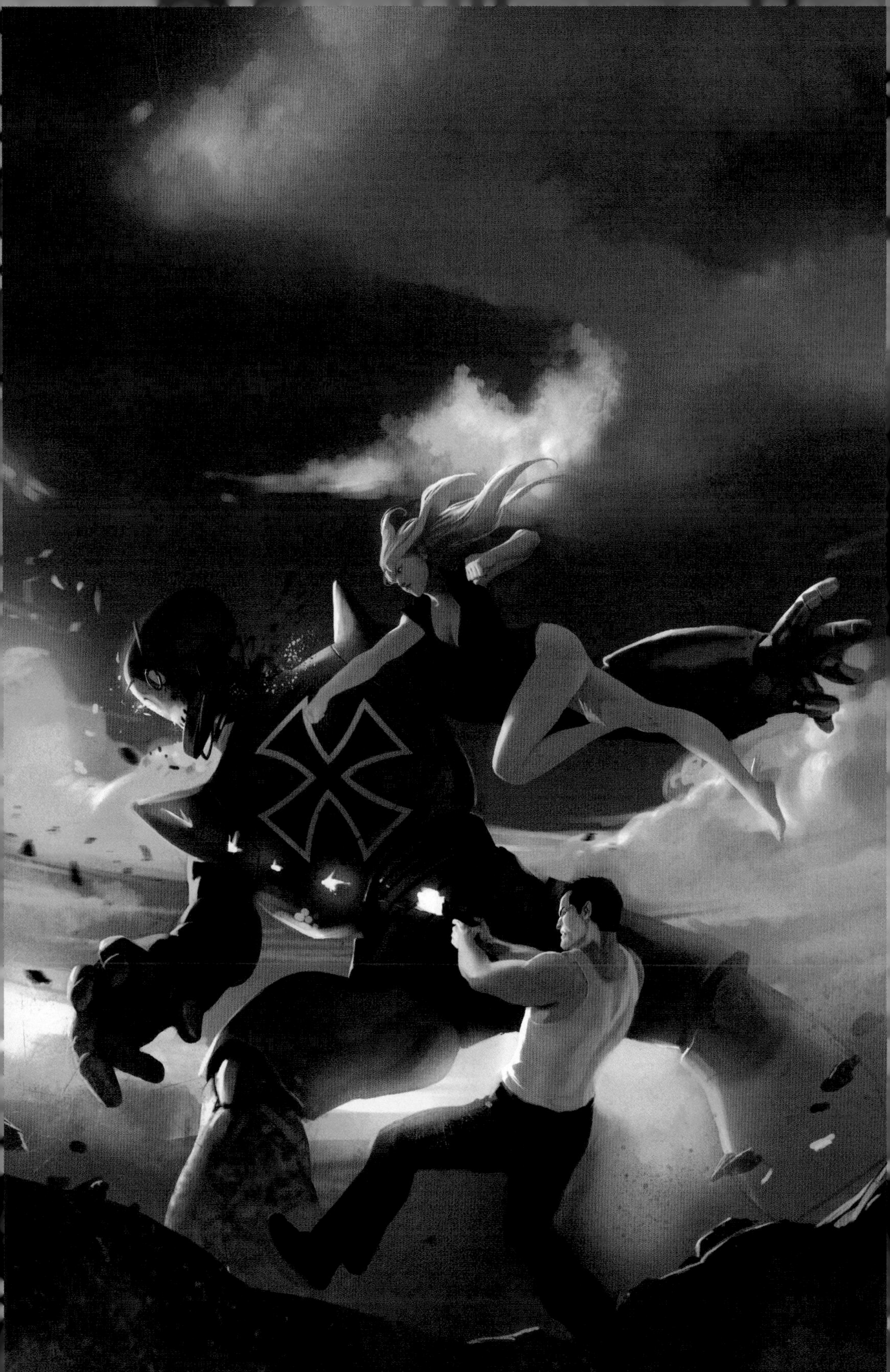

FEAR ITSI FRONT #4

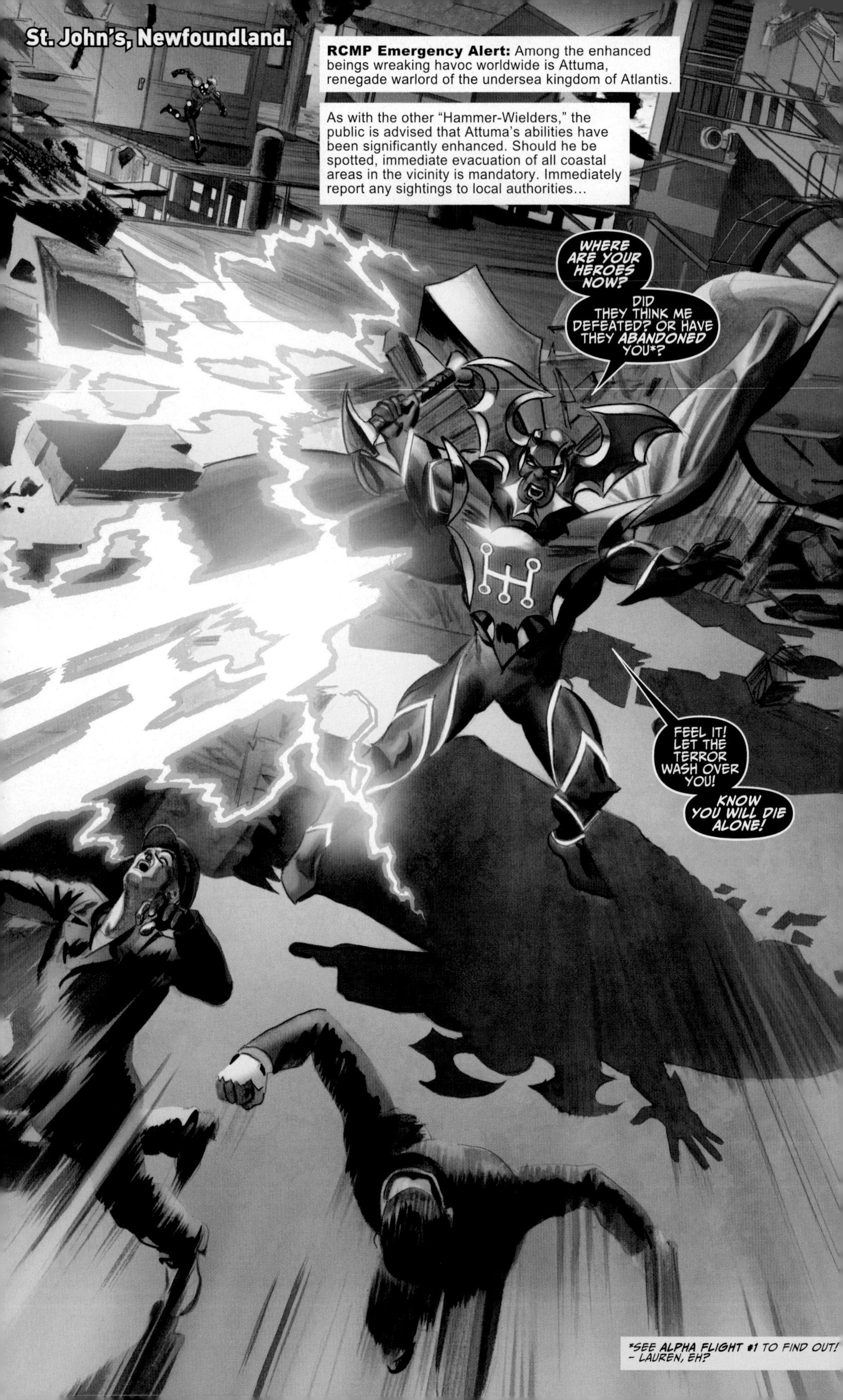
St. John's, Newfoundland.
RCMP Emergency Alert: Among the enhanced beings wreaking havoc worldwide is Attuma, renegade warlord of the undersea kingdom of Atlantis.
As with the other "Hammer-Wielders," the public is advised that Attuma's abilities have been significantly enhanced. Should he be spotted, immediate evacuation of all coastal areas in the vicinity is mandatory. Immediately report any sightings to local authorities...
WHERE ARE YOUR HEROES NOW?
DID THEY THINK ME DEFEATED? OR HAVE THEY ABANDONED YOU*?
FEEL IT! LET THE TERROR WASH OVER YOU!
KNOW YOU WILL DIE ALONE!
*SEE ALPHA FLIGHT #1 TO FIND OUT! – LAUREN, EH?

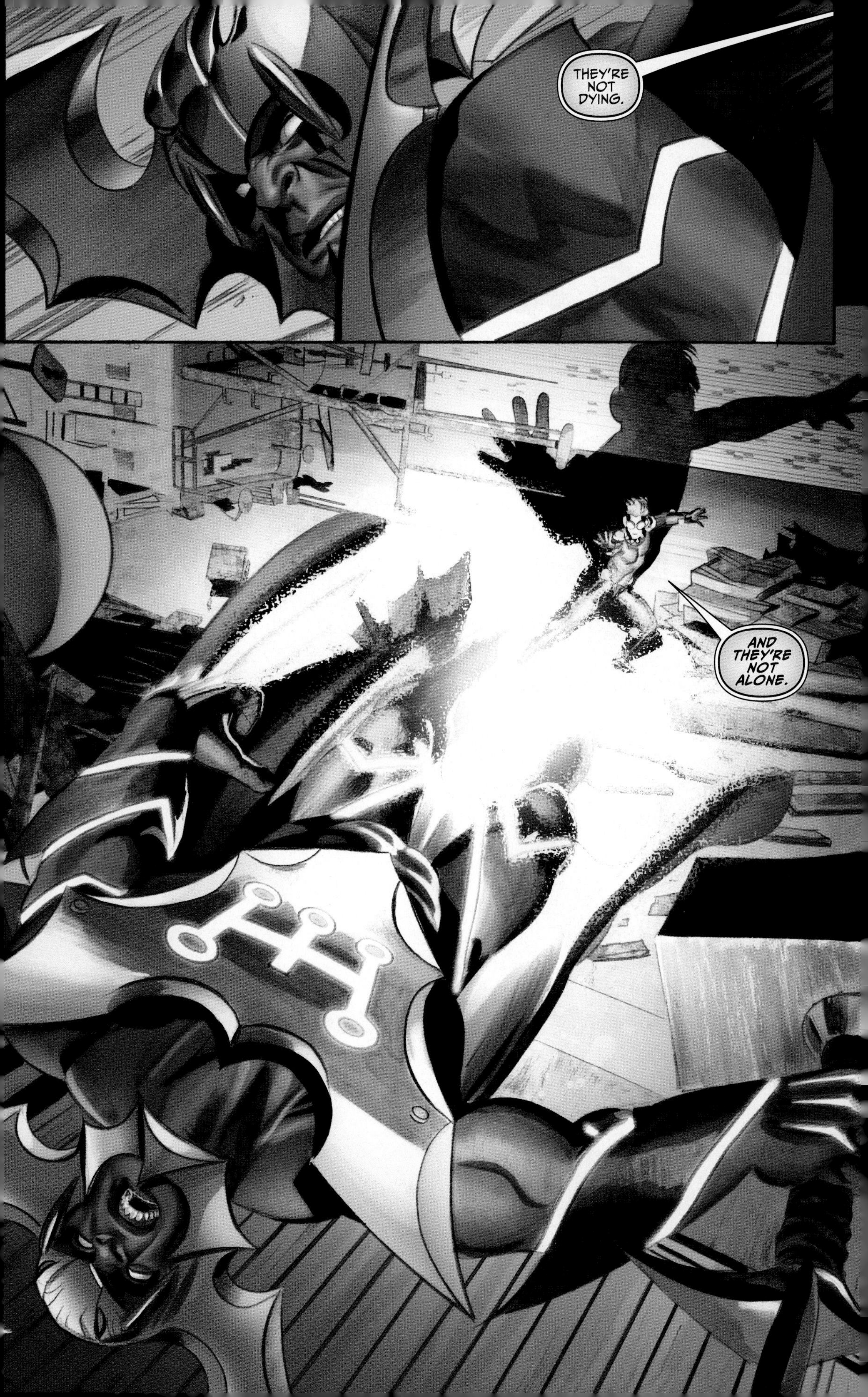
THEY'RE NOT DYING.
AND THEY'RE NOT ALONE.

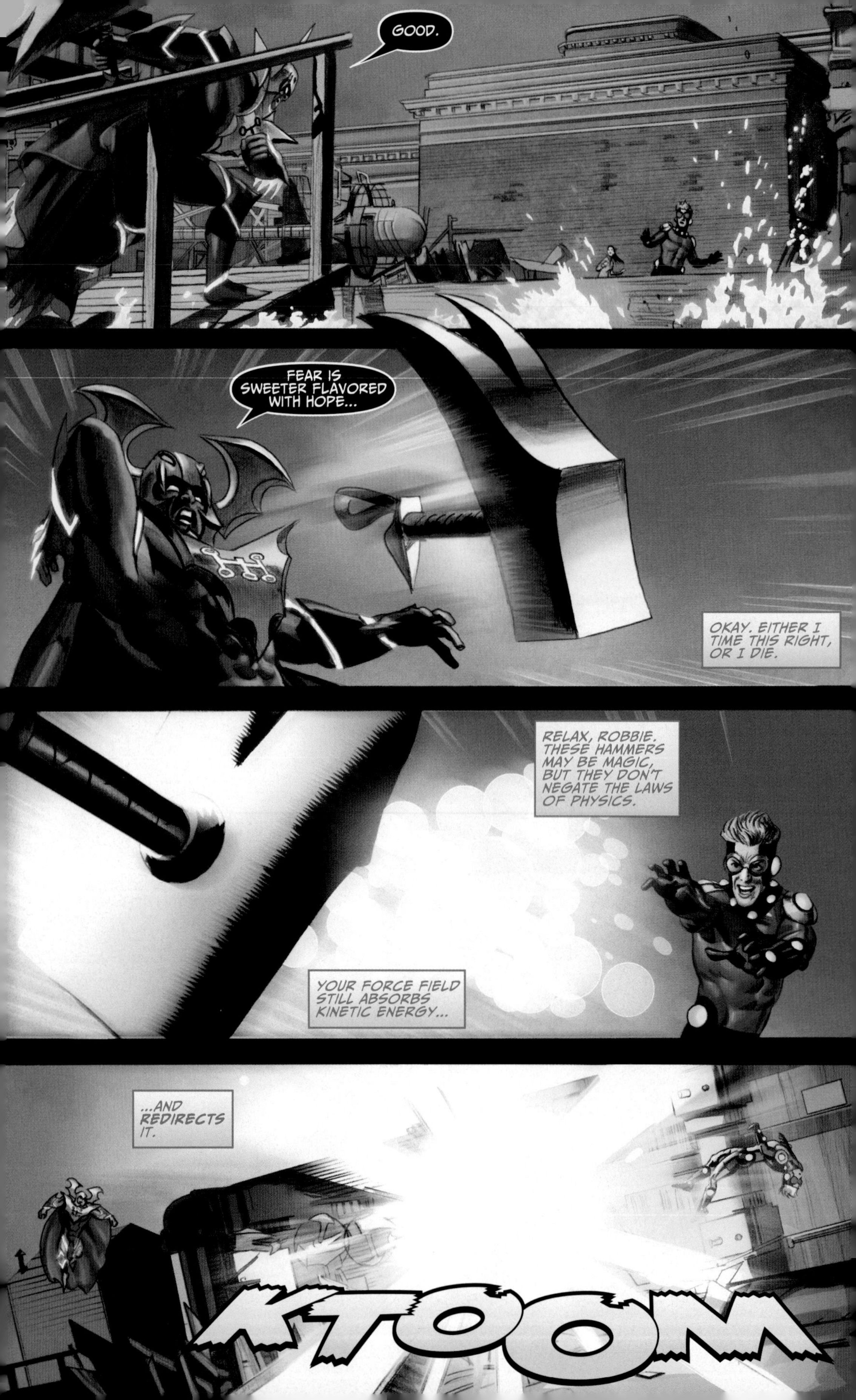
GOOD.
FEAR IS SWEETER FLAVORED WITH HOPE...
OKAY. EITHER I TIME THIS RIGHT, OR I DIE.
RELAX, ROBBIE. THESE HAMMERS MAY BE MAGIC, BUT THEY DON'T NEGATE THE LAWS OF PHYSICS.
YOUR FORCE FIELD STILL ABSORBS KINETIC ENERGY...
...AND REDIRECTS IT.
KTOOM

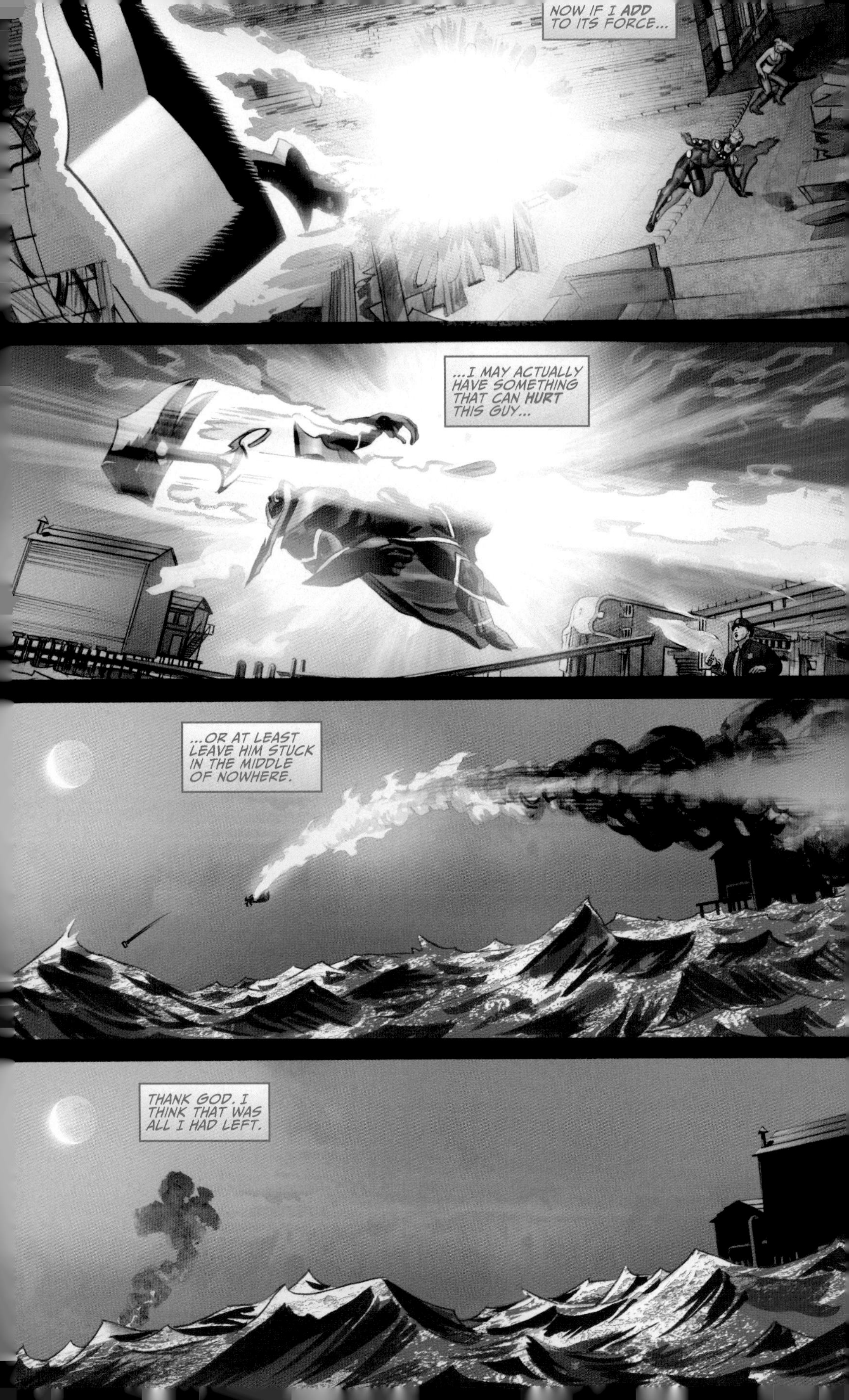
NOW IF I ADD TO ITS FORCE...
...I MAY ACTUALLY HAVE SOMETHING THAT CAN HURT THIS GUY...
...OR AT LEAST LEAVE HIM STUCK IN THE MIDDLE OF NOWHERE.
THANK GOD. I THINK THAT WAS ALL I HAD LEFT.

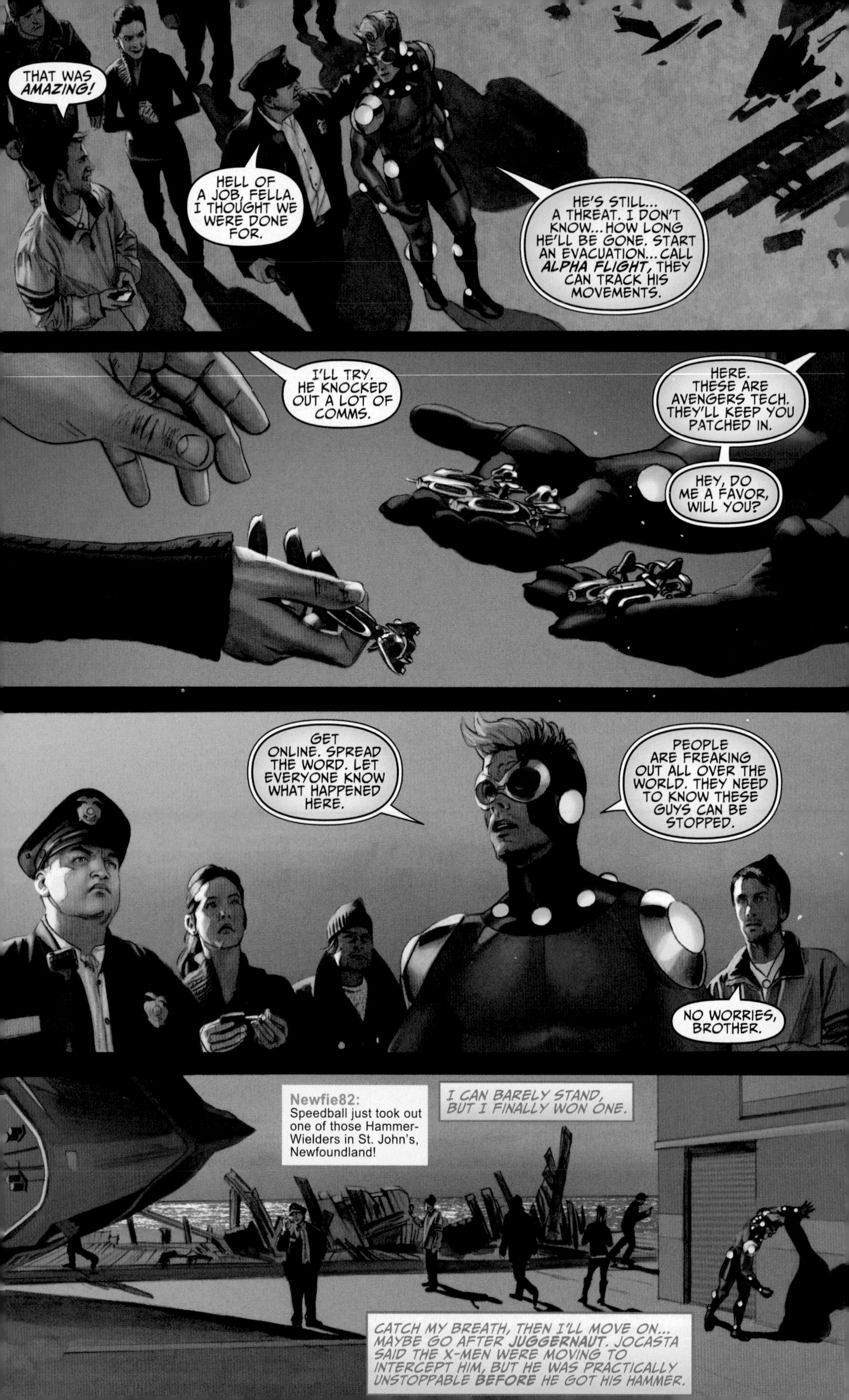
THAT WAS AMAZING!
HELL OF A JOB, FELLA. I THOUGHT WE WERE DONE FOR.
HE'S STILL... A THREAT. I DON'T KNOW... HOW LONG HE'LL BE GONE. START AN EVACUATION... CALL ALPHA FLIGHT, THEY CAN TRACK HIS MOVEMENTS.
I'LL TRY. HE KNOCKED OUT A LOT OF COMMS.
HERE. THESE ARE AVENGERS TECH. THEY'LL KEEP YOU PATCHED IN.
HEY, DO ME A FAVOR, WILL YOU?
GET ONLINE. SPREAD THE WORD. LET EVERYONE KNOW WHAT HAPPENED HERE.
PEOPLE ARE FREAKING OUT ALL OVER THE WORLD. THEY NEED TO KNOW THESE GUYS CAN BE STOPPED.
NO WORRIES, BROTHER.
Newfie82: Speedball just took out one of those Hammer-Wielders in St. John's, Newfoundland!
I CAN BARELY STAND, BUT I FINALLY WON ONE.
CATCH MY BREATH, THEN I'LL MOVE ON... MAYBE GO AFTER JUGGERNAUT. JOCASTA SAID THE X-MEN WERE MOVING TO INTERCEPT HIM, BUT HE WAS PRACTICALLY UNSTOPPABLE BEFORE HE GOT HIS HAMMER.

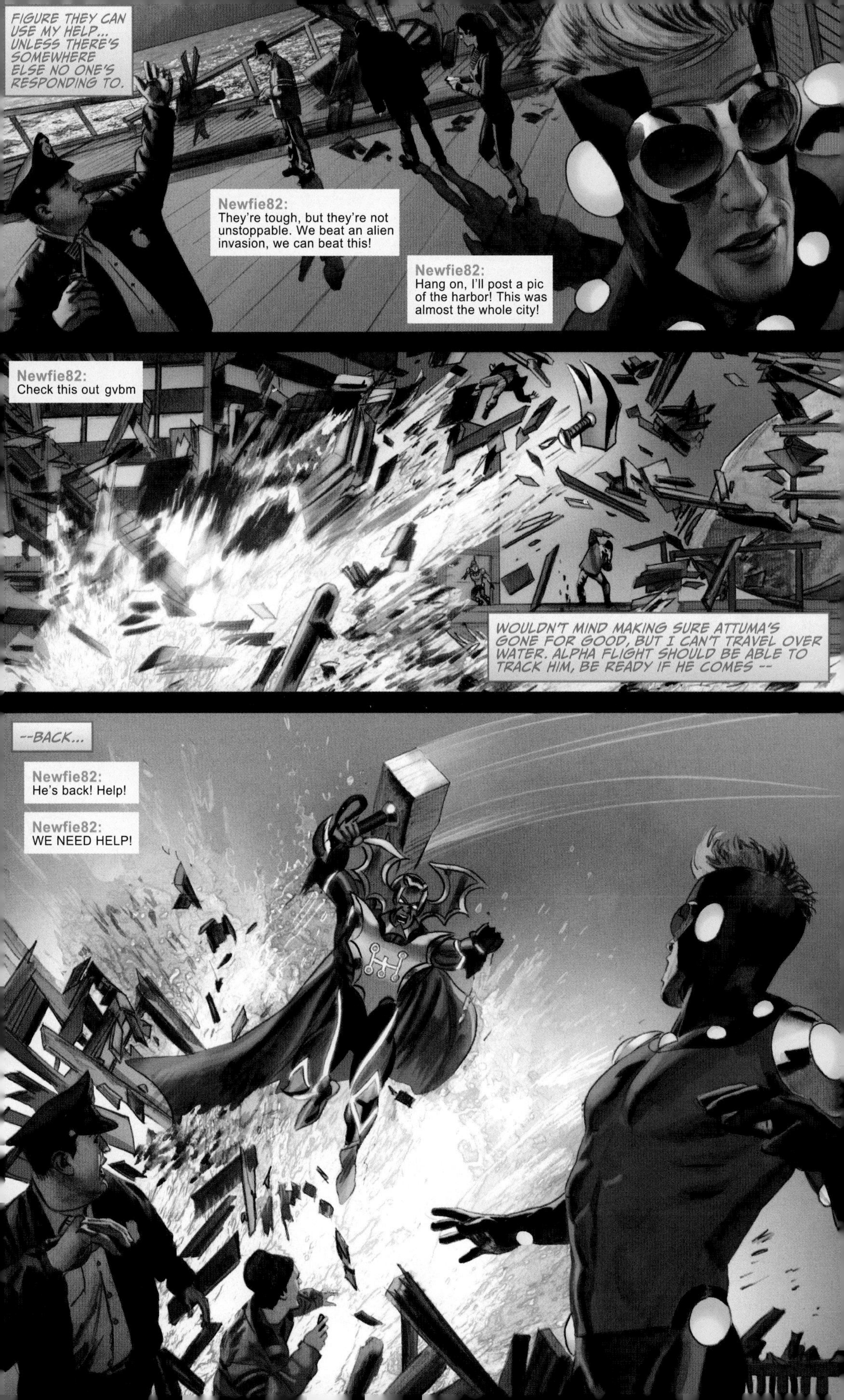
FIGURE THEY CAN USE MY HELP... UNLESS THERE'S SOMEWHERE ELSE NO ONE'S RESPONDING TO.
Newfie82: They're tough, but they're not unstoppable. We beat an alien invasion, we can beat this!
Newfie82: Hang on, I'll post a pic of the harbor! This was almost the whole city!
Newfie82: Check this out gvbm
WOULDN'T MIND MAKING SURE ATTUMA'S GONE FOR GOOD, BUT I CAN'T TRAVEL OVER WATER. ALPHA FLIGHT SHOULD BE ABLE TO TRACK HIM, BE READY IF HE COMES --
--BACK...
Newfie82: He's back! Help!
Newfie82: WE NEED HELP!

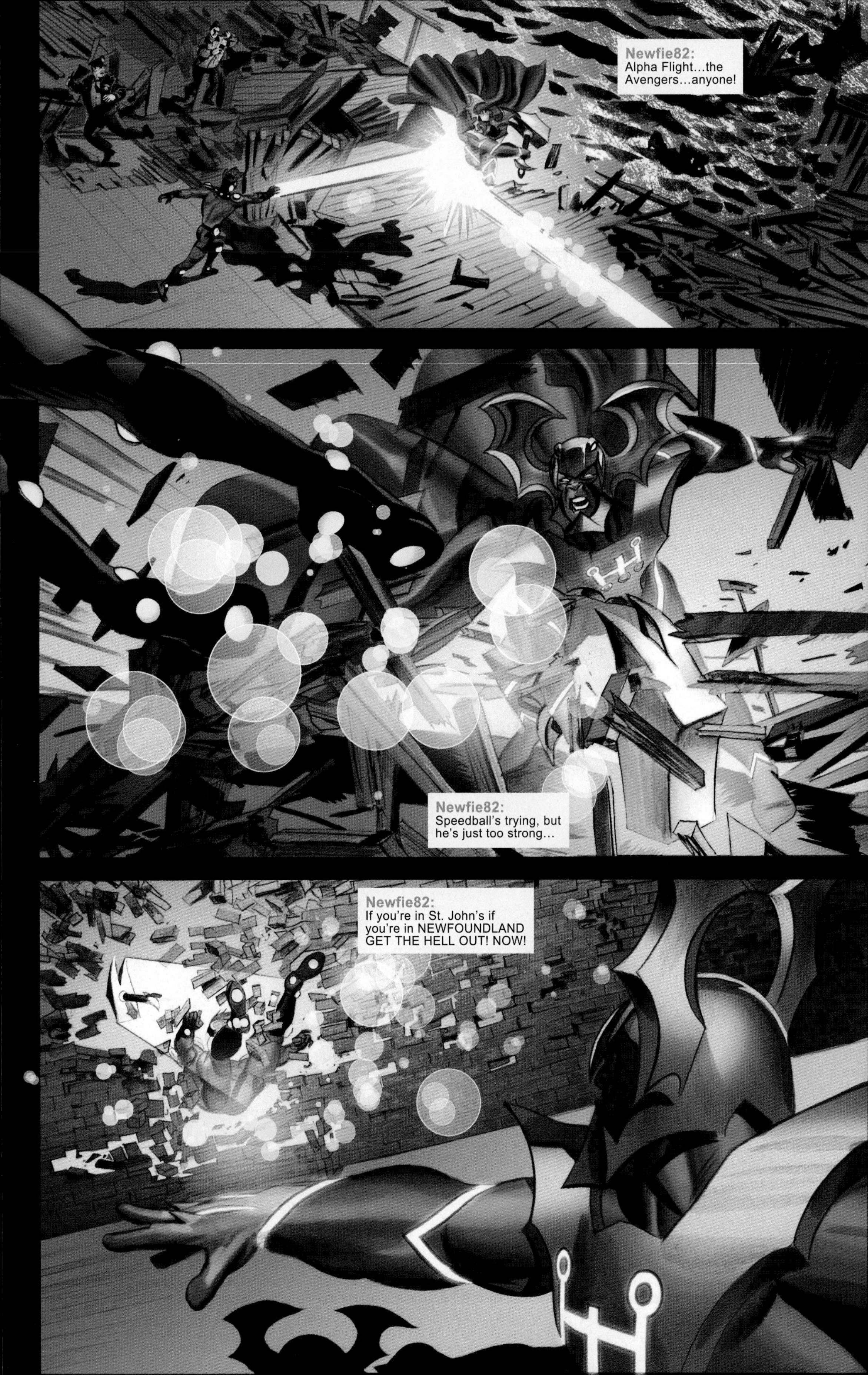
Newfie82:
Alpha Flight…the Avengers…anyone!
Newfie82:
Speedball's trying, but he's just too strong…
Newfie82:
If you're in St. John's if you're in NEWFOUNDLAND GET THE HELL OUT! NOW!

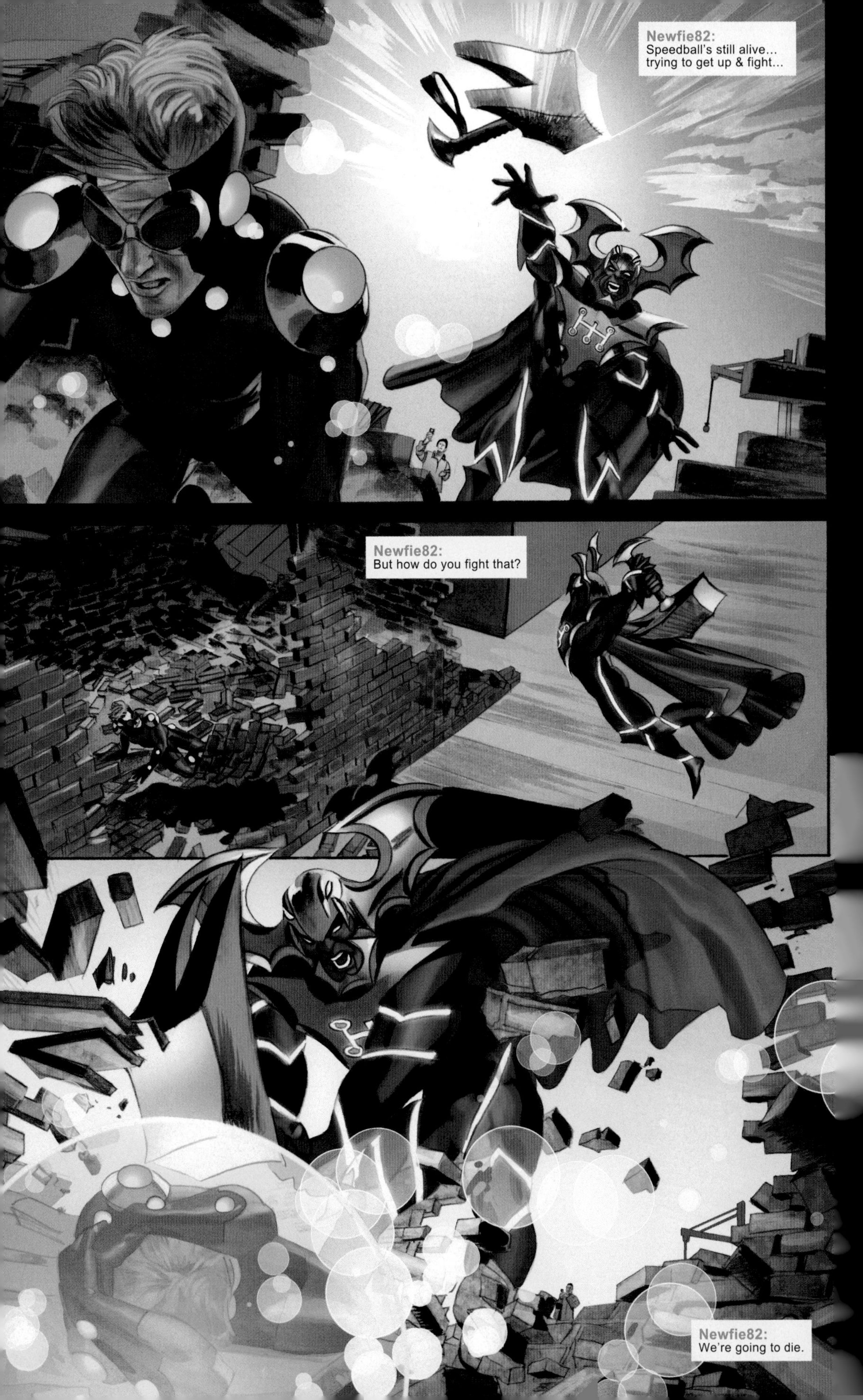
Newfie82:
Speedball's still alive...
trying to get up & fight...
Newfie82:
But how do you fight that?
Newfie82:
We're going to die.

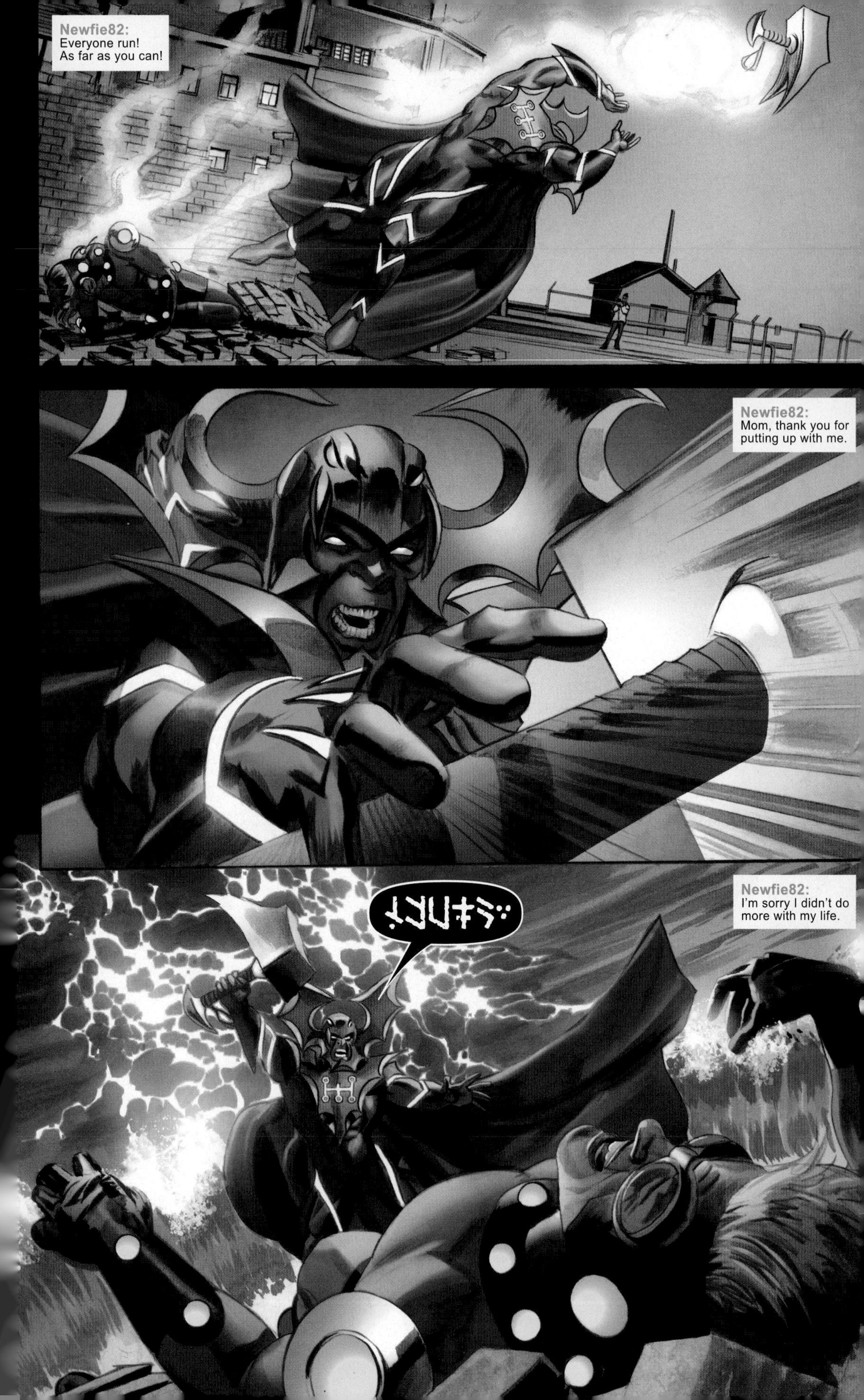

Newfie82:
Everyone run!
As far as you can!
Newfie82:
Mom, thank you for putting up with me.
Newfie82:
I'm sorry I didn't do more with my life.

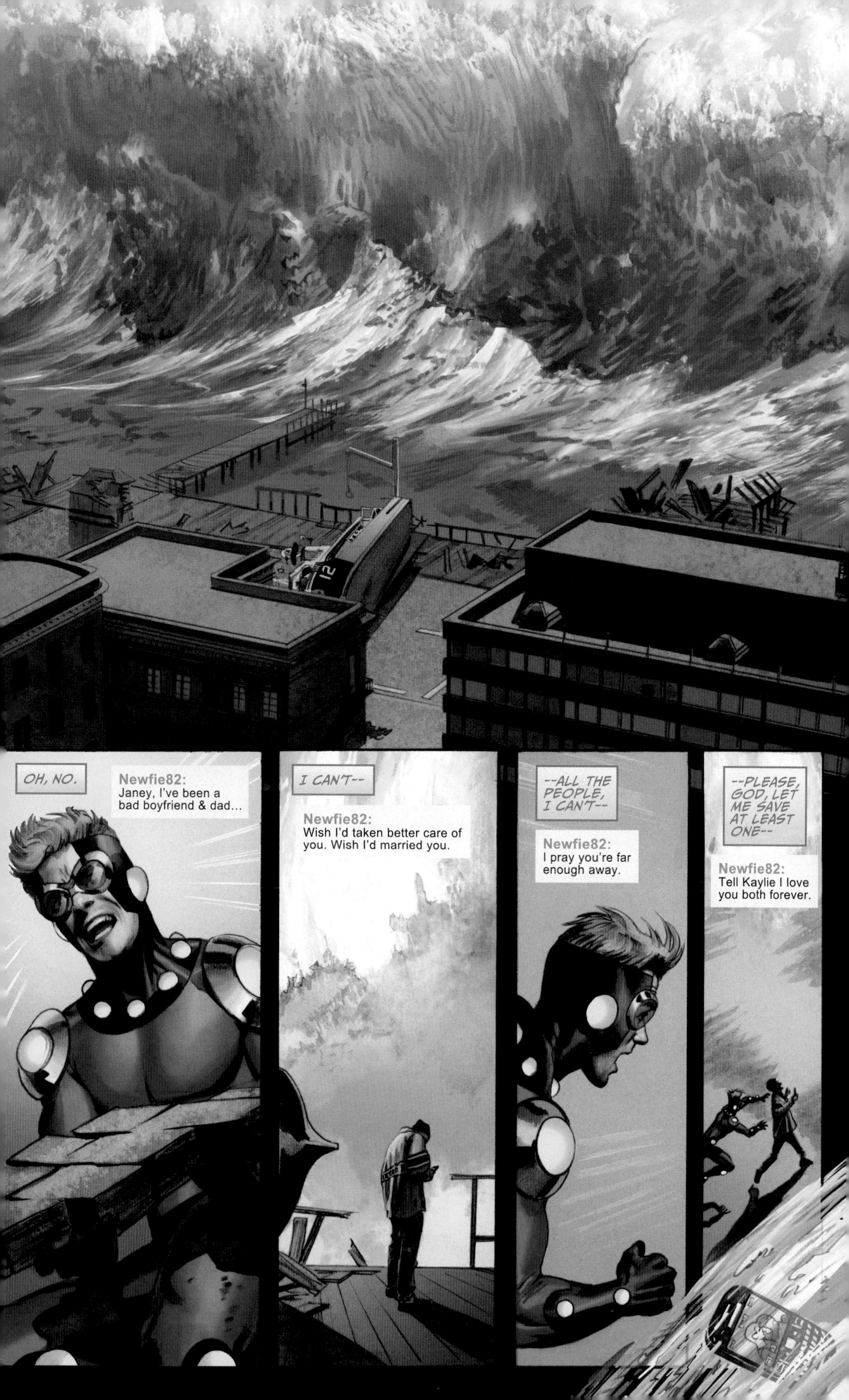
OH, NO.
Newfie82:
Janey, I've been a bad boyfriend & dad...
I CAN'T--
Newfie82:
Wish I'd taken better care of you. Wish I'd married you.
--ALL THE PEOPLE, I CAN'T--
Newfie82:
I pray you're far enough away.
--PLEASE, GOD, LET ME SAVE AT LEAST ONE--
Newfie82:
Tell Kaylie I love you both forever.

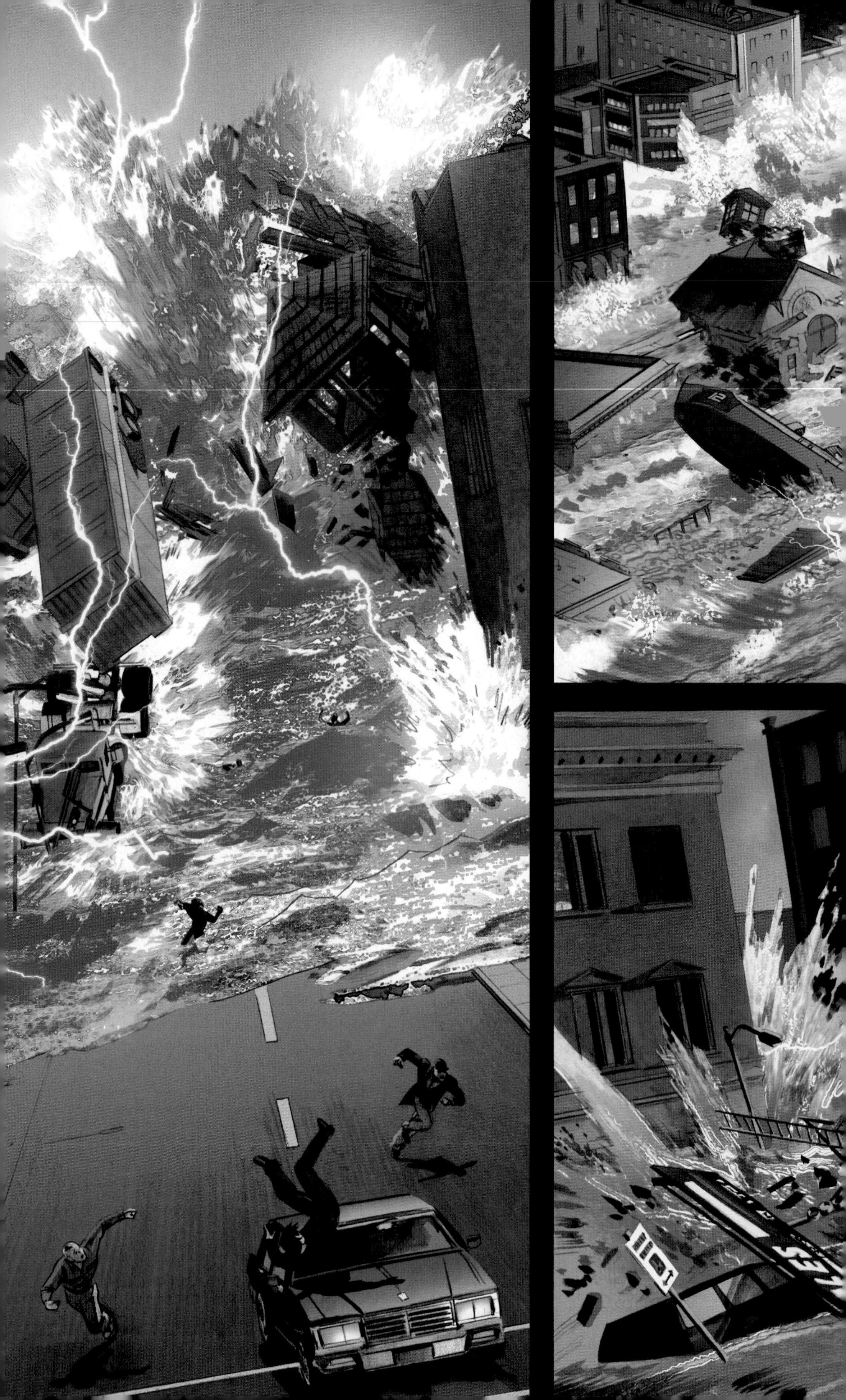

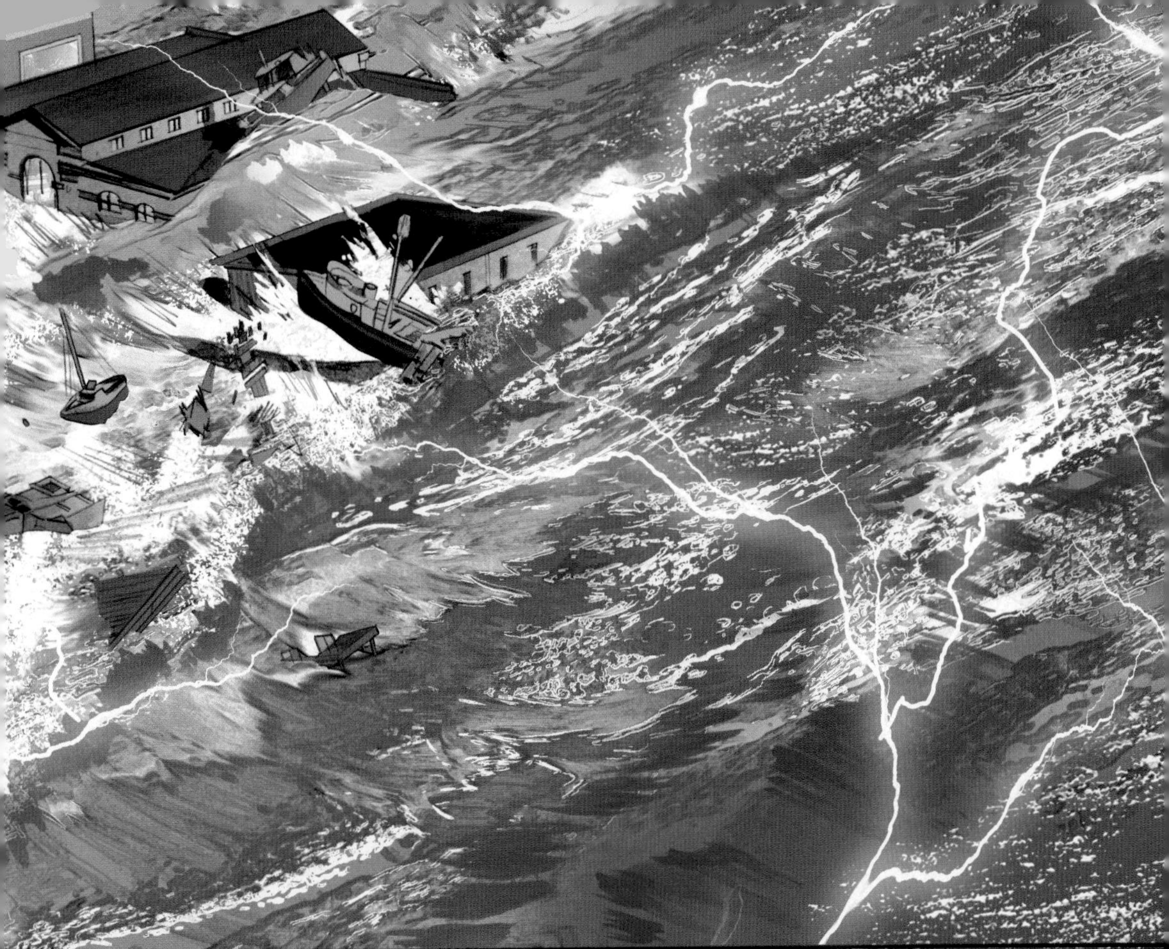

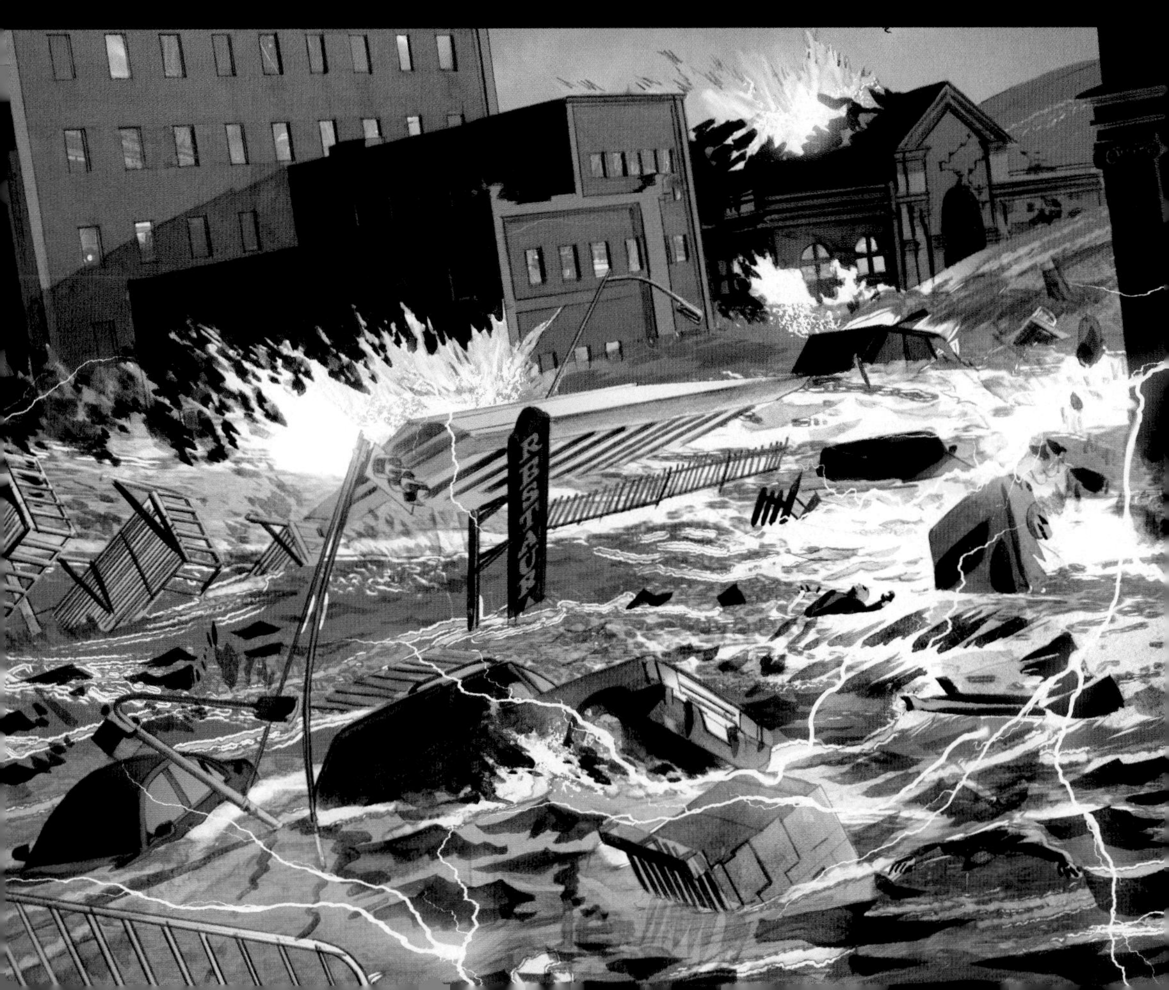
RESTAUR

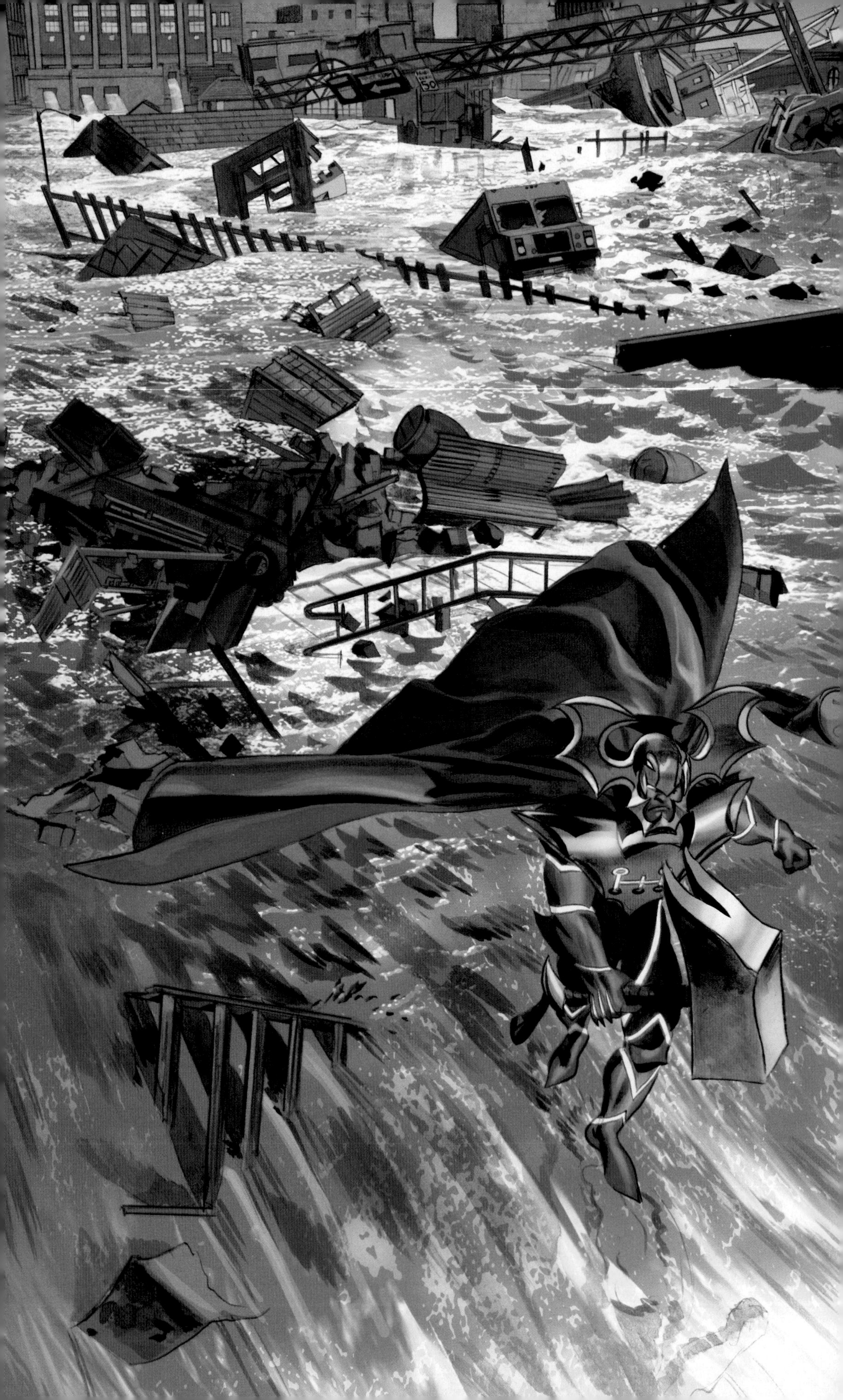
50

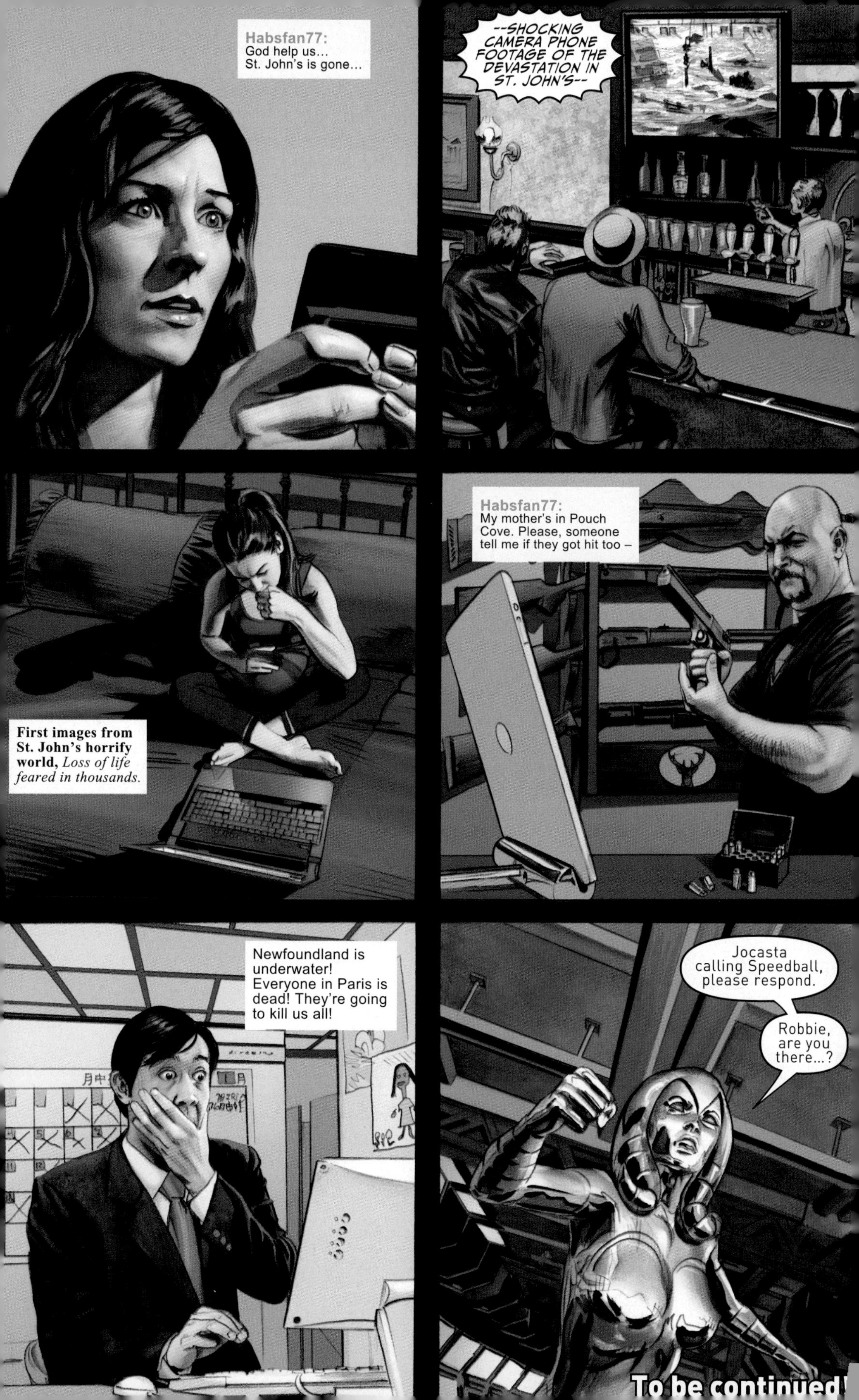
Habsfan77:
God help us... St. John's is gone...
--SHOCKING CAMERA PHONE FOOTAGE OF THE DEVASTATION IN ST. JOHN'S--
First images from St. John's horrify world, *Loss of life feared in thousands.*
Habsfan77:
My mother's in Pouch Cove. Please, someone tell me if they got hit too –
Newfoundland is underwater! Everyone in Paris is dead! They're going to kill us all!
Jocasta calling Speedball, please respond.
Robbie, are you there...?
To be continued!

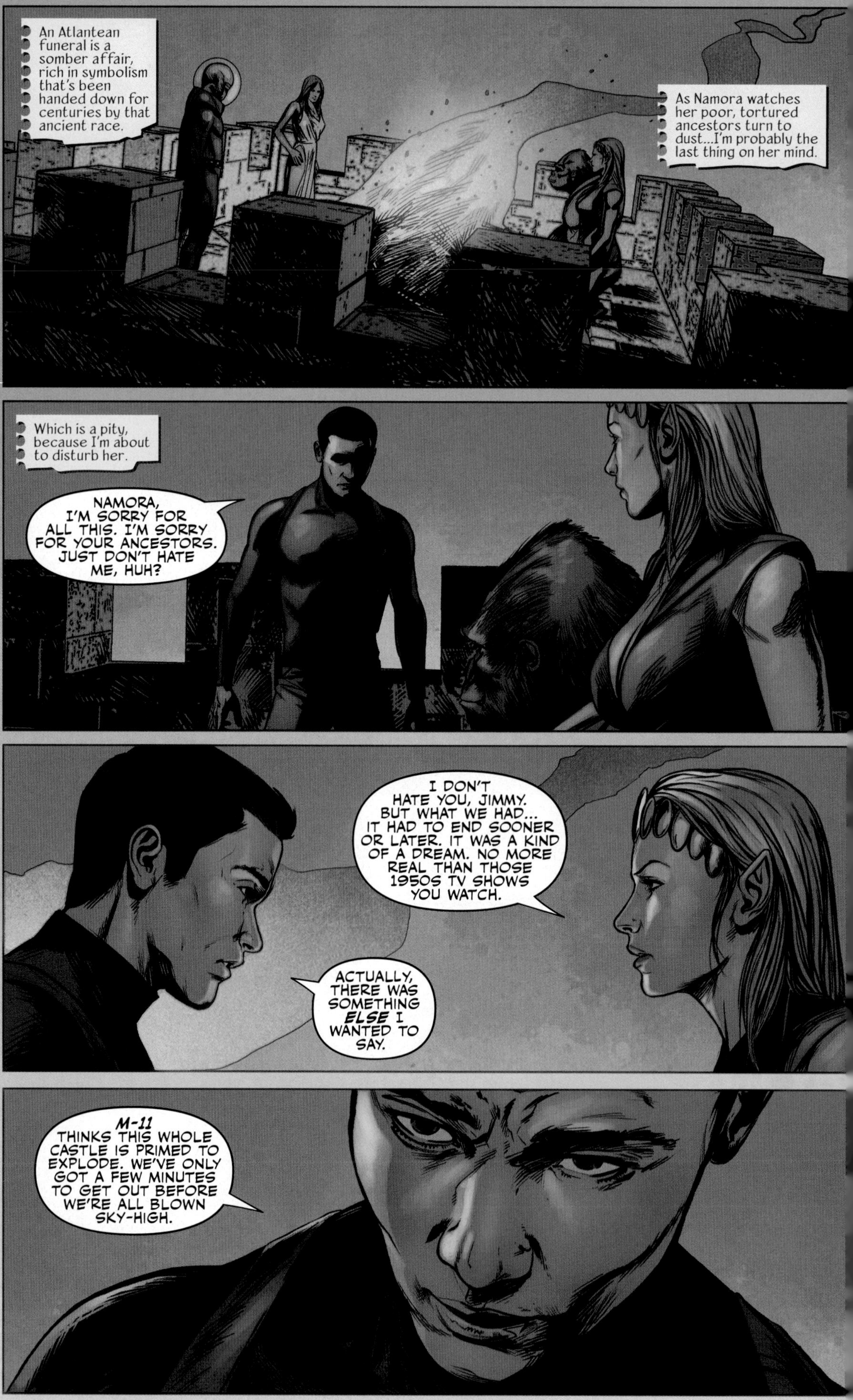
An Atlantean funeral is a somber affair, rich in symbolism that's been handed down for centuries by that ancient race.
As Namora watches her poor, tortured ancestors turn to dust...I'm probably the last thing on her mind.
Which is a pity, because I'm about to disturb her.
NAMORA, I'M SORRY FOR ALL THIS. I'M SORRY FOR YOUR ANCESTORS. JUST DON'T HATE ME, HUH?
I DON'T HATE YOU, JIMMY. BUT WHAT WE HAD... IT HAD TO END SOONER OR LATER. IT WAS A KIND OF A DREAM. NO MORE REAL THAN THOSE 1950S TV SHOWS YOU WATCH.
ACTUALLY, THERE WAS SOMETHING *ELSE* I WANTED TO SAY.
M-11 THINKS THIS WHOLE CASTLE IS PRIMED TO EXPLODE. WE'VE ONLY GOT A FEW MINUTES TO GET OUT BEFORE WE'RE ALL BLOWN SKY-HIGH.

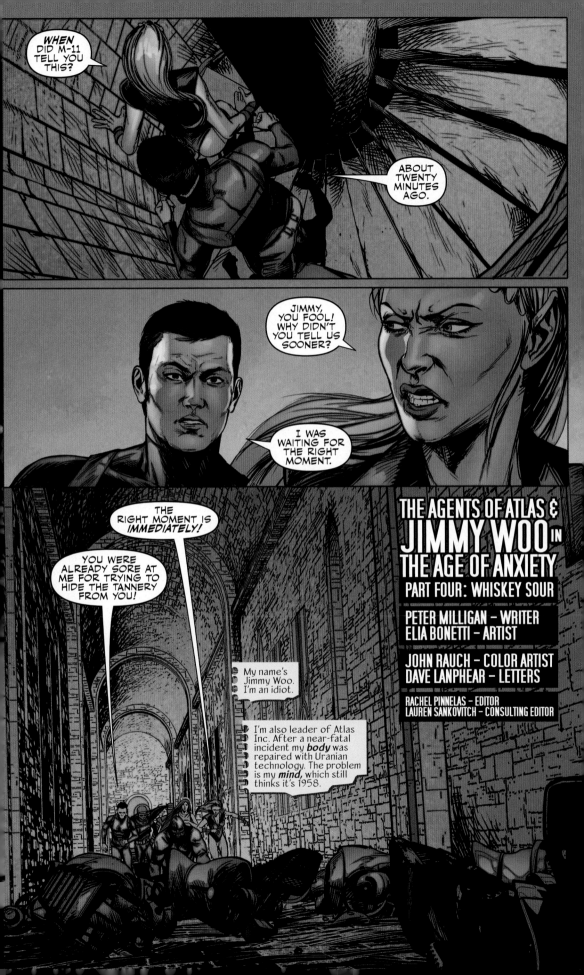

WHEN DID M-11 TELL YOU THIS?

ABOUT TWENTY MINUTES AGO.

JIMMY, YOU FOOL! WHY DIDN'T YOU TELL US SOONER?

I WAS WAITING FOR THE RIGHT MOMENT.

THE RIGHT MOMENT IS *IMMEDIATELY!*

YOU WERE ALREADY SORE AT ME FOR TRYING TO HIDE THE TANNERY FROM YOU!

My name's Jimmy Woo. I'm an idiot.

I'm also leader of Atlas Inc. After a near-fatal incident my *body* was repaired with Uranian technology. The problem is my *mind*, which still thinks it's 1958.

THE AGENTS OF ATLAS & JIMMY WOO IN THE AGE OF ANXIETY
PART FOUR: WHISKEY SOUR

PETER MILLIGAN – WRITER
ELIA BONETTI – ARTIST

JOHN RAUCH – COLOR ARTIST
DAVE LANPHEAR – LETTERS

RACHEL PINNELAS – EDITOR
LAUREN SANKOVITCH – CONSULTING EDITOR

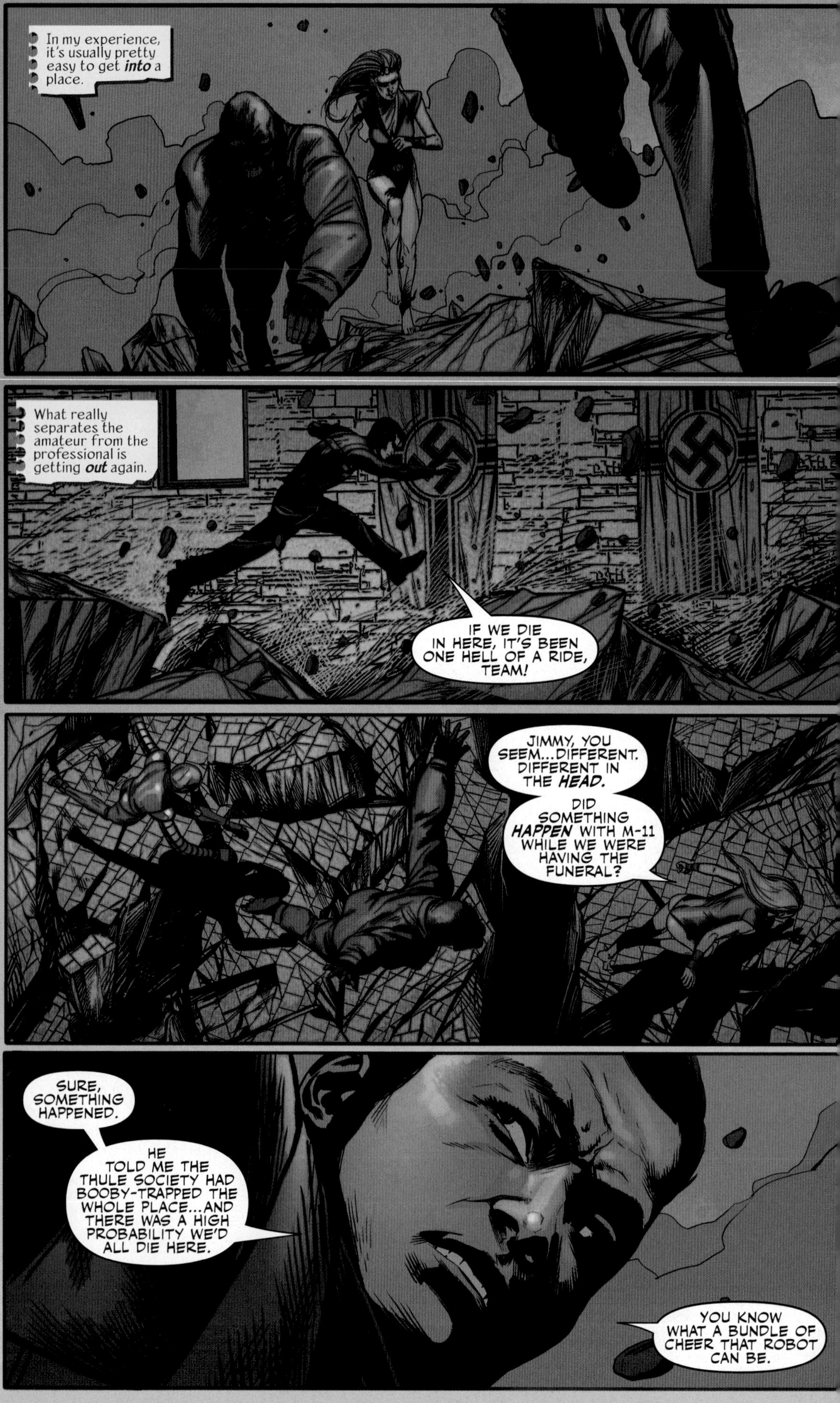

In my experience, it's usually pretty easy to get *into* a place.
What really separates the amateur from the professional is getting *out* again.
IF WE DIE IN HERE, IT'S BEEN ONE HELL OF A RIDE, TEAM!
JIMMY, YOU SEEM...DIFFERENT. DIFFERENT IN THE *HEAD.*
DID SOMETHING *HAPPEN* WITH M-11 WHILE WE WERE HAVING THE FUNERAL?
SURE, SOMETHING HAPPENED.
HE TOLD ME THE THULE SOCIETY HAD BOOBY-TRAPPED THE WHOLE PLACE...AND THERE WAS A HIGH PROBABILITY WE'D ALL DIE HERE.
YOU KNOW WHAT A BUNDLE OF CHEER THAT ROBOT CAN BE.

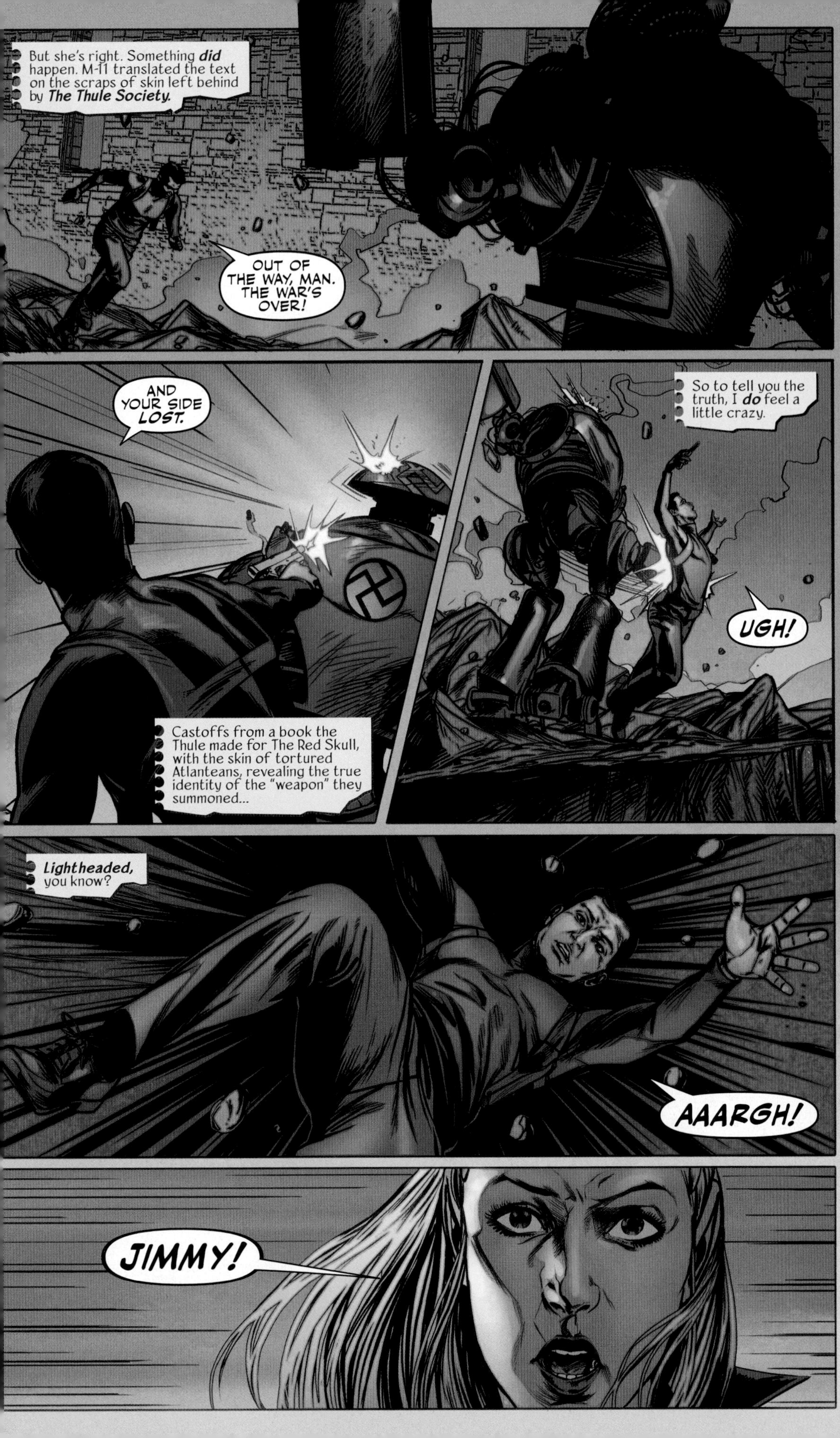

But she's right. Something *did* happen. M-11 translated the text on the scraps of skin left behind by *The Thule Society.*
OUT OF THE WAY, MAN. THE WAR'S OVER!
AND YOUR SIDE *LOST.*
Castoffs from a book the Thule made for The Red Skull, with the skin of tortured Atlanteans, revealing the true identity of the "weapon" they summoned...
So to tell you the truth, I *do* feel a little crazy.
UGH!
Lightheaded, you know?
AAARGH!
JIMMY!

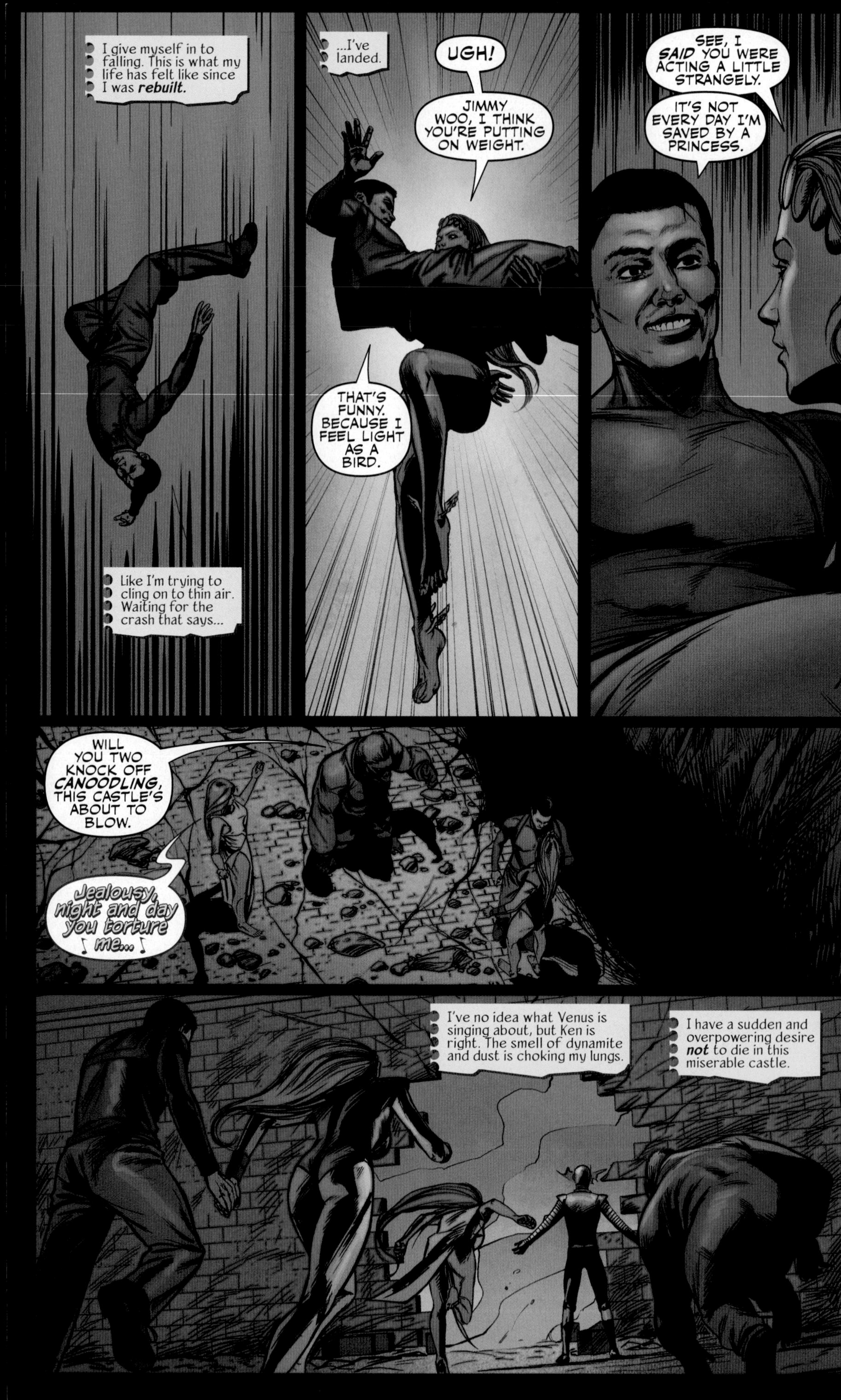

I give myself in to falling. This is what my life has felt like since I was ***rebuilt.***
Like I'm trying to cling on to thin air. Waiting for the crash that says...
...I've landed.
UGH!
JIMMY WOO, I THINK YOU'RE PUTTING ON WEIGHT.
THAT'S FUNNY. BECAUSE I FEEL LIGHT AS A BIRD.
SEE, I ***SAID*** YOU WERE ACTING A LITTLE STRANGELY.
IT'S NOT EVERY DAY I'M SAVED BY A PRINCESS.
WILL YOU TWO KNOCK OFF ***CANOODLING***, THIS CASTLE'S ABOUT TO BLOW.
Jealousy, night and day you torture me...
I've no idea what Venus is singing about, but Ken is right. The smell of dynamite and dust is choking my lungs.
I have a sudden and overpowering desire ***not*** to die in this miserable castle.

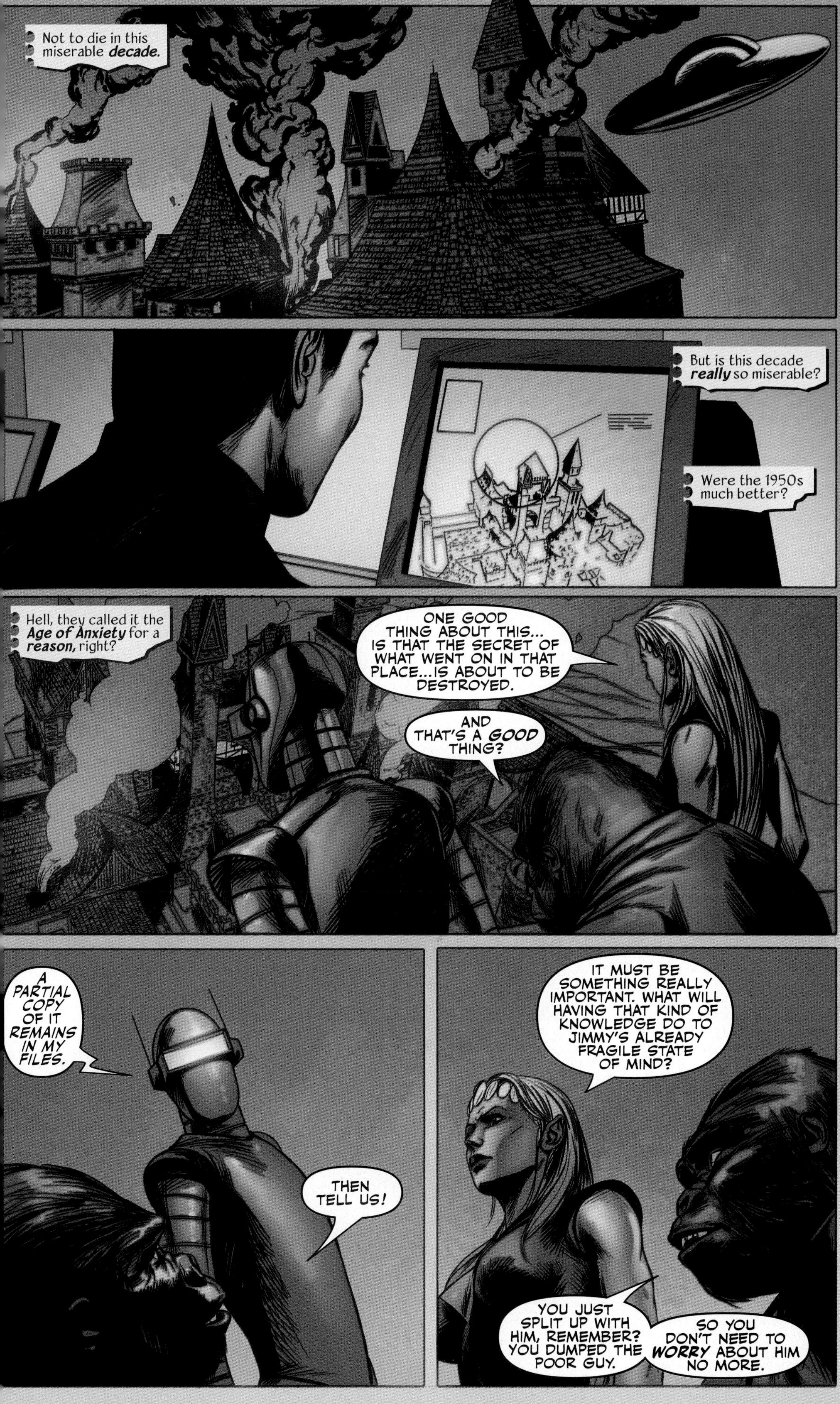

Not to die in this miserable *decade.*
But is this decade *really* so miserable?
Were the 1950s much better?
Hell, they called it the *Age of Anxiety* for a *reason,* right?
ONE GOOD THING ABOUT THIS... IS THAT THE SECRET OF WHAT WENT ON IN THAT PLACE...IS ABOUT TO BE DESTROYED.
AND THAT'S A *GOOD* THING?
A PARTIAL COPY OF IT REMAINS IN MY FILES.
THEN TELL US!
IT MUST BE SOMETHING REALLY IMPORTANT. WHAT WILL HAVING THAT KIND OF KNOWLEDGE DO TO JIMMY'S ALREADY FRAGILE STATE OF MIND?
YOU JUST SPLIT UP WITH HIM, REMEMBER? YOU DUMPED THE POOR GUY.
SO YOU DON'T NEED TO *WORRY* ABOUT HIM NO MORE.

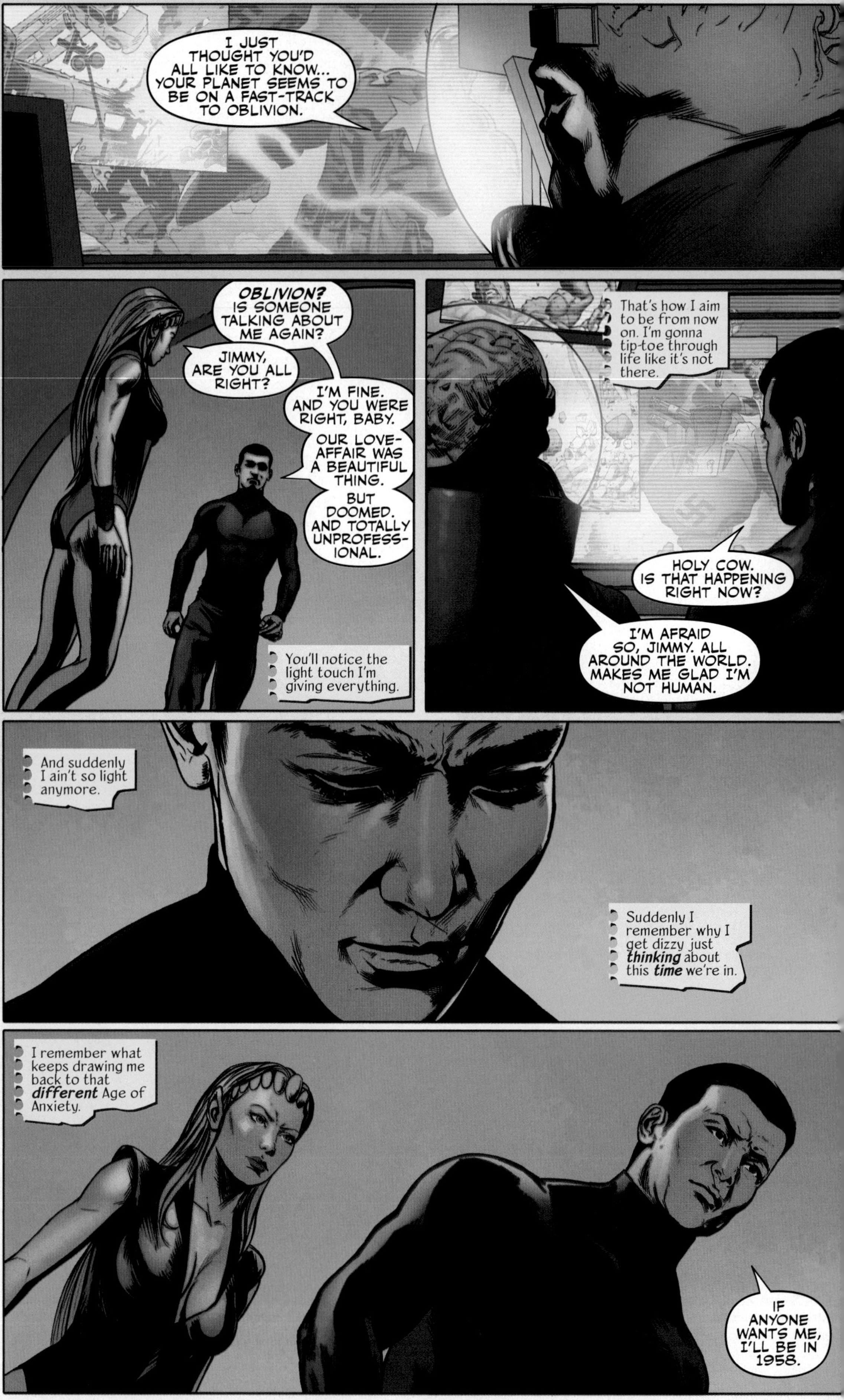
I JUST THOUGHT YOU'D ALL LIKE TO KNOW... YOUR PLANET SEEMS TO BE ON A FAST-TRACK TO OBLIVION.
OBLIVION? IS SOMEONE TALKING ABOUT ME AGAIN?
JIMMY, ARE YOU ALL RIGHT?
I'M FINE. AND YOU WERE RIGHT, BABY.
OUR LOVE-AFFAIR WAS A BEAUTIFUL THING.
BUT DOOMED. AND TOTALLY UNPROFESS-IONAL.
You'll notice the light touch I'm giving everything.
That's how I aim to be from now on. I'm gonna tip-toe through life like it's not there.
HOLY COW. IS THAT HAPPENING RIGHT NOW?
I'M AFRAID SO, JIMMY. ALL AROUND THE WORLD. MAKES ME GLAD I'M NOT HUMAN.
And suddenly I ain't so light anymore.
Suddenly I remember why I get dizzy just *thinking* about this *time* we're in.
I remember what keeps drawing me back to that *different* Age of Anxiety.
IF ANYONE WANTS ME, I'LL BE IN 1958.

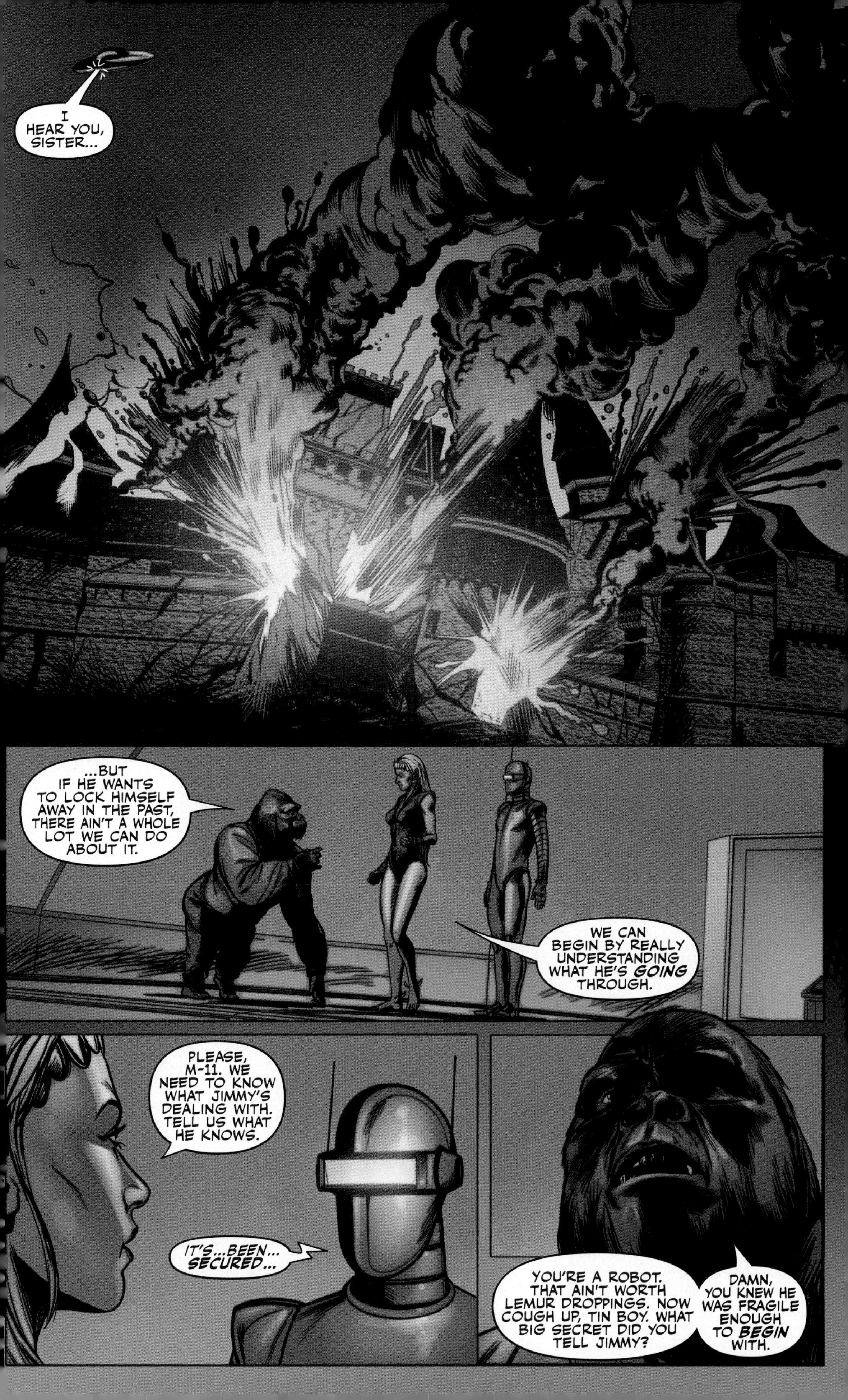
I HEAR YOU, SISTER...
...BUT IF HE WANTS TO LOCK HIMSELF AWAY IN THE PAST, THERE AIN'T A WHOLE LOT WE CAN DO ABOUT IT.
WE CAN BEGIN BY REALLY UNDERSTANDING WHAT HE'S *GOING* THROUGH.
PLEASE, M-11. WE NEED TO KNOW WHAT JIMMY'S DEALING WITH. TELL US WHAT HE KNOWS.
IT'S...BEEN... ***SECURED...***
DAMN, YOU KNEW HE WAS FRAGILE ENOUGH TO ***BEGIN*** WITH.
YOU'RE A ROBOT. THAT AIN'T WORTH LEMUR DROPPINGS. NOW COUGH UP, TIN BOY. WHAT BIG SECRET DID YOU TELL JIMMY?

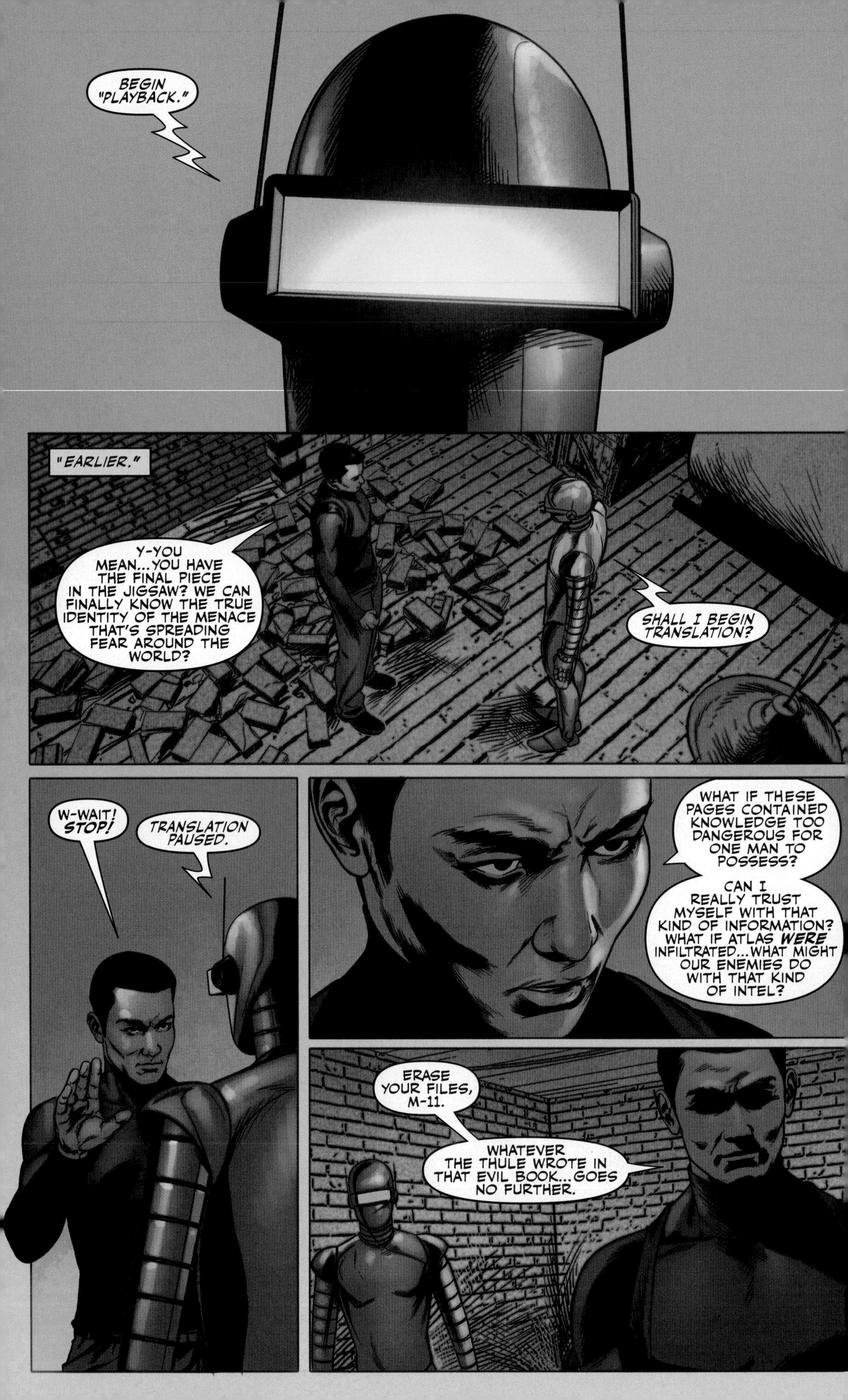
BEGIN "PLAYBACK."
"EARLIER."
Y-YOU MEAN...YOU HAVE THE FINAL PIECE IN THE JIGSAW? WE CAN FINALLY KNOW THE TRUE IDENTITY OF THE MENACE THAT'S SPREADING FEAR AROUND THE WORLD?
SHALL I BEGIN TRANSLATION?
W-WAIT! STOP!
TRANSLATION PAUSED.
WHAT IF THESE PAGES CONTAINED KNOWLEDGE TOO DANGEROUS FOR ONE MAN TO POSSESS?
CAN I REALLY TRUST MYSELF WITH THAT KIND OF INFORMATION? WHAT IF ATLAS WERE INFILTRATED...WHAT MIGHT OUR ENEMIES DO WITH THAT KIND OF INTEL?
ERASE YOUR FILES, M-11.
WHATEVER THE THULE WROTE IN THAT EVIL BOOK...GOES NO FURTHER.

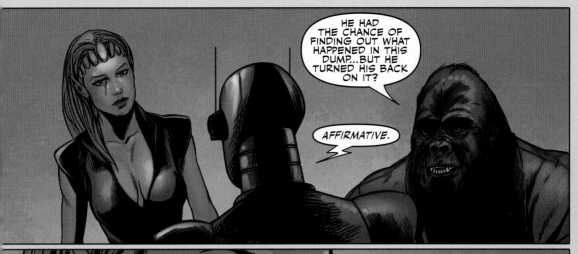

HE HAD THE CHANCE OF FINDING OUT WHAT HAPPENED IN THIS DUMP...BUT HE TURNED HIS BACK ON IT?

AFFIRMATIVE.

FOR SOMEONE LIKE JIMMY... TO SPURN THE CHANCE OF GETTING HIS HANDS ON SUCH KNOWLEDGE...FOR THE SAKE OF THE WORLD...

I DON'T BELIEVE...I'VE EVER HEARD OF ANYTHING QUITE SO... HEROIC.

AND THAT'S ALL FROM TONIGHT'S SHOW. NEXT WEEK, DAISY AND MICKY UNSUSPECTINGLY JOIN A PARTY OF COMMUNISTS...

I DIG DAISY

2011? The Red Skull?

That already feels somehow unreal. Impossibly distant. From a different age.

As the Atlas Saucer speeds home, I make myself comfortable.

And finally get time to have that whiskey sour.

THE END

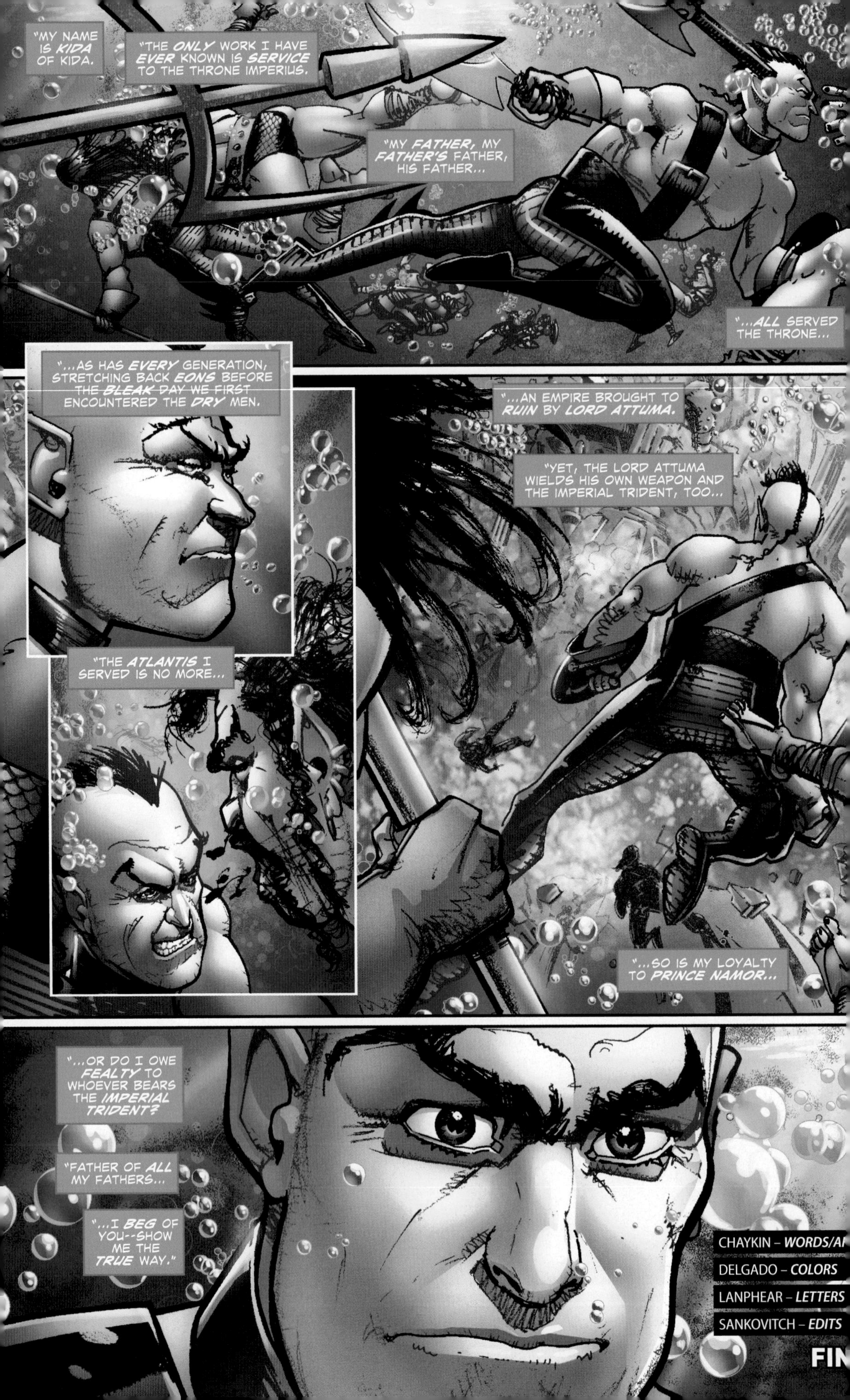
"MY NAME IS KIDA OF KIDA.
"THE ONLY WORK I HAVE EVER KNOWN IS SERVICE TO THE THRONE IMPERIUS.
"MY FATHER, MY FATHER'S FATHER, HIS FATHER...
"...ALL SERVED THE THRONE...
"...AS HAS EVERY GENERATION, STRETCHING BACK EONS BEFORE THE BLEAK DAY WE FIRST ENCOUNTERED THE DRY MEN.
"THE ATLANTIS I SERVED IS NO MORE...
"...AN EMPIRE BROUGHT TO RUIN BY LORD ATTUMA.
"YET, THE LORD ATTUMA WIELDS HIS OWN WEAPON AND THE IMPERIAL TRIDENT, TOO...
"...SO IS MY LOYALTY TO PRINCE NAMOR...
"...OR DO I OWE FEALTY TO WHOEVER BEARS THE IMPERIAL TRIDENT?
"FATHER OF ALL MY FATHERS...
"...I BEG OF YOU--SHOW ME THE TRUE WAY."
CHAYKIN – WORDS/A
DELGADO – COLORS
LANPHEAR – LETTERS
SANKOVITCH – EDITS
FIN

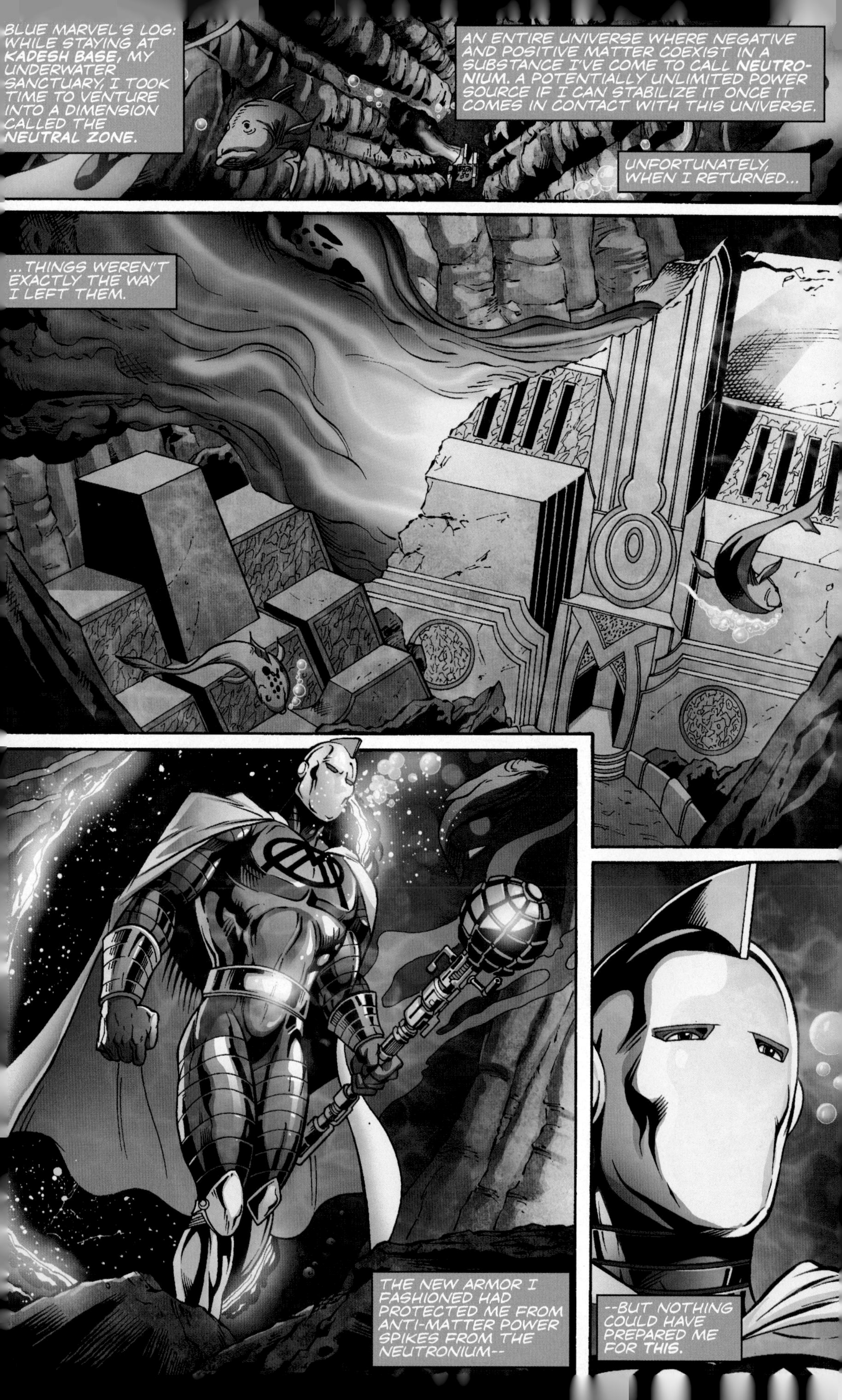
BLUE MARVEL'S LOG: WHILE STAYING AT KADESH BASE, MY UNDERWATER SANCTUARY, I TOOK TIME TO VENTURE INTO A DIMENSION CALLED THE NEUTRAL ZONE.
AN ENTIRE UNIVERSE WHERE NEGATIVE AND POSITIVE MATTER COEXIST IN A SUBSTANCE I'VE COME TO CALL NEUTRONIUM. A POTENTIALLY UNLIMITED POWER SOURCE IF I CAN STABILIZE IT ONCE IT COMES IN CONTACT WITH THIS UNIVERSE.
UNFORTUNATELY, WHEN I RETURNED...
...THINGS WEREN'T EXACTLY THE WAY I LEFT THEM.
THE NEW ARMOR I FASHIONED HAD PROTECTED ME FROM ANTI-MATTER POWER SPIKES FROM THE NEUTRONIUM--
--BUT NOTHING COULD HAVE PREPARED ME FOR THIS.

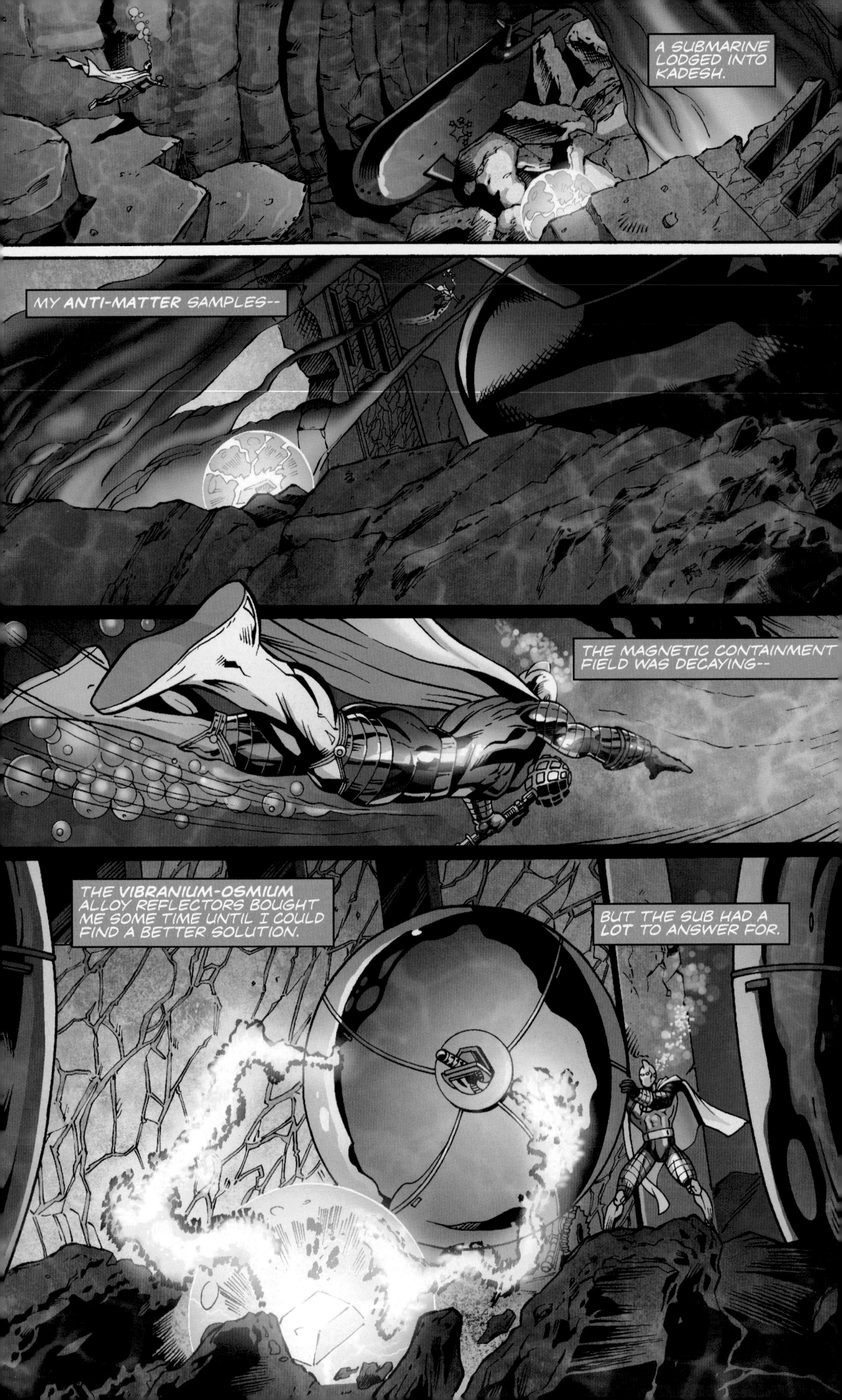
A SUBMARINE LODGED INTO KADESH.
MY ANTI-MATTER SAMPLES--
THE MAGNETIC CONTAINMENT FIELD WAS DECAYING--
THE VIBRANIUM-OSMIUM ALLOY REFLECTORS BOUGHT ME SOME TIME UNTIL I COULD FIND A BETTER SOLUTION.
BUT THE SUB HAD A LOT TO ANSWER FOR.

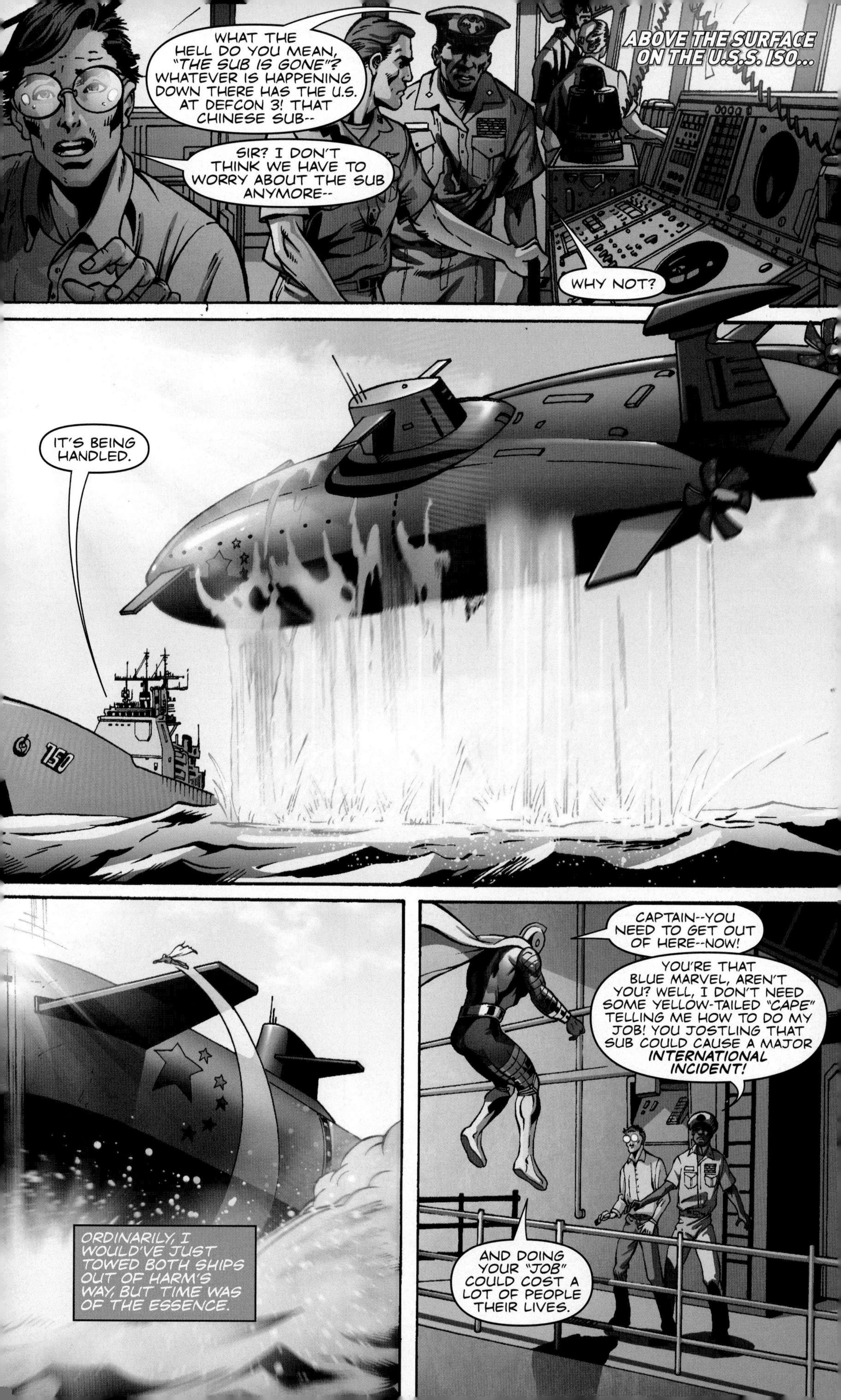
ABOVE THE SURFACE ON THE U.S.S. ISO...
WHAT THE HELL DO YOU MEAN, "THE SUB IS GONE"? WHATEVER IS HAPPENING DOWN THERE HAS THE U.S. AT DEFCON 3! THAT CHINESE SUB--
SIR? I DON'T THINK WE HAVE TO WORRY ABOUT THE SUB ANYMORE--
WHY NOT?
IT'S BEING HANDLED.
750
ORDINARILY, I WOULD'VE JUST TOWED BOTH SHIPS OUT OF HARM'S WAY, BUT TIME WAS OF THE ESSENCE.
CAPTAIN--YOU NEED TO GET OUT OF HERE--NOW!
YOU'RE THAT BLUE MARVEL, AREN'T YOU? WELL, I DON'T NEED SOME YELLOW-TAILED "CAPE" TELLING ME HOW TO DO MY JOB! YOU JOSTLING THAT SUB COULD CAUSE A MAJOR INTERNATIONAL INCIDENT!
AND DOING YOUR "JOB" COULD COST A LOT OF PEOPLE THEIR LIVES.

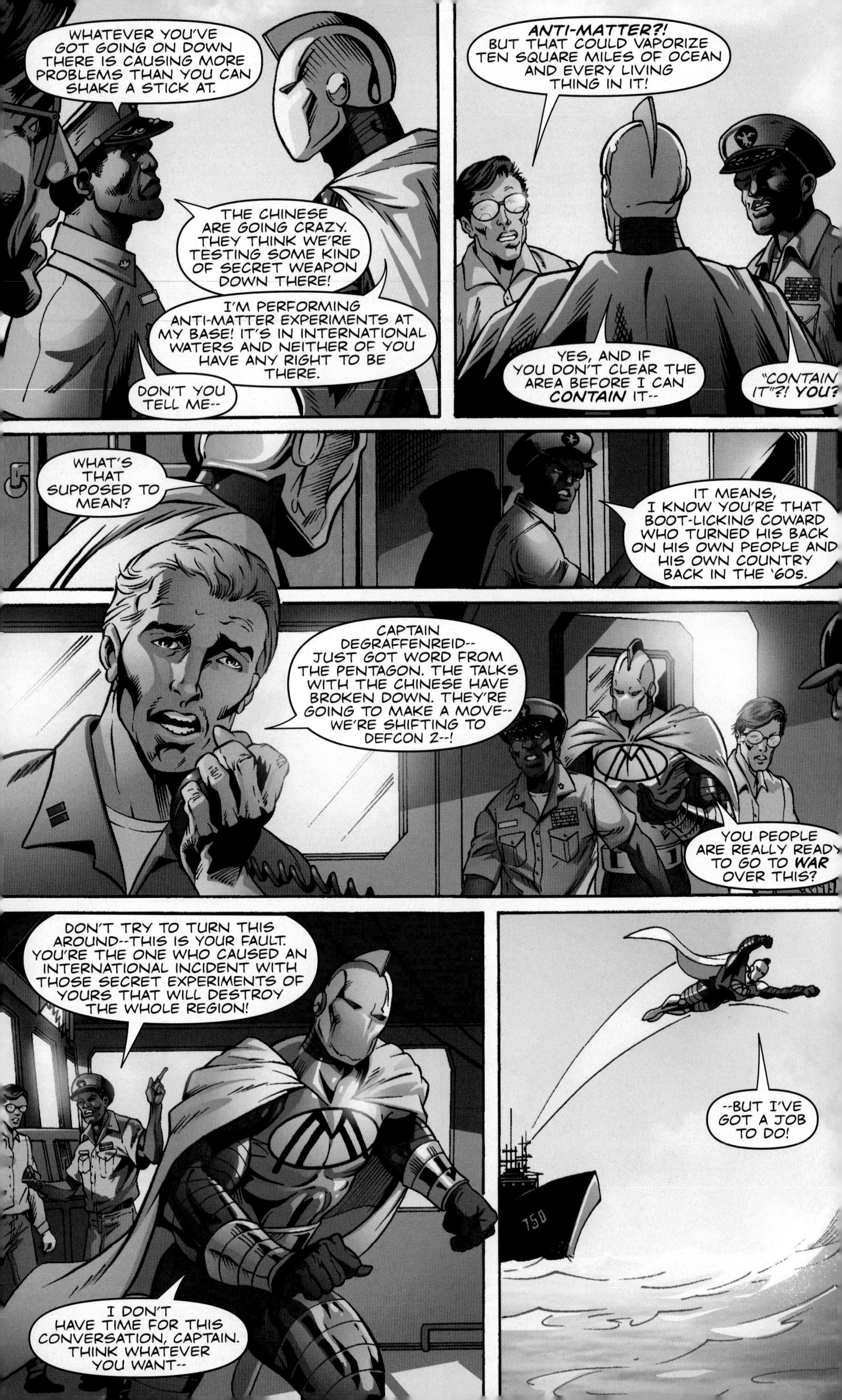

WHATEVER YOU'VE GOT GOING ON DOWN THERE IS CAUSING MORE PROBLEMS THAN YOU CAN SHAKE A STICK AT.
THE CHINESE ARE GOING CRAZY. THEY THINK WE'RE TESTING SOME KIND OF SECRET WEAPON DOWN THERE!
I'M PERFORMING ANTI-MATTER EXPERIMENTS AT MY BASE! IT'S IN INTERNATIONAL WATERS AND NEITHER OF YOU HAVE ANY RIGHT TO BE THERE.
DON'T YOU TELL ME--
ANTI-MATTER?! BUT THAT COULD VAPORIZE TEN SQUARE MILES OF OCEAN AND EVERY LIVING THING IN IT!
YES, AND IF YOU DON'T CLEAR THE AREA BEFORE I CAN CONTAIN IT--
"CONTAIN IT"?! YOU?
WHAT'S THAT SUPPOSED TO MEAN?
IT MEANS, I KNOW YOU'RE THAT BOOT-LICKING COWARD WHO TURNED HIS BACK ON HIS OWN PEOPLE AND HIS OWN COUNTRY BACK IN THE '60s.
CAPTAIN DEGRAFFENREID-- JUST GOT WORD FROM THE PENTAGON. THE TALKS WITH THE CHINESE HAVE BROKEN DOWN. THEY'RE GOING TO MAKE A MOVE-- WE'RE SHIFTING TO DEFCON 2--!
YOU PEOPLE ARE REALLY READY TO GO TO WAR OVER THIS?
DON'T TRY TO TURN THIS AROUND--THIS IS YOUR FAULT. YOU'RE THE ONE WHO CAUSED AN INTERNATIONAL INCIDENT WITH THOSE SECRET EXPERIMENTS OF YOURS THAT WILL DESTROY THE WHOLE REGION!
I DON'T HAVE TIME FOR THIS CONVERSATION, CAPTAIN. THINK WHATEVER YOU WANT--
--BUT I'VE GOT A JOB TO DO!
750

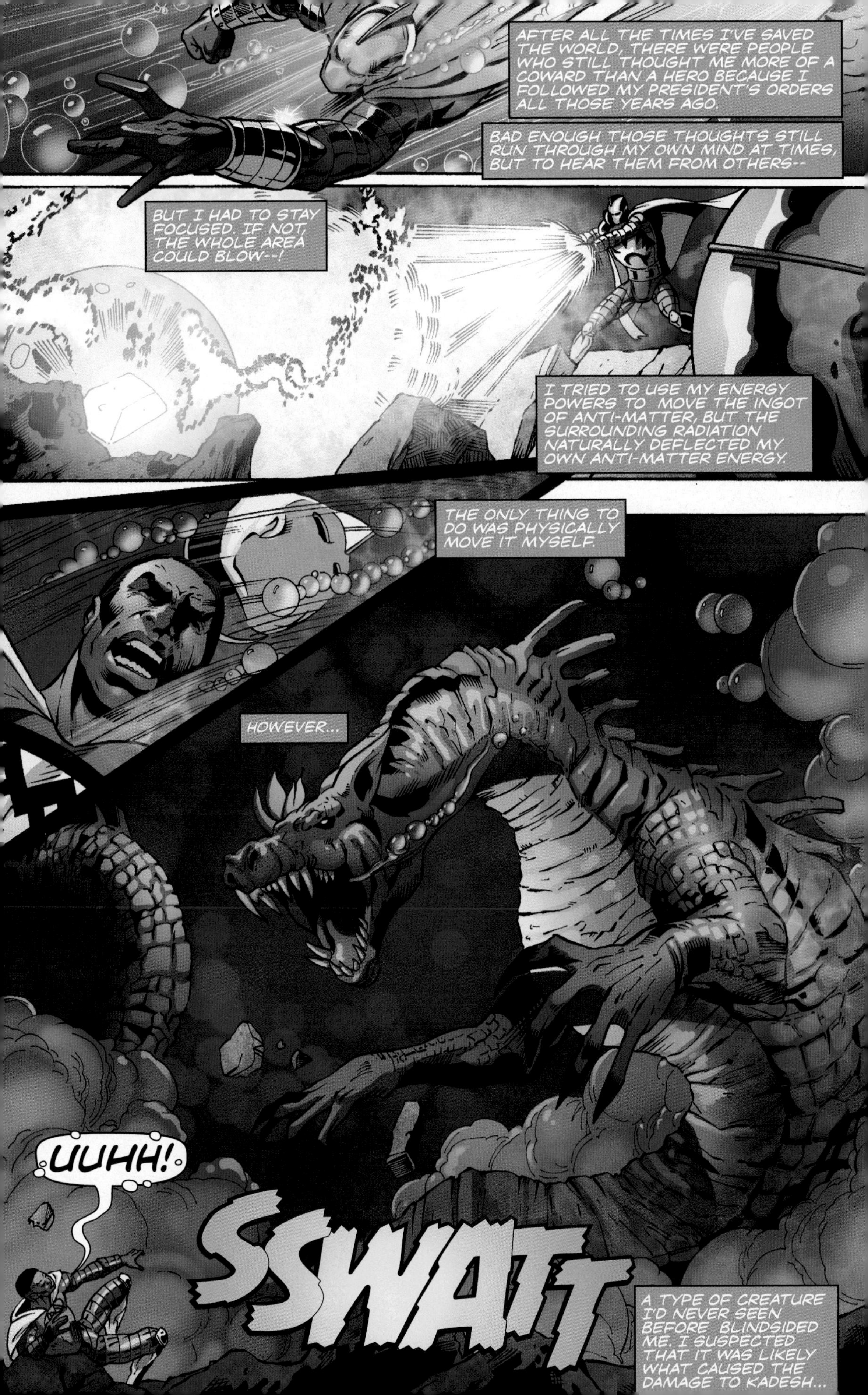
AFTER ALL THE TIMES I'VE SAVED THE WORLD, THERE WERE PEOPLE WHO STILL THOUGHT ME MORE OF A COWARD THAN A HERO BECAUSE I FOLLOWED MY PRESIDENT'S ORDERS ALL THOSE YEARS AGO.
BAD ENOUGH THOSE THOUGHTS STILL RUN THROUGH MY OWN MIND AT TIMES, BUT TO HEAR THEM FROM OTHERS--
BUT I HAD TO STAY FOCUSED. IF NOT, THE WHOLE AREA COULD BLOW--!
I TRIED TO USE MY ENERGY POWERS TO MOVE THE INGOT OF ANTI-MATTER, BUT THE SURROUNDING RADIATION NATURALLY DEFLECTED MY OWN ANTI-MATTER ENERGY.
THE ONLY THING TO DO WAS PHYSICALLY MOVE IT MYSELF.
HOWEVER...
UUHH!
SSWATT
A TYPE OF CREATURE I'D NEVER SEEN BEFORE BLINDSIDED ME. I SUSPECTED THAT IT WAS LIKELY WHAT CAUSED THE DAMAGE TO KADESH...

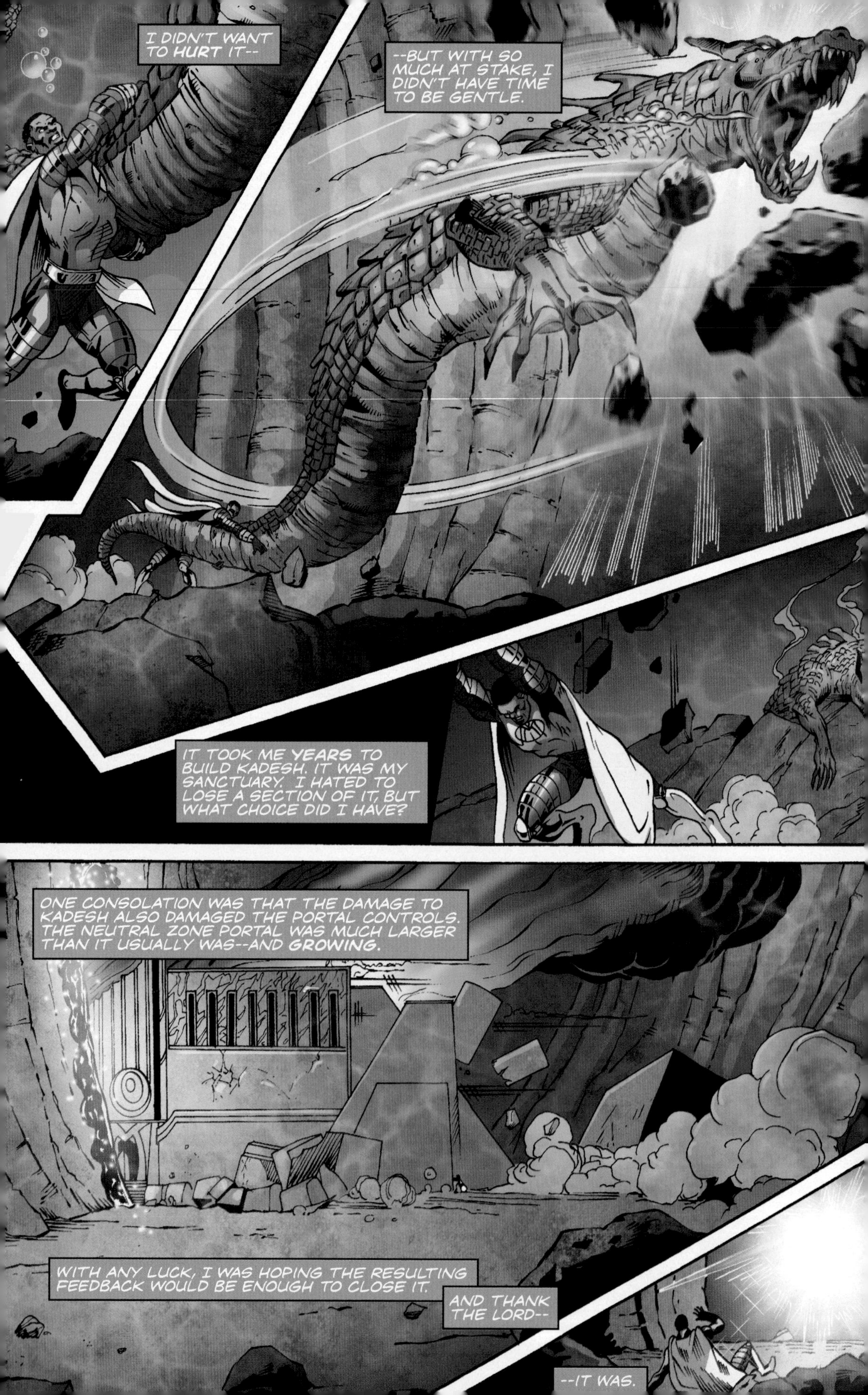
I DIDN'T WANT TO HURT IT--
--BUT WITH SO MUCH AT STAKE, I DIDN'T HAVE TIME TO BE GENTLE.
IT TOOK ME YEARS TO BUILD KADESH. IT WAS MY SANCTUARY. I HATED TO LOSE A SECTION OF IT, BUT WHAT CHOICE DID I HAVE?
ONE CONSOLATION WAS THAT THE DAMAGE TO KADESH ALSO DAMAGED THE PORTAL CONTROLS. THE NEUTRAL ZONE PORTAL WAS MUCH LARGER THAN IT USUALLY WAS--AND GROWING.
WITH ANY LUCK, I WAS HOPING THE RESULTING FEEDBACK WOULD BE ENOUGH TO CLOSE IT.
AND THANK THE LORD--
--IT WAS.

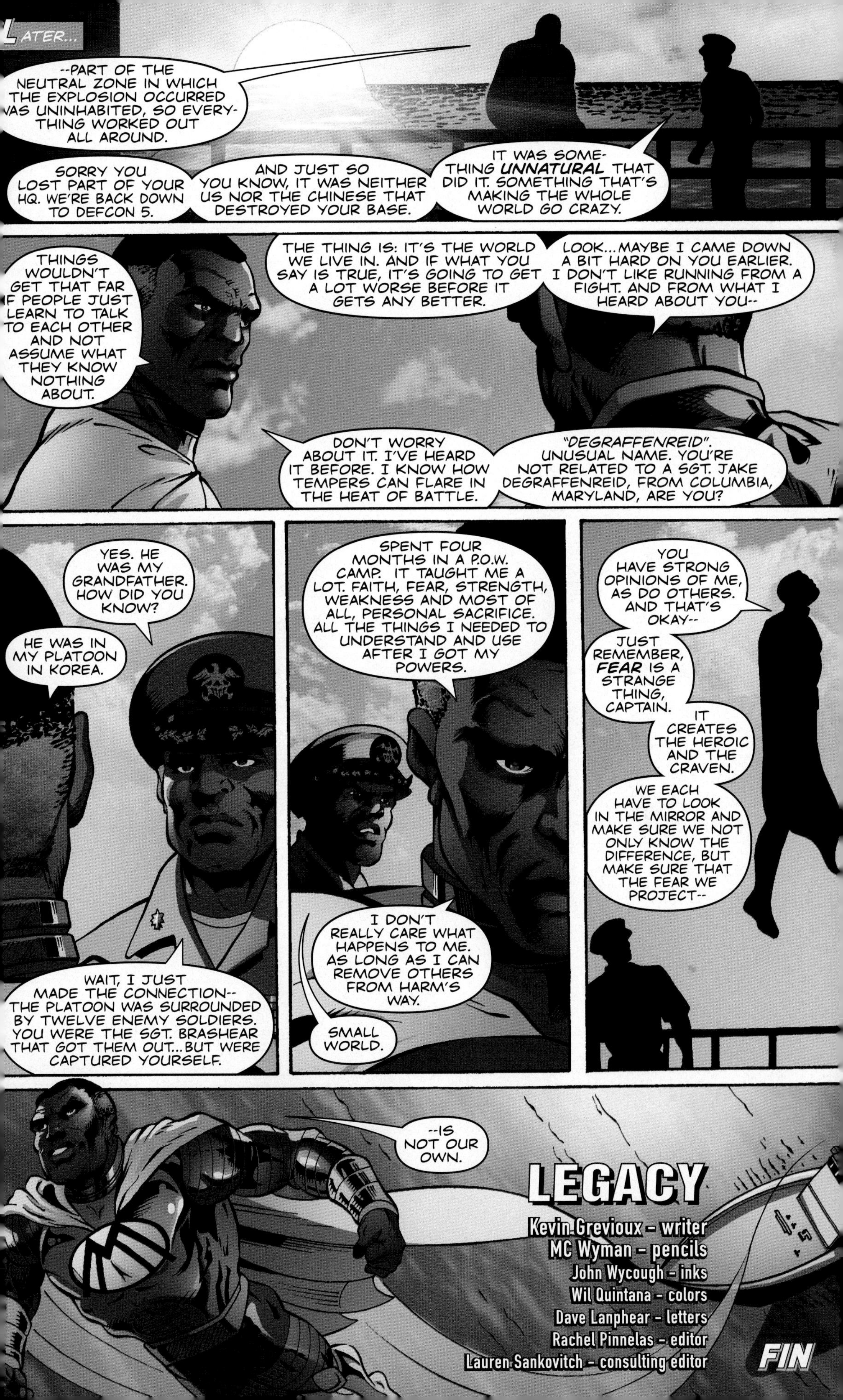
LATER...
--PART OF THE NEUTRAL ZONE IN WHICH THE EXPLOSION OCCURRED WAS UNINHABITED, SO EVERYTHING WORKED OUT ALL AROUND.
SORRY YOU LOST PART OF YOUR HQ. WE'RE BACK DOWN TO DEFCON 5.
AND JUST SO YOU KNOW, IT WAS NEITHER US NOR THE CHINESE THAT DESTROYED YOUR BASE.
IT WAS SOMETHING *UNNATURAL* THAT DID IT. SOMETHING THAT'S MAKING THE WHOLE WORLD GO CRAZY.
THINGS WOULDN'T GET THAT FAR IF PEOPLE JUST LEARN TO TALK TO EACH OTHER AND NOT ASSUME WHAT THEY KNOW NOTHING ABOUT.
THE THING IS: IT'S THE WORLD WE LIVE IN. AND IF WHAT YOU SAY IS TRUE, IT'S GOING TO GET A LOT WORSE BEFORE IT GETS ANY BETTER.
LOOK...MAYBE I CAME DOWN A BIT HARD ON YOU EARLIER. I DON'T LIKE RUNNING FROM A FIGHT. AND FROM WHAT I HEARD ABOUT YOU--
DON'T WORRY ABOUT IT. I'VE HEARD IT BEFORE. I KNOW HOW TEMPERS CAN FLARE IN THE HEAT OF BATTLE.
"DEGRAFFENREID". UNUSUAL NAME. YOU'RE NOT RELATED TO A SGT. JAKE DEGRAFFENREID, FROM COLUMBIA, MARYLAND, ARE YOU?
YES. HE WAS MY GRANDFATHER. HOW DID YOU KNOW?
HE WAS IN MY PLATOON IN KOREA.
WAIT, I JUST MADE THE CONNECTION-- THE PLATOON WAS SURROUNDED BY TWELVE ENEMY SOLDIERS. YOU WERE THE SGT. BRASHEAR THAT GOT THEM OUT...BUT WERE CAPTURED YOURSELF.
SPENT FOUR MONTHS IN A P.O.W. CAMP. IT TAUGHT ME A LOT. FAITH, FEAR, STRENGTH, WEAKNESS AND MOST OF ALL, PERSONAL SACRIFICE. ALL THE THINGS I NEEDED TO UNDERSTAND AND USE AFTER I GOT MY POWERS.
I DON'T REALLY CARE WHAT HAPPENS TO ME. AS LONG AS I CAN REMOVE OTHERS FROM HARM'S WAY.
SMALL WORLD.
YOU HAVE STRONG OPINIONS OF ME, AS DO OTHERS. AND THAT'S OKAY--
JUST REMEMBER, *FEAR* IS A STRANGE THING, CAPTAIN.
IT CREATES THE HEROIC AND THE CRAVEN.
WE EACH HAVE TO LOOK IN THE MIRROR AND MAKE SURE WE NOT ONLY KNOW THE DIFFERENCE, BUT MAKE SURE THAT THE FEAR WE PROJECT--
--IS NOT OUR OWN.
LEGACY
Kevin Grevioux - writer
MC Wyman - pencils
John Wycough - inks
Wil Quintana - colors
Dave Lanphear - letters
Rachel Pinnelas - editor
Lauren Sankovitch - consulting editor
FIN

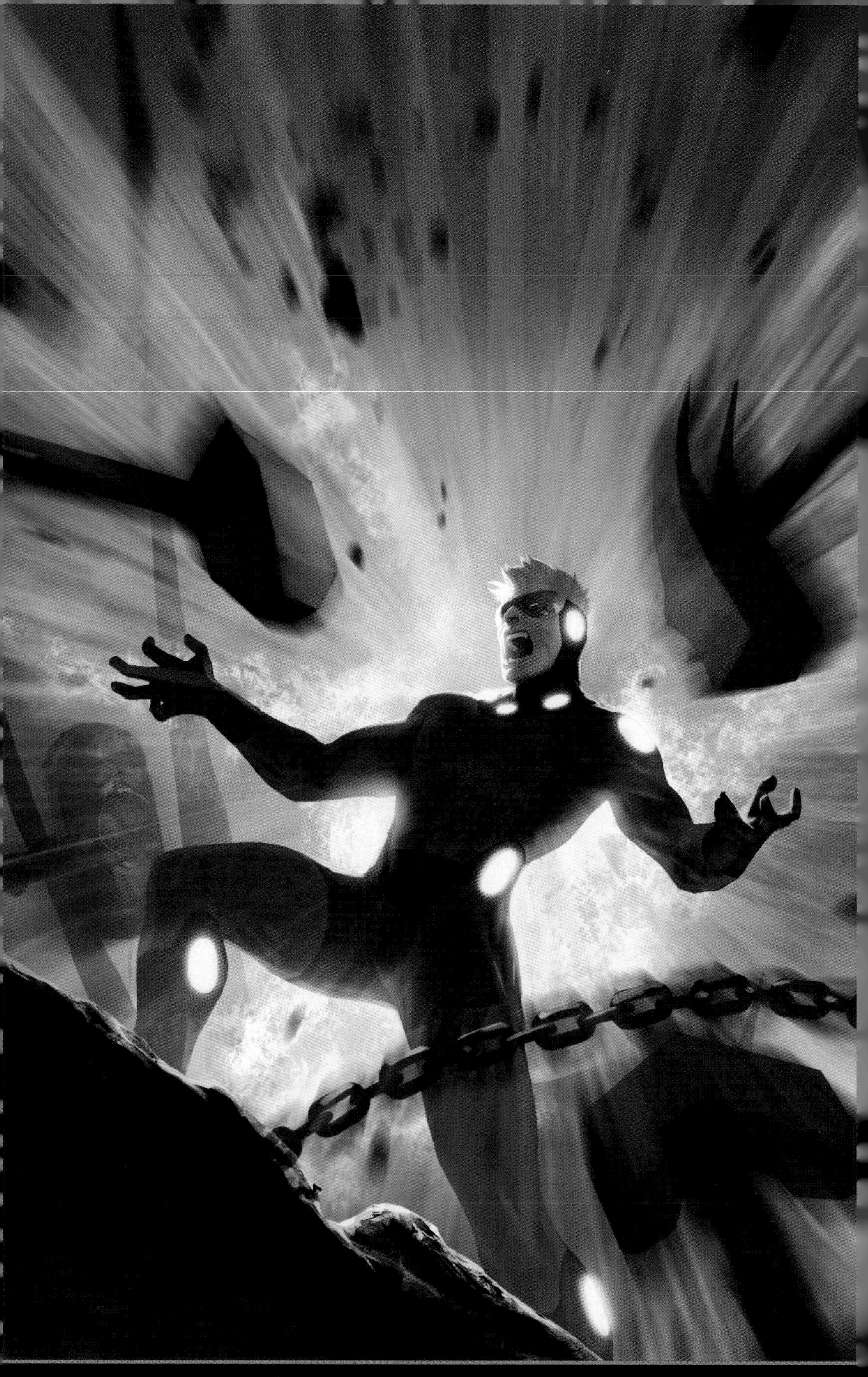

FEAR ITSELF: THE HOME FRONT #5

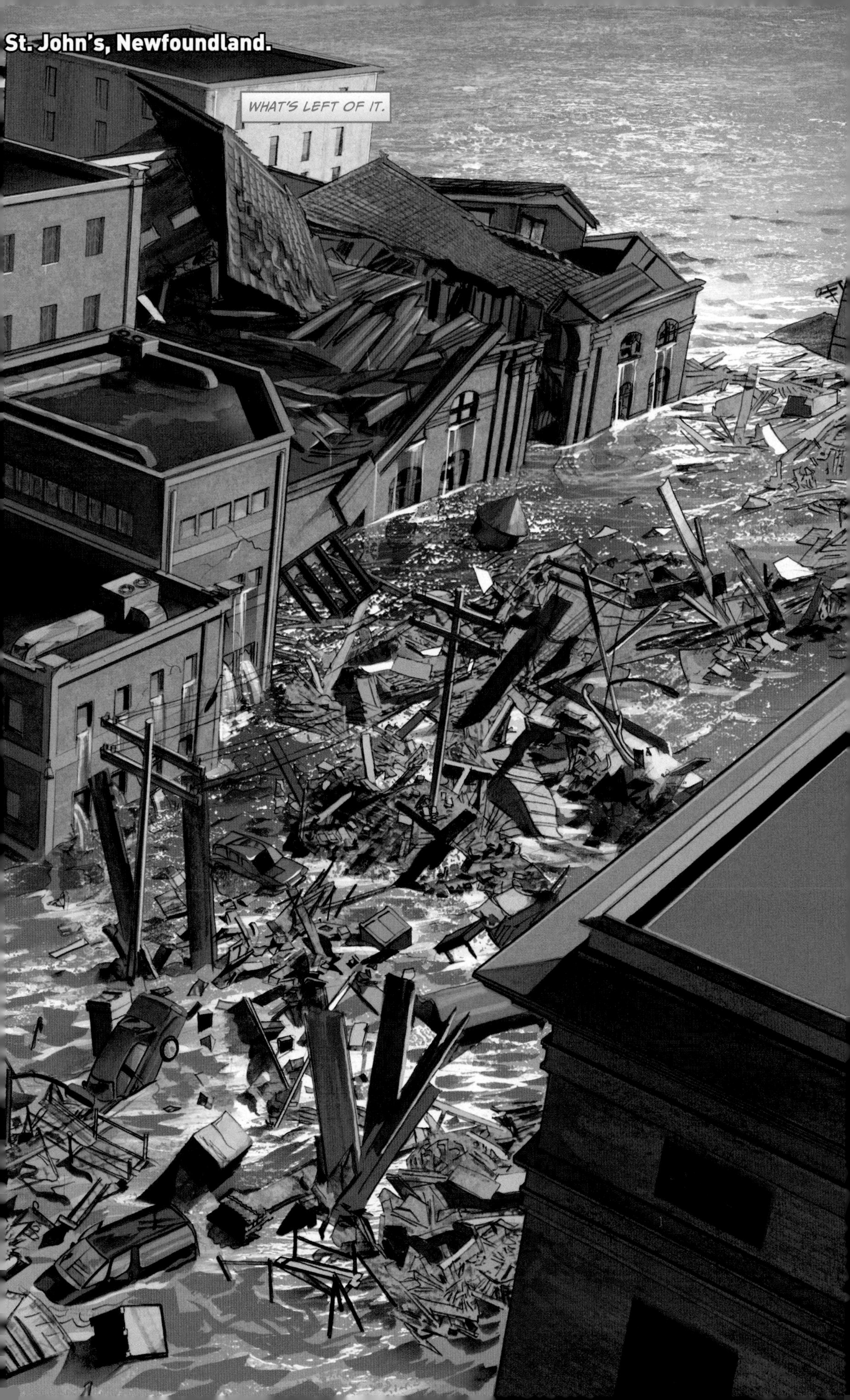
St. John's, Newfoundland.
WHAT'S LEFT OF IT.

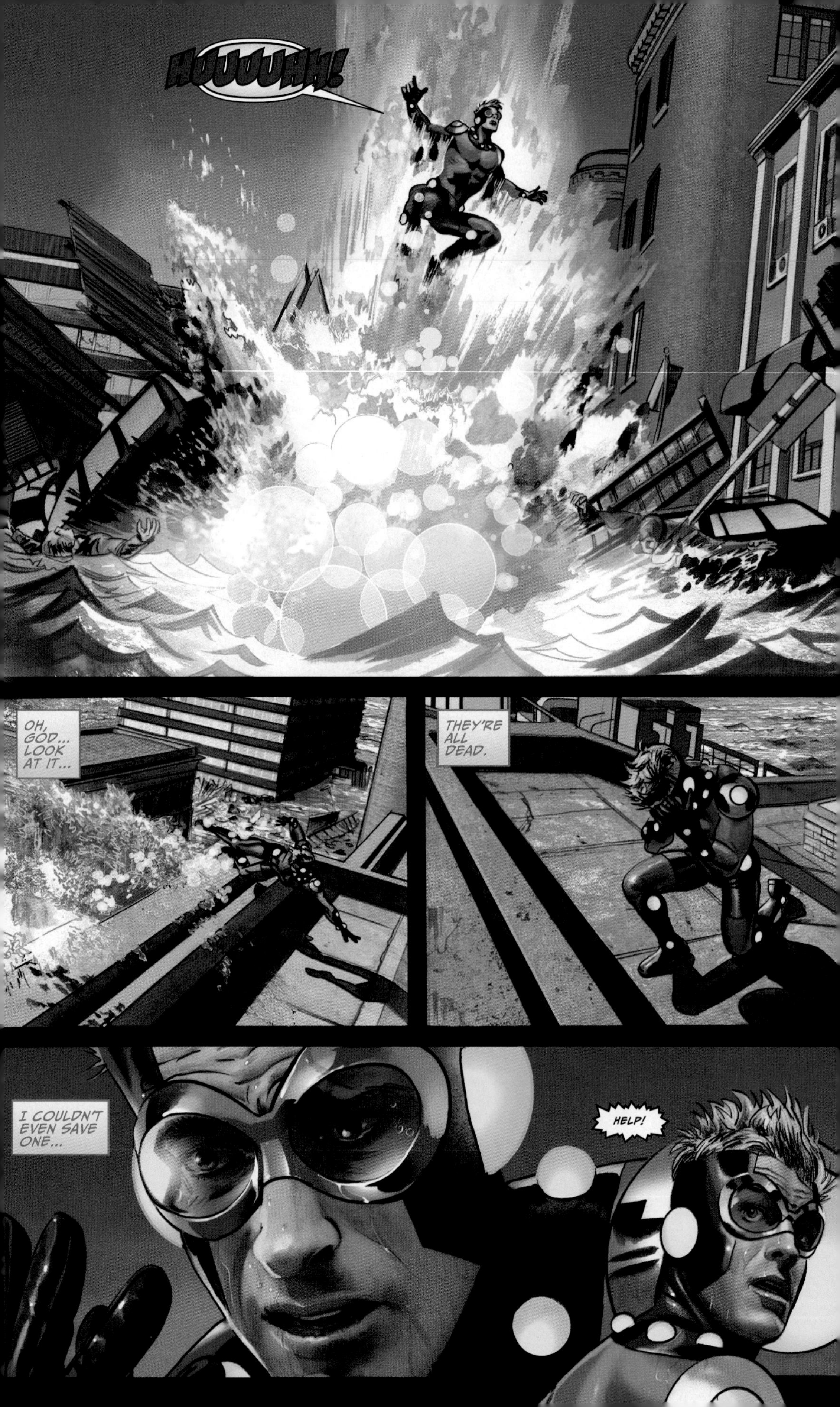
HOUUUUHH!
OH, GOD... LOOK AT IT...
THEY'RE ALL DEAD.
I COULDN'T EVEN SAVE ONE...
HELP!

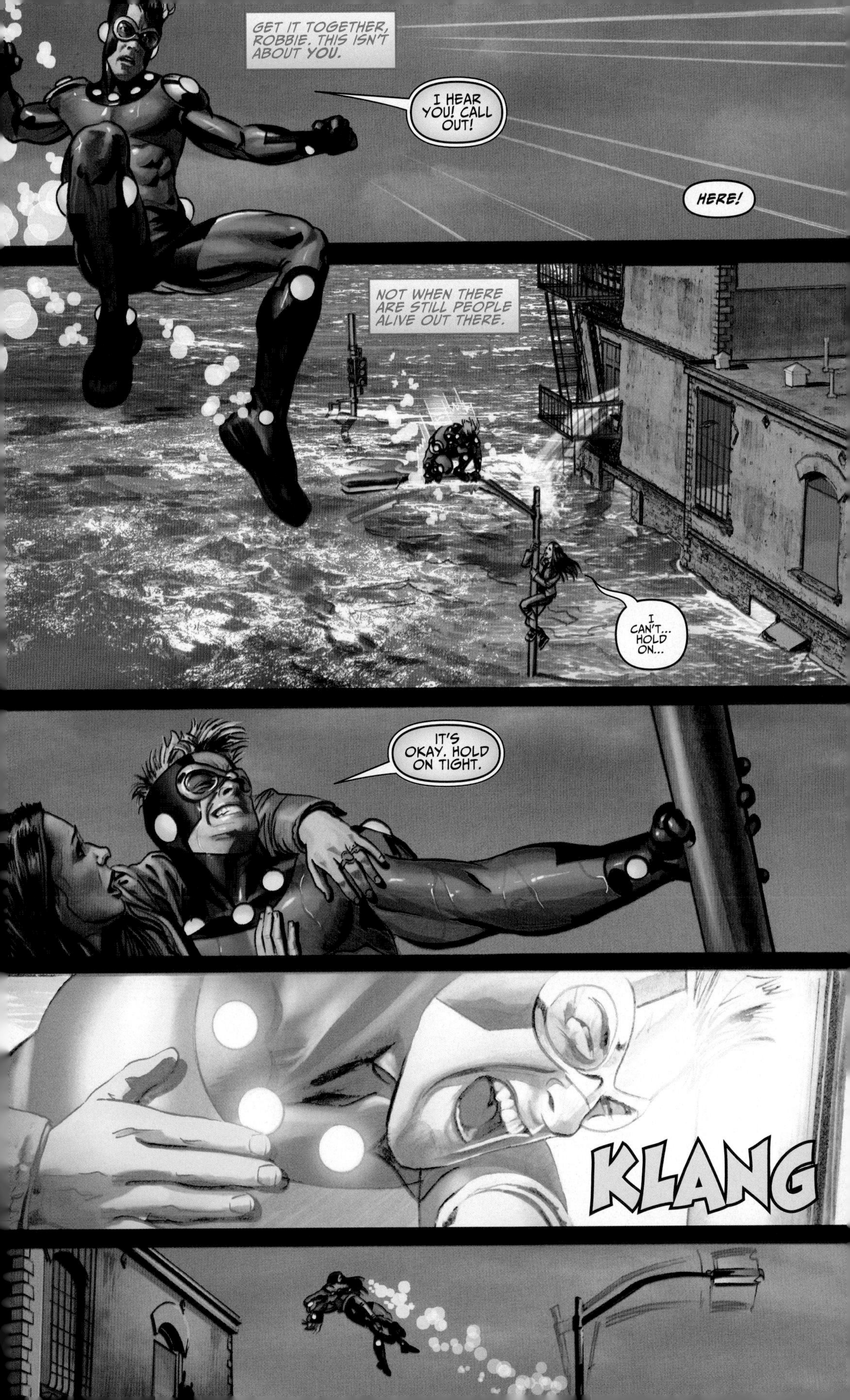
GET IT TOGETHER, ROBBIE. THIS ISN'T ABOUT YOU.
I HEAR YOU! CALL OUT!
HERE!
NOT WHEN THERE ARE STILL PEOPLE ALIVE OUT THERE.
I CAN'T... HOLD ON...
IT'S OKAY. HOLD ON TIGHT.
KLANG

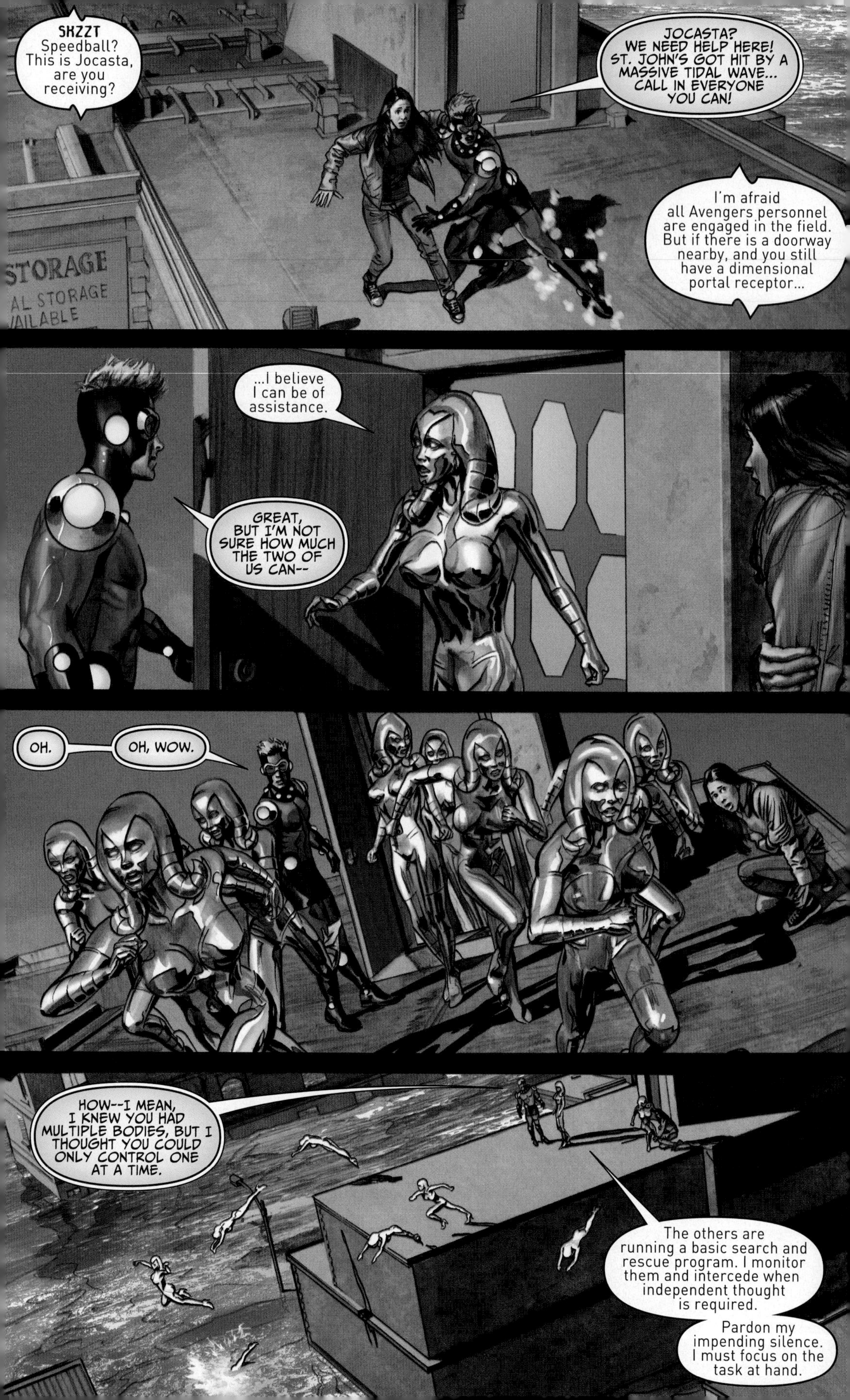
SHZZT Speedball? This is Jocasta, are you receiving?
JOCASTA? WE NEED HELP HERE! ST. JOHN'S GOT HIT BY A MASSIVE TIDAL WAVE... CALL IN EVERYONE YOU CAN!
I'm afraid all Avengers personnel are engaged in the field. But if there is a doorway nearby, and you still have a dimensional portal receptor...
STORAGE
AL STORAGE
AILABLE
...I believe I can be of assistance.
GREAT, BUT I'M NOT SURE HOW MUCH THE TWO OF US CAN--
OH.
OH, WOW.
HOW--I MEAN, I KNEW YOU HAD MULTIPLE BODIES, BUT I THOUGHT YOU COULD ONLY CONTROL ONE AT A TIME.
The others are running a basic search and rescue program. I monitor them and intercede when independent thought is required.
Pardon my impending silence. I must focus on the task at hand.

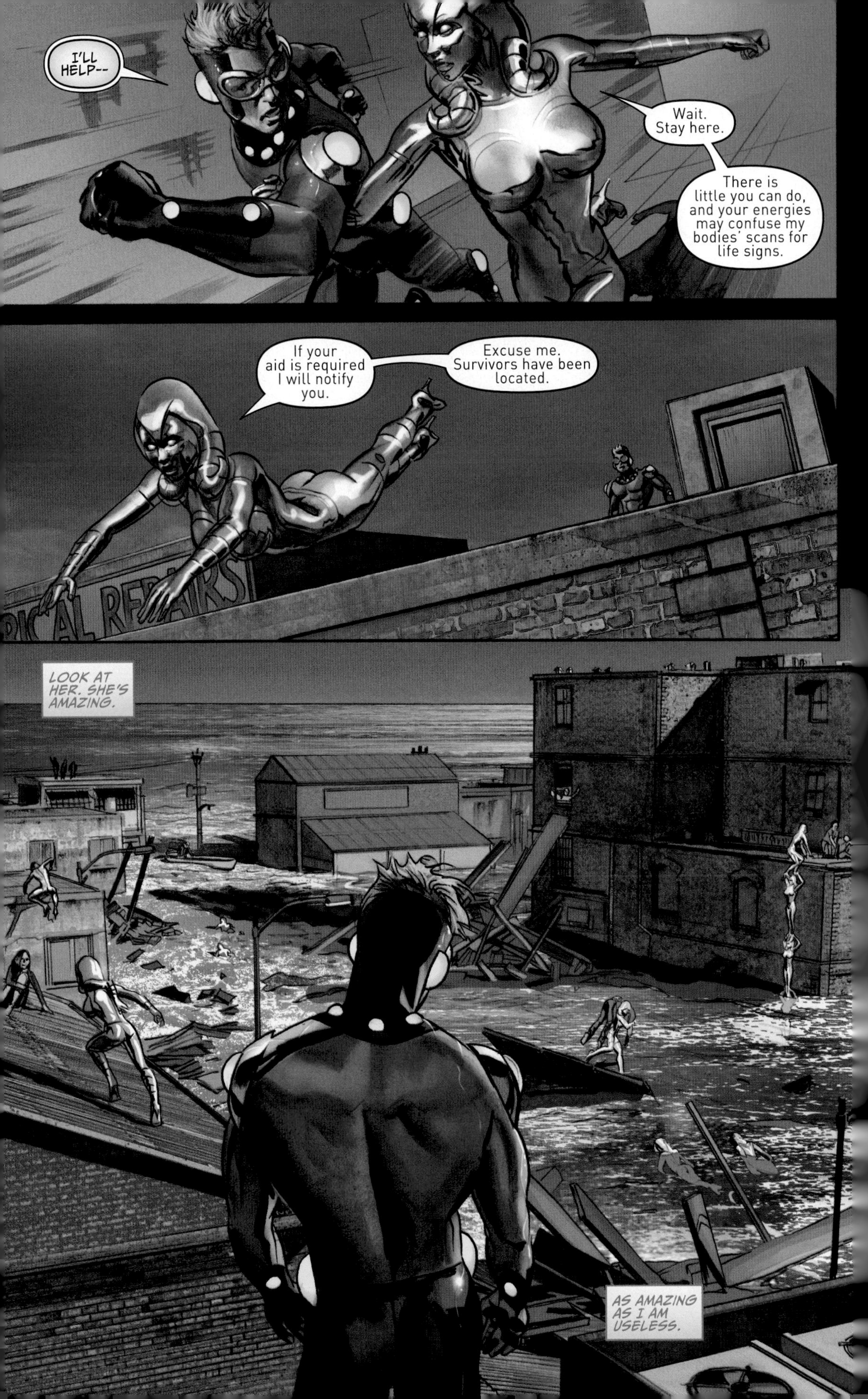
I'LL HELP--
Wait. Stay here.
There is little you can do, and your energies may confuse my bodies' scans for life signs.
If your aid is required I will notify you.
Excuse me. Survivors have been located.
LOOK AT HER. SHE'S AMAZING.
AS AMAZING AS I AM USELESS.

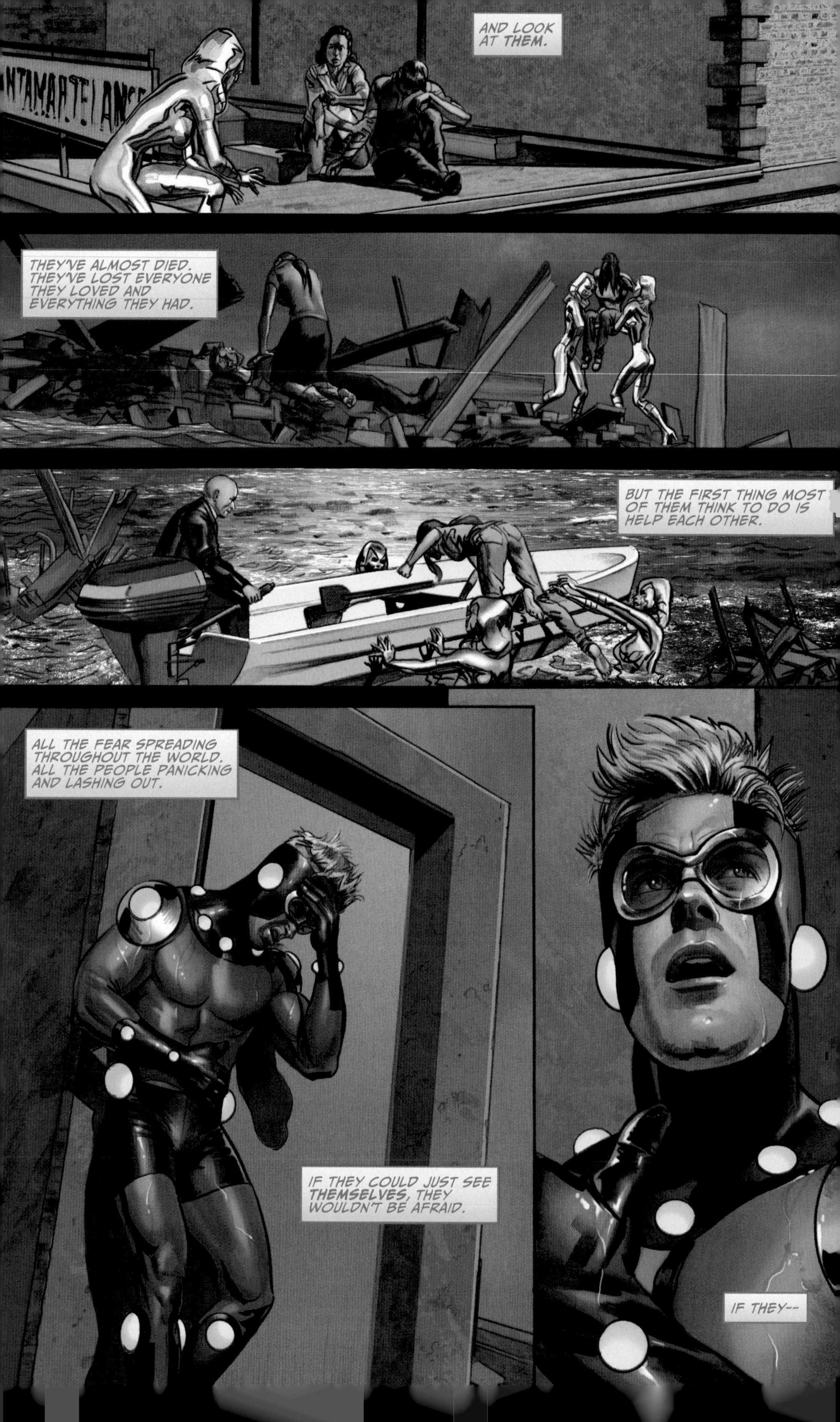
AND LOOK AT THEM.
THEY'VE ALMOST DIED. THEY'VE LOST EVERYONE THEY LOVED AND EVERYTHING THEY HAD.
BUT THE FIRST THING MOST OF THEM THINK TO DO IS HELP EACH OTHER.
ALL THE FEAR SPREADING THROUGHOUT THE WORLD. ALL THE PEOPLE PANICKING AND LASHING OUT.
IF THEY COULD JUST SEE THEMSELVES, THEY WOULDN'T BE AFRAID.
IF THEY--

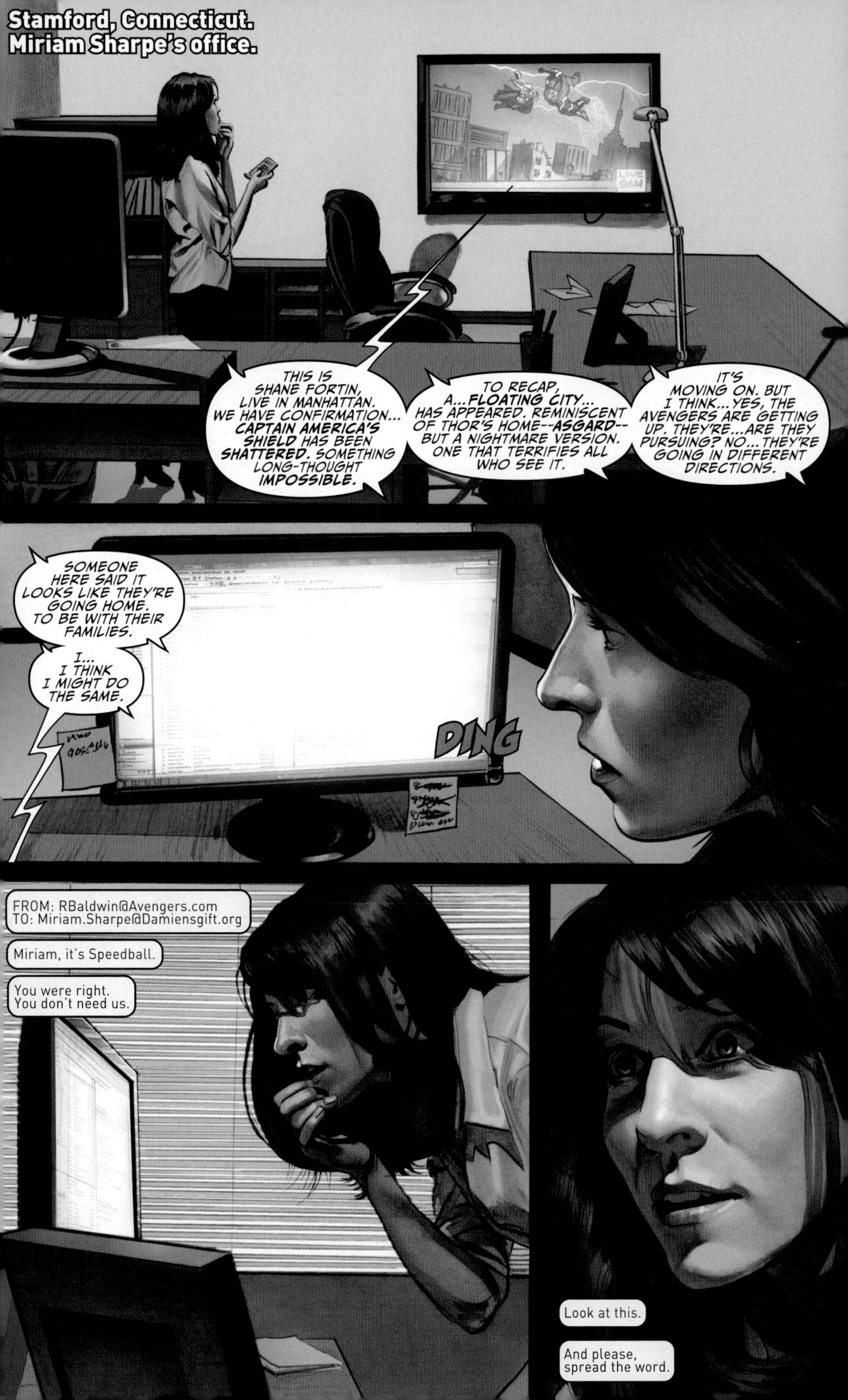
Stamford, Connecticut. Miriam Sharpe's office.
THIS IS SHANE FORTIN, LIVE IN MANHATTAN. WE HAVE CONFIRMATION... CAPTAIN AMERICA'S SHIELD HAS BEEN SHATTERED. SOMETHING LONG-THOUGHT IMPOSSIBLE.
TO RECAP, A...FLOATING CITY... HAS APPEARED. REMINISCENT OF THOR'S HOME--ASGARD-- BUT A NIGHTMARE VERSION. ONE THAT TERRIFIES ALL WHO SEE IT.
IT'S MOVING ON. BUT I THINK...YES, THE AVENGERS ARE GETTING UP. THEY'RE...ARE THEY PURSUING? NO...THEY'RE GOING IN DIFFERENT DIRECTIONS.
SOMEONE HERE SAID IT LOOKS LIKE THEY'RE GOING HOME. TO BE WITH THEIR FAMILIES.
I... I THINK I MIGHT DO THE SAME.
DING
FROM: RBaldwin@Avengers.com
TO: Miriam.Sharpe@Damiensgift.org
Miriam, it's Speedball.
You were right. You don't need us.
Look at this.
And please, spread the word.

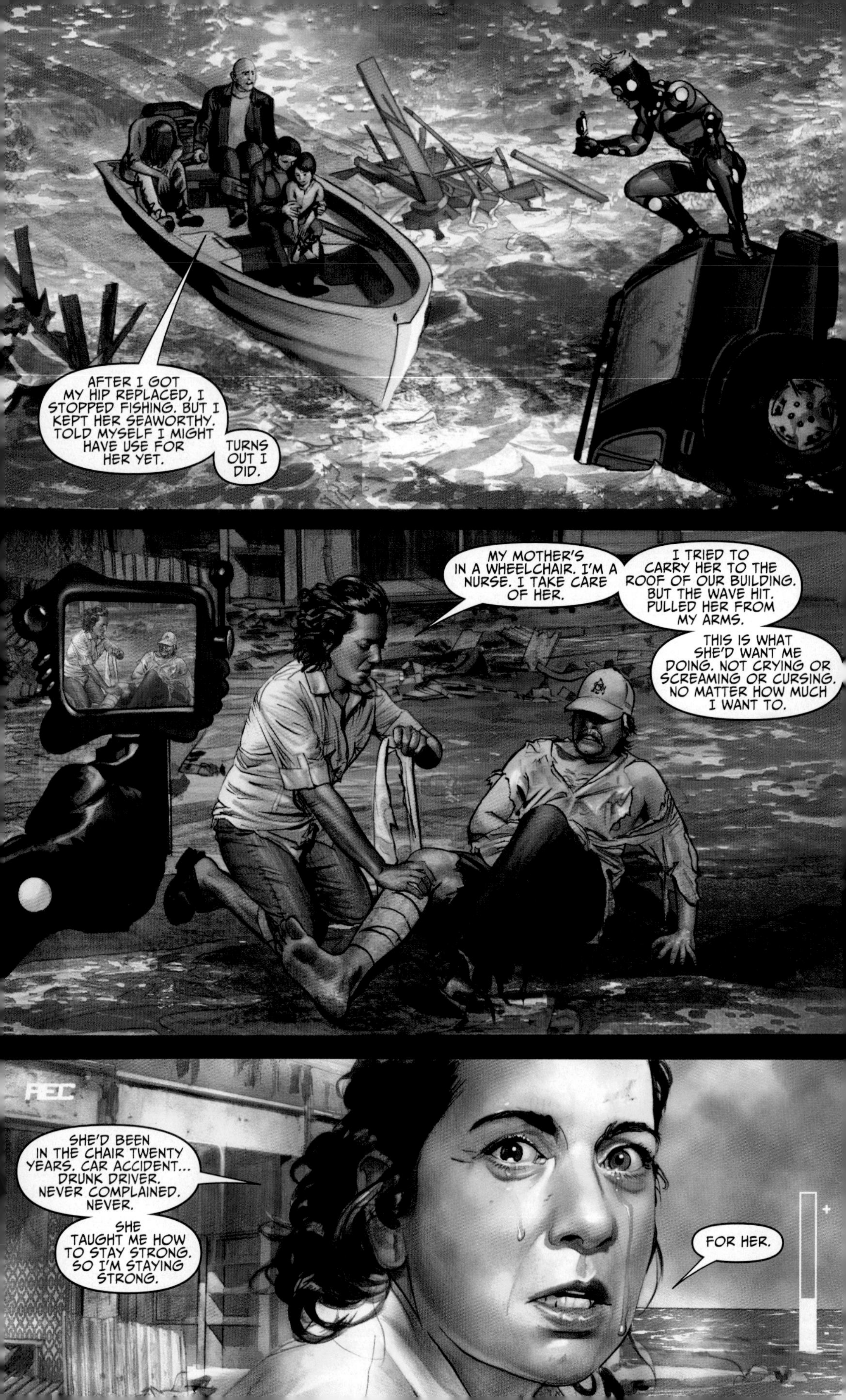
AFTER I GOT MY HIP REPLACED, I STOPPED FISHING. BUT I KEPT HER SEAWORTHY. TOLD MYSELF I MIGHT HAVE USE FOR HER YET.
TURNS OUT I DID.
MY MOTHER'S IN A WHEELCHAIR. I'M A NURSE. I TAKE CARE OF HER.
I TRIED TO CARRY HER TO THE ROOF OF OUR BUILDING. BUT THE WAVE HIT. PULLED HER FROM MY ARMS.
THIS IS WHAT SHE'D WANT ME DOING. NOT CRYING OR SCREAMING OR CURSING. NO MATTER HOW MUCH I WANT TO.
REC.
SHE'D BEEN IN THE CHAIR TWENTY YEARS. CAR ACCIDENT... DRUNK DRIVER. NEVER COMPLAINED. NEVER.
SHE TAUGHT ME HOW TO STAY STRONG. SO I'M STAYING STRONG.
FOR HER.

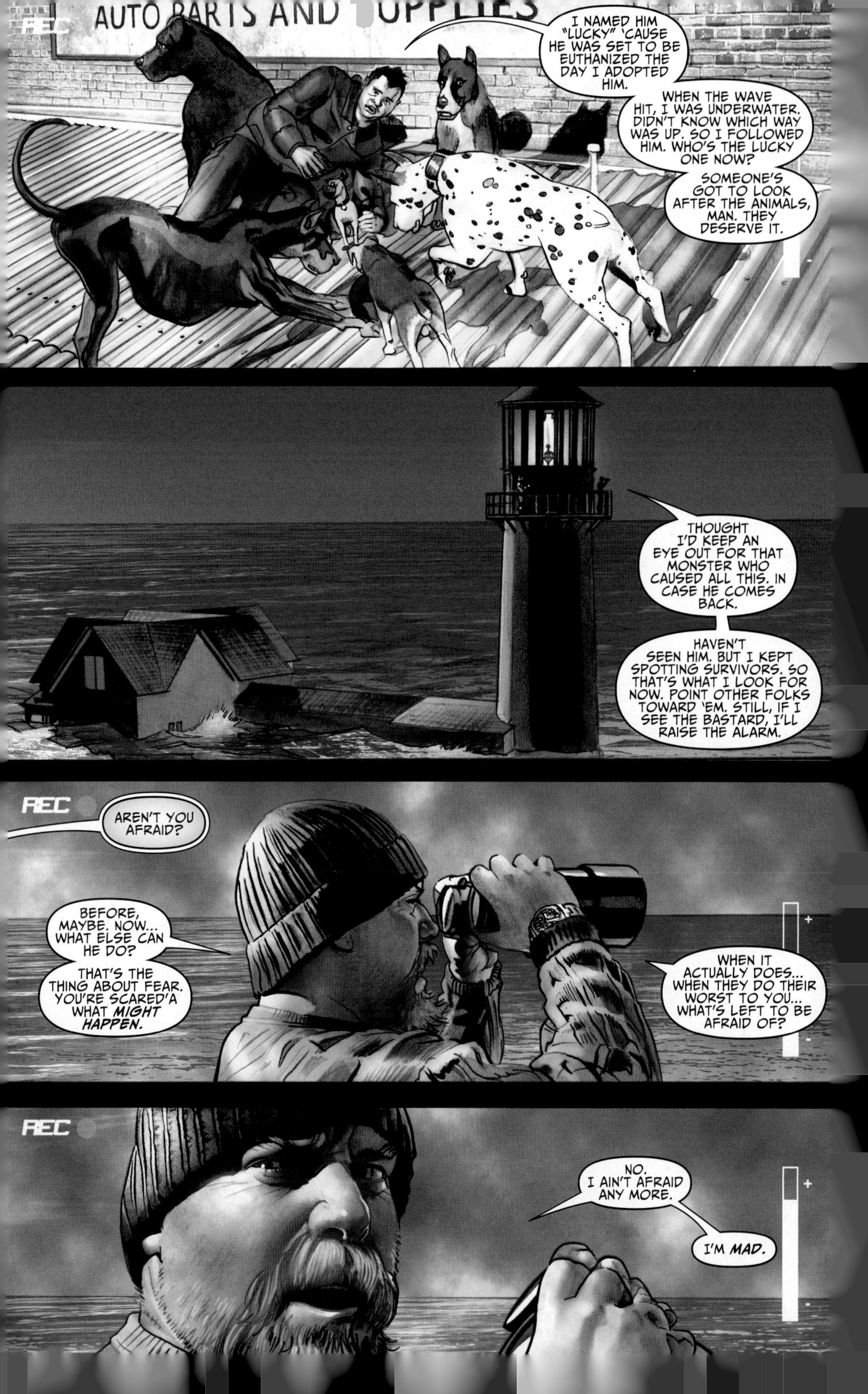
AUTO PARTS AND SUPPLIES
REC
I NAMED HIM "LUCKY" 'CAUSE HE WAS SET TO BE EUTHANIZED THE DAY I ADOPTED HIM.
WHEN THE WAVE HIT, I WAS UNDERWATER. DIDN'T KNOW WHICH WAY WAS UP. SO I FOLLOWED HIM. WHO'S THE LUCKY ONE NOW?
SOMEONE'S GOT TO LOOK AFTER THE ANIMALS, MAN. THEY DESERVE IT.
THOUGHT I'D KEEP AN EYE OUT FOR THAT MONSTER WHO CAUSED ALL THIS. IN CASE HE COMES BACK.
HAVEN'T SEEN HIM. BUT I KEPT SPOTTING SURVIVORS. SO THAT'S WHAT I LOOK FOR NOW. POINT OTHER FOLKS TOWARD 'EM. STILL, IF I SEE THE BASTARD, I'LL RAISE THE ALARM.
REC
AREN'T YOU AFRAID?
BEFORE, MAYBE. NOW... WHAT ELSE CAN HE DO?
THAT'S THE THING ABOUT FEAR. YOU'RE SCARED'A WHAT *MIGHT HAPPEN.*
WHEN IT ACTUALLY DOES... WHEN THEY DO THEIR WORST TO YOU... WHAT'S LEFT TO BE AFRAID OF?
REC
NO. I AIN'T AFRAID ANY MORE.
I'M *MAD.*

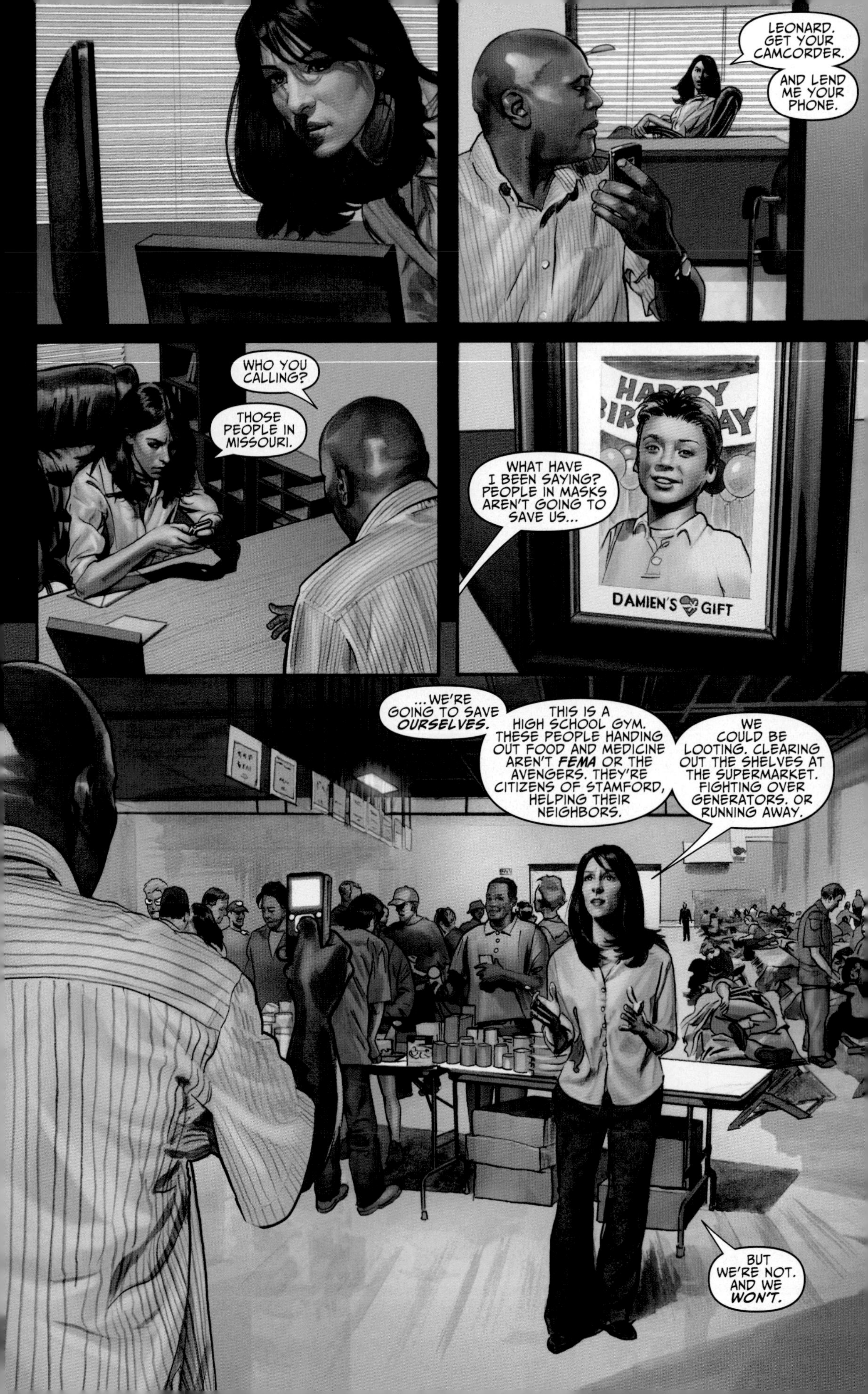
LEONARD. GET YOUR CAMCORDER.
AND LEND ME YOUR PHONE.
WHO YOU CALLING?
THOSE PEOPLE IN MISSOURI.
HAPPY BIRTHDAY
DAMIEN'S GIFT
WHAT HAVE I BEEN SAYING? PEOPLE IN MASKS AREN'T GOING TO SAVE US...
...WE'RE GOING TO SAVE *OURSELVES.*
THIS IS A HIGH SCHOOL GYM. THESE PEOPLE HANDING OUT FOOD AND MEDICINE AREN'T *FEMA* OR THE AVENGERS. THEY'RE CITIZENS OF STAMFORD, HELPING THEIR NEIGHBORS.
WE COULD BE LOOTING. CLEARING OUT THE SHELVES AT THE SUPERMARKET. FIGHTING OVER GENERATORS. OR RUNNING AWAY.
BUT WE'RE NOT. AND WE *WON'T.*

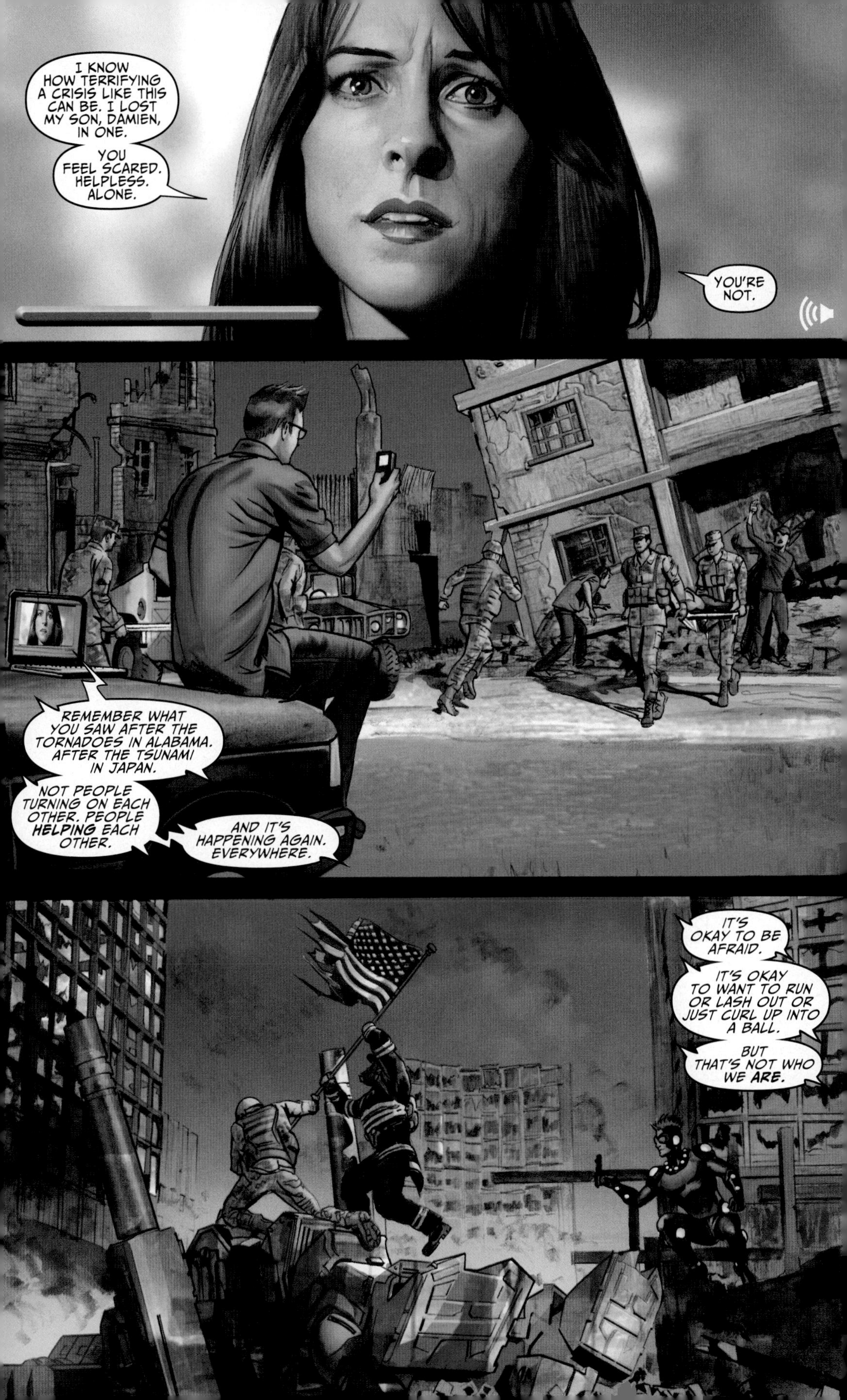
I KNOW HOW TERRIFYING A CRISIS LIKE THIS CAN BE. I LOST MY SON, DAMIEN, IN ONE.
YOU FEEL SCARED. HELPLESS. ALONE.
YOU'RE NOT.
REMEMBER WHAT YOU SAW AFTER THE TORNADOES IN ALABAMA. AFTER THE TSUNAMI IN JAPAN.
NOT PEOPLE TURNING ON EACH OTHER. PEOPLE HELPING EACH OTHER.
AND IT'S HAPPENING AGAIN. EVERYWHERE.
IT'S OKAY TO BE AFRAID.
IT'S OKAY TO WANT TO RUN OR LASH OUT OR JUST CURL UP INTO A BALL.
BUT THAT'S NOT WHO WE ARE.

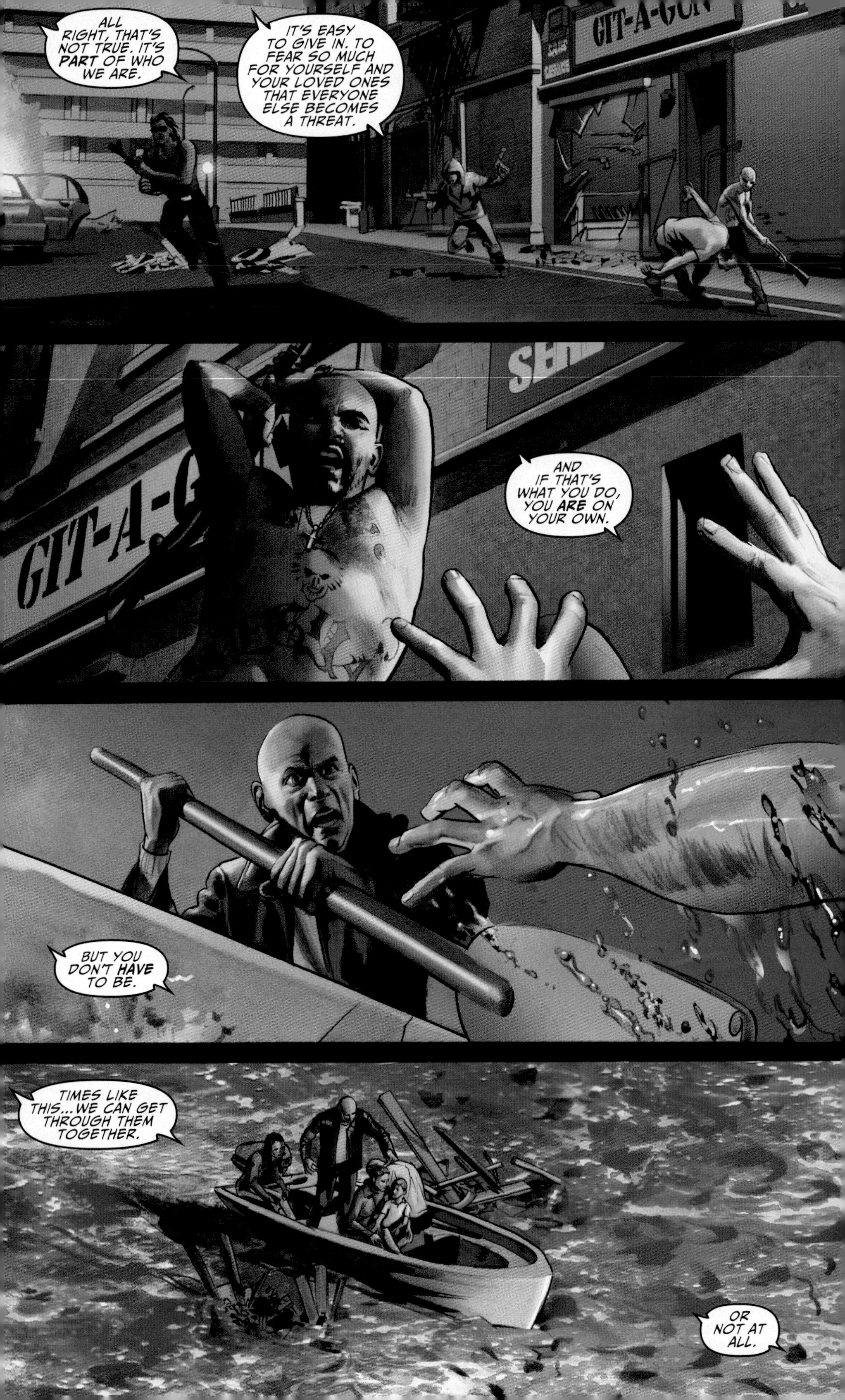
GIT-A-GUN
ALL RIGHT, THAT'S NOT TRUE. IT'S **PART** OF WHO WE ARE.
IT'S EASY TO GIVE IN. TO FEAR SO MUCH FOR YOURSELF AND YOUR LOVED ONES THAT EVERYONE ELSE BECOMES A THREAT.
GIT-A-G
AND IF THAT'S WHAT YOU DO, YOU **ARE** ON YOUR OWN.
BUT YOU DON'T **HAVE** TO BE.
TIMES LIKE THIS...WE CAN GET THROUGH THEM TOGETHER.
OR NOT AT ALL.

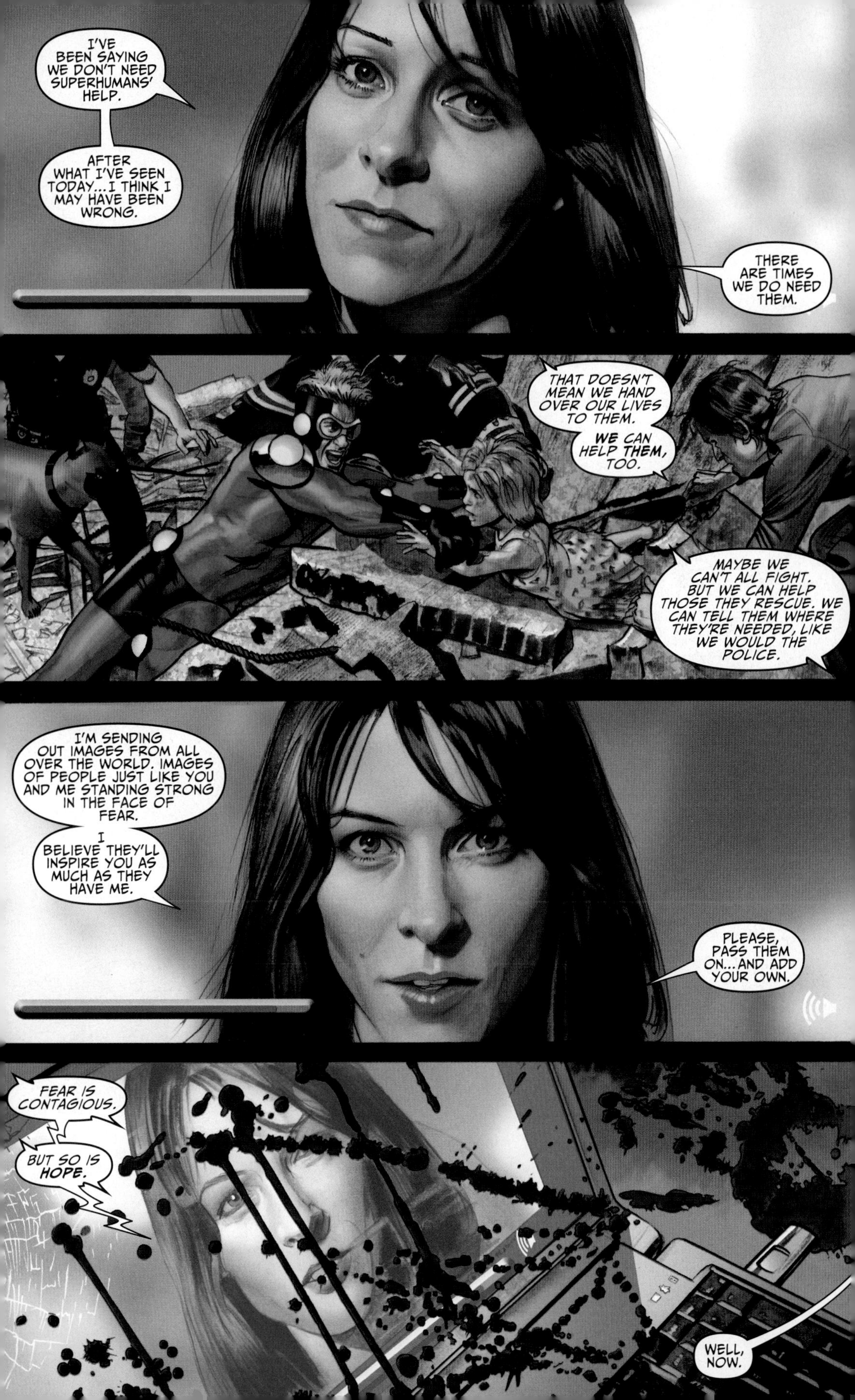
I'VE BEEN SAYING WE DON'T NEED SUPERHUMANS' HELP.
AFTER WHAT I'VE SEEN TODAY... I THINK I MAY HAVE BEEN WRONG.
THERE ARE TIMES WE DO NEED THEM.
THAT DOESN'T MEAN WE HAND OVER OUR LIVES TO THEM.
WE CAN HELP THEM, TOO.
MAYBE WE CAN'T ALL FIGHT. BUT WE CAN HELP THOSE THEY RESCUE. WE CAN TELL THEM WHERE THEY'RE NEEDED, LIKE WE WOULD THE POLICE.
I'M SENDING OUT IMAGES FROM ALL OVER THE WORLD. IMAGES OF PEOPLE JUST LIKE YOU AND ME STANDING STRONG IN THE FACE OF FEAR.
I BELIEVE THEY'LL INSPIRE YOU AS MUCH AS THEY HAVE ME.
PLEASE, PASS THEM ON... AND ADD YOUR OWN.
FEAR IS CONTAGIOUS.
BUT SO IS HOPE.
WELL, NOW.

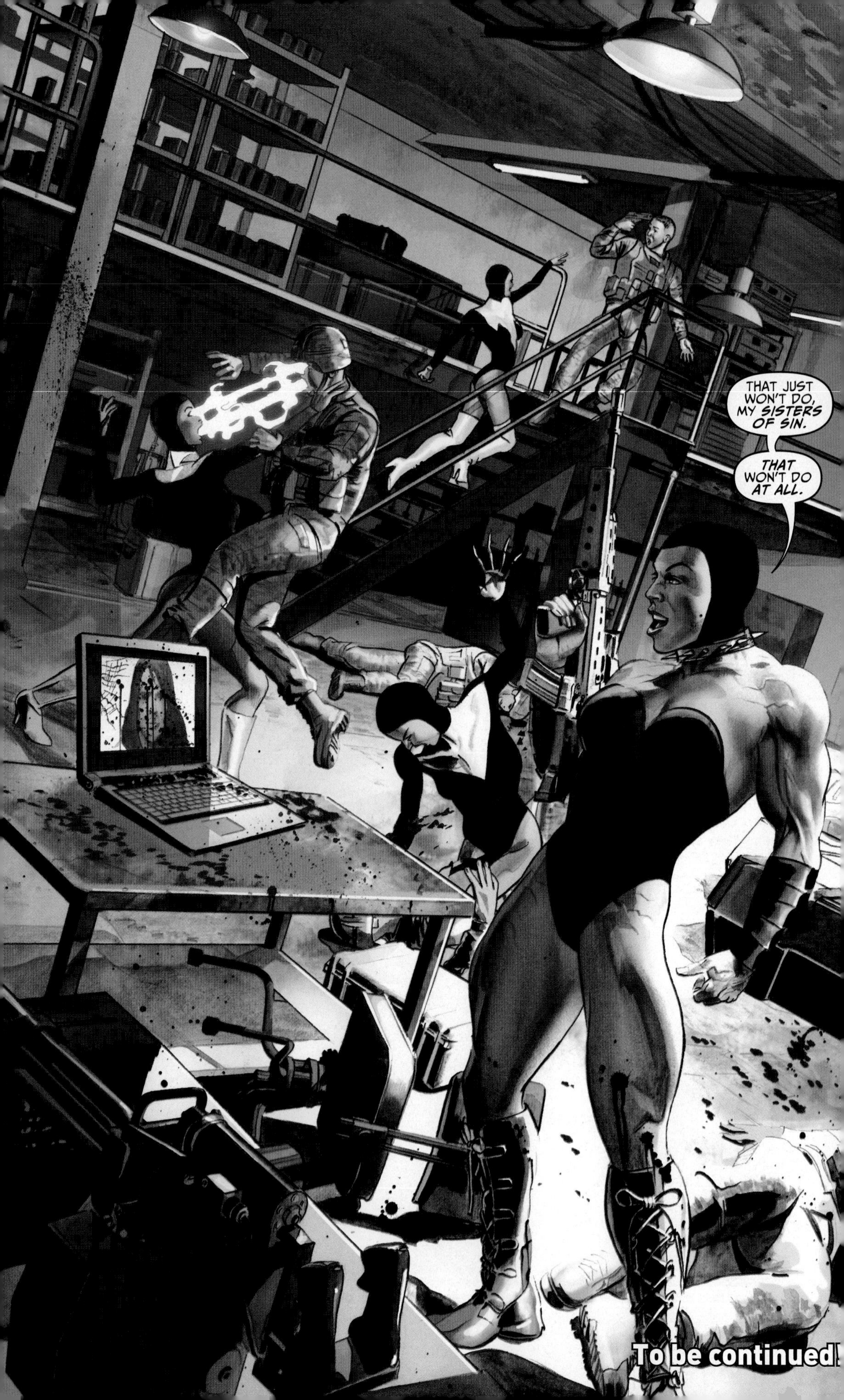
THAT JUST WON'T DO, MY SISTERS OF SIN.
THAT WON'T DO AT ALL.
To be continued!

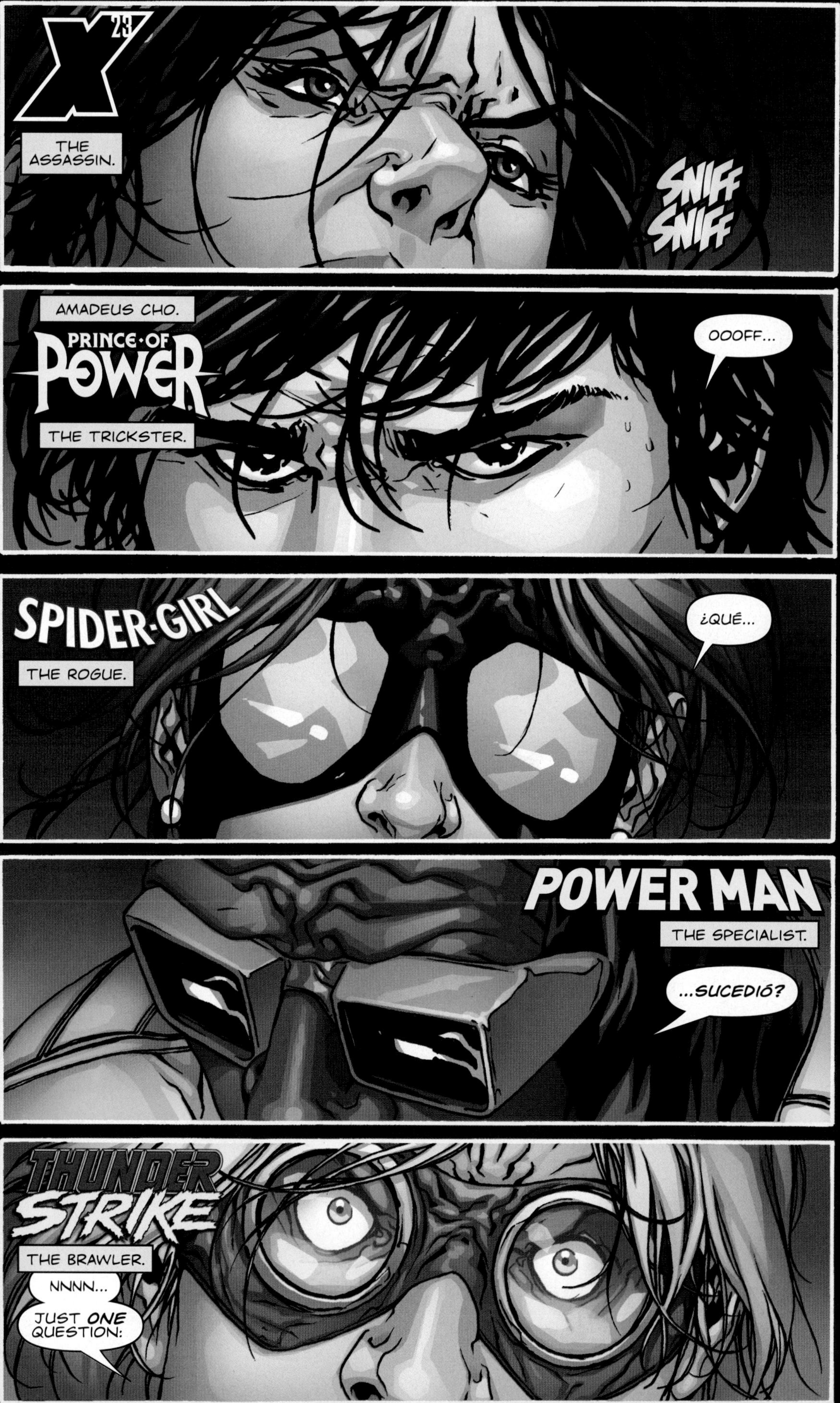
X-23
THE ASSASSIN.
SNIFF SNIFF
AMADEUS CHO.
PRINCE OF POWER
THE TRICKSTER.
OOOFF...
SPIDER-GIRL
THE ROGUE.
¿QUÉ...
POWER MAN
THE SPECIALIST.
...SUCEDIÓ?
THUNDERSTRIKE
THE BRAWLER.
NNNN...
JUST ONE QUESTION:

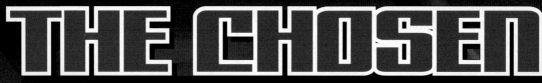

THE CHOSEN

Writer--Fred Van Lente Artist--Alessandro Vitti

Color Artist--Javier Tartaglia Letterer--Dave Lanphear Editor--Lauren Sankovitch

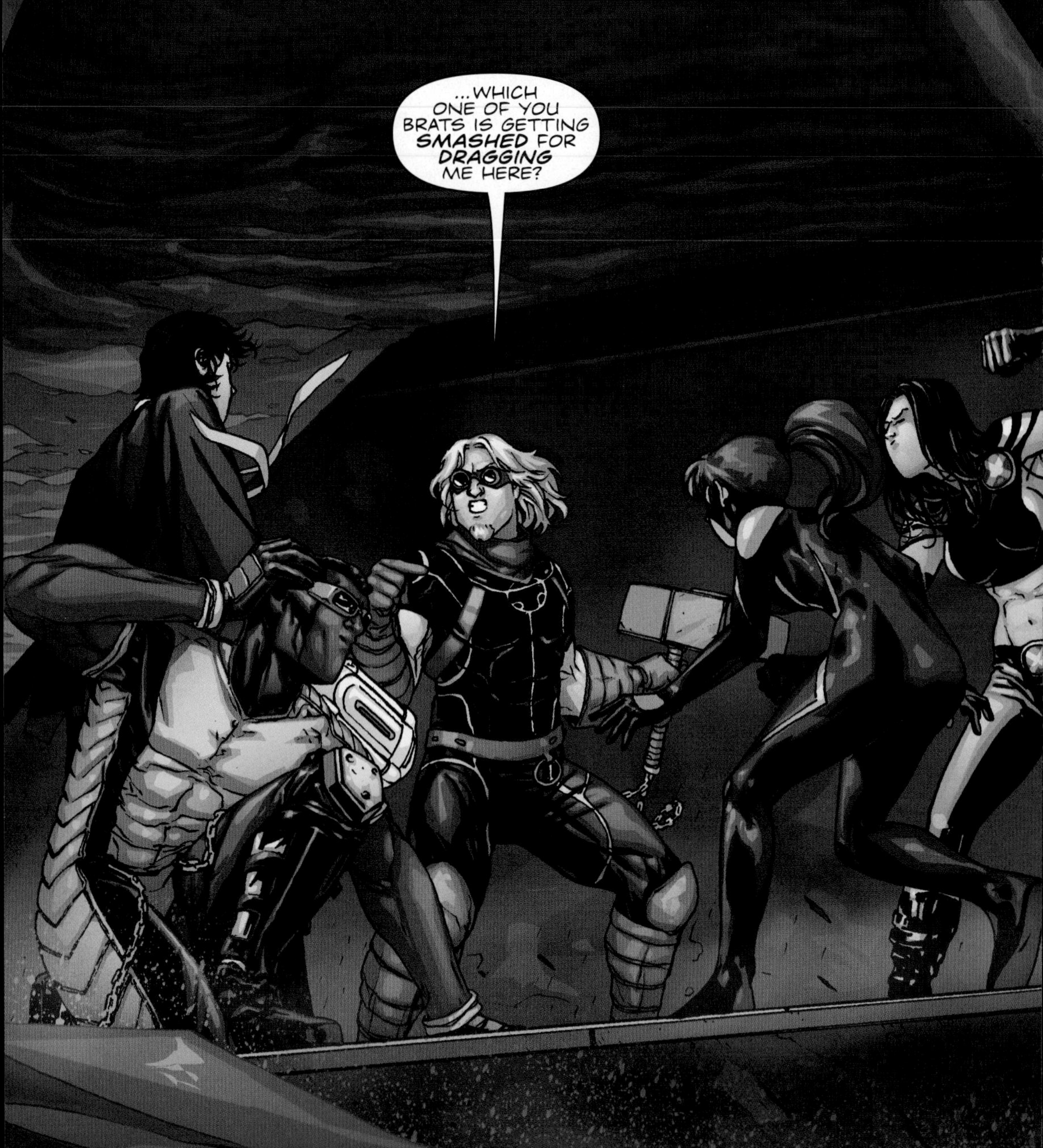
...WHICH ONE OF YOU BRATS IS GETTING SMASHED FOR DRAGGING ME HERE?

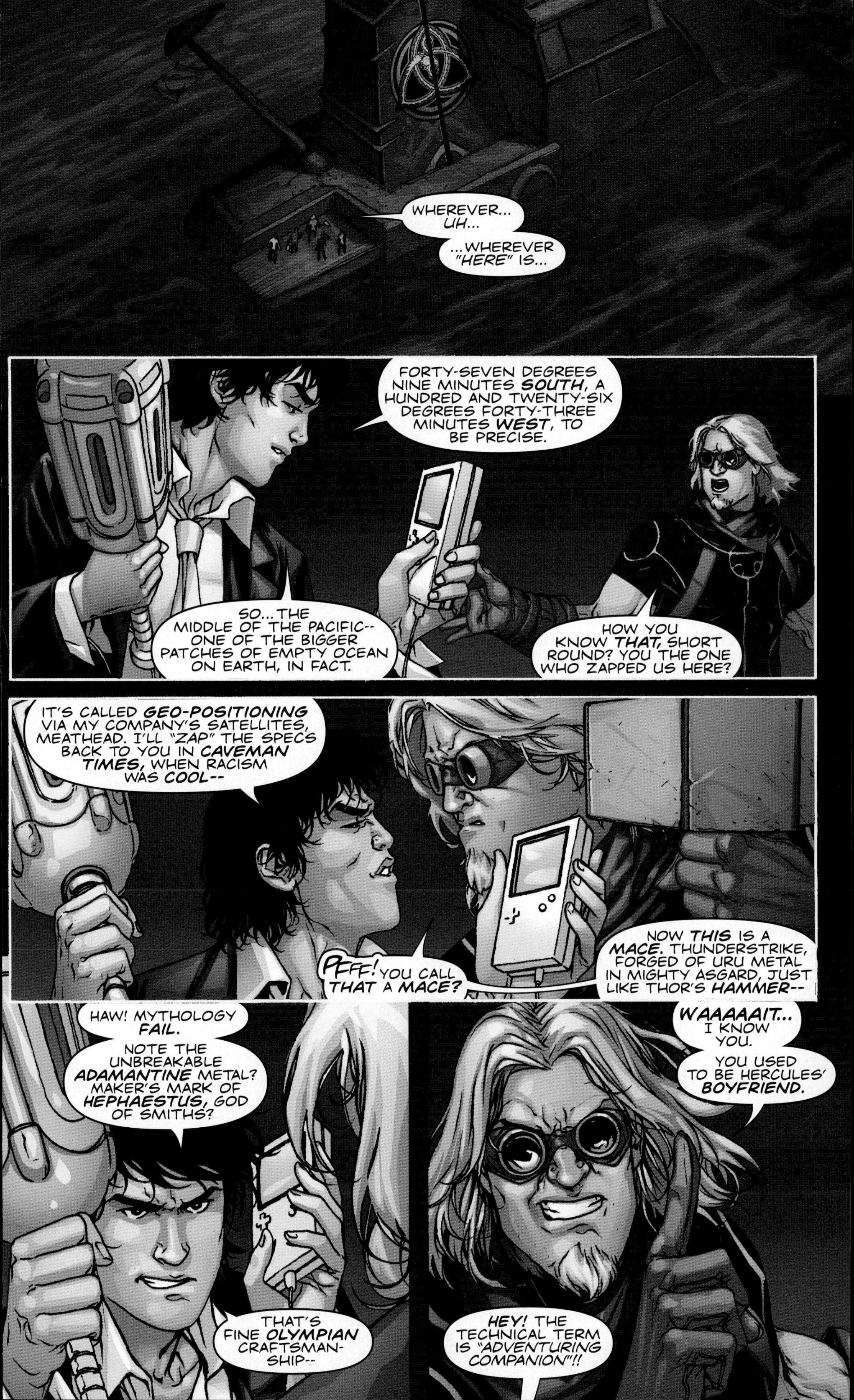
WHEREVER... UH...
...WHEREVER "HERE" IS...
FORTY-SEVEN DEGREES NINE MINUTES SOUTH, A HUNDRED AND TWENTY-SIX DEGREES FORTY-THREE MINUTES WEST, TO BE PRECISE.
SO... THE MIDDLE OF THE PACIFIC-- ONE OF THE BIGGER PATCHES OF EMPTY OCEAN ON EARTH, IN FACT.
HOW YOU KNOW THAT, SHORT ROUND? YOU THE ONE WHO ZAPPED US HERE?
IT'S CALLED GEO-POSITIONING VIA MY COMPANY'S SATELLITES, MEATHEAD. I'LL "ZAP" THE SPECS BACK TO YOU IN CAVEMAN TIMES, WHEN RACISM WAS COOL--
PFFF! YOU CALL THAT A MACE?
NOW THIS IS A MACE. THUNDERSTRIKE, FORGED OF URU METAL IN MIGHTY ASGARD, JUST LIKE THOR'S HAMMER--
HAW! MYTHOLOGY FAIL.
NOTE THE UNBREAKABLE ADAMANTINE METAL? MAKER'S MARK OF HEPHAESTUS, GOD OF SMITHS?
THAT'S FINE OLYMPIAN CRAFTSMANSHIP--
WAAAAAIT... I KNOW YOU.
YOU USED TO BE HERCULES' BOYFRIEND.
HEY! THE TECHNICAL TERM IS "ADVENTURING COMPANION"!!

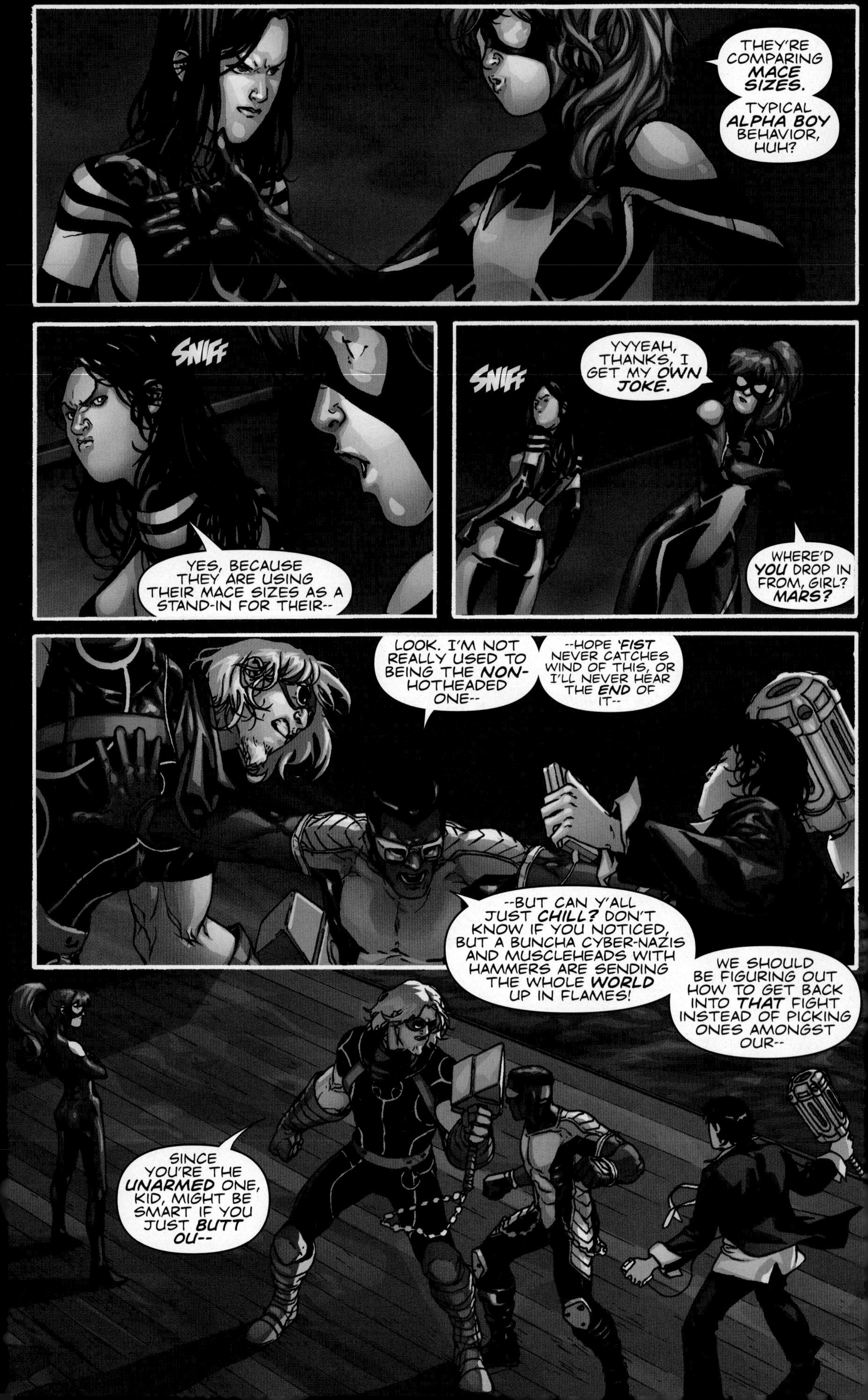
THEY'RE COMPARING MACE SIZES.
TYPICAL ALPHA BOY BEHAVIOR, HUH?
SNIFF
YES, BECAUSE THEY ARE USING THEIR MACE SIZES AS A STAND-IN FOR THEIR--
SNIFF
YYYEAH, THANKS, I GET MY OWN JOKE.
WHERE'D YOU DROP IN FROM, GIRL? MARS?
LOOK. I'M NOT REALLY USED TO BEING THE NON-HOTHEADED ONE--
--HOPE 'FIST NEVER CATCHES WIND OF THIS, OR I'LL NEVER HEAR THE END OF IT--
--BUT CAN Y'ALL JUST CHILL? DON'T KNOW IF YOU NOTICED, BUT A BUNCHA CYBER-NAZIS AND MUSCLEHEADS WITH HAMMERS ARE SENDING THE WHOLE WORLD UP IN FLAMES!
WE SHOULD BE FIGURING OUT HOW TO GET BACK INTO THAT FIGHT INSTEAD OF PICKING ONES AMONGST OUR--
SINCE YOU'RE THE UNARMED ONE, KID, MIGHT BE SMART IF YOU JUST BUTT OU--

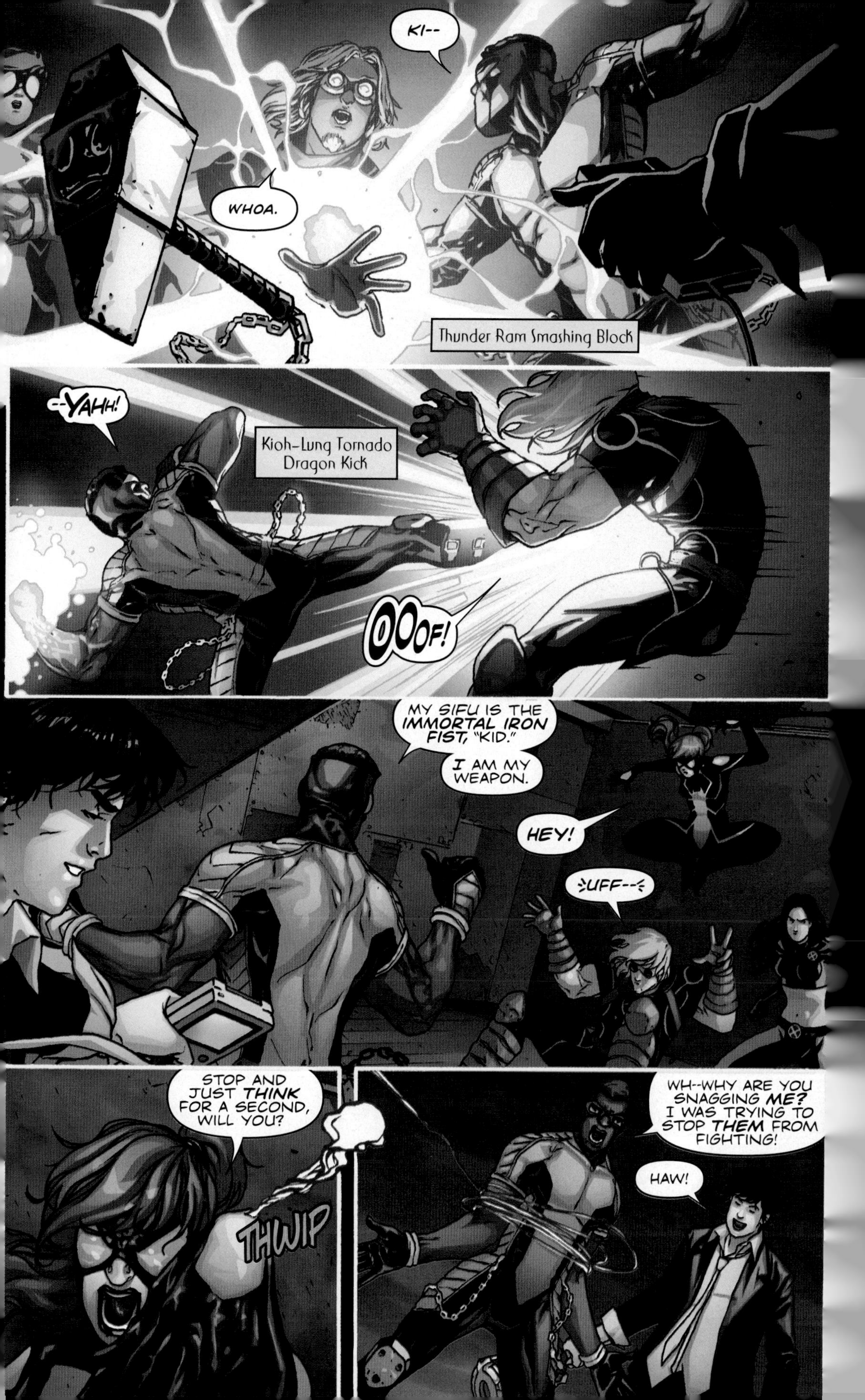

KI--
WHOA.
Thunder Ram Smashing Block
--YAHH!
Kioh-Lung Tornado Dragon Kick
OOOF!
MY SIFU IS THE IMMORTAL IRON FIST, "KID."
I AM MY WEAPON.
HEY!
UFF--
STOP AND JUST THINK FOR A SECOND, WILL YOU?
THWIP
WH--WHY ARE YOU SNAGGING ME? I WAS TRYING TO STOP THEM FROM FIGHTING!
HAW!

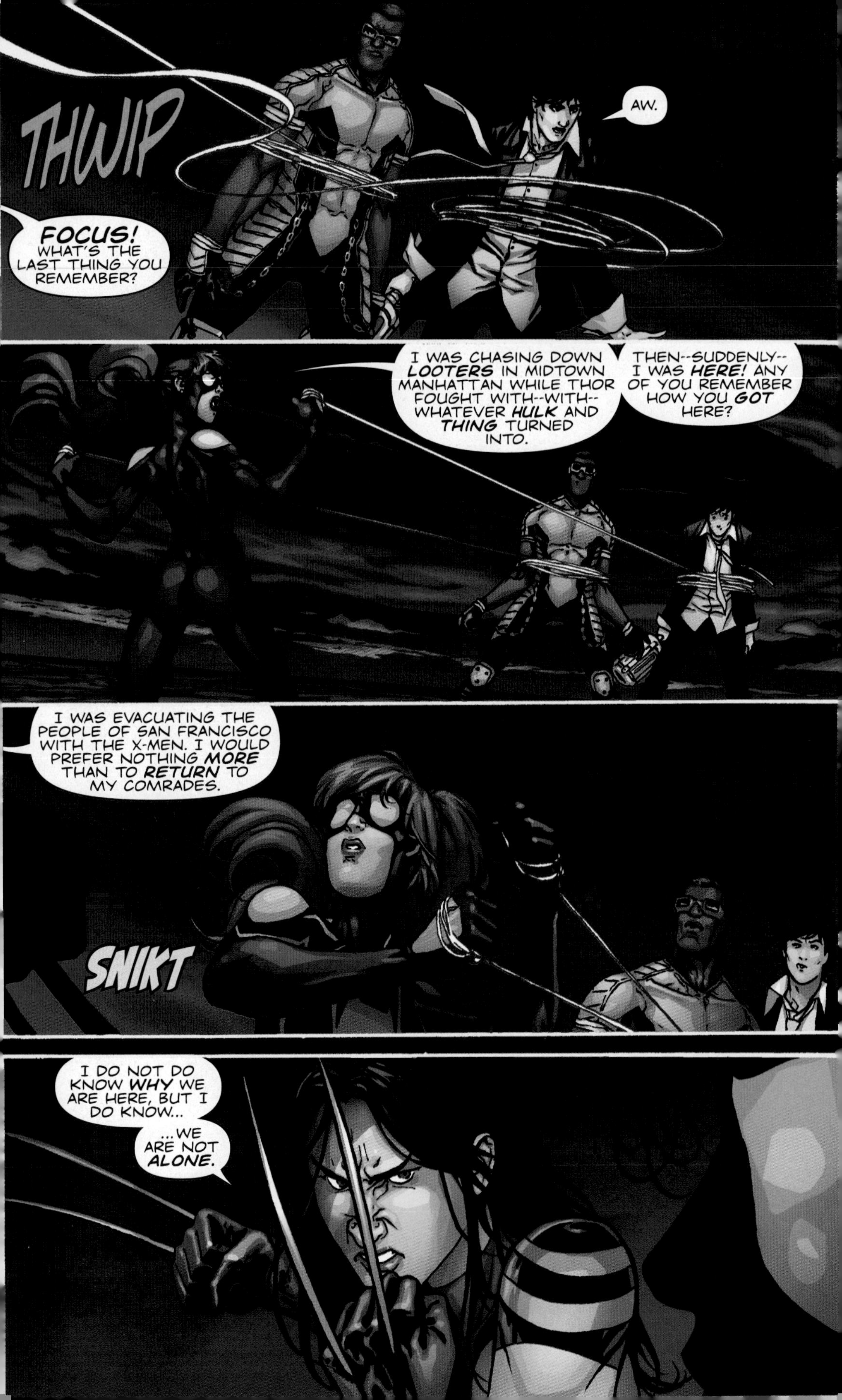
THWIP
AW.
FOCUS! WHAT'S THE LAST THING YOU REMEMBER?
I WAS CHASING DOWN LOOTERS IN MIDTOWN MANHATTAN WHILE THOR FOUGHT WITH--WITH--WHATEVER HULK AND THING TURNED INTO.
THEN--SUDDENLY--I WAS HERE! ANY OF YOU REMEMBER HOW YOU GOT HERE?
I WAS EVACUATING THE PEOPLE OF SAN FRANCISCO WITH THE X-MEN. I WOULD PREFER NOTHING MORE THAN TO RETURN TO MY COMRADES.
SNIKT
I DO NOT DO KNOW WHY WE ARE HERE, BUT I DO KNOW...
...WE ARE NOT ALONE.

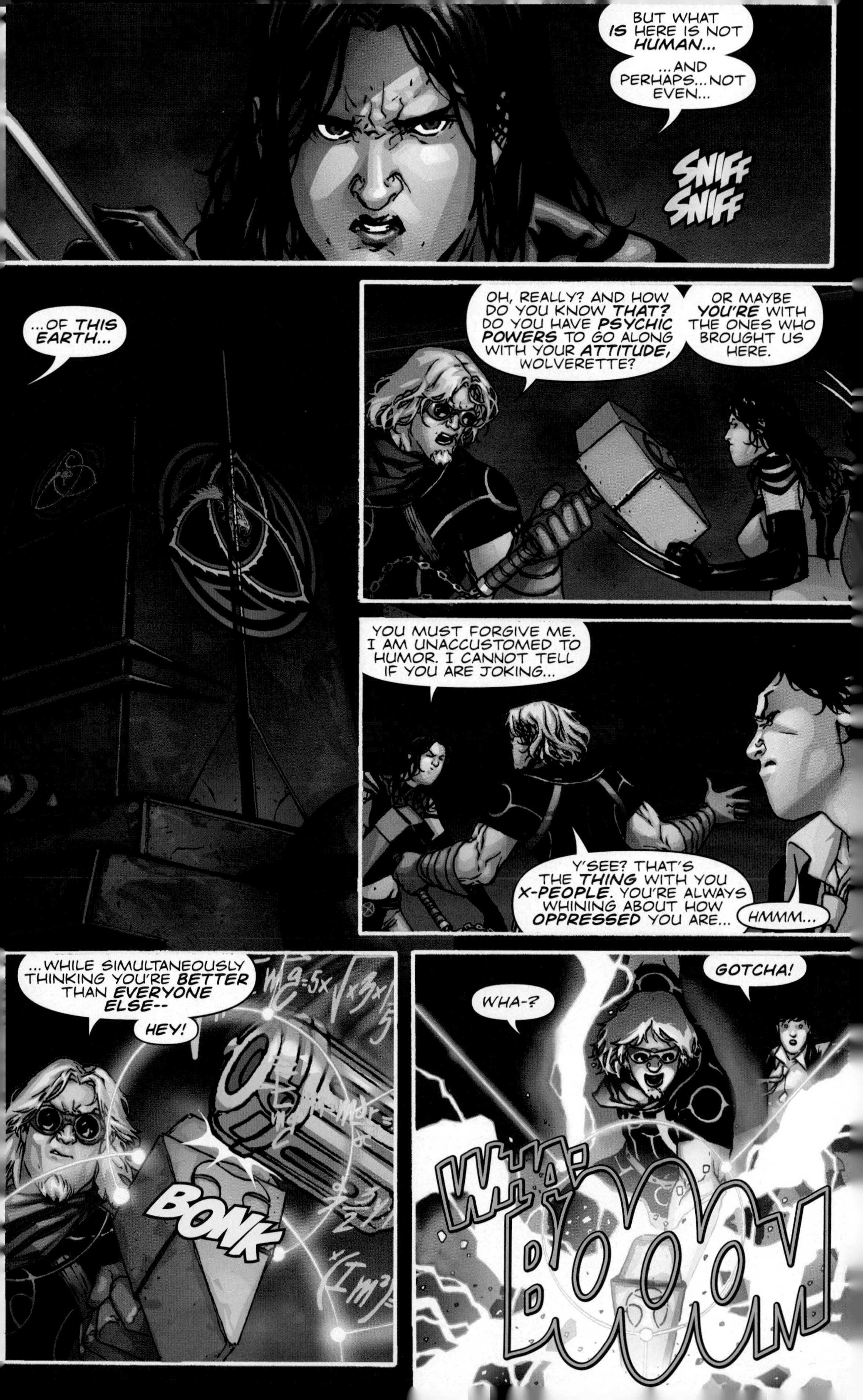
BUT WHAT IS HERE IS NOT HUMAN...
...AND PERHAPS...NOT EVEN...
SNIFF SNIFF
...OF THIS EARTH...
OH, REALLY? AND HOW DO YOU KNOW THAT? DO YOU HAVE PSYCHIC POWERS TO GO ALONG WITH YOUR ATTITUDE, WOLVERETTE?
OR MAYBE YOU'RE WITH THE ONES WHO BROUGHT US HERE.
YOU MUST FORGIVE ME. I AM UNACCUSTOMED TO HUMOR. I CANNOT TELL IF YOU ARE JOKING...
Y'SEE? THAT'S THE THING WITH YOU X-PEOPLE. YOU'RE ALWAYS WHINING ABOUT HOW OPPRESSED YOU ARE...
HMMM...
...WHILE SIMULTANEOUSLY THINKING YOU'RE BETTER THAN EVERYONE ELSE--
HEY!
BONK
WHA-?
GOTCHA!
BOOOOM

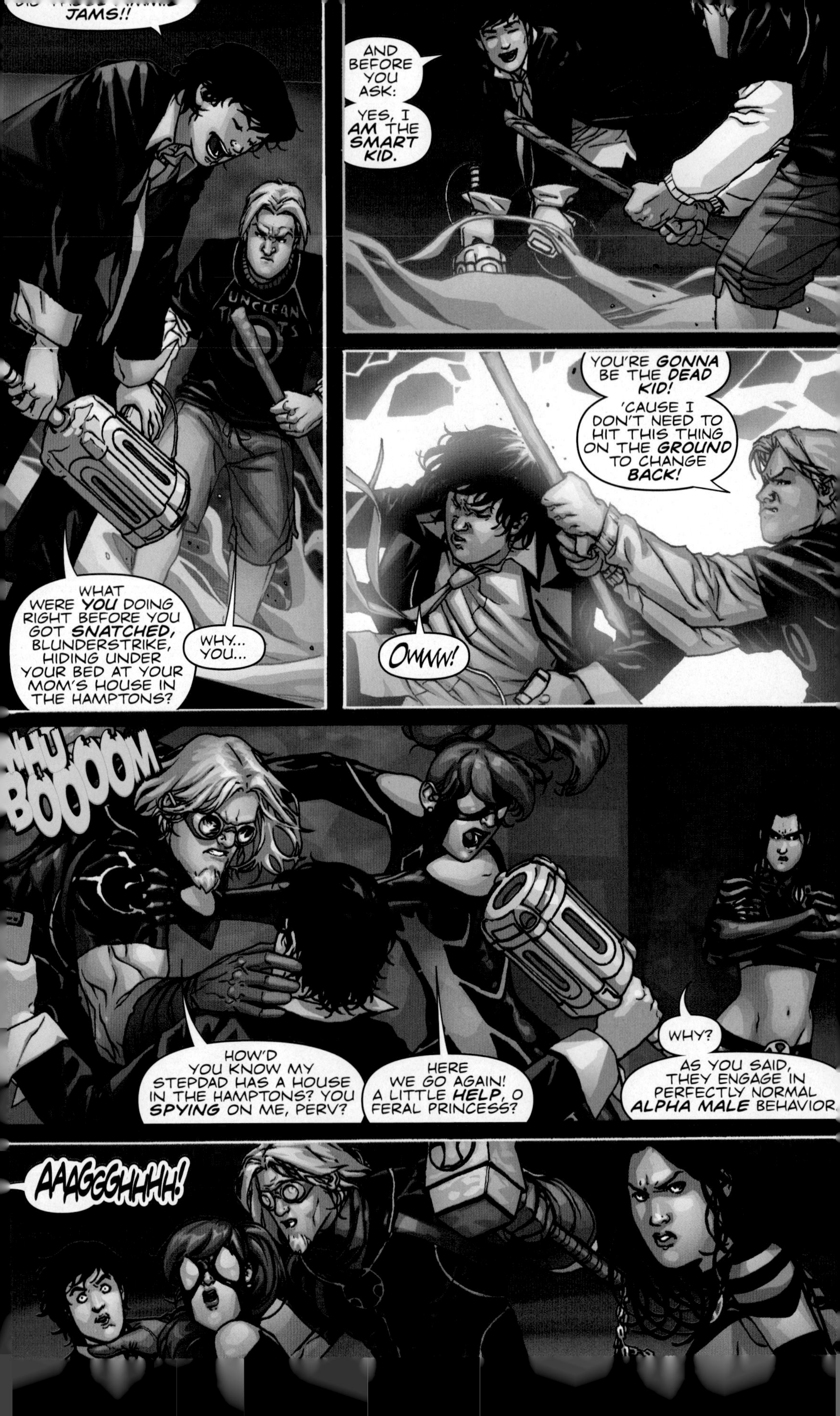
JAMS!!
AND BEFORE YOU ASK:
YES, I AM THE SMART KID.
WHAT WERE YOU DOING RIGHT BEFORE YOU GOT SNATCHED, BLUNDERSTRIKE, HIDING UNDER YOUR BED AT YOUR MOM'S HOUSE IN THE HAMPTONS?
WHY... YOU...
YOU'RE GONNA BE THE DEAD KID!
'CAUSE I DON'T NEED TO HIT THIS THING ON THE GROUND TO CHANGE BACK!
OWWW!
WHU BOOOOM
HOW'D YOU KNOW MY STEPDAD HAS A HOUSE IN THE HAMPTONS? YOU SPYING ON ME, PERV?
HERE WE GO AGAIN! A LITTLE HELP, O FERAL PRINCESS?
WHY?
AS YOU SAID, THEY ENGAGE IN PERFECTLY NORMAL ALPHA MALE BEHAVIOR.
AAAGGGHHHH!

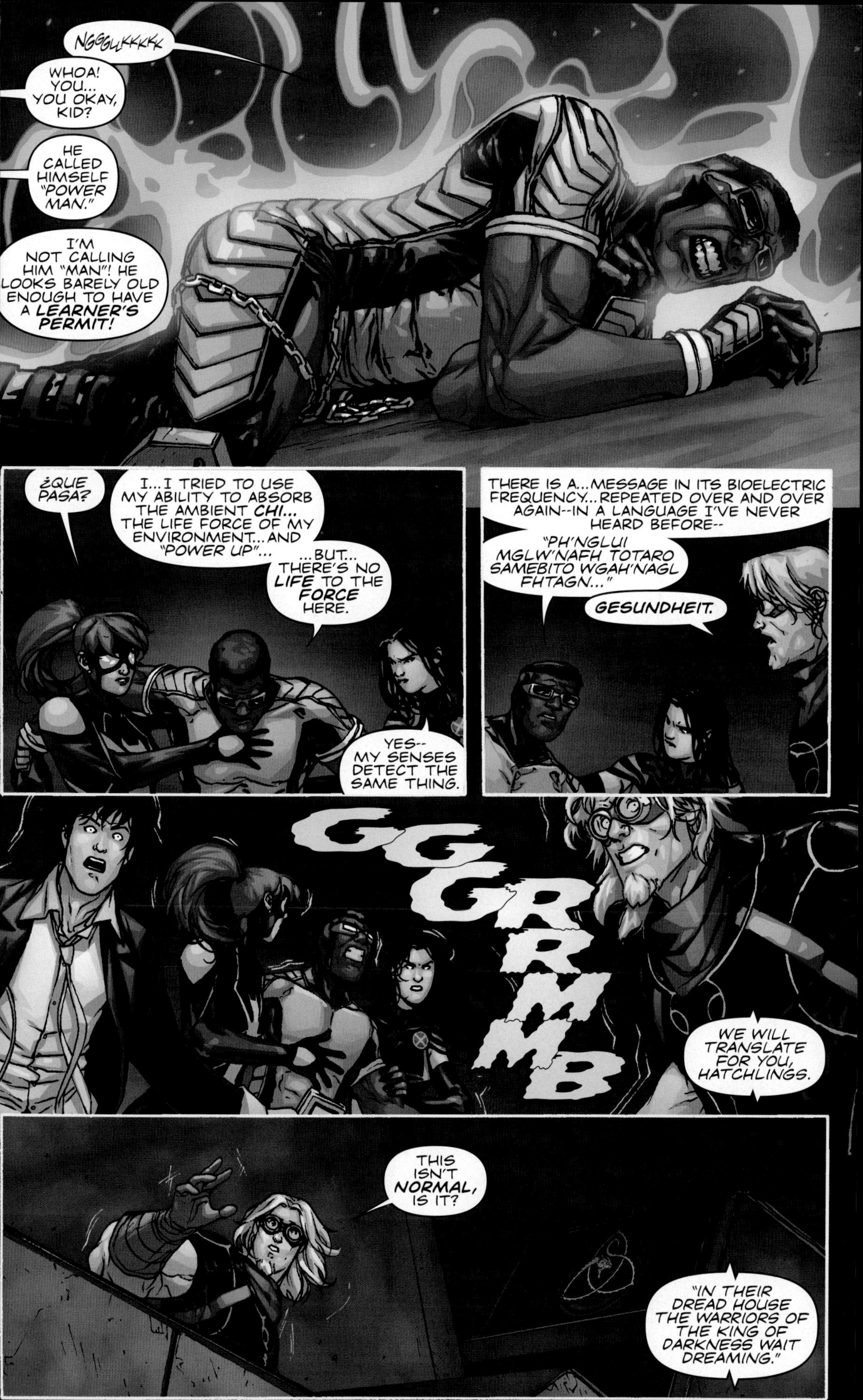
NGGGLLKKKKK
WHOA! YOU... YOU OKAY, KID?
HE CALLED HIMSELF "POWER MAN."
I'M NOT CALLING HIM "MAN"! HE LOOKS BARELY OLD ENOUGH TO HAVE A **LEARNER'S PERMIT!**
¿QUE PASA?
I...I TRIED TO USE MY ABILITY TO ABSORB THE AMBIENT **CHI...** THE LIFE FORCE OF MY ENVIRONMENT...AND "POWER UP"...
...BUT... THERE'S NO **LIFE** TO THE **FORCE** HERE.
YES-- MY SENSES DETECT THE SAME THING.
THERE IS A...MESSAGE IN ITS BIOELECTRIC FREQUENCY...REPEATED OVER AND OVER AGAIN--IN A LANGUAGE I'VE NEVER HEARD BEFORE--
"PH'NGLUI MGLW'NAFH TOTARO SAMEBITO WGAH'NAGL FHTAGN..."
GESUNDHEIT.
GGGRRMMB
WE WILL TRANSLATE FOR YOU, HATCHLINGS.
THIS ISN'T **NORMAL,** IS IT?
"IN THEIR DREAD HOUSE THE WARRIORS OF THE KING OF DARKNESS WAIT DREAMING."

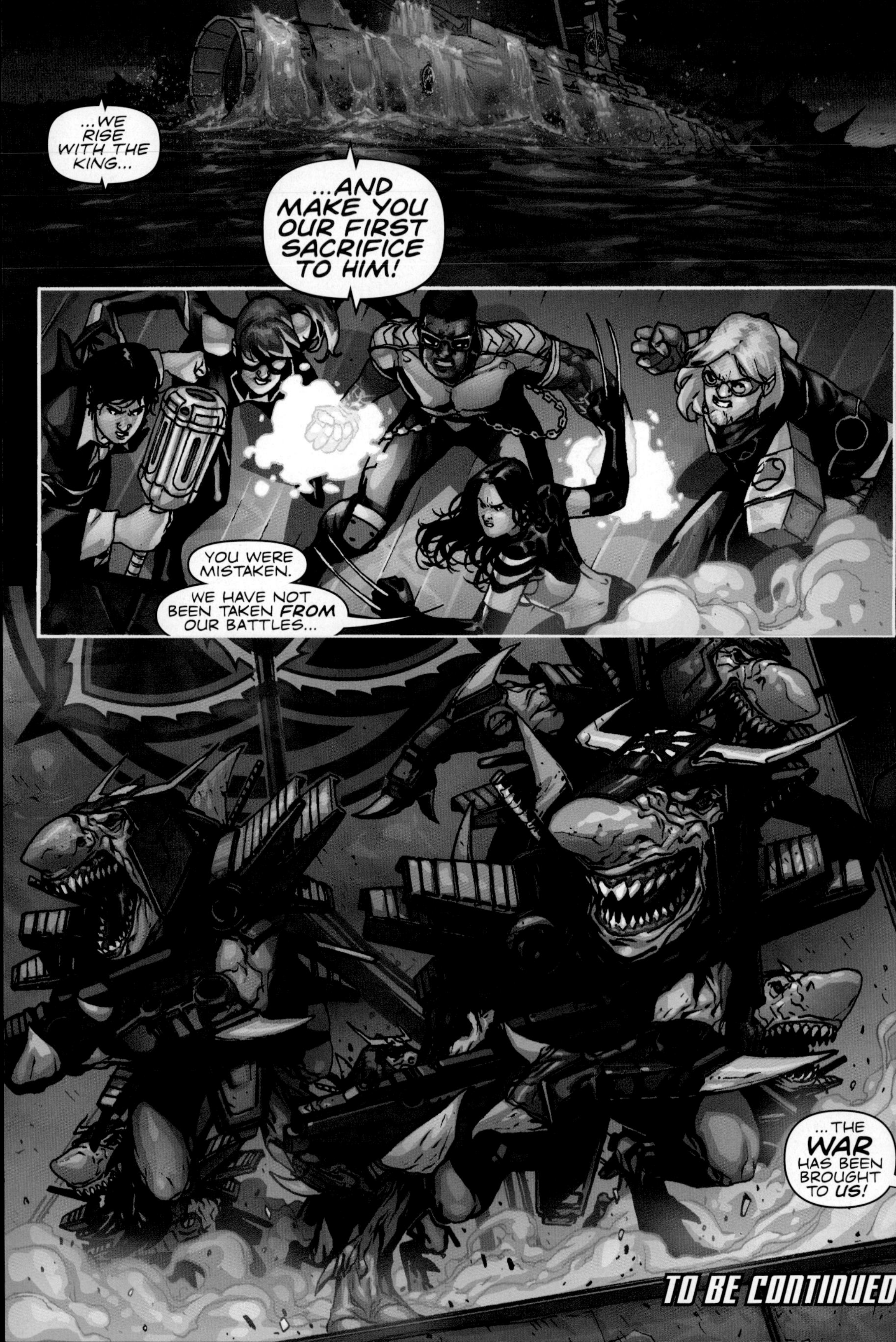
...WE RISE WITH THE KING...
...AND MAKE YOU OUR FIRST SACRIFICE TO HIM!
YOU WERE MISTAKEN.
WE HAVE NOT BEEN TAKEN FROM OUR BATTLES...
...THE WAR HAS BEEN BROUGHT TO US!
TO BE CONTINUED

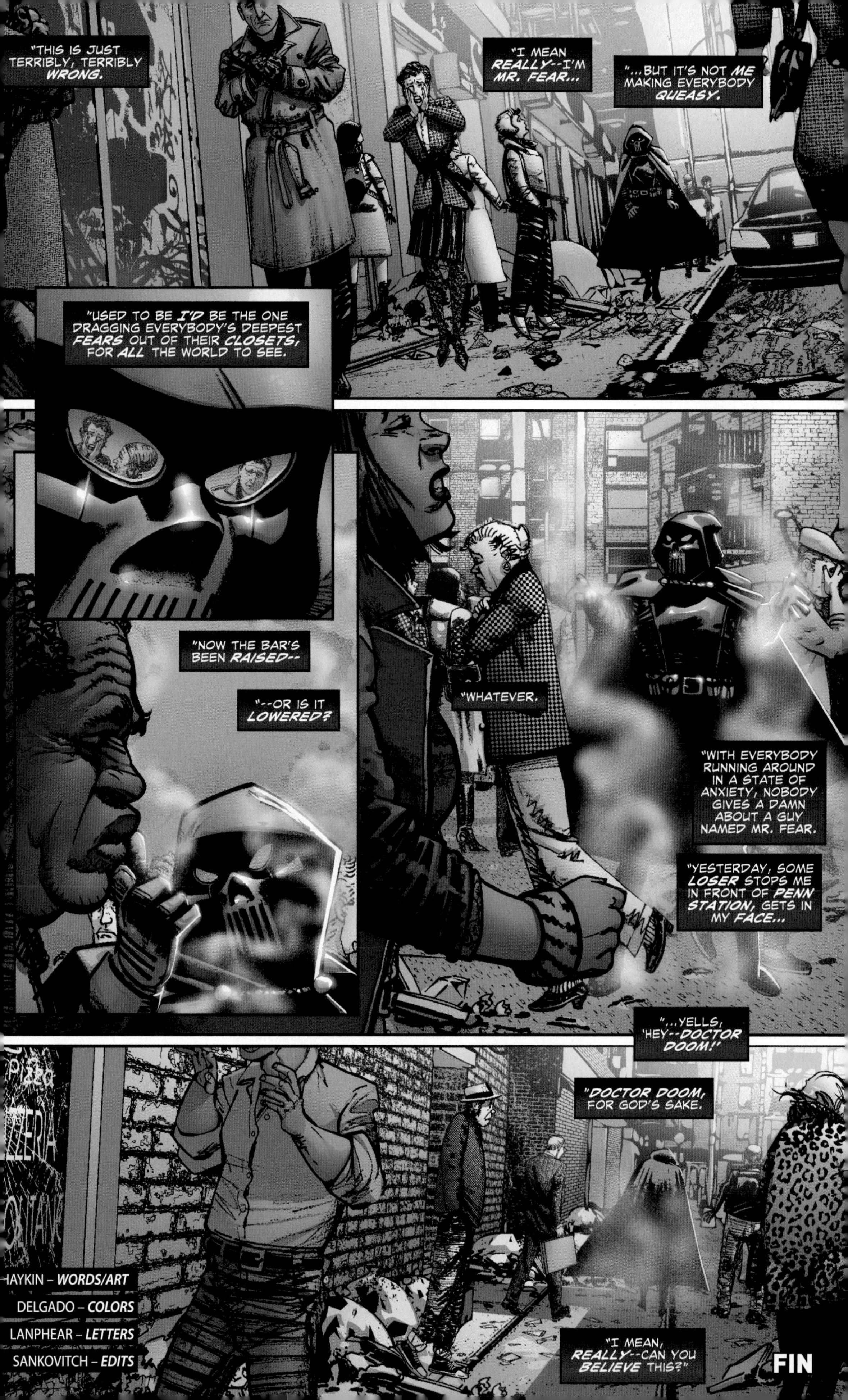
"THIS IS JUST TERRIBLY, TERRIBLY WRONG.
"I MEAN REALLY--I'M MR. FEAR...
"...BUT IT'S NOT ME MAKING EVERYBODY QUEASY.
"USED TO BE I'D BE THE ONE DRAGGING EVERYBODY'S DEEPEST FEARS OUT OF THEIR CLOSETS, FOR ALL THE WORLD TO SEE.
"NOW THE BAR'S BEEN RAISED--
"--OR IS IT LOWERED?
"WHATEVER.
"WITH EVERYBODY RUNNING AROUND IN A STATE OF ANXIETY, NOBODY GIVES A DAMN ABOUT A GUY NAMED MR. FEAR.
"YESTERDAY, SOME LOSER STOPS ME IN FRONT OF PENN STATION, GETS IN MY FACE...
"...YELLS, 'HEY--DOCTOR DOOM!'
"DOCTOR DOOM, FOR GOD'S SAKE.
"I MEAN, REALLY--CAN YOU BELIEVE THIS?"
HAYKIN – WORDS/ART
DELGADO – COLORS
LANPHEAR – LETTERS
SANKOVITCH – EDITS
FIN

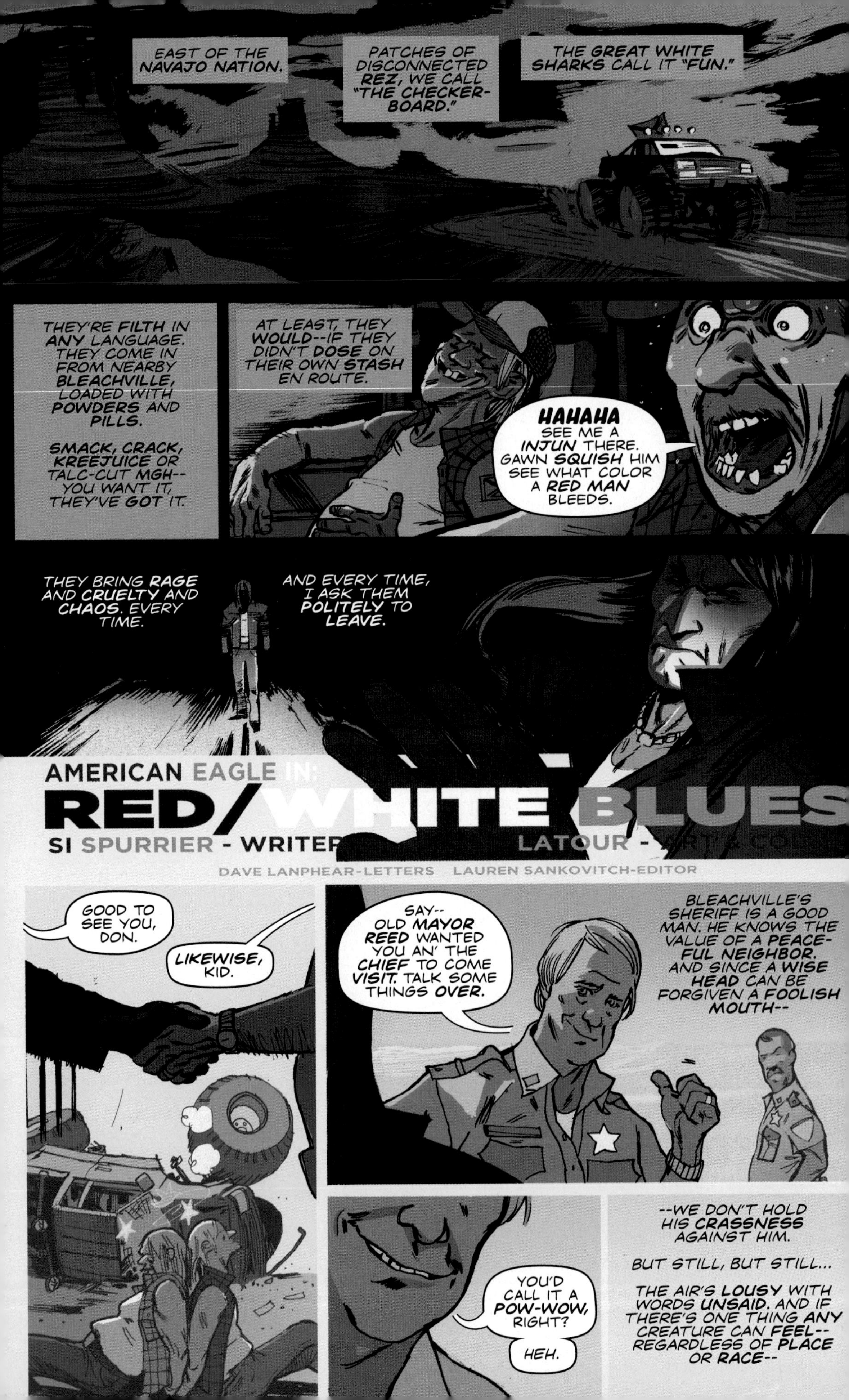
EAST OF THE NAVAJO NATION.
PATCHES OF DISCONNECTED REZ, WE CALL "THE CHECKER-BOARD."
THE GREAT WHITE SHARKS CALL IT "FUN."
THEY'RE FILTH IN ANY LANGUAGE. THEY COME IN FROM NEARBY BLEACHVILLE, LOADED WITH POWDERS AND PILLS.
SMACK, CRACK, KREEJUICE OR TALC-CUT MGH-- YOU WANT IT, THEY'VE GOT IT.
AT LEAST, THEY WOULD--IF THEY DIDN'T DOSE ON THEIR OWN STASH EN ROUTE.
HAHAHA SEE ME A INJUN THERE. GAWN SQUISH HIM SEE WHAT COLOR A RED MAN BLEEDS.
THEY BRING RAGE AND CRUELTY AND CHAOS. EVERY TIME.
AND EVERY TIME, I ASK THEM POLITELY TO LEAVE.
AMERICAN EAGLE IN:
RED/WHITE BLUES
SI SPURRIER - WRITER
LATOUR -
DAVE LANPHEAR-LETTERS LAUREN SANKOVITCH-EDITOR
GOOD TO SEE YOU, DON.
LIKEWISE, KID.
SAY-- OLD MAYOR REED WANTED YOU AN' THE CHIEF TO COME VISIT. TALK SOME THINGS OVER.
BLEACHVILLE'S SHERIFF IS A GOOD MAN. HE KNOWS THE VALUE OF A PEACE-FUL NEIGHBOR. AND SINCE A WISE HEAD CAN BE FORGIVEN A FOOLISH MOUTH--
YOU'D CALL IT A POW-WOW, RIGHT?
HEH.
--WE DON'T HOLD HIS CRASSNESS AGAINST HIM.
BUT STILL, BUT STILL...
THE AIR'S LOUSY WITH WORDS UNSAID. AND IF THERE'S ONE THING ANY CREATURE CAN FEEL-- REGARDLESS OF PLACE OR RACE--

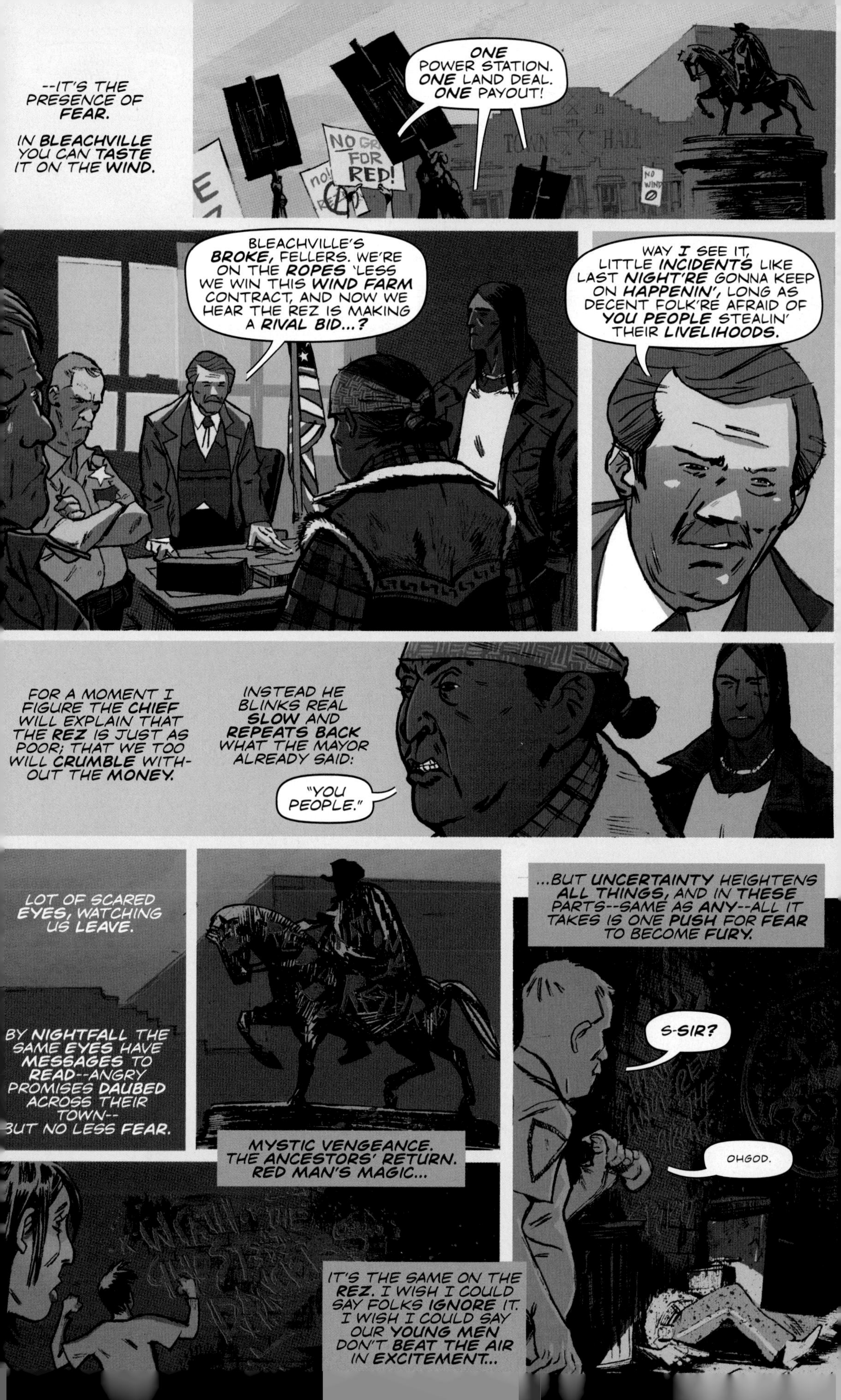
--IT'S THE PRESENCE OF FEAR.
IN BLEACHVILLE YOU CAN TASTE IT ON THE WIND.
ONE POWER STATION. ONE LAND DEAL. ONE PAYOUT!
NO GR FOR RED!
NO WIND
BLEACHVILLE'S BROKE, FELLERS. WE'RE ON THE ROPES 'LESS WE WIN THIS WIND FARM CONTRACT, AND NOW WE HEAR THE REZ IS MAKING A RIVAL BID...?
WAY I SEE IT, LITTLE INCIDENTS LIKE LAST NIGHT'RE GONNA KEEP ON HAPPENIN', LONG AS DECENT FOLK'RE AFRAID OF YOU PEOPLE STEALIN' THEIR LIVELIHOODS.
FOR A MOMENT I FIGURE THE CHIEF WILL EXPLAIN THAT THE REZ IS JUST AS POOR; THAT WE TOO WILL CRUMBLE WITH-OUT THE MONEY.
INSTEAD HE BLINKS REAL SLOW AND REPEATS BACK WHAT THE MAYOR ALREADY SAID:
"YOU PEOPLE."
LOT OF SCARED EYES, WATCHING US LEAVE.
BY NIGHTFALL THE SAME EYES HAVE MESSAGES TO READ--ANGRY PROMISES DAUBED ACROSS THEIR TOWN--
BUT NO LESS FEAR.
MYSTIC VENGEANCE. THE ANCESTORS' RETURN. RED MAN'S MAGIC...
...BUT UNCERTAINTY HEIGHTENS ALL THINGS, AND IN THESE PARTS--SAME AS ANY--ALL IT TAKES IS ONE PUSH FOR FEAR TO BECOME FURY.
S-SIR?
OHGOD.
IT'S THE SAME ON THE REZ. I WISH I COULD SAY FOLKS IGNORE IT. I WISH I COULD SAY OUR YOUNG MEN DON'T BEAT THE AIR IN EXCITEMENT...

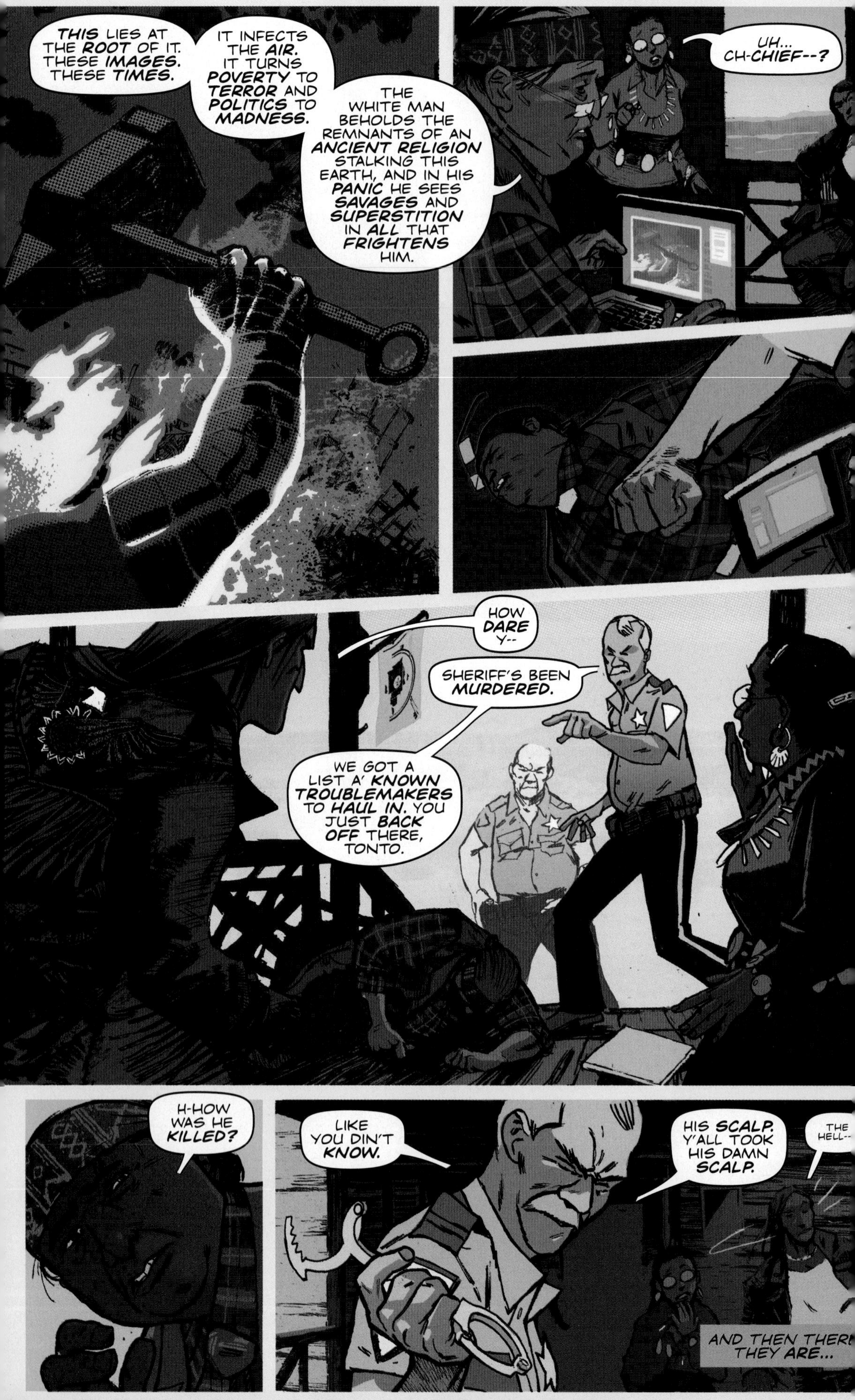

THIS LIES AT THE ROOT OF IT. THESE IMAGES. THESE TIMES.
IT INFECTS THE AIR. IT TURNS POVERTY TO TERROR AND POLITICS TO MADNESS.
THE WHITE MAN BEHOLDS THE REMNANTS OF AN ANCIENT RELIGION STALKING THIS EARTH, AND IN HIS PANIC HE SEES SAVAGES AND SUPERSTITION IN ALL THAT FRIGHTENS HIM.
UH... CH-CHIEF--?
HOW DARE Y--
SHERIFF'S BEEN MURDERED.
WE GOT A LIST A' KNOWN TROUBLEMAKERS TO HAUL IN. YOU JUST BACK OFF THERE, TONTO.
H-HOW WAS HE KILLED?
LIKE YOU DIN'T KNOW.
HIS SCALP. Y'ALL TOOK HIS DAMN SCALP.
THE HELL--
AND THEN THERE THEY ARE...

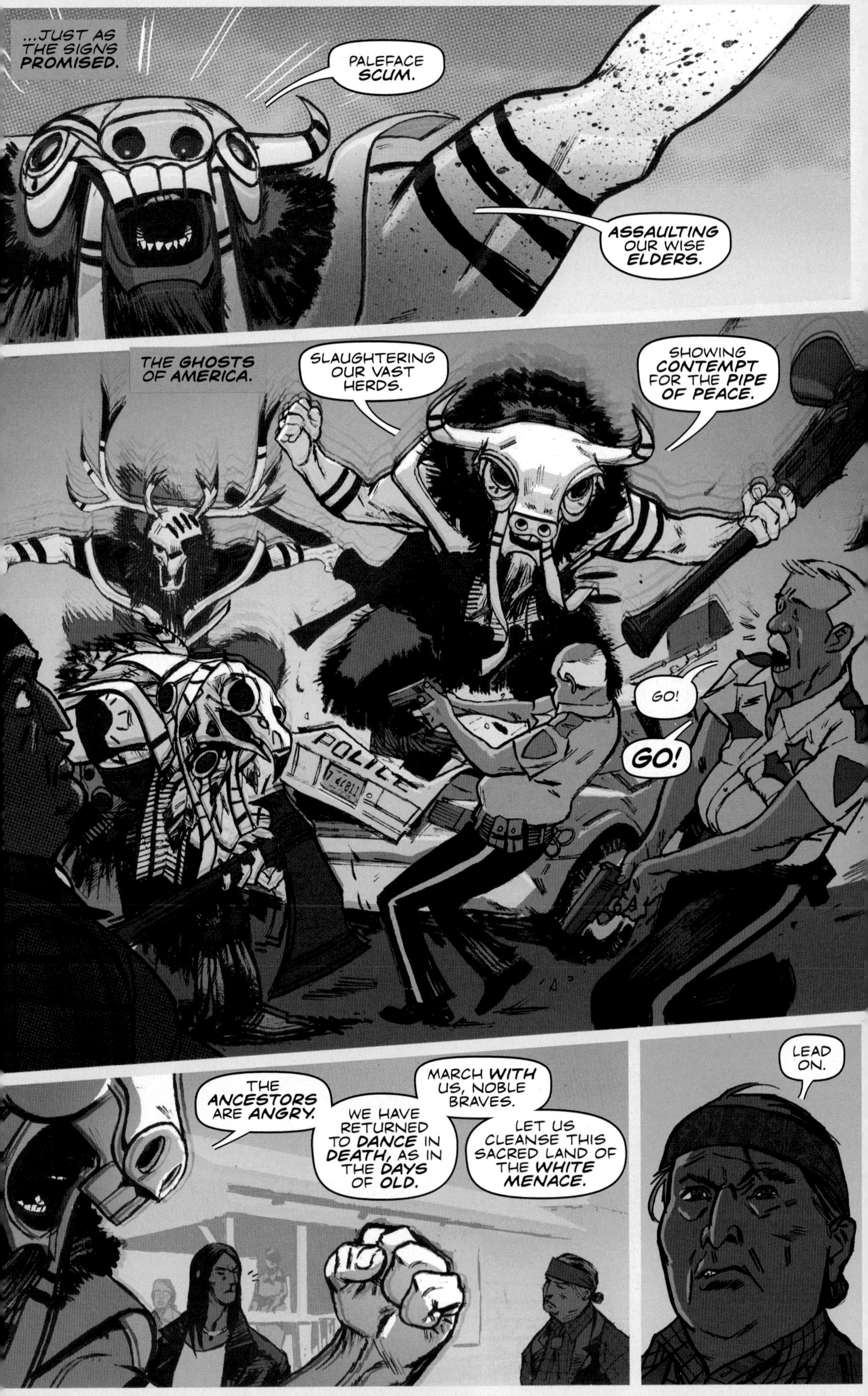
...JUST AS THE SIGNS PROMISED.
PALEFACE SCUM.
ASSAULTING OUR WISE ELDERS.
THE GHOSTS OF AMERICA.
SLAUGHTERING OUR VAST HERDS.
SHOWING CONTEMPT FOR THE PIPE OF PEACE.
POLICE
GO!
GO!
THE ANCESTORS ARE ANGRY.
WE HAVE RETURNED TO DANCE IN DEATH, AS IN THE DAYS OF OLD.
MARCH WITH US, NOBLE BRAVES.
LET US CLEANSE THIS SACRED LAND OF THE WHITE MENACE.
LEAD ON.

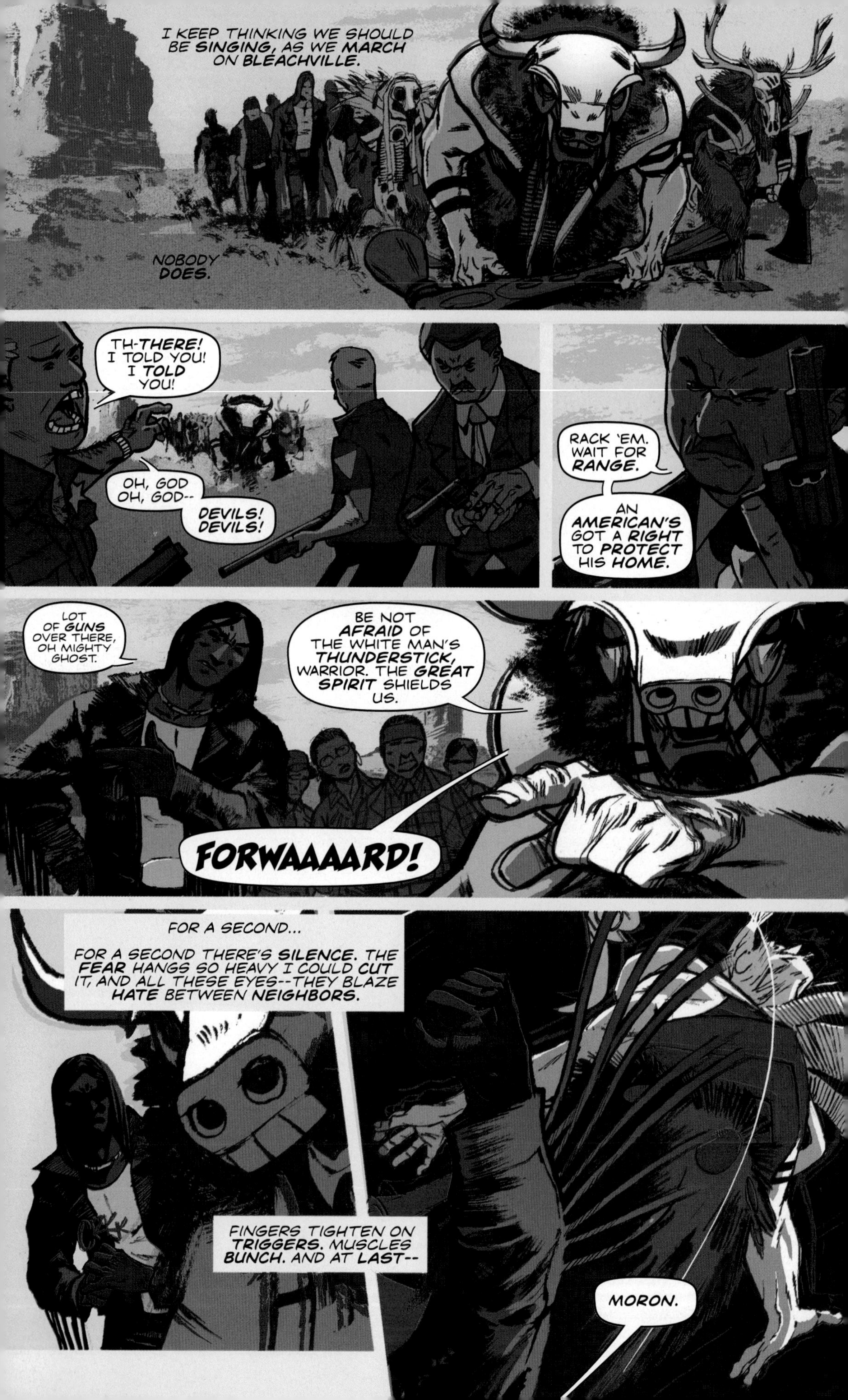
I KEEP THINKING WE SHOULD BE SINGING, AS WE MARCH ON BLEACHVILLE.
NOBODY DOES.
TH-THERE! I TOLD YOU! I TOLD YOU!
OH, GOD OH, GOD--
DEVILS! DEVILS!
RACK 'EM. WAIT FOR RANGE.
AN AMERICAN'S GOT A RIGHT TO PROTECT HIS HOME.
LOT OF GUNS OVER THERE, OH MIGHTY GHOST.
BE NOT AFRAID OF THE WHITE MAN'S THUNDERSTICK, WARRIOR. THE GREAT SPIRIT SHIELDS US.
FORWAAAARD!
FOR A SECOND...
FOR A SECOND THERE'S SILENCE. THE FEAR HANGS SO HEAVY I COULD CUT IT, AND ALL THESE EYES--THEY BLAZE HATE BETWEEN NEIGHBORS.
FINGERS TIGHTEN ON TRIGGERS. MUSCLES BUNCH. AND AT LAST--
MORON.

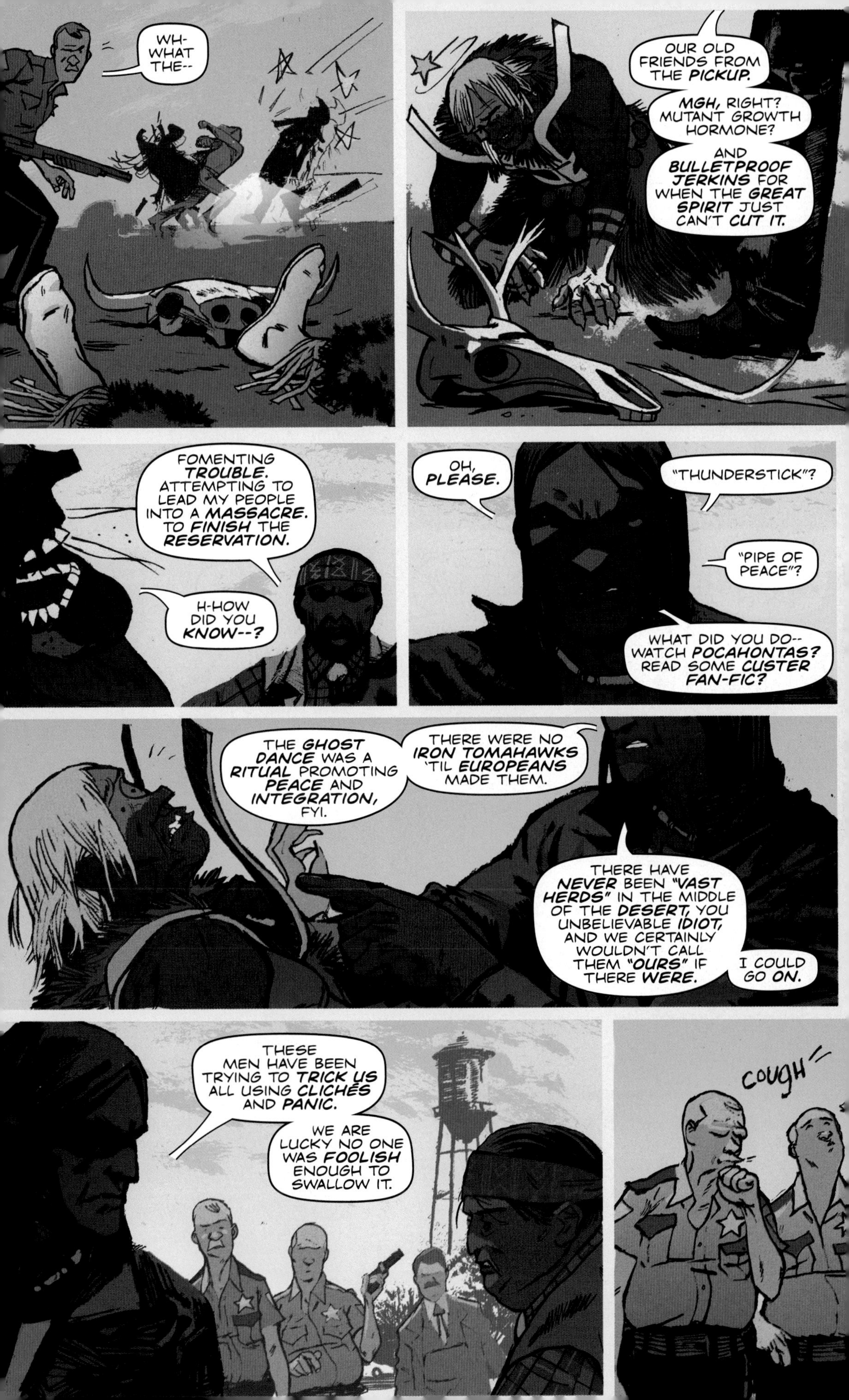
WH-WHAT THE--
OUR OLD FRIENDS FROM THE PICKUP.
MGH, RIGHT? MUTANT GROWTH HORMONE?
AND BULLETPROOF JERKINS FOR WHEN THE GREAT SPIRIT JUST CAN'T CUT IT.
FOMENTING TROUBLE. ATTEMPTING TO LEAD MY PEOPLE INTO A MASSACRE. TO FINISH THE RESERVATION.
H-HOW DID YOU KNOW--?
OH, PLEASE.
"THUNDERSTICK"?
"PIPE OF PEACE"?
WHAT DID YOU DO--WATCH POCAHONTAS? READ SOME CUSTER FAN-FIC?
THE GHOST DANCE WAS A RITUAL PROMOTING PEACE AND INTEGRATION, FYI.
THERE WERE NO IRON TOMAHAWKS 'TIL EUROPEANS MADE THEM.
THERE HAVE NEVER BEEN "VAST HERDS" IN THE MIDDLE OF THE DESERT, YOU UNBELIEVABLE IDIOT, AND WE CERTAINLY WOULDN'T CALL THEM "OURS" IF THERE WERE.
I COULD GO ON.
THESE MEN HAVE BEEN TRYING TO TRICK US ALL USING CLICHÉS AND PANIC.
WE ARE LUCKY NO ONE WAS FOOLISH ENOUGH TO SWALLOW IT.
COUGH

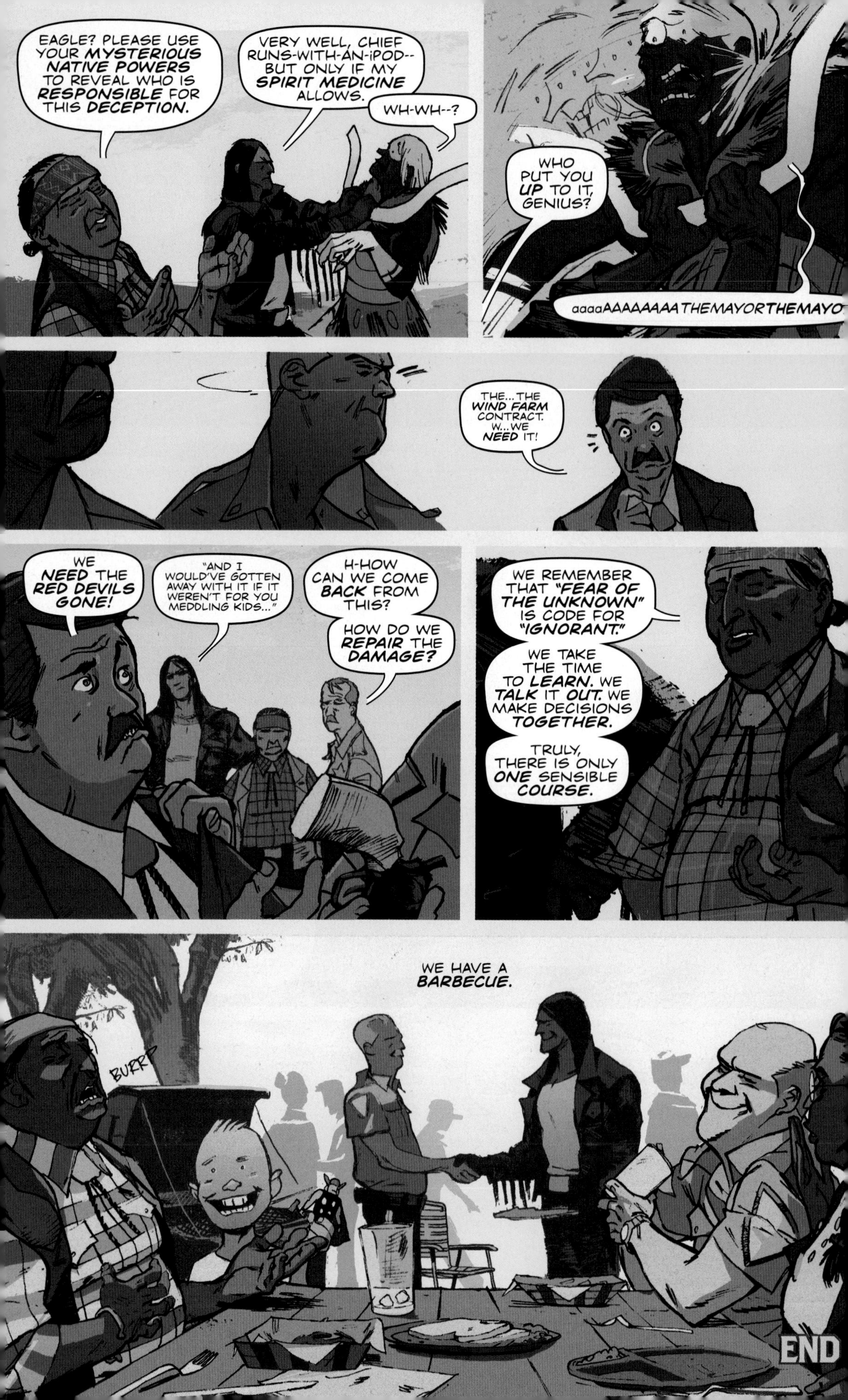
EAGLE? PLEASE USE YOUR MYSTERIOUS NATIVE POWERS TO REVEAL WHO IS RESPONSIBLE FOR THIS DECEPTION.
VERY WELL, CHIEF RUNS-WITH-AN-iPOD-- BUT ONLY IF MY SPIRIT MEDICINE ALLOWS.
WH-WH--?
WHO PUT YOU UP TO IT, GENIUS?
aaaaAAAAAAAATHEMAYORTHEMAYO
THE...THE WIND FARM CONTRACT. W...WE NEED IT!
WE NEED THE RED DEVILS GONE!
"AND I WOULD'VE GOTTEN AWAY WITH IT IF IT WEREN'T FOR YOU MEDDLING KIDS..."
H-HOW CAN WE COME BACK FROM THIS?
HOW DO WE REPAIR THE DAMAGE?
WE REMEMBER THAT "FEAR OF THE UNKNOWN" IS CODE FOR "IGNORANT."
WE TAKE THE TIME TO LEARN. WE TALK IT OUT. WE MAKE DECISIONS TOGETHER.
TRULY, THERE IS ONLY ONE SENSIBLE COURSE.
WE HAVE A BARBECUE.
BURRP
END

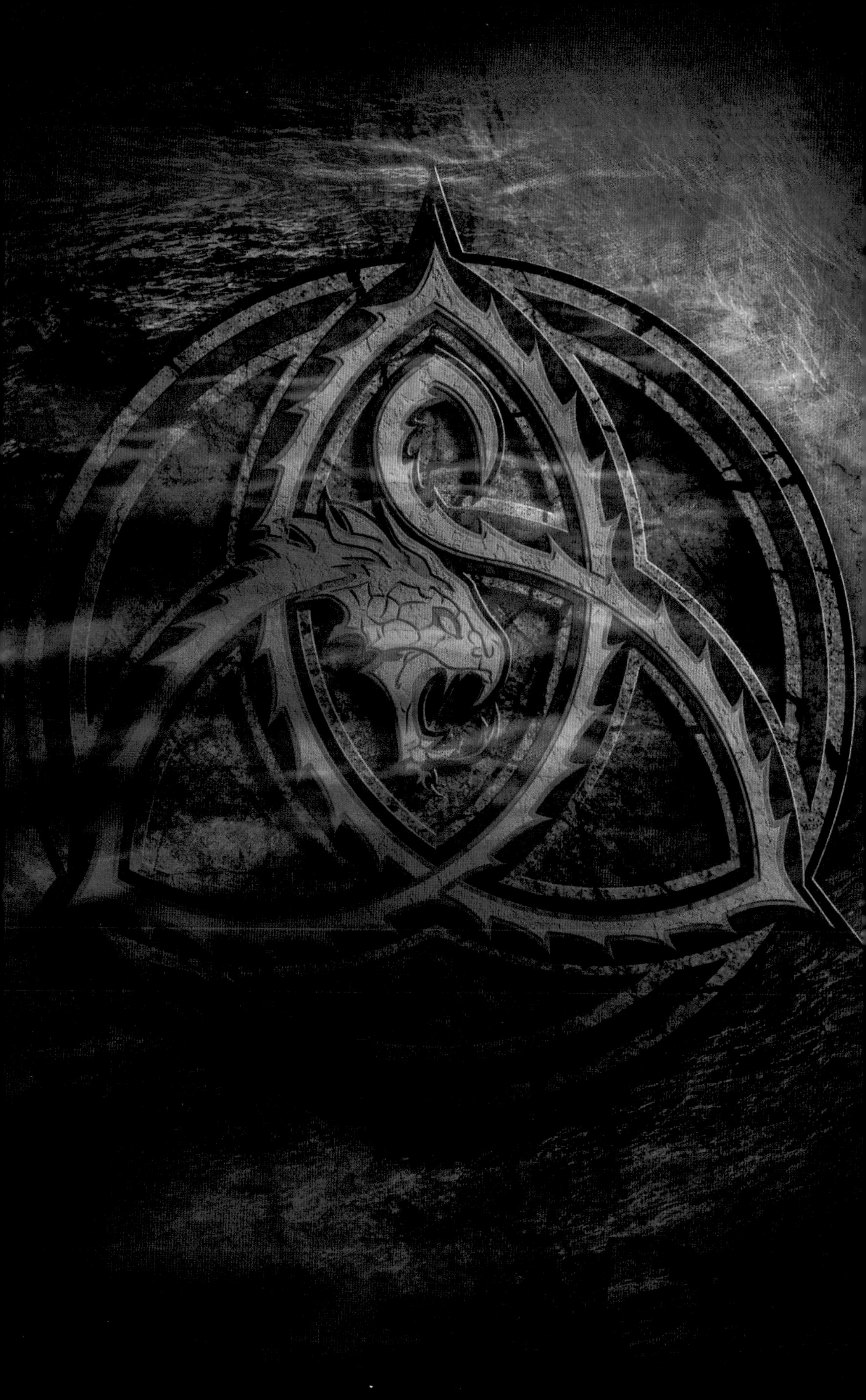

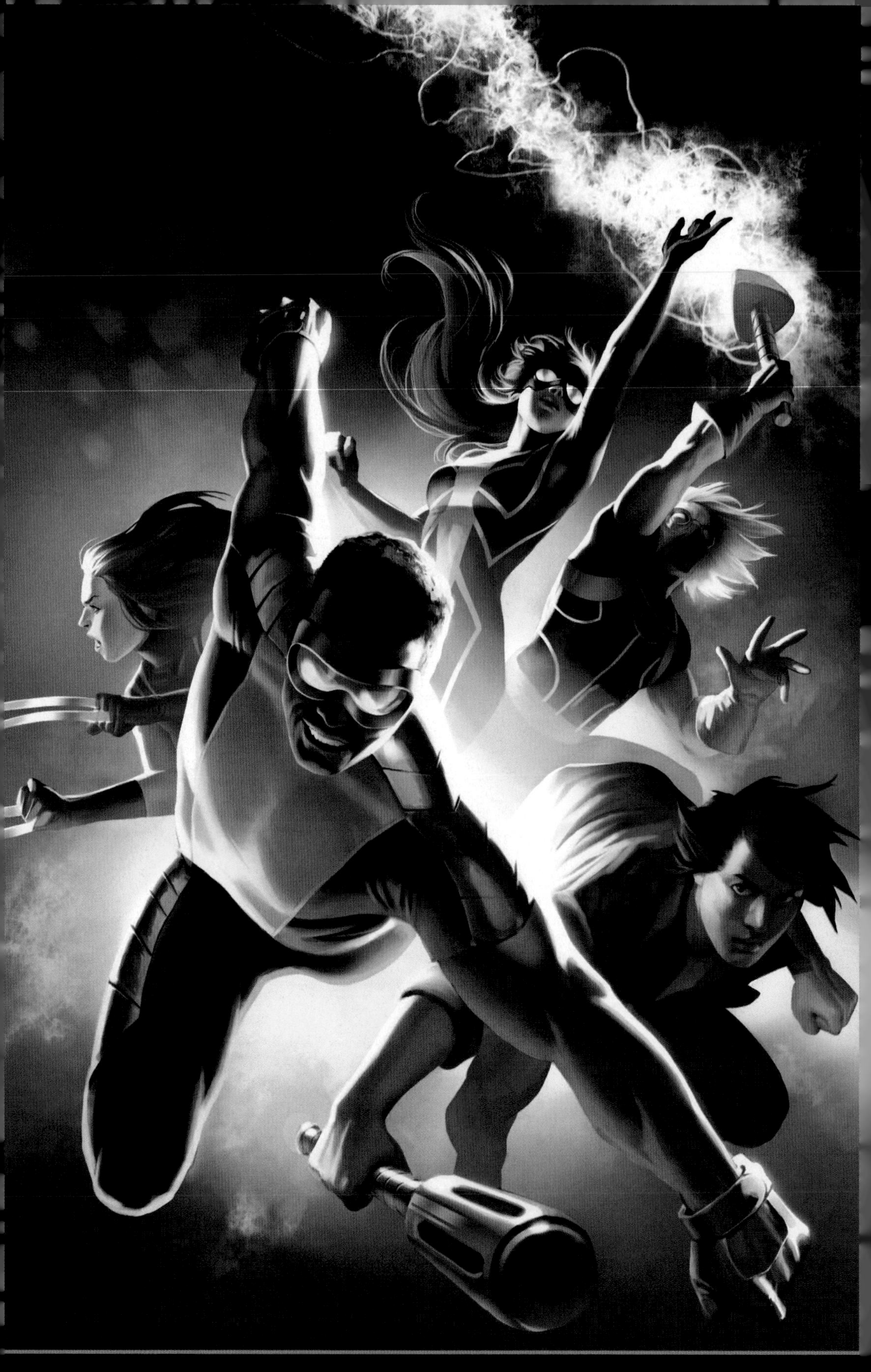

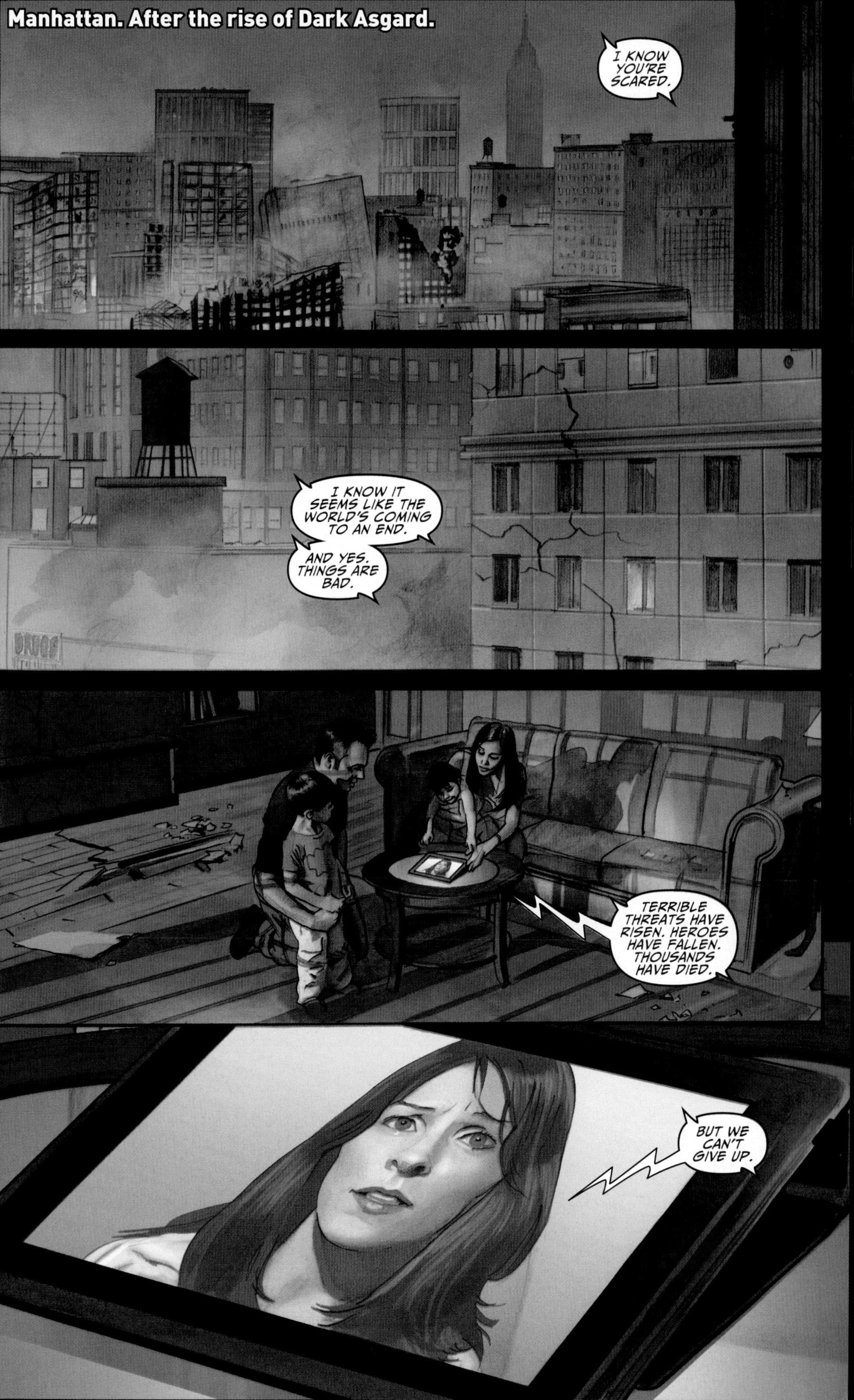
Manhattan. After the rise of Dark Asgard.
I KNOW YOU'RE SCARED.
I KNOW IT SEEMS LIKE THE WORLD'S COMING TO AN END.
AND YES. THINGS ARE BAD.
TERRIBLE THREATS HAVE RISEN. HEROES HAVE FALLEN. THOUSANDS HAVE DIED.
BUT WE CAN'T GIVE UP.

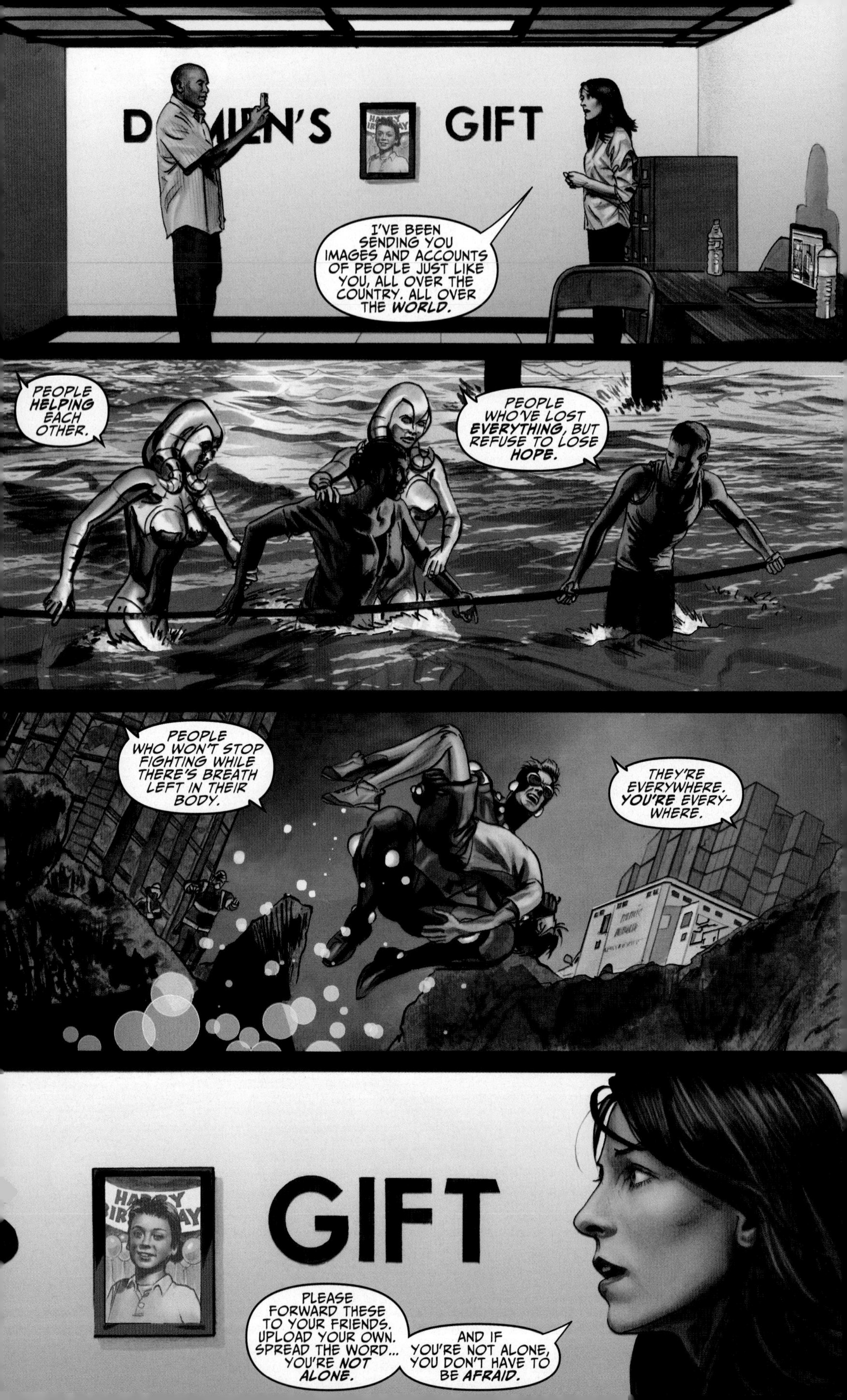
GIFT
I'VE BEEN SENDING YOU IMAGES AND ACCOUNTS OF PEOPLE JUST LIKE YOU, ALL OVER THE COUNTRY. ALL OVER THE WORLD.
PEOPLE HELPING EACH OTHER.
PEOPLE WHO'VE LOST EVERYTHING, BUT REFUSE TO LOSE HOPE.
PEOPLE WHO WON'T STOP FIGHTING WHILE THERE'S BREATH LEFT IN THEIR BODY.
THEY'RE EVERYWHERE. YOU'RE EVERYWHERE.
GIFT
PLEASE FORWARD THESE TO YOUR FRIENDS. UPLOAD YOUR OWN. SPREAD THE WORD... YOU'RE NOT ALONE.
AND IF YOU'RE NOT ALONE, YOU DON'T HAVE TO BE AFRAID.

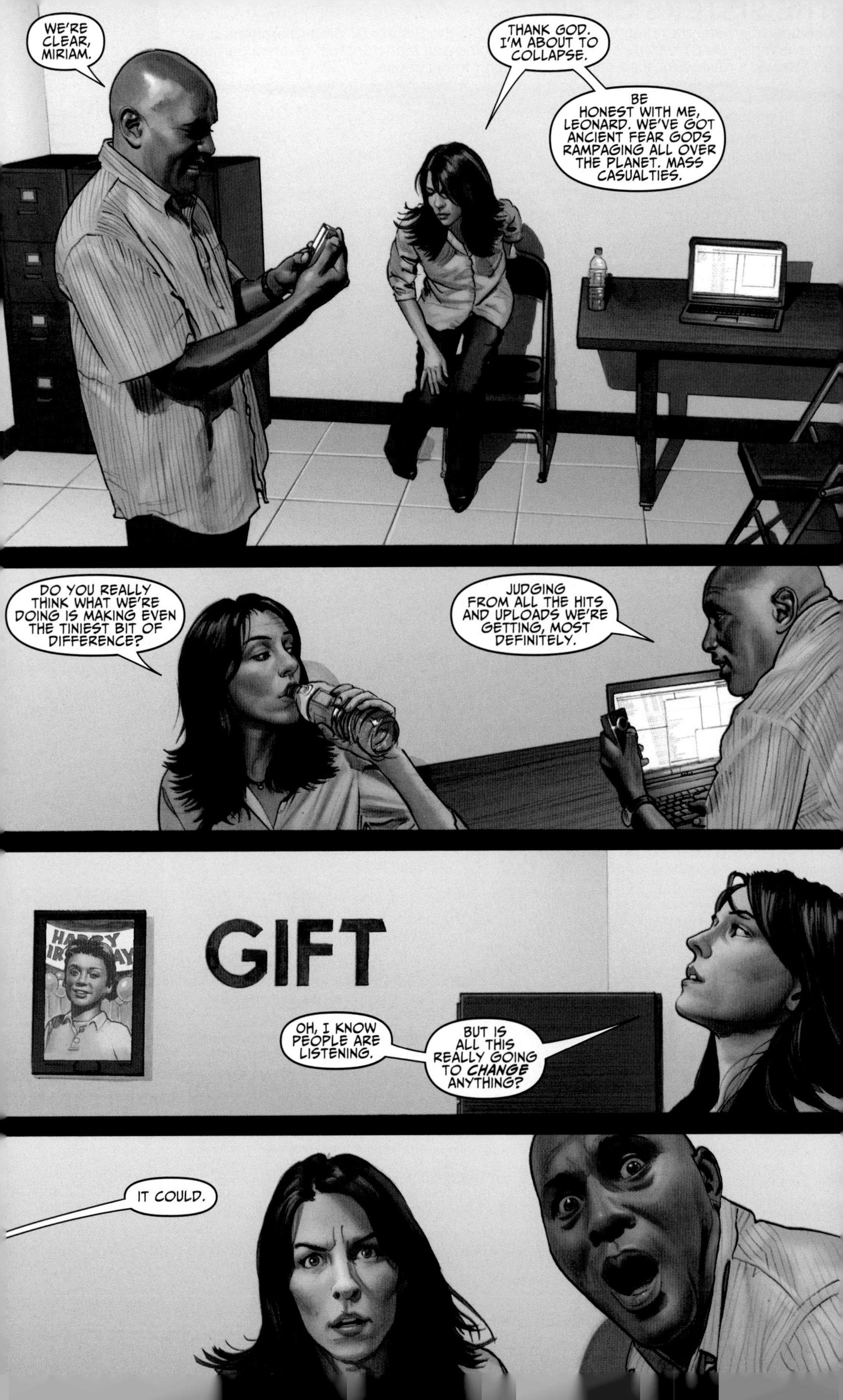
WE'RE CLEAR, MIRIAM.
THANK GOD. I'M ABOUT TO COLLAPSE.
BE HONEST WITH ME, LEONARD. WE'VE GOT ANCIENT FEAR GODS RAMPAGING ALL OVER THE PLANET. MASS CASUALTIES.
DO YOU REALLY THINK WHAT WE'RE DOING IS MAKING EVEN THE TINIEST BIT OF DIFFERENCE?
JUDGING FROM ALL THE HITS AND UPLOADS WE'RE GETTING, MOST DEFINITELY.
GIFT
OH, I KNOW PEOPLE ARE LISTENING.
BUT IS ALL THIS REALLY GOING TO *CHANGE* ANYTHING?
IT COULD.

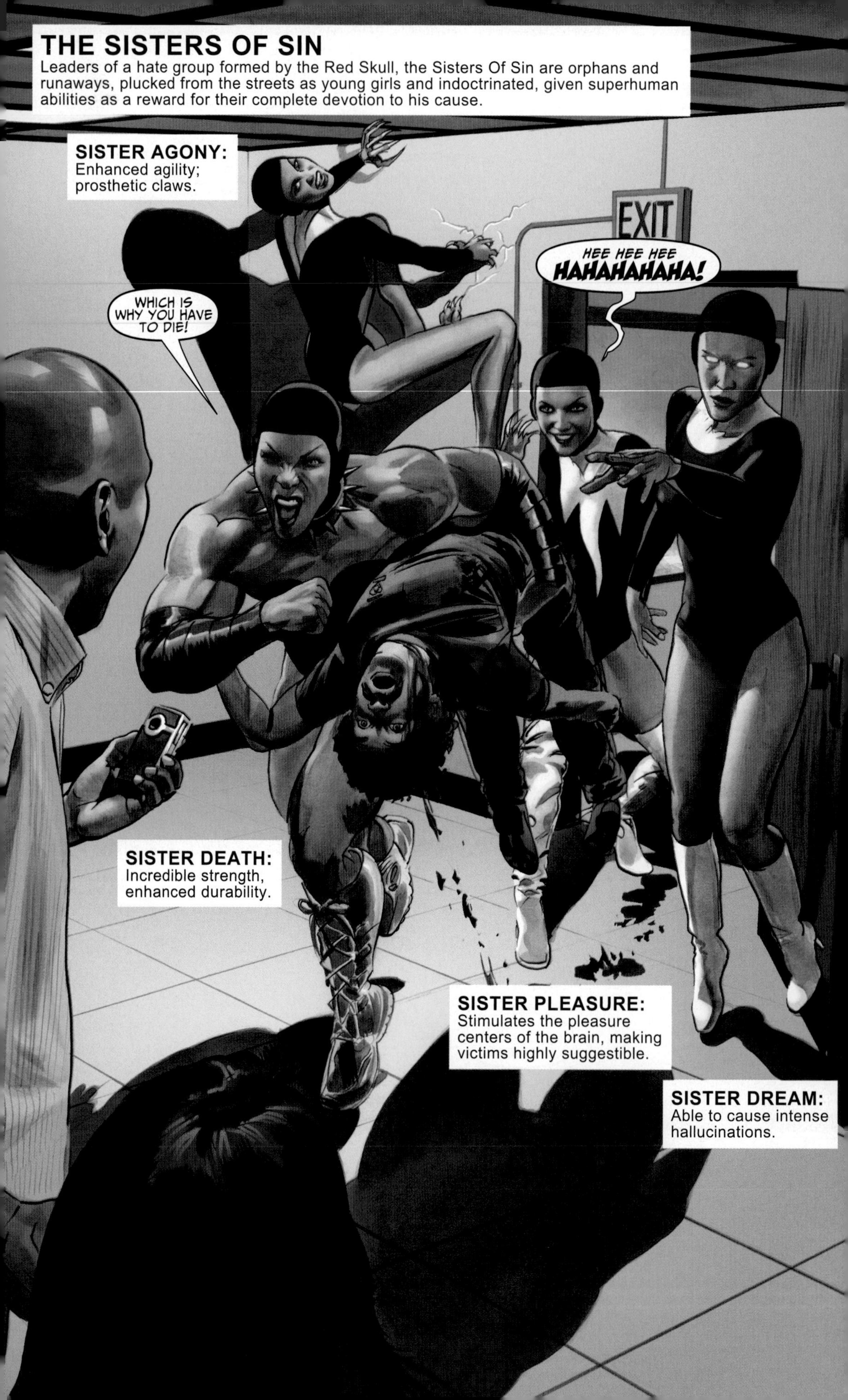
THE SISTERS OF SIN
Leaders of a hate group formed by the Red Skull, the Sisters Of Sin are orphans and runaways, plucked from the streets as young girls and indoctrinated, given superhuman abilities as a reward for their complete devotion to his cause.
SISTER AGONY: Enhanced agility; prosthetic claws.
EXIT
HEE HEE HEE HAHAHAHAHA!
WHICH IS WHY YOU HAVE TO DIE!
SISTER DEATH: Incredible strength, enhanced durability.
SISTER PLEASURE: Stimulates the pleasure centers of the brain, making victims highly suggestible.
SISTER DREAM: Able to cause intense hallucinations.

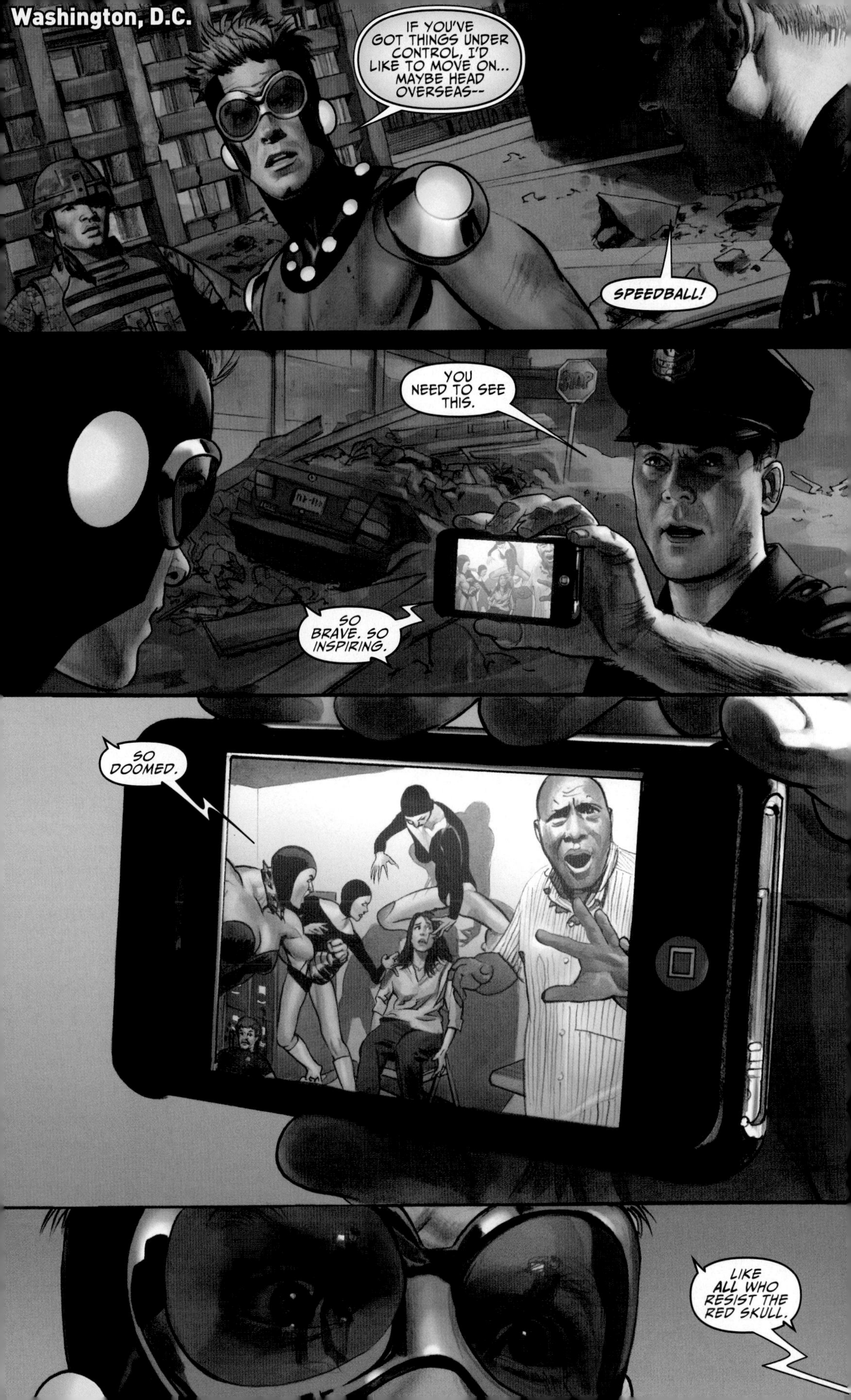
Washington, D.C.
IF YOU'VE GOT THINGS UNDER CONTROL, I'D LIKE TO MOVE ON... MAYBE HEAD OVERSEAS--
SPEEDBALL!
YOU NEED TO SEE THIS.
SO BRAVE. SO INSPIRING.
SO DOOMED.
LIKE ALL WHO RESIST THE RED SKULL.

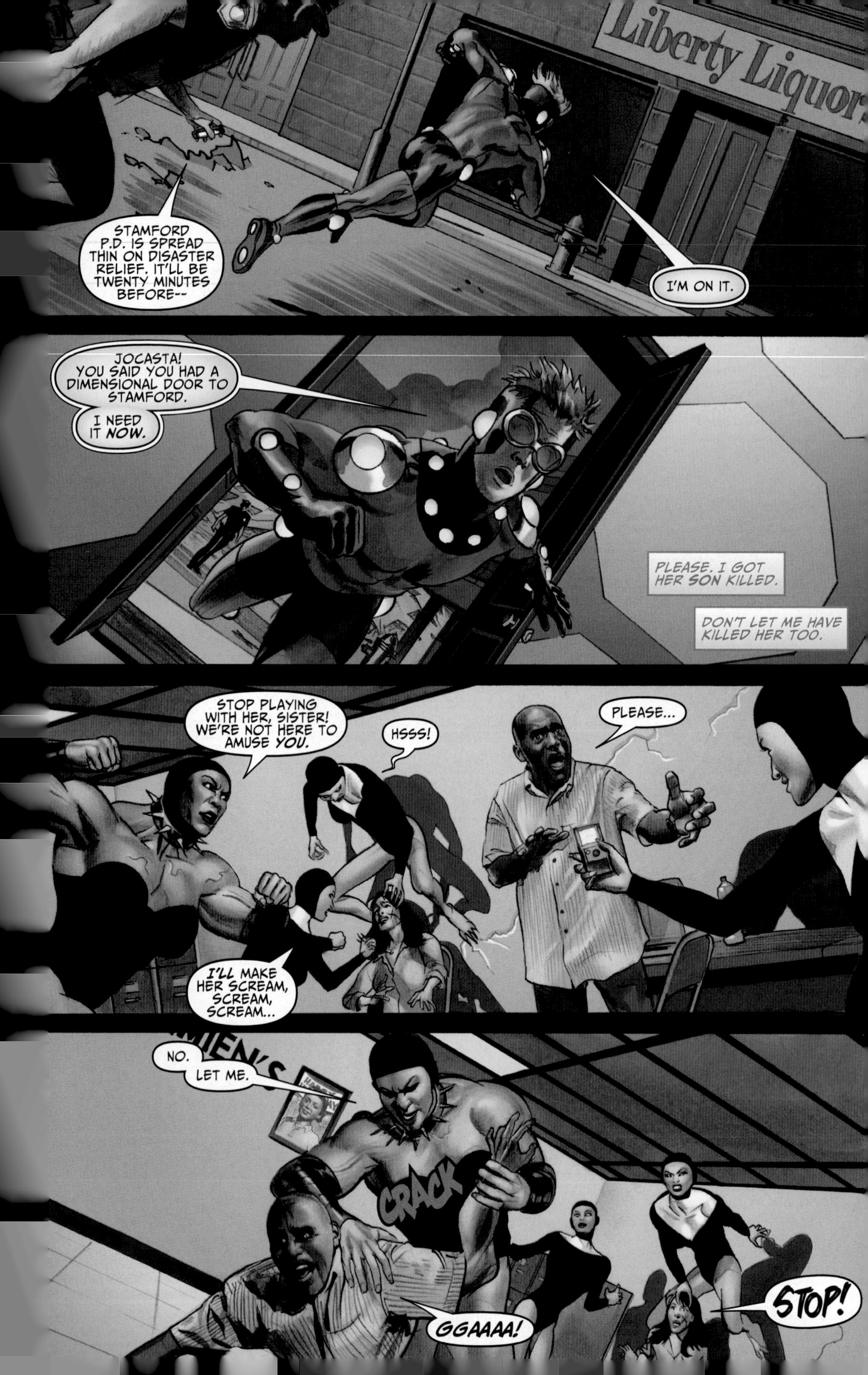
Liberty Liquor
STAMFORD P.D. IS SPREAD THIN ON DISASTER RELIEF. IT'LL BE TWENTY MINUTES BEFORE--
I'M ON IT.
JOCASTA! YOU SAID YOU HAD A DIMENSIONAL DOOR TO STAMFORD.
I NEED IT NOW.
PLEASE. I GOT HER SON KILLED.
DON'T LET ME HAVE KILLED HER TOO.
STOP PLAYING WITH HER, SISTER! WE'RE NOT HERE TO AMUSE YOU.
HSSS!
PLEASE...
I'LL MAKE HER SCREAM, SCREAM, SCREAM...
NO.
LET ME.
CRACK
GGAAAA!
STOP!

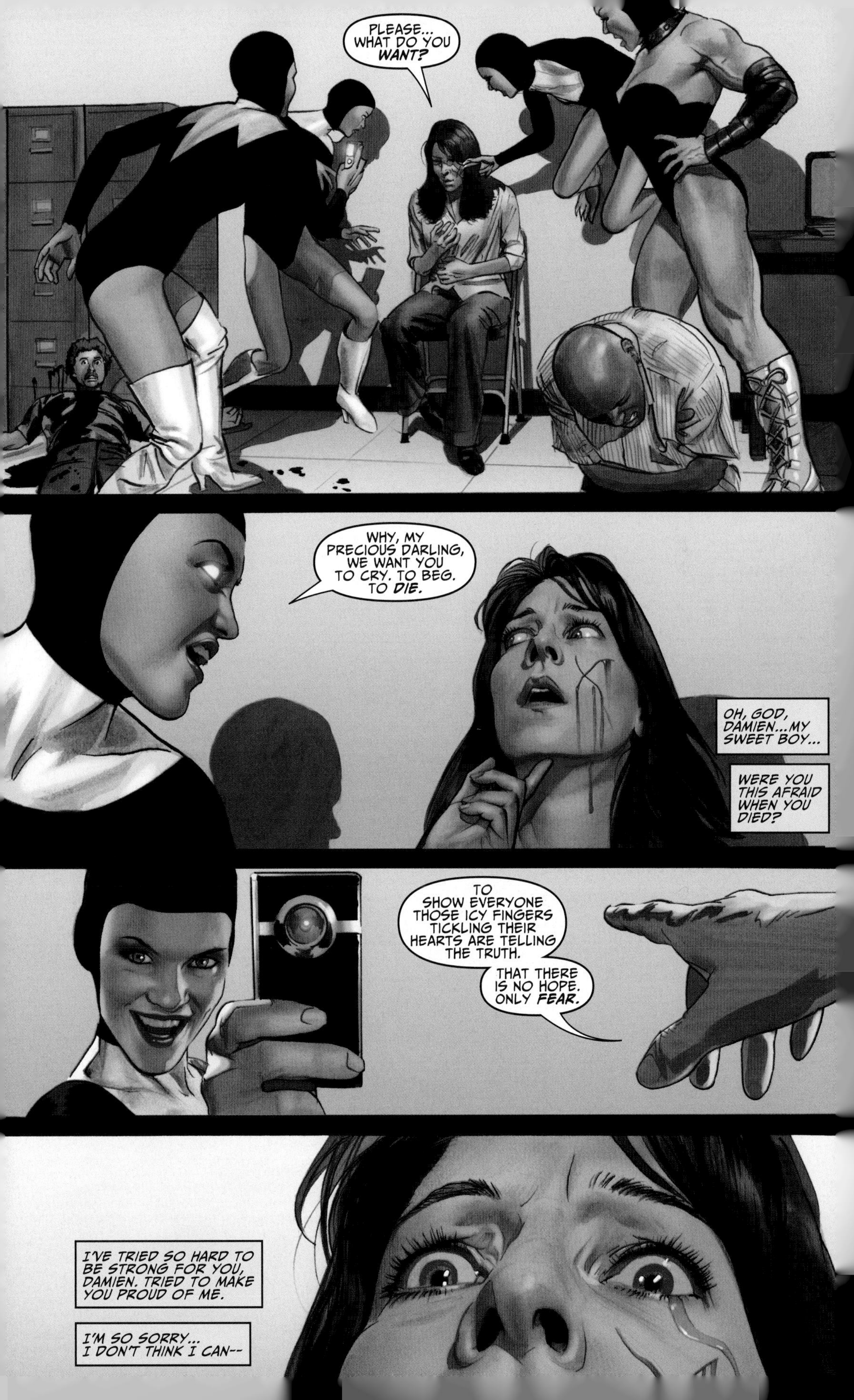
PLEASE... WHAT DO YOU WANT?
WHY, MY PRECIOUS DARLING, WE WANT YOU TO CRY. TO BEG. TO DIE.
OH, GOD, DAMIEN...MY SWEET BOY...
WERE YOU THIS AFRAID WHEN YOU DIED?
TO SHOW EVERYONE THOSE ICY FINGERS TICKLING THEIR HEARTS ARE TELLING THE TRUTH.
THAT THERE IS NO HOPE. ONLY FEAR.
I'VE TRIED SO HARD TO BE STRONG FOR YOU, DAMIEN. TRIED TO MAKE YOU PROUD OF ME.
I'M SO SORRY... I DON'T THINK I CAN--

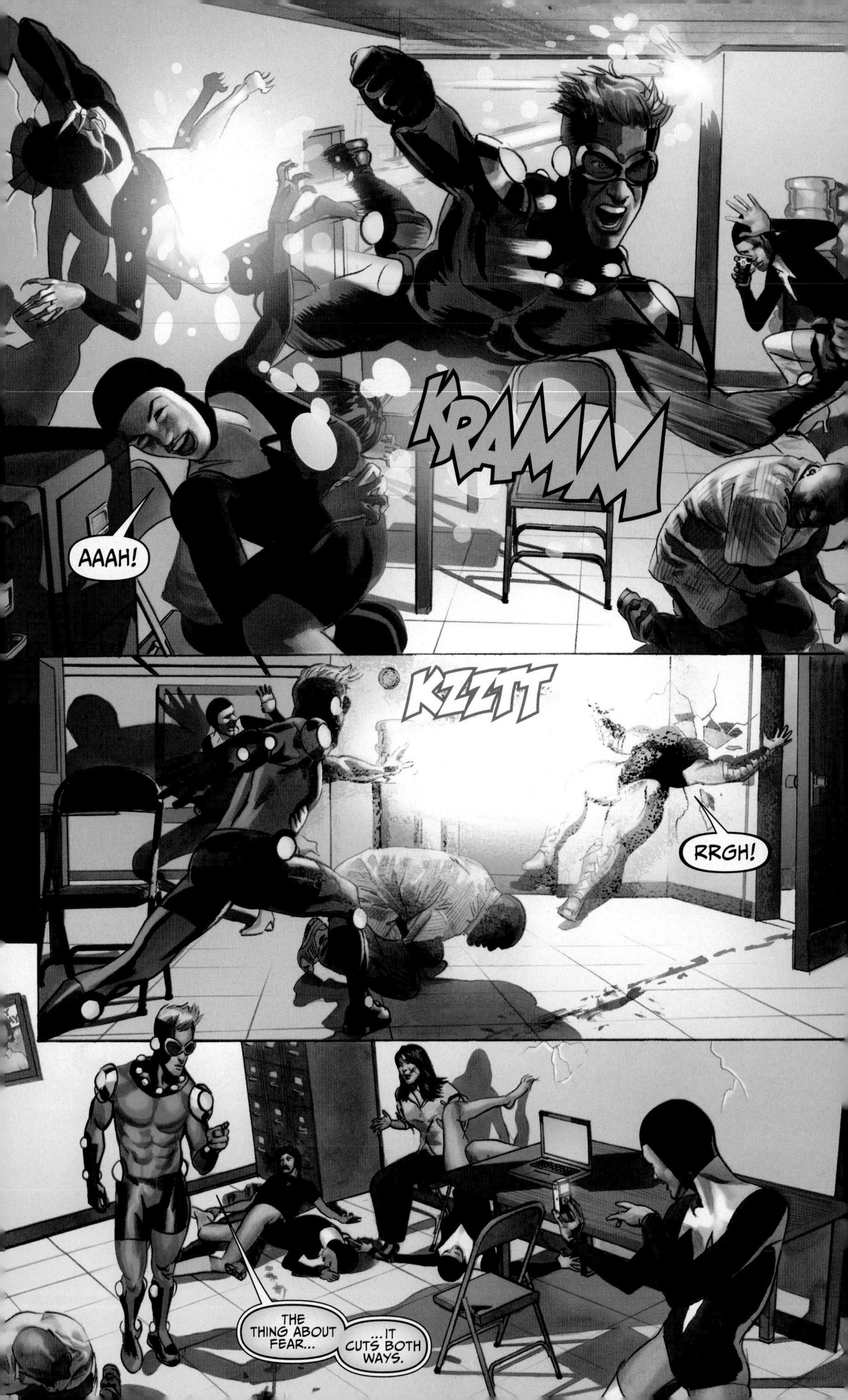
KRAMM
AAAH!
KZZTT
RRGH!
THE THING ABOUT FEAR...
...IT CUTS BOTH WAYS.

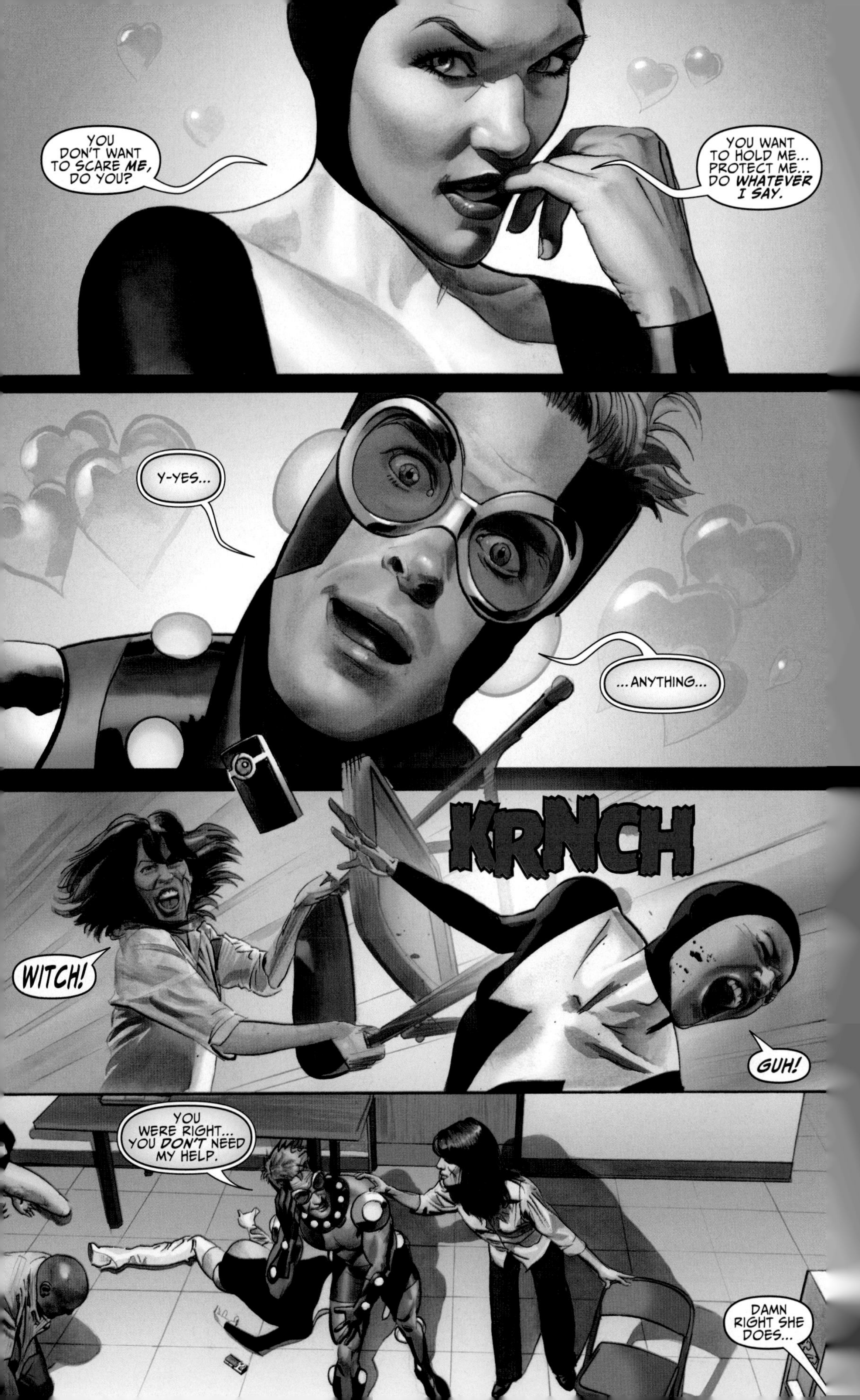
YOU DON'T WANT TO SCARE ME, DO YOU?
YOU WANT TO HOLD ME... PROTECT ME... DO WHATEVER I SAY.
Y-YES...
...ANYTHING...
KRNCH
WITCH!
GUH!
YOU WERE RIGHT... YOU DON'T NEED MY HELP.
DAMN RIGHT SHE DOES...

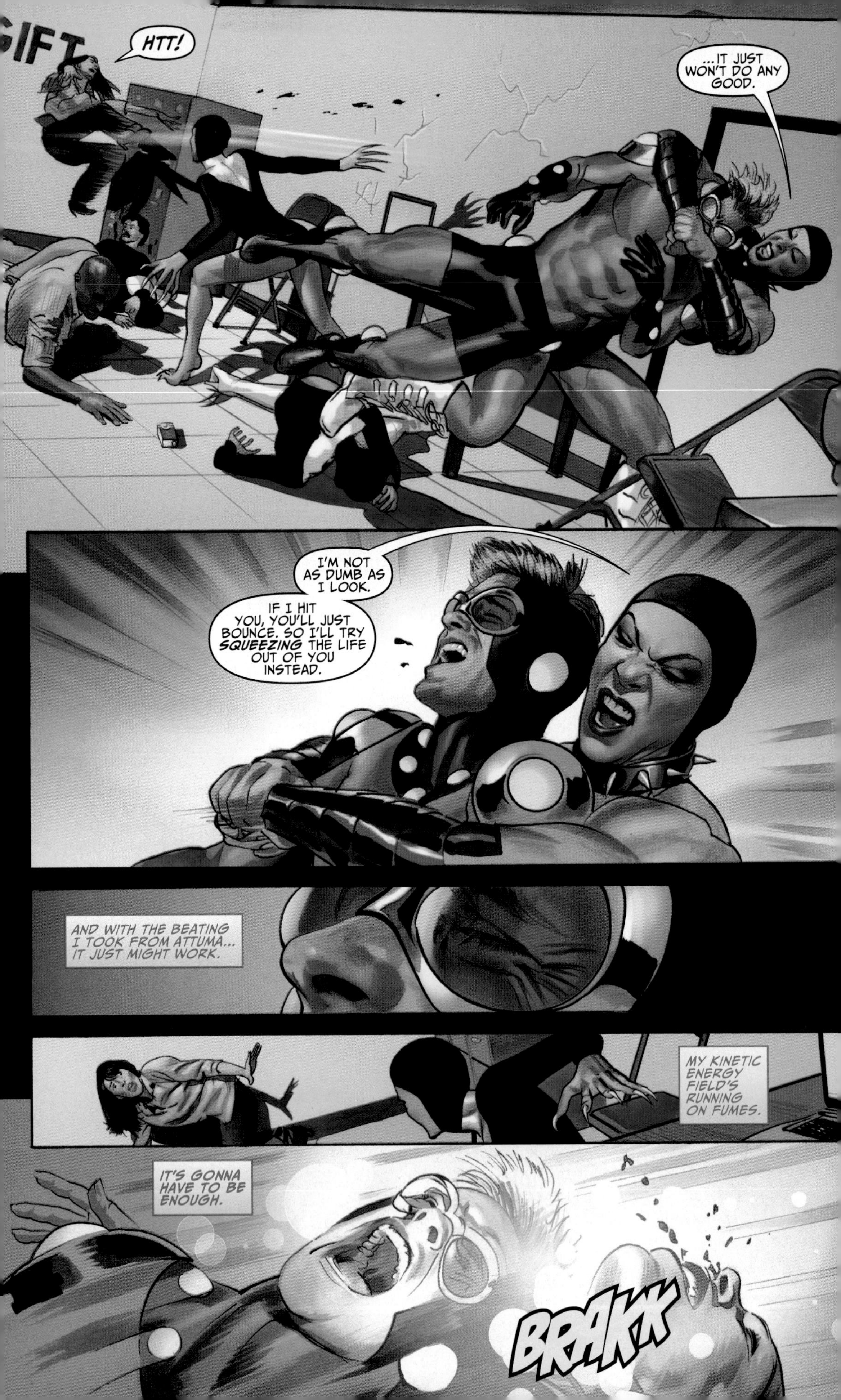

GIFT
HTT!
...IT JUST WON'T DO ANY GOOD.
I'M NOT AS DUMB AS I LOOK.
IF I HIT YOU, YOU'LL JUST BOUNCE. SO I'LL TRY SQUEEZING THE LIFE OUT OF YOU INSTEAD.
AND WITH THE BEATING I TOOK FROM ATTUMA... IT JUST MIGHT WORK.
MY KINETIC ENERGY FIELD'S RUNNING ON FUMES.
IT'S GONNA HAVE TO BE ENOUGH.
BRAKK

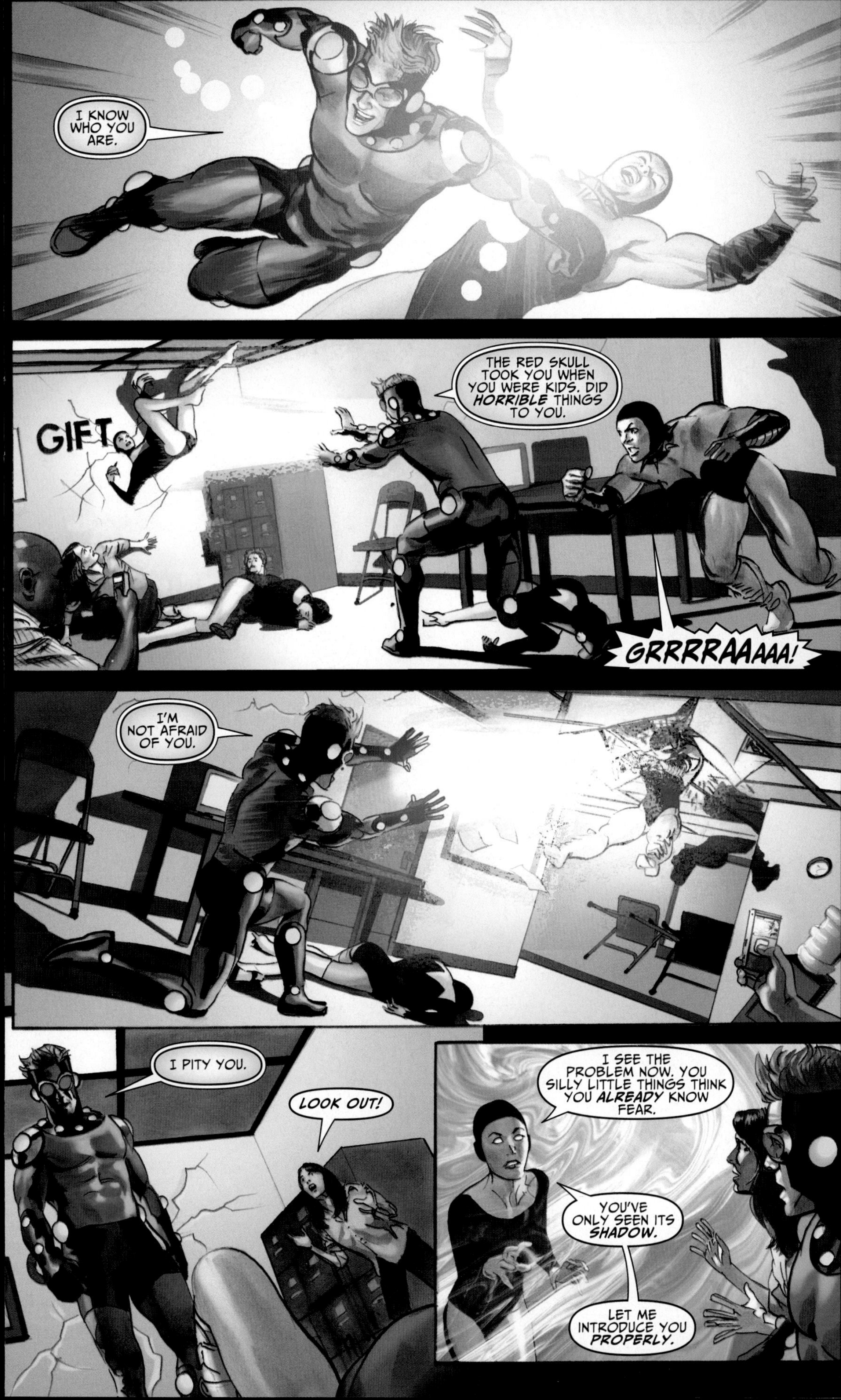
I KNOW WHO YOU ARE.
GIFT
THE RED SKULL TOOK YOU WHEN YOU WERE KIDS. DID HORRIBLE THINGS TO YOU.
GRRRRAAAAA!
I'M NOT AFRAID OF YOU.
I PITY YOU.
LOOK OUT!
I SEE THE PROBLEM NOW. YOU SILLY LITTLE THINGS THINK YOU ALREADY KNOW FEAR.
YOU'VE ONLY SEEN ITS SHADOW.
LET ME INTRODUCE YOU PROPERLY.

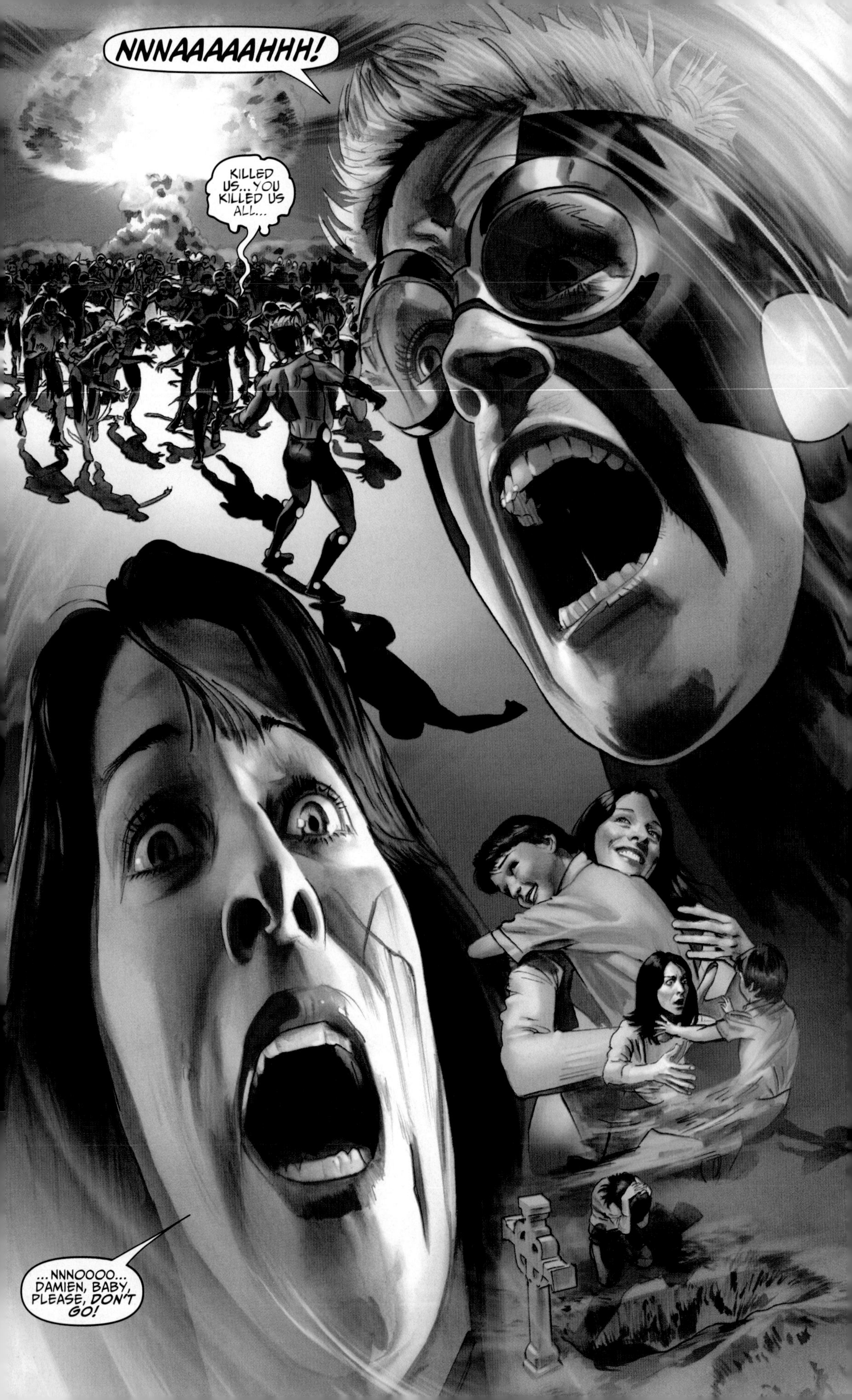
NNNAAAAAHHH!
KILLED US...YOU KILLED US ALL...
...NNNOOOO... DAMIEN, BABY, PLEASE, DON'T GO!

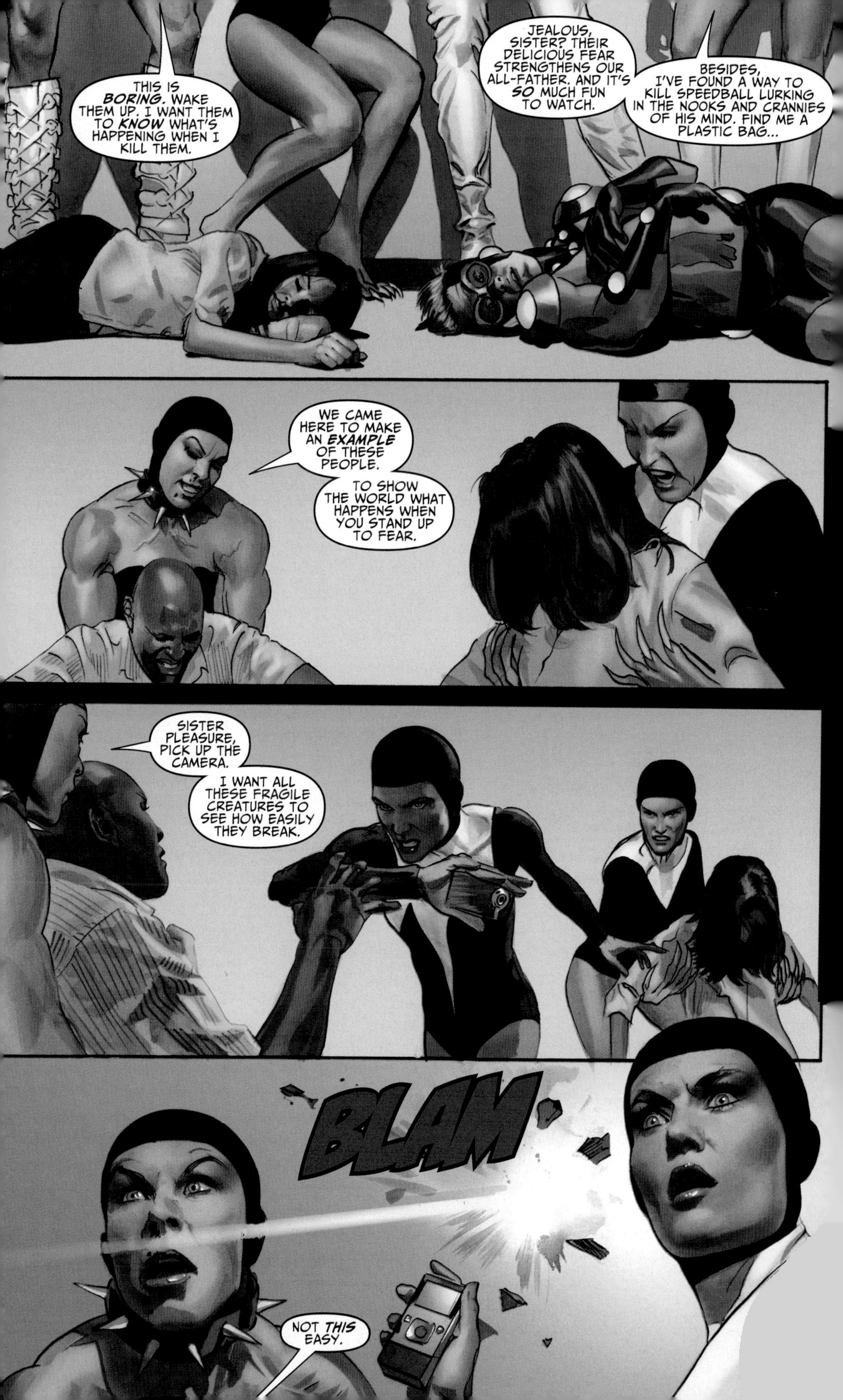
THIS IS BORING. WAKE THEM UP. I WANT THEM TO KNOW WHAT'S HAPPENING WHEN I KILL THEM.
JEALOUS, SISTER? THEIR DELICIOUS FEAR STRENGTHENS OUR ALL-FATHER. AND IT'S SO MUCH FUN TO WATCH.
BESIDES, I'VE FOUND A WAY TO KILL SPEEDBALL LURKING IN THE NOOKS AND CRANNIES OF HIS MIND. FIND ME A PLASTIC BAG...
WE CAME HERE TO MAKE AN EXAMPLE OF THESE PEOPLE.
TO SHOW THE WORLD WHAT HAPPENS WHEN YOU STAND UP TO FEAR.
SISTER PLEASURE, PICK UP THE CAMERA.
I WANT ALL THESE FRAGILE CREATURES TO SEE HOW EASILY THEY BREAK.
BLAM
NOT THIS EASY.

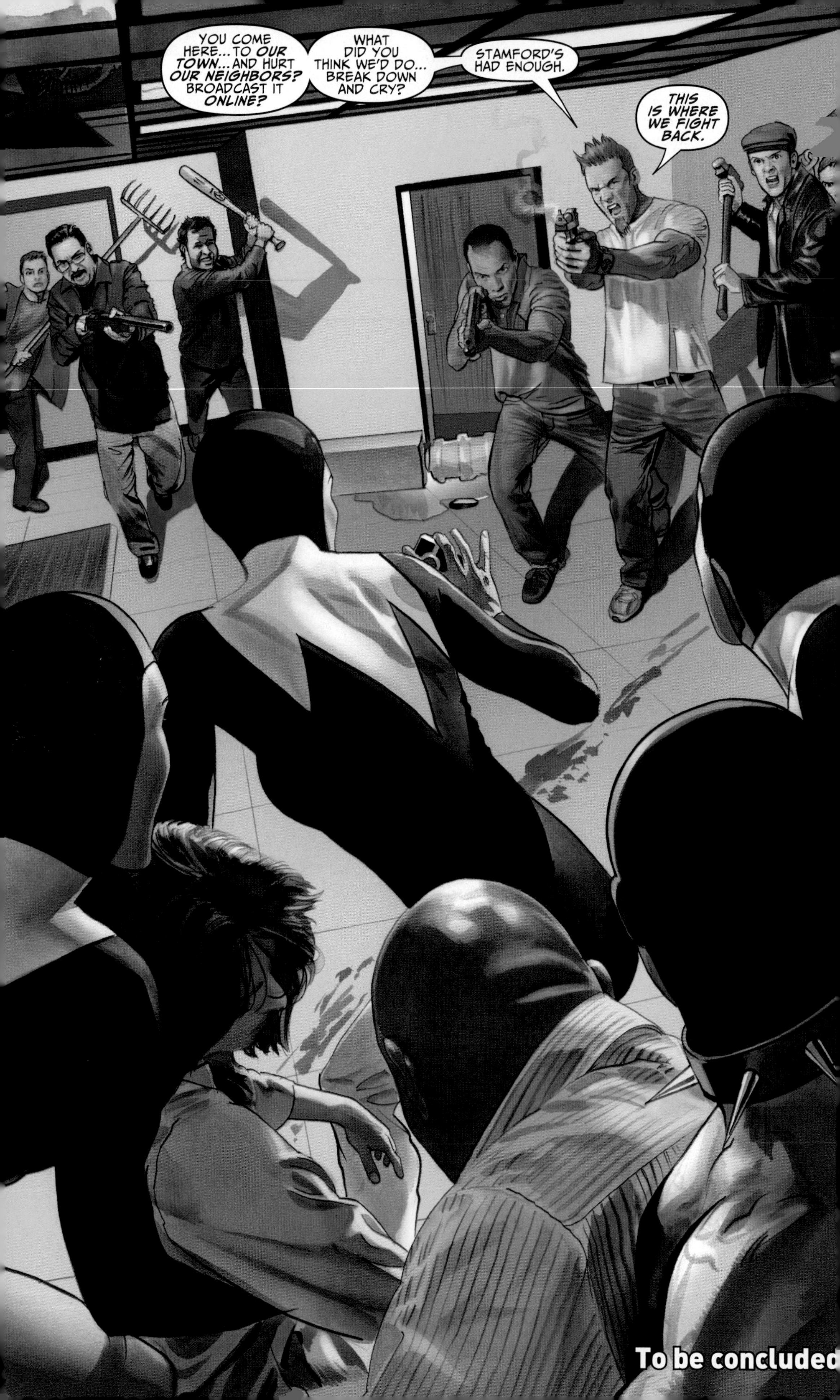

YOU COME HERE... TO OUR TOWN... AND HURT OUR NEIGHBORS? BROADCAST IT ONLINE?
WHAT DID YOU THINK WE'D DO... BREAK DOWN AND CRY?
STAMFORD'S HAD ENOUGH.
THIS IS WHERE WE FIGHT BACK.
To be concluded

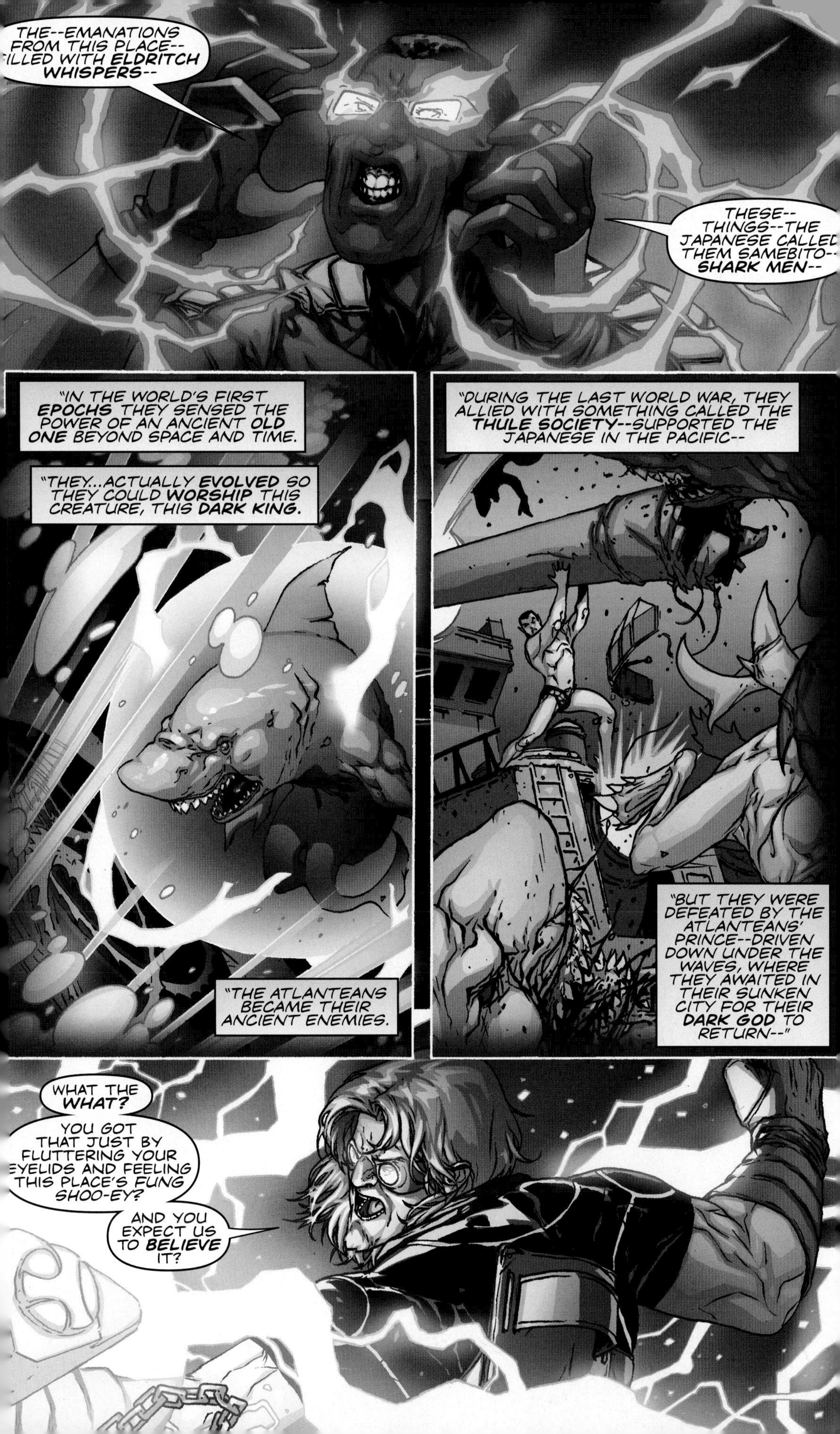

THE--EMANATIONS FROM THIS PLACE--FILLED WITH ELDRITCH WHISPERS--
THESE--THINGS--THE JAPANESE CALLED THEM SAMEBITO--SHARK MEN--
"IN THE WORLD'S FIRST EPOCHS THEY SENSED THE POWER OF AN ANCIENT OLD ONE BEYOND SPACE AND TIME.
"THEY...ACTUALLY EVOLVED SO THEY COULD WORSHIP THIS CREATURE, THIS DARK KING.
"THE ATLANTEANS BECAME THEIR ANCIENT ENEMIES.
"DURING THE LAST WORLD WAR, THEY ALLIED WITH SOMETHING CALLED THE THULE SOCIETY--SUPPORTED THE JAPANESE IN THE PACIFIC--
"BUT THEY WERE DEFEATED BY THE ATLANTEANS' PRINCE--DRIVEN DOWN UNDER THE WAVES, WHERE THEY AWAITED IN THEIR SUNKEN CITY FOR THEIR DARK GOD TO RETURN--"
WHAT THE WHAT?
YOU GOT THAT JUST BY FLUTTERING YOUR EYELIDS AND FEELING THIS PLACE'S FUNG SHOO-EY?
AND YOU EXPECT US TO BELIEVE IT?

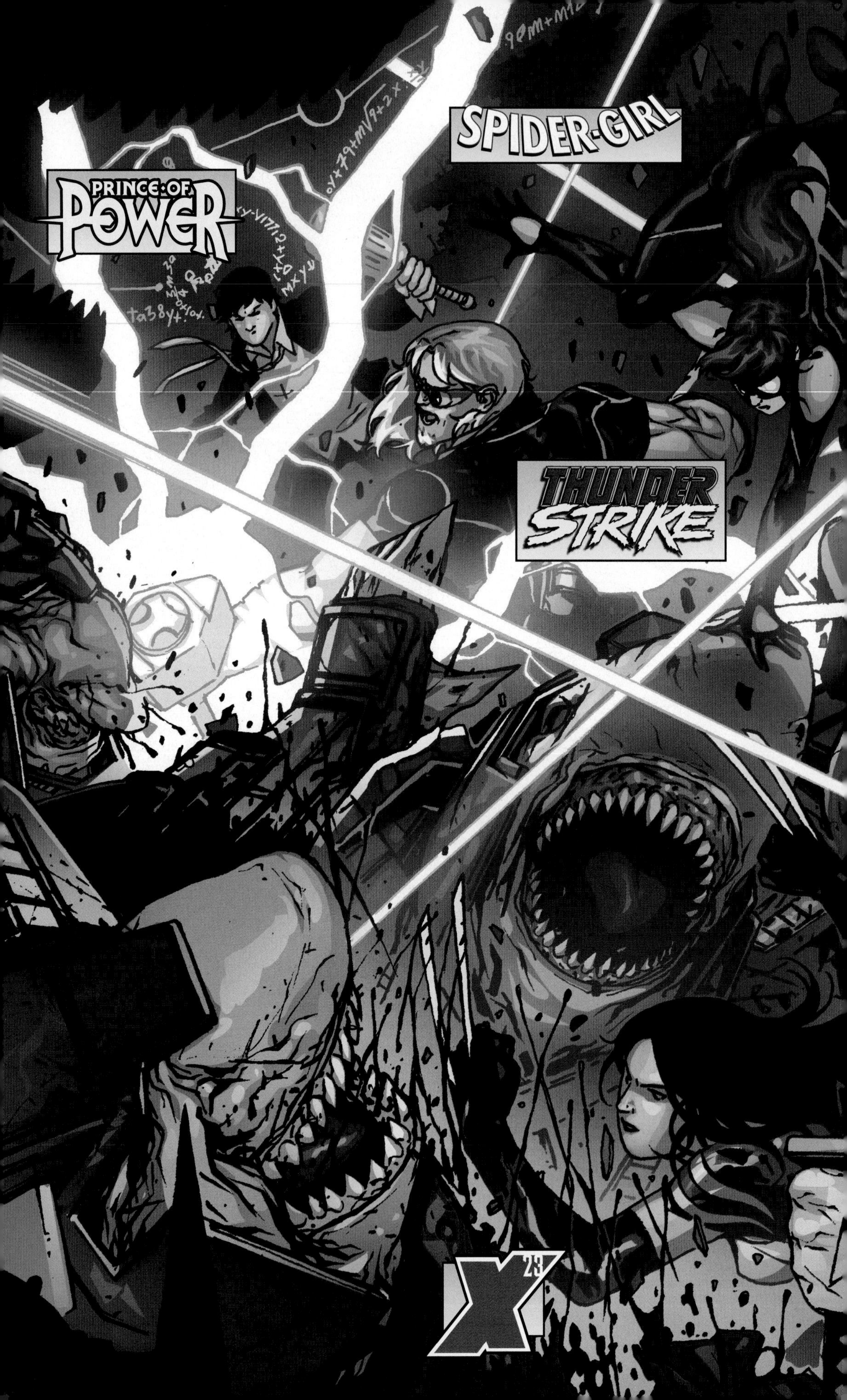
SPIDER-GIRL
PRINCE OF POWER
THUNDER STRIKE
X-23

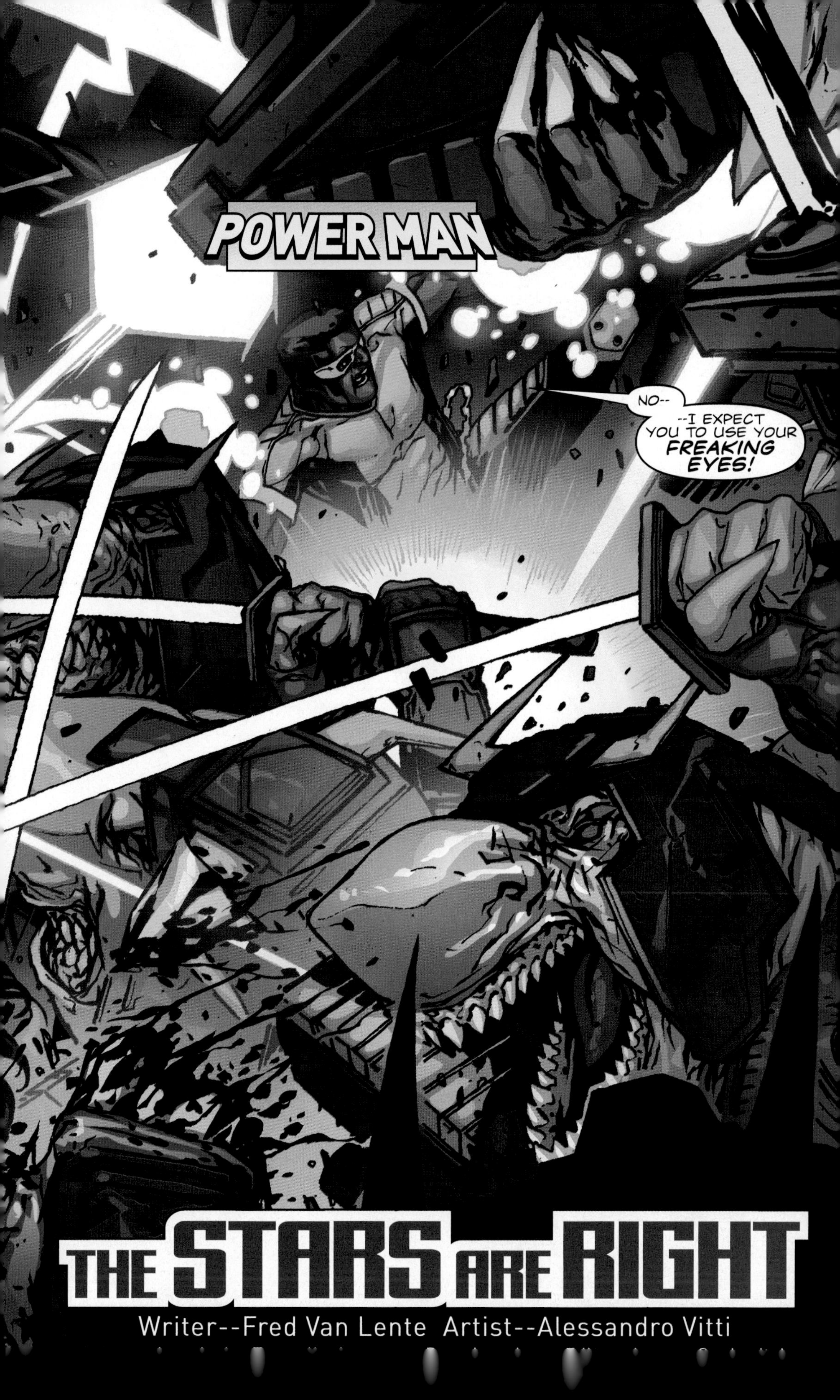
POWER MAN
NO--
--I EXPECT YOU TO USE YOUR FREAKING EYES!
THE STARS ARE RIGHT
Writer--Fred Van Lente Artist--Alessandro Vitti

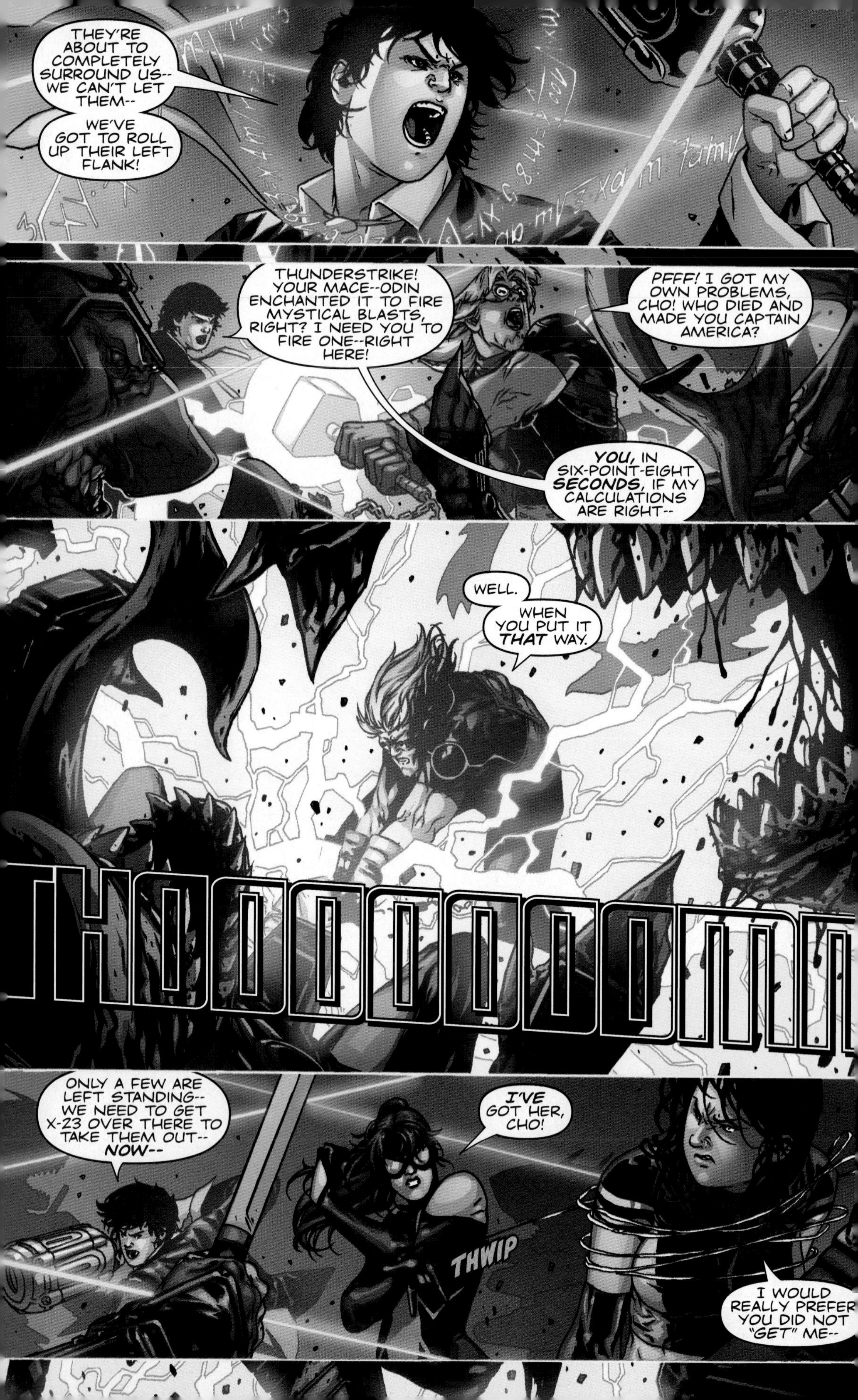
THEY'RE ABOUT TO COMPLETELY SURROUND US-- WE CAN'T LET THEM--
WE'VE GOT TO ROLL UP THEIR LEFT FLANK!
THUNDERSTRIKE! YOUR MACE--ODIN ENCHANTED IT TO FIRE MYSTICAL BLASTS, RIGHT? I NEED YOU TO FIRE ONE--RIGHT HERE!
PFFF! I GOT MY OWN PROBLEMS, CHO! WHO DIED AND MADE YOU CAPTAIN AMERICA?
YOU, IN SIX-POINT-EIGHT SECONDS, IF MY CALCULATIONS ARE RIGHT--
WELL.
WHEN YOU PUT IT THAT WAY.
THOOOOOOMM
ONLY A FEW ARE LEFT STANDING-- WE NEED TO GET X-23 OVER THERE TO TAKE THEM OUT-- NOW--
I'VE GOT HER, CHO!
THWIP
I WOULD REALLY PREFER YOU DID NOT "GET" ME--

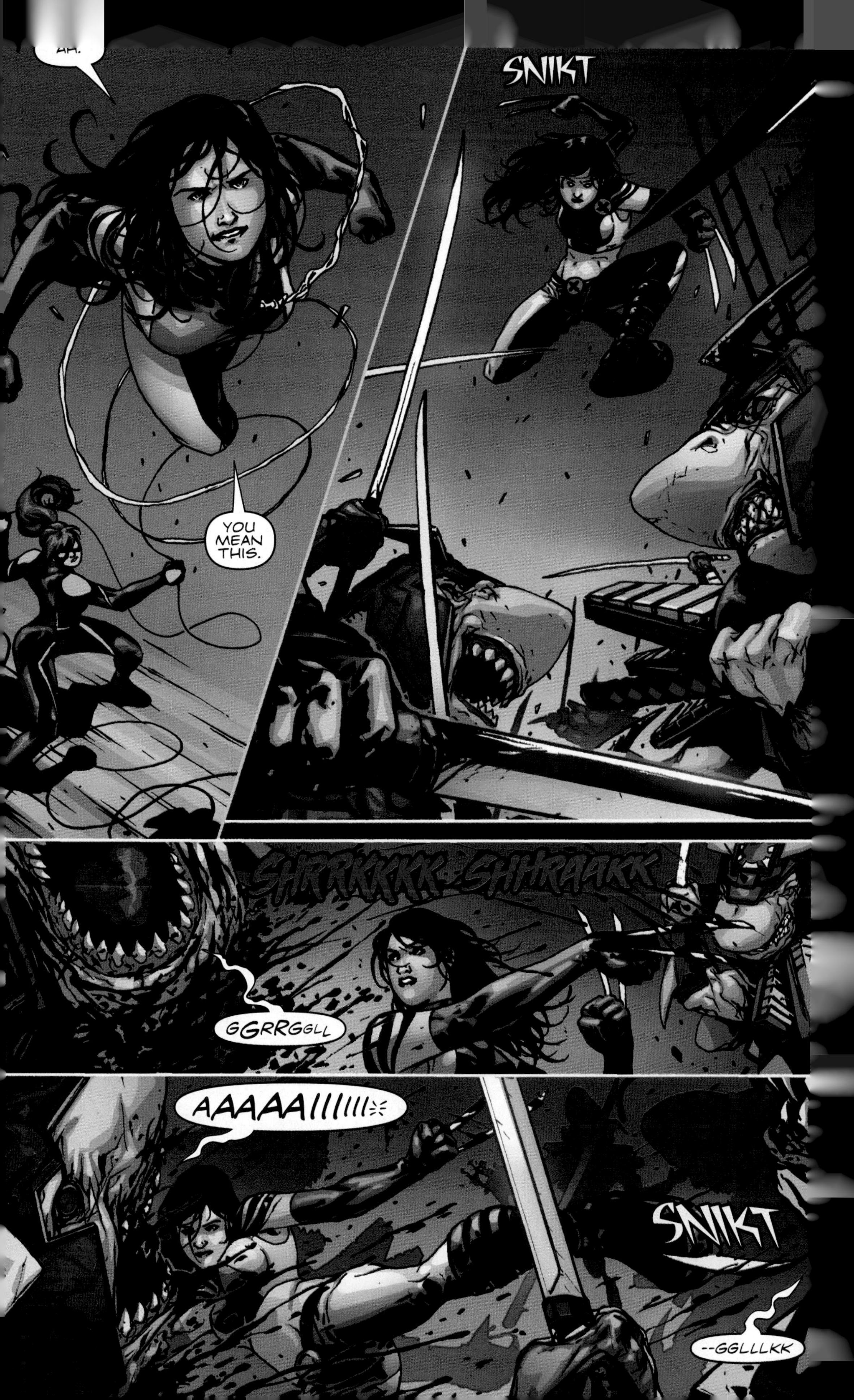
AH.
SNIKT
YOU MEAN THIS.
SHRKKKK SHHRAAKK
GGRRGGLL
AAAAAIIIIII
SNIKT
--GGLLLKK

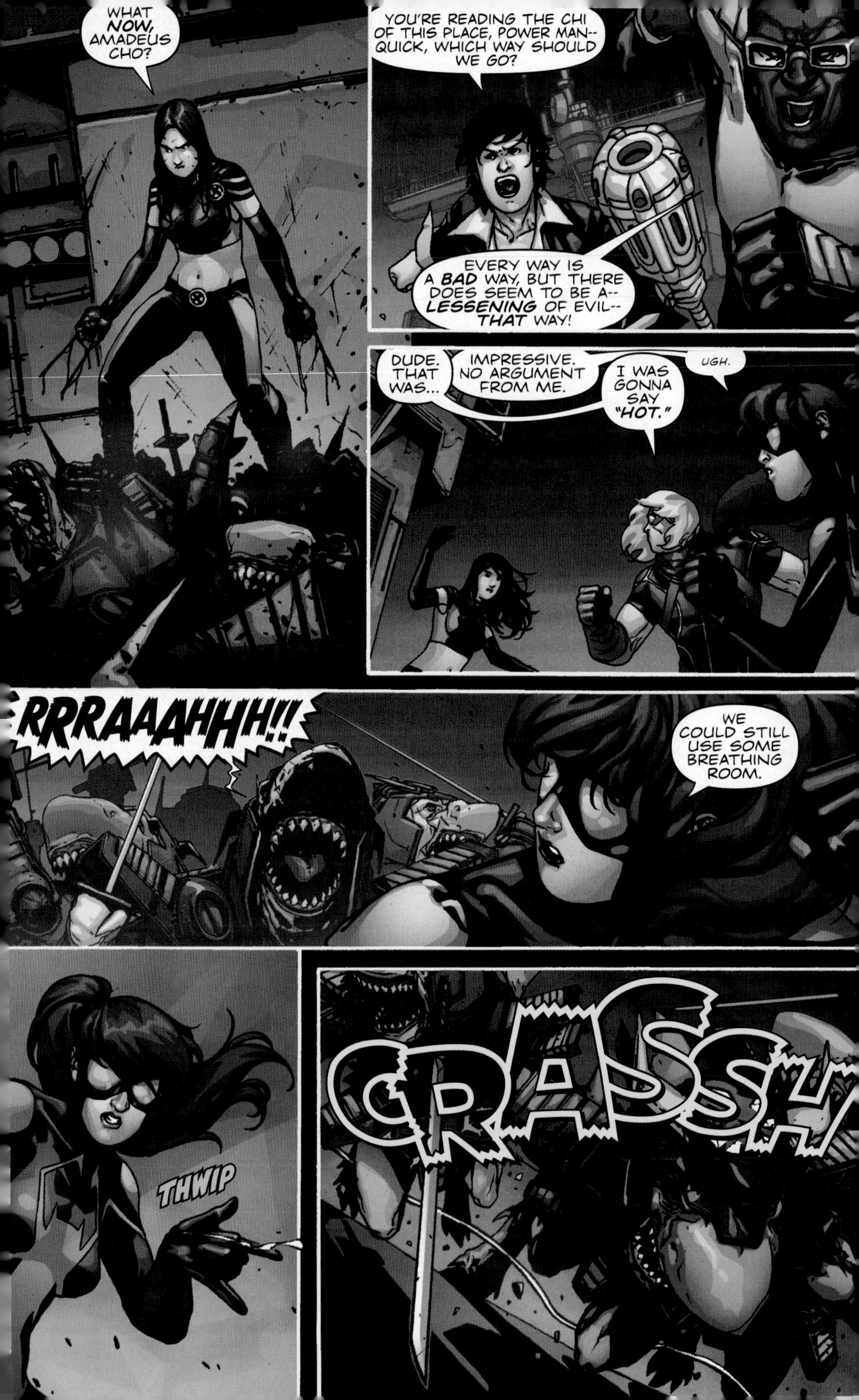
WHAT NOW, AMADEUS CHO?
YOU'RE READING THE CHI OF THIS PLACE, POWER MAN-- QUICK, WHICH WAY SHOULD WE GO?
EVERY WAY IS A BAD WAY, BUT THERE DOES SEEM TO BE A-- LESSENING OF EVIL-- THAT WAY!
DUDE. THAT WAS...
IMPRESSIVE. NO ARGUMENT FROM ME.
I WAS GONNA SAY "HOT."
UGH.
RRRAAAHHH!!
WE COULD STILL USE SOME BREATHING ROOM.
THWIP
CRASSH

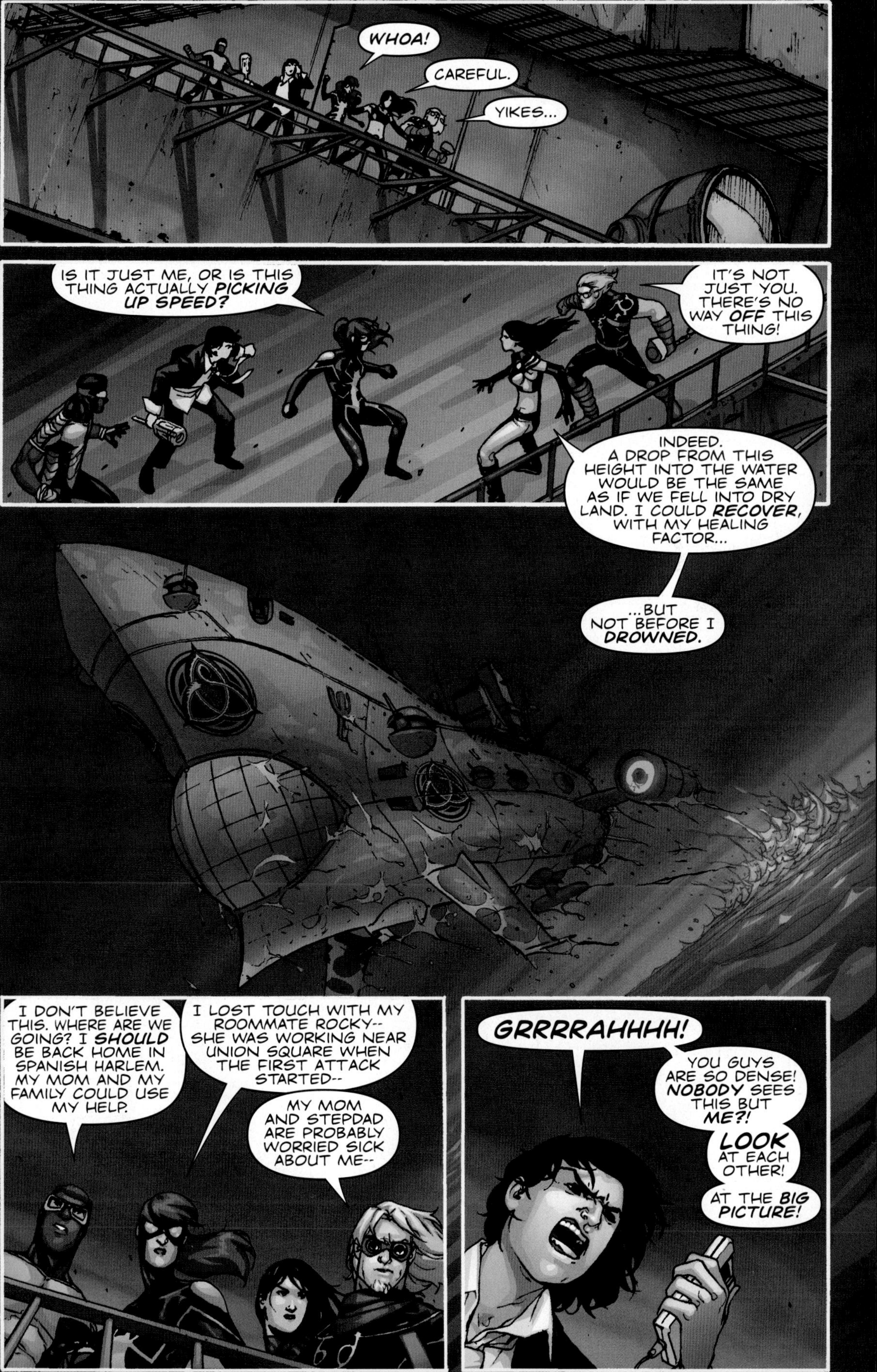
WHOA!
CAREFUL.
YIKES...
IS IT JUST ME, OR IS THIS THING ACTUALLY PICKING UP SPEED?
IT'S NOT JUST YOU. THERE'S NO WAY OFF THIS THING!
INDEED. A DROP FROM THIS HEIGHT INTO THE WATER WOULD BE THE SAME AS IF WE FELL INTO DRY LAND. I COULD RECOVER, WITH MY HEALING FACTOR...
...BUT NOT BEFORE I DROWNED.
I DON'T BELIEVE THIS. WHERE ARE WE GOING? I SHOULD BE BACK HOME IN SPANISH HARLEM. MY MOM AND MY FAMILY COULD USE MY HELP.
I LOST TOUCH WITH MY ROOMMATE ROCKY-- SHE WAS WORKING NEAR UNION SQUARE WHEN THE FIRST ATTACK STARTED--
MY MOM AND STEPDAD ARE PROBABLY WORRIED SICK ABOUT ME--
GRRRRAHHHH!
YOU GUYS ARE SO DENSE! NOBODY SEES THIS BUT ME?!
LOOK AT EACH OTHER!
AT THE BIG PICTURE!

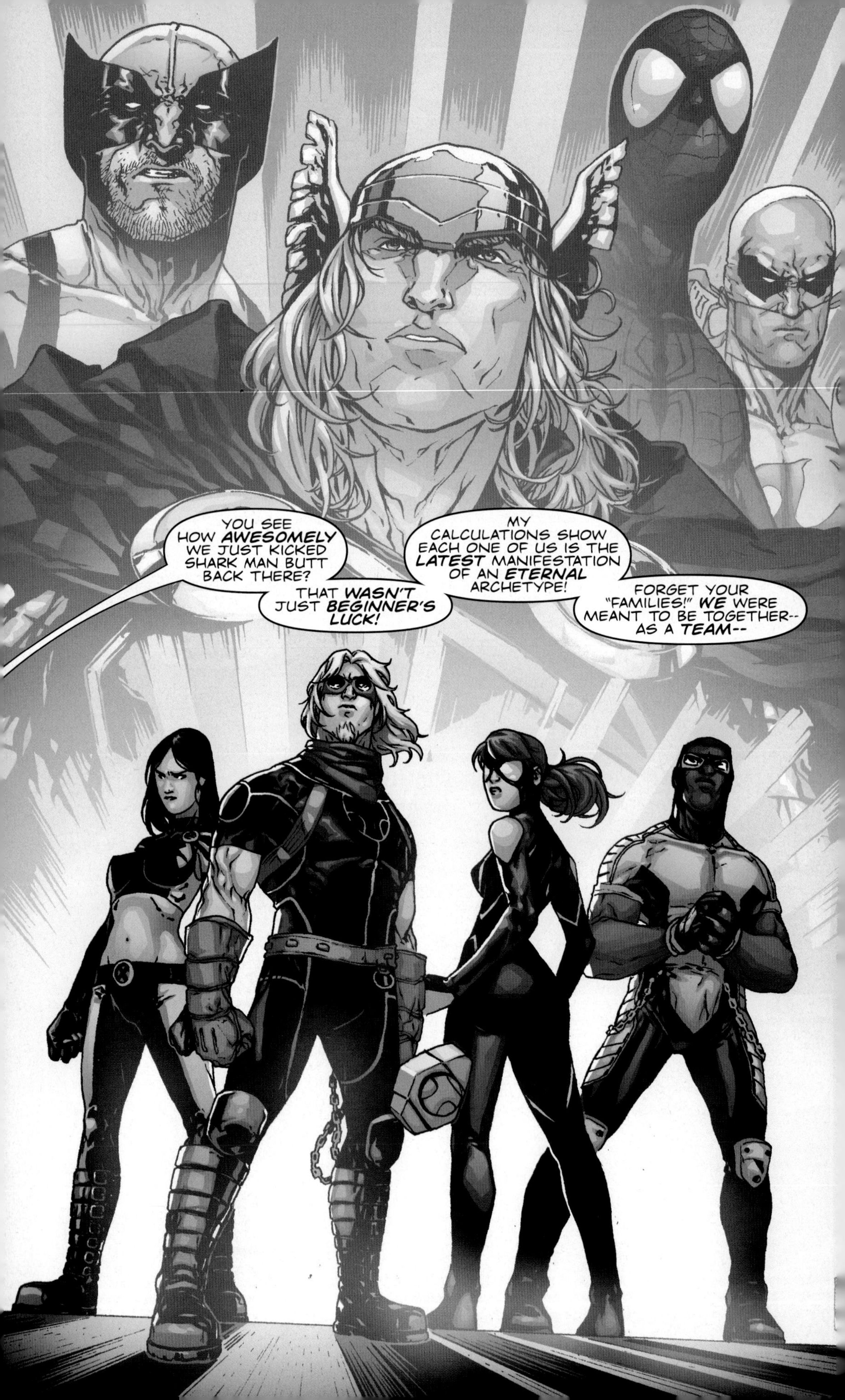
YOU SEE HOW **AWESOMELY** WE JUST KICKED SHARK MAN BUTT BACK THERE?
THAT **WASN'T** JUST **BEGINNER'S LUCK!**
MY CALCULATIONS SHOW EACH ONE OF US IS THE **LATEST** MANIFESTATION OF AN **ETERNAL** ARCHETYPE!
FORGET YOUR "FAMILIES!" **WE** WERE MEANT TO BE TOGETHER-- AS A **TEAM**--

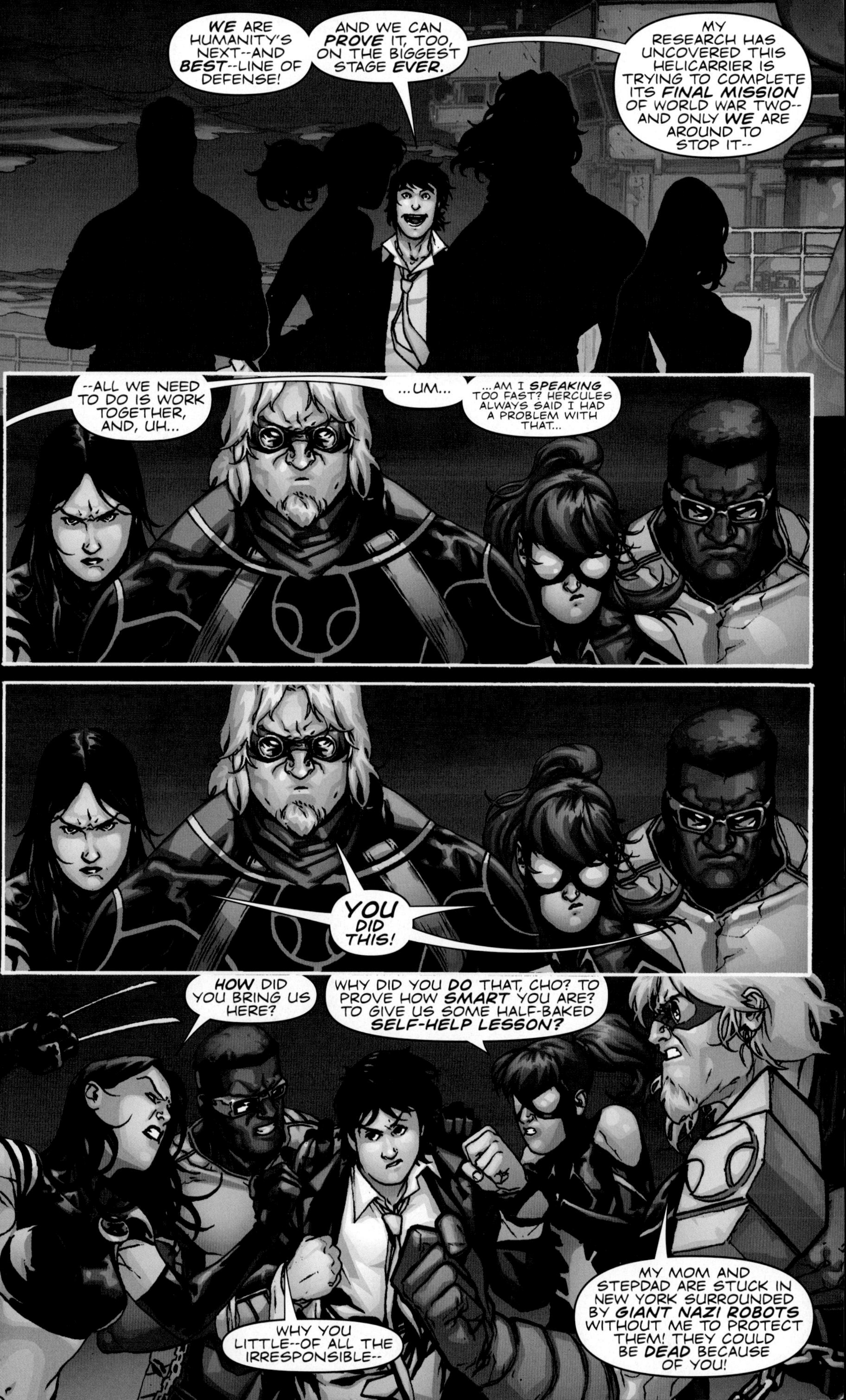
WE ARE HUMANITY'S NEXT--AND BEST--LINE OF DEFENSE!
AND WE CAN PROVE IT, TOO, ON THE BIGGEST STAGE EVER.
MY RESEARCH HAS UNCOVERED THIS HELICARRIER IS TRYING TO COMPLETE ITS FINAL MISSION OF WORLD WAR TWO-- AND ONLY WE ARE AROUND TO STOP IT--
--ALL WE NEED TO DO IS WORK TOGETHER, AND, UH...
...UM...
...AM I SPEAKING TOO FAST? HERCULES ALWAYS SAID I HAD A PROBLEM WITH THAT...
YOU DID THIS!
HOW DID YOU BRING US HERE?
WHY DID YOU DO THAT, CHO? TO PROVE HOW SMART YOU ARE? TO GIVE US SOME HALF-BAKED SELF-HELP LESSON?
WHY YOU LITTLE--OF ALL THE IRRESPONSIBLE--
MY MOM AND STEPDAD ARE STUCK IN NEW YORK SURROUNDED BY GIANT NAZI ROBOTS WITHOUT ME TO PROTECT THEM! THEY COULD BE DEAD BECAUSE OF YOU!

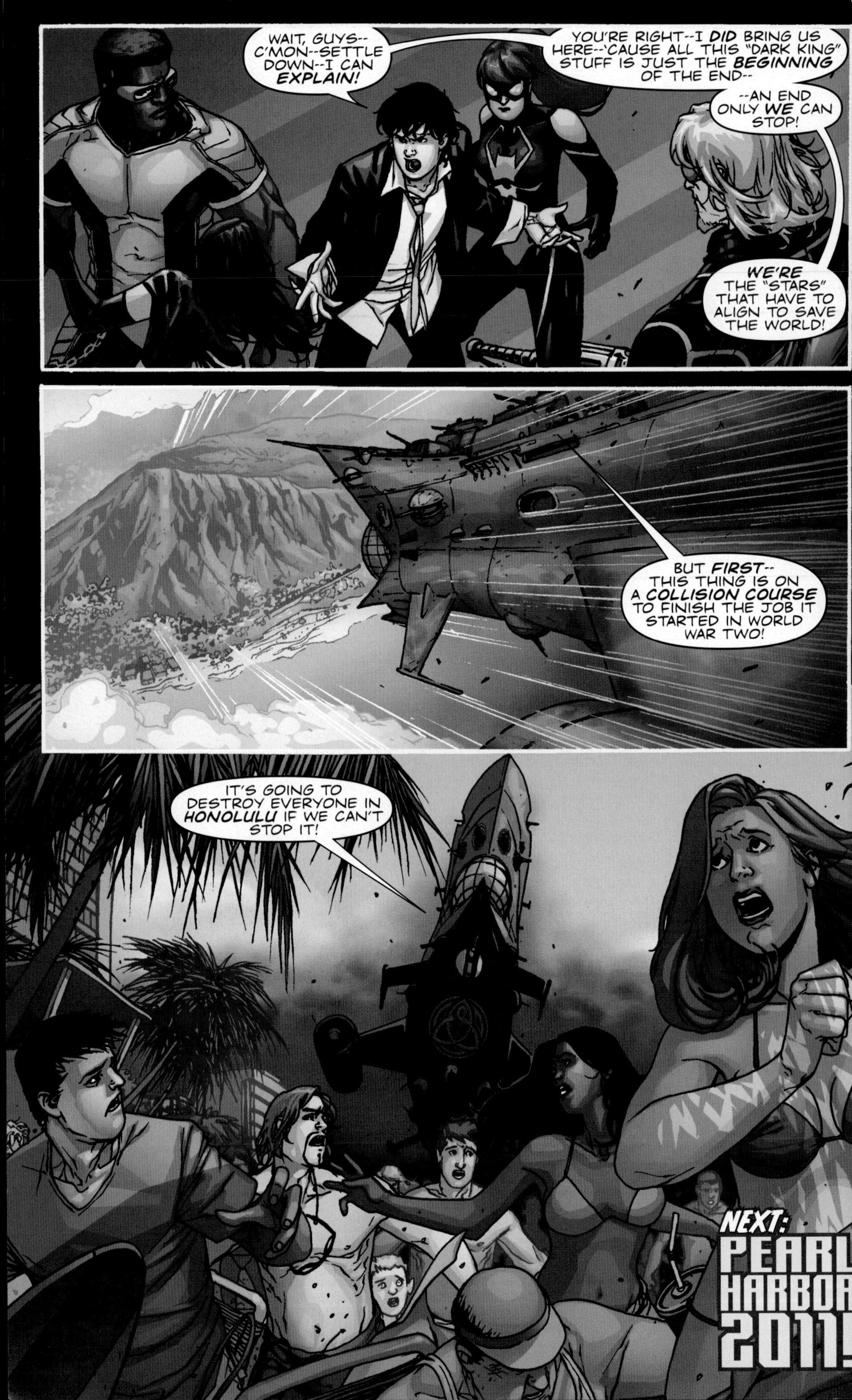
WAIT, GUYS-- C'MON--SETTLE DOWN--I CAN EXPLAIN!
YOU'RE RIGHT--I DID BRING US HERE--'CAUSE ALL THIS "DARK KING" STUFF IS JUST THE BEGINNING OF THE END--
--AN END ONLY WE CAN STOP!
WE'RE THE "STARS" THAT HAVE TO ALIGN TO SAVE THE WORLD!
BUT FIRST-- THIS THING IS ON A COLLISION COURSE TO FINISH THE JOB IT STARTED IN WORLD WAR TWO!
IT'S GOING TO DESTROY EVERYONE IN HONOLULU IF WE CAN'T STOP IT!
NEXT:
PEARL HARBOR 2011!

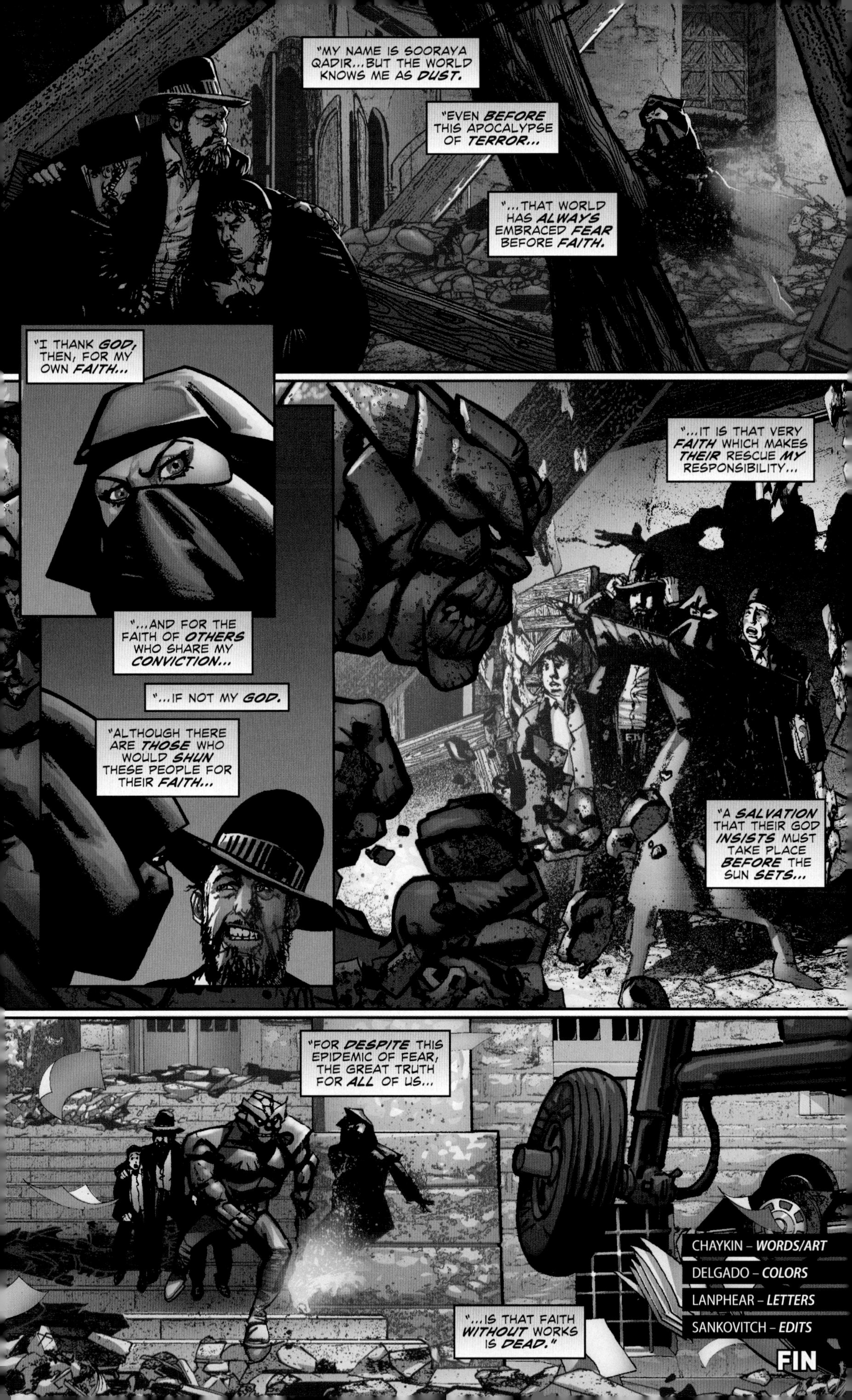

"MY NAME IS SOORAYA QADIR...BUT THE WORLD KNOWS ME AS DUST.
"EVEN BEFORE THIS APOCALYPSE OF TERROR...
"...THAT WORLD HAS ALWAYS EMBRACED FEAR BEFORE FAITH.
"I THANK GOD, THEN, FOR MY OWN FAITH...
"...AND FOR THE FAITH OF OTHERS WHO SHARE MY CONVICTION...
"...IF NOT MY GOD.
"ALTHOUGH THERE ARE THOSE WHO WOULD SHUN THESE PEOPLE FOR THEIR FAITH...
"...IT IS THAT VERY FAITH WHICH MAKES THEIR RESCUE MY RESPONSIBILITY...
"A SALVATION THAT THEIR GOD INSISTS MUST TAKE PLACE BEFORE THE SUN SETS...
"FOR DESPITE THIS EPIDEMIC OF FEAR, THE GREAT TRUTH FOR ALL OF US...
"...IS THAT FAITH WITHOUT WORKS IS DEAD."
CHAYKIN – WORDS/ART
DELGADO – COLORS
LANPHEAR – LETTERS
SANKOVITCH – EDITS
FIN

MILWAUKEE, WISCONSIN. A CITY TIRED OF LIVING IN FEAR.

WE'RE *TIRED* OF LIVING IN FEAR! TIME TO THROW OUT THE GREAT LAKES *AVENGERS!*

I THOUGHT WE WERE THROWING OUT THE GREAT LAKES *DEFENDERS.*

NO, THE GREAT LAKES *X-MEN!*

WE'LL THROW 'EM ALL OUT!

GLA MAKES ME *TOO* SCEARED TO SPELL RITE!

NO GLA!

GLA GET OUT!

SUPER CREEPS NOT WANTED

THE GREAT LAKES AVENGERS/X-MEN/CHAMPIONS/DEFENDERS/POWER PACK
in "FEAR AND SELF-LOATHING IN WISCONSIN"
Elliott Kalan·Writer   Ty Templeton·Artist
David Curiel·Color Artist   Dave Lanphear·Letterer
Lauren Sankovitch·Editor

THEY'VE GOT SOME KIND OF FORCE-FIELD BLOCKING THE DOOR! A SOFT, YELLOW FORCE-FIELD!

SINCE WHEN DO THEY HAVE SOMEONE WITH FORCE-FIELD POWERS?

GLA SUCKS

I REALLY *WISH* WE HAD SOMEONE WITH FORCE-FIELD POWERS. WHAT'S HAPPENED TO THESE PEOPLE? IT'S ALMOST LIKE THEY'RE IN THE GRIP OF FEAR ITSELF!©®™

BIG BERTHA. SECRET SUPERMODEL. FOR REALS.

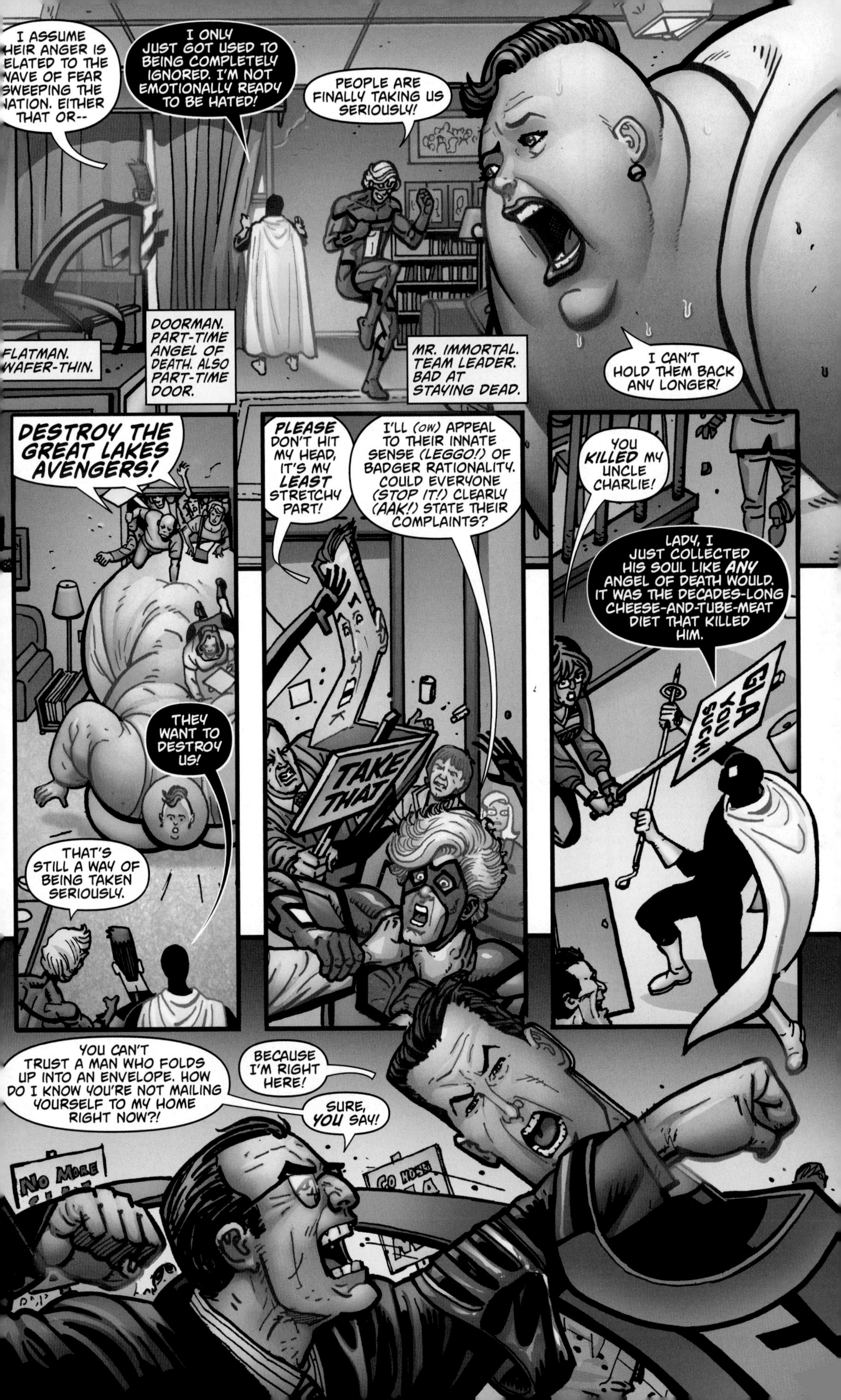
I ASSUME HEIR ANGER IS ELATED TO THE WAVE OF FEAR SWEEPING THE NATION. EITHER THAT OR--
I ONLY JUST GOT USED TO BEING COMPLETELY IGNORED. I'M NOT EMOTIONALLY READY TO BE HATED!
PEOPLE ARE FINALLY TAKING US SERIOUSLY!
FLATMAN. WAFER-THIN.
DOORMAN. PART-TIME ANGEL OF DEATH. ALSO PART-TIME DOOR.
MR. IMMORTAL. TEAM LEADER. BAD AT STAYING DEAD.
I CAN'T HOLD THEM BACK ANY LONGER!
DESTROY THE GREAT LAKES AVENGERS!
THEY WANT TO DESTROY US!
THAT'S STILL A WAY OF BEING TAKEN SERIOUSLY.
PLEASE DON'T HIT MY HEAD, IT'S MY LEAST STRETCHY PART!
I'LL (OW) APPEAL TO THEIR INNATE SENSE (LEGGO!) OF BADGER RATIONALITY. COULD EVERYONE (STOP IT!) CLEARLY (AAK!) STATE THEIR COMPLAINTS?
TAKE THAT
YOU KILLED MY UNCLE CHARLIE!
LADY, I JUST COLLECTED HIS SOUL LIKE ANY ANGEL OF DEATH WOULD. IT WAS THE DECADES-LONG CHEESE-AND-TUBE-MEAT DIET THAT KILLED HIM.
GLA YOU SUCK!
YOU CAN'T TRUST A MAN WHO FOLDS UP INTO AN ENVELOPE. HOW DO I KNOW YOU'RE NOT MAILING YOURSELF TO MY HOME RIGHT NOW?!
BECAUSE I'M RIGHT HERE!
SURE, YOU SAY!
NO MORE

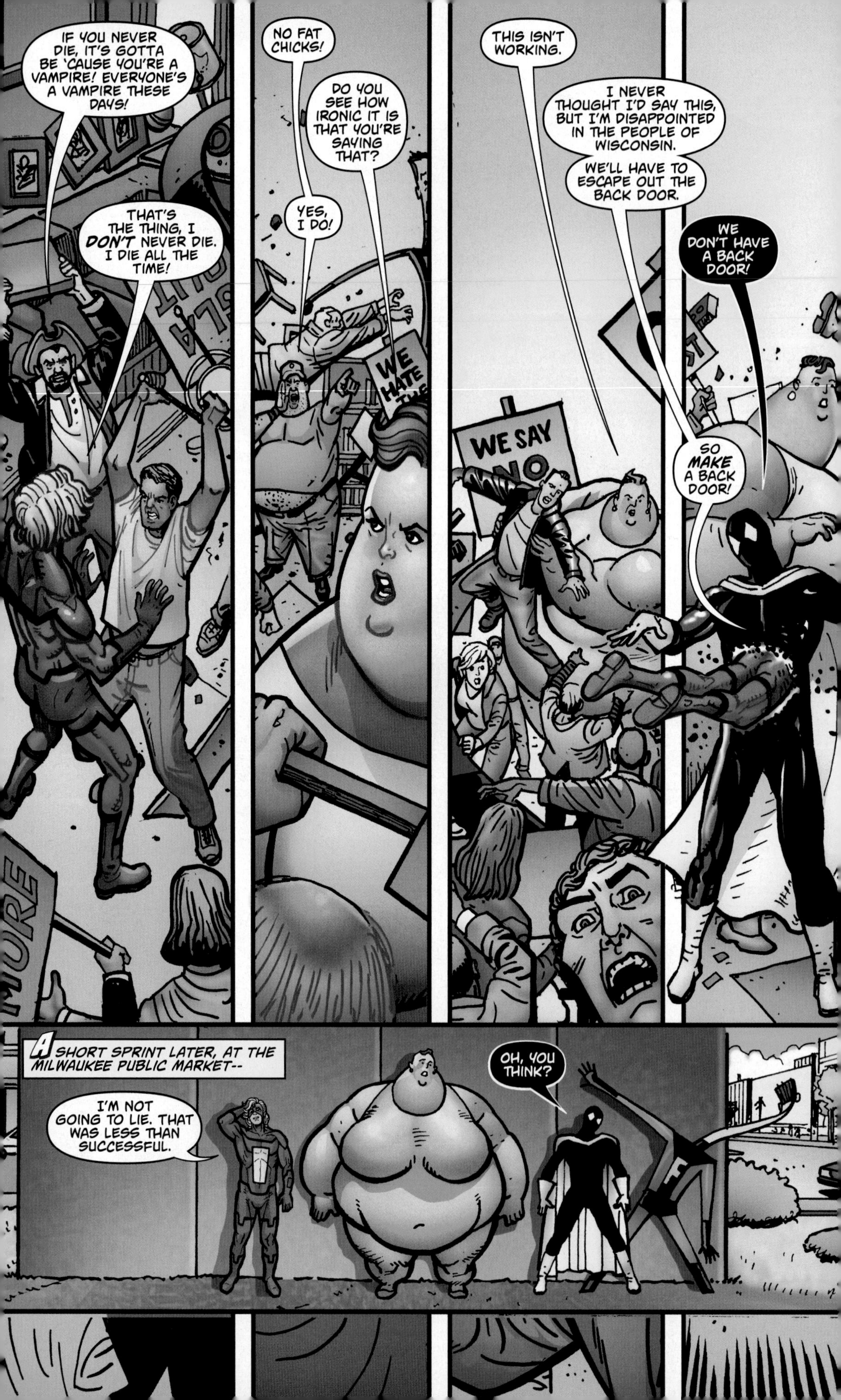

IF YOU NEVER DIE, IT'S GOTTA BE 'CAUSE YOU'RE A VAMPIRE! EVERYONE'S A VAMPIRE THESE DAYS!
THAT'S THE THING, I DON'T NEVER DIE. I DIE ALL THE TIME!
MORE
NO FAT CHICKS!
DO YOU SEE HOW IRONIC IT IS THAT YOU'RE SAYING THAT?
YES, I DO!
WE HATE
THIS ISN'T WORKING.
I NEVER THOUGHT I'D SAY THIS, BUT I'M DISAPPOINTED IN THE PEOPLE OF WISCONSIN.
WE'LL HAVE TO ESCAPE OUT THE BACK DOOR.
WE SAY NO
WE DON'T HAVE A BACK DOOR!
SO MAKE A BACK DOOR!
A SHORT SPRINT LATER, AT THE MILWAUKEE PUBLIC MARKET--
I'M NOT GOING TO LIE. THAT WAS LESS THAN SUCCESSFUL.
OH, YOU THINK?

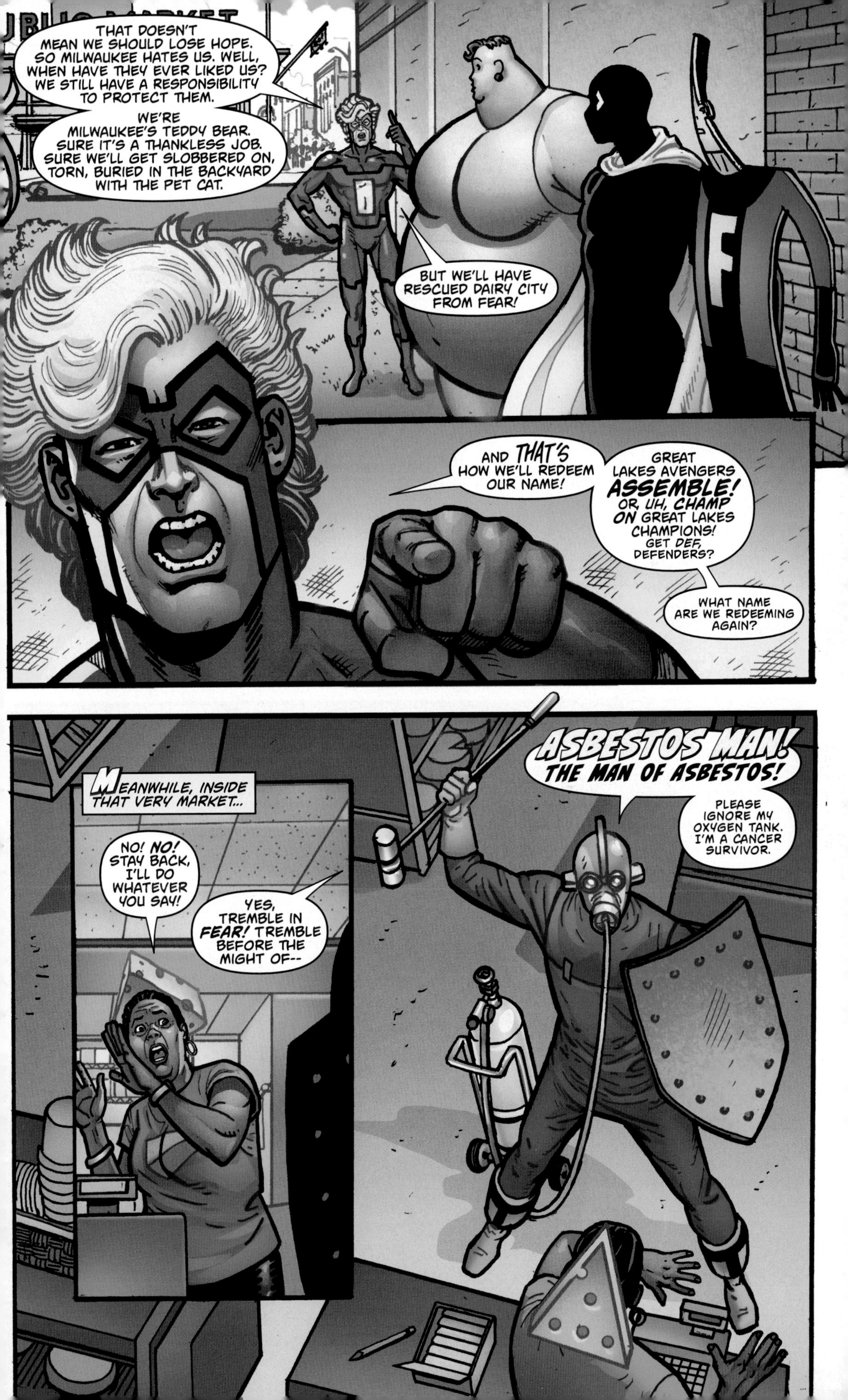

THAT DOESN'T MEAN WE SHOULD LOSE HOPE. SO MILWAUKEE HATES US. WELL, WHEN HAVE THEY EVER LIKED US? WE STILL HAVE A RESPONSIBILITY TO PROTECT THEM.
WE'RE MILWAUKEE'S TEDDY BEAR. SURE IT'S A THANKLESS JOB. SURE WE'LL GET SLOBBERED ON, TORN, BURIED IN THE BACKYARD WITH THE PET CAT.
BUT WE'LL HAVE RESCUED DAIRY CITY FROM FEAR!
AND THAT'S HOW WE'LL REDEEM OUR NAME!
GREAT LAKES AVENGERS ASSEMBLE! OR, UH, CHAMP ON GREAT LAKES CHAMPIONS! GET DEF, DEFENDERS?
WHAT NAME ARE WE REDEEMING AGAIN?
MEANWHILE, INSIDE THAT VERY MARKET...
NO! NO! STAY BACK, I'LL DO WHATEVER YOU SAY!
YES, TREMBLE IN FEAR! TREMBLE BEFORE THE MIGHT OF--
ASBESTOS MAN! THE MAN OF ASBESTOS!
PLEASE IGNORE MY OXYGEN TANK. I'M A CANCER SURVIVOR.

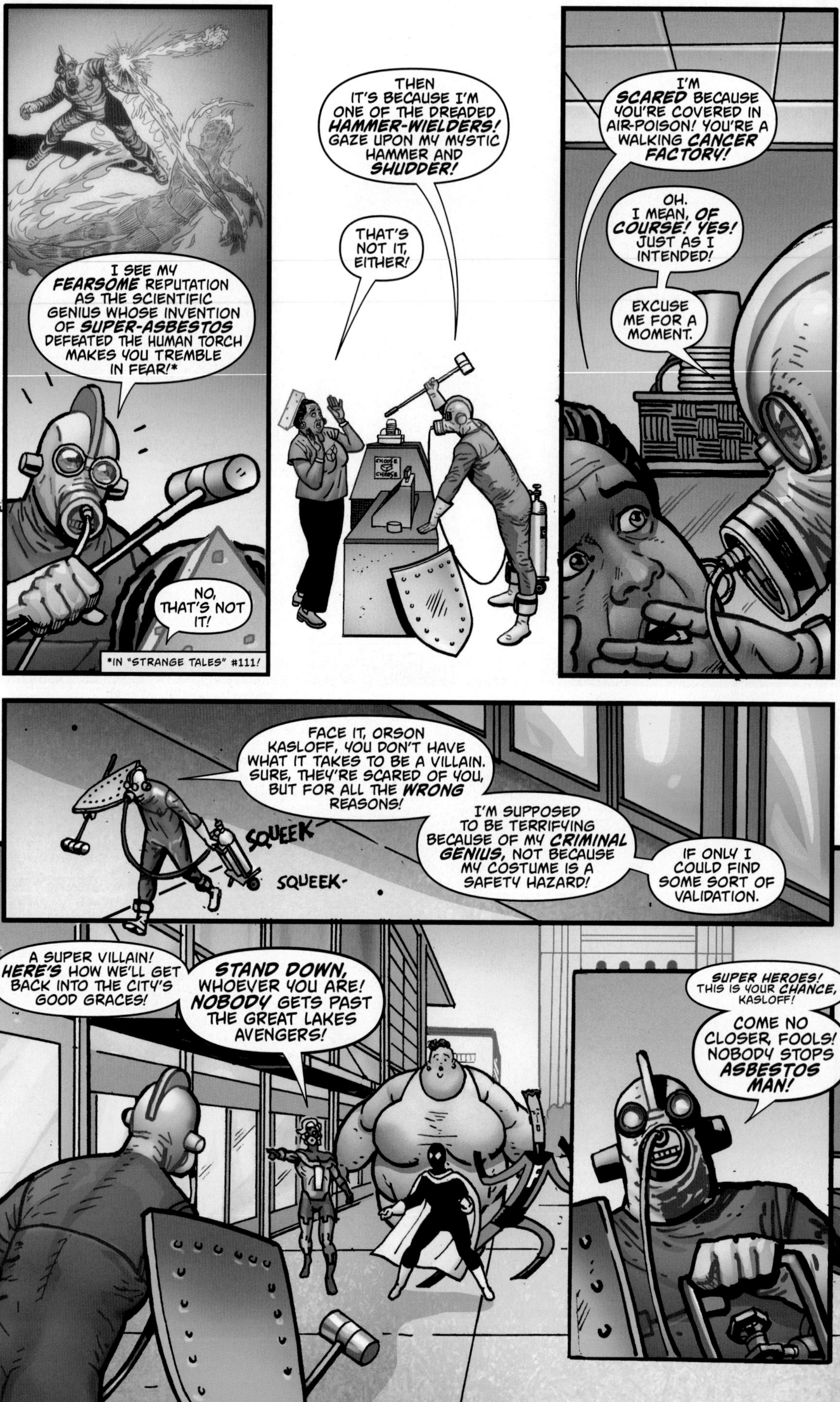
I SEE MY FEARSOME REPUTATION AS THE SCIENTIFIC GENIUS WHOSE INVENTION OF SUPER-ASBESTOS DEFEATED THE HUMAN TORCH MAKES YOU TREMBLE IN FEAR!*
NO, THAT'S NOT IT!
*IN "STRANGE TALES" #111!
THEN IT'S BECAUSE I'M ONE OF THE DREADED HAMMER-WIELDERS! GAZE UPON MY MYSTIC HAMMER AND SHUDDER!
THAT'S NOT IT, EITHER!
I'M SCARED BECAUSE YOU'RE COVERED IN AIR-POISON! YOU'RE A WALKING CANCER FACTORY!
OH. I MEAN, OF COURSE! YES! JUST AS I INTENDED!
EXCUSE ME FOR A MOMENT.
FACE IT, ORSON KASLOFF, YOU DON'T HAVE WHAT IT TAKES TO BE A VILLAIN. SURE, THEY'RE SCARED OF YOU, BUT FOR ALL THE WRONG REASONS!
SQUEEK
SQUEEK
I'M SUPPOSED TO BE TERRIFYING BECAUSE OF MY CRIMINAL GENIUS, NOT BECAUSE MY COSTUME IS A SAFETY HAZARD!
IF ONLY I COULD FIND SOME SORT OF VALIDATION.
A SUPER VILLAIN! HERE'S HOW WE'LL GET BACK INTO THE CITY'S GOOD GRACES!
STAND DOWN, WHOEVER YOU ARE! NOBODY GETS PAST THE GREAT LAKES AVENGERS!
SUPER HEROES! THIS IS YOUR CHANCE, KASLOFF!
COME NO CLOSER, FOOLS! NOBODY STOPS ASBESTOS MAN!

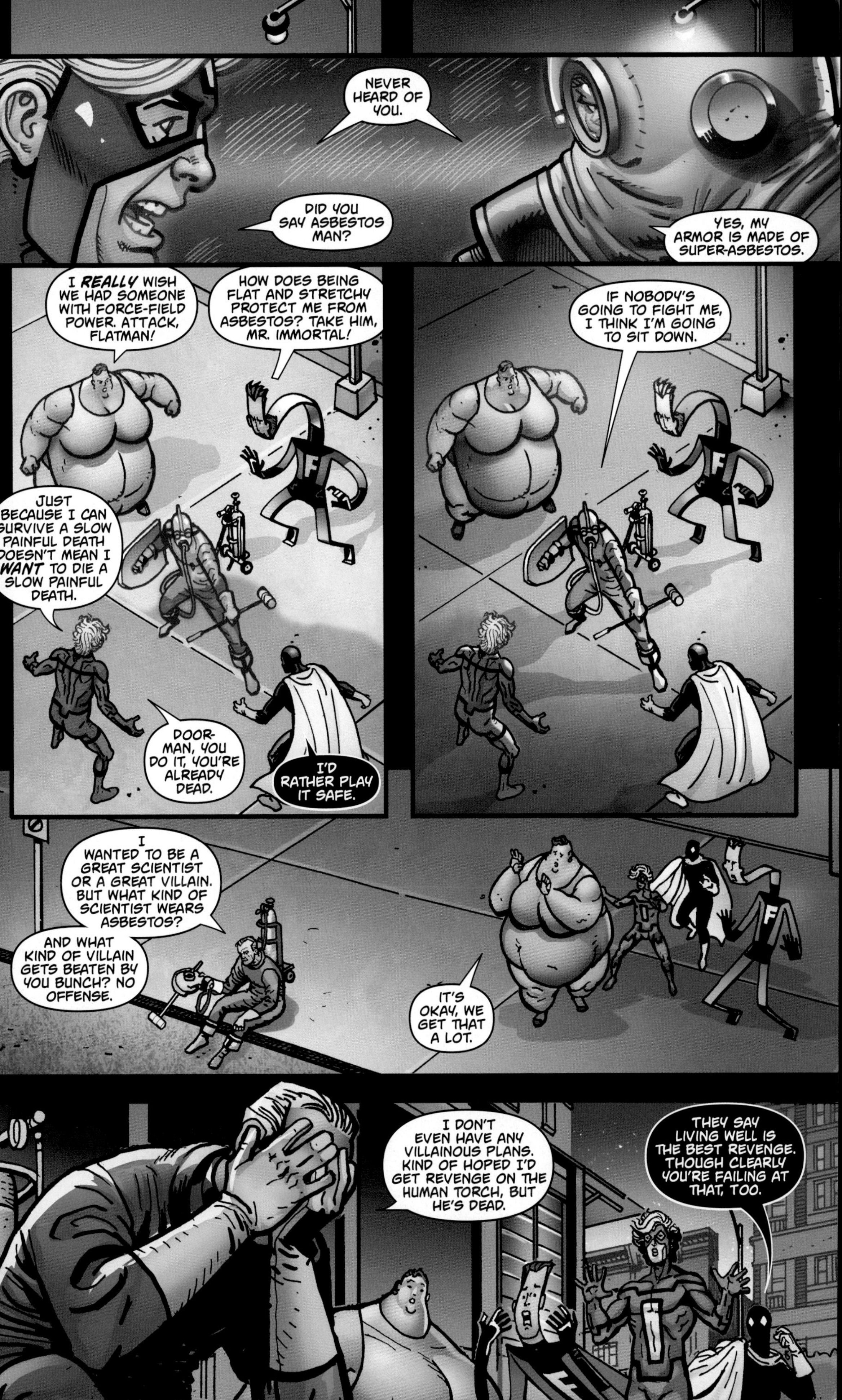
NEVER HEARD OF YOU.
DID YOU SAY ASBESTOS MAN?
YES, MY ARMOR IS MADE OF SUPER-ASBESTOS.
I *REALLY* WISH WE HAD SOMEONE WITH FORCE-FIELD POWER. ATTACK, FLATMAN!
HOW DOES BEING FLAT AND STRETCHY PROTECT ME FROM ASBESTOS? TAKE HIM, MR. IMMORTAL!
JUST BECAUSE I CAN SURVIVE A SLOW PAINFUL DEATH DOESN'T MEAN I *WANT* TO DIE A SLOW PAINFUL DEATH.
DOOR-MAN, YOU DO IT, YOU'RE ALREADY DEAD.
I'D RATHER PLAY IT SAFE.
IF NOBODY'S GOING TO FIGHT ME, I THINK I'M GOING TO SIT DOWN.
I WANTED TO BE A GREAT SCIENTIST OR A GREAT VILLAIN. BUT WHAT KIND OF SCIENTIST WEARS ASBESTOS?
AND WHAT KIND OF VILLAIN GETS BEATEN BY YOU BUNCH? NO OFFENSE.
IT'S OKAY, WE GET THAT A LOT.
I DON'T EVEN HAVE ANY VILLAINOUS PLANS. KIND OF HOPED I'D GET REVENGE ON THE HUMAN TORCH, BUT HE'S DEAD.
THEY SAY LIVING WELL IS THE BEST REVENGE. THOUGH CLEARLY YOU'RE FAILING AT THAT, TOO.

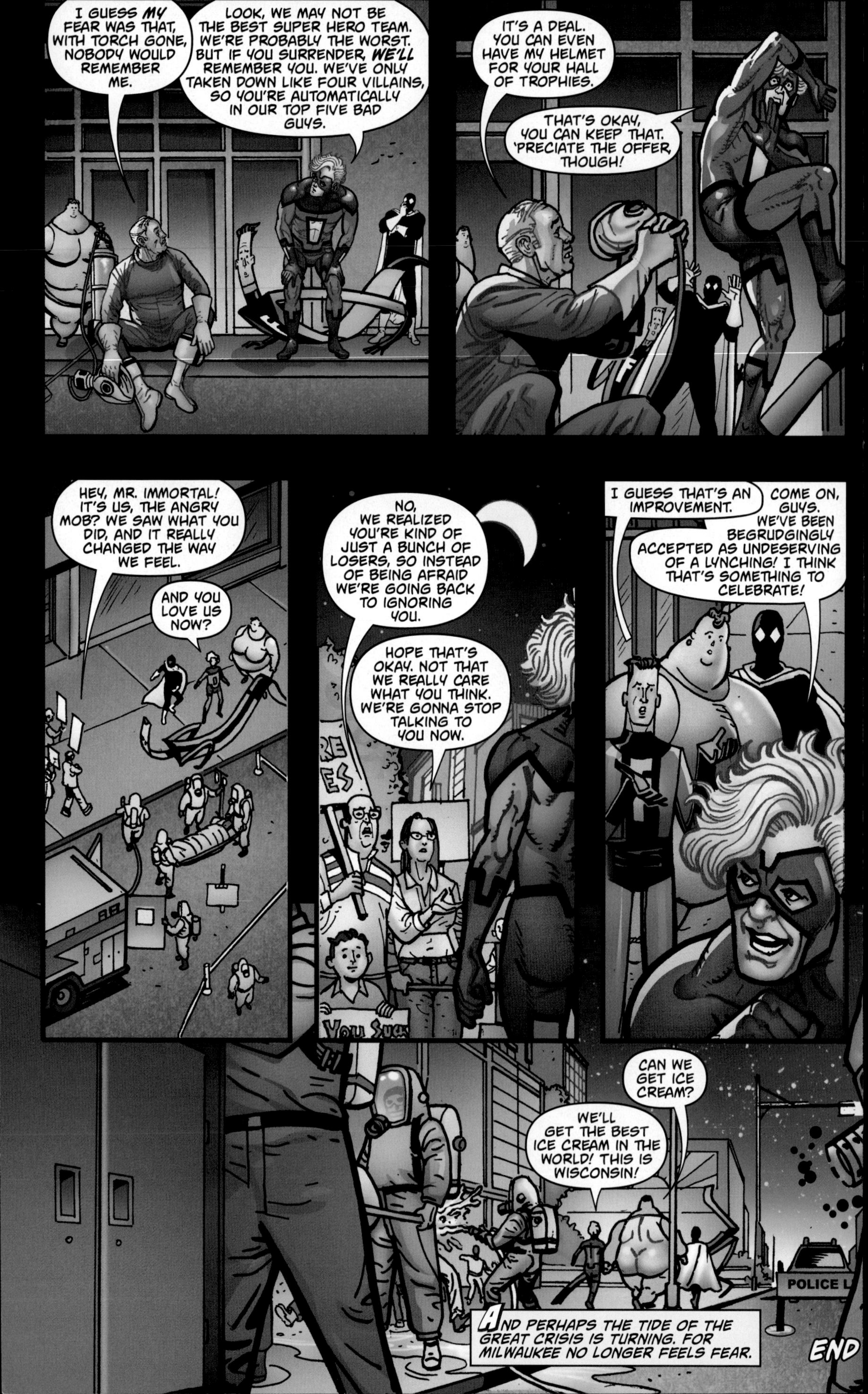
I GUESS MY FEAR WAS THAT, WITH TORCH GONE, NOBODY WOULD REMEMBER ME.
LOOK, WE MAY NOT BE THE BEST SUPER HERO TEAM. WE'RE PROBABLY THE WORST. BUT IF YOU SURRENDER, WE'LL REMEMBER YOU. WE'VE ONLY TAKEN DOWN LIKE FOUR VILLAINS, SO YOU'RE AUTOMATICALLY IN OUR TOP FIVE BAD GUYS.
IT'S A DEAL. YOU CAN EVEN HAVE MY HELMET FOR YOUR HALL OF TROPHIES.
THAT'S OKAY, YOU CAN KEEP THAT. 'PRECIATE THE OFFER, THOUGH!
HEY, MR. IMMORTAL! IT'S US, THE ANGRY MOB? WE SAW WHAT YOU DID, AND IT REALLY CHANGED THE WAY WE FEEL.
AND YOU LOVE US NOW?
NO, WE REALIZED YOU'RE KIND OF JUST A BUNCH OF LOSERS, SO INSTEAD OF BEING AFRAID WE'RE GOING BACK TO IGNORING YOU.
HOPE THAT'S OKAY. NOT THAT WE REALLY CARE WHAT YOU THINK. WE'RE GONNA STOP TALKING TO YOU NOW.
I GUESS THAT'S AN IMPROVEMENT.
COME ON, GUYS. WE'VE BEEN BEGRUDGINGLY ACCEPTED AS UNDESERVING OF A LYNCHING! I THINK THAT'S SOMETHING TO CELEBRATE!
CAN WE GET ICE CREAM?
WE'LL GET THE BEST ICE CREAM IN THE WORLD! THIS IS WISCONSIN!
AND PERHAPS THE TIDE OF THE GREAT CRISIS IS TURNING. FOR MILWAUKEE NO LONGER FEELS FEAR.
END

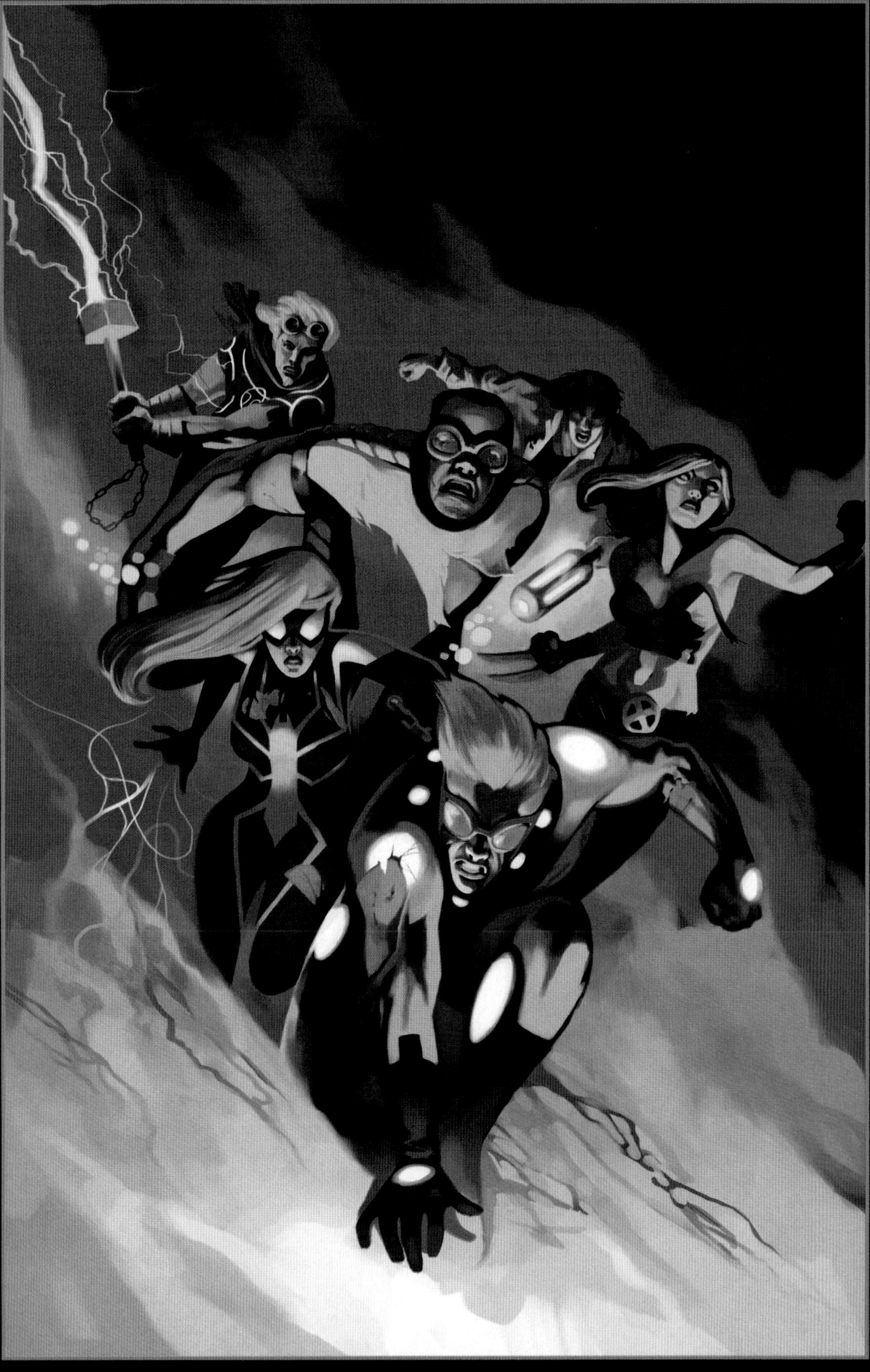

FEAR ITSELF: THE HOME FRONT #7

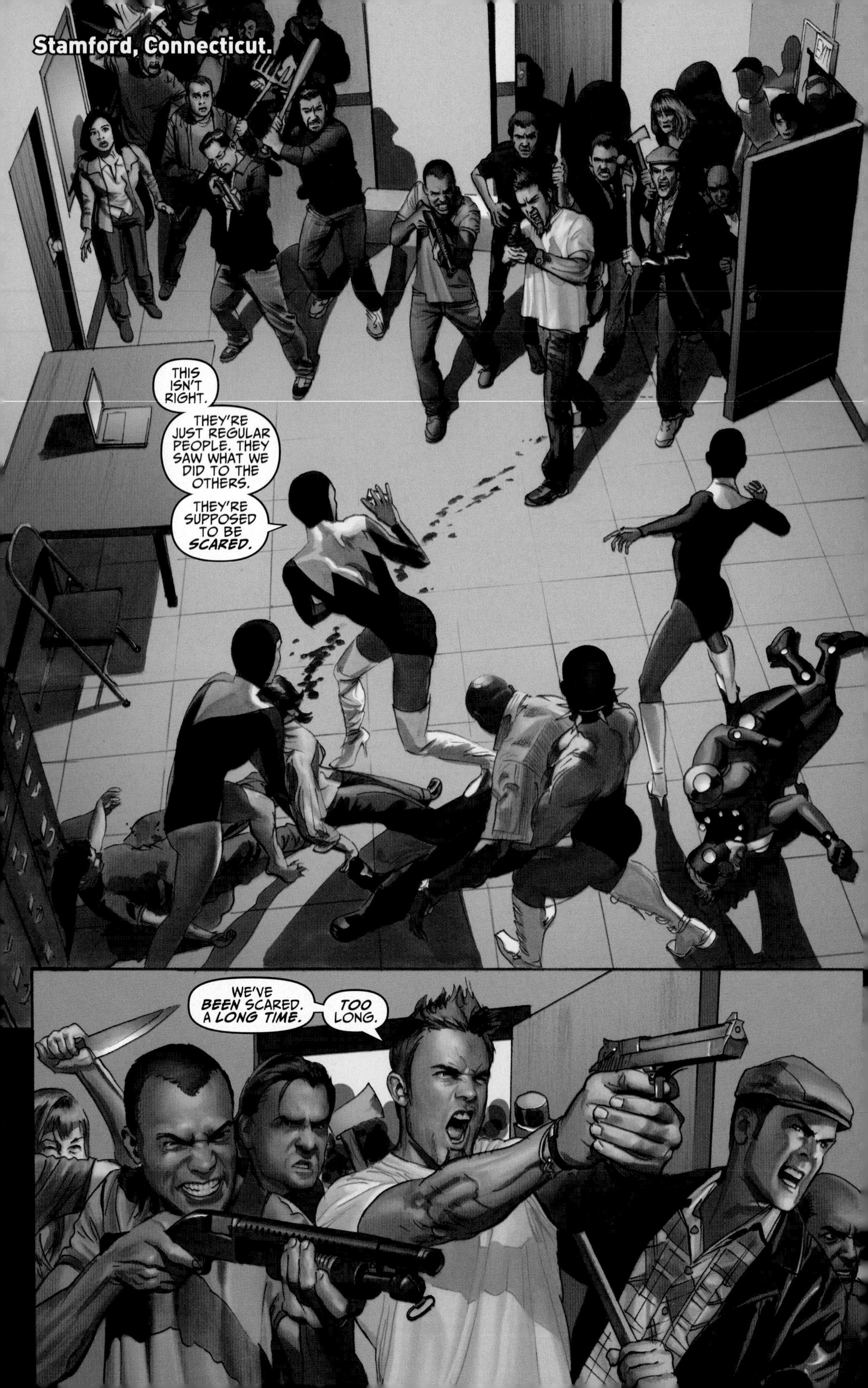

Stamford, Connecticut.
THIS ISN'T RIGHT.
THEY'RE JUST REGULAR PEOPLE. THEY SAW WHAT WE DID TO THE OTHERS.
THEY'RE SUPPOSED TO BE SCARED.
WE'VE BEEN SCARED. A LONG TIME.
TOO LONG.
EXIT

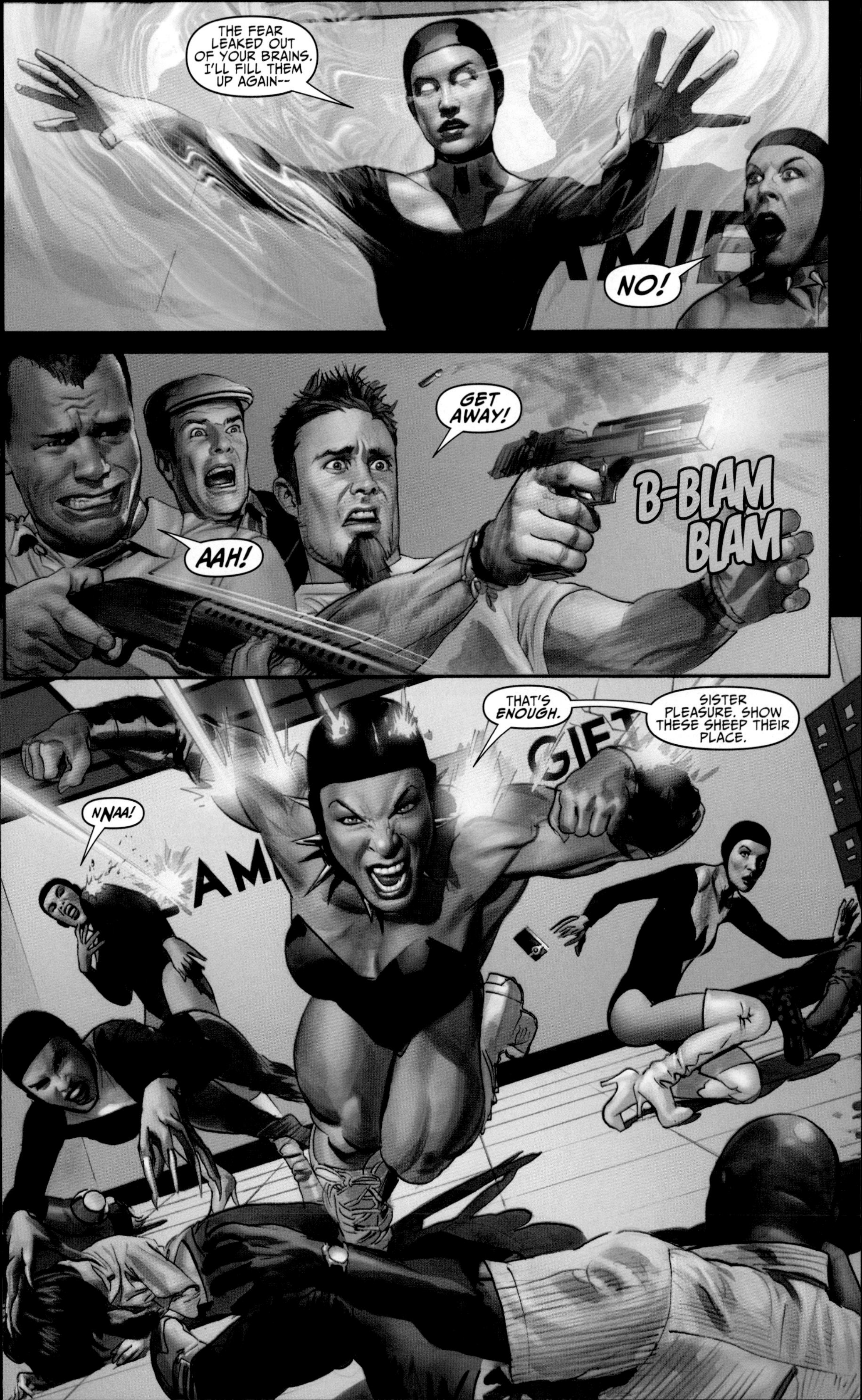

THE FEAR LEAKED OUT OF YOUR BRAINS. I'LL FILL THEM UP AGAIN--
NO!
GET AWAY!
AAH!
B-BLAM BLAM
THAT'S ENOUGH.
SISTER PLEASURE. SHOW THESE SHEEP THEIR PLACE.
NNAA!

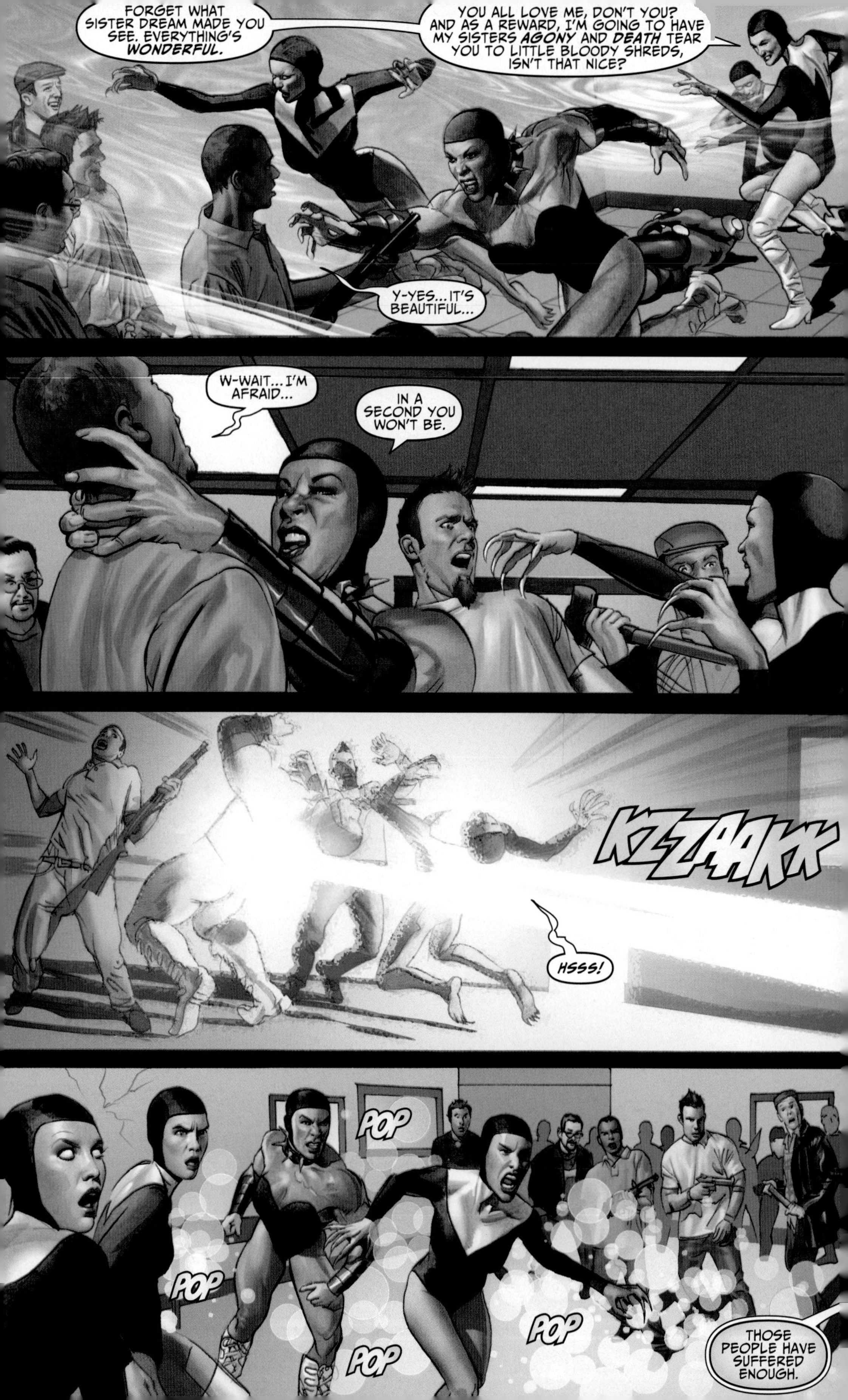
FORGET WHAT SISTER DREAM MADE YOU SEE. EVERYTHING'S *WONDERFUL.*
YOU ALL LOVE ME, DON'T YOU? AND AS A REWARD, I'M GOING TO HAVE MY SISTERS *AGONY* AND *DEATH* TEAR YOU TO LITTLE BLOODY SHREDS, ISN'T THAT NICE?
Y-YES... IT'S BEAUTIFUL...
W-WAIT... I'M AFRAID...
IN A SECOND YOU WON'T BE.
KZZAAKK
HSSS!
POP
POP
POP
POP
THOSE PEOPLE HAVE SUFFERED ENOUGH.

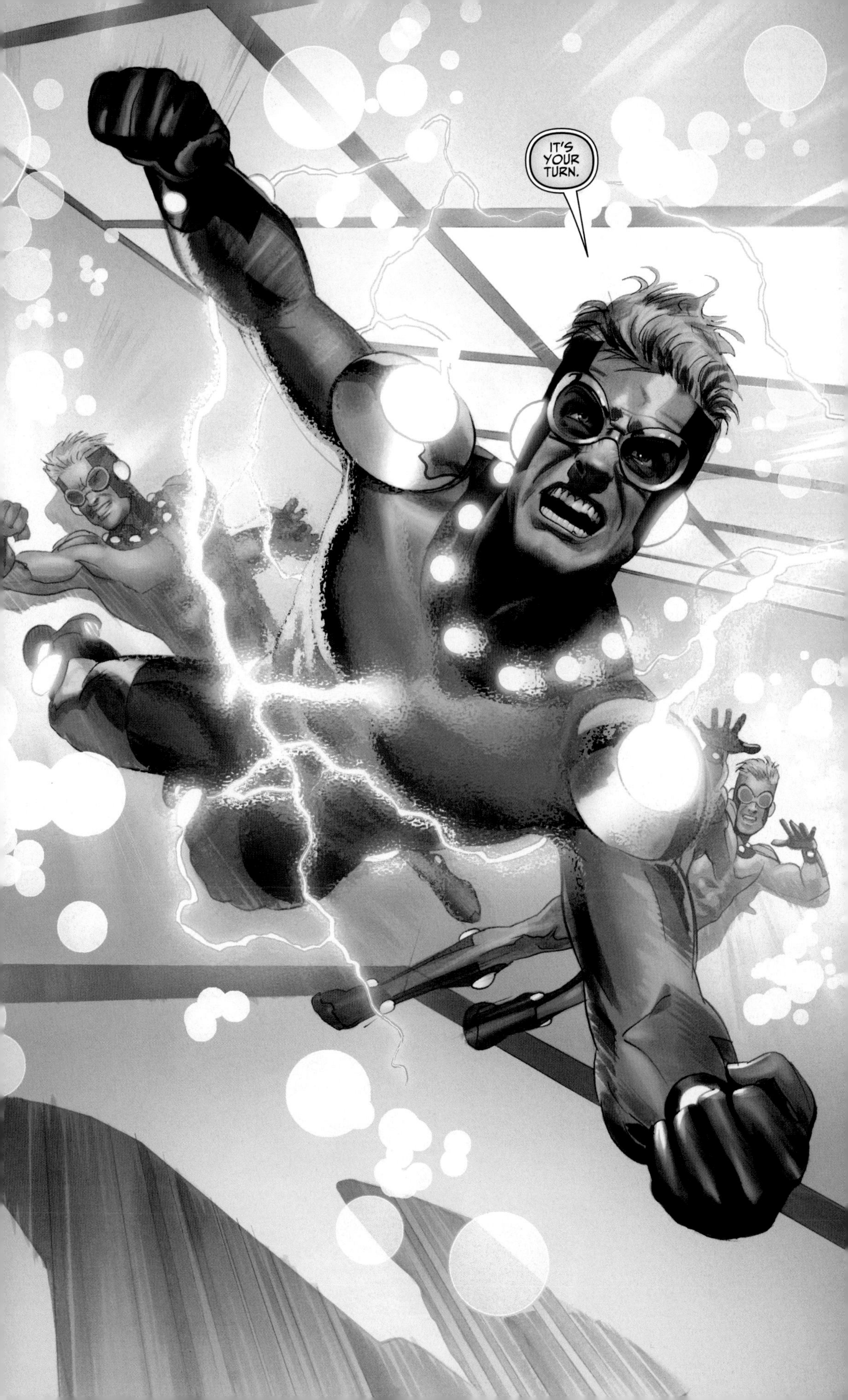
IT'S YOUR TURN.

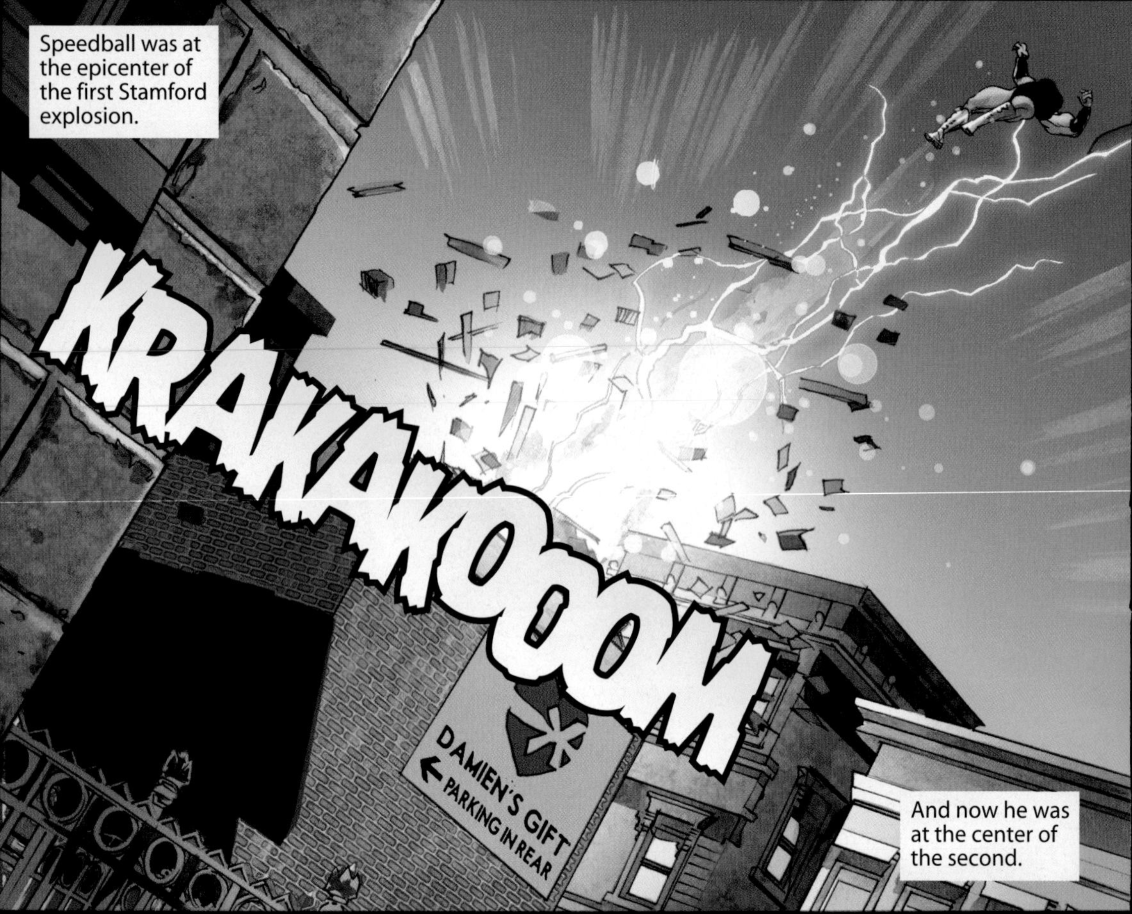
Speedball was at the epicenter of the first Stamford explosion.
KRAKAKOOOOM
DAMIEN'S GIFT
PARKING IN REAR
And now he was at the center of the second.

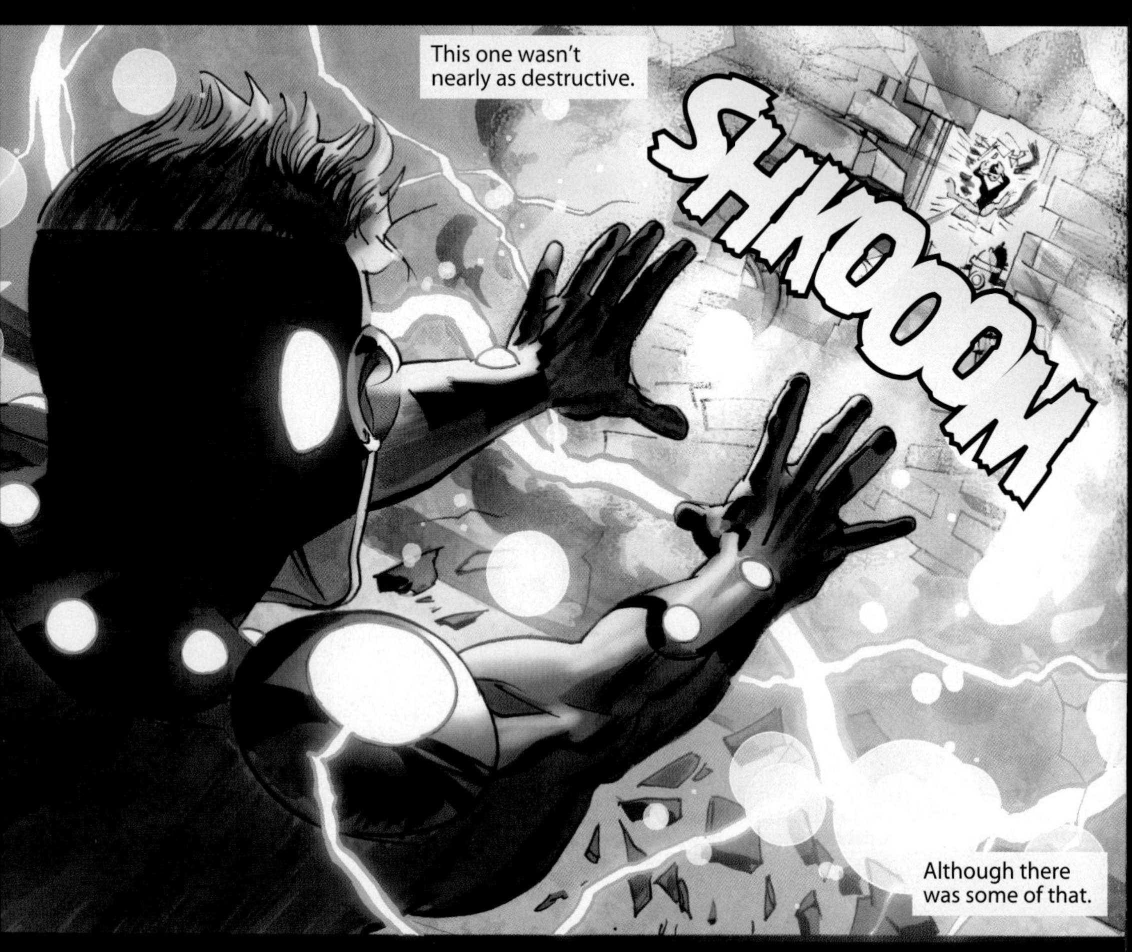
This one wasn't nearly as destructive.
SHKOOOM
Although there was some of that.

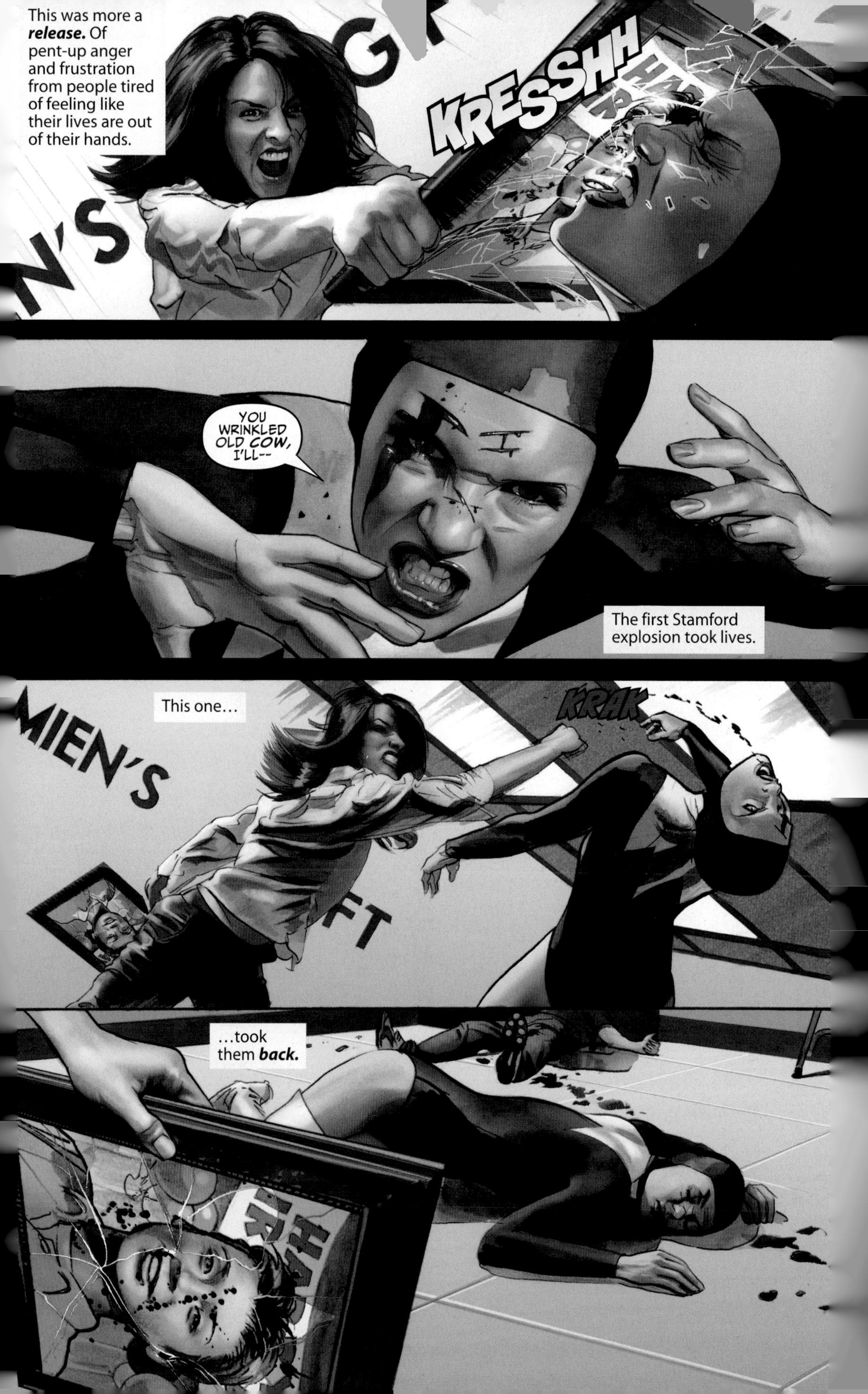
This was more a ***release.*** Of pent-up anger and frustration from people tired of feeling like their lives are out of their hands.
KRESSHH
YOU WRINKLED OLD *COW*, I'LL--
The first Stamford explosion took lives.
This one…
KRAK
…took them ***back.***

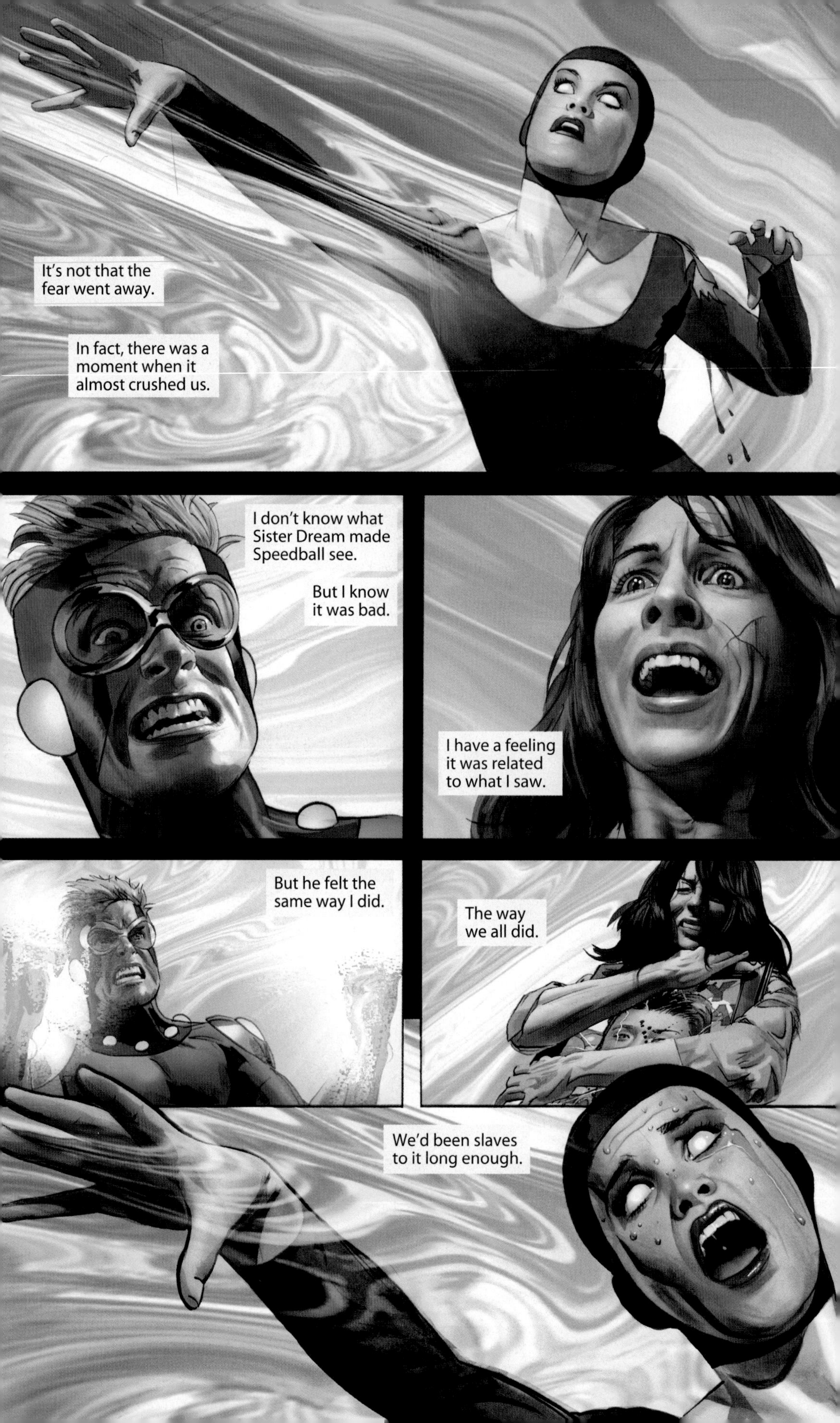
It's not that the fear went away.
In fact, there was a moment when it almost crushed us.
I don't know what Sister Dream made Speedball see.
But I know it was bad.
I have a feeling it was related to what I saw.
But he felt the same way I did.
The way we all did.
We'd been slaves to it long enough.

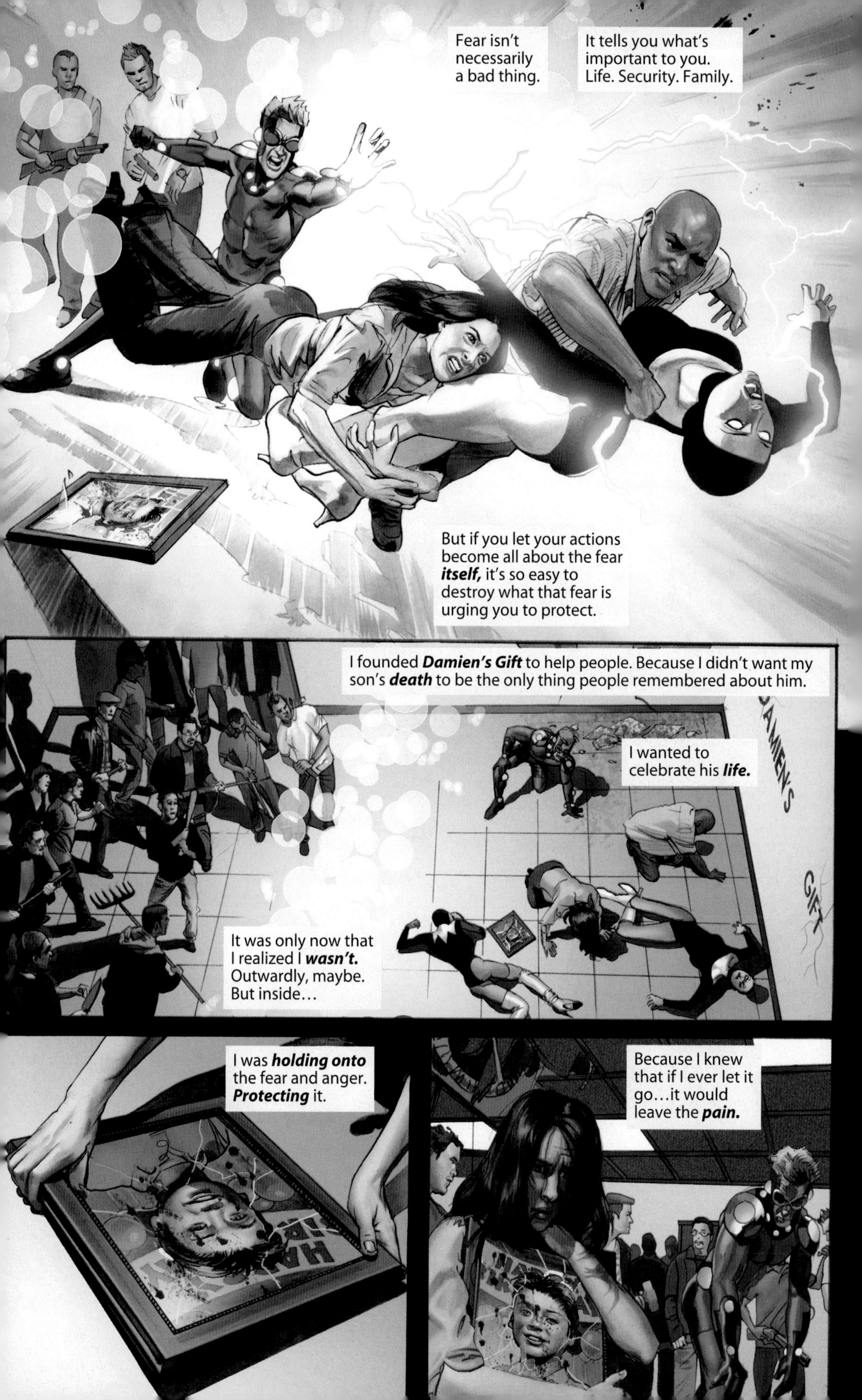
Fear isn't necessarily a bad thing.
It tells you what's important to you. Life. Security. Family.
But if you let your actions become all about the fear *itself,* it's so easy to destroy what that fear is urging you to protect.
I founded *Damien's Gift* to help people. Because I didn't want my son's *death* to be the only thing people remembered about him.
I wanted to celebrate his *life.*
It was only now that I realized I *wasn't.* Outwardly, maybe. But inside…
I was *holding onto* the fear and anger. *Protecting* it.
Because I knew that if I ever let it go…it would leave the *pain.*

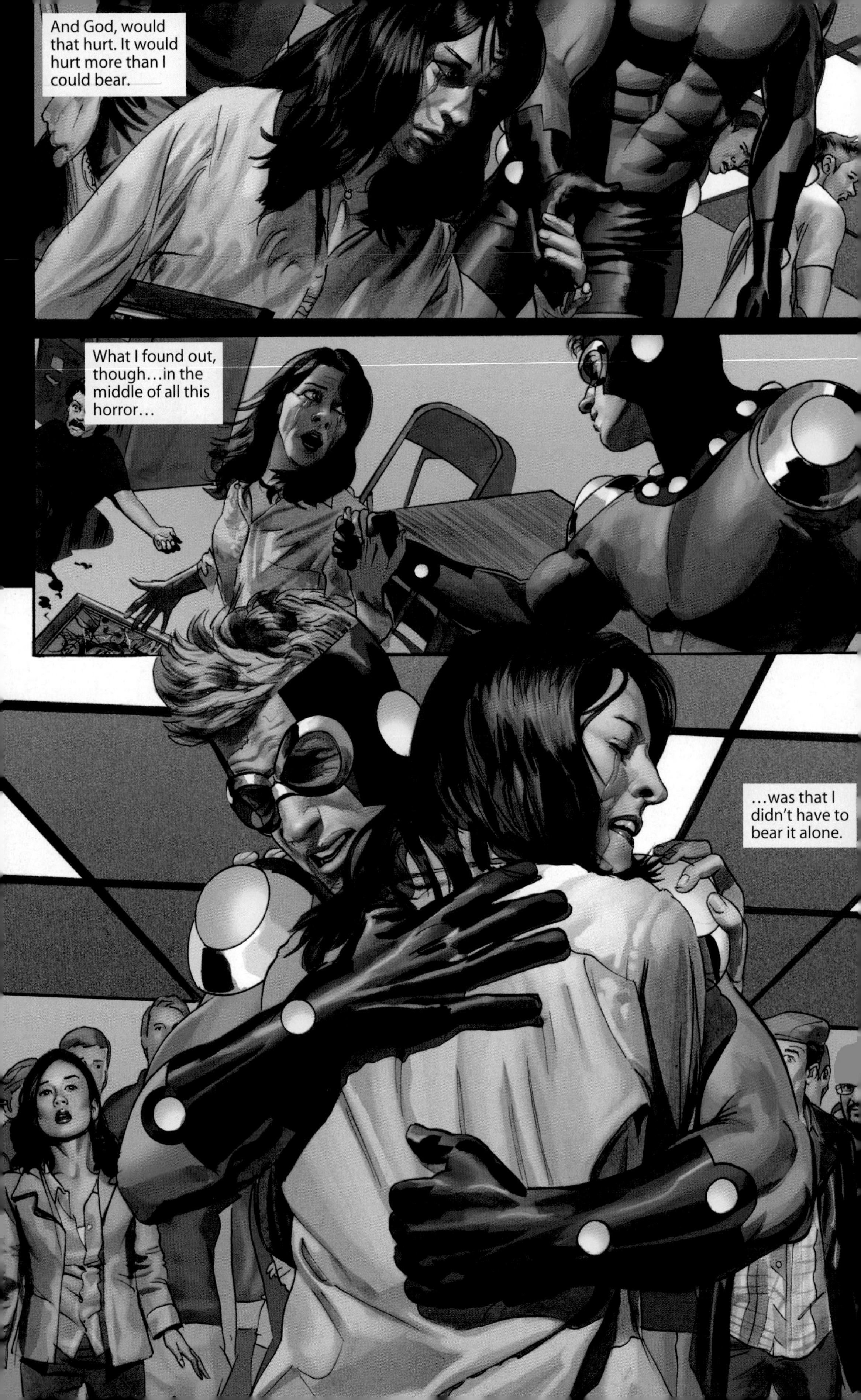
And God, would that hurt. It would hurt more than I could bear.
What I found out, though…in the middle of all this horror…
…was that I didn't have to bear it alone.

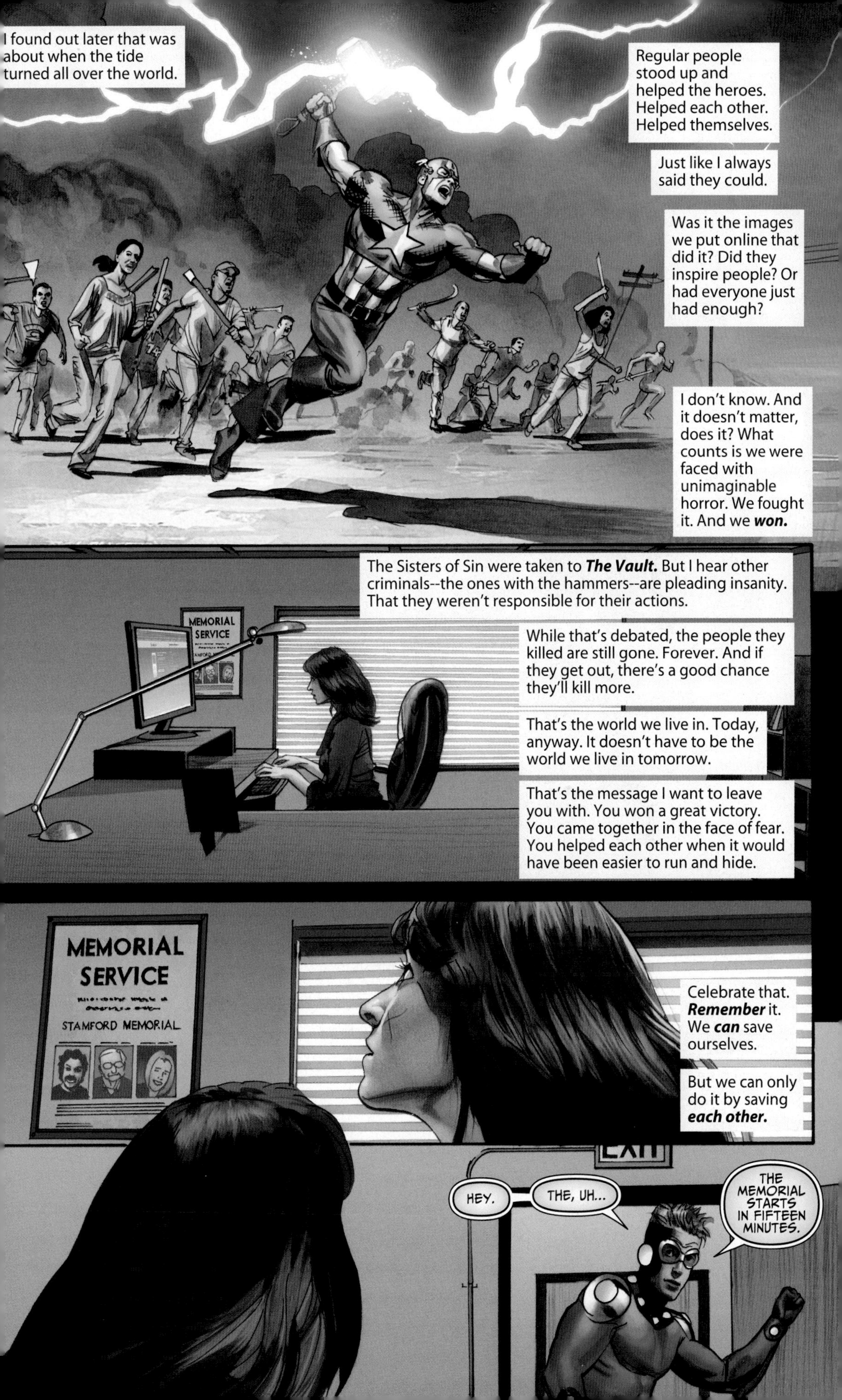

I found out later that was about when the tide turned all over the world.
Regular people stood up and helped the heroes. Helped each other. Helped themselves.
Just like I always said they could.
Was it the images we put online that did it? Did they inspire people? Or had everyone just had enough?
I don't know. And it doesn't matter, does it? What counts is we were faced with unimaginable horror. We fought it. And we ***won.***
The Sisters of Sin were taken to ***The Vault.*** But I hear other criminals--the ones with the hammers--are pleading insanity. That they weren't responsible for their actions.
While that's debated, the people they killed are still gone. Forever. And if they get out, there's a good chance they'll kill more.
That's the world we live in. Today, anyway. It doesn't have to be the world we live in tomorrow.
That's the message I want to leave you with. You won a great victory. You came together in the face of fear. You helped each other when it would have been easier to run and hide.
MEMORIAL SERVICE
STAMFORD MEMORIAL
Celebrate that. ***Remember*** it. We ***can*** save ourselves.
But we can only do it by saving ***each other.***
HEY.
THE, UH...
THE MEMORIAL STARTS IN FIFTEEN MINUTES.

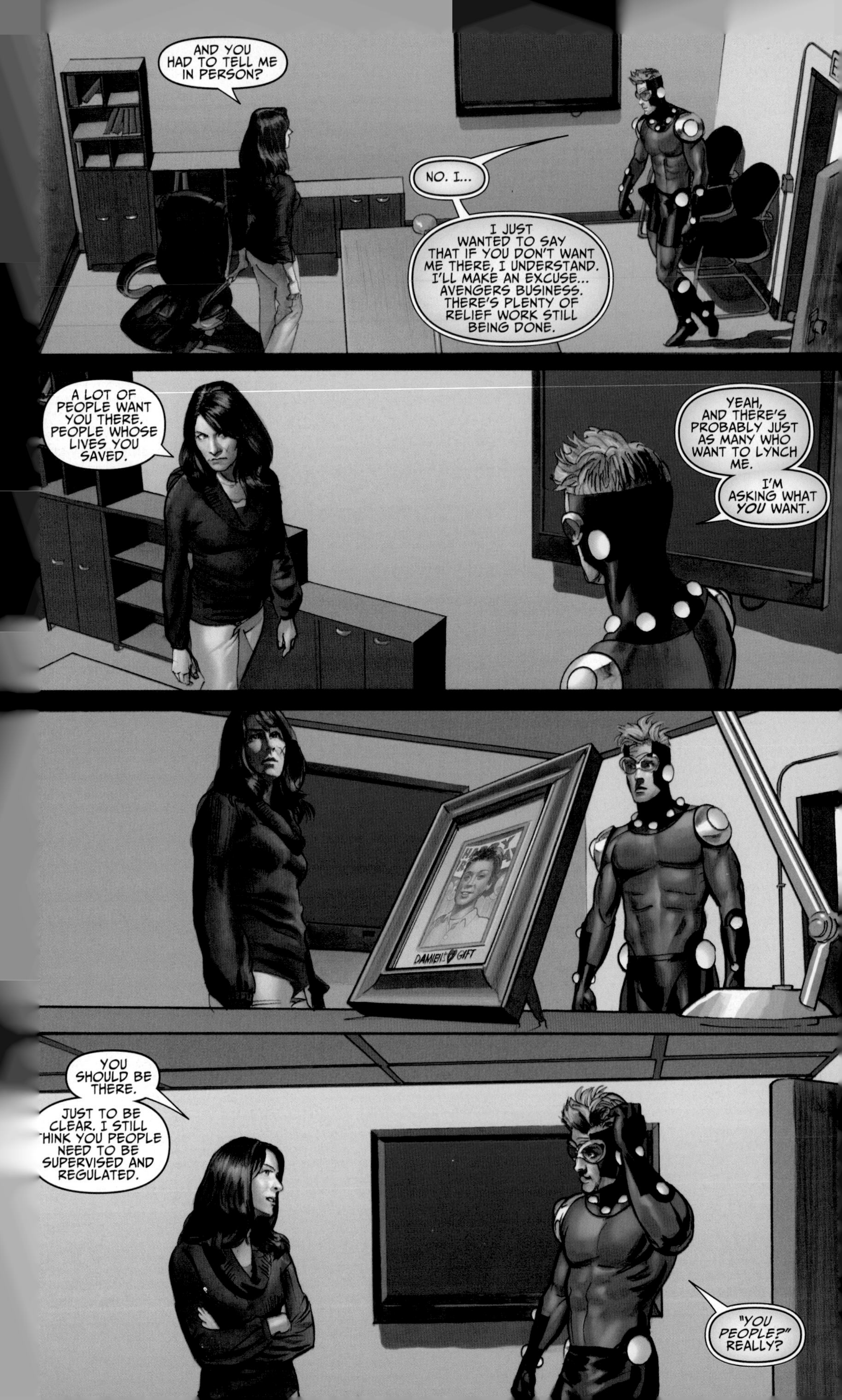

AND YOU HAD TO TELL ME IN PERSON?
NO. I...
I JUST WANTED TO SAY THAT IF YOU DON'T WANT ME THERE, I UNDERSTAND. I'LL MAKE AN EXCUSE... AVENGERS BUSINESS. THERE'S PLENTY OF RELIEF WORK STILL BEING DONE.
A LOT OF PEOPLE WANT YOU THERE. PEOPLE WHOSE LIVES YOU SAVED.
YEAH, AND THERE'S PROBABLY JUST AS MANY WHO WANT TO LYNCH ME.
I'M ASKING WHAT *YOU* WANT.
DAMIEN'S GIFT
YOU SHOULD BE THERE.
JUST TO BE CLEAR. I STILL THINK YOU PEOPLE NEED TO BE SUPERVISED AND REGULATED.
"YOU PEOPLE?" REALLY?

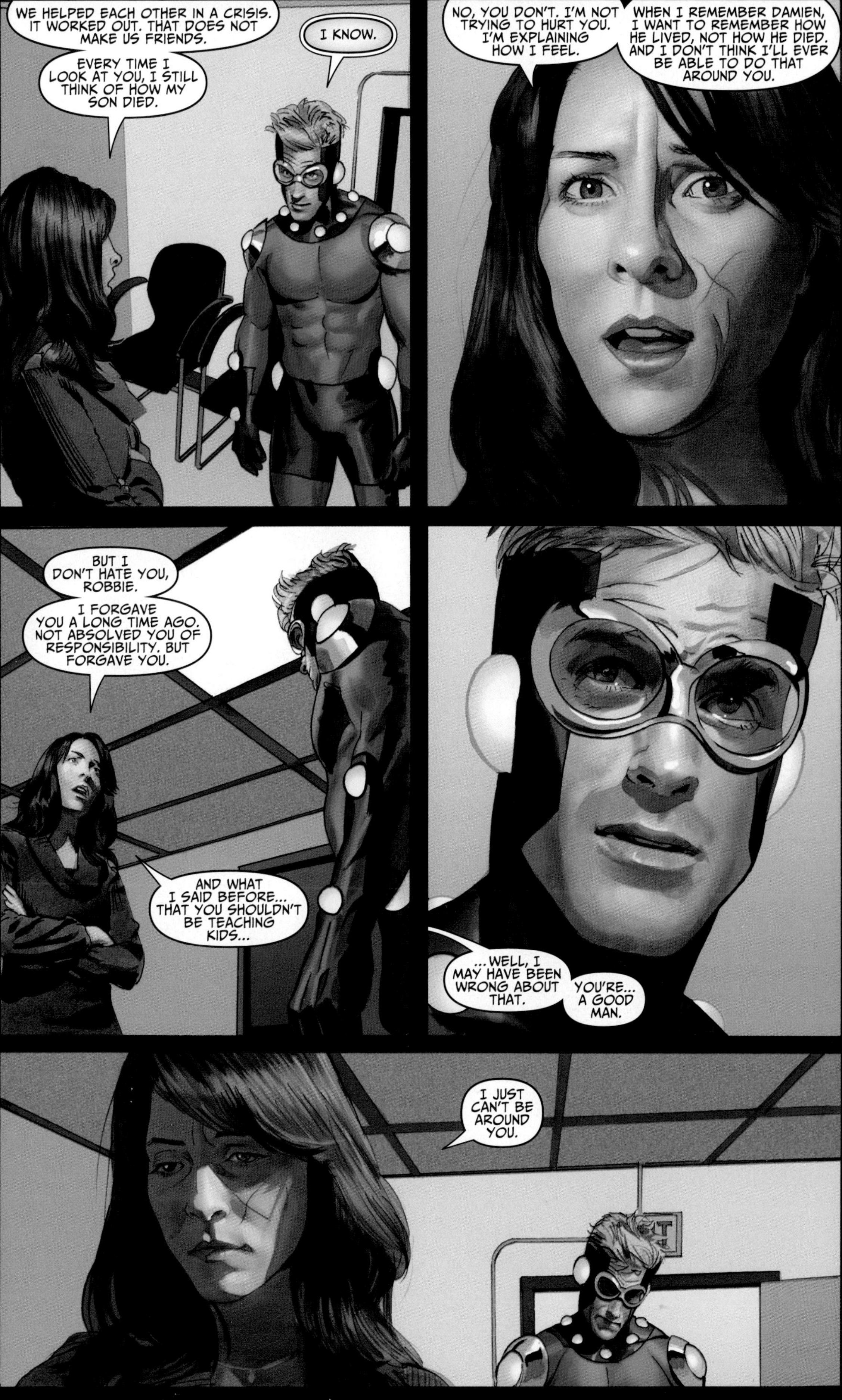
WE HELPED EACH OTHER IN A CRISIS. IT WORKED OUT. THAT DOES NOT MAKE US FRIENDS.
EVERY TIME I LOOK AT YOU, I STILL THINK OF HOW MY SON DIED.
I KNOW.
NO, YOU DON'T. I'M NOT TRYING TO HURT YOU. I'M EXPLAINING HOW I FEEL.
WHEN I REMEMBER DAMIEN, I WANT TO REMEMBER HOW HE LIVED, NOT HOW HE DIED. AND I DON'T THINK I'LL EVER BE ABLE TO DO THAT AROUND YOU.
BUT I DON'T HATE YOU, ROBBIE.
I FORGAVE YOU A LONG TIME AGO. NOT ABSOLVED YOU OF RESPONSIBILITY. BUT FORGAVE YOU.
AND WHAT I SAID BEFORE... THAT YOU SHOULDN'T BE TEACHING KIDS...
...WELL, I MAY HAVE BEEN WRONG ABOUT THAT.
YOU'RE... A GOOD MAN.
I JUST CAN'T BE AROUND YOU.

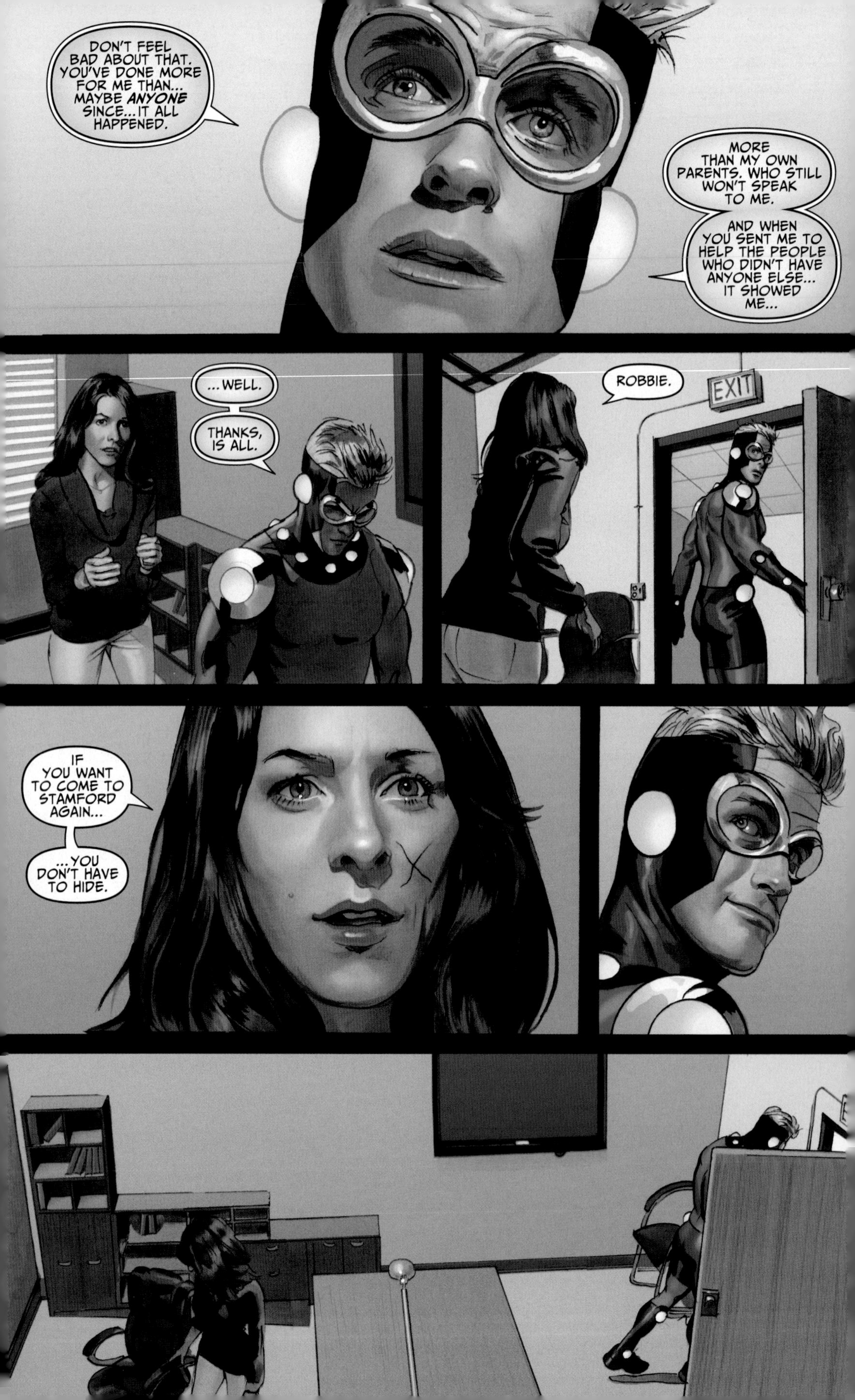
DON'T FEEL BAD ABOUT THAT. YOU'VE DONE MORE FOR ME THAN... MAYBE ANYONE SINCE...IT ALL HAPPENED.
MORE THAN MY OWN PARENTS. WHO STILL WON'T SPEAK TO ME.
AND WHEN YOU SENT ME TO HELP THE PEOPLE WHO DIDN'T HAVE ANYONE ELSE... IT SHOWED ME...
...WELL.
THANKS, IS ALL.
ROBBIE.
EXIT
IF YOU WANT TO COME TO STAMFORD AGAIN...
...YOU DON'T HAVE TO HIDE.

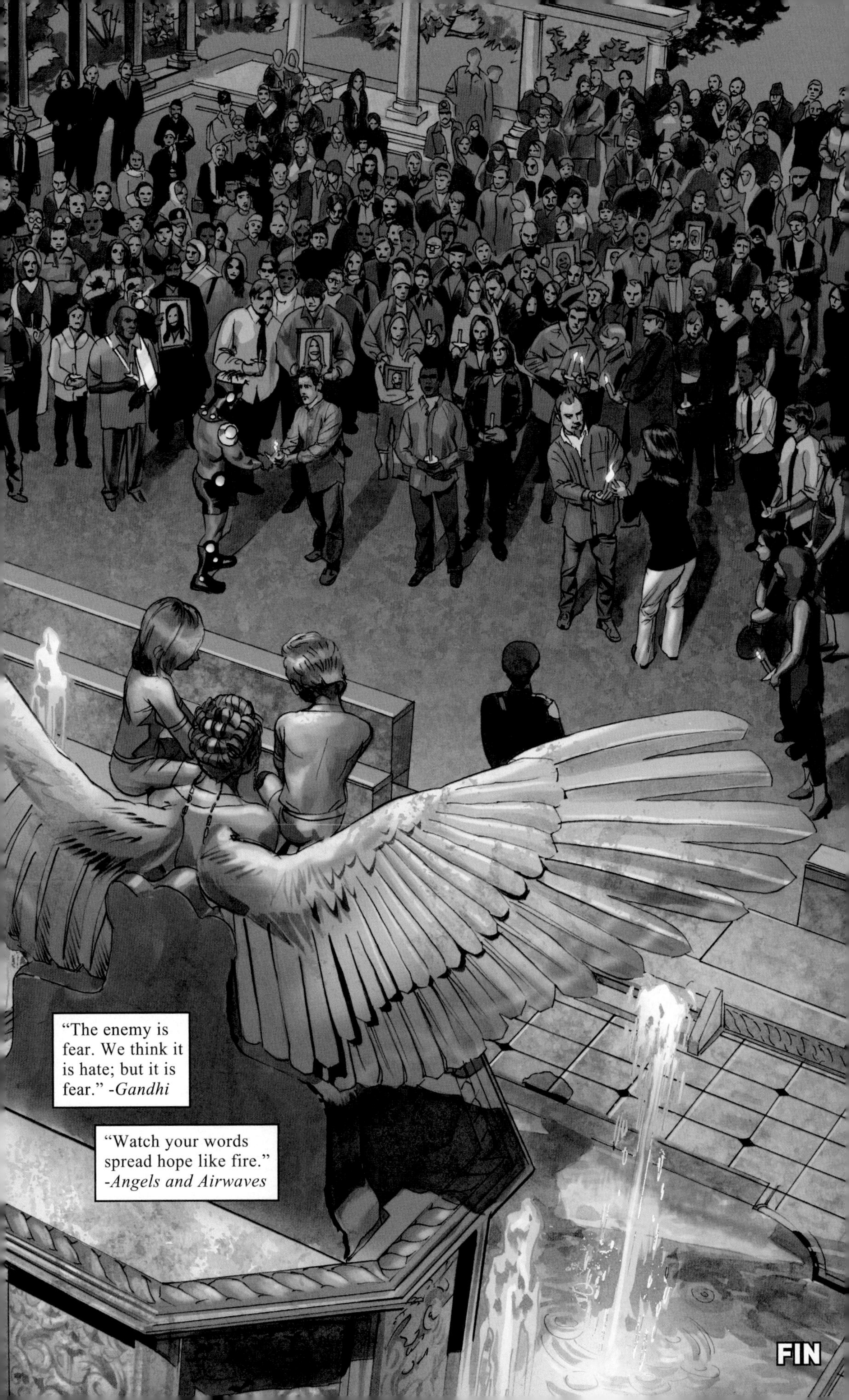
"The enemy is fear. We think it is hate; but it is fear." -Gandhi
"Watch your words spread hope like fire." -Angels and Airwaves
FIN

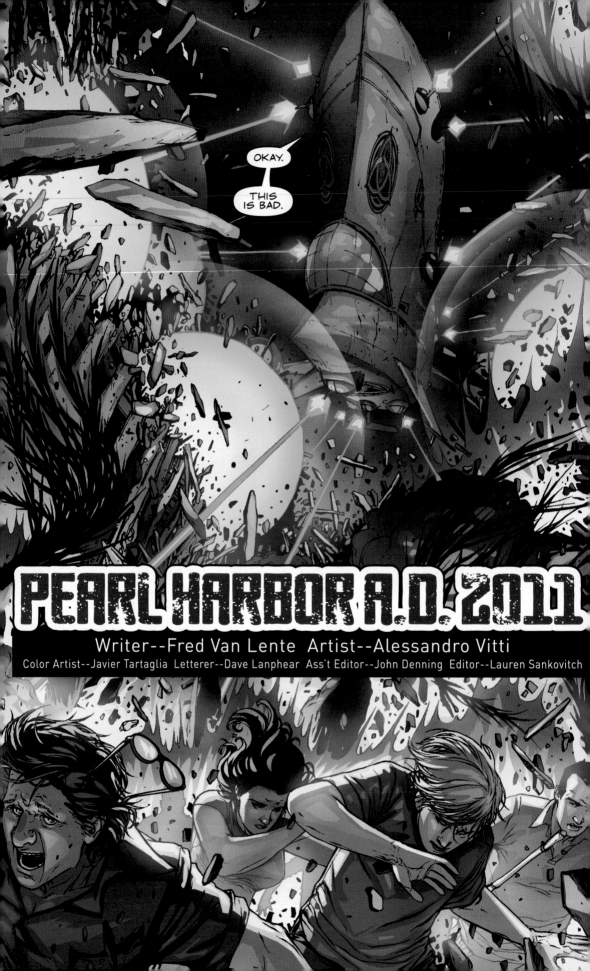

PEARL HARBOR A.D. 2011

Writer--Fred Van Lente Artist--Alessandro Vitti

Color Artist--Javier Tartaglia Letterer--Dave Lanphear Ass't Editor--John Denning Editor--Lauren Sankovitch

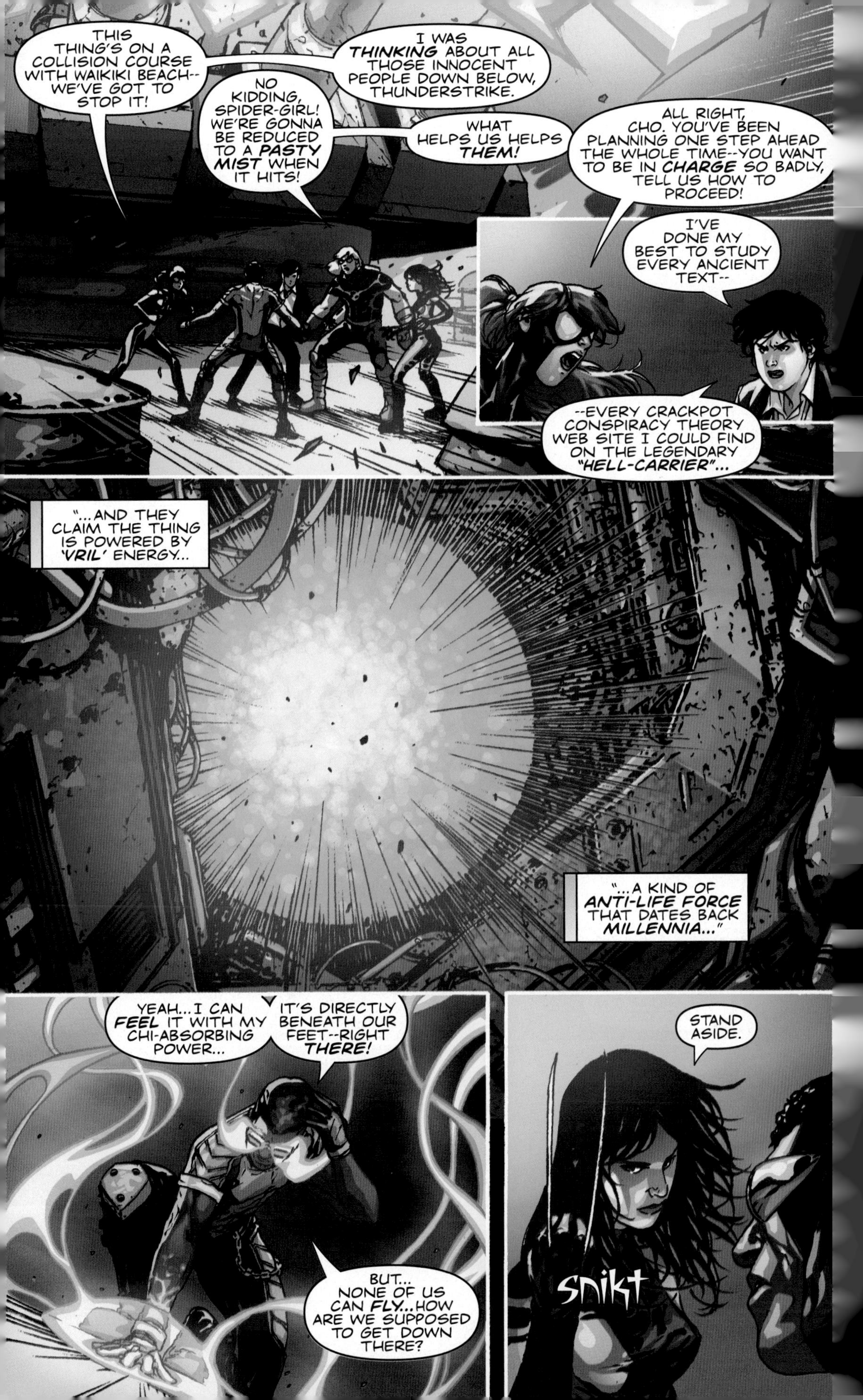
THIS THING'S ON A COLLISION COURSE WITH WAIKIKI BEACH--WE'VE GOT TO STOP IT!
I WAS THINKING ABOUT ALL THOSE INNOCENT PEOPLE DOWN BELOW, THUNDERSTRIKE.
NO KIDDING, SPIDER-GIRL! WE'RE GONNA BE REDUCED TO A PASTY MIST WHEN IT HITS!
WHAT HELPS US HELPS THEM!
ALL RIGHT, CHO. YOU'VE BEEN PLANNING ONE STEP AHEAD THE WHOLE TIME--YOU WANT TO BE IN CHARGE SO BADLY, TELL US HOW TO PROCEED!
I'VE DONE MY BEST TO STUDY EVERY ANCIENT TEXT--
--EVERY CRACKPOT CONSPIRACY THEORY WEB SITE I COULD FIND ON THE LEGENDARY "HELL-CARRIER"...
"...AND THEY CLAIM THE THING IS POWERED BY 'VRIL' ENERGY...
"...A KIND OF ANTI-LIFE FORCE THAT DATES BACK MILLENNIA..."
YEAH...I CAN FEEL IT WITH MY CHI-ABSORBING POWER...
IT'S DIRECTLY BENEATH OUR FEET--RIGHT THERE!
BUT... NONE OF US CAN FLY...HOW ARE WE SUPPOSED TO GET DOWN THERE?
STAND ASIDE.
SNIKT

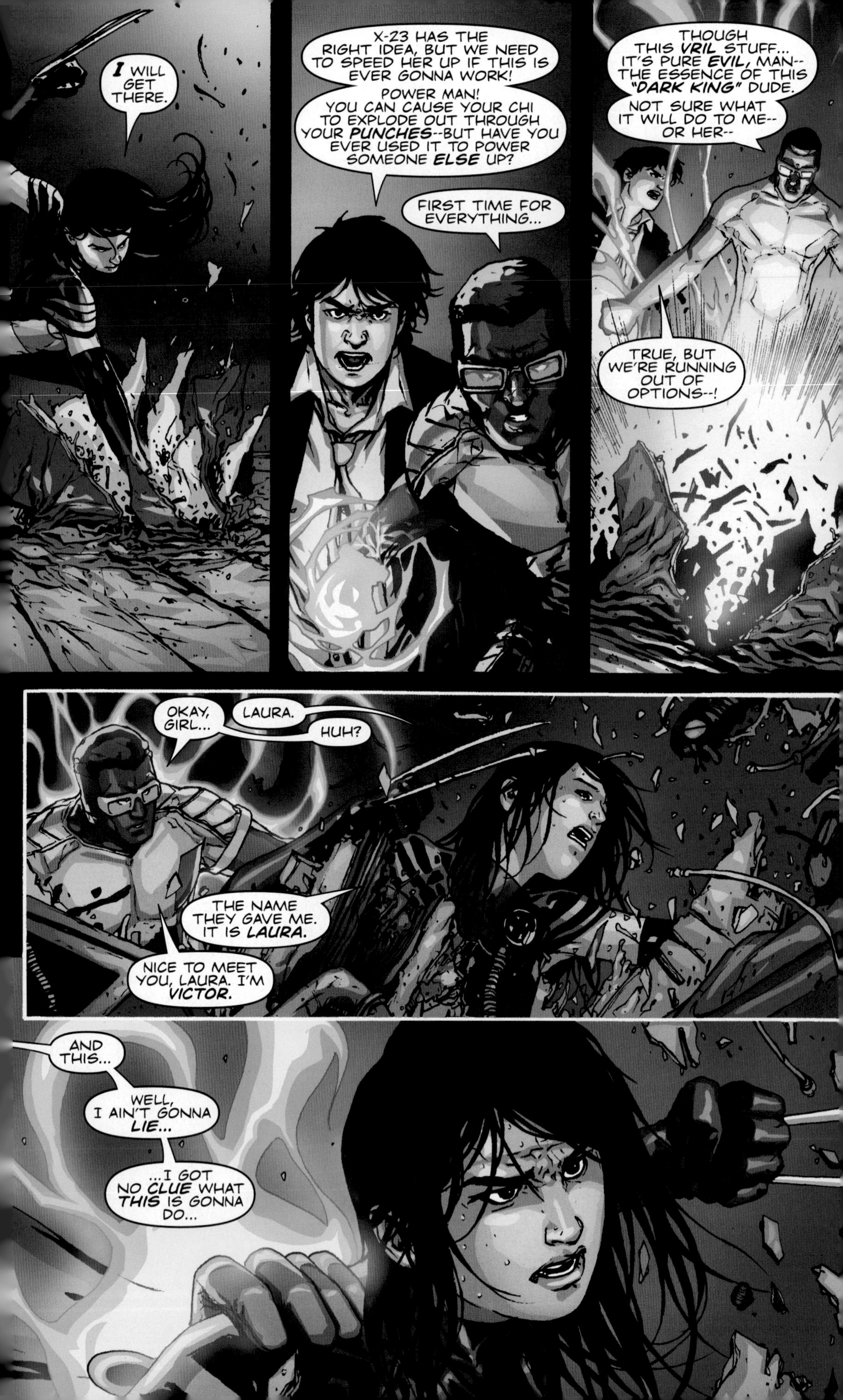

I WILL GET THERE.
X-23 HAS THE RIGHT IDEA, BUT WE NEED TO SPEED HER UP IF THIS IS EVER GONNA WORK!
POWER MAN! YOU CAN CAUSE YOUR CHI TO EXPLODE OUT THROUGH YOUR PUNCHES--BUT HAVE YOU EVER USED IT TO POWER SOMEONE ELSE UP?
FIRST TIME FOR EVERYTHING...
THOUGH THIS VRIL STUFF... IT'S PURE EVIL, MAN-- THE ESSENCE OF THIS "DARK KING" DUDE.
NOT SURE WHAT IT WILL DO TO ME-- OR HER--
TRUE, BUT WE'RE RUNNING OUT OF OPTIONS--!
OKAY, GIRL...
LAURA.
HUH?
THE NAME THEY GAVE ME. IT IS LAURA.
NICE TO MEET YOU, LAURA. I'M VICTOR.
AND THIS...
WELL, I AIN'T GONNA LIE...
...I GOT NO CLUE WHAT THIS IS GONNA DO...

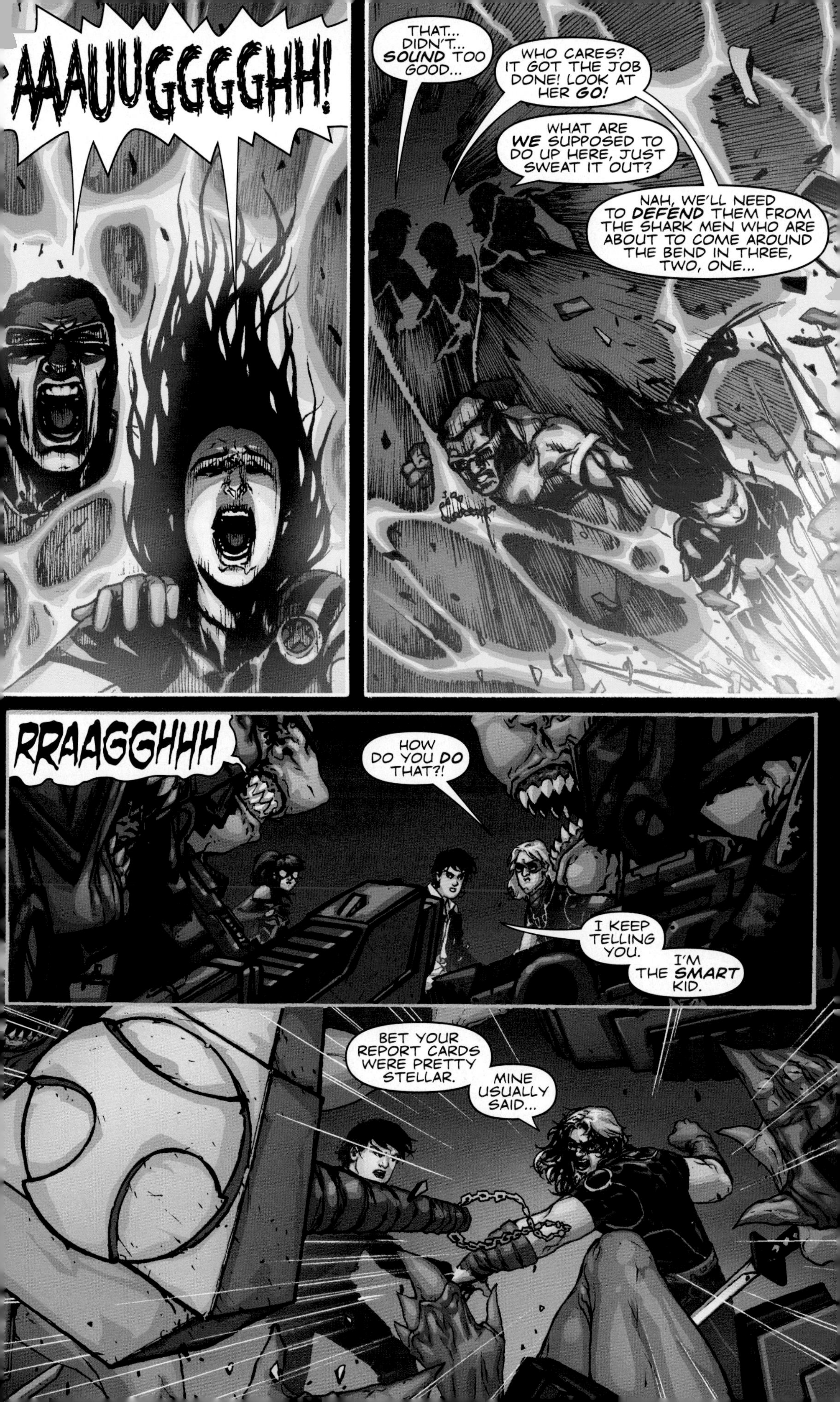

AAAUUGGGGHH!
THAT... DIDN'T... SOUND TOO GOOD...
WHO CARES? IT GOT THE JOB DONE! LOOK AT HER GO!
WHAT ARE WE SUPPOSED TO DO UP HERE, JUST SWEAT IT OUT?
NAH, WE'LL NEED TO DEFEND THEM FROM THE SHARK MEN WHO ARE ABOUT TO COME AROUND THE BEND IN THREE, TWO, ONE...
RRAAGGHHH
HOW DO YOU DO THAT?!
I KEEP TELLING YOU.
I'M THE SMART KID.
BET YOUR REPORT CARDS WERE PRETTY STELLAR.
MINE USUALLY SAID...

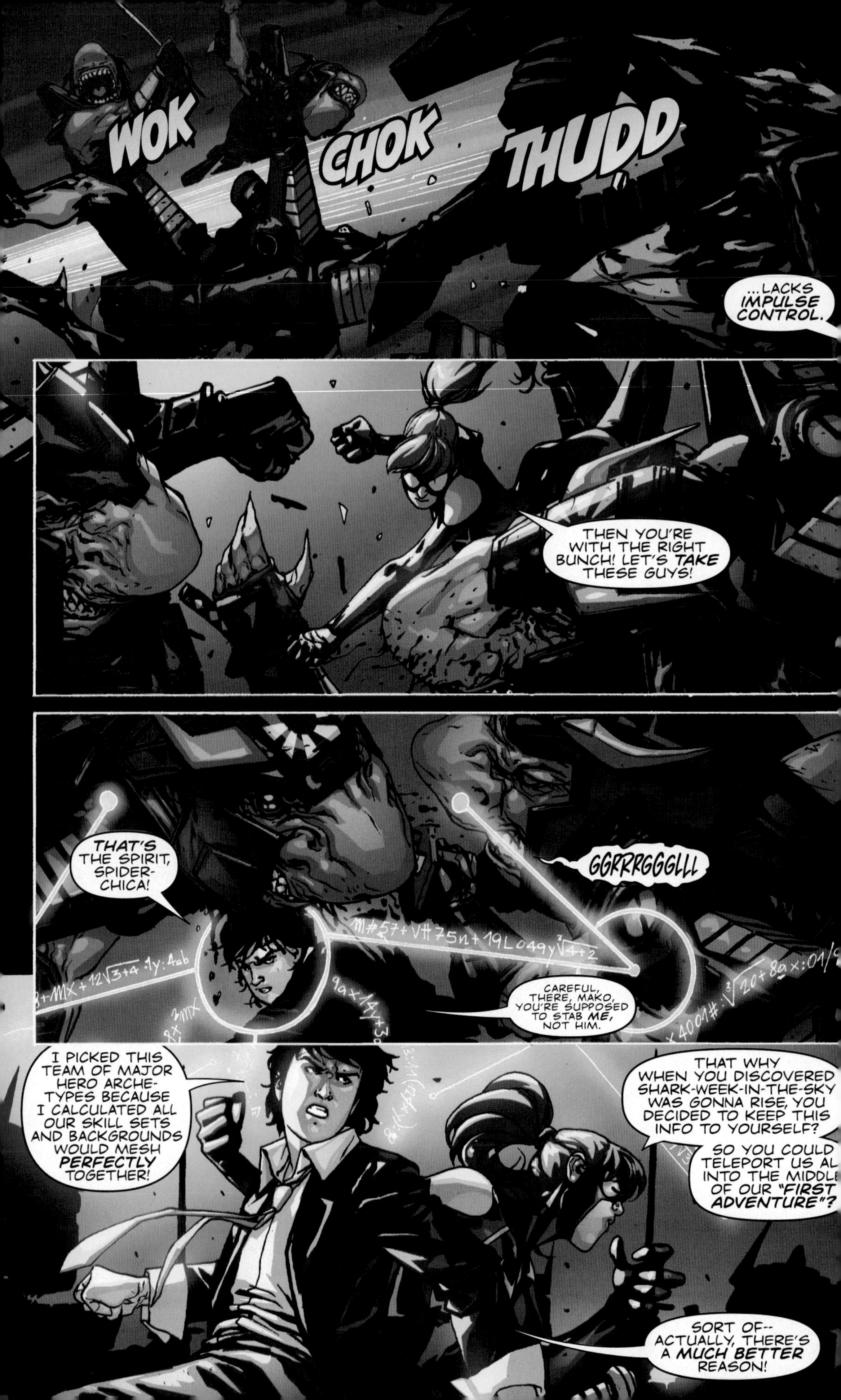

WOK
CHOK
THUDD
...LACKS IMPULSE CONTROL.
THEN YOU'RE WITH THE RIGHT BUNCH! LET'S TAKE THESE GUYS!
THAT'S THE SPIRIT, SPIDER-CHICA!
GGRRRGGGLLL
CAREFUL, THERE, MAKO, YOU'RE SUPPOSED TO STAB ME, NOT HIM.
I PICKED THIS TEAM OF MAJOR HERO ARCHE-TYPES BECAUSE I CALCULATED ALL OUR SKILL SETS AND BACKGROUNDS WOULD MESH PERFECTLY TOGETHER!
THAT WHY WHEN YOU DISCOVERED SHARK-WEEK-IN-THE-SKY WAS GONNA RISE, YOU DECIDED TO KEEP THIS INFO TO YOURSELF?
SO YOU COULD TELEPORT US AL INTO THE MIDDLE OF OUR "FIRST ADVENTURE"?
SORT OF-- ACTUALLY, THERE'S A MUCH BETTER REASON!

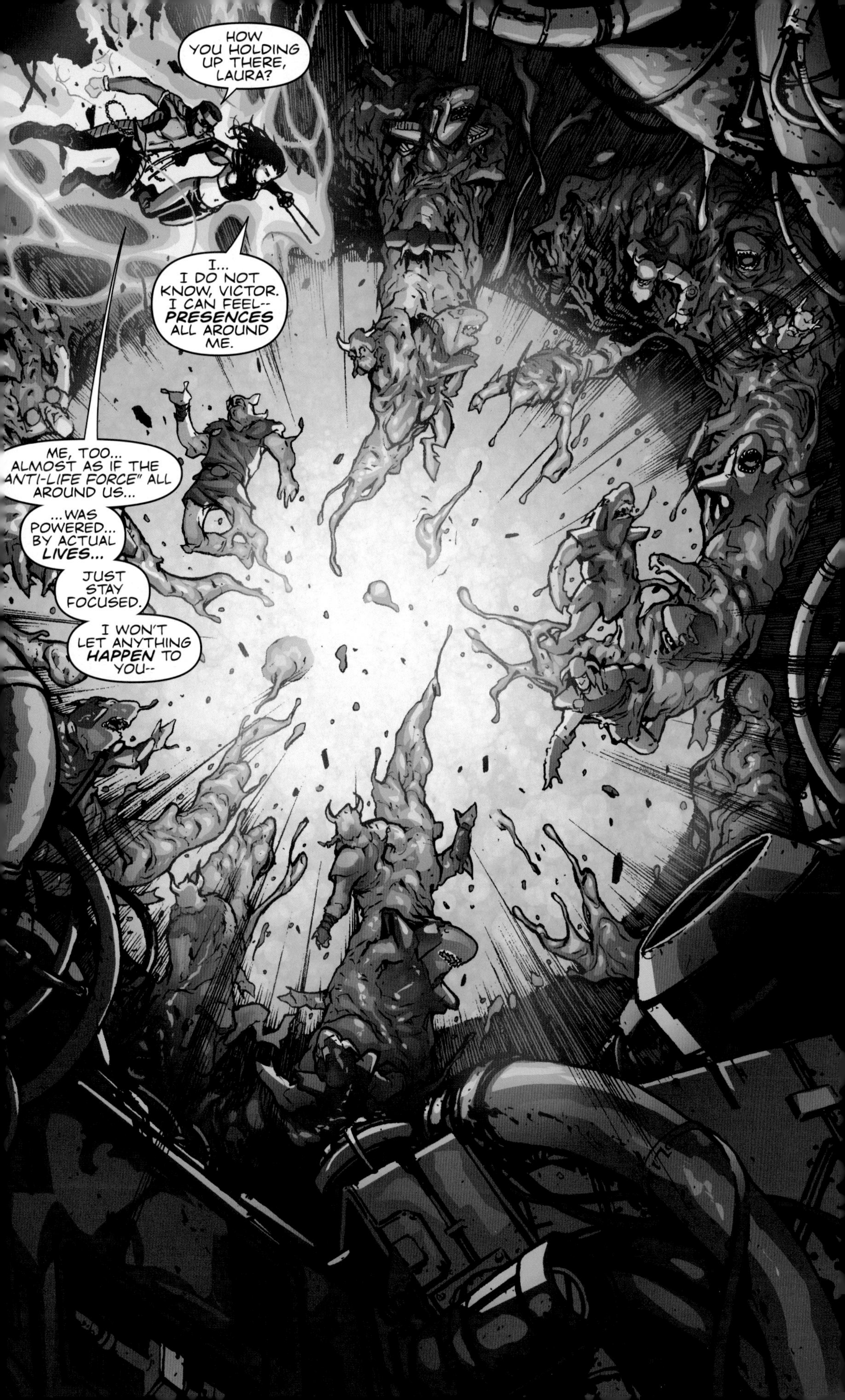
HOW YOU HOLDING UP THERE, LAURA?
I... I DO NOT KNOW, VICTOR. I CAN FEEL-- **PRESENCES** ALL AROUND ME.
ME, TOO... ALMOST AS IF THE ANTI-LIFE FORCE" ALL AROUND US...
...WAS POWERED... BY ACTUAL **LIVES...**
JUST STAY FOCUSED.
I WON'T LET ANYTHING **HAPPEN** TO YOU--

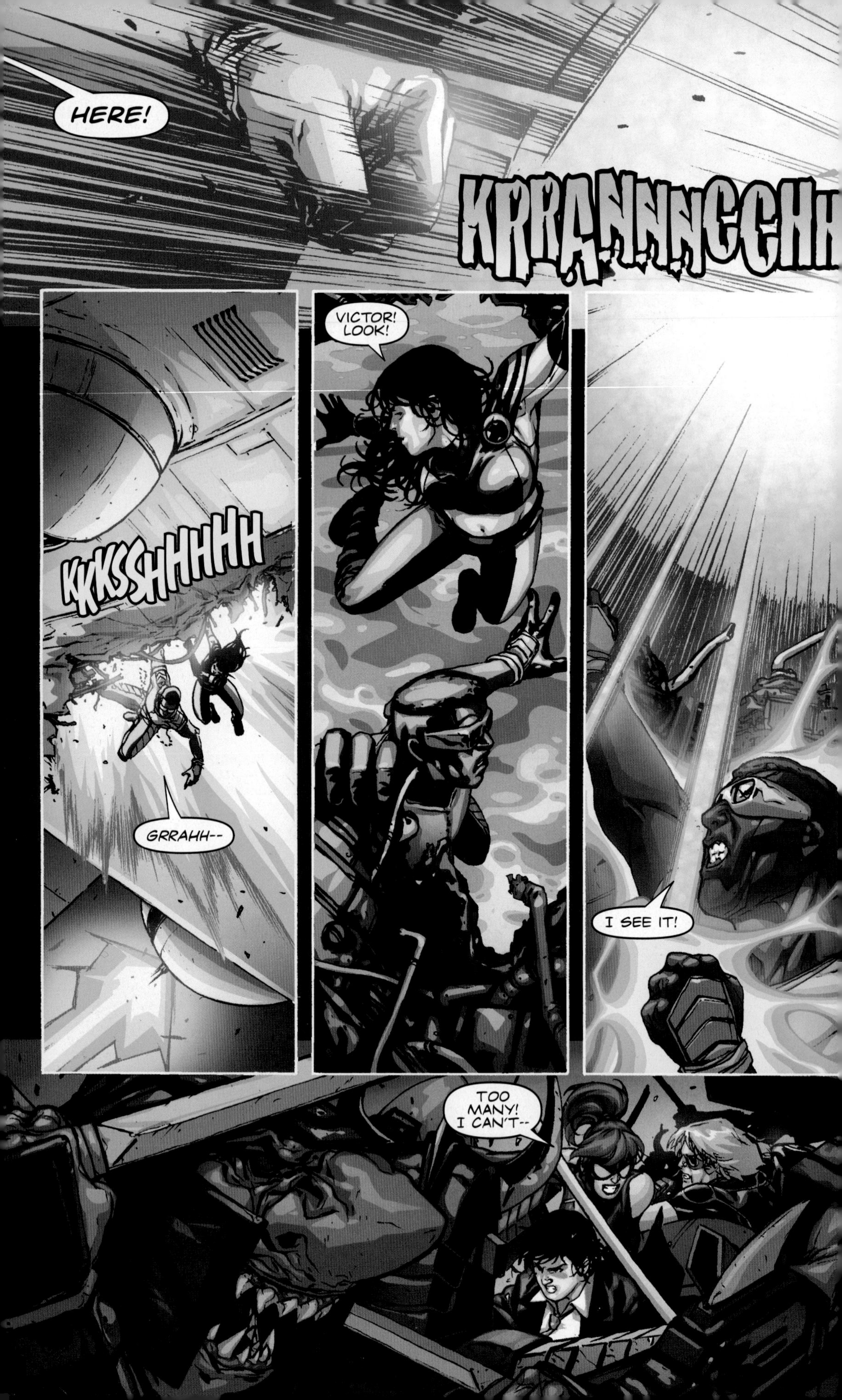
HERE!
KRRANNNCCHH
KKKSSHHHHH
GRRAHH--
VICTOR! LOOK!
I SEE IT!
TOO MANY! I CAN'T--

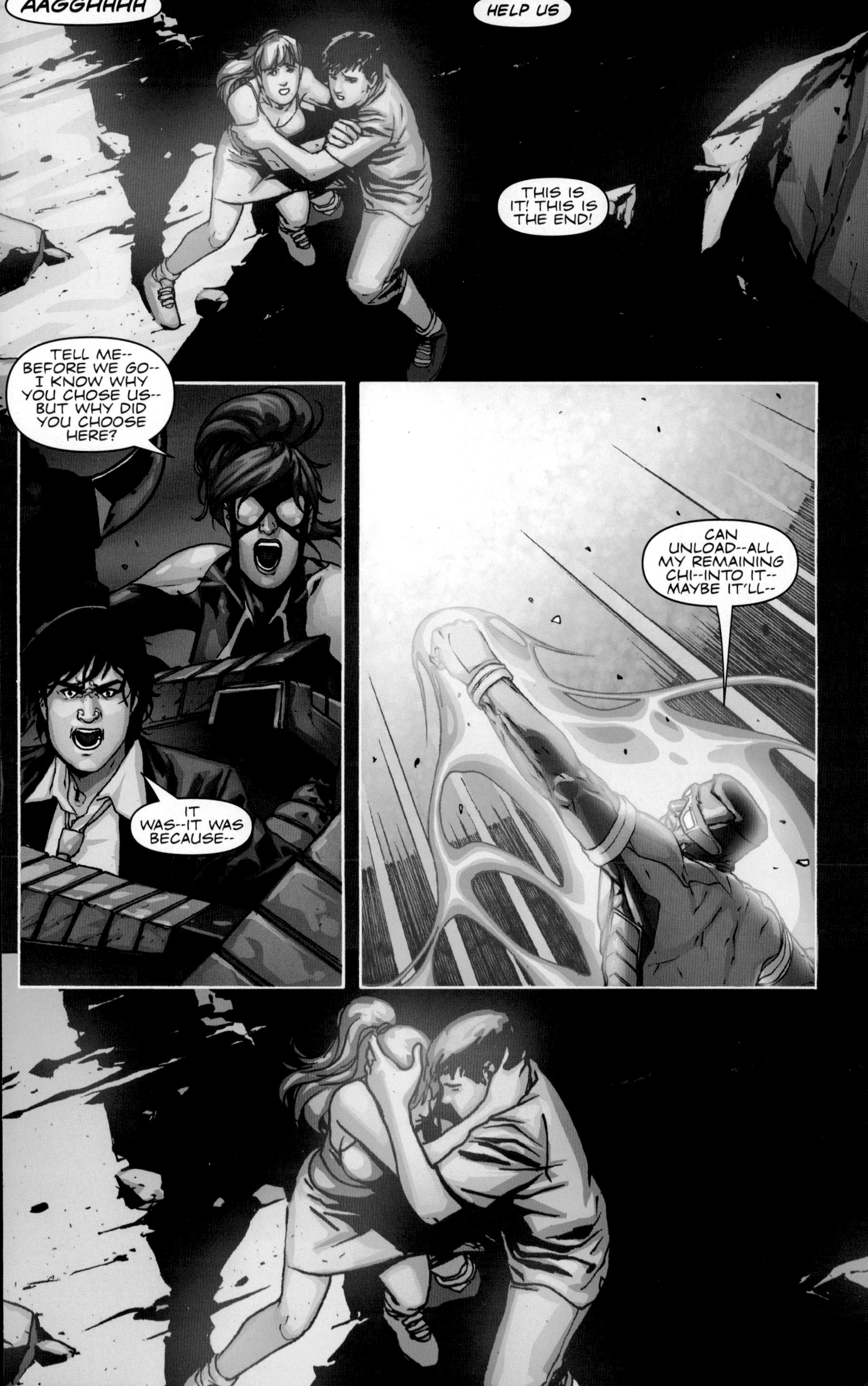
AAGGHHHH
HELP US
THIS IS IT! THIS IS THE END!
TELL ME-- BEFORE WE GO-- I KNOW WHY YOU CHOSE US-- BUT WHY DID YOU CHOOSE HERE?
IT WAS--IT WAS BECAUSE--
CAN UNLOAD--ALL MY REMAINING CHI--INTO IT-- MAYBE IT'LL--

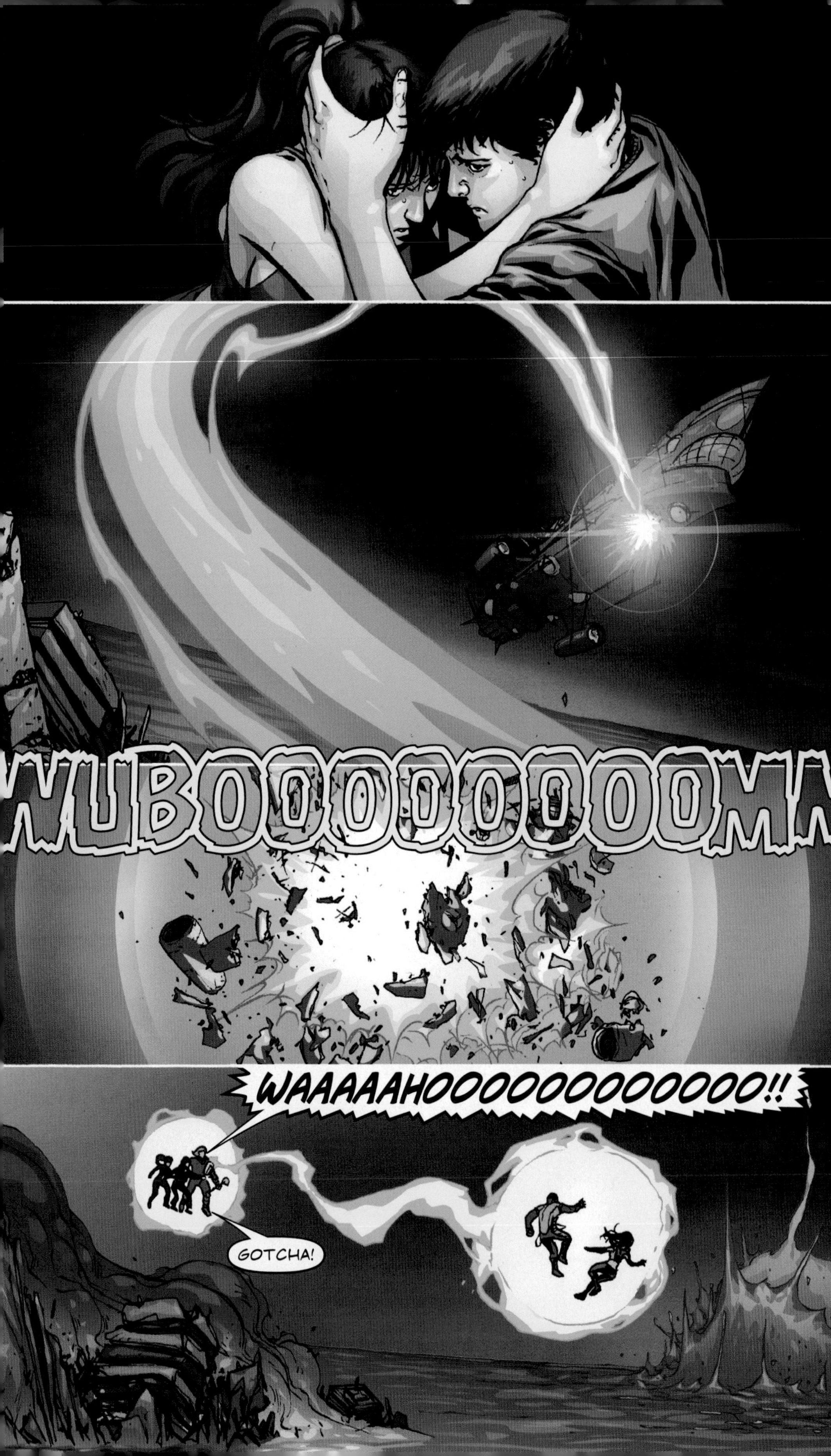
WUBOOOOOOOOOMM
WAAAAAHOOOOOOOOOOOOO!!
GOTCHA!

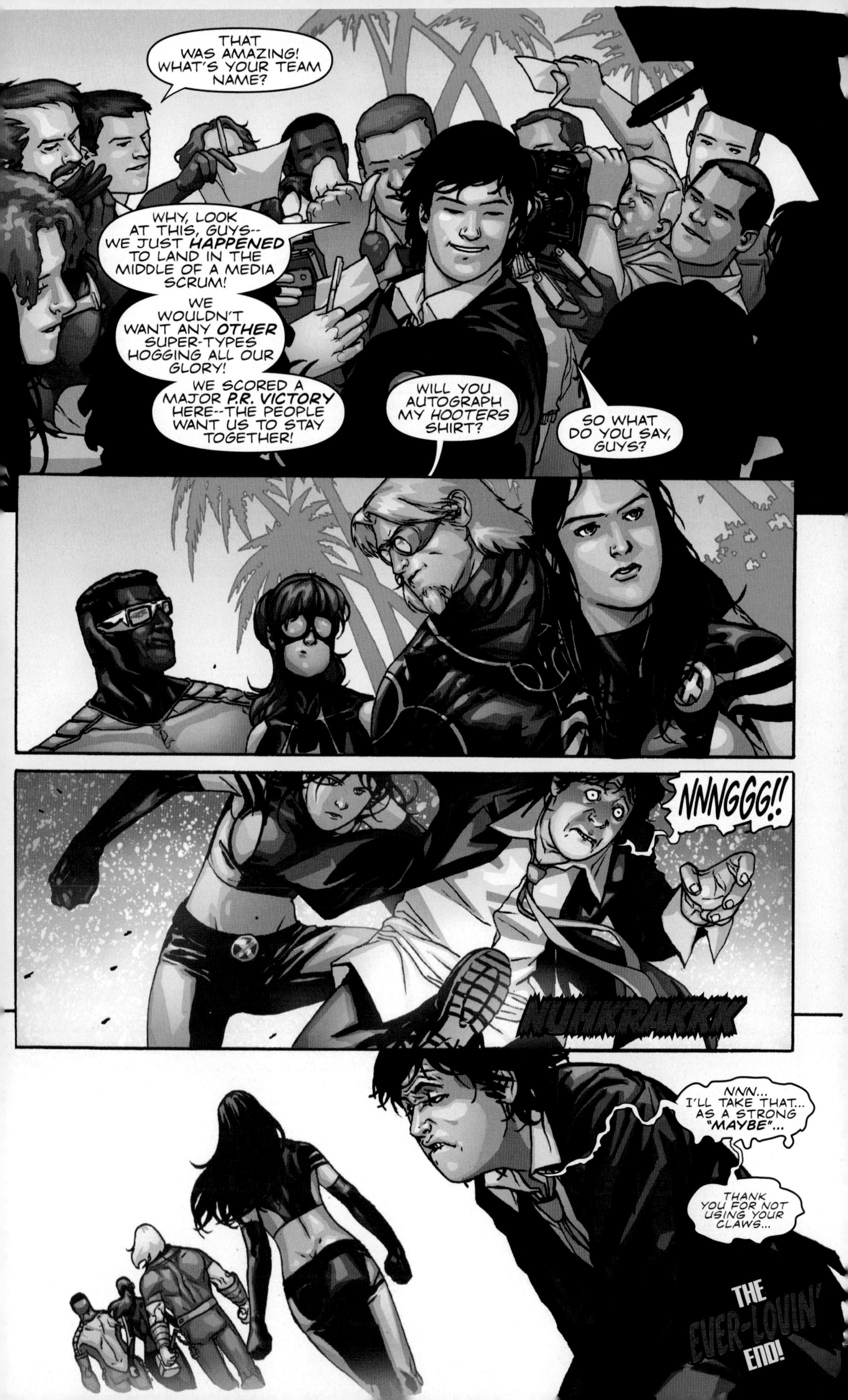

THAT WAS AMAZING! WHAT'S YOUR TEAM NAME?
WHY, LOOK AT THIS, GUYS-- WE JUST HAPPENED TO LAND IN THE MIDDLE OF A MEDIA SCRUM!
WE WOULDN'T WANT ANY OTHER SUPER-TYPES HOGGING ALL OUR GLORY!
WE SCORED A MAJOR P.R. VICTORY HERE--THE PEOPLE WANT US TO STAY TOGETHER!
WILL YOU AUTOGRAPH MY HOOTERS SHIRT?
SO WHAT DO YOU SAY, GUYS?
NNNGGG!!
NUHKRAKKK
NNN... I'LL TAKE THAT... AS A STRONG "MAYBE"...
THANK YOU FOR NOT USING YOUR CLAWS...
THE EVER-LOVIN' END!

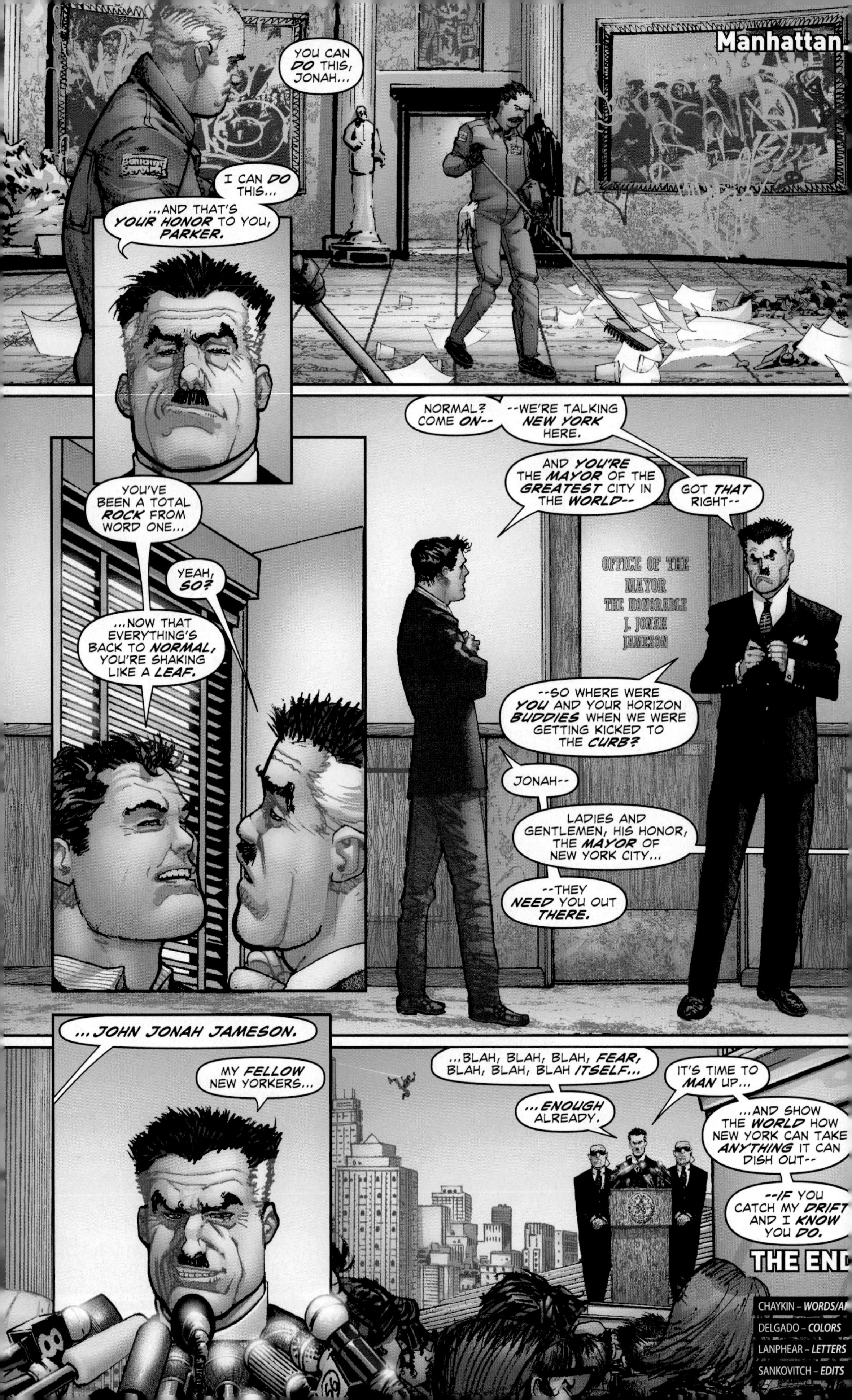
Manhattan.
YOU CAN DO THIS, JONAH...
I CAN DO THIS...
...AND THAT'S YOUR HONOR TO YOU, PARKER.
YOU'VE BEEN A TOTAL ROCK FROM WORD ONE...
YEAH, SO?
...NOW THAT EVERYTHING'S BACK TO NORMAL, YOU'RE SHAKING LIKE A LEAF.
NORMAL? COME ON--
--WE'RE TALKING NEW YORK HERE.
AND YOU'RE THE MAYOR OF THE GREATEST CITY IN THE WORLD--
GOT THAT RIGHT--
OFFICE OF THE MAYOR THE HONORABLE J. JONAH JAMESON
--SO WHERE WERE YOU AND YOUR HORIZON BUDDIES WHEN WE WERE GETTING KICKED TO THE CURB?
JONAH--
LADIES AND GENTLEMEN, HIS HONOR, THE MAYOR OF NEW YORK CITY...
--THEY NEED YOU OUT THERE.
...JOHN JONAH JAMESON.
MY FELLOW NEW YORKERS...
...BLAH, BLAH, BLAH, FEAR, BLAH, BLAH, BLAH ITSELF...
...ENOUGH ALREADY.
IT'S TIME TO MAN UP...
...AND SHOW THE WORLD HOW NEW YORK CAN TAKE ANYTHING IT CAN DISH OUT--
--IF YOU CATCH MY DRIFT AND I KNOW YOU DO.
THE END
CHAYKIN – WORDS/A
DELGADO – COLORS
LANPHEAR – LETTERS
SANKOVITCH – EDITS

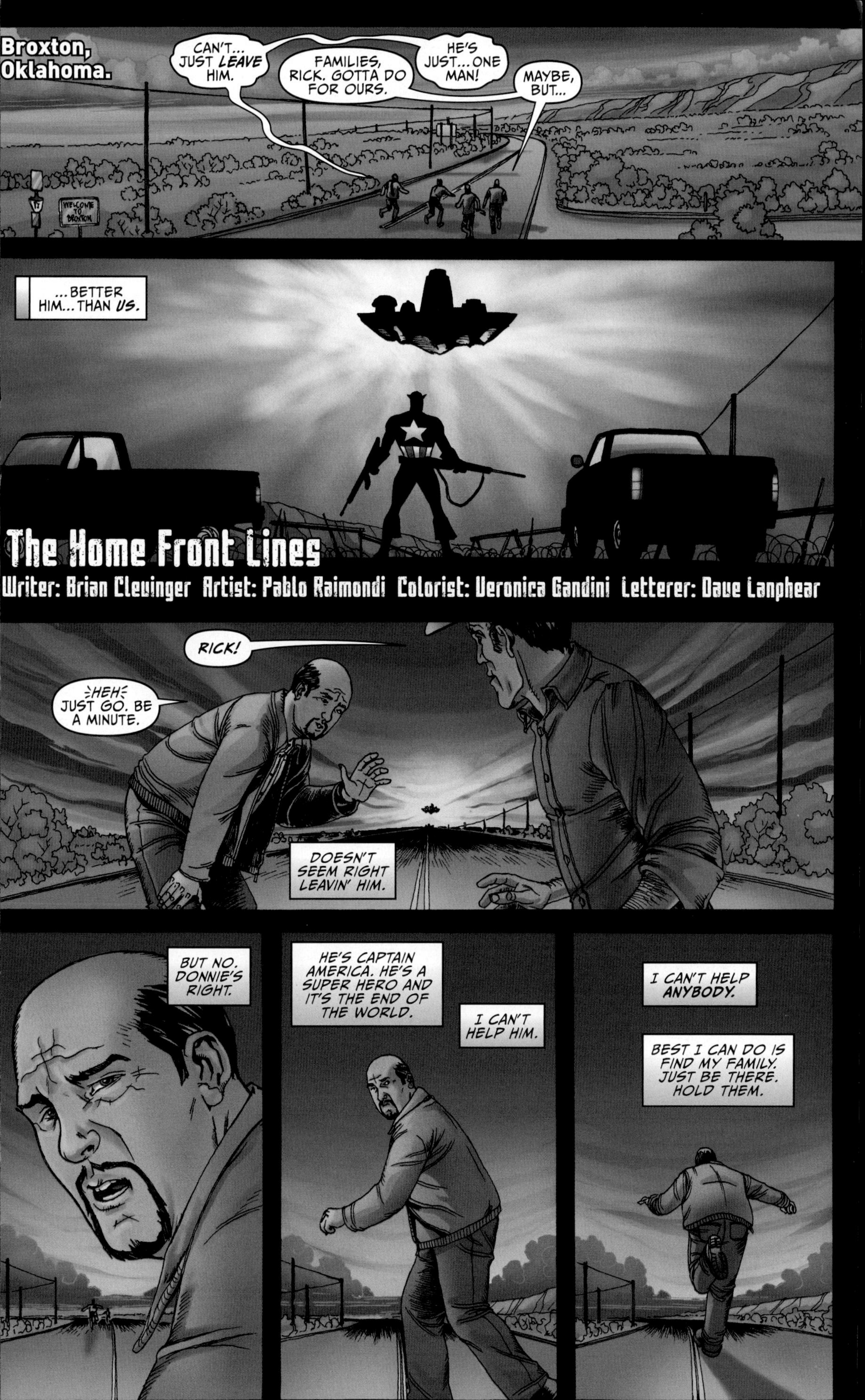
Broxton, Oklahoma.
CAN'T... JUST LEAVE HIM.
FAMILIES, RICK. GOTTA DO FOR OURS.
HE'S JUST... ONE MAN!
MAYBE, BUT...
WELCOME TO BROXTON
...BETTER HIM... THAN US.
The Home Front Lines
Writer: Brian Clevinger Artist: Pablo Raimondi Colorist: Veronica Gandini Letterer: Dave Lanphear
RICK!
HEH JUST GO. BE A MINUTE.
DOESN'T SEEM RIGHT LEAVIN' HIM.
BUT NO. DONNIE'S RIGHT.
HE'S CAPTAIN AMERICA. HE'S A SUPER HERO AND IT'S THE END OF THE WORLD.
I CAN'T HELP HIM.
I CAN'T HELP ANYBODY.
BEST I CAN DO IS FIND MY FAMILY. JUST BE THERE. HOLD THEM.

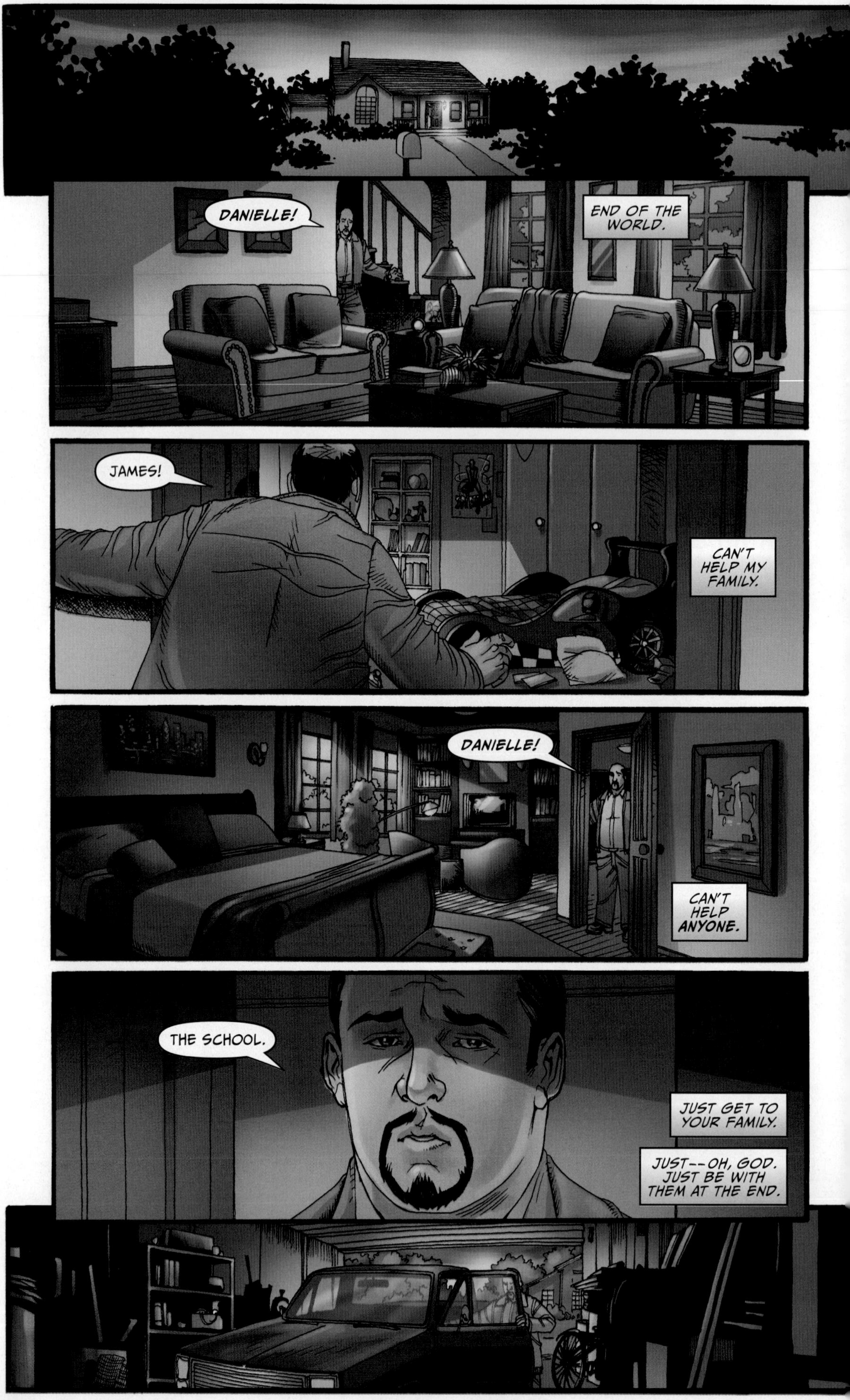
DANIELLE!
END OF THE WORLD.
JAMES!
CAN'T HELP MY FAMILY.
DANIELLE!
CAN'T HELP ANYONE.
THE SCHOOL.
JUST GET TO YOUR FAMILY.
JUST--OH, GOD. JUST BE WITH THEM AT THE END.

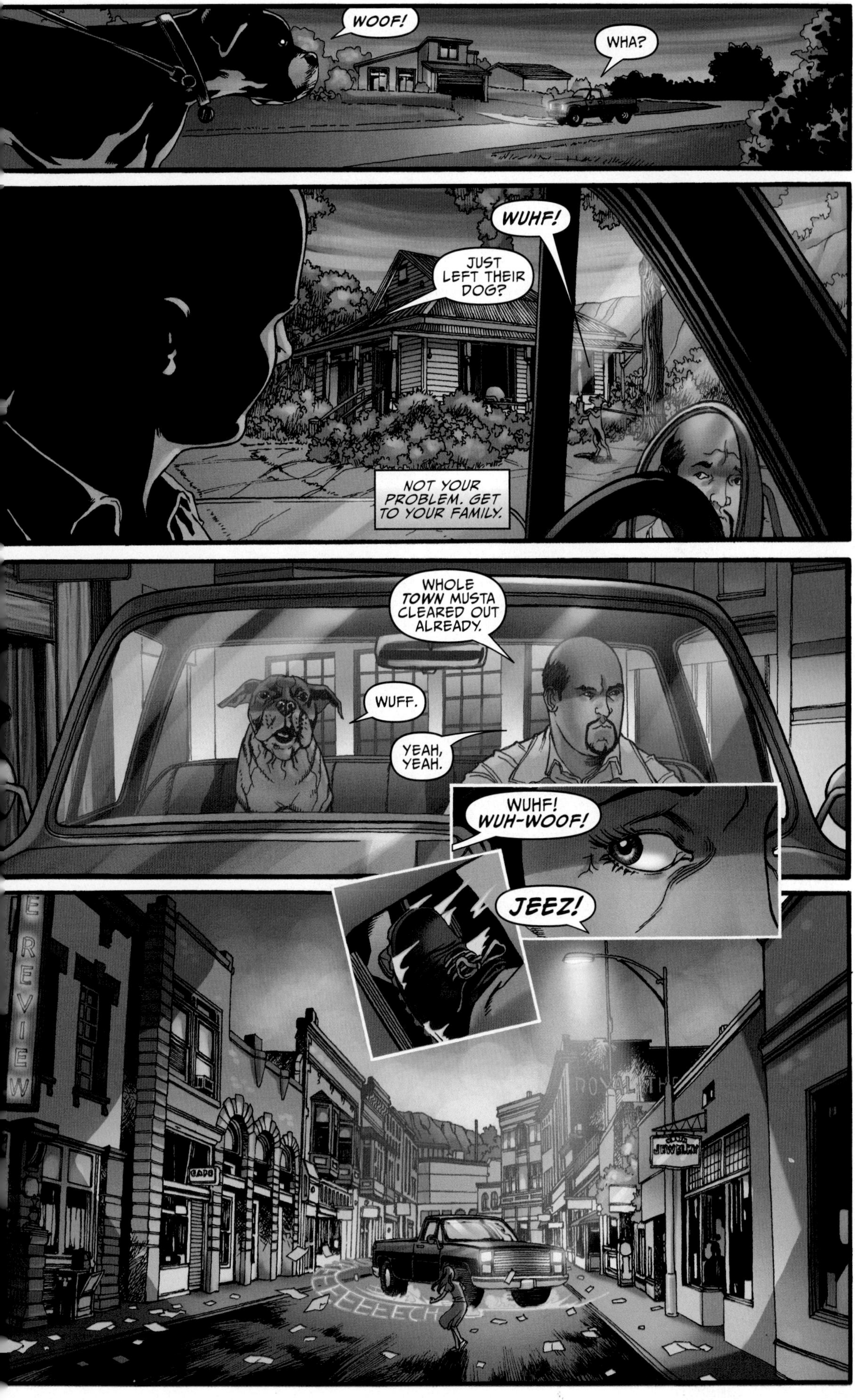
WOOF!
WHA?
WUHF!
JUST LEFT THEIR DOG?
NOT YOUR PROBLEM. GET TO YOUR FAMILY.
WHOLE TOWN MUSTA CLEARED OUT ALREADY.
WUFF.
YEAH, YEAH.
WUHF! WUH-WOOF!
JEEZ!

CAN YOU HELP MY GRAMPA?

END OF THE WORLD. CAN'T HELP ANYONE.

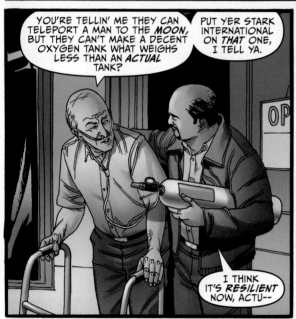

YOU'RE TELLIN' ME THEY CAN TELEPORT A MAN TO THE *MOON*, BUT THEY CAN'T MAKE A DECENT OXYGEN TANK WHAT WEIGHS LESS THAN AN *ACTUAL* TANK?

PUT YER STARK INTERNATIONAL ON *THAT* ONE, I TELL YA.

I THINK IT'S *RESILIENT* NOW, ACTU--

RESILIENT'S WHAT WE WERE IN THE *WAR*.

NOW LOOK AT US.

SIR?

WHAT'S YER DOG'S NAME, MISTER?

ER, SHE'S THE *NEIGHBOR'S* DOG. I THINK IT'S *DAISY*?

SHE'S *REAL* FRIENDLY.

YUP. SHE'S A GOOD DOG.

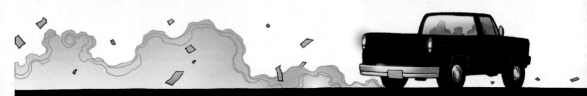

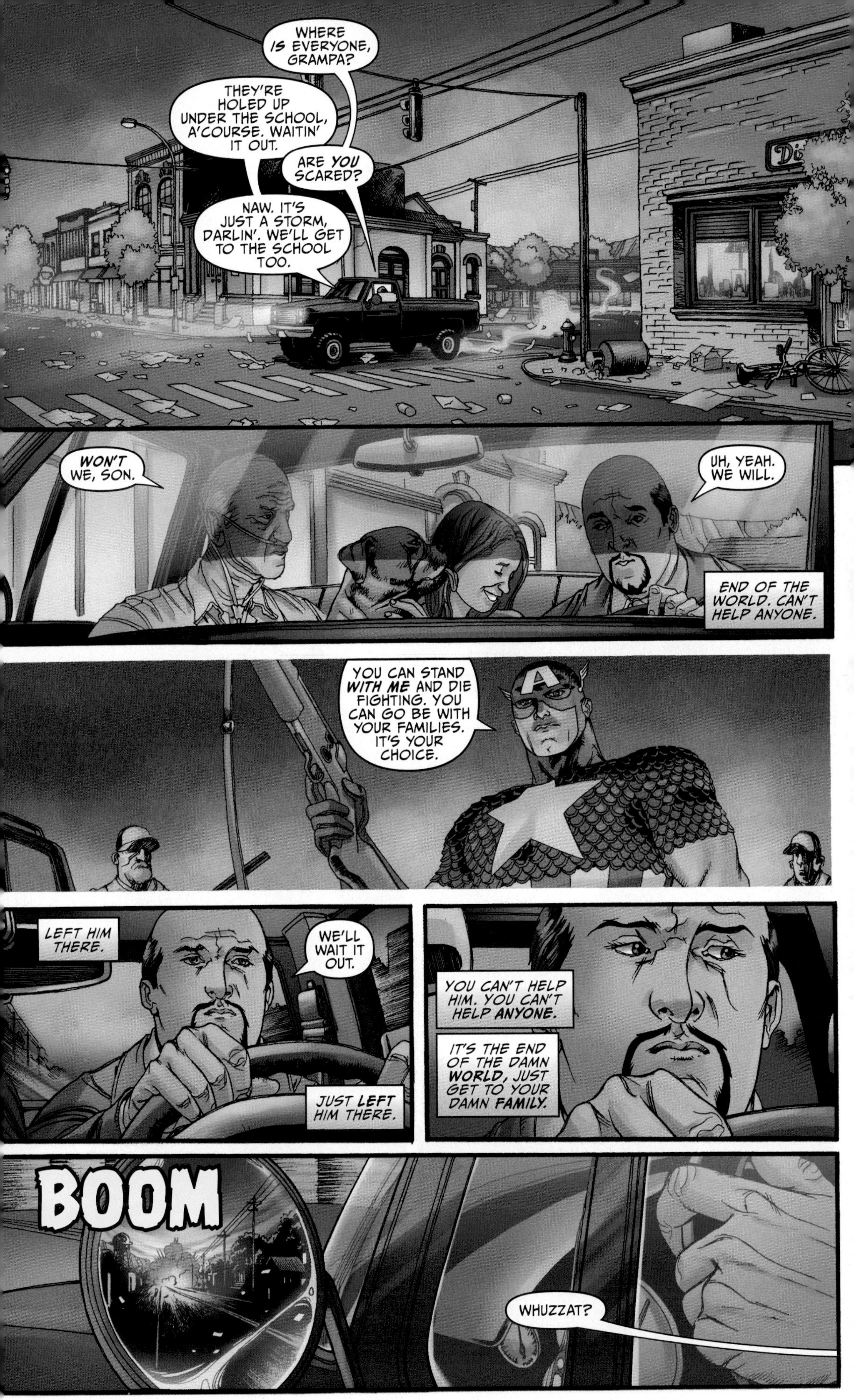
WHERE IS EVERYONE, GRAMPA?
THEY'RE HOLED UP UNDER THE SCHOOL, A'COURSE. WAITIN' IT OUT.
ARE YOU SCARED?
NAW. IT'S JUST A STORM, DARLIN'. WE'LL GET TO THE SCHOOL TOO.
WON'T WE, SON.
UH, YEAH. WE WILL.
END OF THE WORLD. CAN'T HELP ANYONE.
YOU CAN STAND WITH ME AND DIE FIGHTING. YOU CAN GO BE WITH YOUR FAMILIES. IT'S YOUR CHOICE.
LEFT HIM THERE.
WE'LL WAIT IT OUT.
JUST LEFT HIM THERE.
YOU CAN'T HELP HIM. YOU CAN'T HELP ANYONE.
IT'S THE END OF THE DAMN WORLD, JUST GET TO YOUR DAMN FAMILY.
BOOM
WHUZZAT?

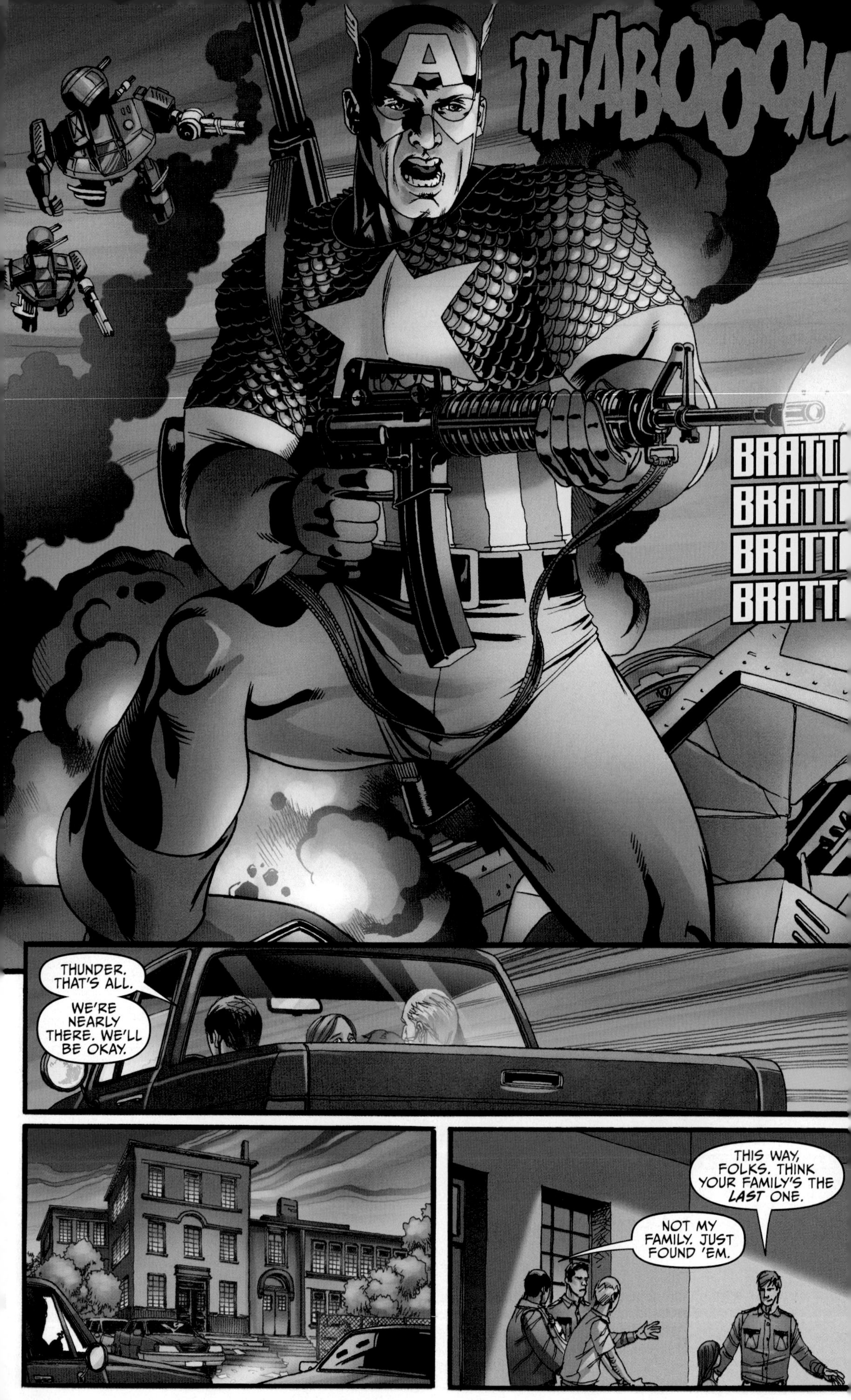
THABOOOM
BRATT
BRATT
BRATT
BRATT
THUNDER. THAT'S ALL.
WE'RE NEARLY THERE. WE'LL BE OKAY.
THIS WAY, FOLKS. THINK YOUR FAMILY'S THE *LAST* ONE.
NOT MY FAMILY. JUST FOUND 'EM.

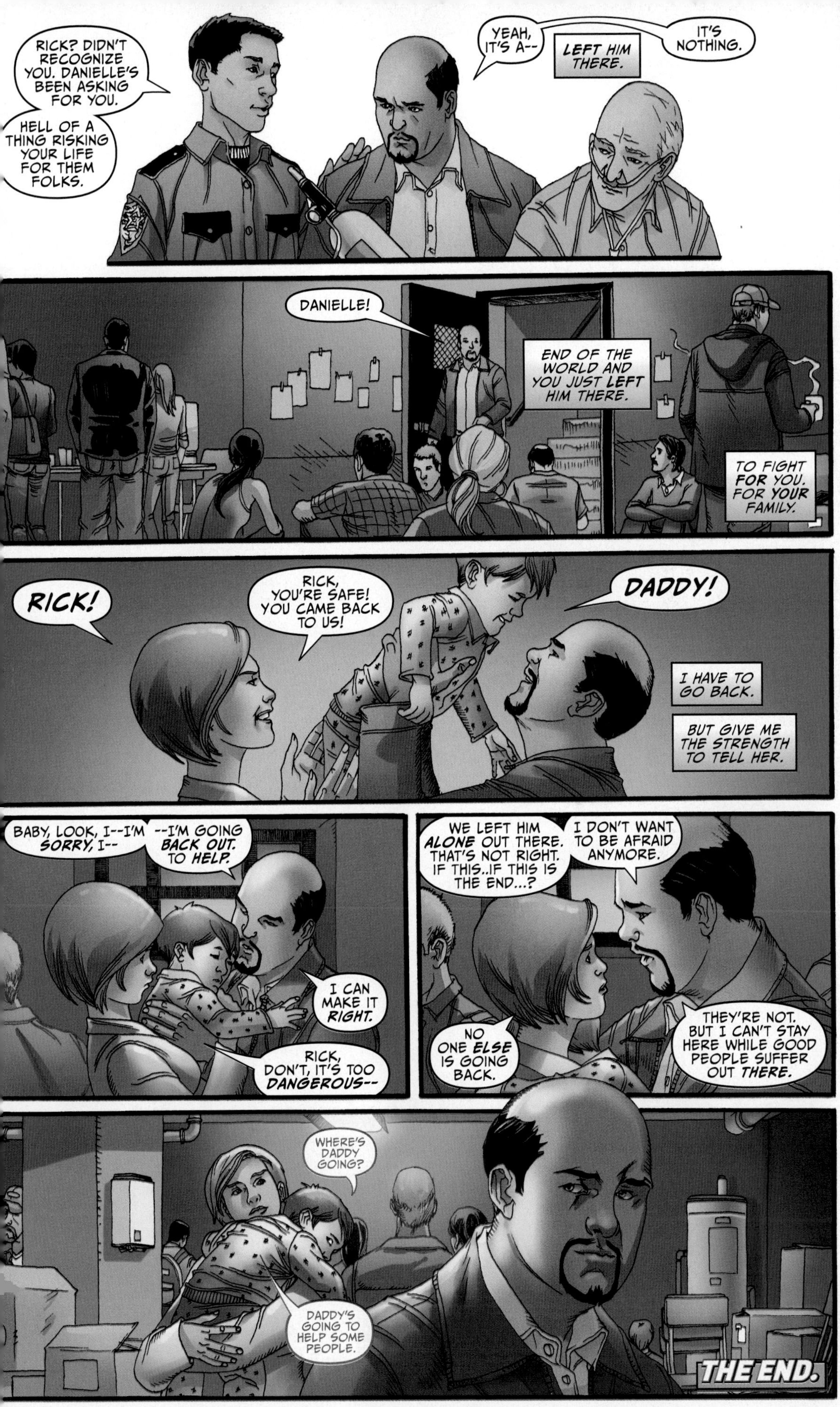
RICK? DIDN'T RECOGNIZE YOU. DANIELLE'S BEEN ASKING FOR YOU.
HELL OF A THING RISKING YOUR LIFE FOR THEM FOLKS.
YEAH, IT'S A--
IT'S NOTHING.
LEFT HIM THERE.
DANIELLE!
END OF THE WORLD AND YOU JUST LEFT HIM THERE.
TO FIGHT FOR YOU. FOR YOUR FAMILY.
RICK!
RICK, YOU'RE SAFE! YOU CAME BACK TO US!
DADDY!
I HAVE TO GO BACK.
BUT GIVE ME THE STRENGTH TO TELL HER.
BABY, LOOK, I--I'M SORRY, I--
--I'M GOING BACK OUT. TO HELP.
I CAN MAKE IT RIGHT.
RICK, DON'T, IT'S TOO DANGEROUS--
WE LEFT HIM ALONE OUT THERE. THAT'S NOT RIGHT. IF THIS..IF THIS IS THE END...?
I DON'T WANT TO BE AFRAID ANYMORE.
NO ONE ELSE IS GOING BACK.
THEY'RE NOT. BUT I CAN'T STAY HERE WHILE GOOD PEOPLE SUFFER OUT THERE.
WHERE'S DADDY GOING?
DADDY'S GOING TO HELP SOME PEOPLE.
THE END.

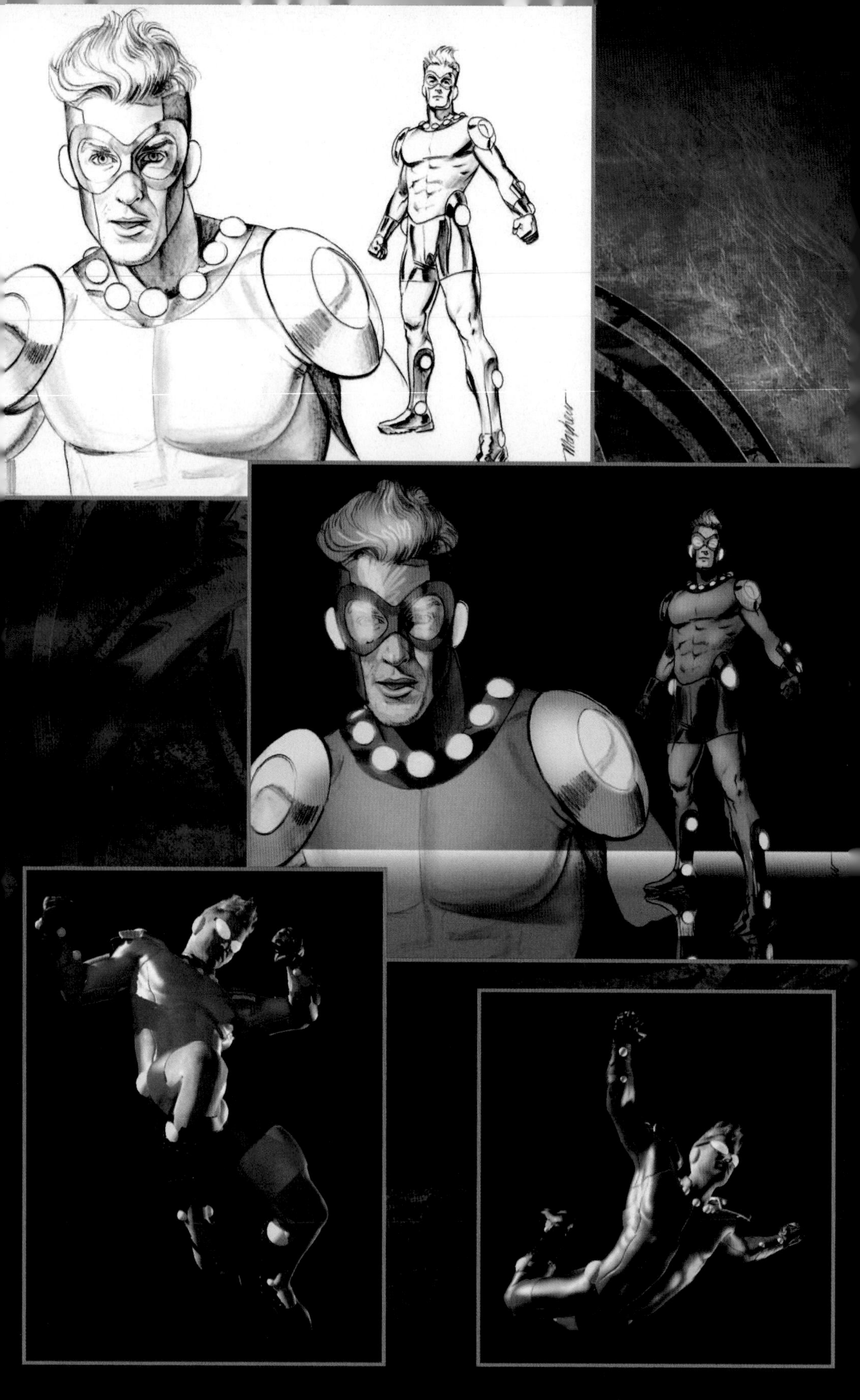

SPEEDBALL CHARACTER TESTS BY MIKE MAYHEW

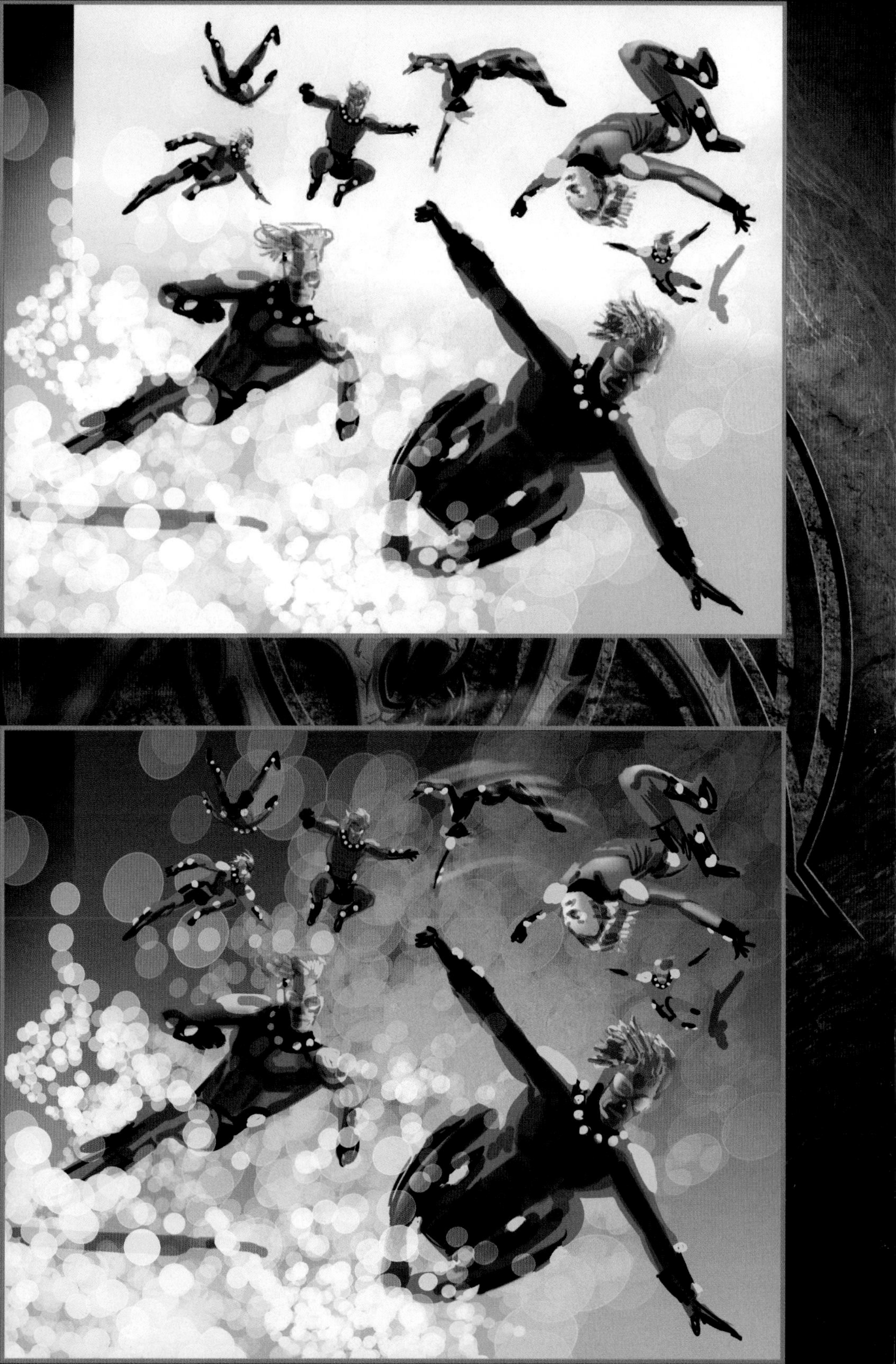

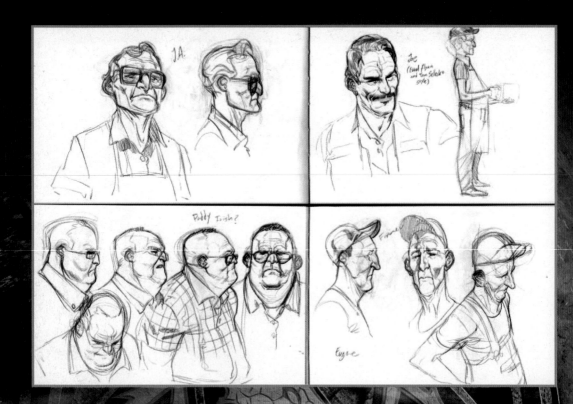

CHARACTER STUDIES BY PEPE LARRAZ

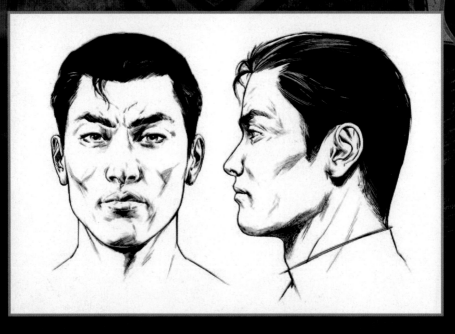

JIMMY WOO CHARACTER STUDY BY ELIA BONETTI

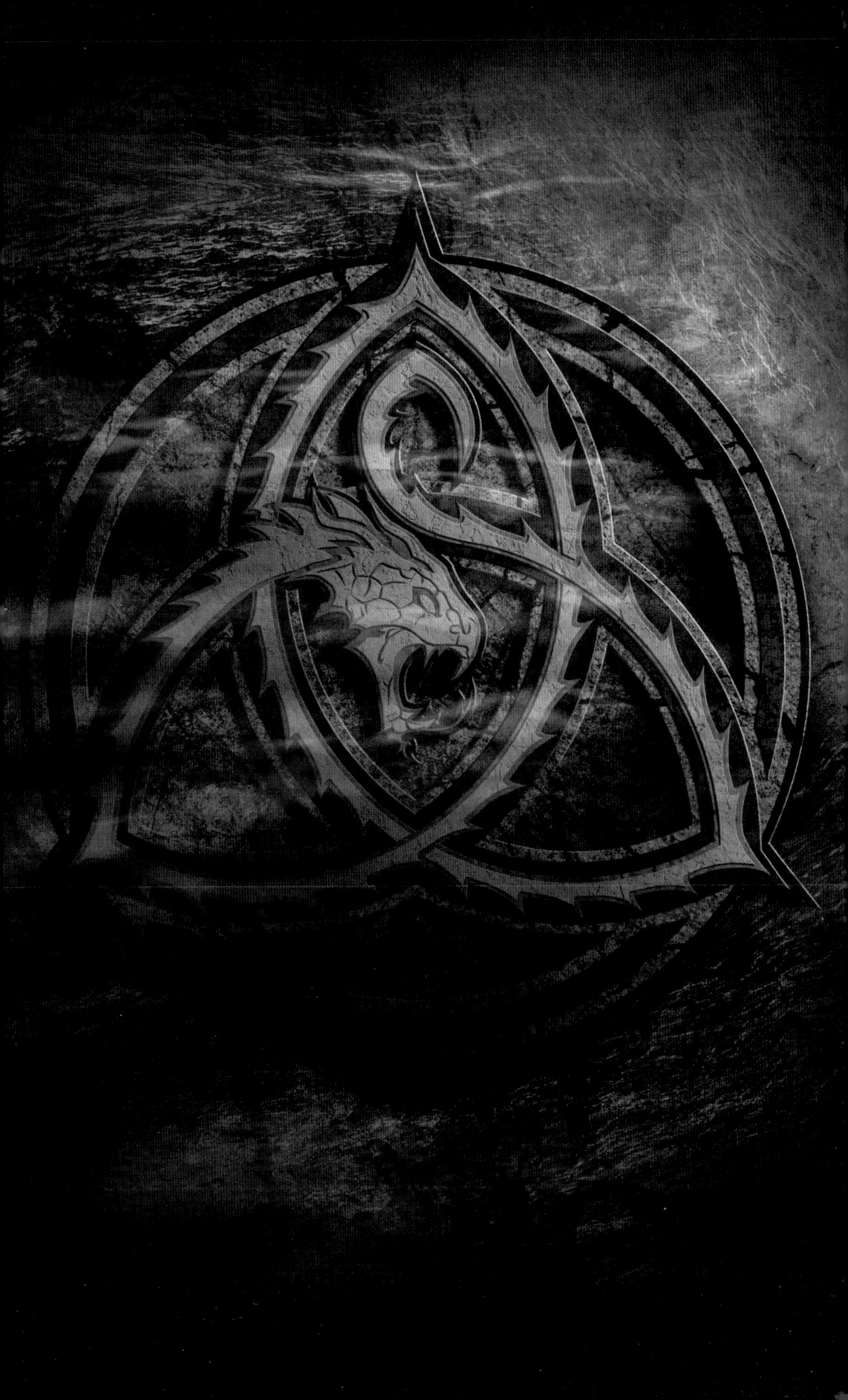

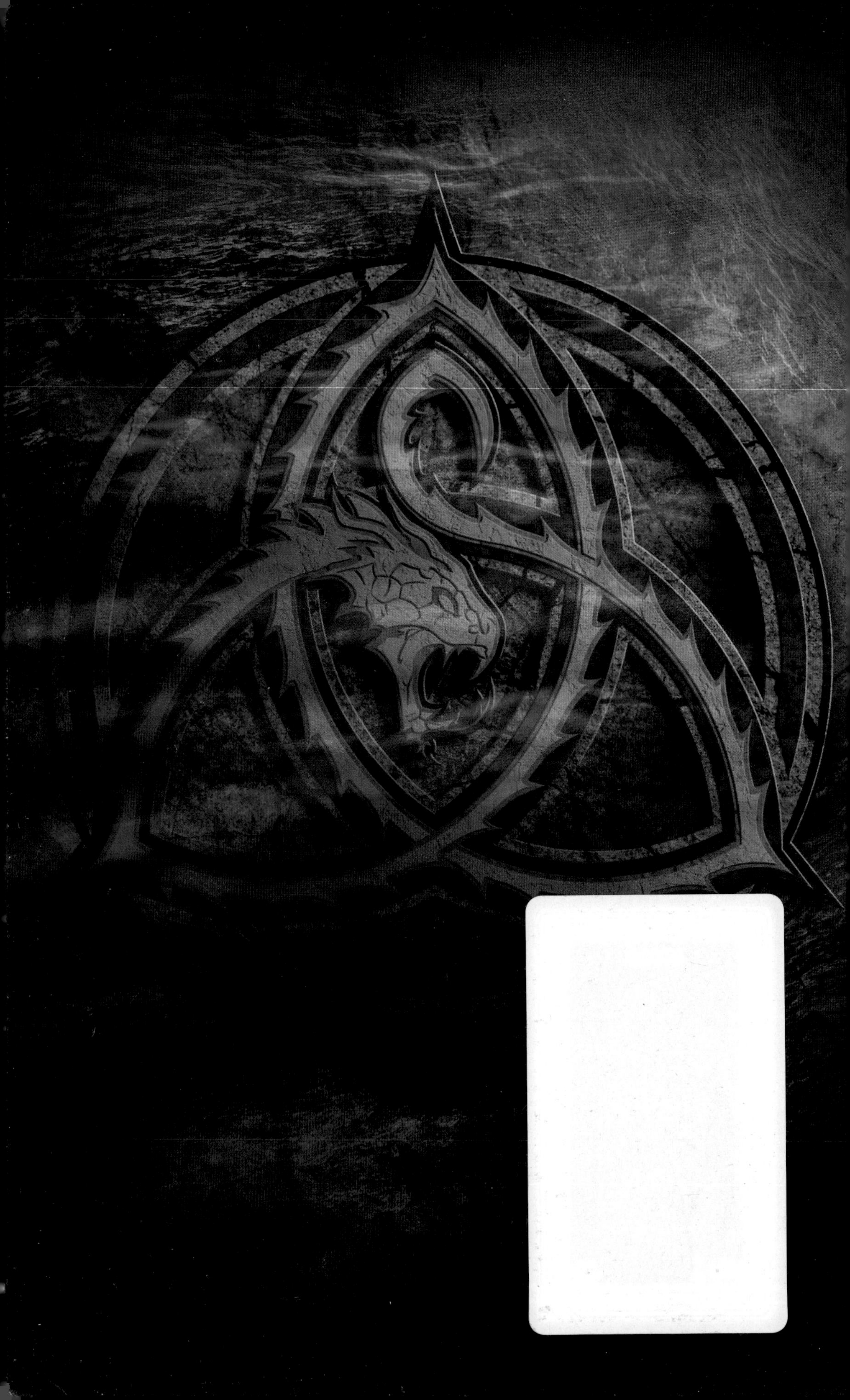